Web Development with Oracle® Portal

Mohamed El-Mallah

Prentice Hall PTR
Upper Saddle River, NJ 07458
www.phptr.com

Library of Congress Cataloging-in-Publication Data
A CIP catalog record for this book can be obtained from the Library of Congress.

Editorial Production/Composition: *G&S Typesetters, Inc.*
Acquisitions Editor: *Mark Taub*
Editorial Assistant: *Sarah Hand*
Cover Design: *Nina Scuderi*
Cover Director: *Jerry Votta*
Marketing Manager: *Debby Van Dijk*
Buyer: *Maura Zaldivar*
Project Coordinator: *Anne R. Garcia*

Prentice-Hall, Inc.
Upper Saddle River, New Jersey 07458

Prentice Hall books are widely used by corporations and government agencies for training, marketing, and resale. The publisher offers discounts on this book when ordered in bulk quantities. For more information, contact:

Corporate S]ales Department
Prentice Hall PTR
One Lake Street
Upper Saddle River, NJ 07458
Phone: 800-382-3419; FAX: 201-236-7141
E-mail (Internet): corpsales@prenhall.com

Printed in the United States of America

10 9 8 7 6 5 4 3 2 1

ISBN 0-13-060037-7

Pearson Education Ltd.
Pearson Education Australia PTY, Ltd.
Pearson Education Singapore, Pte. Ltd.
Pearson Education North Asia Ltd.
Pearson Education Canada, Ltd.
Pearson Educación de Mexico, S.A. de C.V.
Pearson Education—Japan
Pearson Education Malaysia, Pte. Ltd.
Pearson Education, Upper Saddle River, New Jersey

To my beloved father, Mostafa El-Mallah.

May God accept his good deeds, forgive him, and have mercy on him.

Brief Contents

Detailed Contents

Preface

Web Development with Oracle Portal is intended as an Oracle9*i*AS Portal tutorial. To get the most out of the book, you need to have basic knowledge of relational database concepts and SQL programming. Familiarity with HTML and PL/SQL will also help you understand the simple HTML and PL/SQL code inserted in some of the book examples. Chapter 16 examples require basic Java and Java Server Pages knowledge.

This book covers O9*i*AS Portal from both developmental and administrative points of view. Even though some chapters demonstrate the developmental capabilities of O9*i*AS Portal by building a simple demo Web site (i.e., Employee Information), most of the chapters were written so they can be read individually. So if you need information about a specific feature, you can read just the related chapter.

You can download the latest CD-ROM contents from *http://www.el-mallah.com* (username: wdwop; password: prenhall).

Acknowledgments

In the name of Allah, The Most Compassionate, The Most Merciful; all my thanks and praises are to Him. After God, I would like to thank several people. My mother has always been there for me without waiting for anything in return. I love you, Mom. My wife, Nesrin, has been patient night after night for almost a year while I worked on my laptop. You are wonderful. I also thank my manager in Oracle Support Services, Ken Haldane, for his continuing support. You are one of the best managers I have had.

I thank the people at Prentice Hall who helped me throughout the process of writing this book: Tim Moore, who gave me this opportunity; Russ Hall, who has been there guiding me through; Mike Meehan, who kept reminding me of the book schedule. Thanks, Mike. I also thank Anne Garcia, Alison Rainey, Michael Stowe, and Joshua Goodman. Guys and gals, you are great.

I thank the people who had a positive effect on my career through the years. Hamid B. Soubh was my mentor while I was working in the Diwan Amiri, Qatar. Professor Hussam Rashwan was the first one to introduce me to Oracle database and development tools. I also thank Professors Mohamed Marouf and Salah Selim and all my professors in the computer science department, Engineering College, Alexandria University, Egypt.

Finally, I thank my friends at Advanced Sequel Technologies, Inc. (sequeltechs.com) and my great community members at the Islamic Center of San Diego (icsd.org).

PART I

Getting Started

CHAPTER 1

Introduction to Portals

Introduction

This chapter introduces you to the corporate portal concepts and describes how portals can be built. Corporate portals are also known as Enterprise Information Portals, or EIPs. You can think of a corporate portal as a single point of access to the enterprise information sources, integrating heterogeneous data systems and providing users with the capability to personalize and optionally manage their data contents. Also, this chapter explains the architecture of Oracle Portal and how it can be used to build corporate portals.

Why Do You Need a Portal?

Any company in this computer age has a significant number of computer hardware systems, ranging from personal computers to mainframes. These systems can have different operating systems (e.g., Windows, Linux, Solaris, etc.), as well as software applications, which include electronic office/personal documents (e.g., text files, word documents, spreadsheet documents, etc.), maps or spatial information, databases, Web servers, HTML files, and so forth. These different sources of information have the following characteristics:

1. It is hard to search for what you need across all these information sources.
2. It is difficult to integrate these systems to provide end-users with a consolidated system.
3. In a large number of corporations, each system is developed and maintained separately. And hence the systems are Web-enabled separately, which adds more Web sites to the corporate intranet without easily integrating them. Therefore end-users do not have a common access gateway to these systems.

What Is an EIP?

An EIP is conceptually similar to an Internet portal such as My Yahoo! or My Netscape. It is where end-users first go to use applications and access information in their day-to-day activities. The EIP and the Internet portal should be easy to use and can be used out of the box without customization. Also, if the portal's end-users prefer, they can choose what they want to include in their portals, using the portal customization features. The difference between an EIP/corporate portal and an Internet portal is that the Internet portal—in general—does not include any business-specific information. EIPs can be considered as a super set of the Internet portals, because EIPs can include generic information—usually offered by Internet portal providers—such as stocks, weather, and so on, as well as internal business information, such as payroll and company sales.

EIP Characteristics

EIPs have the following characteristics:

- An EIP is simple to use. Users can learn how to use it without manuals. Nevertheless, it is helpful to have a small reference listing the advanced features, inside tips and hints, and capabilities. This reference can be offered in the format of online help or tutorials.
- EIPs offer a single point of access to information inside the corporation (i.e., intranet) or outside the corporation (i.e., Internet).
- EIPs can be personalized. Once authenticated to the portal, the end-user should be able to customize not only the layout (fonts, color, location, etc.) of the information in his or her Web page(s) but also the contents of these pages (e.g., how many orders are displayed and how they are sorted).
- If the portal is deployed in different languages, the portal has to be localized in the language the user prefers.
- EIPs are centrally administered. The portal content managers, data administrators, and portal administrators do not need to jump from one administration tool to the other to do their jobs.
- EIPs are secure. The data entered and accessed by portal end-users has to be protected. For example, the end-user should be authenticated to the portal through a password-protected account. Also, secure Internet and networking protocols should be used to protect the data while it is entered, sent, and saved through different layers of the architecture.

Why Oracle Portal?

Oracle Portal is a browser-based development tool for building, deploying, and administering EIPs. Oracle Portal provides the following advantages as an EIP development tool:

- Single Sign-On: Oracle Portal provides a login server, which can be used to simplify access to different information sources inside and outside the corporation.

- Consolidated backup and recovery: The portals developed using Oracle Portal are generated and saved inside Oracle databases. This means both the corporate data and the portal Web sites can be backed up and restored using the same tools and techniques and utilizing the existing inhouse Oracle database expertise.
- Browser-based development and administration: Portal administrators and developers do not have to install any client tools to be able to work on their portals. They can log in remotely to the Oracle Portal through a browser and customize and develop their portals.
- Rich and diverse development capabilities allow the development of unique portals: Some Web page design tools generate similar look-and-feel Web pages, and you can tell right away that they were developed by such-and-such a tool. Oracle Portal makes it easier for companies to develop Web pages with a unique look.

Oracle *internet* Application Server

Oracle Portal is a product inside Oracle *internet* Application Server (O*i*AS; Figure 1.1). Oracle8*i* Application Server (version 1.0.0) is the first release of O*i*AS, and it includes Oracle Portal 2

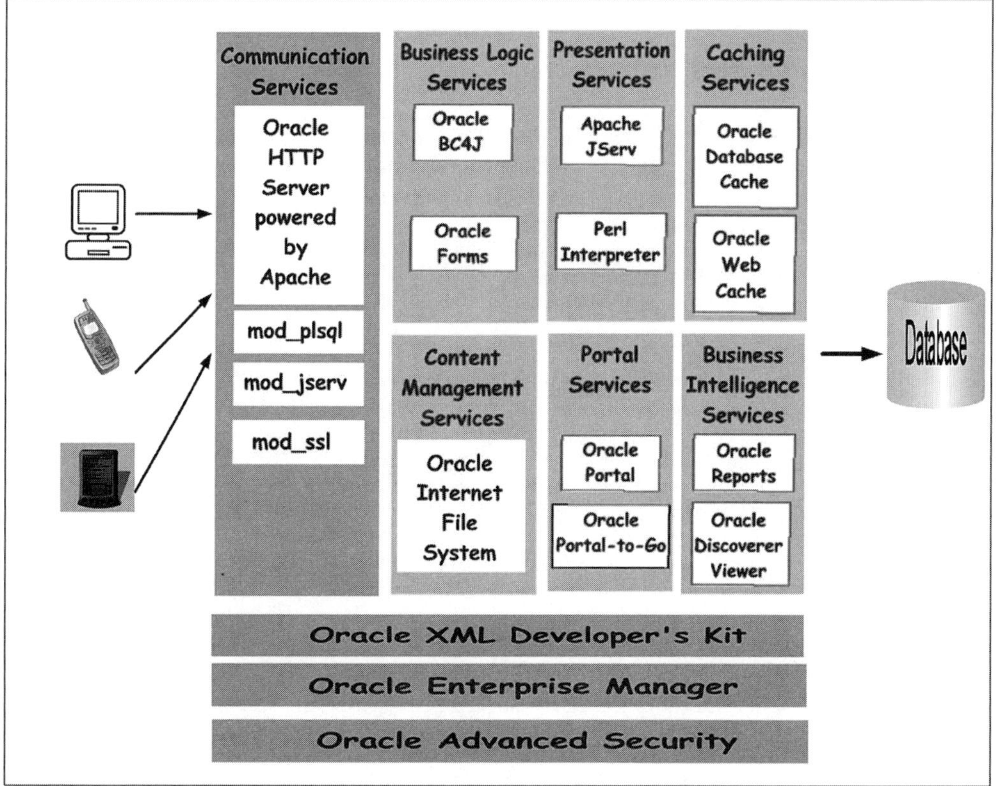

Figure 1.1 Oracle *internet* Application Server Architecture Overview.

(formerly known as Oracle WebDB). The second release of the O*i*AS is version 1.0.2, which includes Oracle Portal 3, and this is the version mainly covered in this book. This book refers to the product as both Oracle9*i*AS and O9*i*AS. I will also cover migration from WebDB 2.x to Portal 3.

O*i*AS Services

O*i*AS has a set of services to provide administrators and developers with different components that can be assembled to build an integrated set of applications. Oracle categorizes O*i*AS services based on their main capabilities. A brief description of these categories follows.

Communication Services

The main communication service in the O*i*AS is the Oracle HTTP server, which is the Apache Web listener with Oracle modules added to it. One of the most important modules is the mod_plsql, which routes the PL/SQL requests to the database PL/SQL engine to execute PL/SQL stored procedures.

Content Management Services

These services make all of your contents—regardless of the file type—accessible in one heterogeneous file hierarchy via Web browsers, email clients, and FTP (file transfer protocol) clients. In addition, you can use these services to configure sophisticated file searching capability, event-triggered alerts, and check-in–check-out functionality to support collaborative projects. The main service is the Oracle Internet File System, which is a file system service that stores files in an Oracle8*i* database. From the end-user's viewpoint, Oracle Internet File System appears as any other file system accessible through Microsoft Windows networking, a Web browser, FTP, or an email client. The fact that files are stored in the database is transparent to users because users do not directly interact with the database.

Business Logic Services

These services support your application logic. Using Business Logic Services, you can build and run your Web applications. The main services are Oracle BC4J (Business Components for Java) and Oracle Forms.

Presentation Services

These services deliver dynamic content to client browsers, supporting servlets, Java Server Pages (JSP), Perl/CGI scripts, PL/SQL Pages, forms, and business intelligence. Using Presentation Services, you can build your presentation layer for your Web applications.

Caching Services

Caching services include Oracle Web Cache and Oracle Database Cache. Oracle Web Cache is a content-aware cache that improves the performance, scalability, and availability of Web sites by caching both static and dynamic Web pages. Oracle Database Cache is a middle-tier database cache that reduces the load on the back-end database instance by caching frequently requested data and avoiding unnecessary network round-trips.

System Services

To provide system management and security services, Oracle Internet Application Server includes Oracle Enterprise Manager and Oracle Advanced Security. These system services provide a comprehensive management framework for your entire Oracle environment and network security via SSL (Secure Sockets Layer)-based encryption and authentication facilities.

Business Intelligence Services

To understand what is happening in your business and on your Web site every day, you can use these services to deploy and share business intelligence over the Web or over your corporate intranet. The main services are Oracle Reports and Oracle Discoverer. Oracle9*i*AS Discoverer in O9*i*AS version 1.0.2.2 contains Oracle9*i*AS Discoverer4*i* Plus Oracle9*i*AS Discoverer4*i* Viewer.

Portal Services

There are two main types of portal services; the first is Oracle Portal, which is the main target product for this book, and Oracle Portal-to-Go. Oracle Portal-to-Go is considered the wireless edition of O9*i*AS, and is a portal service for delivering information and applications to mobile devices. Using Portal-to-Go, you can create custom portal sites that use different kinds of content, including Web pages, custom Java applications, and XML-based applications. Portal-to-Go makes this diverse information accessible to mobile devices without your having to rewrite the content for each target device platform.

Developer's Kits

These kits are included in the O9*i*AS. They contain libraries and tools to support application development and deployment. Oracle XML Developer's Kit (XDK) is an example of the developer's kits.

Oracle Portal Architecture

To help you understand the Oracle Portal architecture, I start by introducing some Oracle Portal terms that are used throughout this book.

Portlets and Pages

Portlets and pages are two of the most important new concepts introduced in Oracle Portal 3. Oracle Portal displays its information organized in pages. Each Oracle Portal page is composed of small areas of display; these areas are called portlets (Figure 1.2). A portlet is a reusable, pluggable component that displays information from a data source (Figure 1.3). Portlets are

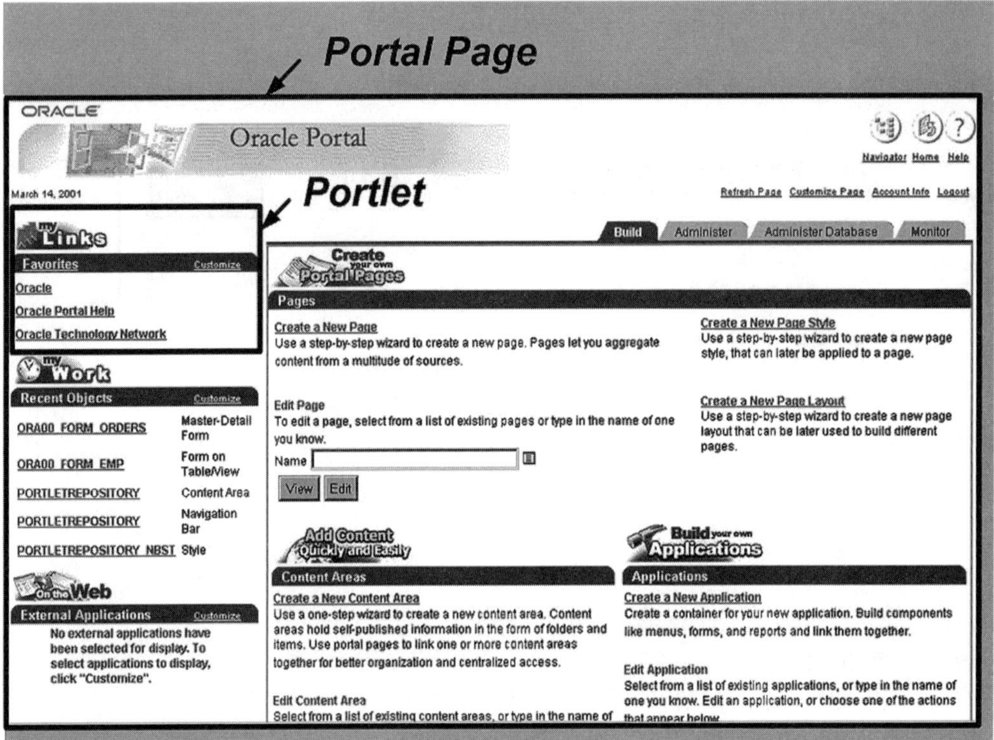

Figure 1.2 Oracle Portal Pages and Portlets.

arranged in vertical and horizontal table cells. Actually, portlets are implemented using HTML table cells.

There are different types of portlets, such as built-in and programmable portlets. I will explain these in detail in Chapter 13.

Portlet Providers

A provider is an entity that provides information to one or more portlets. For example, Oracle Portal comes prebuilt with a provider that owns the Recent Objects portlet. This provider allows only logged-on users to view and access recent objects. Public users do not have the privilege to run this portlet.

There are two main types of providers: database providers and Web providers. Database providers are either written in Java or PL/SQL. They are saved in the Oracle database. The call to the provider is done over Oracle Net8. In the Web provider's case, the calls to the provider methods are performed over HTTP. The Web providers can be implemented in any Web development environment such as JSP or Java.

Figure 1.3 A Portlet Example.

Servicing HTTP Requests in Oracle Portal

Oracle Portal is designed around a three-tier architecture. The most common architecture has a dedicated database server acting as your Oracle Portal node. The Oracle Portal node performs the communication with other business databases over database links. And, in the middleware you have a server with O9*i*AS (Figure 1.4).

When users request a portal page by typing its URL or by clicking on its hyperlink, they retrieve an HTML page with different pieces of information. The flow of a request is as follows:

1. A request is made from the browser to retrieve a portal page.
2. The Oracle HTTP server receives the HTTP request.
3. The Oracle HTTP server translates the request by mapping the virtual path specified in the URL (i.e., pls) to mod_plsql.
4. Mod_plsql sends the request to the Oracle instances acting as the Oracle Portal node.
5. The portal node contains the page definition, the code that shows the page, and the page user's customizations. If authentication is needed for the page portlets, the Oracle Portal node authenticates to the login server.
6. The request goes to the Parallel Page Engine (i.e., Parallel Servlet), which resides in the middle tier as part of the O9*i*AS.

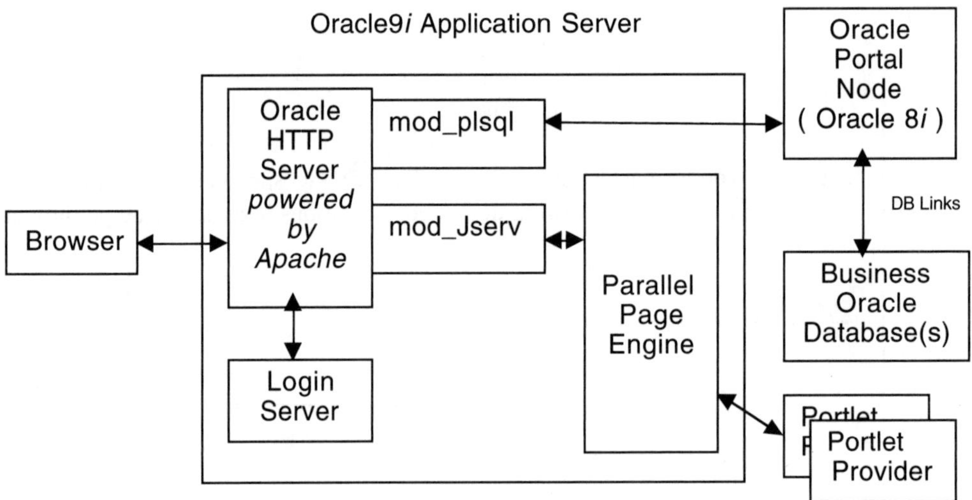

Figure 1.4 Oracle Portal Architecture Overview.

7. The Page Engine accepts the page definition and issues show portlet requests to the portlets' providers. These requests are performed in parallel to speed the page rendering process.
8. The providers return their portlets' output to the Page Engine, which in return assembles the outputs into a single page and passes it to the Oracle HTTP server.
9. The Oracle HTTP server sends the HTML page to the browser.

Portal Development Cycle

This section explains briefly the typical phases involved in portal software development. Software development is a quite detailed process, and there are many methodologies used that are beyond the scope of this book. This section only highlights the main development stages without going into details of these stages or differences between the available methodologies.

Portal Analysis

This phase is also called the system requirements or data gathering phase. Here you identify the portal system requirements by knowing the corporate business and by identifying the portal users and their tasks.

Portal Design

One important guideline you need to remember when designing your portal is to keep it simple. Keeping the design simple helps both the developers in building the portal and the end-users in using the portal. Simplicity of the portal GUI (graphical user interface) and functionality makes it easier to handle performance tuning and maintenance issues, especially in a large-scale deployment environment. Keep the following design considerations in mind as you go through the design process:

- Support personalized views: The portal may provide users with the ability to customize their portal view. For example, users can choose not to display a certain portlet, change the color of another portlet, or choose a different language.
- Support self-service applications: You will identify the self-publishing areas where you give users the ability to add contents to the portal.
- Provide easily manageable architecture: You can integrate other related and needed corporate systems (Web applications, client-server applications, and mainframe applications).
- Provide secure access to the portal information (information included in the portal itself and information in the external integrated applications as well) and protect your information from being hacked. Each group of users gets access to its relevant information (nothing more and nothing less).

You can break down the design phase into three processes, discussed in the following sections.

Portal User Interface Design

The user interface (UI) design is where you come up with your portal Web pages, how the navigation is done, what UI components will be used for interaction with the user, and so on.

You start here by identifying your portal navigation model, portlets, banners, and so forth. When you design a portal user interface, try to follow these guidelines:

1. Be different: You need to provide your portal with a unique and attractive look that is not identical to other Web sites or portals.
2. Use consistent and clear terminology: To avoid confusing portal users, use the same terms across the whole portal. Portal users should validate these terms. If abbreviations must be used, all users should understand them.
3. Use a consistent navigation model: The goal is for users to be able to move easily back and forth from one portal area to another. Try to avoid redundant shortcuts because they tend to confuse the user more than help him or her. There is one exception to that guideline: The redundant shortcut may be needed to simplify a task and should be kept, as much as possible, consistent. Always have a home link, which takes the user back to his or her home page.

4. Organize your portal for all types of users: If your portal is used by different groups of users, the portal obviously should convey who the intended groups of users of each portal area are. For example, you could have a portal with three different groups of users accessing it: customers, webmasters, and partners.
5. Be consistent and careful in using graphics: Each graphic in the portal has to serve a purpose. Do not include graphic items that have no purpose. Such items tend to distract users from the main objective of the portal and will slow your portal display time.
6. Decide what your users (before authentication) or public users will see when they navigate to your portal.
7. Consider all your deployment devices: Browsers, PDAs, and cellular phones all have different displays, which affects your interface design.

Portal Data Design

In this part you design your database (if it does not already exist). This phase is similar to traditional database application design, where you need to identify your table, views, indexes, sequences, constraints, and so forth.

Portal Functional Design

In this part you will need to design the objects, functions, or packages needed to implement your Web providers and server-side business logic.

Portal Building

Build a pilot or a prototype first and then run it by the end-users. Based on users' feedback, revisit your design and analysis. This book mainly covers building and delivering portals.

Portal Testing

Testing should be considered up front. A test plan should be developed and followed to quality-assure the portal. The testing process should start in the design phase by cross-checking the design with the system requirements to make sure that there are no requirements left out. If more than one developer is building the portal, each should test his or her portal units. Also, an integration testing should be performed to make sure that all of these portal units work correctly together to satisfy the portal system requirements.

Portal Delivery

When you think you have covered all of the main portal system requirements, you can deliver your portal to its users, or what we can call deploying the portal. This does not mean that the development is over. Usually, due to budget limitations, time constraints, market competition, and so on, not all the requirements make it to the building phase, so the development is broken down into stages, editions, phases, or releases. So after the first stage is done, you start monitoring your portal, collecting feedback from its users and incorporating this information into the second phase requirements.

Portal Maintenance

You are not done yet. Even though your portal is in production and your end-users are starting to use it, this does not mean you are no longer responsible for it. You need to monitor your portal, collect usage statistics, get user feedback, fix bugs, and upgrade hardware and software pieces as needed.

Now you have an idea about portals and Oracle Portal. Let's start by installing the software.

CHAPTER 2

Installing Oracle 9*i* Application Server and Configuring Oracle Portal on Microsoft Windows NT/2000

Introduction

A database instance is needed to host your Oracle Portal objects; for Oracle Portal 3 this instance needs to be Oracle Database 8.1.6.2 Enterprise Edition (Oracle8*i* EE Release 2), Oracle Database 8.1.7 Standard Edition (Oracle8*i* SE Release 3), Oracle Database 8.1.7 Enterprise Edition, or Oracle 9*i* Database. Oracle 8.0 is not supported; you need an Oracle8*i* database as your Oracle Portal node because Oracle Portal makes extensive use of Oracle8*i* PL/SQL features like native dynamic SQL, bulk collect, autonomous transactions, and nested tables and objects in addition to new features that are exposed through Java.

This chapter takes you through the database installation and configuration to prepare it for the Oracle Portal. This chapter covers the installation of Oracle9*i* Application Server—which includes Oracle Portal—on Windows NT/2000. The installation of Oracle9*i* Application Server on UNIX is covered in Chapter 17.

Important

If you need to go with the 8.1.6 database as your Oracle Portal node, you need to apply the 8.1.6.2 patch or a later patch, because Oracle9*i* Application Server version 1.0.2 is certified with 8.1.6.2.

Getting Prepared

There are some points to take care of before we proceed with the database installation and then the O9*i* Application Server installation. These details are needed to avoid problems in the installation (especially in the O*i*9AS installation).

Hostname

The hostname of the machine that will hold your O9*i*AS needs to be in lowercase letters. You can check your hostname either by going to the DOS prompt and executing the command HOSTNAME, or by going to Control Panel → System → Network Identification tab (Figure 2.1). If you need to change your hostname, this is the right time. Click on "Properties" in the Network Identification tab (Figure 2.2). Also, if your server is part of a network domain (e.g., elmallah.com) you need to make sure it is specified in lowercase letters by clicking on the "More" button (Figure 2.3). If you are not part of a network domain, leave this primary DNS (domain name system) suffix empty.

Now your full computer name is in lowercase letters (e.g., myportal.elmallah.com).

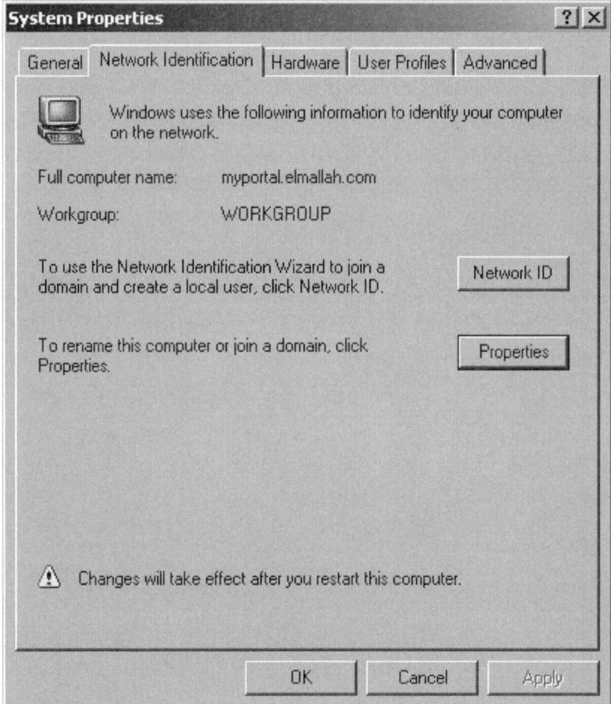

Figure 2.1 Windows 2000 Control Panel: System: Network Identification.

Note

If you changed the server name or its DNS suffix, you will need to reboot the server.

Figure 2.2 Windows 2000 Control Panel: System: Network Identification Properties.

DNS Suffix and NetBIOS Computer Name

Primary DNS suffix of this computer:

elmallah.com

Change primary DNS suffix when domain membership changes

NetBIOS computer name:

MYPORTAL

This name is used for interoperability with older computers and services.

OK Cancel

Figure 2.3 Network Identification Properties: DNS Suffix.

Important

On Microsoft Windows NT 4.0, you can change the computer name by going to Control Panel → Network → Identification tab. By clicking on the "Change" button, you can specify a different name for the computer. Also, you can change the hostname and its domain by going to the Protocols tab and choosing the TCP/IP Protocol. Click on the "Properties" button, then change the Host Name and the Domain values in the DNS tab.

Hardware Requirements

- 128MB RAM or more
- From 1GB–5GB free disk space (refer to the section on installation types)

Software Requirements

- Microsoft Windows NT/2000 or Microsoft NT 4.0 with Service Pack 3 or higher (except Service Pack 4 because it has some TCP/IP issues)
- Oracle9*i*AS version 1.0.2.2 requires Windows 2000 Service Pack 1
- 360MB or more virtual memory (You can change the virtual memory on Windows NT 4.0 by going to Control Panel → System → Performance tab and on Windows NT/2000 by going to Control Panel → System → Advanced → Performance Options.)

Database Installation

Before installing Oracle Portal you need an Oracle database to store the Oracle Portal objects. This section takes you through installing the Oracle database server and creating an Oracle database. If you already have an Oracle database up and running, you can skip this section and go to the section on configuring a database for Oracle Portal.

This section is intended to provide you with the detailed step-by-step experience of installing the Oracle 8*i* Enterprise Edition Release 3 (version 8.1.7) database on Windows 2000. If you will be installing another version of the database, such as Oracle8*i* Release 2 or Oracle9*i*, the process should be very similar. In Chapter 17, I will cover installing Oracle8*i* and O9*i*AS on UNIX. Once you insert the Oracle CD, the autorun starts (Figure 2.4). If for any reason the autorun screen does not come up, you can run the Windows Explorer and double click on ***setup.exe*** on the CD.

Next, click on "Install/Deinstall Products". This starts the Oracle Universal Installer (Figure 2.5). Unless you want to deinstall products or look up the current installed products, you should proceed by clicking on "Next" to choose a name and location of your Oracle Home (Figure 2.6). By default, the Oracle Home name given by the Oracle Installer is OraHome81, and the drive chosen is the drive with the largest free space. Earlier versions of the Oracle installers name the default Oracle home "DEFAULT_HOME". The default Oracle Home location is

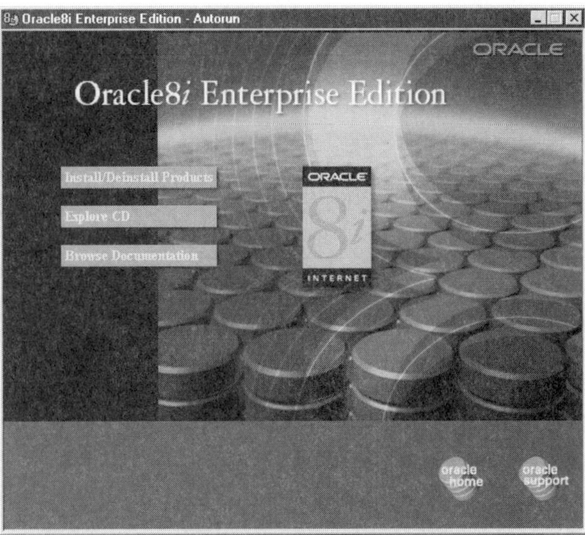

Figure 2.4 Oracle8*i* CD Autorun.

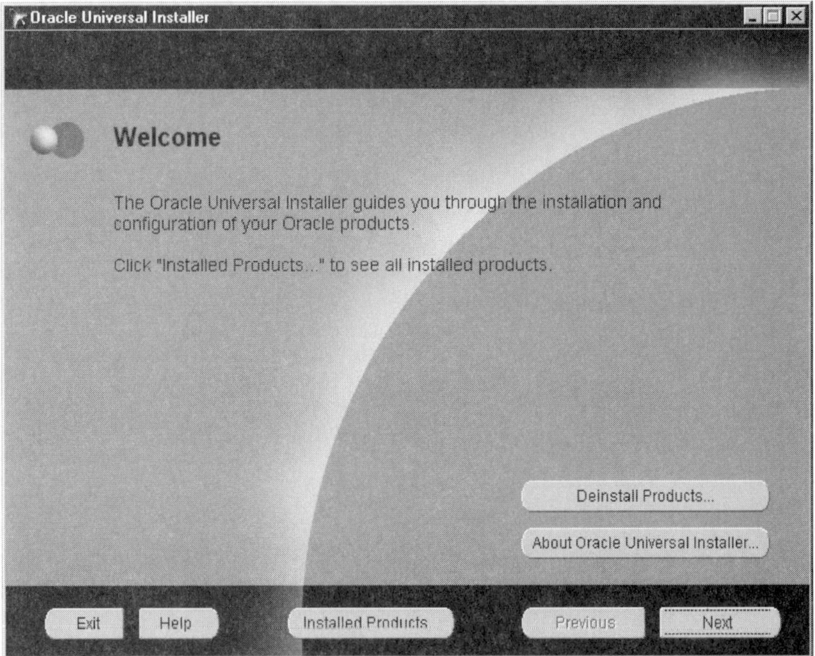

Figure 2.5 Oracle Universal Installer: Welcome.

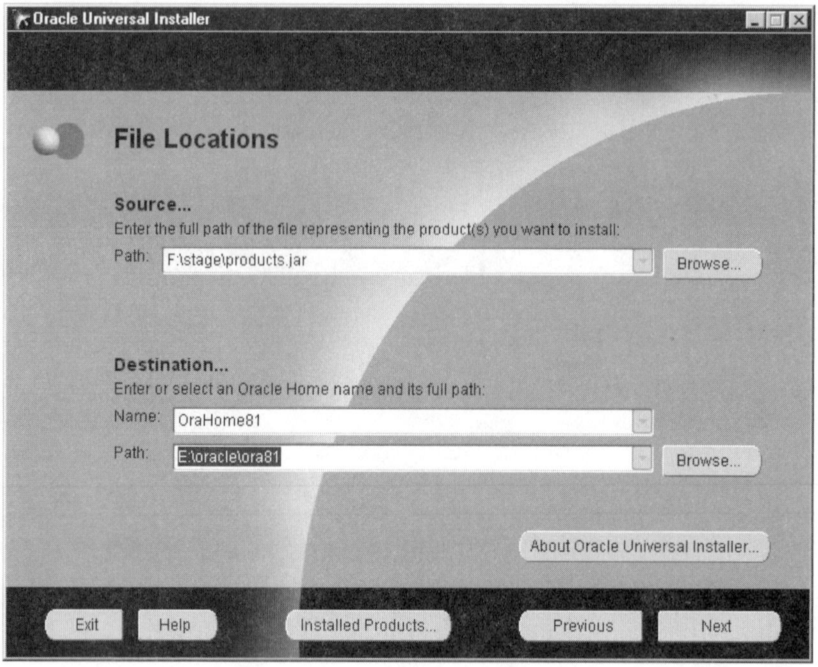

Figure 2.6 Oracle Universal Installer: File Locations.

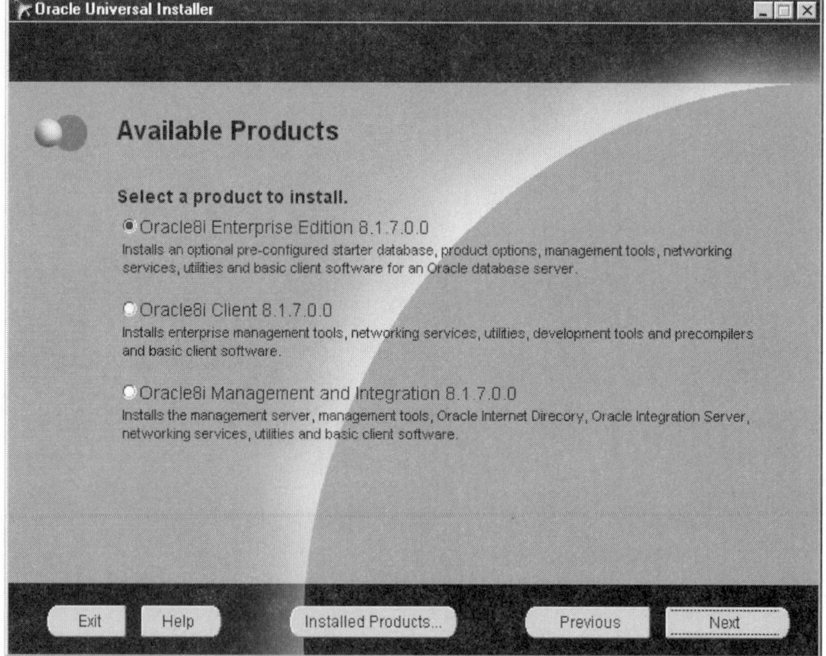

Figure 2.7 Oracle Universal Installer: Available Products.

<C>:\Oracle\Ora81. Unless you want to change the name or the location, you should proceed by clicking on "Next"; the Oracle Installer takes a minute or two to load the products list, and then it displays the Available Products screen (Figure 2.7). The Oracle Home of the Database (e.g., c:\Oracle\Ora81) is referred to as <DB_ORACLE_HOME> throughout this book.

You need to keep the default choice, which is "Oracle8*i* Enterprise Edition 8.1.7.0.0", to install the server software and create the starter database that will be used as the Oracle Portal node. By clicking on "Next", you are taken to Installation Types. For the sake of simplicity, choose Typical installation (Figure 2.8). I recommend having around 2GB of free space in your installation drive before you install Oracle8*i* EE Release 3. This space is needed for both the Oracle Server installation as well as the typical database that will be created. The minimum required free space is less than 2GB, but having extra free space is always a good idea for future upgrades and database expansion. These 2GB do not include the space needed for the O9*i*AS.

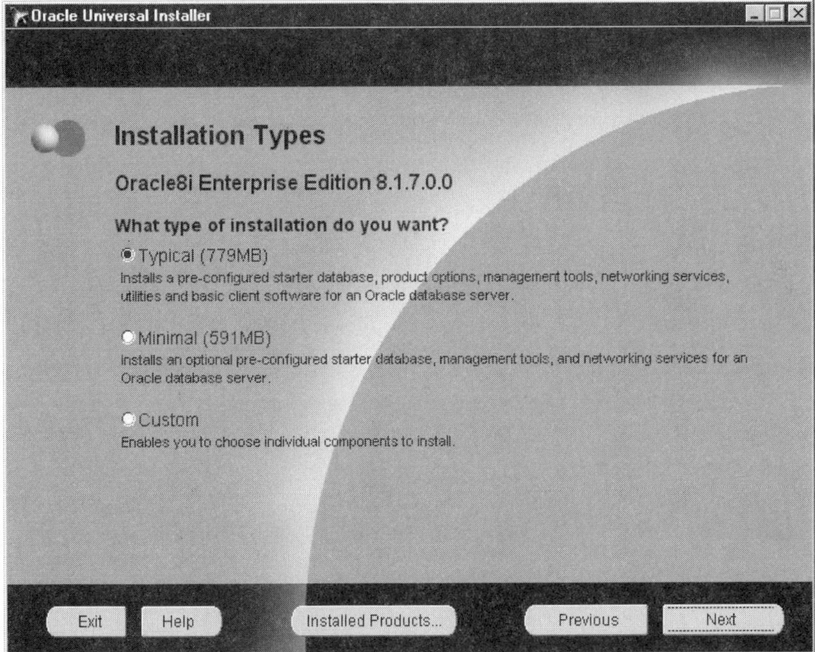

Figure 2.8 Oracle Universal Installer: Installation Types.

Note

If your ORACLE HOME is not on the same drive as your Windows system files, you need to have around 100MB of free space on the Windows system drive (e.g., C:).

Once you click "Next" the installer starts setting up the installation types and executing prerequisites to prepare a list of the products to be installed as part of your typical installation. This process may take a few minutes depending on your hardware speed. Then you are prompted to supply the global database name, which includes the domain name. ORCL.WORLD is used as the global database name in this book. The installer is smart enough to pick only the first portion of the global name (i.e., ORCL) and assign it to the Oracle SID (System IDentifier) automatically (Figure 2.9).

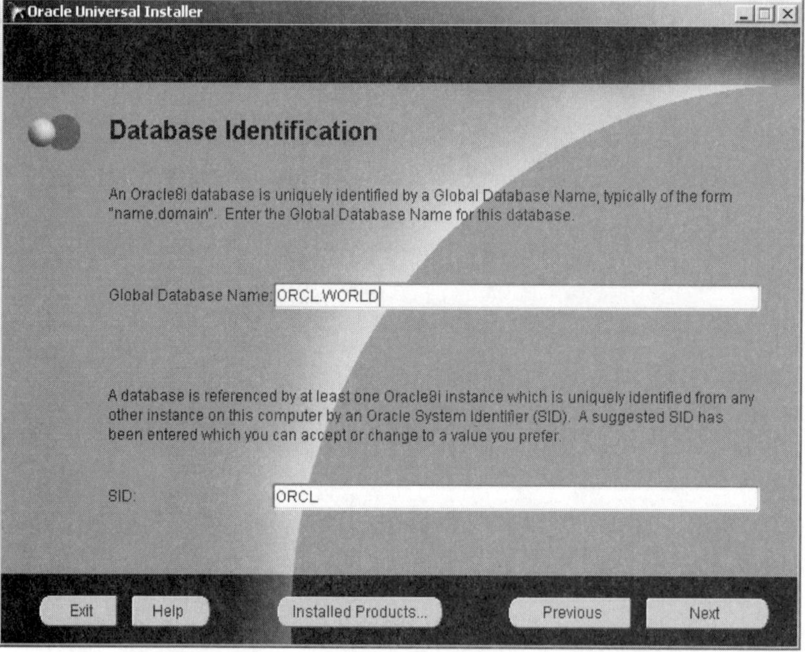

Figure 2.9 Oracle Universal Installer: Database Identification.

When you click on "Next", a summary of the products to be installed is displayed (Figure 2.10). By clicking on "Install", the installation process starts copying the software to your machine (Figure 2.11). The installation process may take about 30 minutes, depending on your hardware. Then the typical installation automatically launches both the Net8 Configuration Assistant and the Oracle Database Configuration Assistant. These tools configure the networking

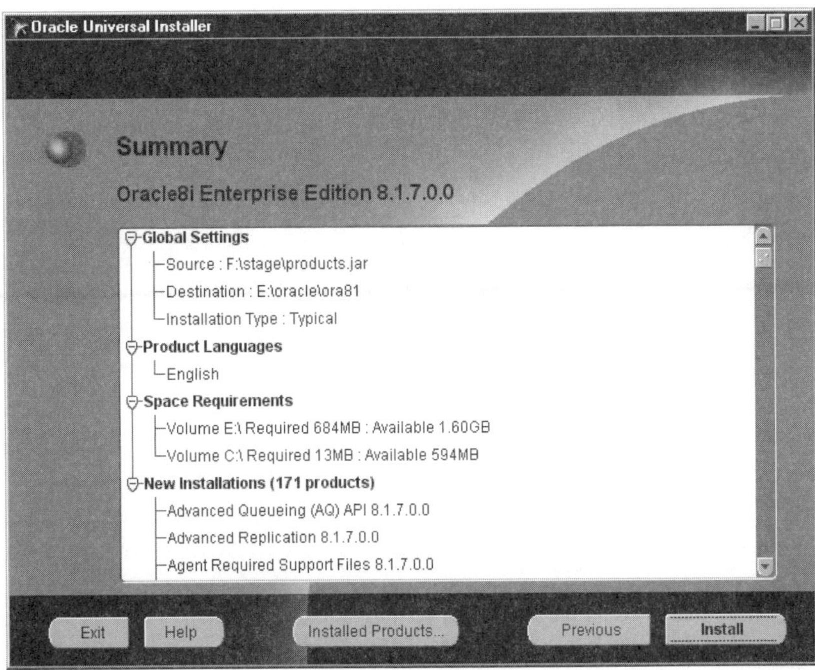

Figure 2.10 Oracle Universal Installer: Summary.

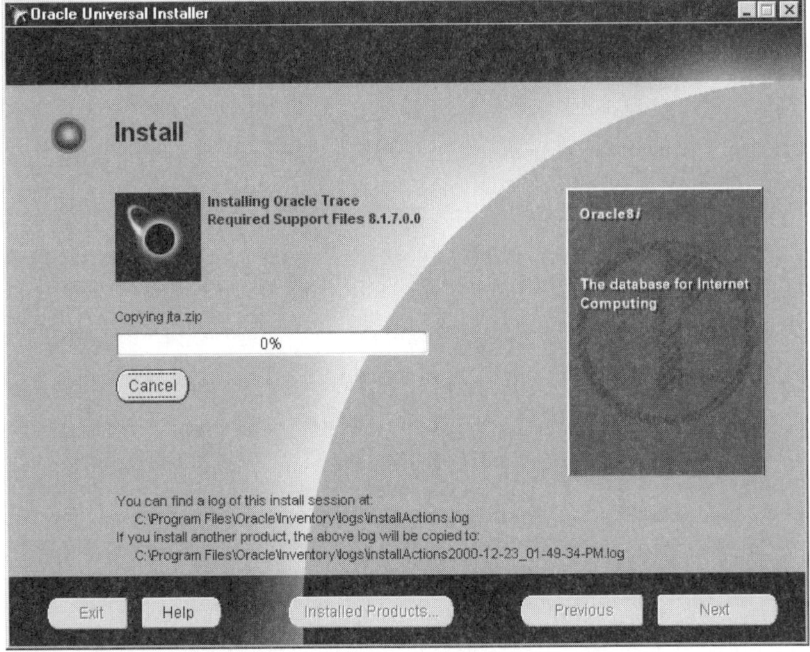

Figure 2.11 Oracle Universal Installer: Install.

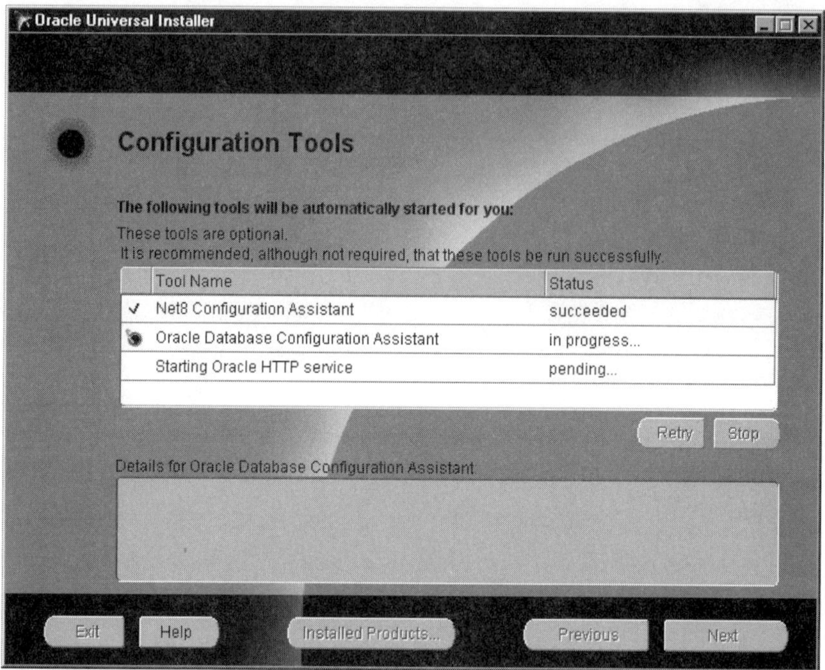

Figure 2.12 Oracle Universal Installer: Configuration Tools.

services and create the database (Figure 2.12). The Oracle Database Configuration Assistant copies the database starter files from the Oracle8*i* CD to the hard disk (Figure 2.13). Usually this operation is faster than creating the files from scratch, because the files are restored from the CD with all the default options preinstalled (e.g., Procedural and Java Option) rather than running the installation scripts (e.g., catproc.sql and initjvm.sql).

Important

Oracle Server 8.1.7 has an Oracle HTTP service, which does not exist in earlier database versions. This service is not needed for Oracle Portal, because Oracle Portal—as a part of Oracle *internet* Application Server—comes with its own Oracle HTTP service. I recommend you stop this service and make sure that it does not start automatically when the server is rebooted, as it can cause port numbers to conflict with the O9*i* Application Server HTTP service. Also, when this installation session is finished, you can uninstall this HTTP server. Click on "Deinstall Products" and select only the "Oracle HTTP Server" check box. It is a good idea to delete the Apache directory under <DB_ORACLE_HOME>.

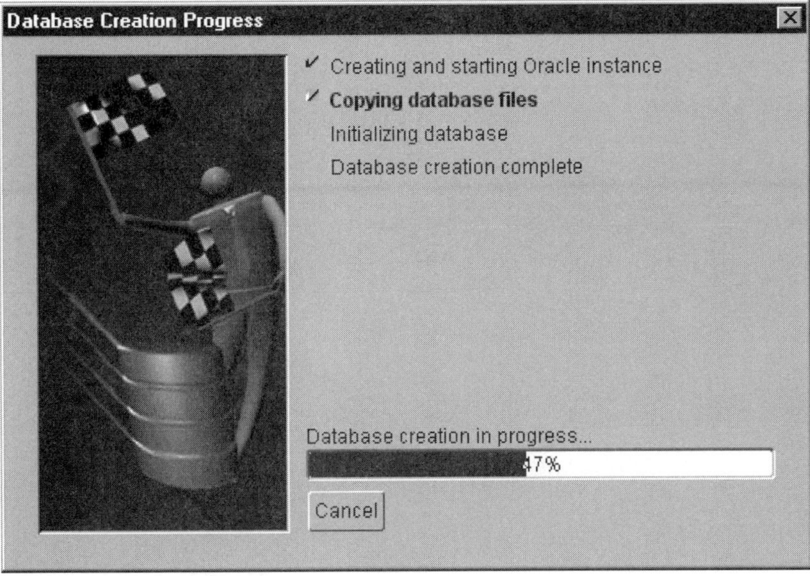

Figure 2.13 Database Creation Progress.

If the database creation and server installation are performed successfully, the installer prompts you with success messages (Figure 2.14 and Figure 2.15). To confirm that the database installation was performed successfully, you can test the connection to the database by logging on using the SQL*Plus (Figure 2.16, Figure 2.17, and Figure 2.18).

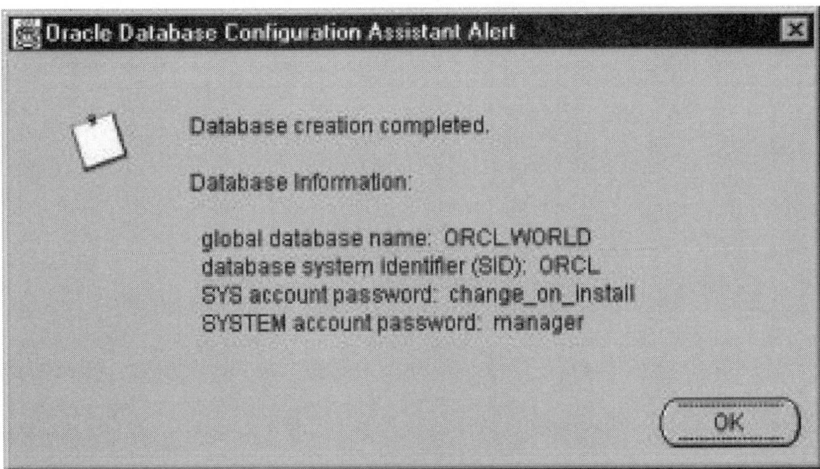

Figure 2.14 Database Creation Completed.

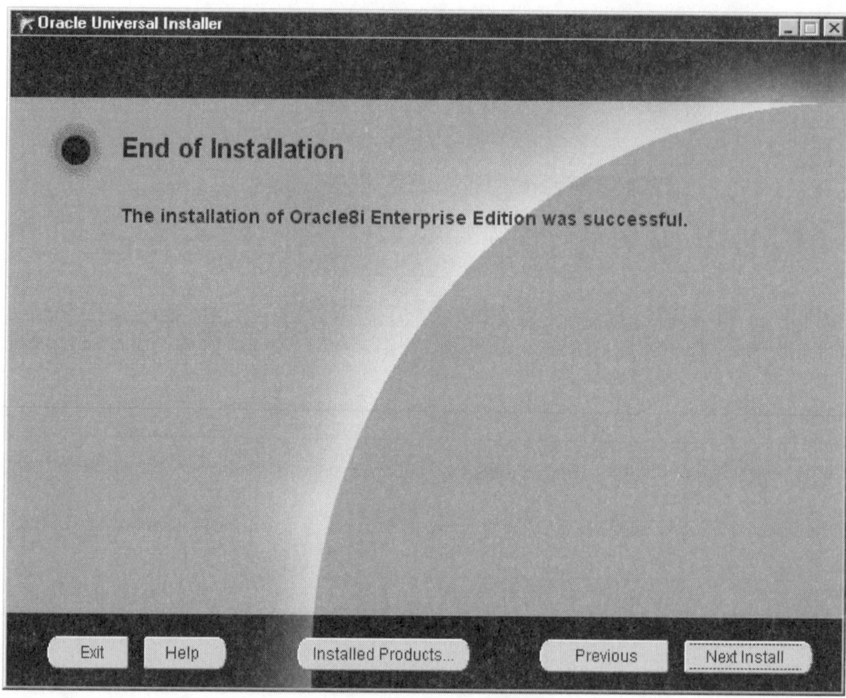

Figure 2.15 Oracle Universal Installer: End of Installation.

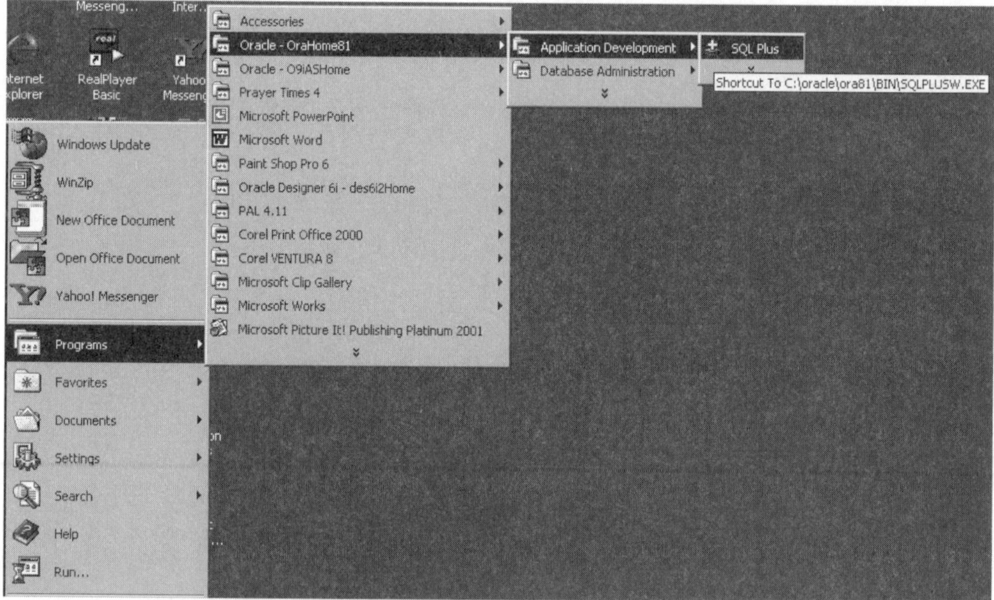

Figure 2.16 Starting SQL*Plus.

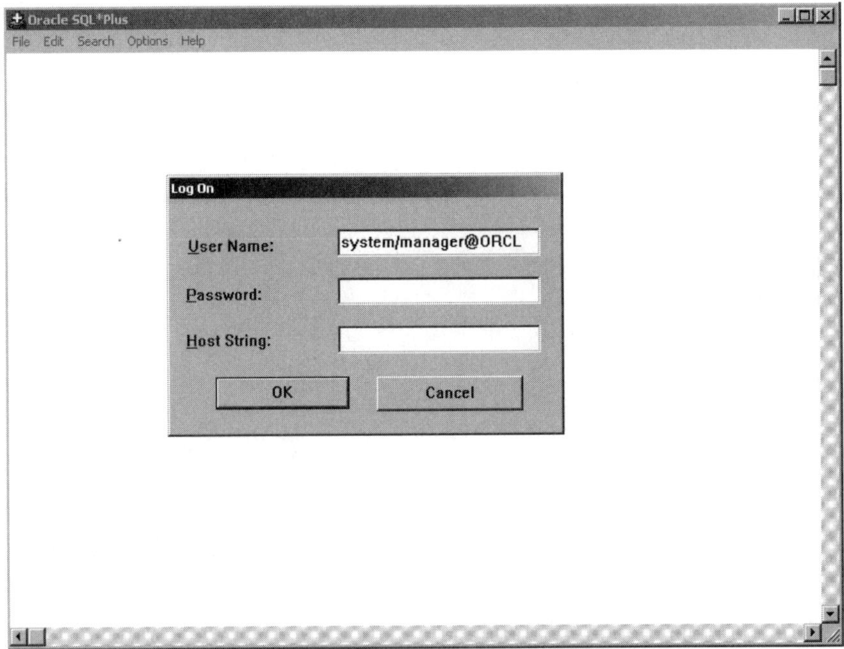

Figure 2.17 SQL*Plus Log On.

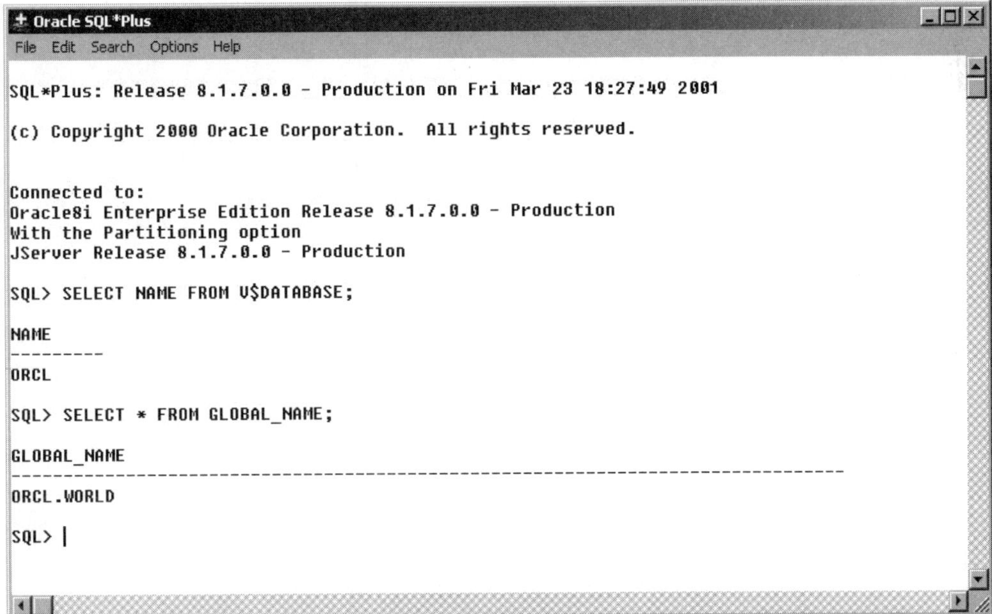

Figure 2.18 SQL*Plus: Checking Database Connectivity.

Configuring a Database for Oracle Portal

In this section you prepare the database for Oracle Portal installation. You can consider this section as Oracle Portal preinstallation instructions. This section uses the Oracle DBA studio to perform the needed administration tasks (Figure 2.19).

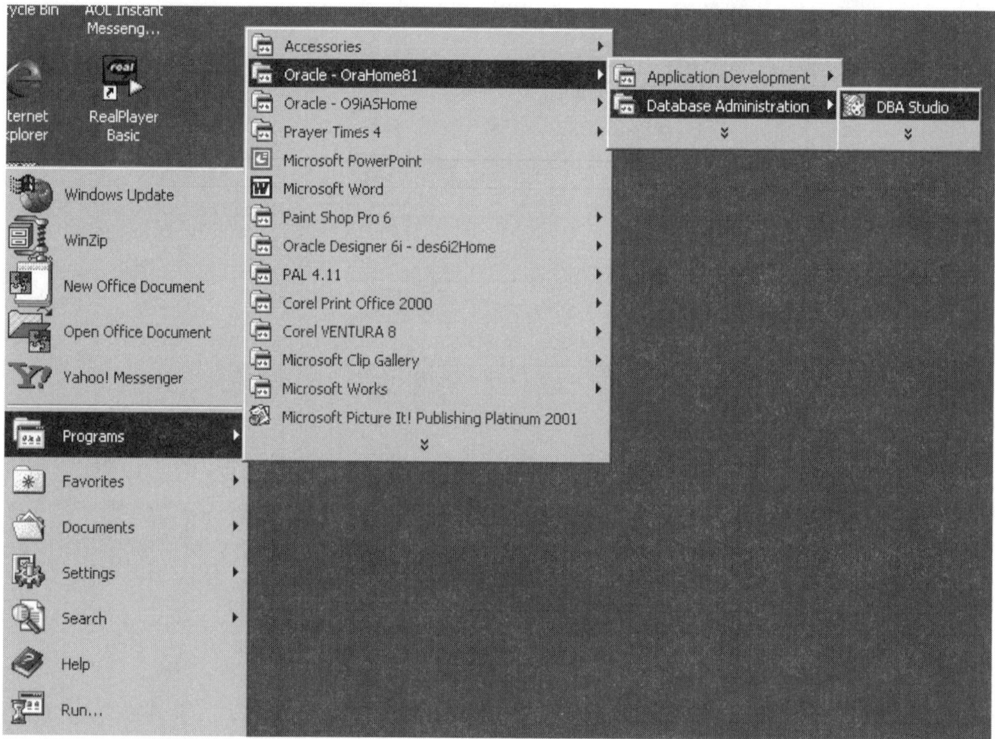

Figure 2.19 Running DBA Studio.

Start the DBA studio in standalone mode. If you have set up Oracle Management Server, you can use the "Login to the Oracle Management Server" option (Figure 2.20). By clicking on "OK" the DBA studio displays the current services defined in the local tnsnames.ora file (Figure 2.21). Once you click "OK" in the listener services, you are routed to the DBA studio main navigator. When you click on the ORCL instance node, you are prompted to log on to the database. Use a DBA account (e.g., SYSTEM), because you need to perform administration tasks on the database, such as expanding the SYSTEM tablespace (Figure 2.22). You can check the "Save As Local Preferred Credentials" check box, which saves the username and password encrypted locally so you do not have to log in each time you run DBA studio.

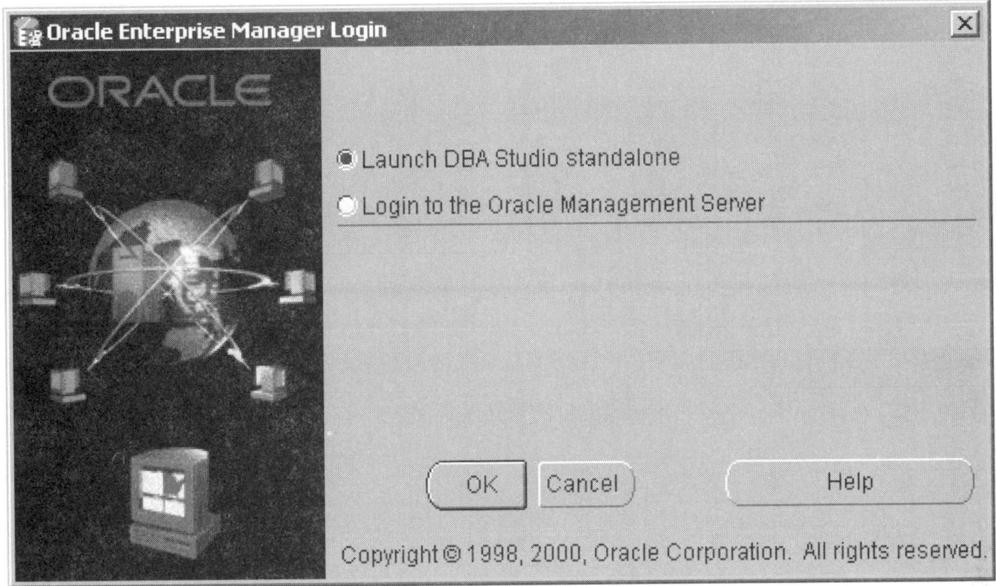

Figure 2.20 DBA Studio Login.

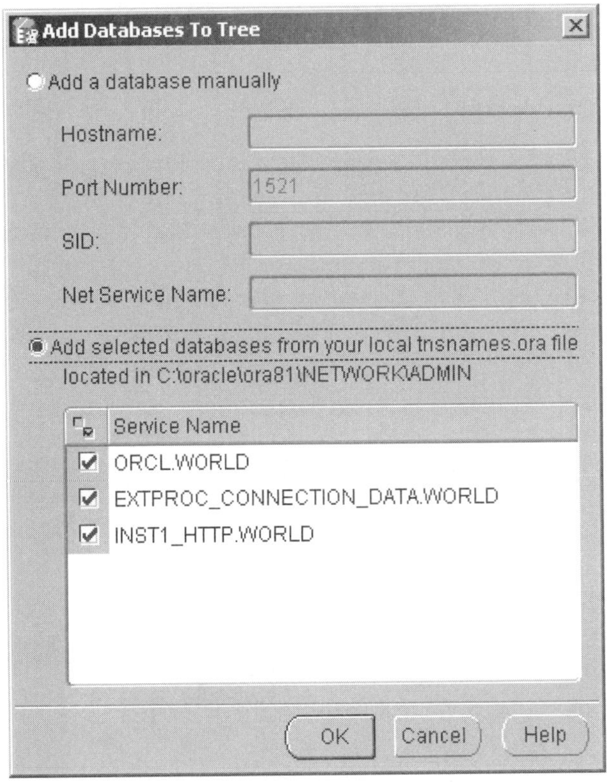

Add Databases To Tree

Add a database manually

Hostname:

Port Number: 1521

SID:

Net Service Name:

Add selected databases from your local tnsnames.ora file located in C:\oracle\ora81\NETWORK\ADMIN

	Service Name
☑	ORCL.WORLD
☑	EXTPROC_CONNECTION_DATA.WORLD
☑	INST1_HTTP.WORLD

OK Cancel Help

Figure 2.21
DBA Studio Services Selection.

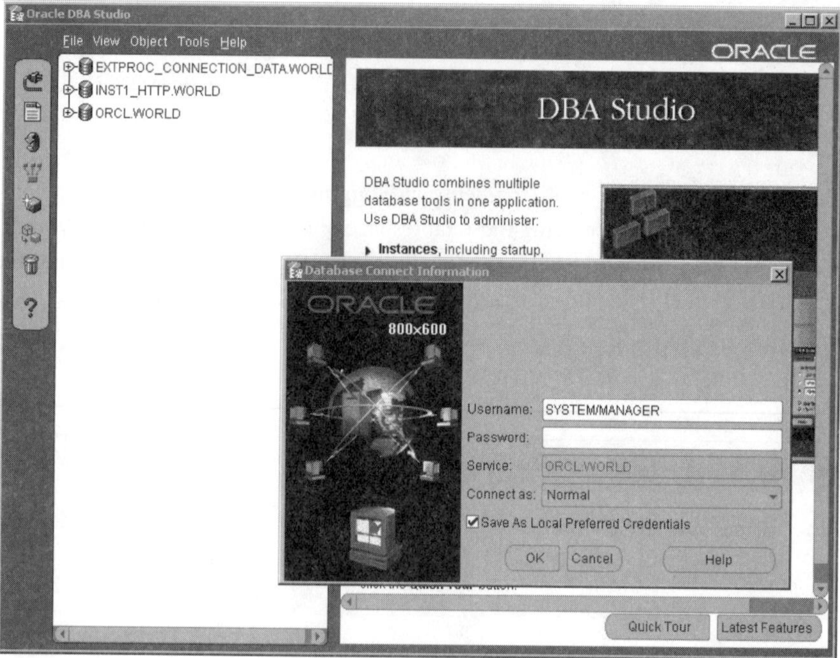

Figure 2.22 DBA Studio: Database Authentication.

When you click on the ORCL instance, Storage node, and then the Tablespaces nodes, a list of the instance tablespaces is displayed (Figure 2.23). The initial sizes of the tablespaces are different based on the database version and options chosen during the database creation. You need to add a new tablespace to be the default tablespace for the Oracle Portal schema (the default portal schema name is PORTAL30). The minimum size of this tablespace is 150MB. Give yourself more space to move in by creating a 200MB tablespace, because you will be creating Oracle Portal objects that will reside in this tablespace. You can name this tablespace any name you want as

Name	Type	Extent Management	Size (M)	Used (M)	Used %
DRSYS	PERMANENT	DICTIONARY	20.000	4.133	20.66
INDX	PERMANENT	DICTIONARY	20.000	0.008	0.04
RBS	PERMANENT	DICTIONARY	50.000	28.008	56.02
SYSTEM	PERMANENT	DICTIONARY	274.000	265.953	97.06
TEMP	TEMPORARY	DICTIONARY	20.000	0.258	1.29
TOOLS	PERMANENT	DICTIONARY	10.000	0.008	0.08
USERS	PERMANENT	DICTIONARY	20.000	0.008	0.04

Figure 2.23 DBA Studio: Initial Tablespaces.

long as it conforms to the Oracle tablespace naming rules (e.g., the name must not exceed 30 characters). In the book installation example, this tablespace is called OP30_DEF.

Create a separate tablespace for the Oracle Portal documents (e.g., OP30_DOC) and another tablespace for the Oracle Portal Logging (e.g., OP30_LOG). There is no minimum size for these two tablespaces; their sizes depend on how many objects will be created in them. Actually, you can use the OP30_DEF as your documents and logging tablespaces, but it is good practice to separate these tablespaces. By placing these tablespaces into different hard disks, you distribute your reads/writes load. Even if you do not have more than one hard disk, separating the tablespaces is still a good idea for administrative ease. A good starting size for these two tablespaces is 20MB. Also, you need to increase the size of the SYSTEM tablespace, to have a minimum of 150MB free space. Again, give yourself more space to move in and add a 200MB free space in the SYSTEM tablespace.

Note

The minimum tablespace values mentioned are applicable to Oracle Portal 3.0.7.x, 3.0.8.x, and 3.0.9.x, which are part of O9*i*AS 1.0.2.0.x, 1.0.2.1, and 1.0.2.2, respectively. You need to check the installation manual for newer releases. Also, the tablespaces will need to be increased in size as you start creating Oracle Portal objects.

Note

It is a good idea at this time to increase the size of both your TEMP and RBS tablespaces, especially if multi-users will use this Oracle Portal node.

Now your tablespaces list should look something like Figure 2.24.

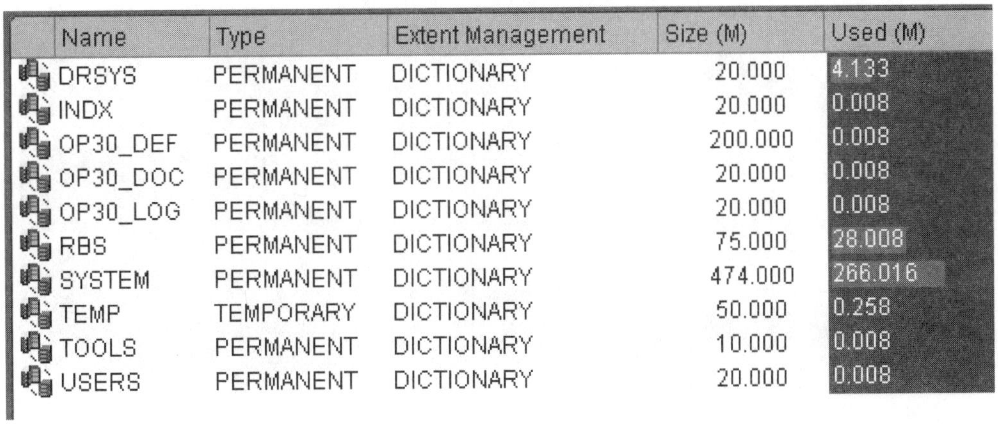

Name	Type	Extent Management	Size (M)	Used (M)
DRSYS	PERMANENT	DICTIONARY	20.000	4.133
INDX	PERMANENT	DICTIONARY	20.000	0.008
OP30_DEF	PERMANENT	DICTIONARY	200.000	0.008
OP30_DOC	PERMANENT	DICTIONARY	20.000	0.008
OP30_LOG	PERMANENT	DICTIONARY	20.000	0.008
RBS	PERMANENT	DICTIONARY	75.000	28.008
SYSTEM	PERMANENT	DICTIONARY	474.000	266.016
TEMP	TEMPORARY	DICTIONARY	50.000	0.258
TOOLS	PERMANENT	DICTIONARY	10.000	0.008
USERS	PERMANENT	DICTIONARY	20.000	0.008

Figure 2.24 DBA Studio: New Tablespaces.

Table 2.1 Initialization Parameter Values Required by Oracle Portal

Parameter Name	Minimum Value	Recommended Value
max_enabled_roles	25	100
open_cursors	50	500
Compatible	8.1.0	8.1.0
java_pool_size	20000000	30000000

The final preinstallation step is to set some of the database initialization parameters. Edit your init.ora file, which is located by default in c:\oracle\admin\ORCL\ pfile. Table 2.1 shows the parameters in need of change. These recommended values are mainly to avoid running out of resources later on while using Oracle Portal. For these new values to take effect, you need to bounce (i.e., reboot) the database. You can stop and start the database from the Windows 2000 services (Control Panel → Administrative Tools → Services), or from SQL*Plus or Server Manager command line (Figure 2.25).

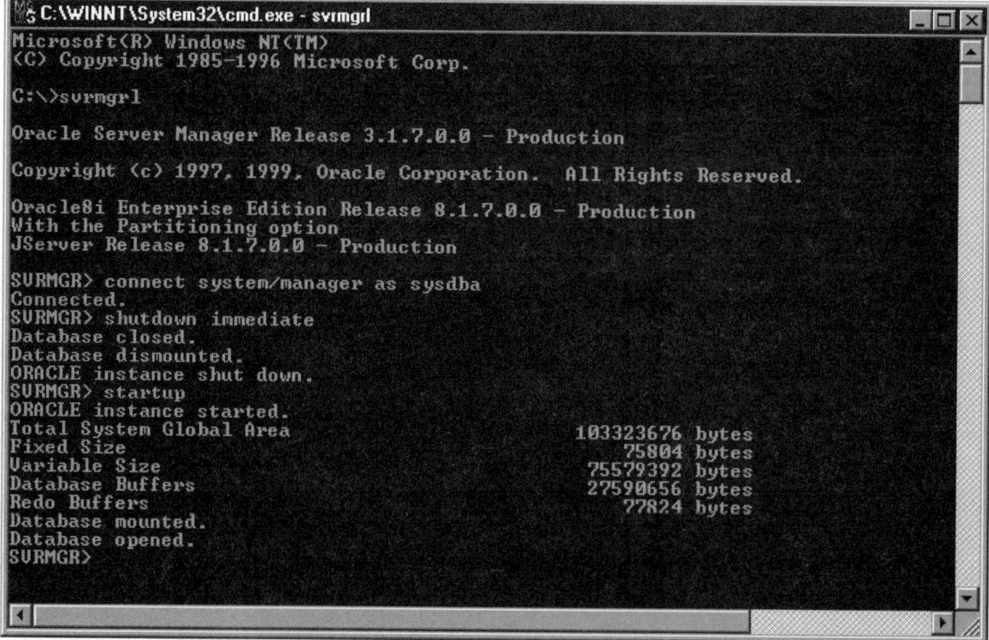

Figure 2.25 Rebooting the Oracle Portal Database.

Oracle Portal Installation

Now it is time to install the Oracle Portal 3 software. As mentioned in Chapter 1, Oracle Portal is part of Oracle9*i* Application Server. When you insert the first O9*i*AS CD, the autorun starts the Oracle Universal Installer automatically, displaying the Welcome window; otherwise it can start by running ***setup.exe*** (Figure 2.26). Click on "Next" and the File Locations window is displayed. Here give the O9*i* Application Server a name and specify its directory location. It is good practice to install the O9*i* Application Server in its own Oracle Home to simplify future O9*i*AS upgrades. O9*i*AS 1.0.2 and Oracle Database Server 8.1.7 can be installed in the same Oracle Home, but upgrading one product will affect the other. O9*i*AS 1.0.2 cannot be installed in the same Oracle Home as Oracle Database Server 8.1.6 because of different versions of library files.

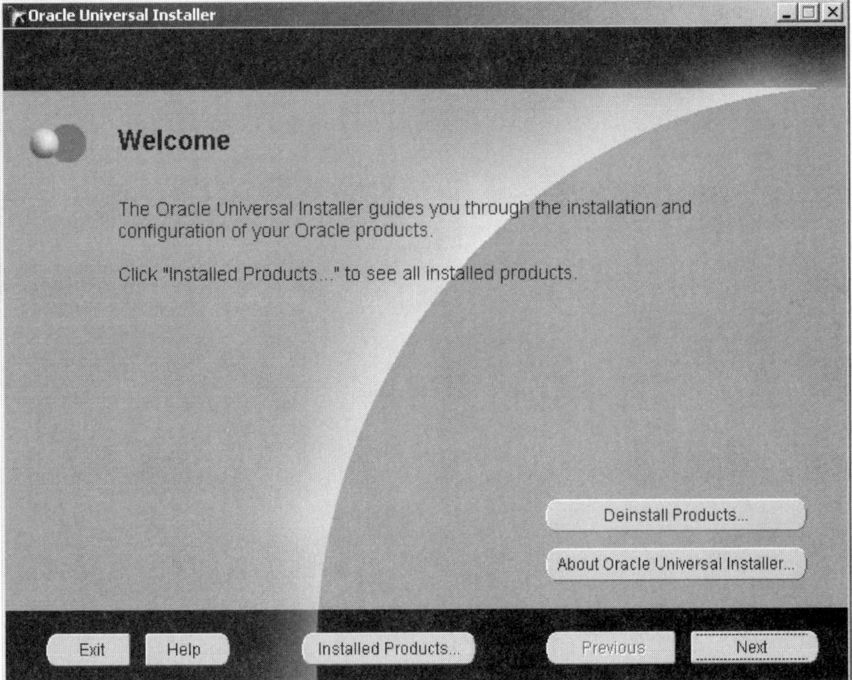

Figure 2.26 O9*i*AS: Oracle Universal Installer: Welcome.

Note

Oracle9*i* Application Server version 1.0.2.2 installer starts by displaying an installation overview screen where you can choose to display additional help during installation.

In the book installation exercise, the D:\Oracle\O9iAS directory was chosen as the O9*i*AS Oracle Home (Figure 2.27). The Oracle Home of Oracle *internet* Application Server is referred to as <iAS_ORACLE_HOME> throughout the book.

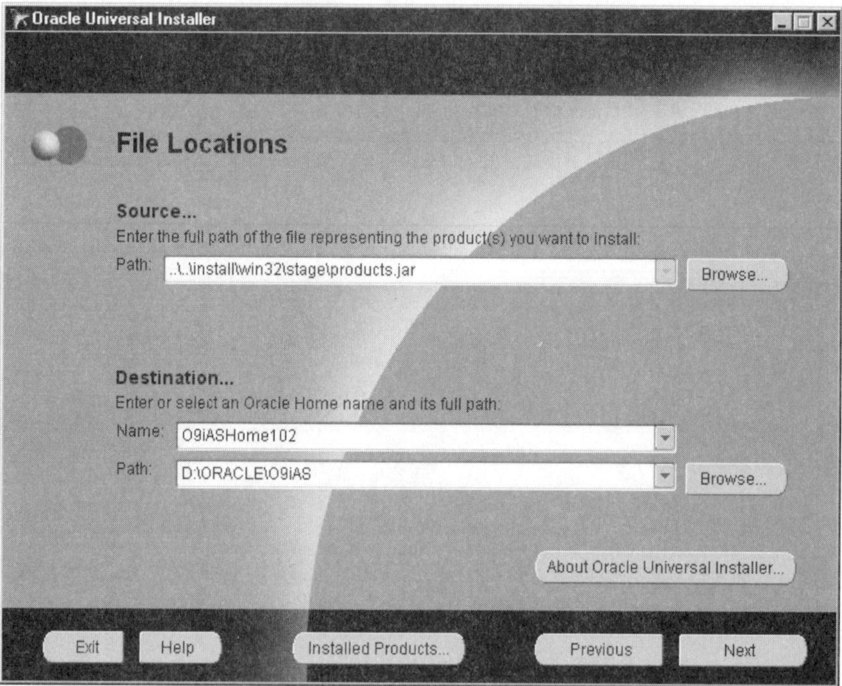

Figure 2.27 O9*i*AS: Oracle Universal Installer: File Locations.

Note

Oracle9*i*AS version 1.0.2.2 renames the File Locations screen Destination Oracle Home and asks for the Oracle Home name.

Next, the installer asks you to choose from three installation types (Figure 2.28). O9*i*AS is composed of many different components, so choose the most suitable type based on what you think you will need. Table 2.2 shows you what components are available with each type. Because Chapter 16 explains how to integrate forms and reports modules into your Oracle Portal, I suggest you choose the Enterprise Edition installation type. The installer displays the minimum space required for each installation type. I recommend having double this space available before you start the installation. This extra free space is needed for the operating system and the O9*i*AS installer to move in (e.g., for expanding files). So, you need to have around 7GB of free space. You do not want your hard disk to be 100% full after you finish your installation, especially if this disk is your system drive (i.e., C:\WINNT).

Note

The exact amount of minimum space required for the different installation types depends on the O9*i*AS version and operating system.

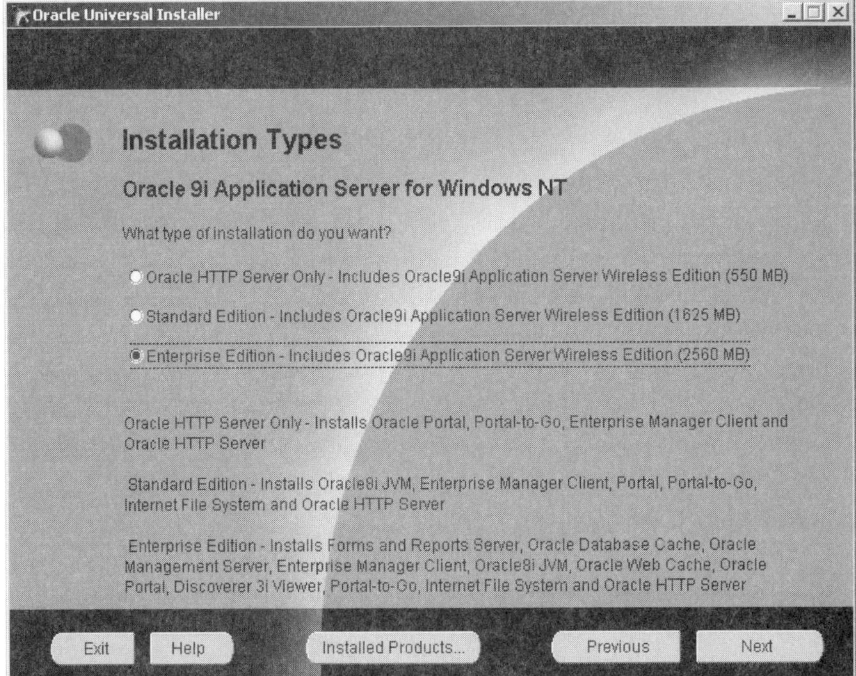

Figure 2.28 O9*i*AS: Oracle Universal Installer: Installation Types.

Note

If you choose Enterprise Edition installation in Oracle9*i*AS version 1.0.2.2, the installer prompts you for the Oracle Home for the 8.0.6-based products (e.g., forms, reports, etc.).

Table 2.2 O9*i*AS Installation Types Comparison

Component	Oracle HTTP Server Only*	Standard Edition	Enterprise Edition
Oracle HTTP Server *powered by Apache*	X	X	X
Oracle Portal	X	X	X
Oracle Portal-to-Go (Oracle9*i*AS wireless)	X	X	X
Oracle Database Cache			X
Oracle Web Cache			X
Oracle Forms Services			X
Oracle Reports Services			X
Oracle Discoverer			X
Oracle Business Components for Java (BC4J)	X	X	X
Oracle Management Server			X
Oracle Enterprise Manager Client	X	X	X
Oracle Internet File System		X	X
Oracle Advanced Security		X	X
Oracle XML Developer's Kit	X	X	X
Oracle LDAP Developer's Kit†		X	X
Oracle8*i* JVM		X	X
Oracle Database Client Developer's Kit	X	X	X
Oracle Plug-in for Microsoft IIS	X	X	X

*In Oracle9*i* Application Server version 1.0.2.2, Oracle HTTP Server Only is called Minimal Edition.
†In Oracle9*i*AS version 1.0.2.2, Oracle LDAP Developer's Kit is available in the Minimal Edition.

The Oracle9*i*AS version 1.0.2.0 installation is a two-step procedure. In the first step, Oracle Universal Installer (OUI) installs some Windows system required files and then reboots the server (Figure 2.29 and Figure 2.30). When rebooted, Windows automatically starts the second installation step by running the OUI again to do the rest of the product installation. The first installation session (i.e., before the reboot) should not take more than a couple of minutes. If the first installation just finishes without rebooting the machine, go ahead and reboot the machine manually. In Oracle9*i*AS version 1.0.2.2, you do not need to reboot Windows in the middle of the installation.

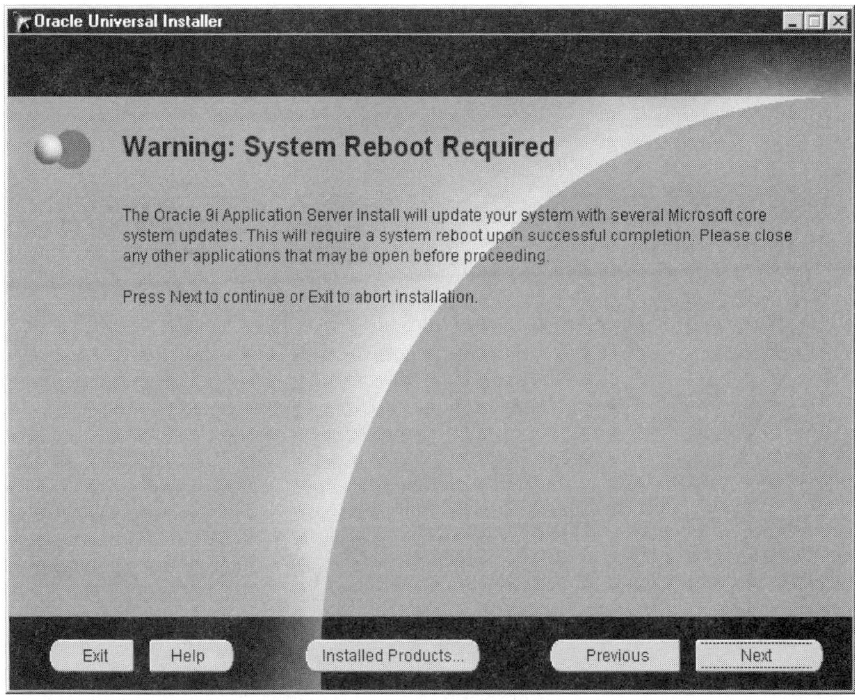

Figure 2.29 Oracle Universal Installer: O9*i*AS: System Reboot Required.

Figure 2.30 Oracle Universal Installer: O9*i*AS: First Installation Session.

Next, the installer starts asking you questions to gather information to be passed to the configuration assistant programs, which will start automatically at the end of the installation. You need to specify the name of the Oracle Portal Data Access Descriptor (DAD). The portal DAD basically defines how the Apache Web server can connect to the database. The default portal DAD name is PORTAL30, and it is created later on by the Oracle Portal Configuration Assistant. For the first-time installation, it is good practice to try to keep the default values until you are more familiar with the product installation. You also need to provide the portal schema name. The portal schema is created later on by the Oracle Portal Configuration Assistant to hold the portal objects. You also need to provide the TNS connect string to connect to the database created earlier to act as the Oracle Portal node (i.e., ORCL; Figure 2.31).

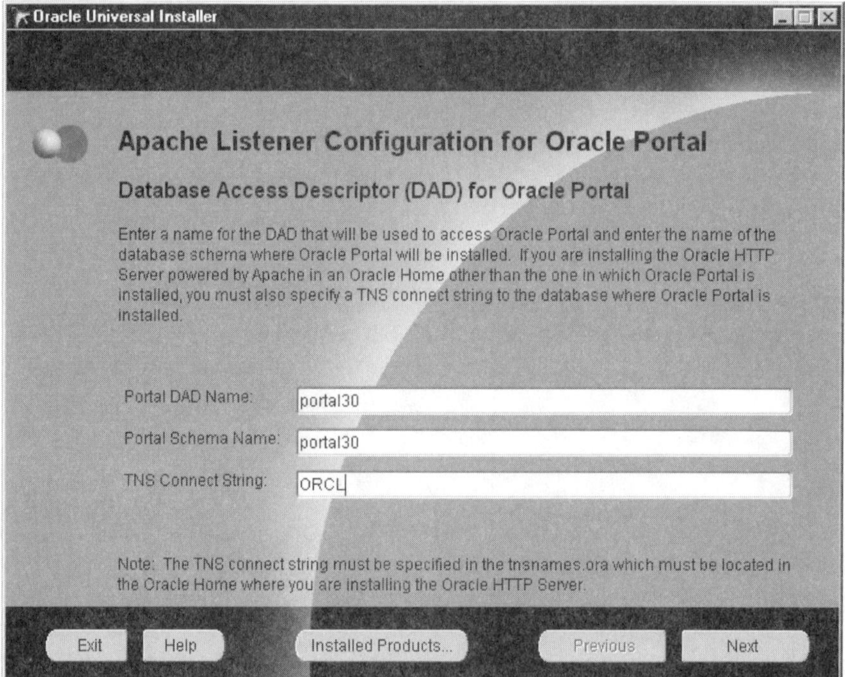

Figure 2.31 Oracle Universal Installer: Apache Listener Configuration: Portal DAD.

Next, you need to specify the name of the Login Server Data Access Descriptor. The Login Server DAD defines how the Apache Web server can connect to the Login Server administration pages. The default Login Server DAD name is PORTAL30_SSO (SSO stands for Single Sign-On). You also need to provide the Login Server schema name. The portal schema is created later on by the Oracle Portal Configuration Assistant to hold the Login Server objects. You also

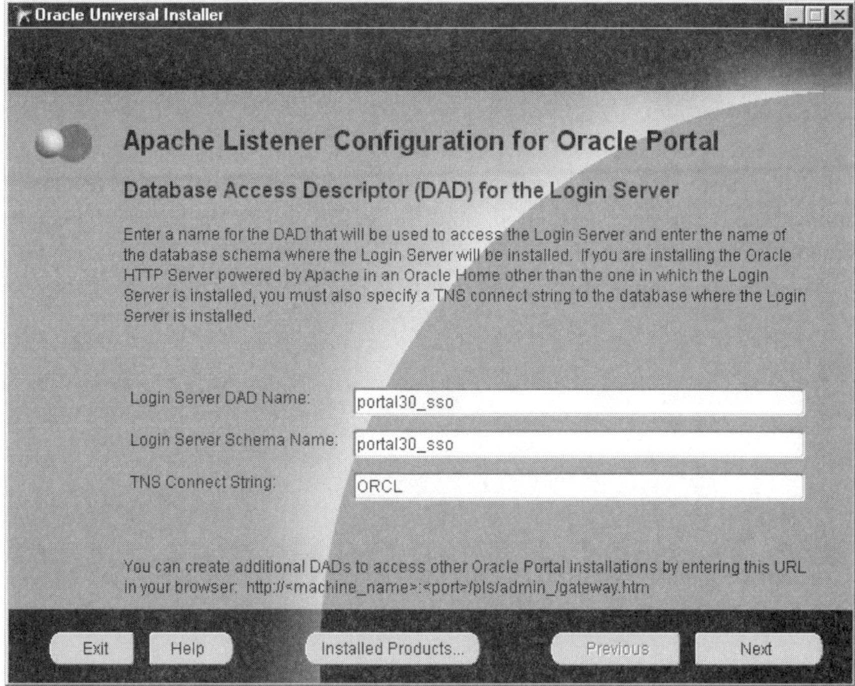

Figure 2.32 Oracle Universal Installer: Apache Listener Configuration: Portal Login Server DAD.

need to provide the TNS connect string to connect to the database that will hold your Login Server (e.g., ORCL; Figure 2.32). For the O9*i*AS products to connect to the Oracle8*i* database created earlier, you need to copy the database connect string entry (i.e., ORCL) from the *<DB_ORACLE_HOME>\network\admin\tnsadmin.ora* to *<iAS_ORACLE_HOME>\network\admin\tnsadmin.ora.*

Here is an example of the ORCL entry:

```
ORCL =
  (DESCRIPTION =
    (ADDRESS_LIST =
      (ADDRESS = (PROTOCOL = TCP)(HOST = myportal)(PORT = 1521))
    )
    (CONNECT_DATA =
      (SERVICE_NAME = ORCL)
    )
  )
```

Oracle Universal Installer

Portal-to-Go repository information

Please enter the hostname.domain, Net8 listener port number and SID of the database where you will install the Portal-to-Go repository.

Hostname MYPORTAL

Port 1521

SID ORCL

Exit Help Installed Products... Previous Next

Figure 2.33 Oracle Universal Installer: Portal-to-Go Repository Information.

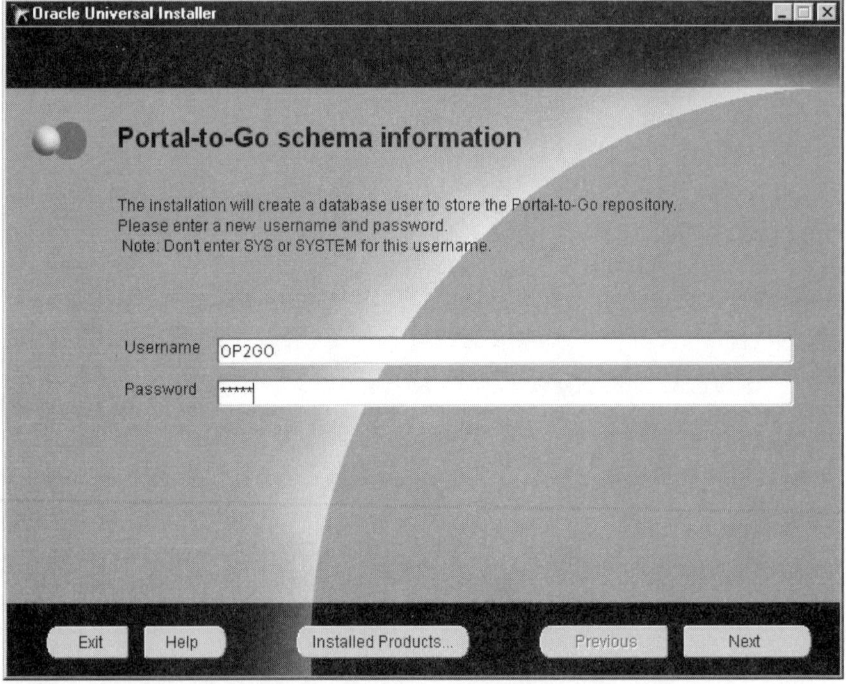

Figure 2.34 Oracle Universal Installer: Portal-to-Go Schema Information.

The next three screens are about Portal-to-Go (i.e., Wireless Edition), which is a different product than Oracle Portal. Even if you are not interested in using Portal-to-Go, provide the information to avoid warnings or errors in the installation. You need to provide the hostname, Net8 listener port (i.e., 1521), and SID of the database that will hold the Portal-to-Go repository (e.g., ORCL; Figure 2.33). Then you need to specify the Portal-to-Go schema username and password. The installer creates this schema to hold the Portal-to-Go objects (Figure 2.34). The installer needs the SYSTEM password (Figure 2.35) to be able to create the Portal-to-Go schema.

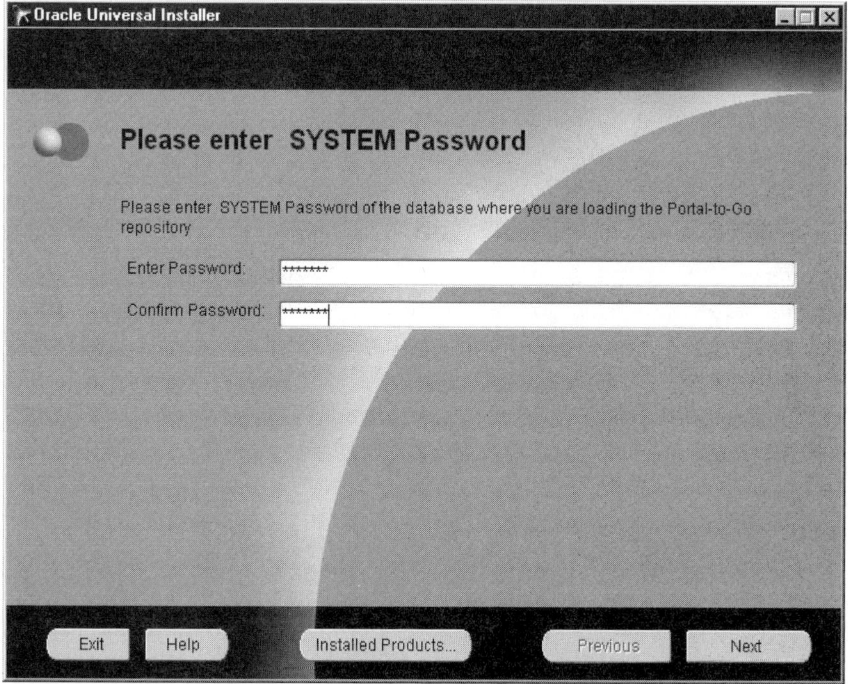

Figure 2.35 Oracle Universal Installer: Portal-to-Go Schema Creation: SYSTEM Password.

When you click on "Next", a Summary screen is displayed with a list of products to be installed (Figure 2.36). By clicking on "Install", the installation process is started (Figure 2.37). This installation (i.e., after the reboot) takes longer than the first installation session. Depending on your server speed, this installation session might take from 15 to 45 minutes. In the second installation session, you are asked to insert the second CD of the O9*i* Application Server (Figure 2.38). Depending on the version of the Oracle9*i*AS, there might be three disks to install. When the installer finishes copying files to the disk, it starts running the configuration tools (Figure 2.39).

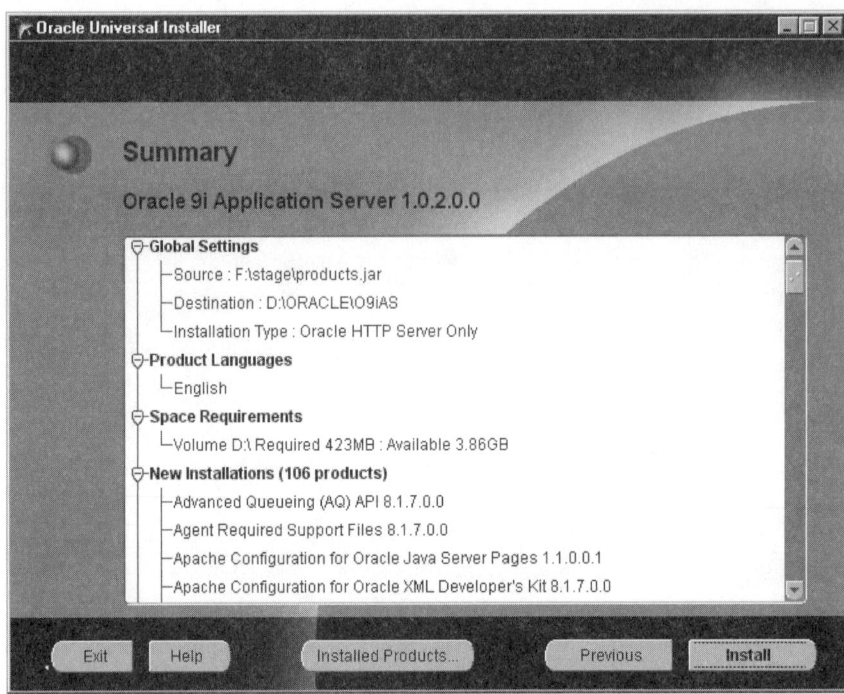

Figure 2.36 Oracle Universal Installer: O9*i*AS: Summary.

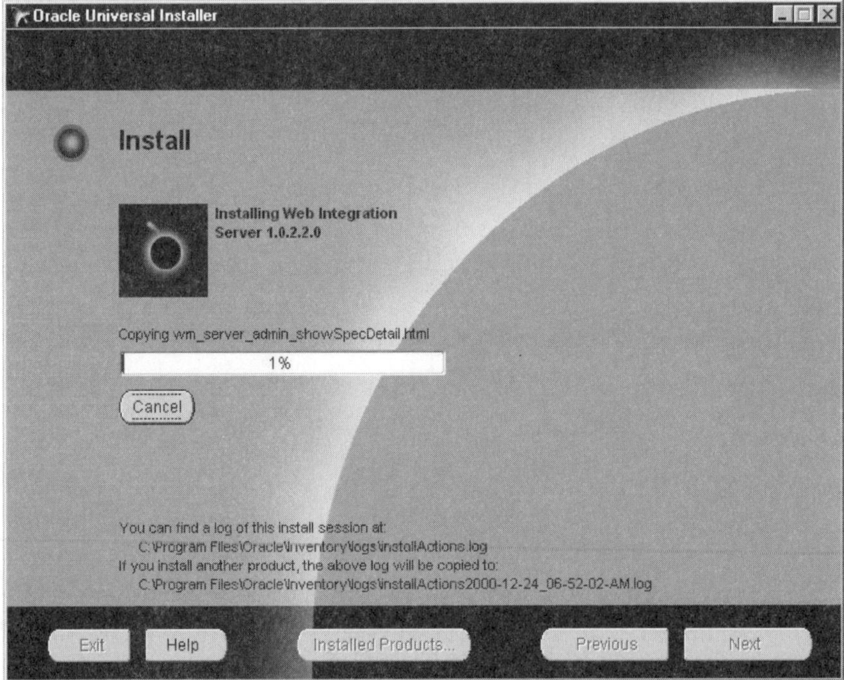

Figure 2.37 Oracle Universal Installer: O9*i*AS: Second Installation Session.

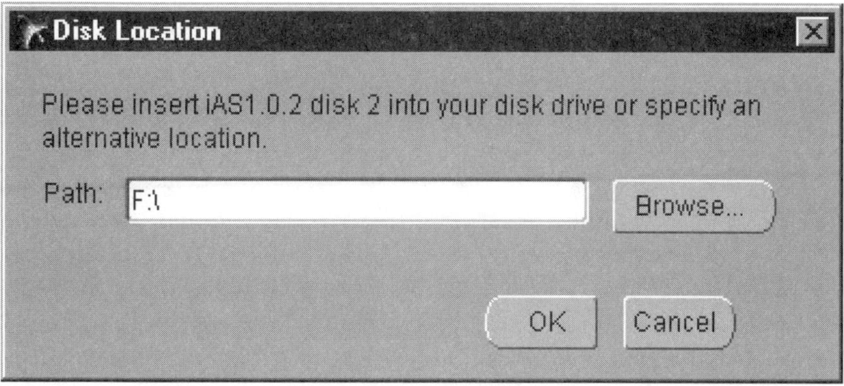

Figure 2.38 Oracle Universal Installer: Second Disk.

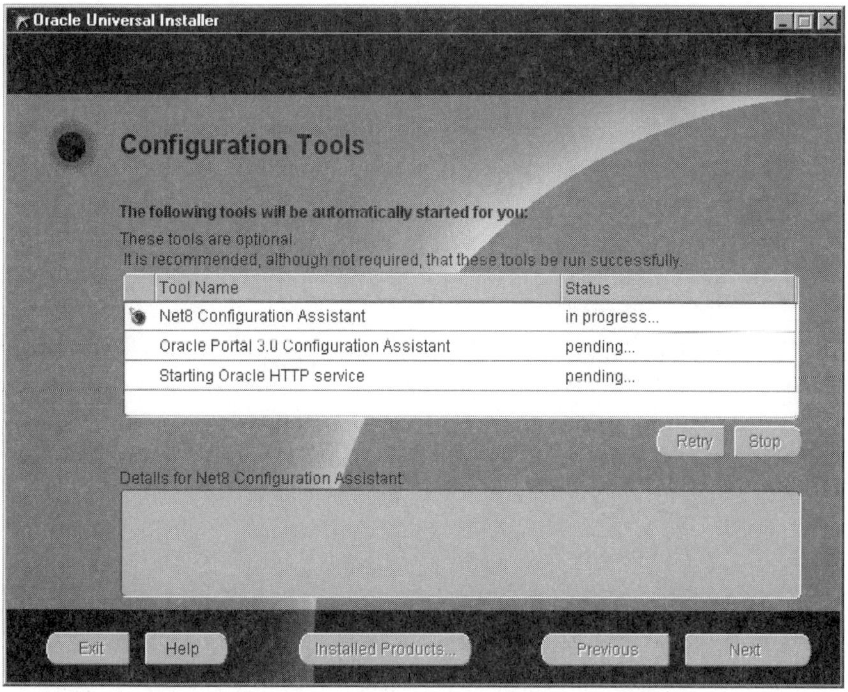

Figure 2.39 Oracle Universal Installer: O9*i*AS: Configuration Tools.

You do not have to configure the O9*i* Application Server Net8 manually. Just make sure that the "Perform typical configuration" check box is checked before you click "Next" (Figure 2.40). The bulk of the Oracle Portal installation is performed by the Oracle Portal Configuration Assistant because the assistant connects to the Oracle Portal database node and creates the Oracle Portal schema and the Login Server schema and their objects (e.g., packages).

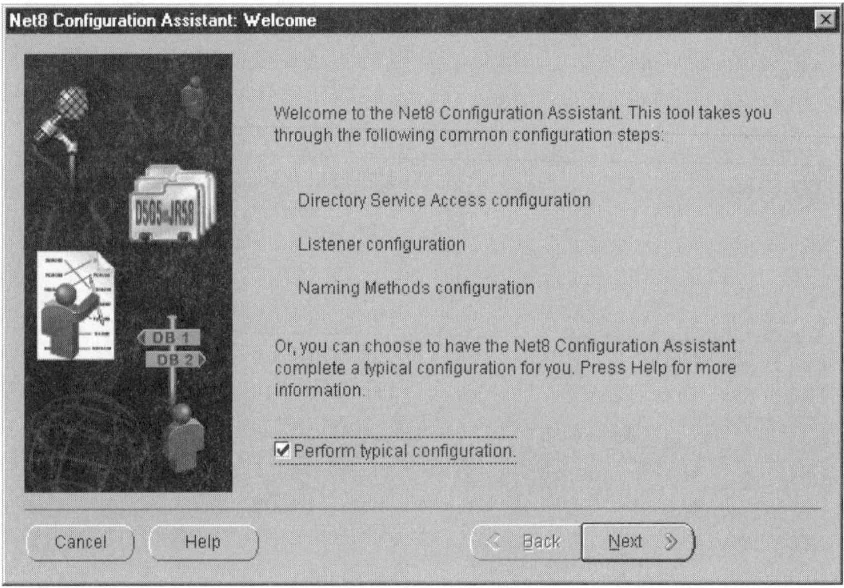

Figure 2.40 Oracle Universal Installer: O9*i*AS: Net8 Configuration Assistant.

The Oracle Portal Configuration Assistant starts by asking if you want to install or drop the Oracle Portal and the Login Server. Keep the default option, which is "Install Oracle Portal and the Login Server", and click "Next" (Figure 2.41). The next step is to provide the database authentication information so the Oracle Portal can log in to the database as the SYS user, to be able to create the schemas and the packages needed by the Oracle9*i*AS portal. The default SYS password is "change_on_install", and the connect information must be specified in the following format: HOSTNAME:Net8 PORT:SID (e.g., myportal:1521:ORCL; Figure 2.42). In step 3 you specify the schema information; the schema name is defaulted from the value specified in the Oracle Installer Portal DAD configuration schema name (Figure 2.43). In step 4 you specify the Single Sign-On schema information; the schema name is defaulted from the value specified in the Oracle Installer Login Server DAD name (Figure 2.44). In step 5 you choose the tablespaces

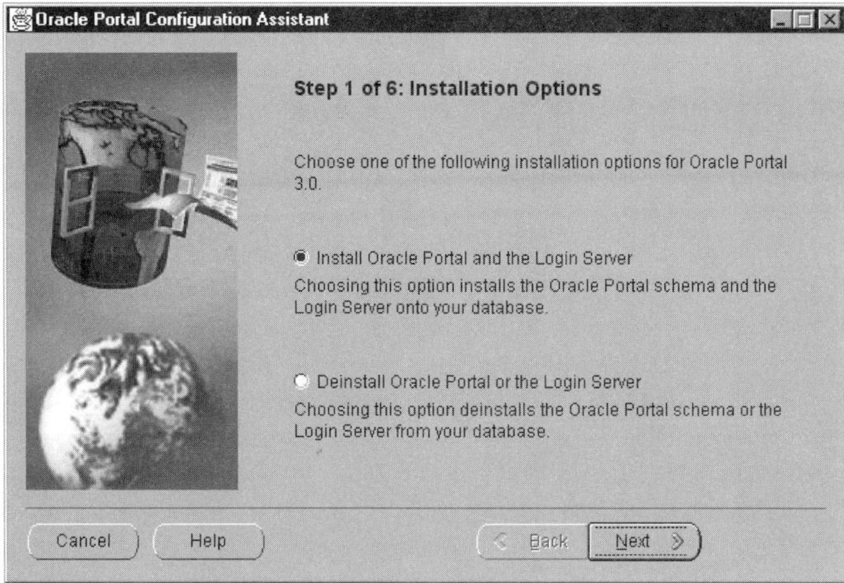

Figure 2.41 Oracle Portal Configuration Assistant: Install Options.

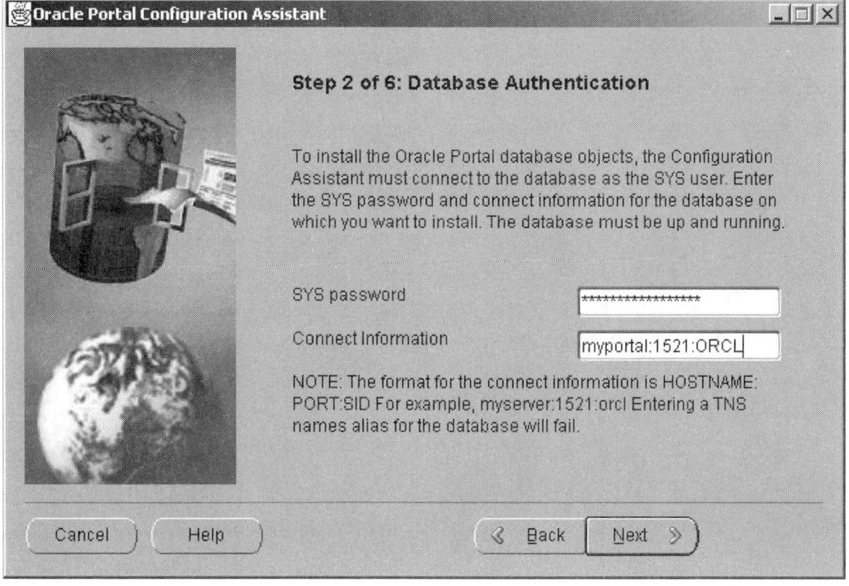

Figure 2.42 Oracle Portal Configuration Assistant: Database Authentication.

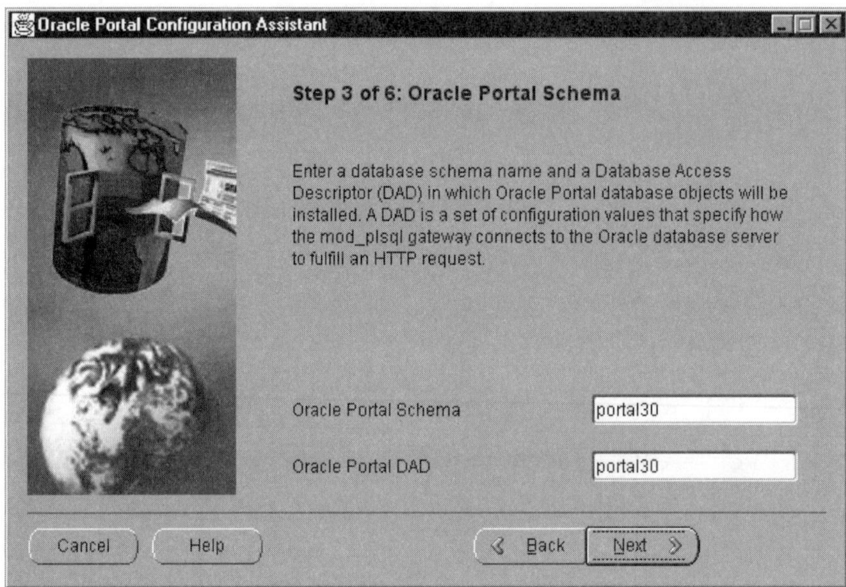

Figure 2.43 Oracle Portal Configuration Assistant: Oracle Portal Schema Information.

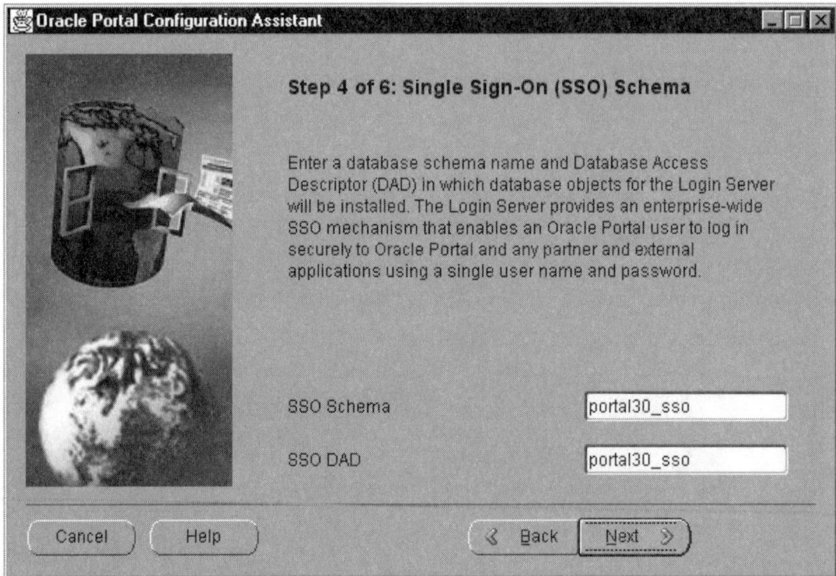

Figure 2.44 Oracle Portal Configuration Assistant: Single Sign-On Schema Information.

for the Oracle Portal installation. Pick OP30_DEF tablespace as the default tablespace, TEMP as the temporary tablespace, OP30_DOC as the document tablespace, and OP30_LOG as the logging tablespace (Figure 2.45).

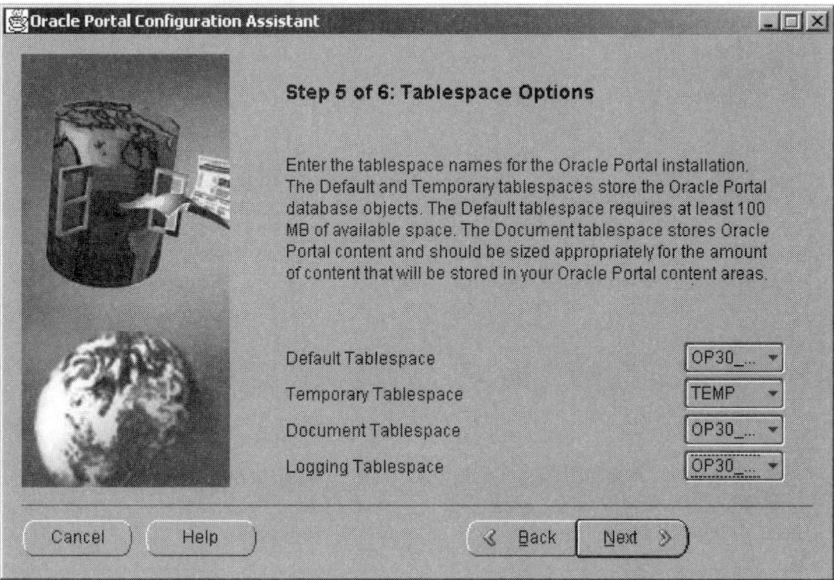

Figure 2.45 Oracle Portal Configuration Assistant: Tablespace Options.

Now it is time to install the PL/SQL Web Toolkit, which is a group of PL/SQL packages used by Oracle Portal to generate HTML from the database. In an earlier version of Oracle Application Server, you had the choice of specifying the owner of these packages. O9*i*AS 1.0.2 installs these packages under the SYS schema. Also, these packages are included in the Oracle 8.1.7 database by default under SYS. This is why the Oracle Portal Configuration Assistant generates a prompt when it detects the 8.1.7 PL/SQL Web Toolkit. Go ahead and click on "Yes" to overwrite the 8.1.7 PL/SQL Web Toolkit with the O9*i*AS PL/SQL Web Toolkit (Figure 2.46). When you respond to the PL/SQL Web Toolkit alert, the Oracle Portal installation starts creating the schemas (i.e., PORTAL30, PORTAL30_SSO) and their objects. The installation can take from 45 minutes to 4 hours, depending on your machine speed. Now might be a good time for a cup of tea.

The percentage may stay at 0% for a few seconds before it starts incrementing (Figure 2.47). While the installation is taking place, it is a good idea to keep checking its log file from time to time. The log file is *<iAS_ORACLE_HOME>\assistants\opca\install.log*.

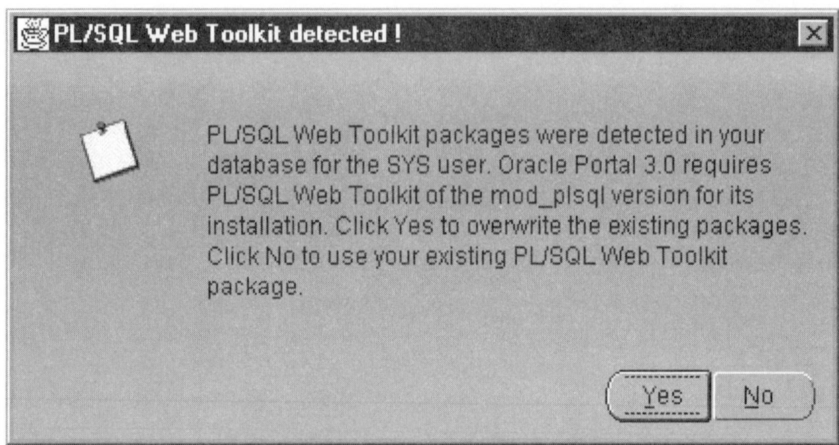

Figure 2.46 Oracle Portal Configuration Assistant: PL/SQL Web Toolkit Detected.

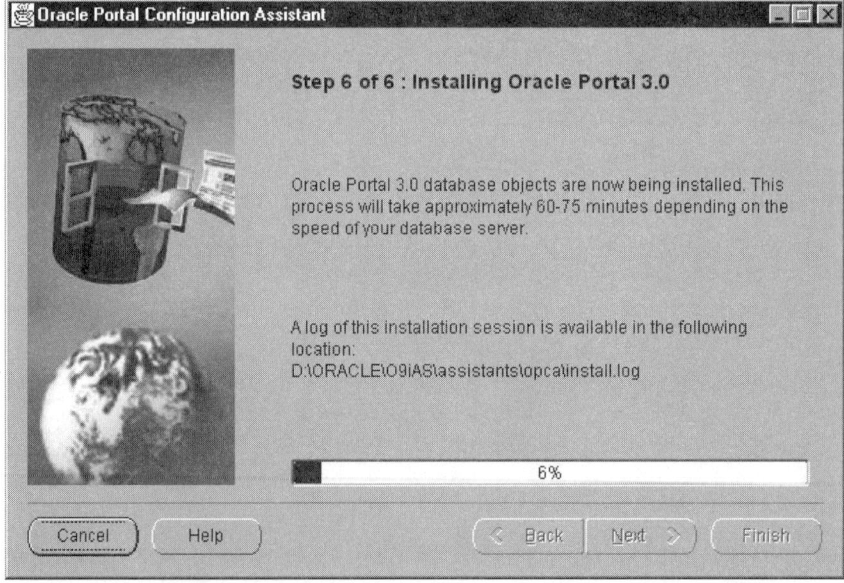

Figure 2.47 Oracle Portal Configuration Assistant: Installing.

If you open the *install.log* file with ***notepad.exe,*** there are no carriage returns, which makes it hard to read the file. Also, ***wordpad.exe*** cannot open the file because the configuration assistant is writing it. If you have Microsoft Word installed, ***winword.exe*** can open the file in a readable read-only format.

Ideally, there should be no errors in the log files except "object does not exist" errors after DROP commands and "name is already used by an existing object" errors. Most of the time these are okay. If you have different types of errors, refer to Chapter 20 on troubleshooting. When the installation is done, you see 100% in the status bar, and the "Finish" button is enabled. When you click on the "Finish" button, a confirmation window is displayed (Figure 2.48).

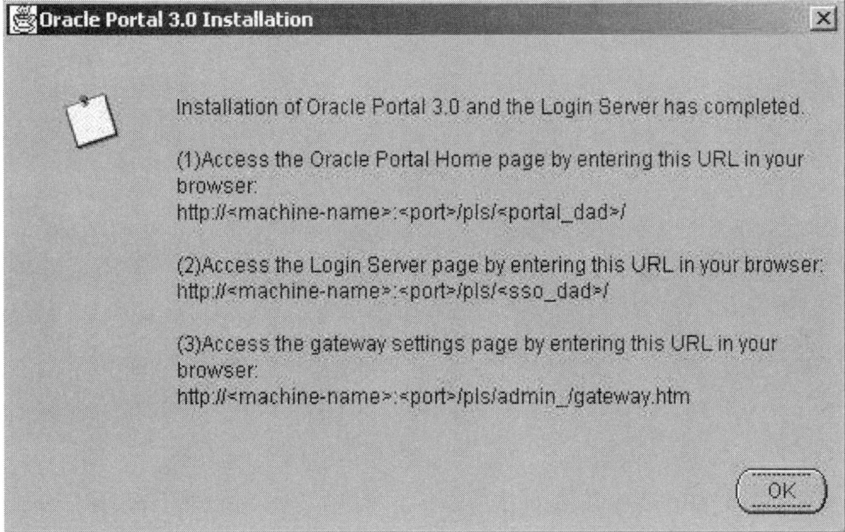

Figure 2.48 Oracle Portal Configuration Assistant: Installation Complete.

You can run the Oracle Portal Configuration Assistant separately (not from Oracle Installer; Figure 2.49). It is useful if you decided to create another Oracle Portal node without reinstalling O9*i* Application Server executables. Also, you can use the assistant to drop an existing portal schema. For example, dropping a schema might be needed if the assistant ran out of space while creating the Oracle Portal schema. A faster alternative to drop an existing Portal schema is to shut down the portal database and delete all of its files. Then create a new database using the database configuration assistant, choosing to copy the database files from the CD. This can be done if you do not have any other application data in the portal database.

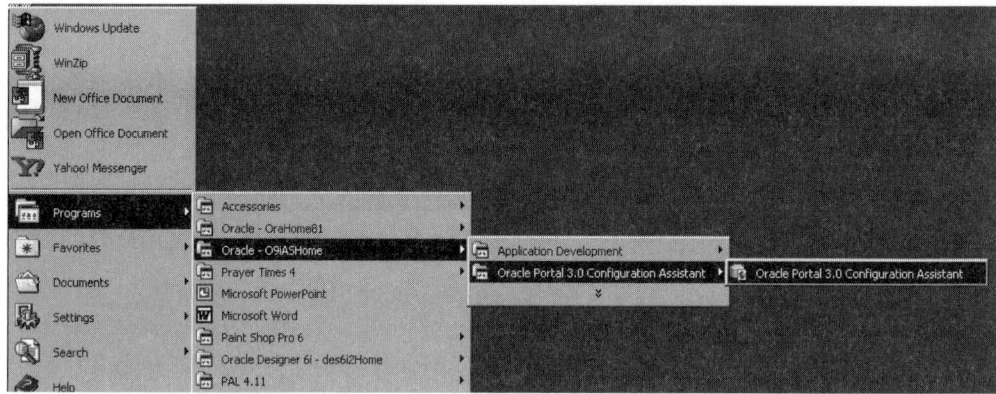

Figure 2.49 Starting Oracle Portal Configuration Assistant Manually.

You should now check the database to make sure that there are no INVALID objects by connecting to the database using the portal schema owner account (i.e., PORTAL30) and running the following SELECT statement:

```
SELECT OBJECT_TYPE, OBJECT_NAME
FROM   USER_OBJECTS
WHERE  STATUS <> 'VALID'
ORDER  BY OBJECT_TYPE, OBJECT_NAME;
```

Ideally, there will be no INVALID objects. If there are any, complete this chapter and then check the troubleshooting chapter for suggested solutions.

You complete this chapter by logging on to the Oracle Portal. Use one of the following Web browsers: Netscape 4.0.8, 4.72, or later, or Microsoft Internet Explorer 4.0.1 with Service Pack 1, 5.0.1, or later.

Before you navigate to the Oracle Portal home page, it is a good idea to check whether the Oracle HTTP server (i.e., Apache) is running. It should be running because the O9*i*AS Installer is supposed to start it as the last configuration step. To check the Apache, type the following URL in your Web browser:

```
http://<Hostname>:<ApachePortNo>
```

Because Oracle HTTP Server for Windows NT/2000 uses port 80 by default, you do not need to include the port number in the URL. So, for the book installation example, the Apache URL is just

```
http://myportal
```

If Apache is running, the Oracle HTTP Server home page will be displayed (Figure 2.50). If you get an error, refer to the troubleshooting chapter.

Figure 2.50 Oracle HTTP Server Home Page.

Note

The Oracle HTTP Server home page might look different, depending on the Oracle-9*i*AS version.

The next step is to go to the Oracle Portal home page:

```
http://<Hostname>:<ApachePortNo>/pls/<PortalDADname>
```

Using the book installation example, the home page URL is

```
http://myportal/pls/portal30
```

The PORTAL30 DAD is set up by the configuration assistant to be the default DAD, so you can go to the Oracle Portal home page by just typing

```
http://myportal/pls
```

A welcome screen is displayed first with the "Login" link. Click on the "Login" link in the top-right corner (Figure 2.51).

Note

The Oracle Portal Web pages might differ from one O9*i*AS version to the next and from one platform to the next. The pages displayed here and in the rest of the chapters are from Oracle Portal 3.0.7, part of Oracle9*i* Application Server 1.0.2.0 for Windows NT 4.0/2000.

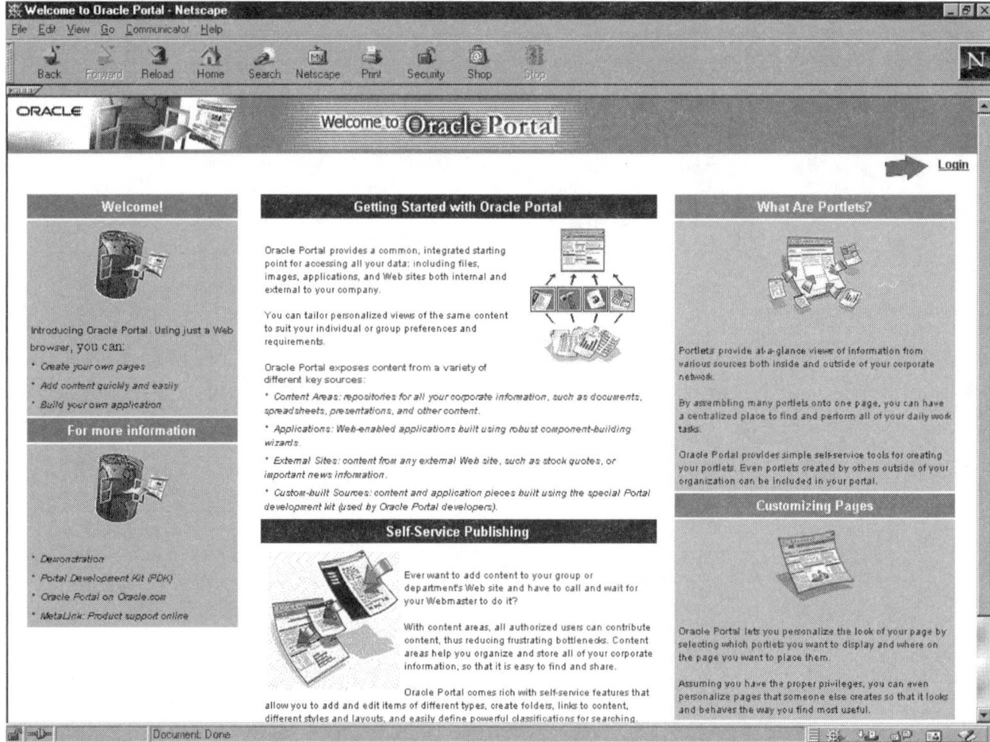

Figure 2.51 Oracle Portal Welcome Screen.

Next you need to log in to the Oracle Portal using the Oracle Portal schema name (portal30) and password (portal30) to go to the Oracle Portal home page (Figure 2.52). If you get an error message, check the troubleshooting chapter. The Oracle Portal user password is case-sensitive but not the username. If the installation is successful, you should be able to log in to the Oracle Portal, and you get the Oracle Portal home page (Figure 2.53).

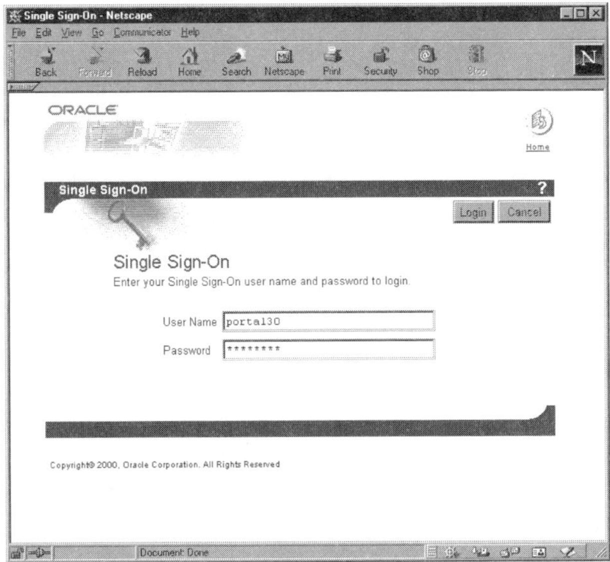

Figure 2.52
Oracle Portal Login.

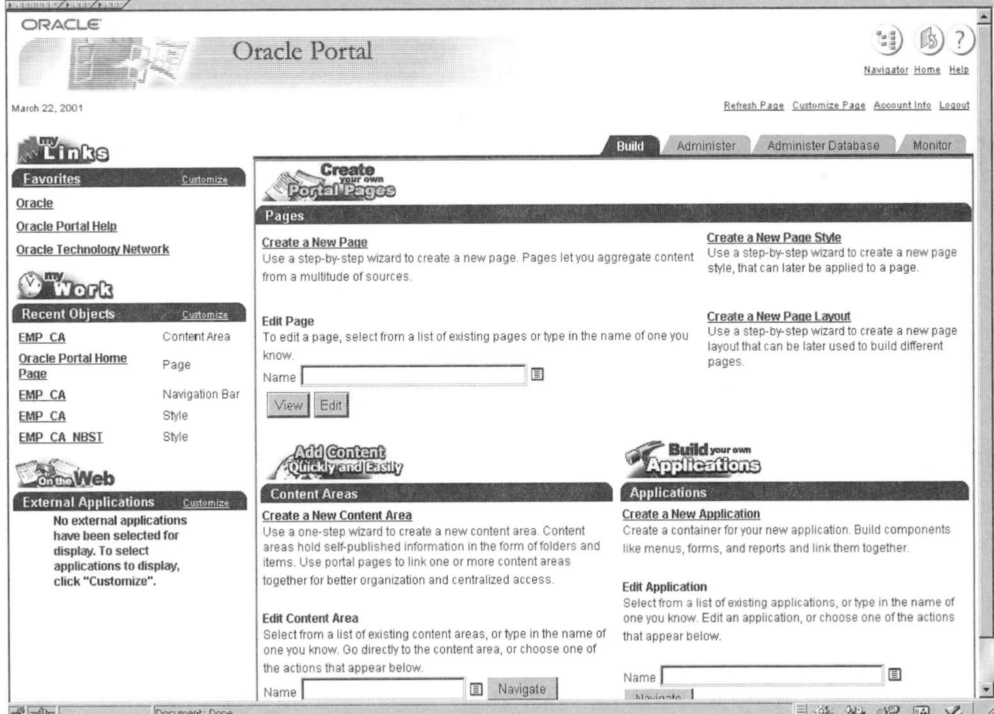

Figure 2.53 Oracle Portal Home Page.

Note

Oracle9*i*AS Portal version 3.0.9 displays an additional Developer News portlet under the Favorites portlet.

Now that your installation is complete and tested, Chapter 3 covers how to build your first portal.

CHAPTER 3

Building Your First Portal

Introduction

This chapter guides you through building your first simple portal. I will not go into details of the components used; this is covered in later chapters. But I will take you through creating a portal page and show you how to add portlets to the page.

Creating Your First Page

For your first hands-on experience using the Oracle Portal, you can log on user PORTAL30 for creating components. Later on, Chapter 12 shows you how to create Oracle Portal users. Using PORTAL30 for development is not a good idea; it is like using the SYSTEM database account for development (e.g., creating tables and running SELECT statements, etc.). If somebody logged on as PORTAL30 and dropped an object by mistake, it might bring the Oracle Portal node down. You can create a new page by clicking on the "Create a New Page" link in the Oracle Portal home page (Figure 3.1).

Note

This book refers to the Oracle Portal schema owner by PORTAL30, but you can choose a different Oracle Portal schema name in the Oracle Portal Configuration Assistant during installation and use it instead of PORTAL30.

The Create Page wizard is displayed, which takes you step by step through the page creation process. You can know where you are in the process by looking at the status bar on the top (e.g., Step 1 of 4). To create a portal page, you need to specify the page name (e.g., EMPLOYEE_PAGE) and the page display name (e.g., Employees Information). The page name is the page identifier and cannot contain spaces. The page display name is what end-users see when they dis-

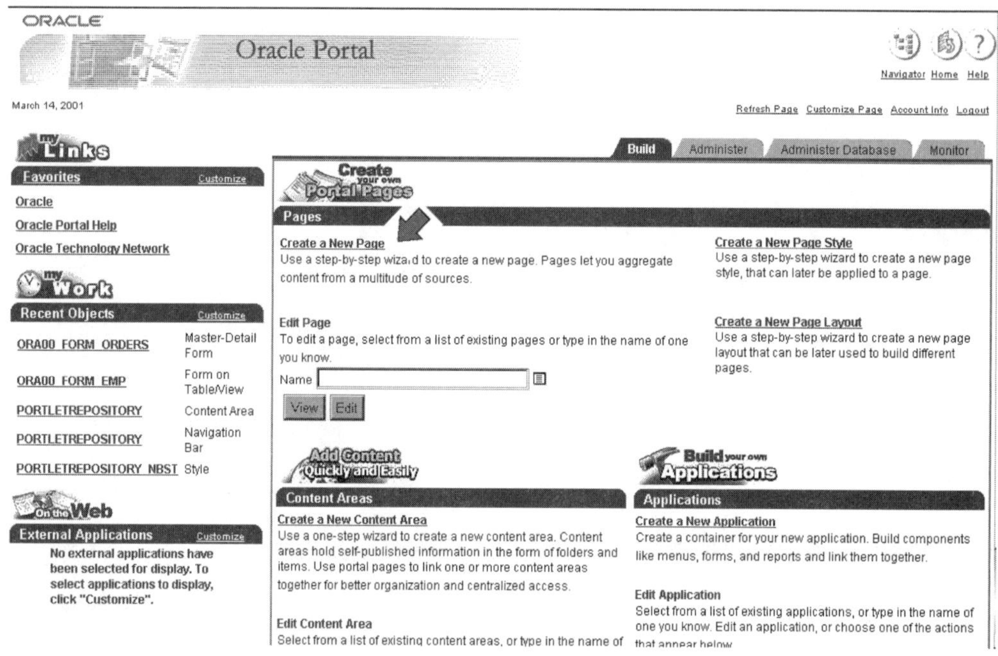

Figure 3.1 Oracle Portal Home Page: Create a New Page.

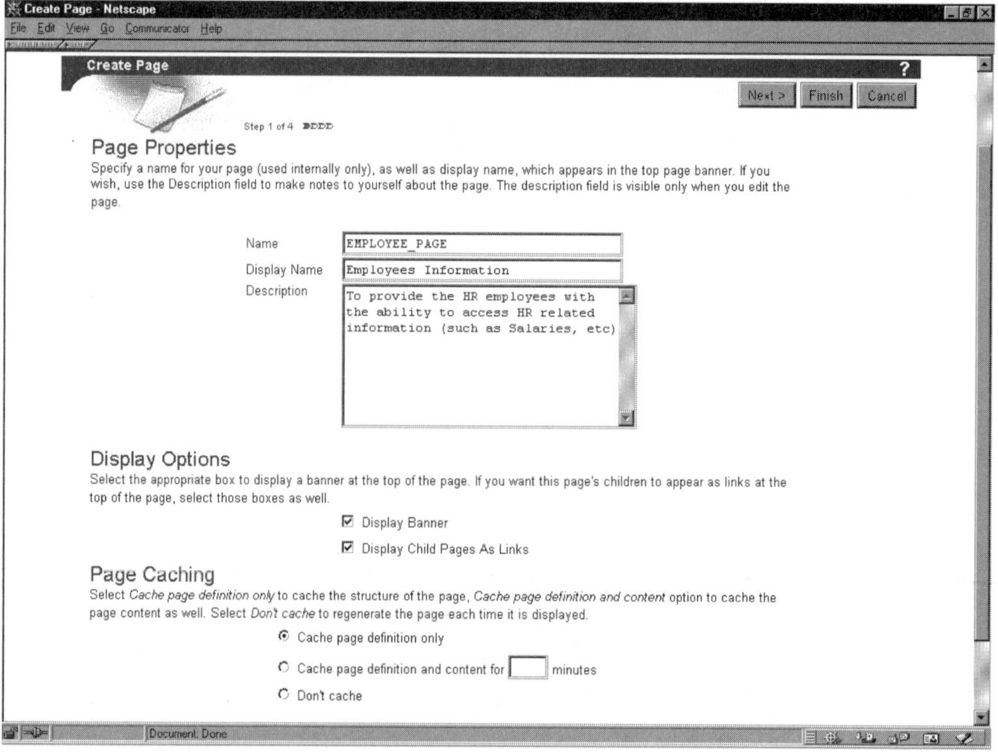

Figure 3.2 Create Page: Page Properties.

play the page. Page description is optional. You can use the description to add comments, because end-users do not see it (Figure 3.2).

Note

To learn more about each property, you can click on the help icon on the top-right side.

Note

Oracle9*i*AS Portal 3.0.9 has added the ability to choose a template for the page in the display options.

You can leave the display and page caching options without changes, and click on the "Finish" button to create the page without going through the remaining three steps. By clicking on the "Finish" button, you are accepting all the default values for the remaining properties. The other option is to click on the "Next >" button to go to the second step of the Create Page wizard. In the second step you can alter the layout and the style of the page (Figure 3.3).

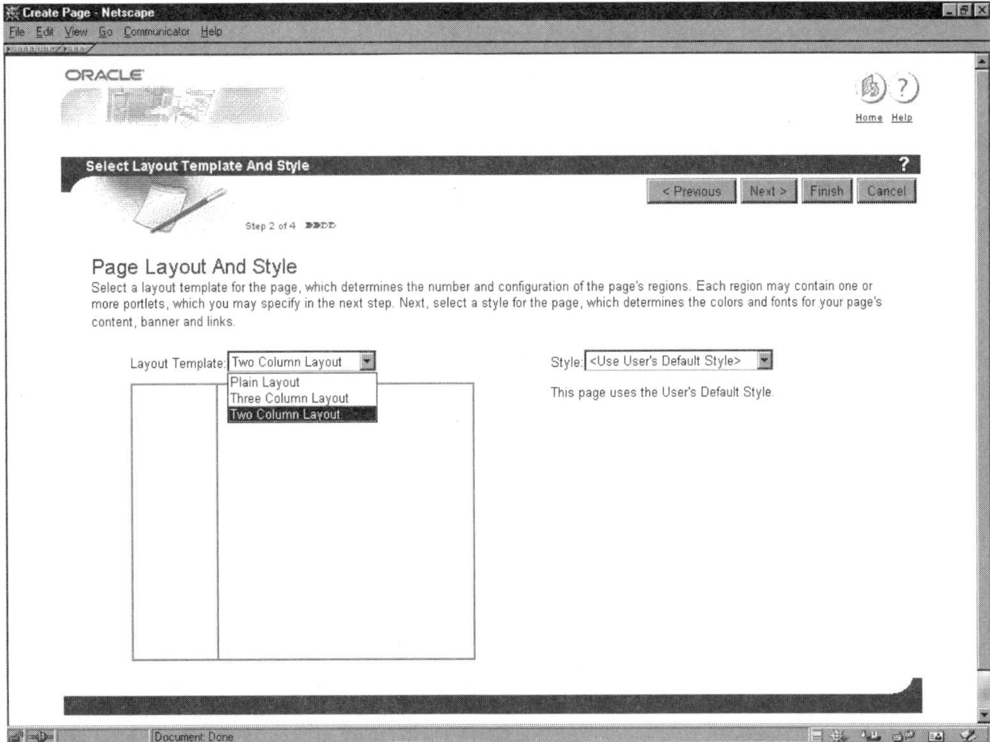

Figure 3.3 Create Page: Page Layout and Style.

The page layout defines how the pages are split into regions. The regions can be horizontal or vertical. The page by default is assigned to the plain layout, where the page is just one region. A Page Style is a group of interface characteristics that defines how the page components are displayed (e.g., text colors, background image, etc.). By default the Create Page wizard creates a new page style to be associated with the new page. You can assign a different existing layout and style to the page. Chapter 11 will explain in detail how you can create new page layouts and styles. Choose the "Two Column Layout" and click on "Next >" to go to the third step in the page creation. In step 3 you can add, edit, and delete regions, tabs, and portlets (Figure 3.4).

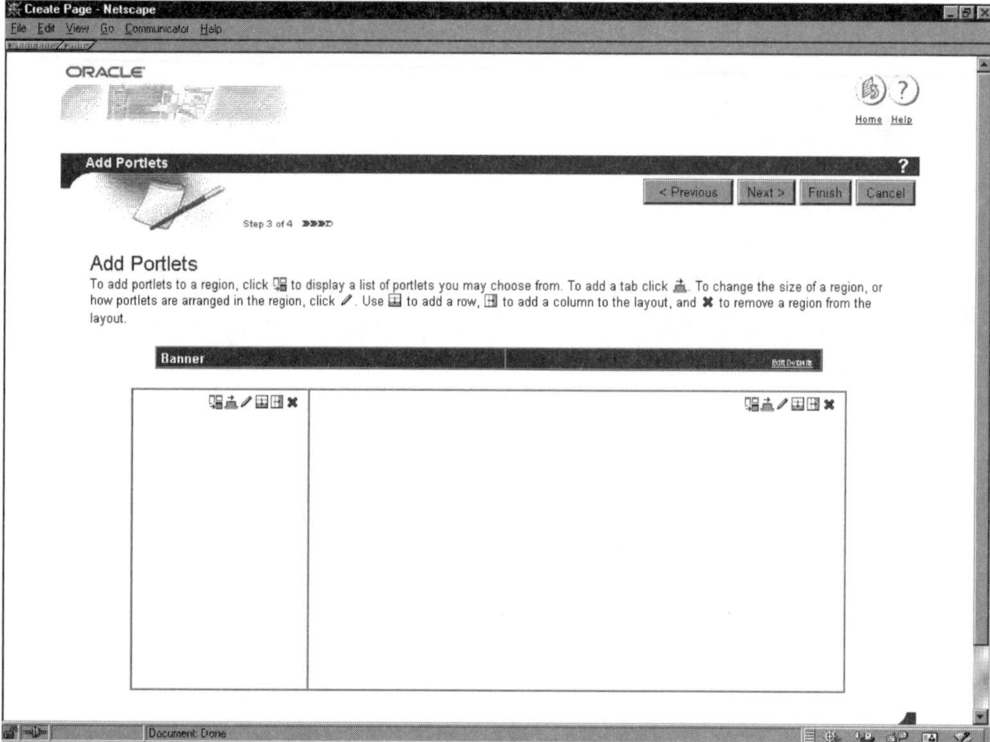

Figure 3.4 Create Page: Add Portlets.

You can try creating and deleting rows and columns. The columns and rows created are new regions added to the page. The icons used in the page customization are explained in Table 3.1.

In Oracle9*i*AS Portal version 3.0.9, the Add Portlets step is called "Modify the Contents of the Page", and the functionality of this step has been enhanced in four ways.

1. Four action push buttons have been added: Hide, Show, Delete, and Move. These buttons allow you to manipulate multiple portlets at the same time.

Table 3.1 Page Customization Icons

Icon	Function	Icon	Function
	Add portlets to a region		Move a portlet
	Add a tab to a region		Show the portlet or the tab by default
	Edit region or tab properties		Hide the portlet or the tab by default
	Add a row (horizontal region)		Move a tab to the left
	Add a column (vertical region)		Select portlet from the repository
	Delete a region, a tab, or a portlet		

2. The portlet's check box does not hide or show the portlet; it includes the portlet in the portlet's selection list upon which the action buttons operate.
3. A new icon is added to the regions' icons, that is "Arrange", which allows you to reorder the portlets within a region.
4. The portlets are not displayed in the Edit page, to preserve space while working on the page design.

Click on the "Add Portlets" icon on the left region to display the Portlet Repository window (Figure 3.5). The repository contains a set of built-in (i.e., out-of-the-box) portlets. In following chapters you will add new portlets to the repository.

By default the portlets are organized in the repository by their providers. You can display them organized by category by changing the "View By" list. A provider is the code component residing in the Oracle Portal node supplying its portlets with the information required for displaying them. You can choose a portlet from the Portlet Repository one of two ways. The first is to click on the arrow on the left side of the portlet name; this adds the portlet directly to the selected portlets list on the right side. The second way is to click on the name of the portlet to preview the

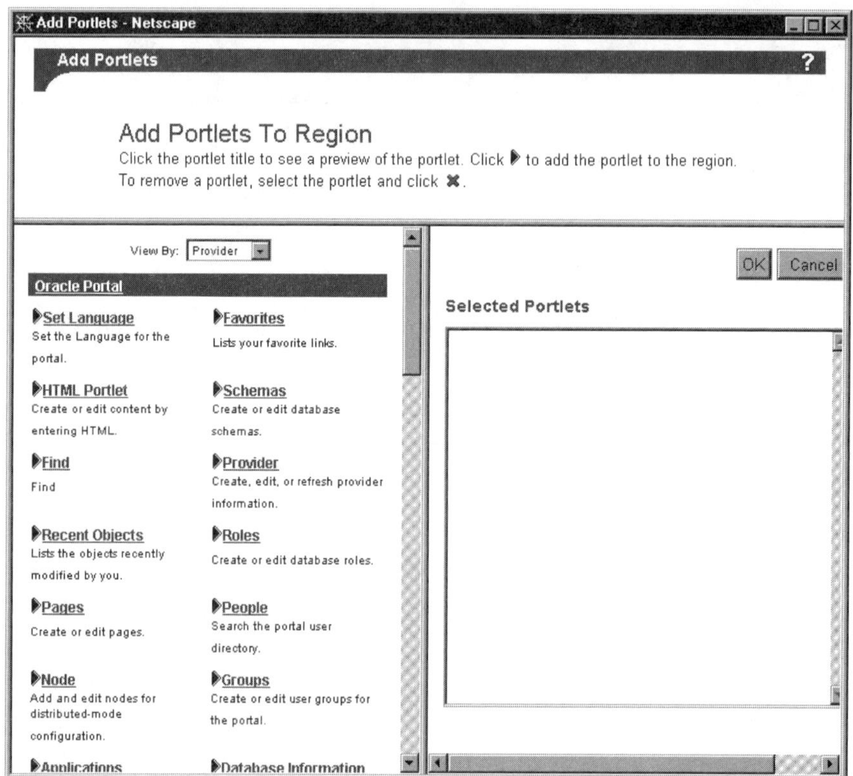

Figure 3.5 Create Page: Add Portlets: Portlet Repository.

portlet before adding it (Figure 3.6). Try adding the Favorites portlet to the EMPLOYEE_PAGE by clicking on the "OK" button of the Portlet Repository window (Figure 3.7).

In Oracle9*i*AS Portal version 3.0.9, the Portlet Repository displays first the providers' names only without displaying their portlet information, to preserve space and to help you find the portlet you are looking for more easily. The built-in providers are called Seeded Providers. By clicking on a provider name, such as "Oracle Portal", the portlets of that provider, such as Favorites and Recent Object, are displayed. You can select a portlet by just clicking on its name. The Select right arrow icon is not available in Portal 3.0.9. To preview a portlet, click on the new preview icon that is displayed on the right side of each portlet. A new window is displayed with a preview of the portlet.

You can change the region's properties by clicking on the Edit Region icon just below the upper border of the region. The Edit Region properties window is displayed (Figure 3.8). You can set the width percentage of the region relative to the whole page width. When you add a new column region, Oracle Portal adjusts the width percentages of the region being split into halves. But if you changed a width percentage manually for one region, Oracle Portal does not change

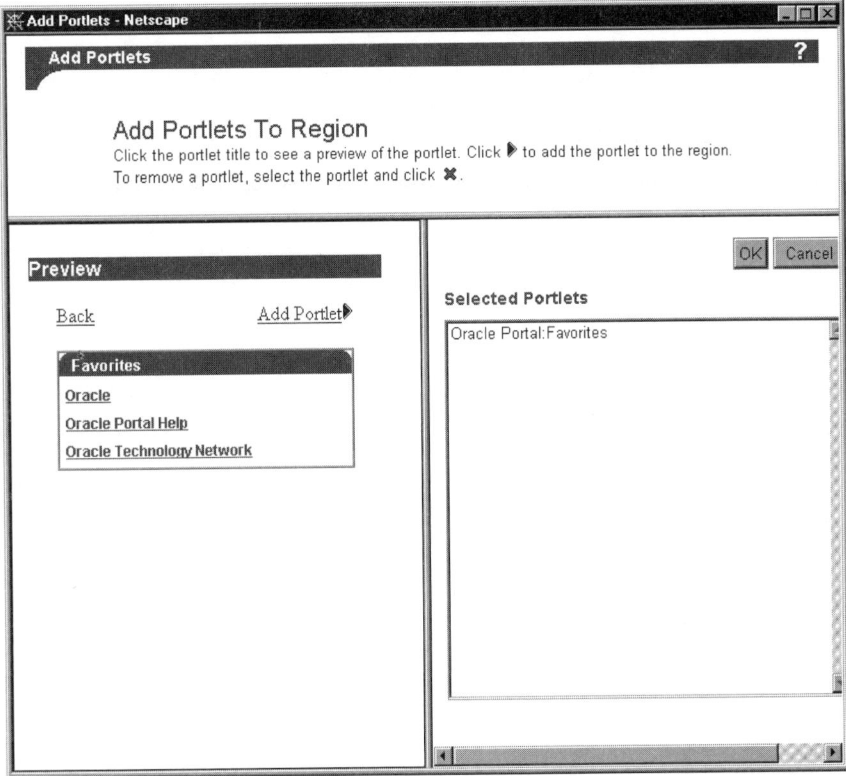

Figure 3.6 Create Page: Add Portlets: Portlet Repository: Favorites Portlet Review.

the other percentages. So it is good practice when you change one region width to adjust other horizontal regions to add up to 100%.

Another region property that can be changed is the way your portlets are displayed in your region. You can choose rows or columns. This is important as you can add more than one portlet to a region. You can also hide all the portlet headers in the region. By hiding the portlet headers, you are hiding the "Customize" links of the portlets as well. Also, the default is to show borders around the portlets; you can uncheck this property for all the portlets in a region to be displayed without borders.

Important

Some Oracle Portal dialogues have both "Apply" and "OK" buttons. In this case clicking "OK" first will both apply changes and dismiss the dialogue. Other dialogues have "Apply" and "Close" buttons. In this case you need to click "Apply" before you close the dialogue. If you do not apply your changes before you dismiss (i.e., close), you will lose them.

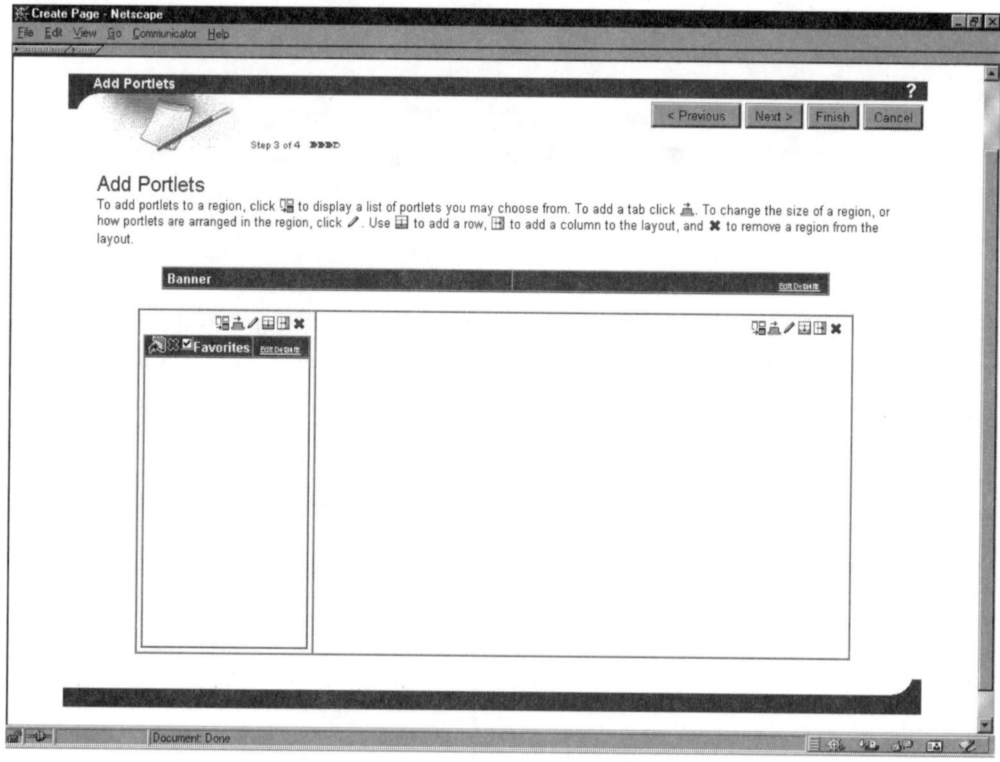

Figure 3.7 Create Page: Add Portlets: Add the Favorites Portlet.

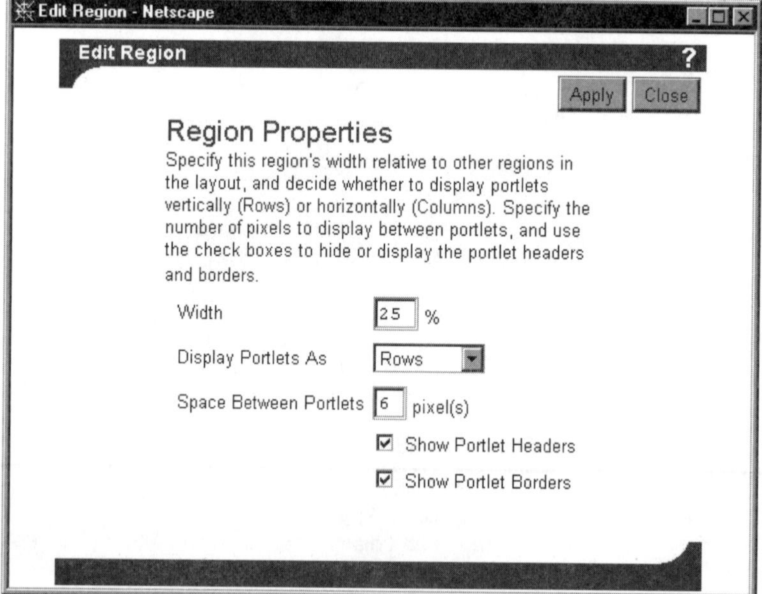

Figure 3.8 Create Page: Edit Region Properties.

Note

You will find another property in Oracle9*i*AS Portal version 3.0.9, Space Around Portlets. This defines the number of pixels between the border of the portlet and the border of its region.

Click on "Next >" to go to the last step of the page creation, which is the control access properties (Figure 3.9). You can leave the properties without changes for now; Chapter 12 will deal with security and controlling access in Oracle Portal. For now, notice the following points:

- By default the page can be accessed by public users.
- Even the page is composed of portlets; the page itself can be published as a portlet and added to another page.
- If you created the page while logged on as PORTAL30, PORTAL30 has the "Manage" privilege on the page.

Figure 3.9 Create Page: Control Access.

Note

In Oracle9*i*AS Portal version 3.0.9, a new "Edit Page" link has been added to the sub-links at the top right corner. The "Customize" link is still available, but only for personal customization of a page. The new "Edit Page" link is used to change the page for everybody (i.e., customize for others).

Clicking on the "Finish" button creates the page, and then the page is displayed (Figure 3.10). The page banner contains the following:

- In the middle: the page display name (e.g., Employees Information)
- On the left side: a default Oracle Portal logo and the system date
- On the right side: Navigator, Home, and Help icons and links as well as "Customize Page", "Account Info", and "Logout" links

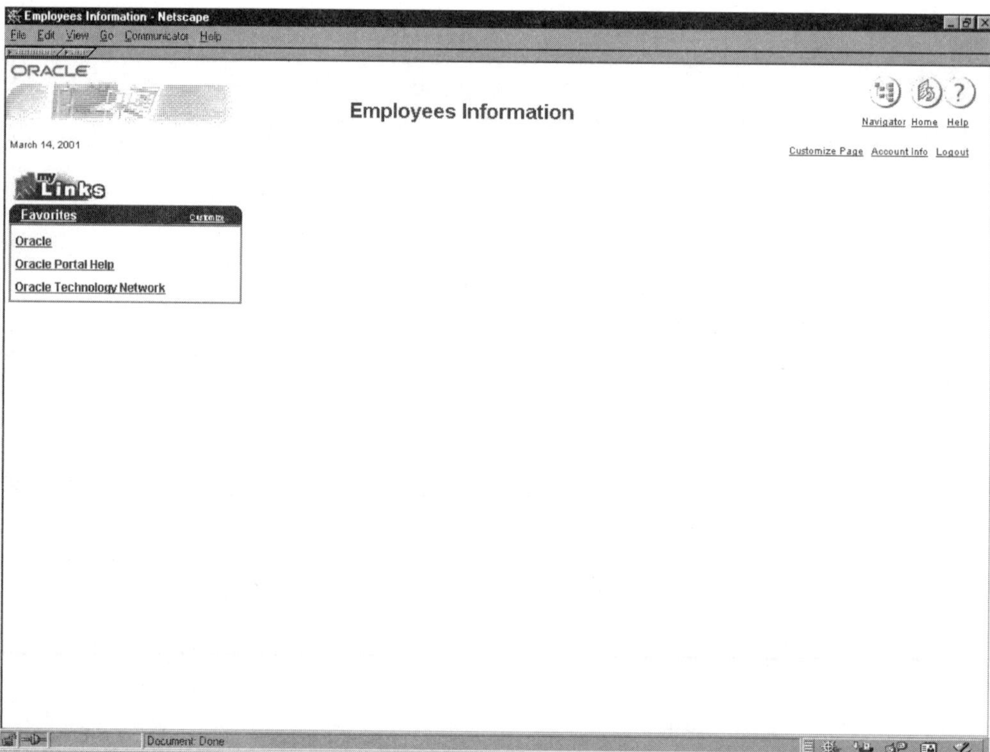

Figure 3.10 Display the Page.

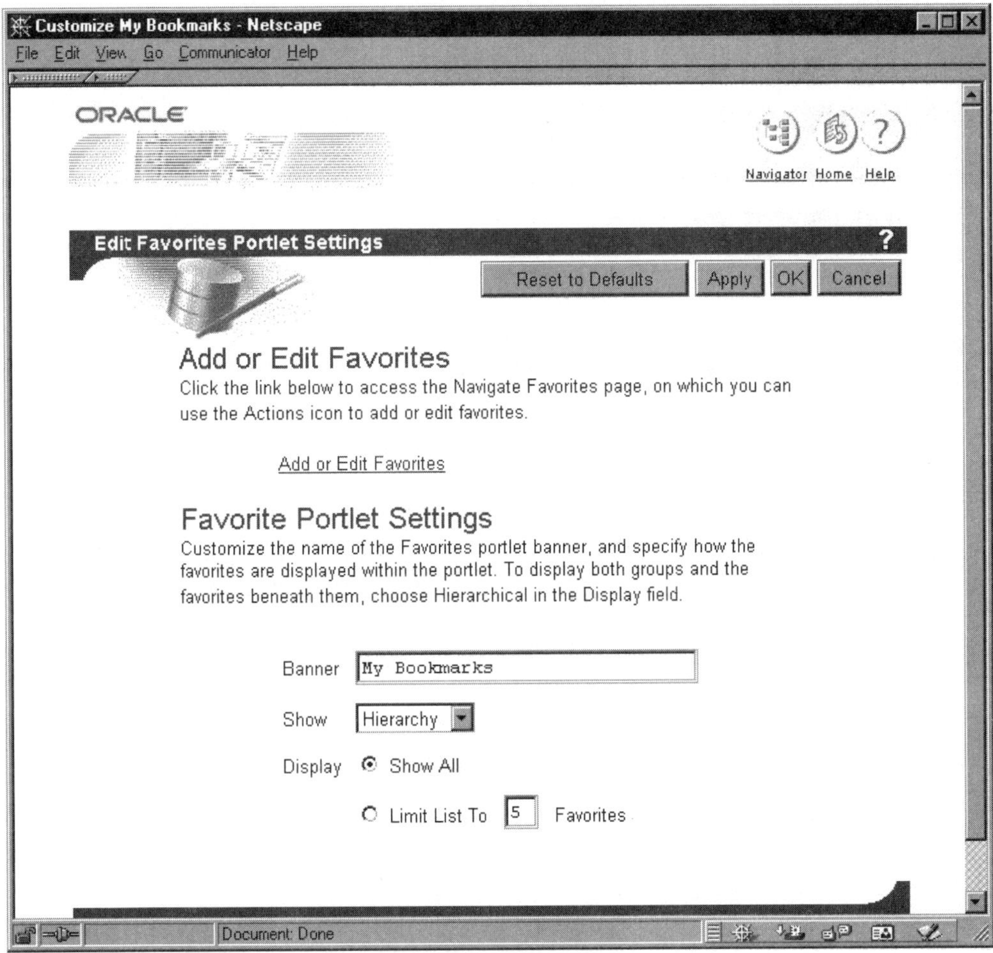

Figure 3.11 Customizing the Favorites Portlet.

You can customize the Favorites portlet by clicking on its "Customize" link in its header (i.e., portlet banner; Figure 3.11). This is where you can change some of the Favorites portlet display settings such as its header text and the number of favorites displayed. You can also add and edit the Favorites links in the portlet from the "Customize" link or by clicking on the portlet header text (i.e., Favorites). There is an example of adding a link to the Favorites portlet at the end of this chapter. When you customize the portlet from the page, you are only customizing it for your account and not for everybody else. So, for example, if you changed the portlet banner text to "My Bookmarks", only you will see "My Bookmarks" as the banner text. The rest of the users will still see "Favorites". This was mentioned earlier as a feature of an EIP, which is to provide end-users with the ability to personalize the pages that they access.

You can edit the page by clicking on the "Customize Page" link on the right side of the page banner where you can navigate between four tabs: Main, Style, Portlets, and Access. As an exercise, create two tabs on the right region by clicking on its Create Tab icon (Figure 3.12).

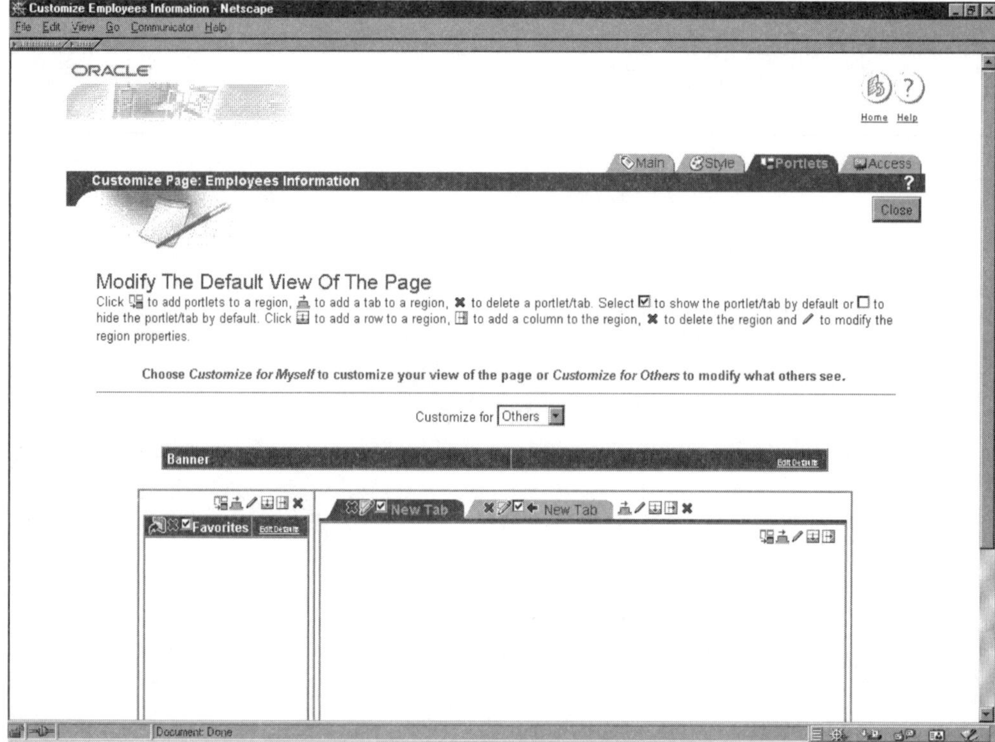

Figure 3.12 Customize Page: Add Tabs to a Region.

After creating the two tabs, you can edit their properties by clicking on their Edit Tab icon (Figure 3.13). Set the first tab's display name to "Departments" and the second tab's display name to "Employees Salaries". You can assign two images to each tab. These images are the active and inactive images. The active image is displayed whenever its tab is the current tab displayed, and the rest of the tabs in the region display their inactive images.

You can click on the Advanced Options tab in the Tab Properties to set access settings for each tab (Figure 3.14). By default the tabs inherit their access settings from their page, but, if

Edit Tab - Netscape

Main | Advanced Options

Edit Tab: Departments ?

Apply | Close

Tab Properties

Enter a display name for the tab. If you supply tab images, the display name is not used. To activate the rollover effect (that is, switching between active and inactive images as the cursor moves over the tabs), check the appropriate box in Tabbed Region Properties.

Display Name: Departments

Active Tab Image: Browse...

Inactive Tab Image: Browse...

Figure 3.13 Customize Page: Edit Tab: Main Properties.

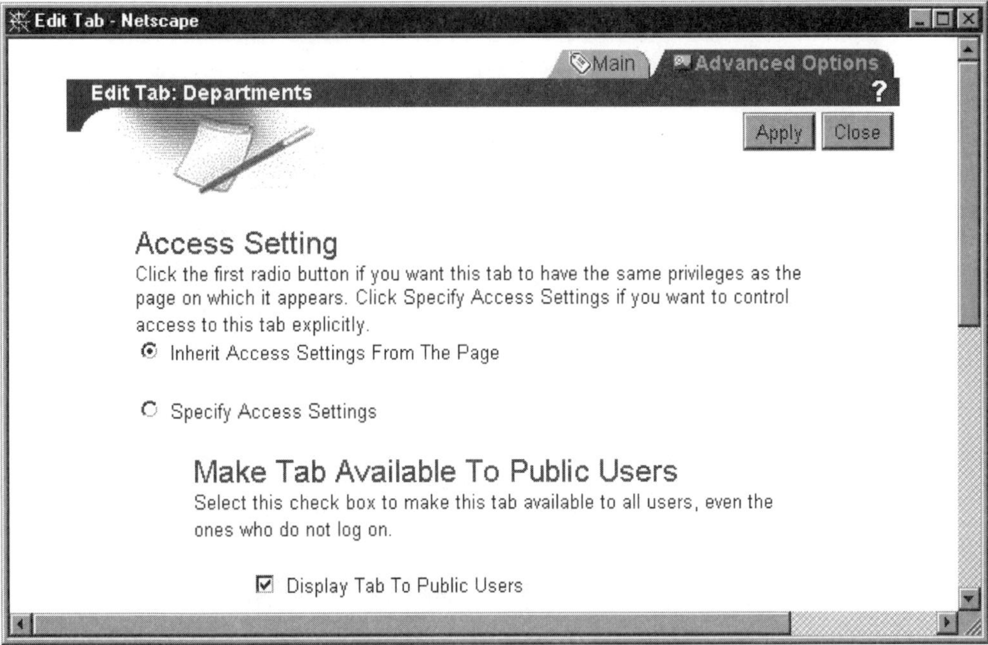

Figure 3.14 Customize Page: Edit Tab: Advanced Options.

needed, you can change each tab's access setting differently so the portal end-users access only the tabs they are allowed to access. When you apply and then close the Tab Properties window, you should return to the "Customize Page" (Figure 3.15).

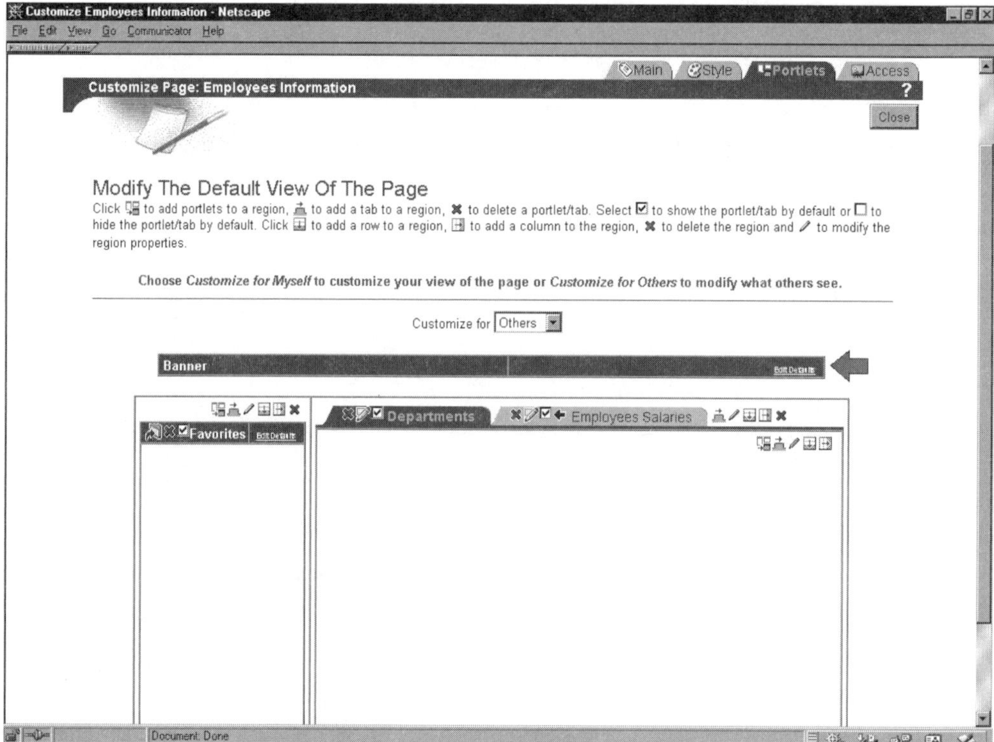

Figure 3.15 Customize Page: Adding Two Tabs and Banner Edit Defaults.

Note

Whenever you customize a page, you have the option to customize it for everybody—this is the default option—or you can customize it just for yourself by changing the "Customize for" list box to "Myself" rather than "Others".

Note

In Oracle9*i*AS Portal version 3.0.9, there is no "Customize for" list because it is replaced by the new "Edit Page" link.

You can also change the page banner properties by clicking on the banner "Edit Defaults". By editing the defaults of the banner, you can specify a page greeting rather than the page display name, or you can even show a greeting image. Also, you can specify a background image for the whole banner. This is useful when you want one background image to cover your entire portal page. You split the image into two pieces. You specify the bottom piece as the background image of your page in the page style. Then you specify the upper piece as the background image of your banner.

In the banner logo settings, you can delete the default Oracle Portal logo by clicking on the delete icon on the logo's left side. Also, you can replace the default banner logo by another logo (Figure 3.16). The default logo URL value is portal30.home, which is a PL/SQL procedure owned by Oracle Portal schema owner that takes you to the Oracle Portal home page. So, whenever you click on the banner logo, it routes you to the Oracle Portal home page. The URL entered in is appended to your full Oracle Portal URL (e.g., *http://myportal/pls/portal30*). If you need to specify an absolute URL, such as *www.oracle.com,* you need to specify "http://" at the beginning of the URL (i.e., *http://www.oracle.com*).

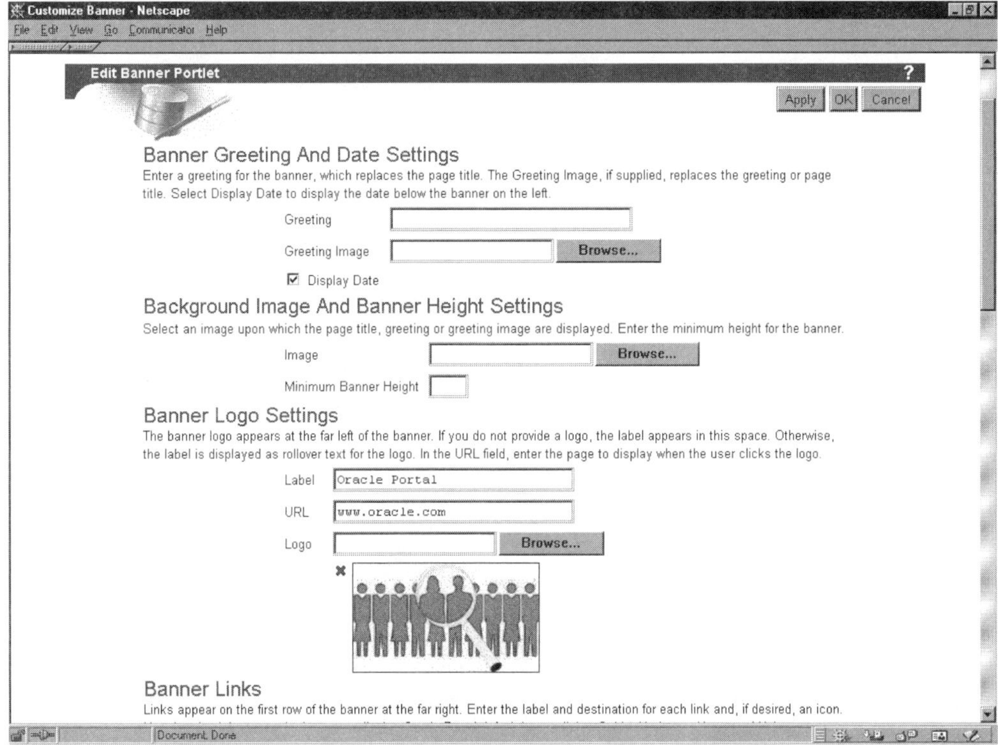

Figure 3.16 Customize Page: Banner: Edit Defaults (1 of 3).

Note

In Oracle9*i*AS Portal version 3.0.9, the Banner Logo URL has the default value #HOMELINK#, which points to the portal home page.

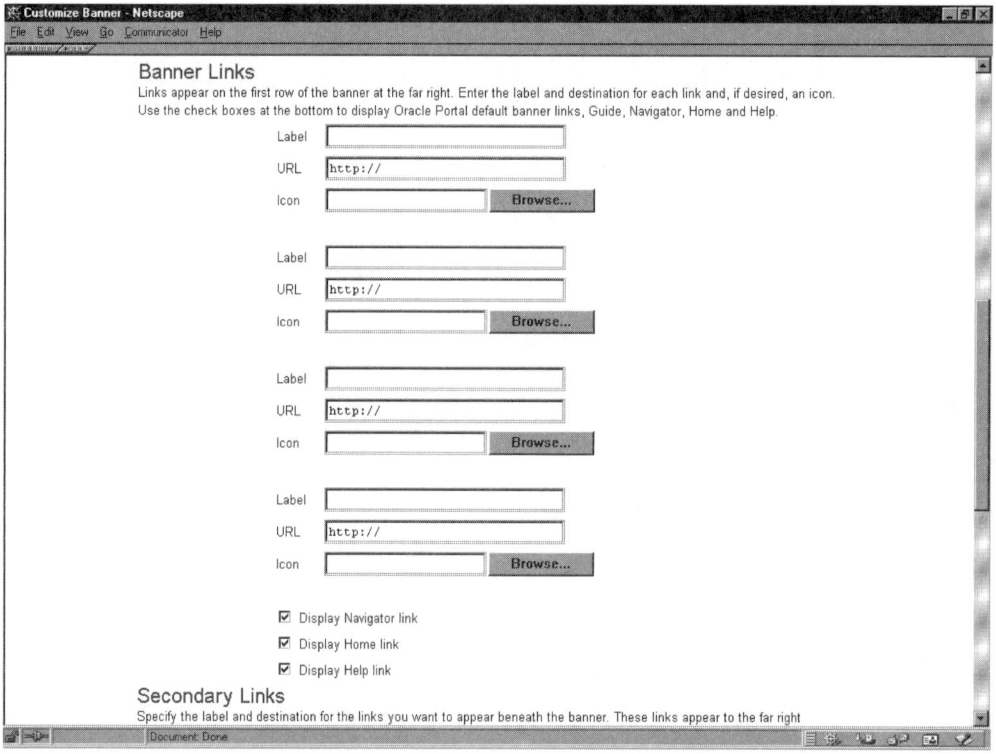

Figure 3.17 Customize Page: Banner: Edit Defaults (2 of 3).

You can add more banner links to the default three links (Navigator, Home, and Help). If you wish, you can hide any or all of these three default links (Figure 3.17). Also, you can add more secondary links to the default secondary links (Refresh, Customize, Account, and Login/Logout). If you wish, you can hide any or all of these default secondary links (Figure 3.18). The default secondary links displayed depends on the portal version. For example, Oracle Portal version 3.0.9 pages have four secondary links: Edit Page, Customize, Account Info, and Login/Logout. Also, in Oracle Portal version 3.0.9, you can decide to hide a link from the primary and display it in the secondary, and vice versa.

By clicking on the "OK" buttons, the changes are committed and the Employees Information page is displayed (Figure 3.19).

Customize Banner - Netscape

File Edit View Go Communicator Help

Secondary Links

Specify the label and destination for the links you want to appear beneath the banner. These links appear to the far right directly below the banner links and on the same line as the date, if displayed. Use the check boxes at the bottom to display Oracle Portal default secondary links, Refresh Page, Customize Page, Account Information, and Login/Logout.

Label

URL http://

Label

URL http://

Label

URL http://

Label

URL http://

☑ Display Refresh Page link(shown only when page caching option is set to *Page Definition and Content*)

☑ Display Customize Page link

☑ Display Account Information link

☑ Display Login/Logout link

Document: Done

Figure 3.18 Customize Page: Banner: Edit Defaults (3 of 3).

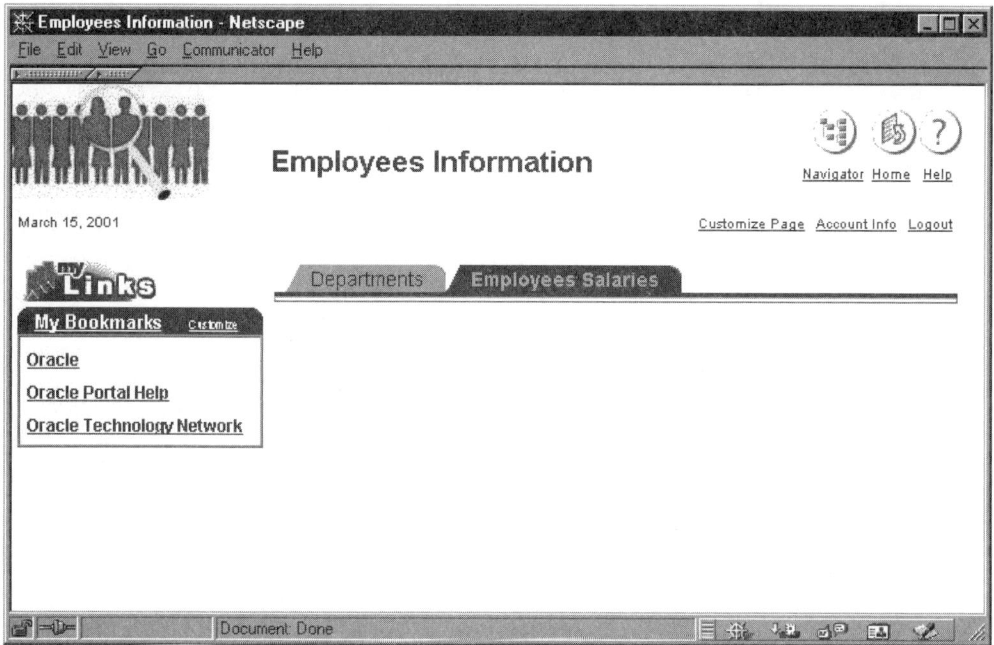

Figure 3.19 Employees Information Page with the New Banner Logo.

Displaying Oracle Portal Pages

Now that you have created your first page, this section explains the different methods available to access it. You can perform any of the following to access the Employees Information page:

- Type the page URL directly into your Web browser:

  ```
  http://<Hostname>:<portno>/pls/<DADname>/url/page/<PageName>
  ```

  So the URL for the Employees Information page is:

  ```
  http://myportal/pls/portal30/url/page/employee_page
  ```

- You can use the Oracle Portal Navigator to access and edit your page. The portal navigator is covered in detail in Chapter 4.

  For now you can click on the Portal Navigator icon, make sure the Pages tab is highlighted, click on the "My Pages" link, and then click on the page name to display it.

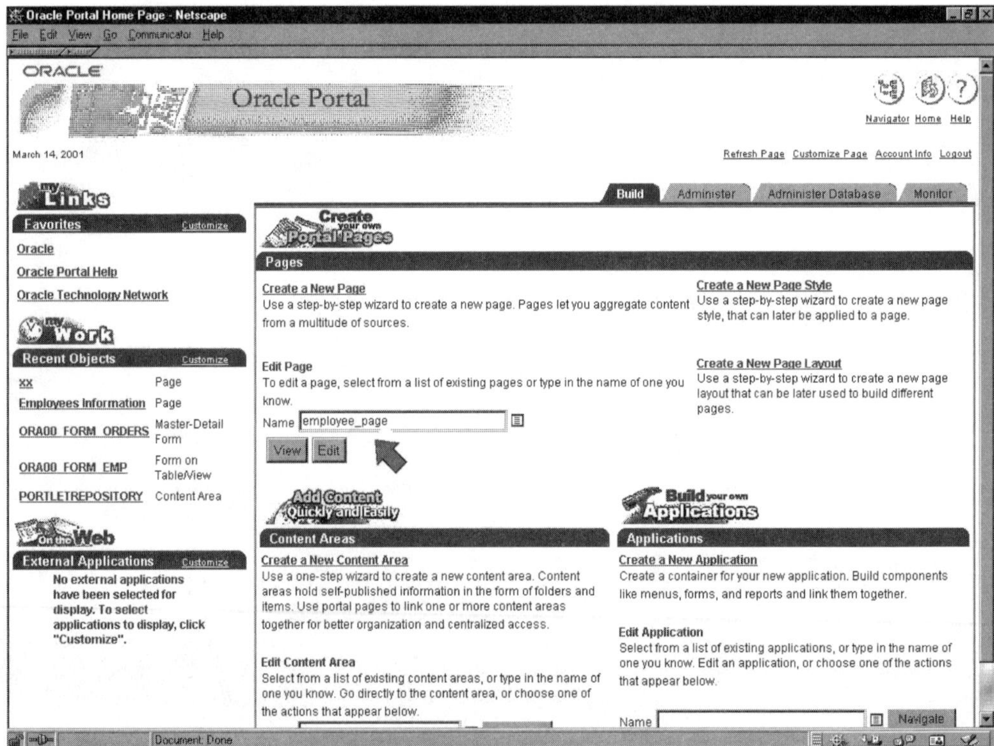

Figure 3.20 Oracle Portal Home Page: Edit Page.

- Go to the Oracle Portal home page. There is a Recent Objects portlet (under the Favorites portlet). This portlet keeps a list of the recently modified objects in Oracle Portal. It displays five objects by default (you can modify the number by customizing the portlet). You should find a link to the new page in this portlet that can be used until you start creating more objects.
- Go to the Oracle Portal home page by clicking on the home icon . Type the page name in the page portlet, then click "View" or "Edit" (Figure 3.20). Or, if you do not remember the page name, you can click on the list of values icon to display the pages' list of values. Expand the "My Pages" node, and then select the page desired (Figure 3.21).
- You can add your page's URL to the Favorites portlet. In the Oracle Portal home page, click on the "Customize" link in the Favorites portlet header to display the Customize Favorites window, and then click on the "Add or Edit Favorites" link to display the Navigate Favorites window (Figure 3.22). Click on "Create Favorite" to display the Create Favorite window, and specify the new favorite information (Figure 3.23). When you submit the new favorite,

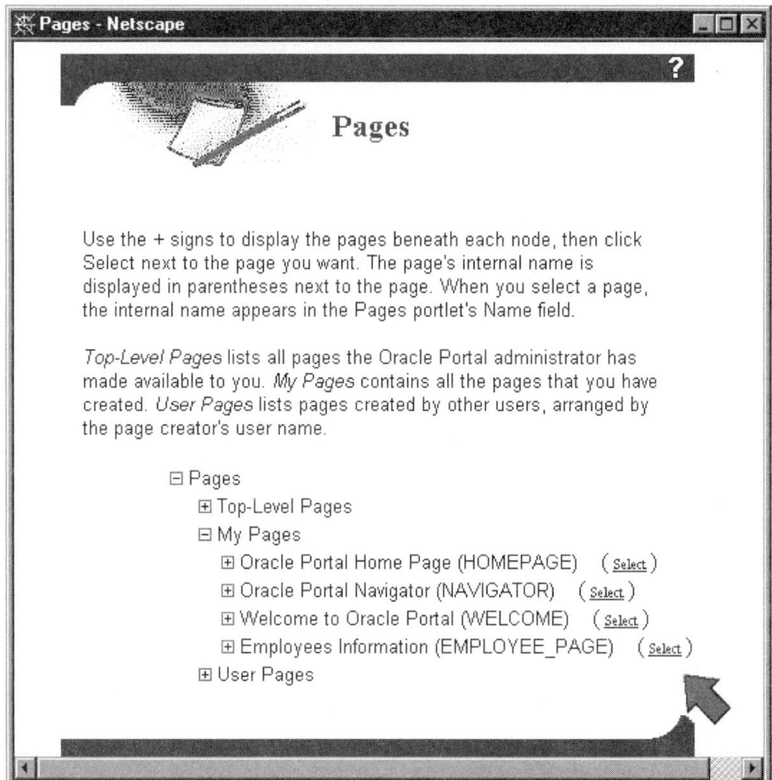

Figure 3.21 Edit Page: List of Values.

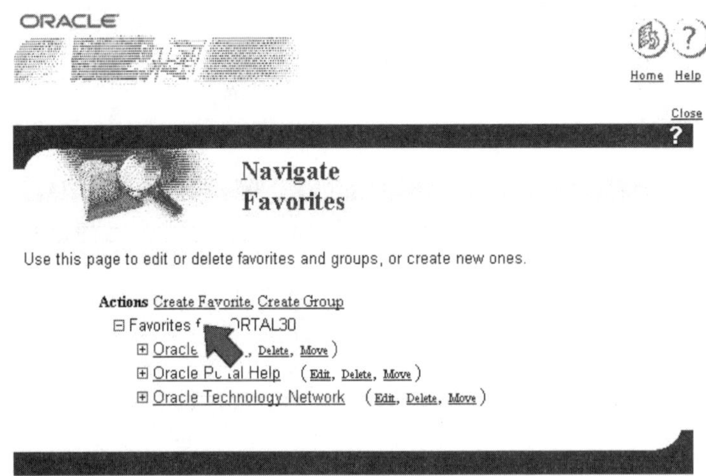

Figure 3.22 Navigate Favorites.

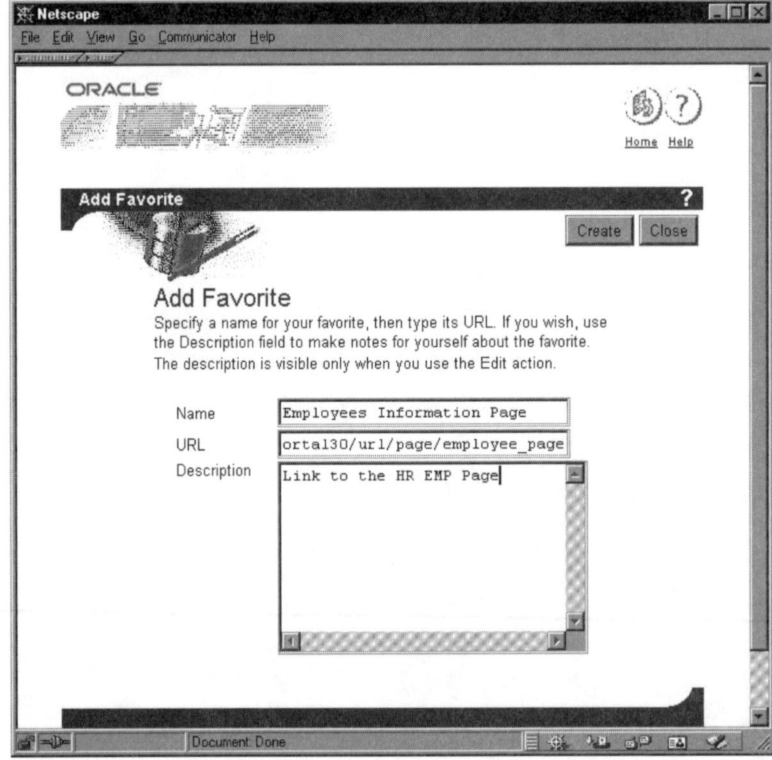

Figure 3.23 Add a Favorite to the Favorites Portlet (1 of 2).

the window is not dismissed, so you can keep adding other favorites (Figure 3.24). Click on "Close" to dismiss it. Now the Favorites portlet has the new link on the top; if you wish you can customize it and move links to reorder them (Figure 3.25).

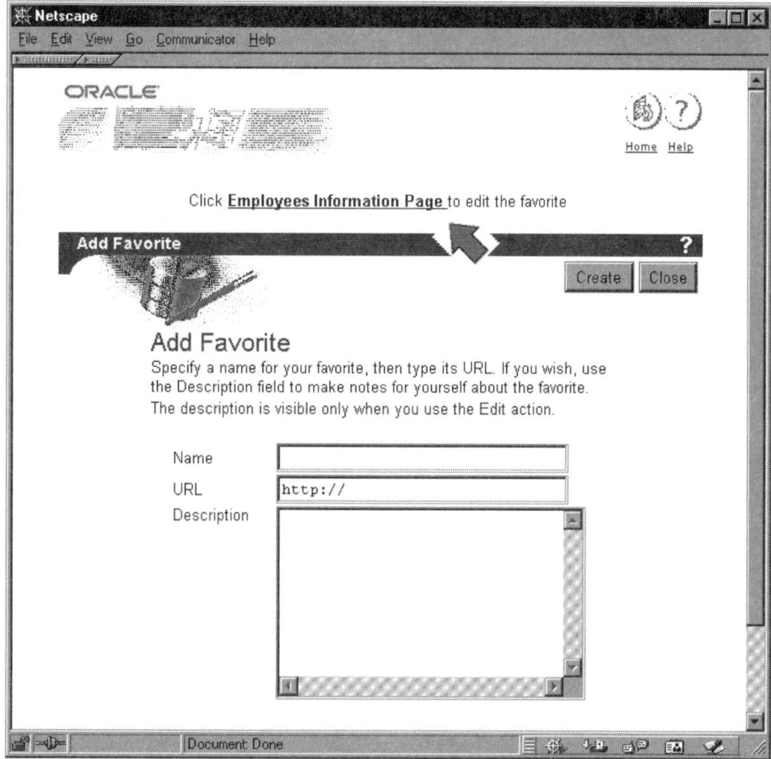

Figure 3.24 Add a Favorite to the Favorites Portlet (2 of 2).

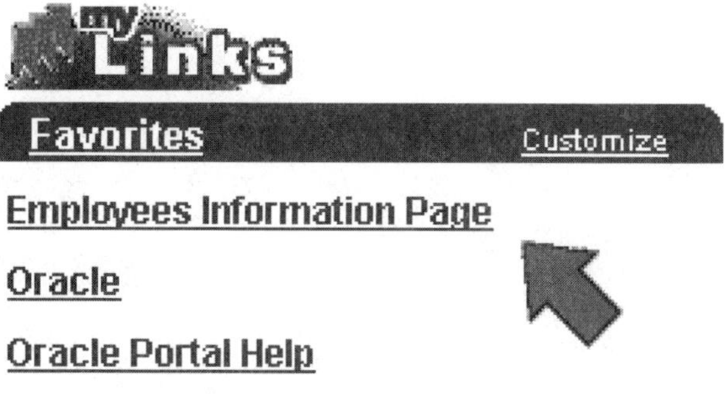

Figure 3.25
The Favorites Portlet after the Addition of a New Favorite.

You can use relative URLs in your Favorites, which means that you can enter just

```
url/page/employee_page
```

and portal will prefix it with the Oracle Portal home page URL (i.e., http://myportal/pls/portal30).

Chapter 4 shows you how to use the Oracle Portal Navigator to create and maintain Oracle Portal objects.

CHAPTER 4

Oracle Portal Navigator

Introduction

This chapter introduces the Oracle Portal Navigator, which allows you to access, create, and maintain Oracle Portal objects. The navigator is fairly easy to use. Knowing how to use the navigator at this time is essential for the next chapters, because in some cases the navigator is the only way to perform a certain task. I will also take you through an exploration tour to get to know different Oracle Portal objects. Some of the actions are performed similarly on different objects types, so they are explained only once.

To go to the Oracle Portal Navigator, click on the Navigator icon, which is available in most of the Oracle Portal Web pages (Figure 4.1). Oracle Portal Navigator displays the objects information in a tabular format. The columns displayed are object type, object name, object available actions, object owner name, and the object last modification date. By default the objects are displayed in the ascending alphabetical order of the object names. This is indicated by the small green up arrow adjacent to the object name column header. If you want to reorder the objects using a different column, you can use the down or up arrows on the column headers to sort the objects in ascending or descending order, respectively. One feature of Oracle Portal Navigator is that when you navigate to a certain level inside it, the navigator remembers your last location, so the next time you click on the Oracle Portal Navigator icon it will take you to the same location as long as you did not log out.

Note

If the order by page name does not seem to be working, do not worry. You might be running into a bug that is fixed in a later version.

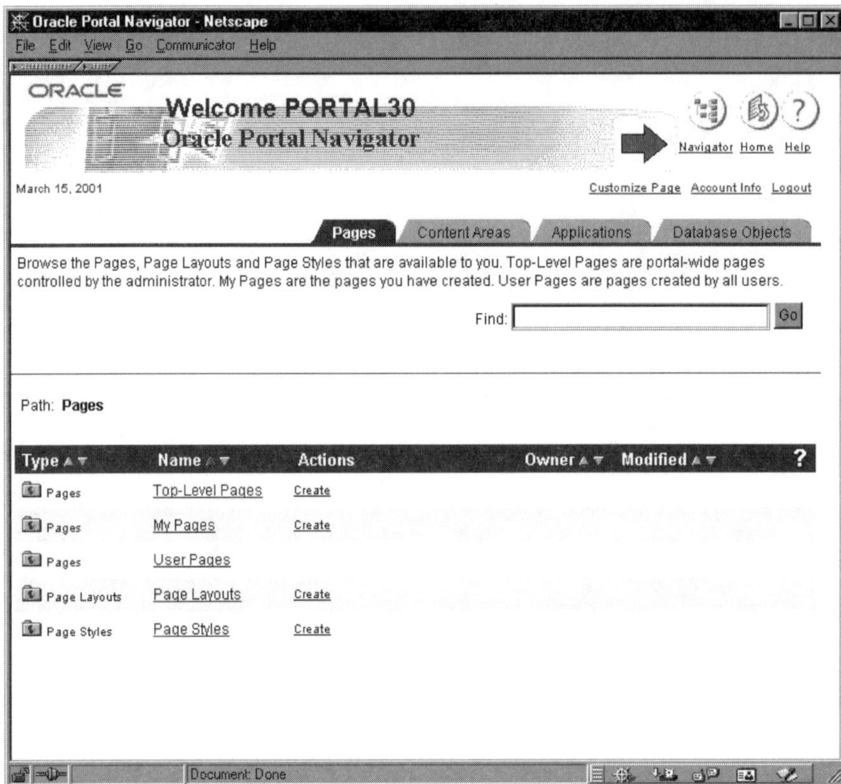

Figure 4.1 Oracle Portal Navigator: Pages Tab.

Pages Navigation

By default, the Oracle Portal Navigator displays the Pages tab. The pages categories are displayed, and you can create new objects in any of these categories. There are five categories under the Pages tab: Top-Level Pages, My Pages, User Pages, Page Layouts, and Page Styles. Top-Level Pages are portal-wide pages (designated for a wide viewing audience and controlled by the portal administrators). My Pages are the pages that have been created by the currently logged-on user. User Pages are pages that have been created by other users, and the current logged-on user has access to them. They are ordered by their owner's username. Page Layouts and Page Styles are covered in Chapter 11.

By clicking on a page category, the list of objects under this category is displayed. Click on "My Pages" (Figure 4.2). Each object that is displayed in Oracle Portal Navigator acts as a link. By clicking on the page name, the page itself is displayed. By using the Path you can tell your location in Oracle Portal Navigator. Also, you can jump back to an upper level (e.g., from My Pages to Pages; Figure 4.3).

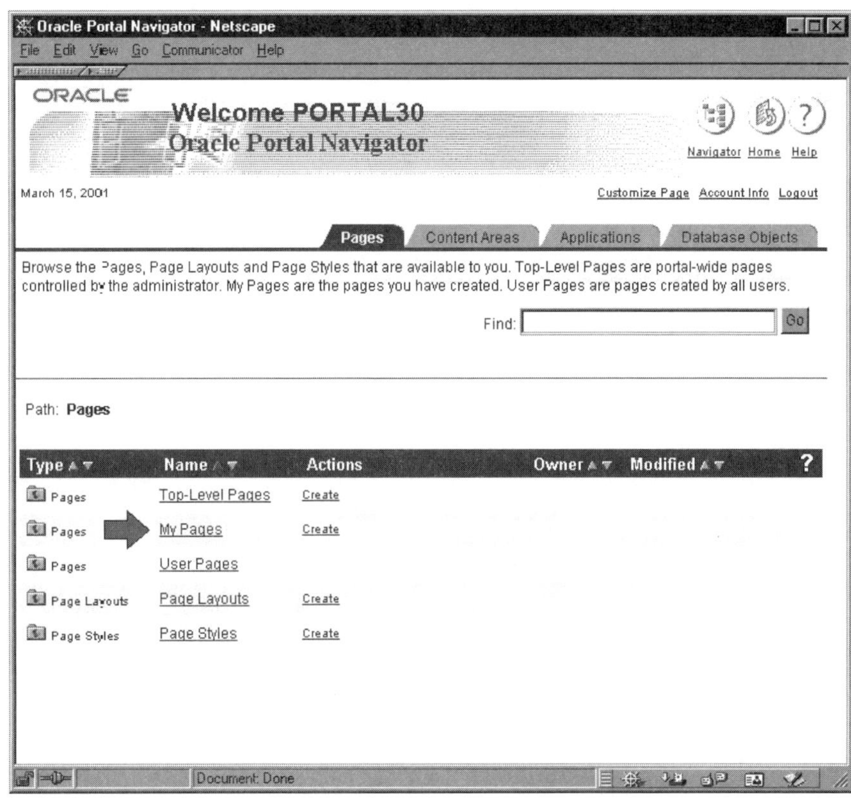

Figure 4.2 Oracle Portal Navigator: Pages Tab: My Pages.

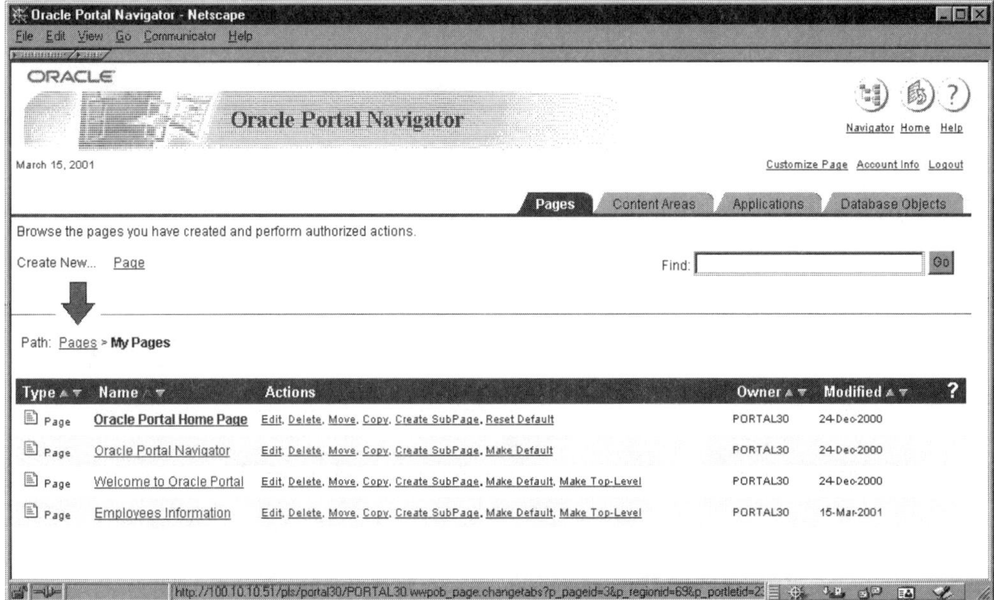

Figure 4.3 Oracle Portal Navigator: Pages: My Pages: Path.

Pages

Each page, page layout, and page style has a list of actions on its right side. This section explains the action applicable to each of these objects.

Page : Create

You can create a new page by clicking on the "Create" link on the right side of the Pages category, where your page will be created. Also, you can create a new page by clicking on the "Page" link on the right side of "Create New" (Figure 4.4).

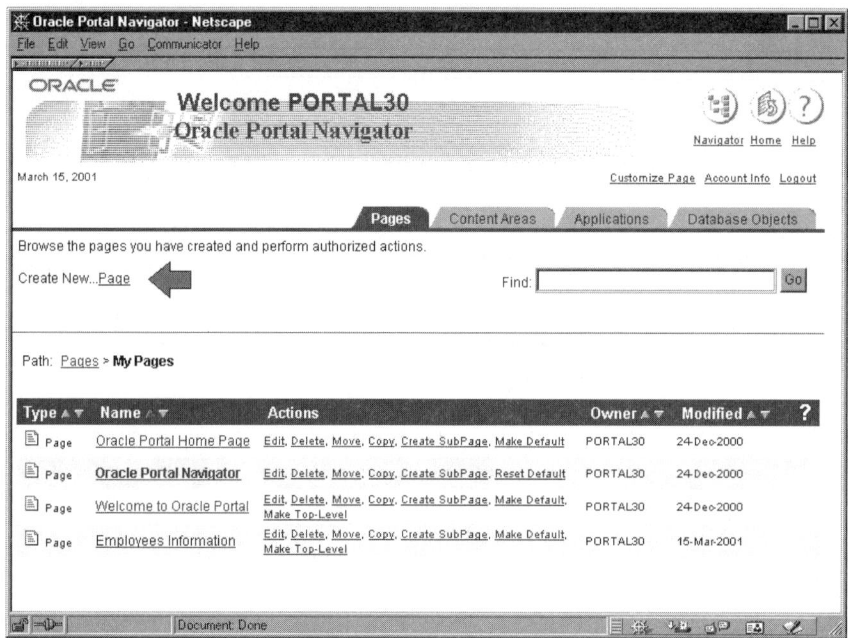

Figure 4.4 Oracle Portal Navigator: Pages: My Pages: Create New Page.

Page : SubPages

If the page has subpages, the action "SubPages" will be displayed on the right side of the page name. By clicking on the "SubPages" link, the Oracle Portal Navigator displays the list of pages beneath this page. The idea of having subpages is to create a hierarchy of pages. You can display subpages as links in the main page so you can navigate easily from a page to its subpages.

Page : Edit

To modify a certain page, click on the "Edit" link on the right side of the page name that you want to edit (Figure 4.5).

Note

In Oracle9*i*AS Portal version 3.0.9, there is another action called "Customize" that allows you to customize a page for yourself, whereas the Edit action modifies the page for everybody.

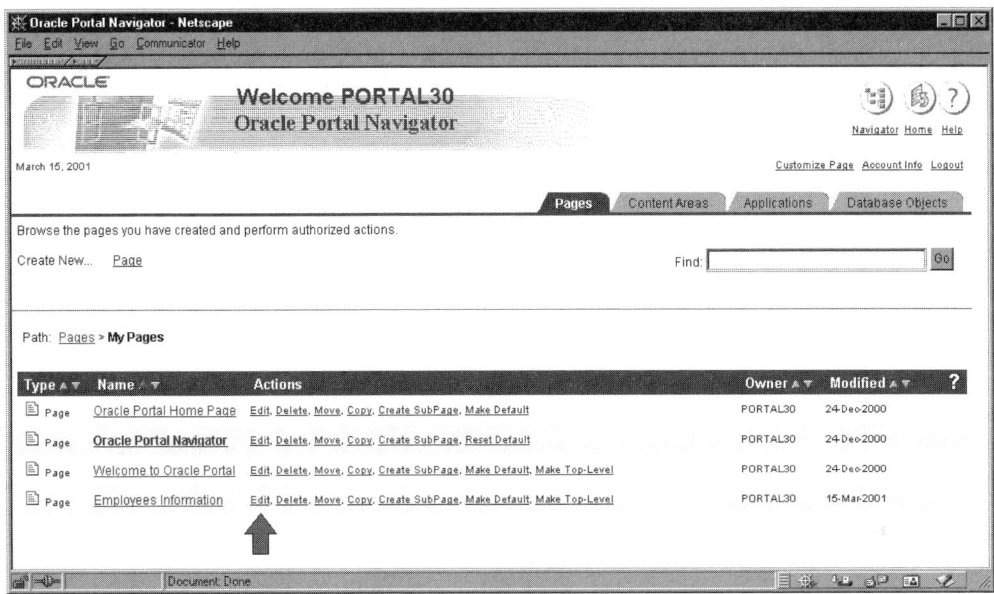

Figure 4.5 Oracle Portal Navigator: Pages: My Pages: Edit.

Page : Delete

If you do not need a page any more (and you do not think that you will need it in the future), you can delete it by clicking on the "Delete" link. You will be prompted to confirm the delete operation (Figure 4.6).

Note

Oracle Portal Design-Time pages (e.g., Oracle Portal home page) cannot be deleted.

Page : Move

You can move a page to be a subpage of another existing page. When you click on the "Move" link, Oracle Portal displays a page list so you can choose the destination parent page (Figure 4.7). Once the page is moved under the selected parent page, you can display all the pages under this parent page by clicking on its "SubPages" link.

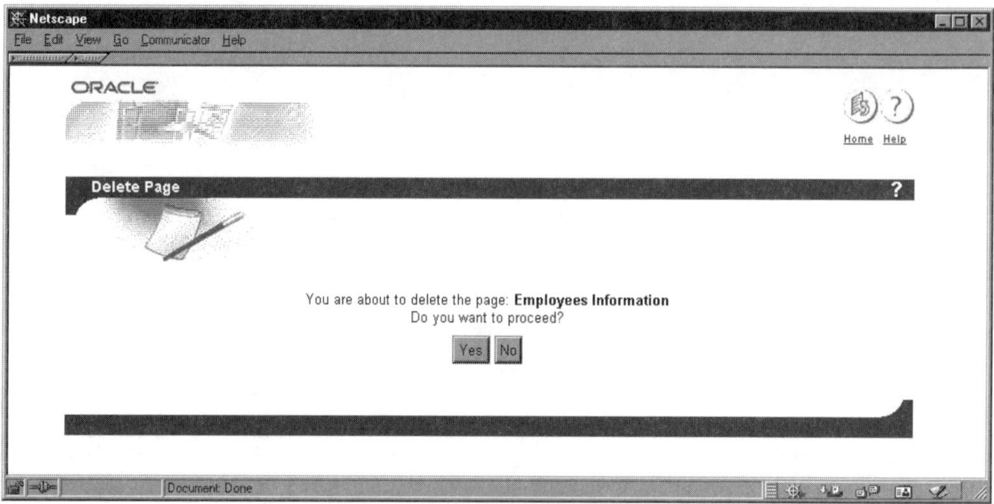

Figure 4.6 Delete Page.

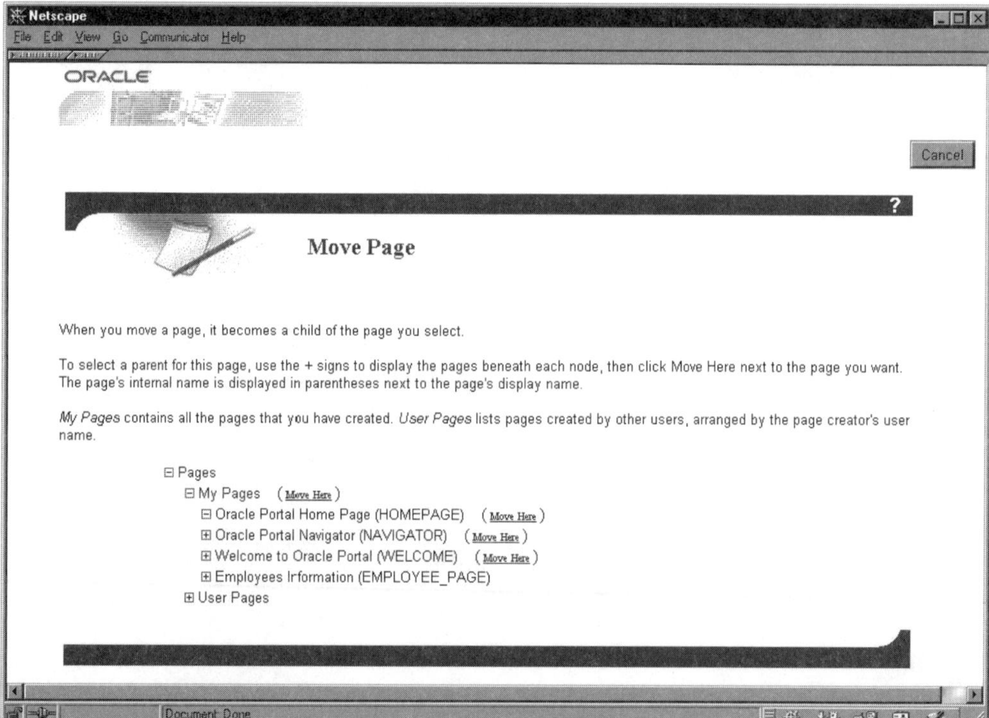

Figure 4.7 Move a Page.

Note

You cannot move a page underneath itself.

Page: Copy

You can copy a page and give it a different name (Figure 4.8).

Note

The page copy operation creates the new page under "My Pages".

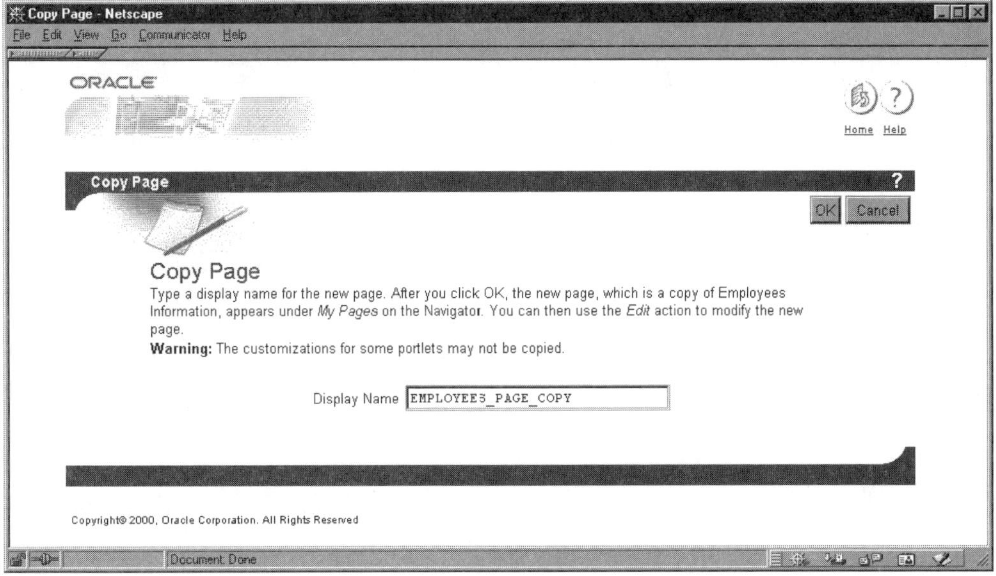

Figure 4.8 Copy a Page.

Page: Create SubPage

The "Create SubPage" link allows you to create a subpage (i.e., child page) under your page (i.e., parent page) by starting the Create Page wizard.

Page: Make Default

By clicking on the "Make Default" link on the right side of a certain page, you make this page your home page. So the next time you log on to Oracle Portal, this page is displayed as your home page.

Note

The home page name is in a boldface font.

Page : Reset Default

Your current default page has a "Reset Default" action link on its right side and all the other pages have "Make Default" actions. When you click on "Reset Default", the factory default page is set instead (i.e., Oracle Portal home page for PORTAL30 user).

Page : Make Top-Level

This action is available only to portal administrators. It copies the page to the Top-Level Pages category. This action does not appear for the pages that are already top-level pages.

Page Layout : Edit, Delete, and Copy

These three actions are the only actions applicable to Page Layouts. You will learn more about Page Layouts and styles in Chapter 11.

Page Style : Edit, Delete, and Copy

These three actions and the make/reset default actions are the only actions applicable to Page Styles.

Page Style : Make Default

You can make a page style the default page style for the current user (e.g., PORTAL30) by clicking on the "Make Default" link on the right side of the style.

Page Style : Reset Default

You can reset your current user default page style to the factory default page style by clicking on the "Reset Default" action link on the right side of your current default page style.

Note

All the non-default styles have the "Make Default" action, and the default style has the "Reset Default" action.

Content Areas Navigation

Content Areas are covered in Chapter 8. The Content Areas tab includes content areas and shared objects (Figure 4.9). By clicking on the content area name, the content area is displayed. You can't click on the Shared Objects entry in the main level, but you are able to drill down to its contents. Each content area and shared object has a list of actions on its right side. You can create a new content area by clicking on the "Content Area" link on the top of the Content Area table. This section explains each action on each content area object.

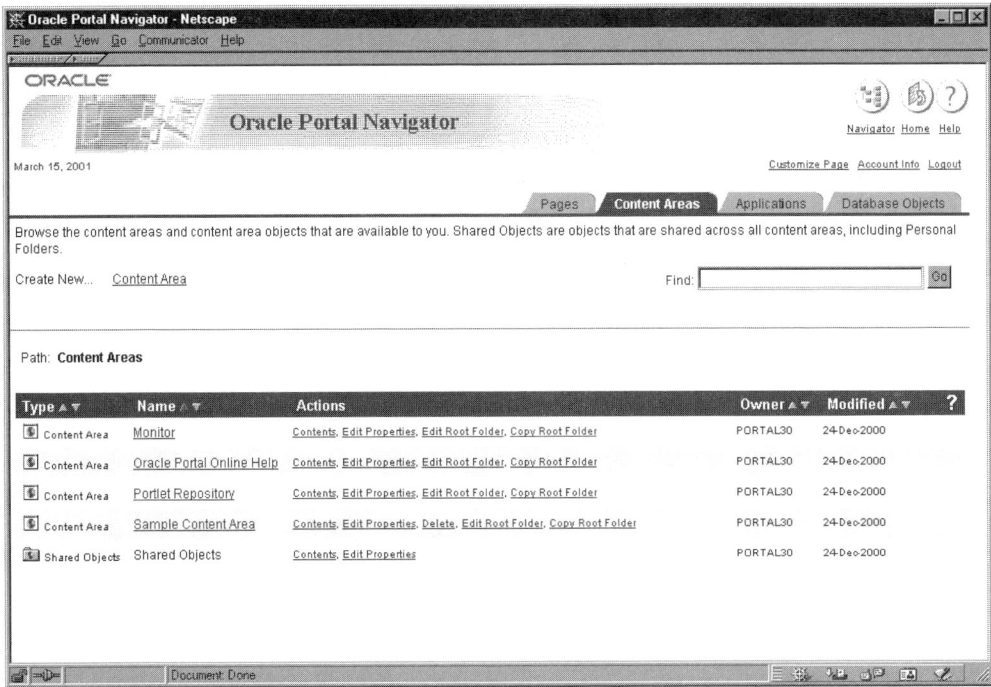

Figure 4.9 Oracle Navigation Portal: Content Areas Tab.

Content Area : Edit Properties

By changing these properties, you can make content-area-wide changes.

Content Area : Delete

This action deletes the content area as well as all of its contents.

Content Area : Edit Root Folder

The root folder is not listed under the folders node of the content area. This action allows you to edit the root folder of a content area.

Content Area : Copy Root Folder

This action copies the root folder to another subfolder in the same content area.

Content Area : Contents

The contents of a content area are Folders, Categories, Navigation Bars, Perspectives, Styles, and Custom Types. You can create new objects of any of these by clicking on its "Create"

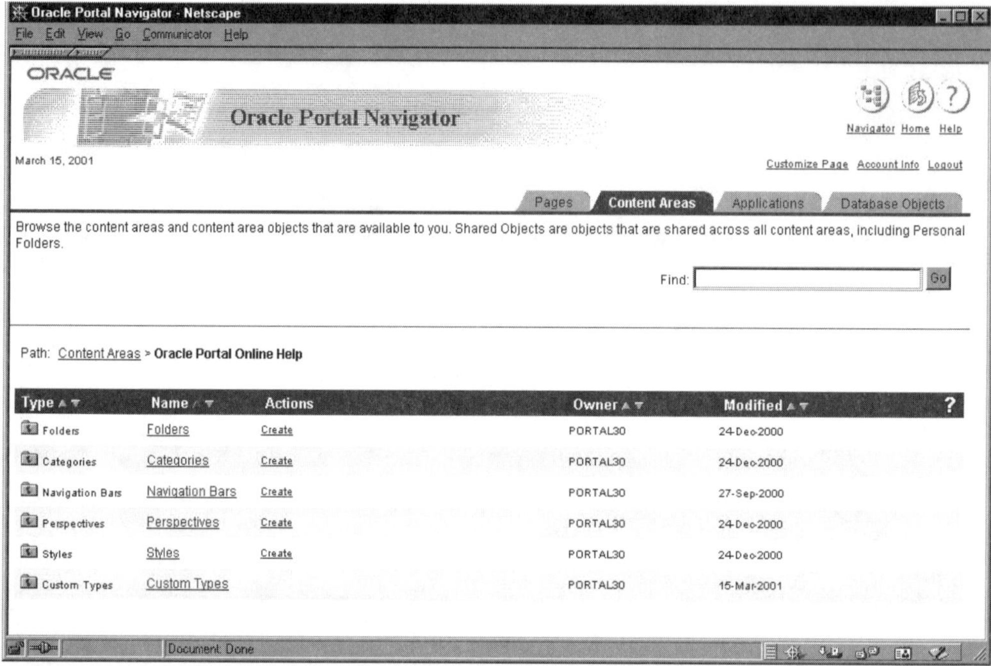

Figure 4.10 Oracle Navigation Portal: Content Areas: Contents.

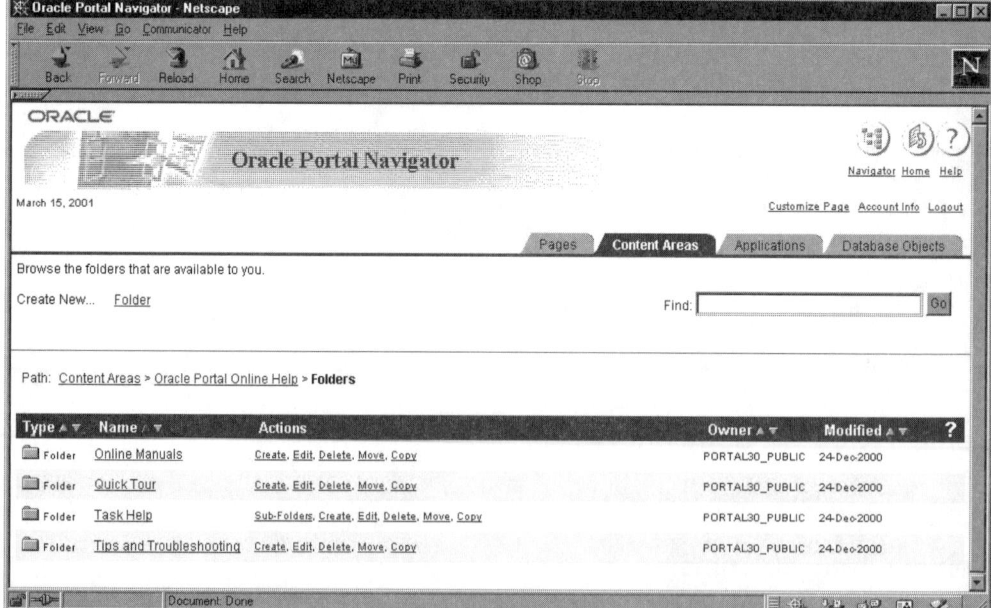

Figure 4.11 Oracle Navigation Portal: Content Areas: Contents: Folders.

action link (Figure 4.10). You can also create new objects under any of these types by drilling down to the specific content type screen.

Folders

The following actions can be performed on folders: create (sub-folders), edit, delete, move, and copy (Figure 4.11). Content areas and folders are explained in detail in Chapters 8 and 9.

Note

In Oracle9*i*AS Portal version 3.0.9, there is a new action called "Bulk action" that can be invoked on folders, categories, and perspectives to perform bulk deletes, copies, and attributes assignment on multiple selected objects.

Categories

The following actions can be performed on categories: create (sub-categories), edit, and delete (Figure 4.12).

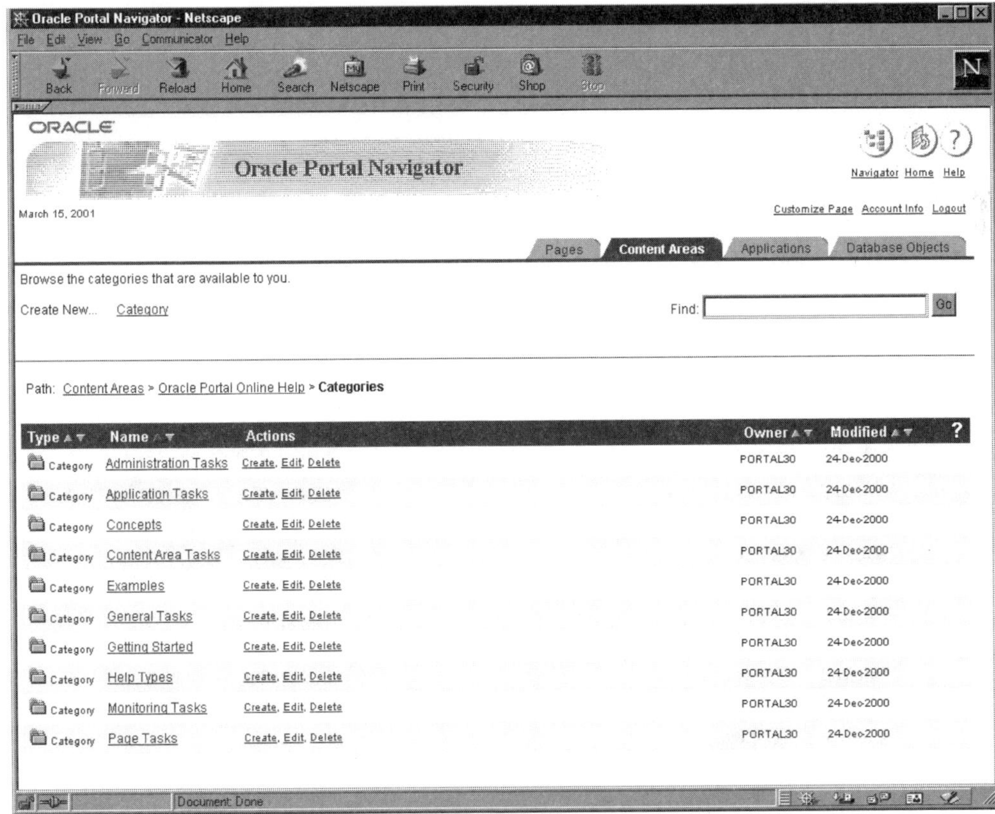

Figure 4.12 Oracle Navigation Portal: Content Areas: Contents: Categories.

Oracle Portal Navigator - Netscape
File Edit View Go Communicator Help
Back Forward Reload Home Search Netscape Print Security Shop Stop
ORACLE
Oracle Portal Navigator
Navigator Home Help
March 15, 2001
Customize Page Account Info Logout
Pages Content Areas Applications Database Objects
Browse the navigation bars that you have created, as well as those you are authorized to use for your folders.
Create New... Navigation Bar
Find: Go
Path: Content Areas > Oracle Portal Online Help > Navigation Bars
Type Name Actions Owner Modified ?
Navigation Bar Navbar 1 Edit, Delete PORTAL30_PUBLIC 27-Sep-2000
Navigation Bar Sample Content Area Navbar Edit, Delete PORTAL30_PUBLIC 8-Aug-2000
Document: Done

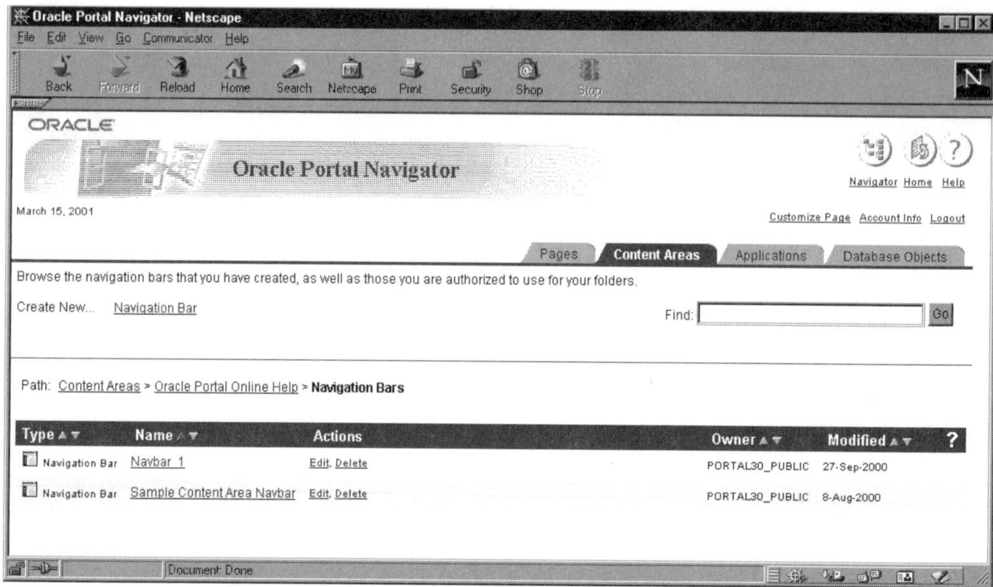

Figure 4.13 Oracle Navigation Portal: Content Areas: Contents: Navigation Bars.

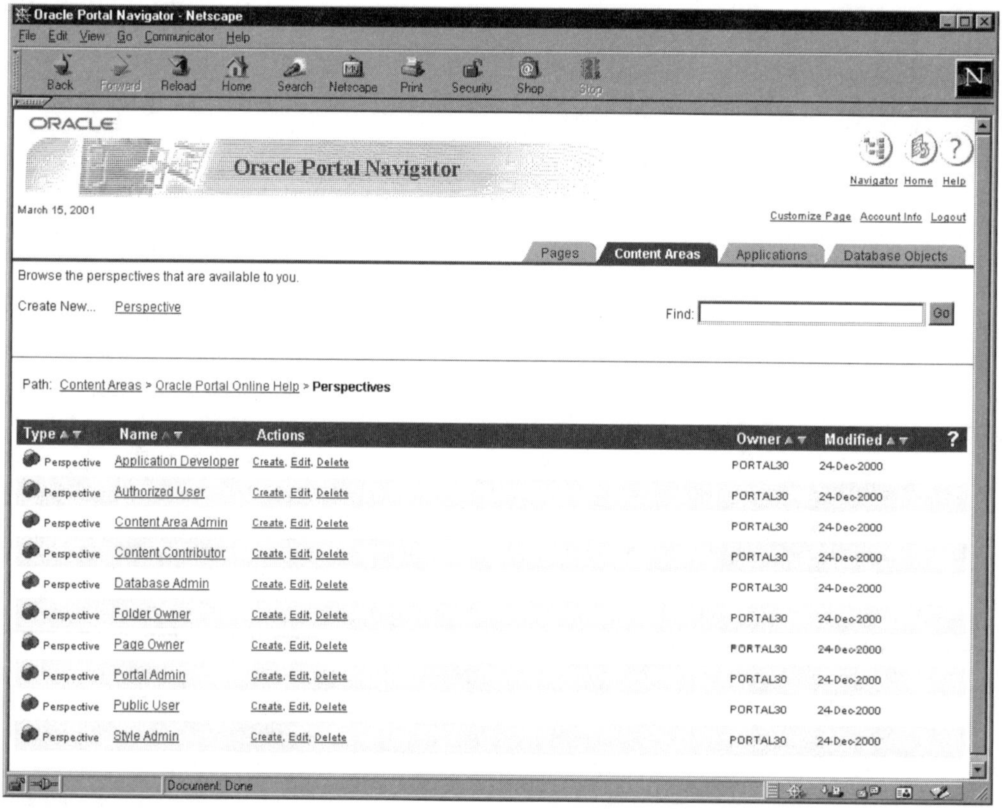

Oracle Portal Navigator - Netscape
File Edit View Go Communicator Help
Back Forward Reload Home Search Netscape Print Security Shop Stop
ORACLE
Oracle Portal Navigator
Navigator Home Help
March 15, 2001
Customize Page Account Info Logout
Pages Content Areas Applications Database Objects
Browse the perspectives that are available to you.
Create New... Perspective
Find: Go
Path: Content Areas > Oracle Portal Online Help > Perspectives
Type Name Actions Owner Modified ?
Perspective Application Developer Create, Edit, Delete PORTAL30 24-Dec-2000
Perspective Authorized User Create, Edit, Delete PORTAL30 24-Dec-2000
Perspective Content Area Admin Create, Edit, Delete PORTAL30 24-Dec-2000
Perspective Content Contributor Create, Edit, Delete PORTAL30 24-Dec-2000
Perspective Database Admin Create, Edit, Delete PORTAL30 24-Dec-2000
Perspective Folder Owner Create, Edit, Delete PORTAL30 24-Dec-2000
Perspective Page Owner Create, Edit, Delete PORTAL30 24-Dec-2000
Perspective Portal Admin Create, Edit, Delete PORTAL30 24-Dec-2000
Perspective Public User Create, Edit, Delete PORTAL30 24-Dec-2000
Perspective Style Admin Create, Edit, Delete PORTAL30 24-Dec-2000
Document: Done

Figure 4.14 Oracle Navigation Portal: Content Areas: Contents: Perspectives.

Navigation Bars

The following actions can be performed on navigation bars: edit and delete (Figure 4.13). You will learn more about navigation bars, perspectives, and categories in Chapter 9.

Perspectives

The following actions can be performed on perspectives: create (sub-perspectives), edit, and delete (Figure 4.14).

Styles

Styles elements define how the content areas and their navigation bars look. The following actions can be performed on styles: edit and delete (Figure 4.15).

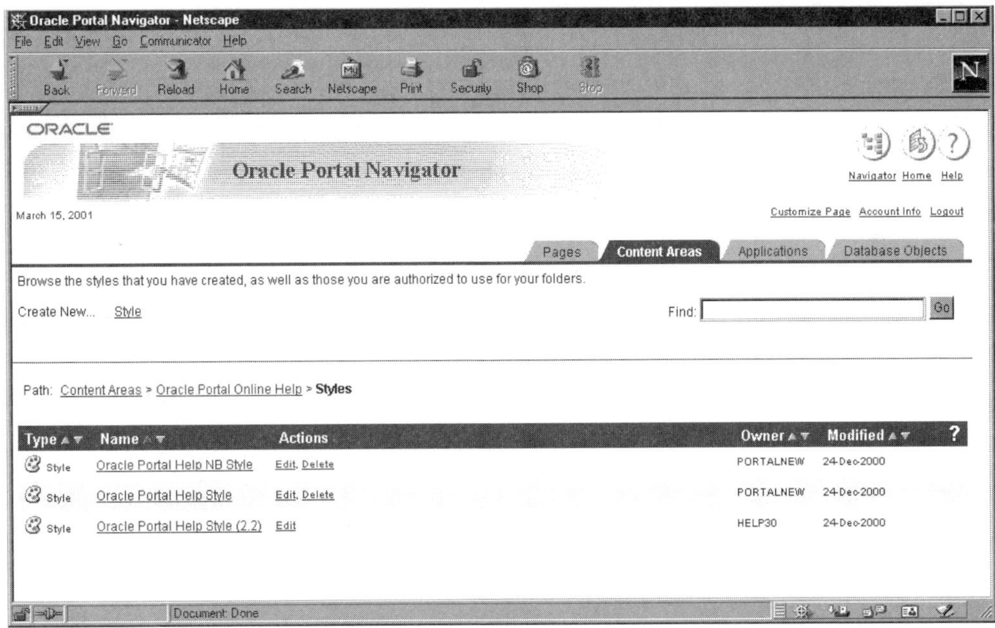

Figure 4.15 Oracle Navigation Portal: Content Areas: Contents: Styles.

Custom Types

Custom types include the following: Attributes, Folder Types, and Item Types (Figure 4.16). You can create a new object in one of these types by clicking on its "Create" action link. An explanation and examples of custom types can be found in Chapter 8.

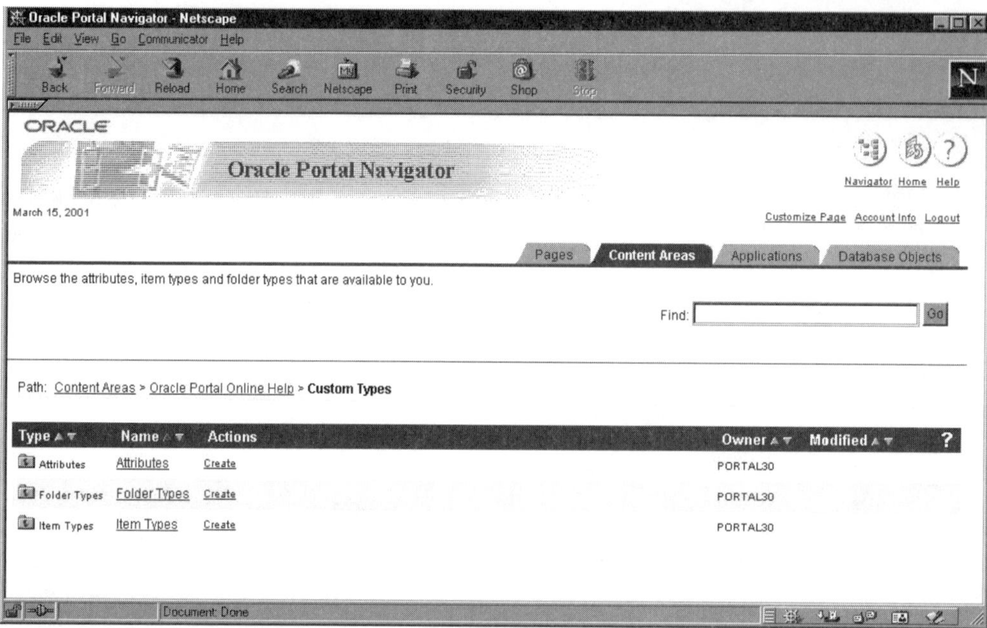

Figure 4.16 Oracle Navigation Portal: Content Areas: Contents: Custom Types.

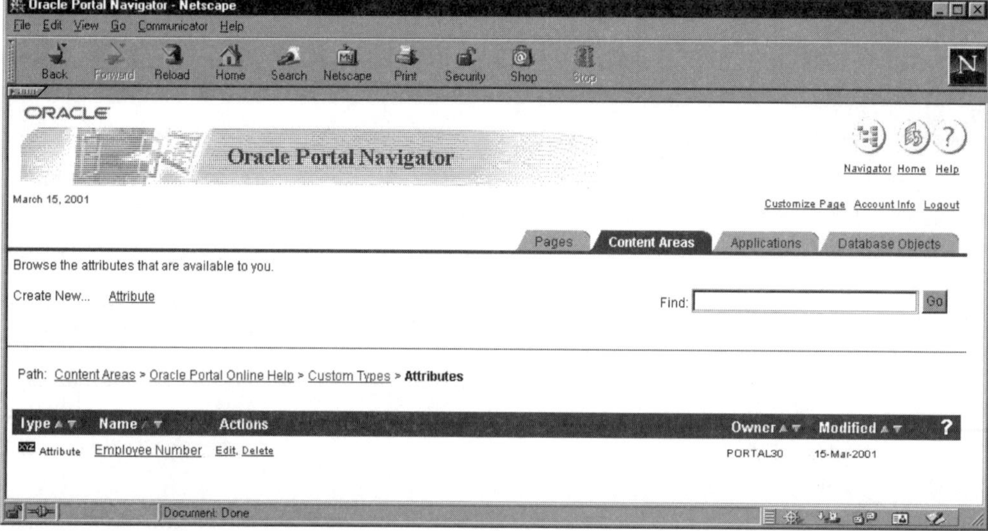

Figure 4.17 Oracle Navigation Portal: Content Areas: Contents: Custom Types: Attributes.

Attributes The following actions can be performed on attributes: edit and delete (Figure 4.17). Clicking on the attribute name has the same effect as editing the attribute. Do not worry if you get no attribute entries when you click on the attributes. Chapter 8 explains attributes and how they can be created and used.

Folder Types The following actions can be performed on folder types: edit and delete (Figure 4.18). Clicking on the folder type name has the same effect as editing the folder type.

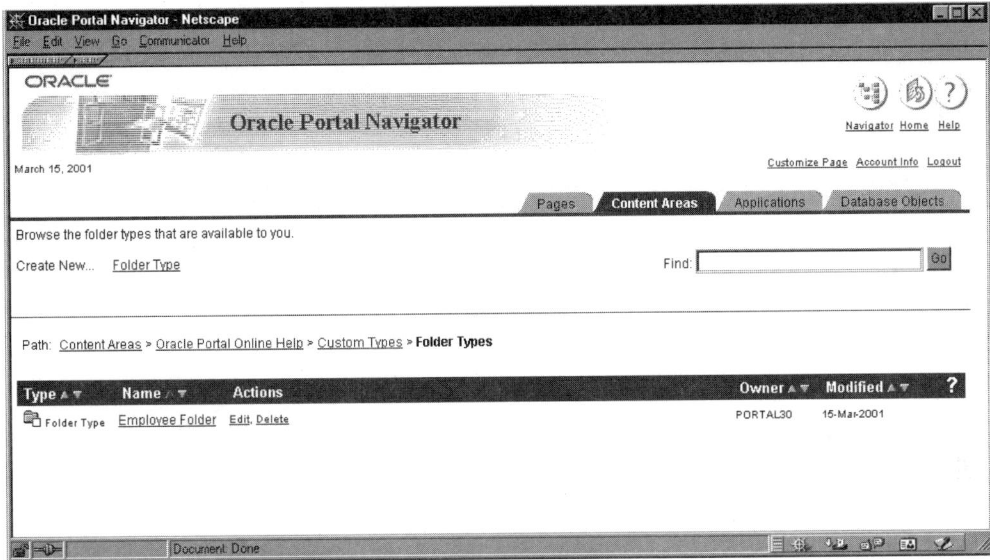

Figure 4.18 Oracle Navigation Portal: Content Areas: Contents: Custom Types: Folder Types.

Item Types The following actions can be performed on item types: edit and delete (Figure 4.19). Clicking on the item type name has the same effect as editing the item type.

Shared Objects: Contents

By creating objects under this node, these objects are available to be used in other content areas. You can consider the shared object as a global content area. Shared Objects include Personal Folders, Categories, Navigation Bars, Perspectives, Styles, and Custom Types, all of which have been covered here except Personal Folders (Figure 4.20).

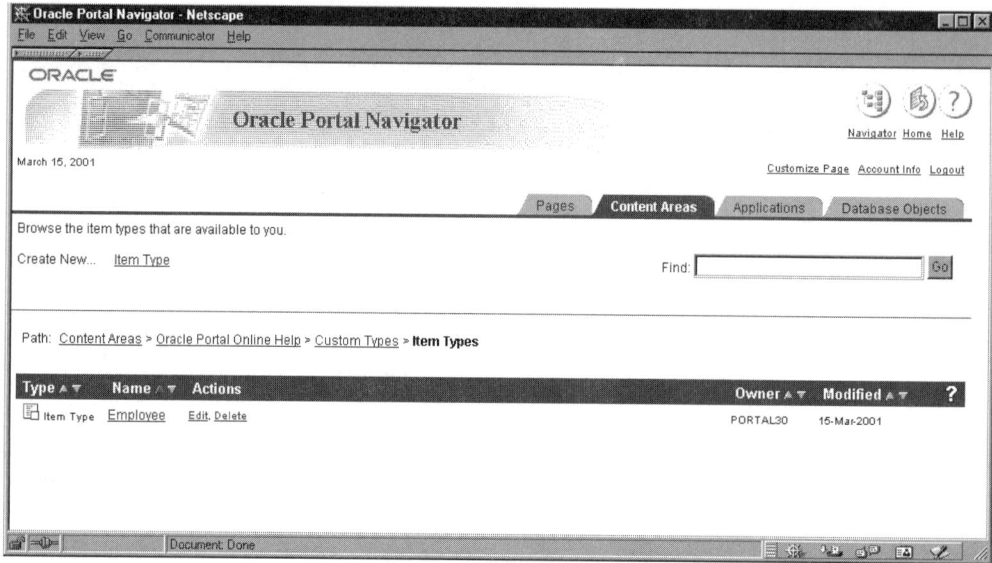

Figure 4.19 Oracle Navigation Portal: Content Areas: Contents: Custom Types: Item Types.

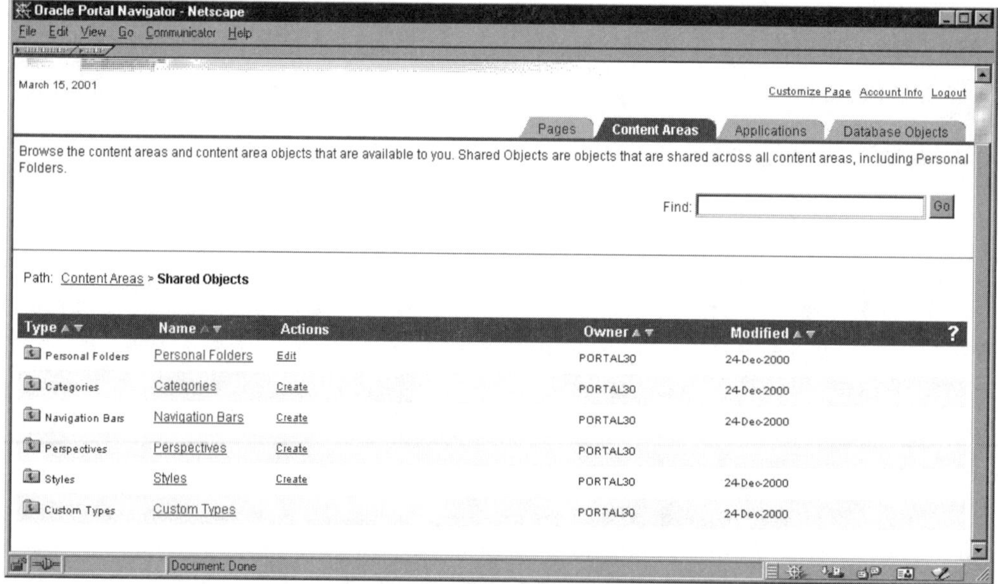

Figure 4.20 Oracle Navigation Portal: Content Areas: Contents: Shared Objects: Contents.

Personal Folders

Personal folders can be used as a storage space by users to keep their personal items, rather than keeping them under the content area folders that are usually accessed by many users. The Personal Folders content area displays the Personal Folders indexed by their owners (Figure 4.21).

Shared Objects: Edit Properties

You can change the properties of the content area that contains all the shared objects.

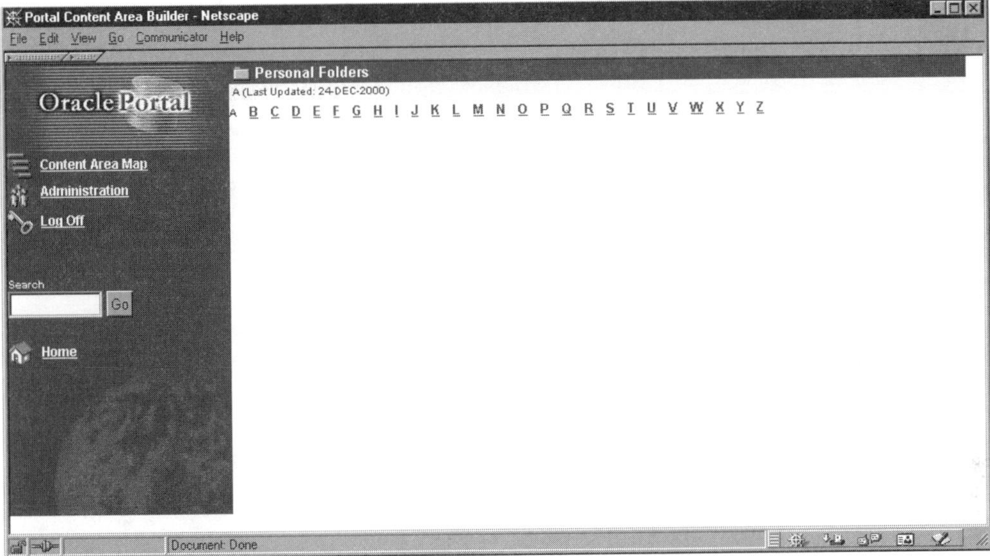

Figure 4.21 Oracle Navigation Portal: Content Areas: Contents: Shared Objects: Personal Folders.

Applications Navigation

The Applications tab in Oracle Portal Navigator includes applications and shared components (Figure 4.22). Applications in Oracle Portal are similar to packages storing PL/SQL subroutines; they contain components that can be used as portlets. Applications are described in Chapter 5.

Application : Open

By clicking on the name or on the open action of a certain application (e.g., EXAMPLE_APP), the list of components of this application is displayed (Figure 4.23). An application component can be any of the following: Form, Report, Chart, Calendar, Dynamic Page, Hierarchy, Menu, Frame Driver, Link, and List of Values. You can perform the following actions on each

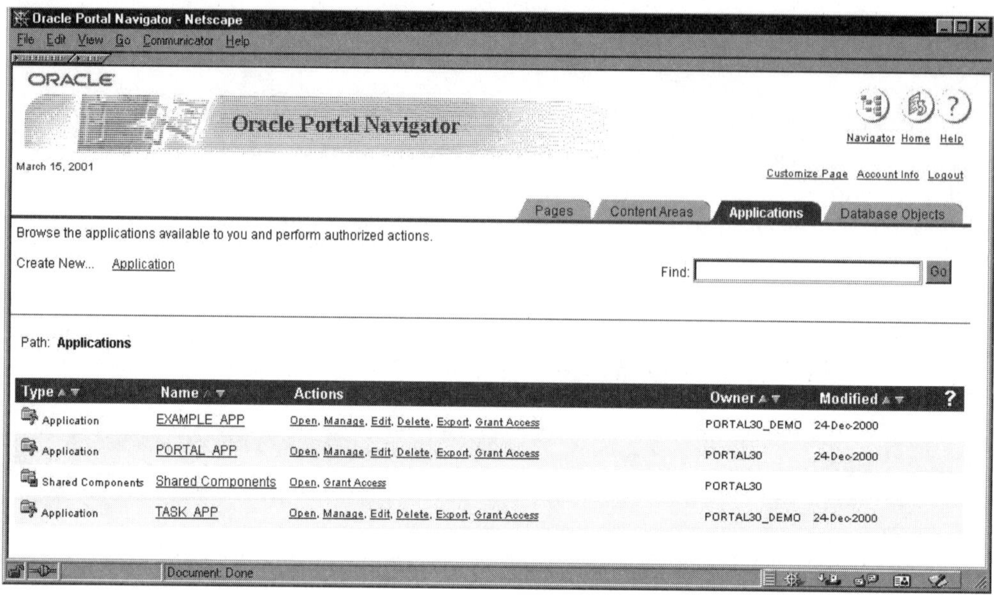

Figure 4.22 Oracle Navigation Portal: Applications Tab.

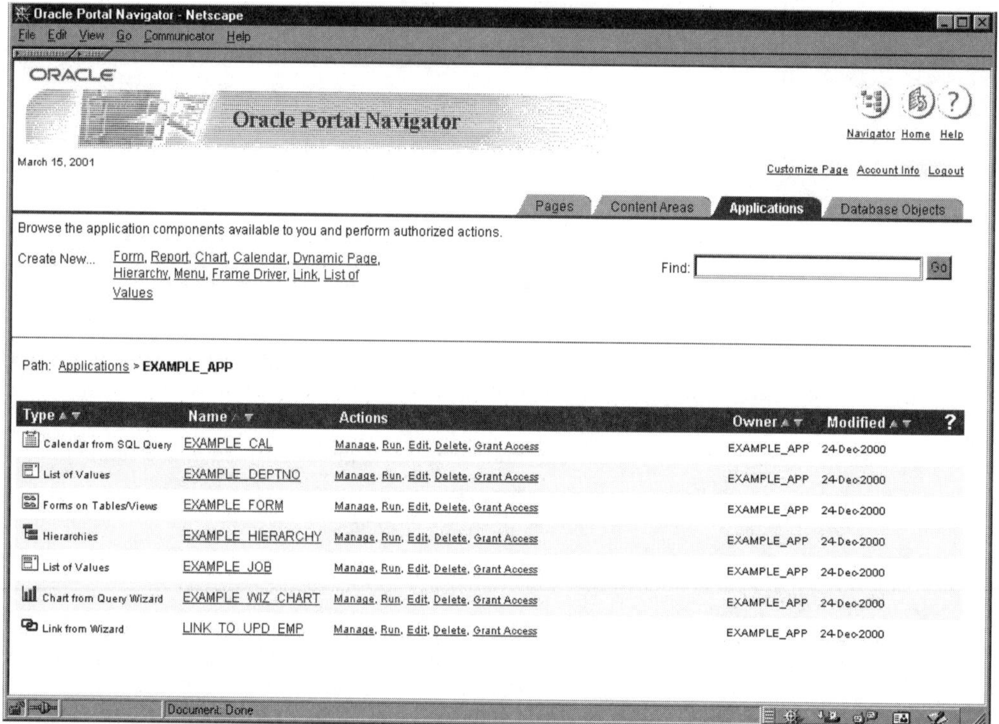

Figure 4.23 Oracle Navigation Portal: Applications: Open.

component: manage, run, edit, delete, and grant access. Chapter 5 goes into detail on how to create and maintain these components.

Shared Components : Open

By clicking on the "Shared Components" link or its open action link, a list of the shared components is displayed that includes Colors, Fonts, Images, JavaScripts, and User Interface Templates (Figure 4.24). For each type you can open and export its objects.

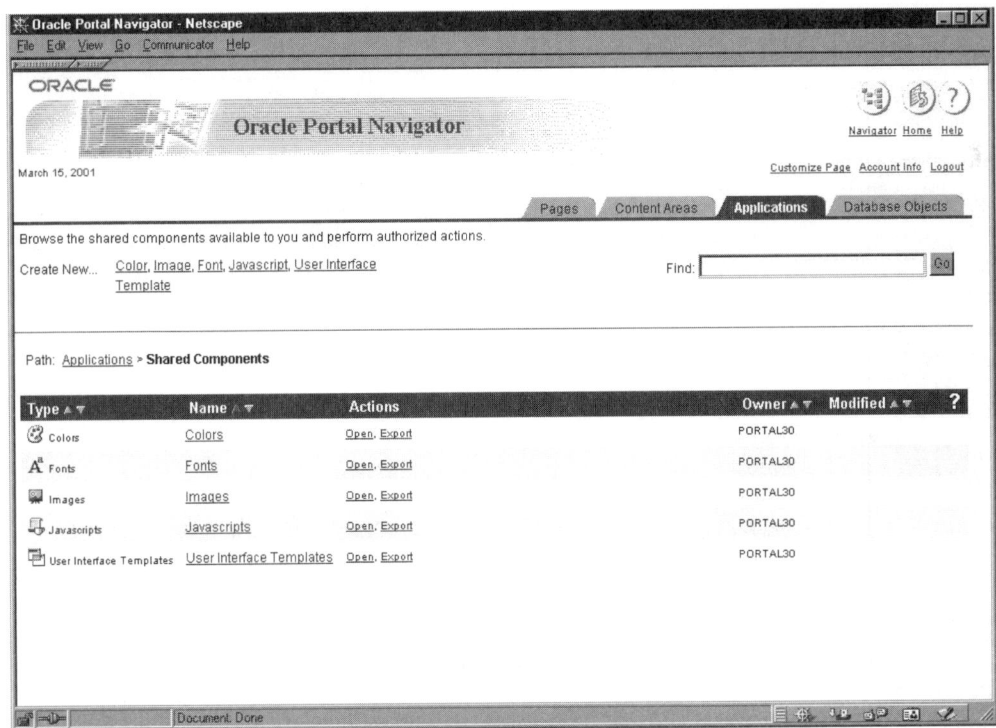

Figure 4.24 Oracle Navigation Portal: Applications: Shared Components: Open.

Applications' shared components mostly deal with user interfaces. They can be created here and then accessed from other applications' components (such as forms and charts). They are explained in Chapter 7.

Database Objects Navigation

The Database Objects tab in Oracle Portal Navigator includes a list of database schemas (Figure 4.25). You can use the Oracle Portal navigator to maintain database objects, especially if you are logging on as a DBA account, such as portal30. It is a handy tool, because you can perform maintenance operations remotely from a PC with a browser and with no SQL*Plus.

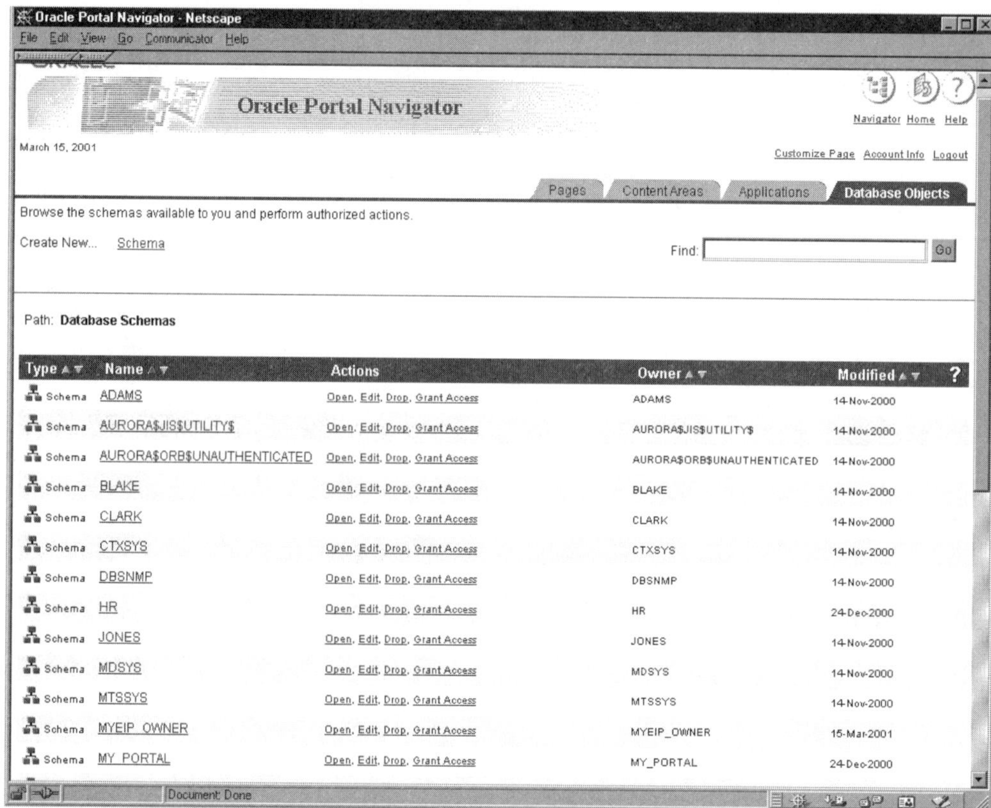

Figure 4.25 Oracle Navigation Portal: Database Objects Tab.

Schema

You can perform the following actions on a schema: open, edit, drop, and grant access.

Schema : Open

The open action displays the database objects owned by the schema (Figure 4.26). Object types displayed are Table, View, Procedure, Function, Package, Sequence, Synonym, Index, Trigger, Database Link, and Java Object. Depending on the database object type, there is a list of

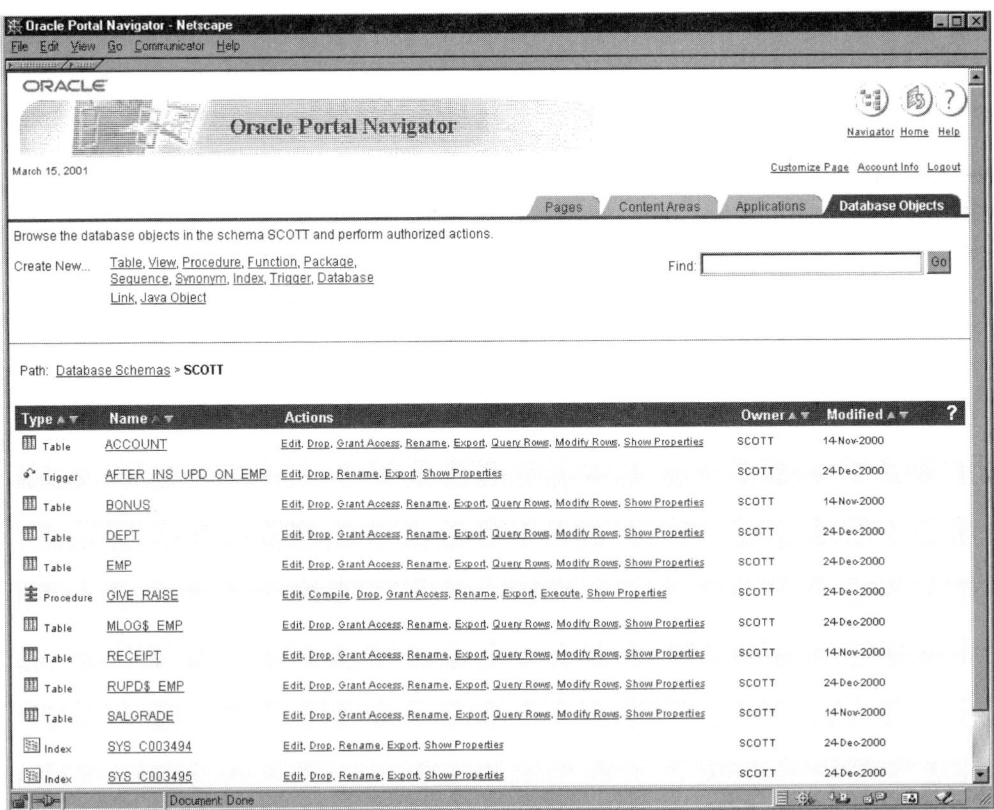

Figure 4.26 Oracle Navigation Portal: Database Objects: Open.

applicable actions displayed for each database object. These actions can be edit, drop, grant access, rename, export, query rows, modify rows, and show properties. If you click on the object name or the "Edit" link, an Edit screen is displayed to allow you to modify the object.

Chapter 5 shows you how to create your own application components and how to add them to your pages.

PART II

Building Application Components and Content Areas

CHAPTER 5

Forms and Reports

Introduction

This chapter explores building different application components using Oracle Portal built-in creation wizards. The chapter demonstrates building form components and report components.

What Is an Application Component?

Oracle Portal comes with wizards that help you create pieces of your EIP. These wizards allow you to create components through an easy-to-use, step-by-step process. When a wizard starts, you specify information about the component you want to create. When you finish the wizard creation process, it generates a database-stored PL/SQL package with the same name as the component. This component package utilizes the PL/SQL Web Toolkit packages to query the Oracle Portal schema and generates HTML back to the client through the Apache server.

Oracle Portal introduces the concept of portal applications, which can be considered as containers used to group the related components together for easier maintenance and administration. Applications in a portal are similar to folders in a disk. Each portal application maps to a database schema that owns the PL/SQL packages of the application components.

Oracle Portal comes with some prebuilt portal applications, such as EXAMPLE_APP and PORTAL_APP. You can start creating components under one of these applications, but for the purpose of modularity, in this chapter you create a new Oracle Portal application with the name "MYEIP_APP" to hold the components created throughout the book. Before creating the MYEIP_APP application, it is a good idea to create a new database schema to hold the database objects of the MYEIP_APP's components.

Create a New Schema

Click on the Administer Database tab in the Oracle Portal home page, and then click on the "Create New Schemas" link to create a new database user named MYEIP_OWNER, which will act as the application schema (Figure 5.1). If needed, change the tablespaces and database user profile settings, and remember to select the "Application Schema" check box so the MYEIP_OWNER schema is added to the schema choices available to the Oracle Portal applications. Then, click on the "Create" button to create the database user (Figure 5.2). Each Oracle Portal user connects to the Oracle Portal database (i.e., ORCL), but the Oracle Portal user does not have to be a database user. Each Oracle Portal user is associated with a database user, so you can get more than one Oracle Portal user connecting to the same database user (e.g., PORTAL30_PUBLIC). If you need your new schema (e.g., MYEIP_OWNER) to be available for association with Oracle Portal users, select the "Use this Schema for Portal Users" check box.

The new schema, by default, has both connect and resource roles granted to it. Also, by default, the new schema has unlimited tablespace quota, which means it can create tables and index in any tablespace in the database.

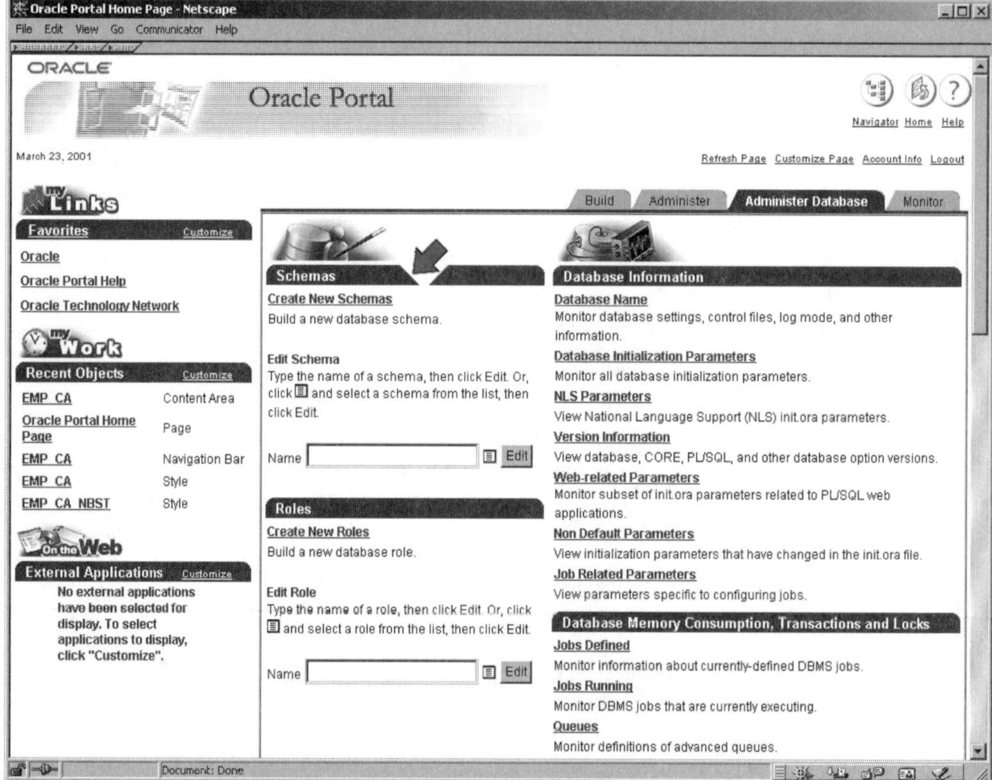

Figure 5.1 Oracle Portal Home Page: Administer Database Tab.

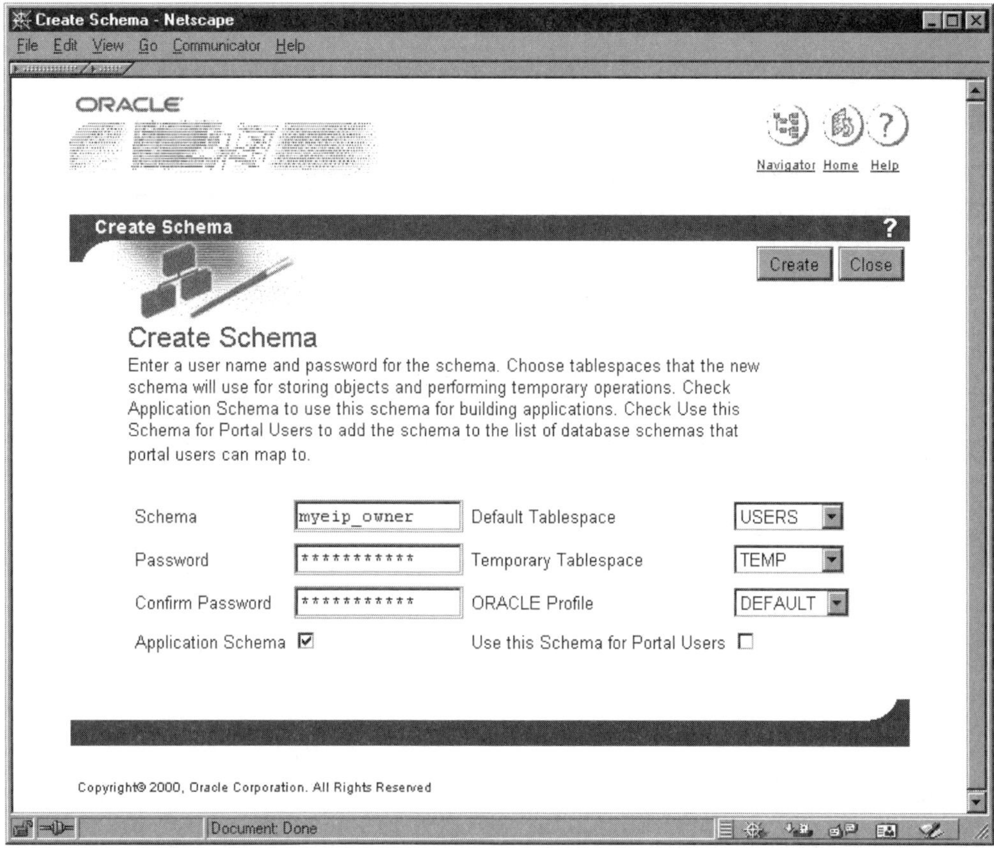

Figure 5.2 Create a Schema.

Note

In Oracle9*i*AS Portal version 3.0.9, there is no check box for "Application Schema". By default, all the schemas in the database can be used as application schemas.

Create a New Application

The new application will hold the new components created in this book. Return to the Oracle Portal home page, and click on the "Create a New Application" link (Figure 5.3). To create the new application, you need to specify an application name (e.g., MYEIP_APP), application display name (e.g., MyEIP Application), and the owner schema created in the previous step (e.g., MYEIP_OWNER; Figure 5.4). When you click on "OK", an application is created and the Manage Application screen is displayed (Figure 5.5). You can edit, delete, or export your application. You can also perform these actions later on from the Oracle Portal Navigator.

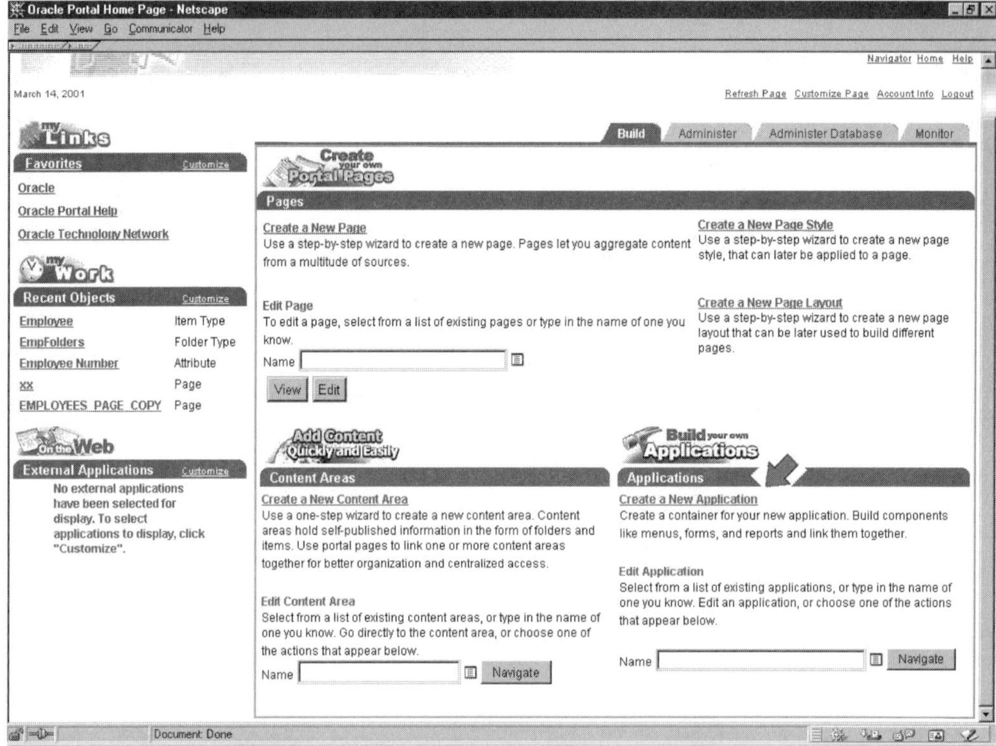

Figure 5.3 Oracle Portal Home Page: Build Tab.

Create Application - Netscape

File Edit View Go Communicator Help

ORACLE

Navigator Home Help

APP_0316075745

OK Cancel

Application Name and Schema

Enter a name and display name for the application and choose the schema that will own it. The Application Name identifies the application to Oracle Portal and the Application Navigator. The Application Display Name identifies the application to end users and appears in the Application Providers list.

The database schemas that you can choose are those in which you have been granted privileges by the Oracle Portal DBA.

Application Name MYEIP_APP

Display Name MyEIP Application

Schema MYEIP_OWNER

Document: Done

Figure 5.4 Create Applications.

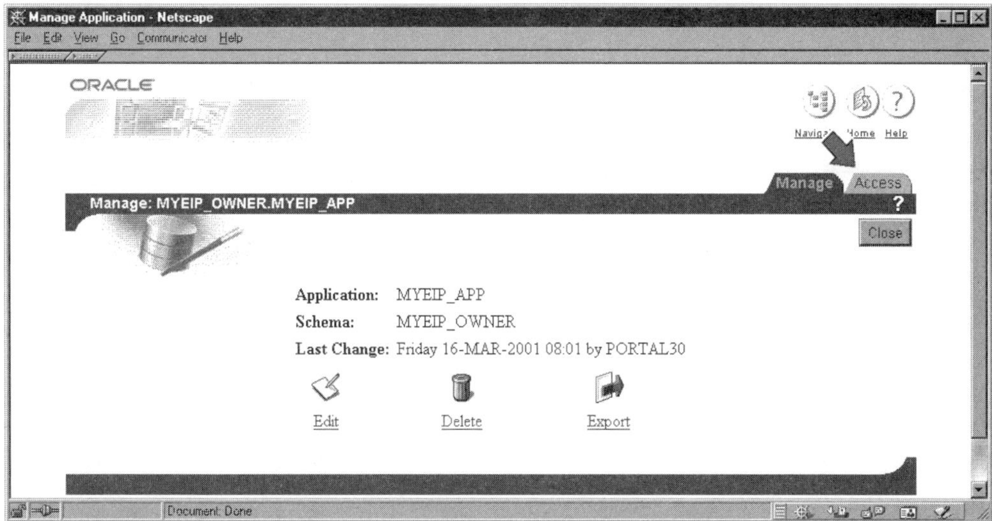

Figure 5.5 Manage Applications.

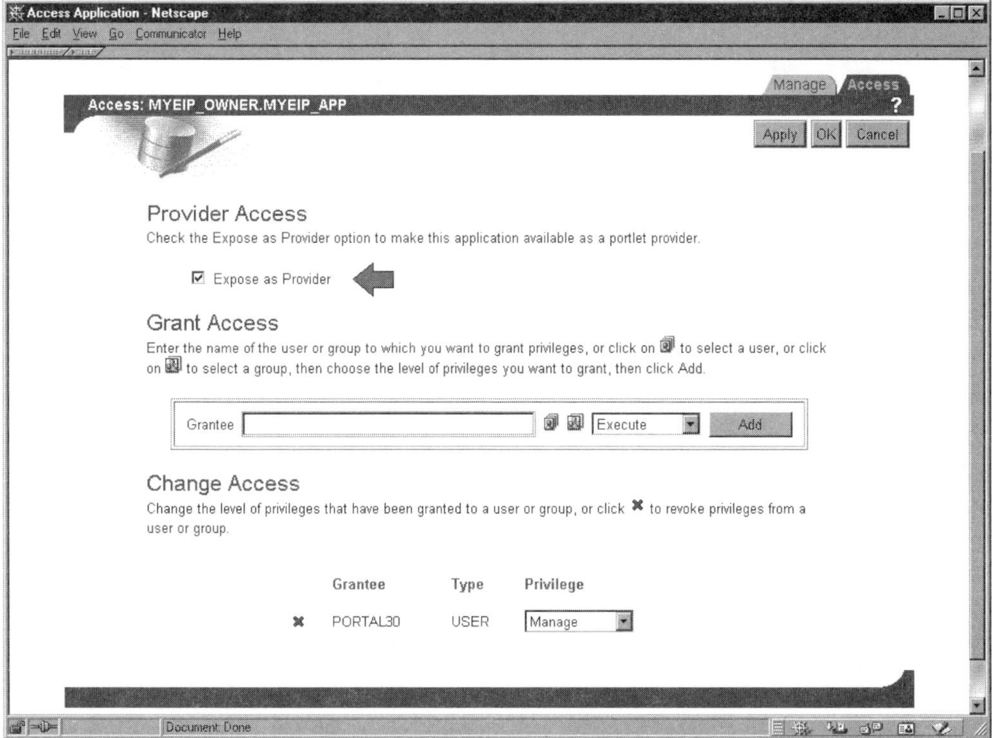

Figure 5.6 Manage Application: Access Tab.

Now you can create application components that reside in this new application. But to be able to add these application components as portlets to your portal page, the application has to be acting as a provider. To do that, click on the Access tab of the Manage Application window and select the "Expose as Provider" check box (Figure 5.6).

Create a Form Component

To create a component, go to the Oracle Portal Navigator and click on the Applications tab. Click on the "MYEIP_APP" link to drill down to its components; there should not be any components for now (Figure 5.7). Click on the "Form" link (Figure 5.8). The Oracle Navigator path should be: Applications > MYEIP_APP.

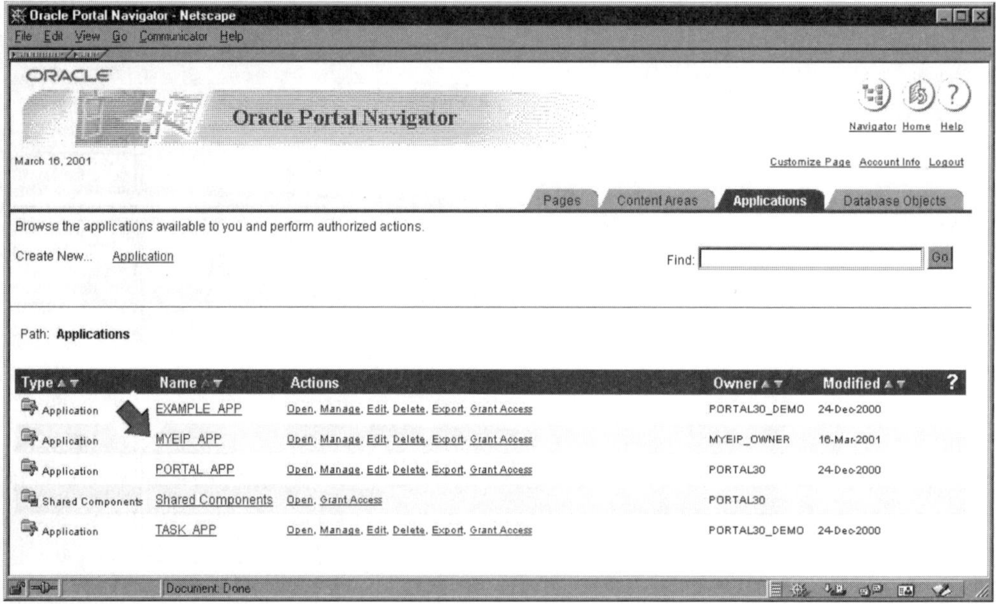

Figure 5.7 Oracle Portal Navigator: Applications Tab.

There are three different types of forms:

1. Forms based on a table or a view: To create one, you choose one table or one view and the creation wizard displays all the columns of this table/view. Then you can exclude some of the columns.
2. Master-detail form: To create one, you choose two tables, one master and one detail. Then you define the join conditions.
3. Form based on procedures: To create one, you choose a database PL/SQL procedure. Now the form acts as an interface to the procedure.

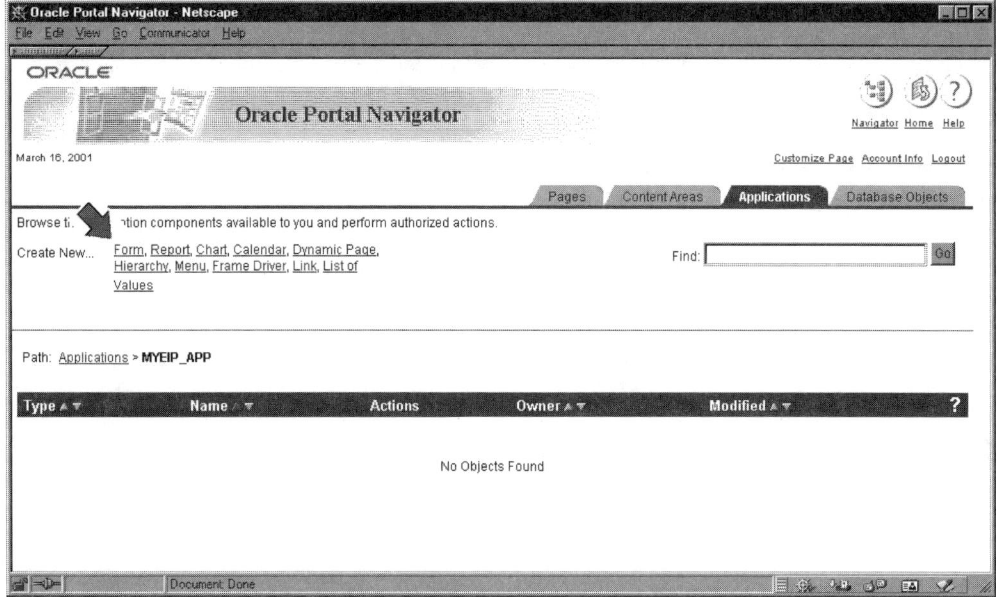

Figure 5.8 Oracle Portal Navigator: Application: MyEIP Application.

Start with Forms On Tables (Figure 5.9). When you click on the "Form based on table or view" link, Oracle Portal starts the Forms creation wizard. The next section explains the wizard creation steps.

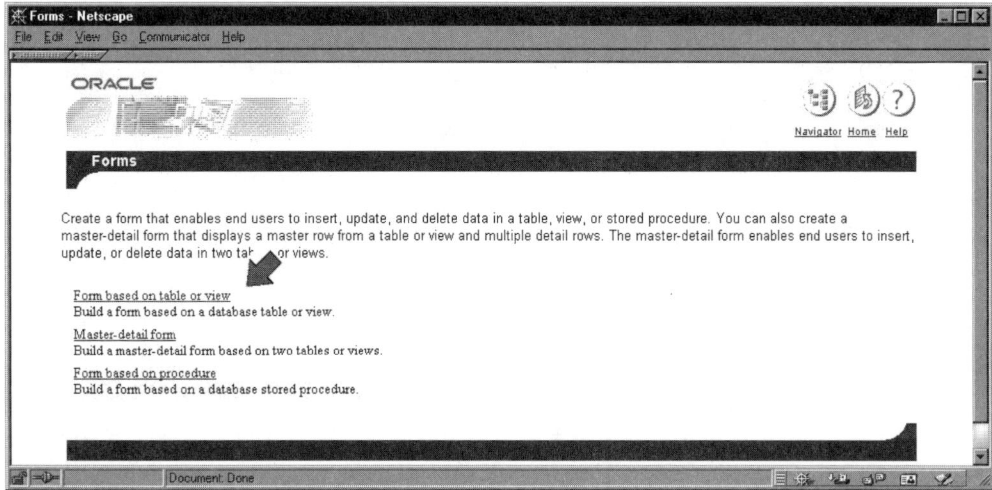

Figure 5.9 Oracle Portal Navigator: Create a Form Component.

Form Based on Table or View

The form created in this section allows Oracle Portal users to enter and maintain employee data. For practice, name your form "EMP_FORM". Note that your form application is MYEIP_APP because you are creating the form under it (Figure 5.10). Click "Next" to provide the table or the view name upon which this form will be based. You can type the table name directly in the field using the <Schema Name>.<Table Name> format (e.g., SCOTT.EMP; Figure 5.11). Also,

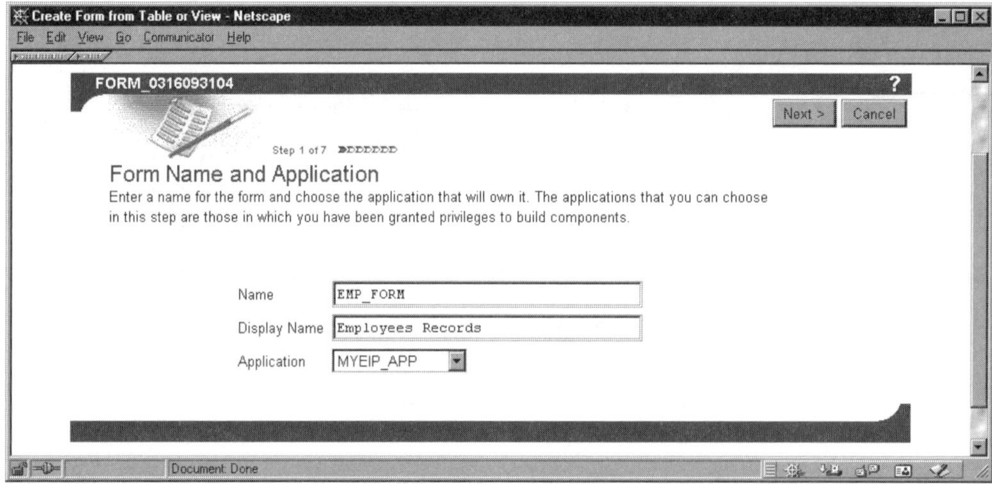

Figure 5.10 Create a Form: Form Name and Application (Step 1 of 7).

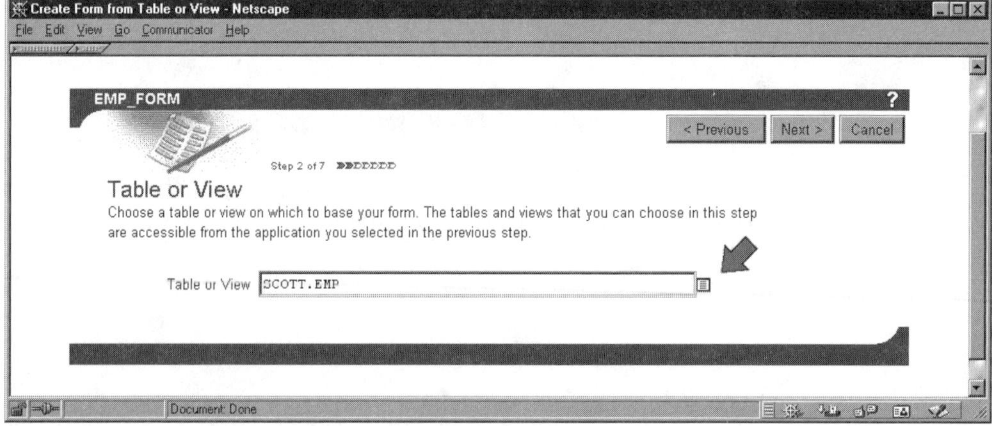

Figure 5.11 Create a Form: Table or View (Step 2 of 7).

you can click on the List of Values icon to search for tables or views. By default the List of Values displays a list of tables and views accessible by the logged-on user. PORTAL30 is granted the DBA database role, which includes the SELECT ANY TABLE system privilege.

You can search for tables and views using pattern search. Similar to the usage of the LIKE operator in SQL statements, you can use the wild cards "%" and "_" to specify your search pattern for any character and one character, respectively. For example, you can get a list of the tables owned by user SCOTT by specifying "SCOTT.%" in the find box (Figure 5.12).

Note

When you choose a table or view for the form, you can finish the creation at this step by clicking on the "Finish" button. All the remaining options are set to the default values.

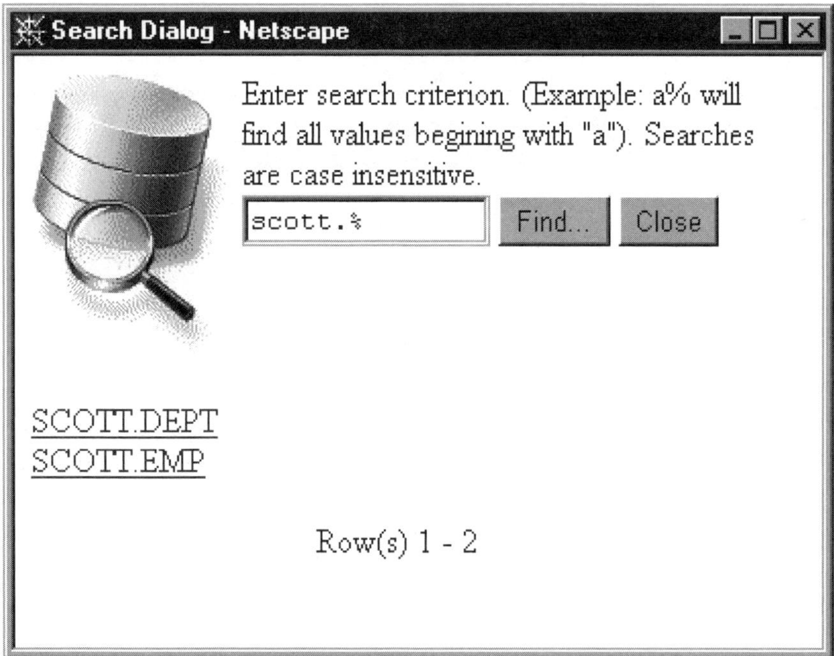

Figure 5.12 Create a Form: Table or View (Step 2 of 7): List of Values.

Click on "Next" to specify the form layout. Tabular form layout is based on the layout options you specify in the creation wizard. Custom form layout is based on HTML code. For practice, leave the EMP_FORM with Tabular layout (Figure 5.13).

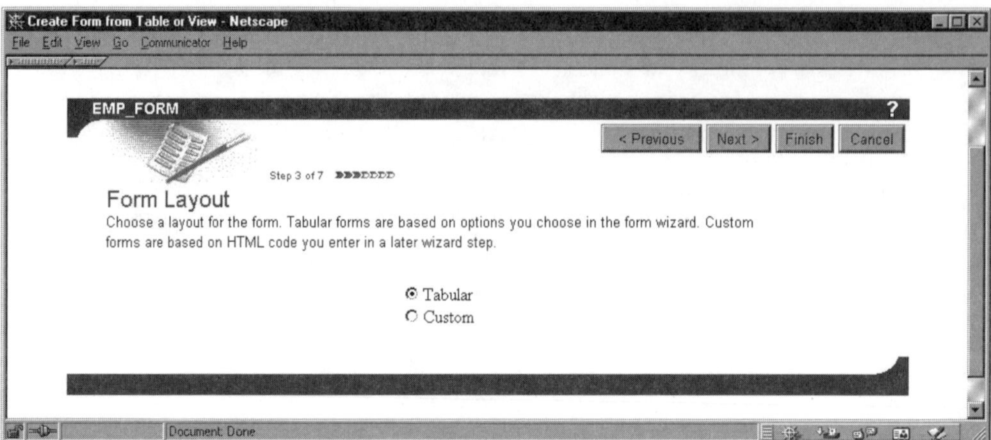

Figure 5.13 Create a Form: Form Layout (Step 3 of 7).

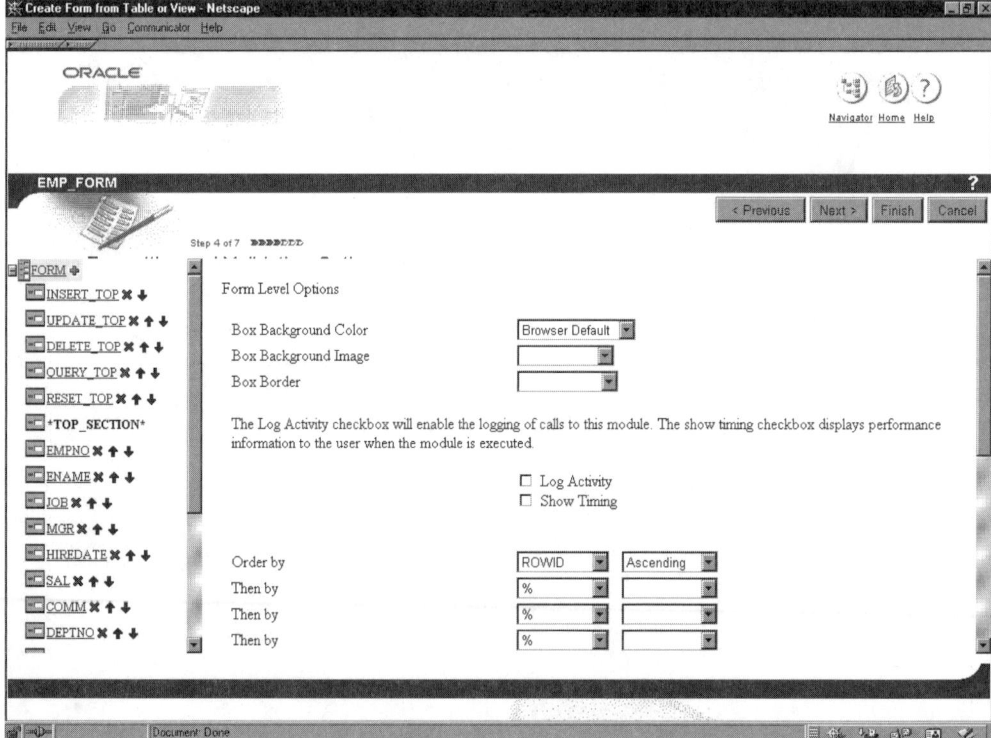

Figure 5.14 Create a Form: Form Layout: Formatting and Validation Options (Step 4 of 7).

Click "Next" to go to the Formatting and Validation Options step, where you get to choose which columns to be displayed and in which order. Also, you get to decide which control push buttons are displayed along with the form (e.g., insert and update). For your first form creation, you can leave all the values as defaults. As you become more familiar with the wizards, you can change the form properties one by one to understand how each property affects the form output. The page is split into two frames, the Navigation frame on the left side and the Options frame on the right side (Figure 5.14). By default the Form Level Options are displayed (e.g., box border, etc.). By clicking on an item in the Navigation frame, the related options are displayed in the Options frame. You can also delete any of the items by clicking on the delete icon. You can reorder the items in the Navigation frame using the up and down arrows. There are more examples on how to use the form's formatting and validation options in this section.

The next step is number 6 of 7 (we skipped step 5, the Custom Form Layout Editor). In step 6, Form Text, you get to customize your form by changing the Form Template or adding HTML code. You can try putting a simple HTML code (e.g., text, <CENTER>, and <H2> tags) and changing the Form Template (Figure 5.15). A Form Template defines the header, the footer,

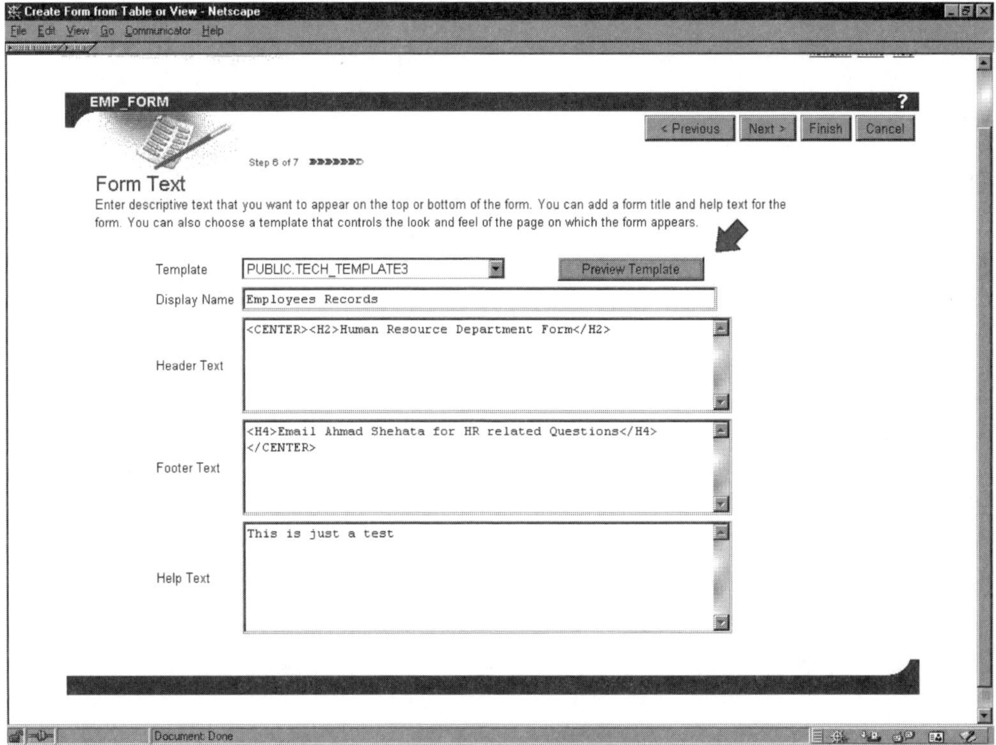

Figure 5.15 Create a Form: Form Layout: Form Text (Step 6 of 7).

and the background image for a form component when it is not running as a portlet. You can preview the templates before choosing them by clicking on the "Preview" button (Figure 5.16).

Note

The default template used depends on the Oracle Portal version. So, you might get a different template when you run the form in full page mode.

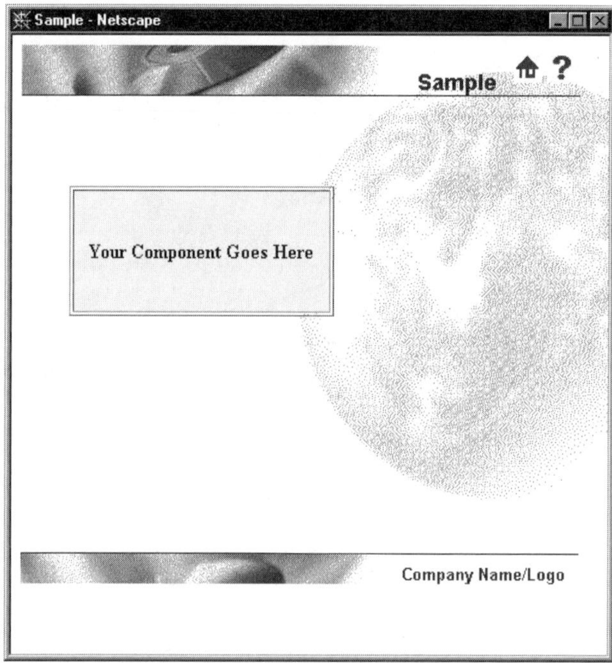

Figure 5.16 Create a Form: Form Layout: Form Text (Step 6 of 7): Preview Template.

The last step in the creation wizard is the Additional PL/SQL Code, where you get to add your own PL/SQL code to generate HTML in different times of the form run time. You have the chance to add some PL/SQL code while editing the form later in this section (Figure 5.17).

When you are done with the creation of a component, Oracle Portal displays the Manage Component screen where you can perform maintenance operations on the component (Figure 5.18).

Click on the "Run" link to test the form (Figure 5.19). The "Run" link opens a new Web browser window displaying the form output. The mandatory field prompts are in red. The mandatory fields are based on the NOT NULL database columns, such as the columns of the Primary and Unique Keys. You can query existing records and then update or delete these retrieved records (Figure 5.20).

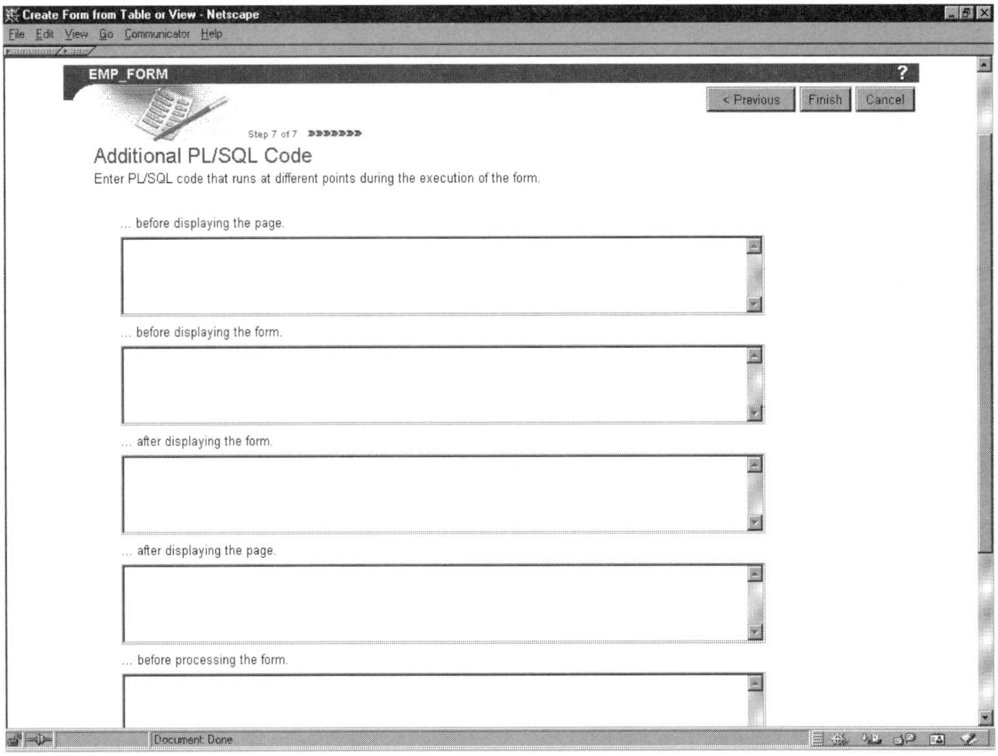

Create Form from Table or View - Netscape
File Edit View Go Communicator Help
EMP_FORM
< Previous
Finish
Cancel
Step 7 of 7
Additional PL/SQL Code
Enter PL/SQL code that runs at different points during the execution of the form.
... before displaying the page.
... before displaying the form.
... after displaying the form.
... after displaying the page.
... before processing the form.
Document: Done

Figure 5.17 Create a Form: Form Layout: Additional PL/SQL (Step 7 of 7).

Manage Component - Netscape
File Edit View Go Communicator Help
Develop
Manage
Access
Develop: MYEIP_APP.EMP_FORM
Close
Form on Table EMP_FORM
Application MYEIP_APP
Version(s) Status 1 (PRODUCTION with VALID Package)
Last Changed Friday 16-MAR-2001 11:36 by PORTAL30
Run Link PORTAL30.wwa_app_module.new_instance?p_moduleid=1217597706
PL/SQL source Package Spec, Package Body
Call Interface Show
Edit
Run
Run as Portlet
Customize
Add to Favorites
About
Delete
Document: Done

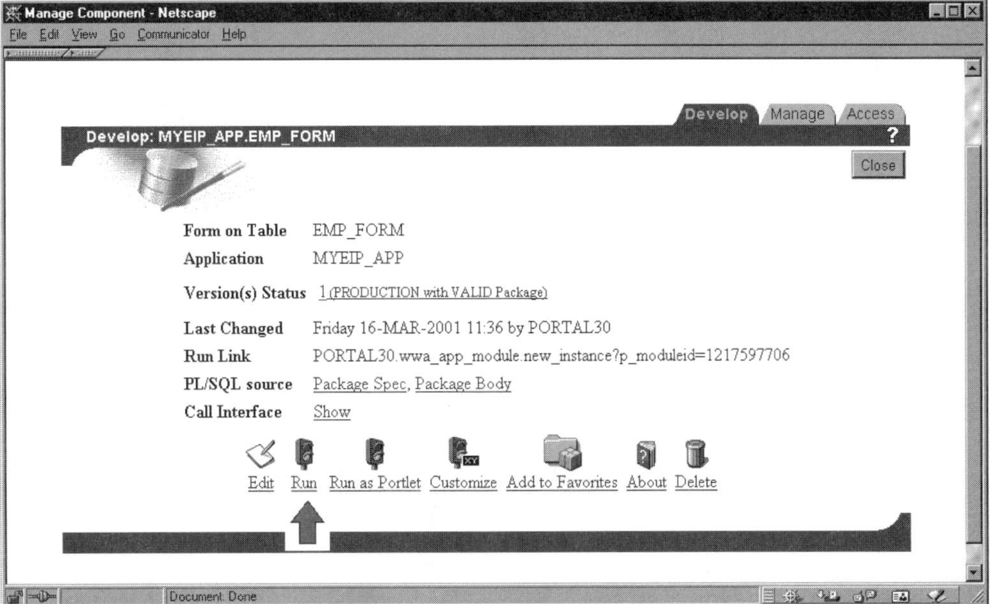

Figure 5.18 Manage Form: Develop Tab.

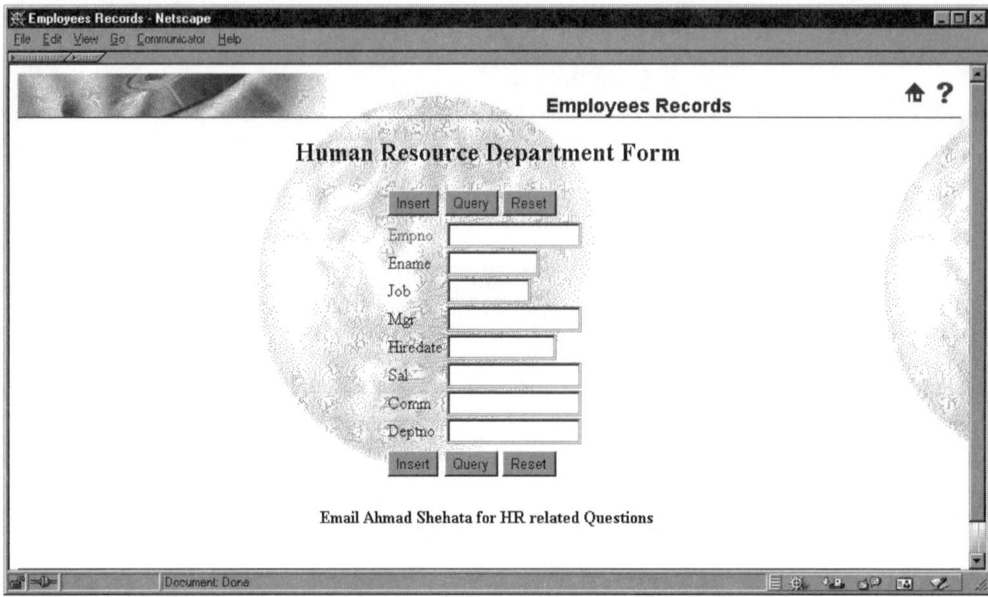

Figure 5.19 Run a Form.

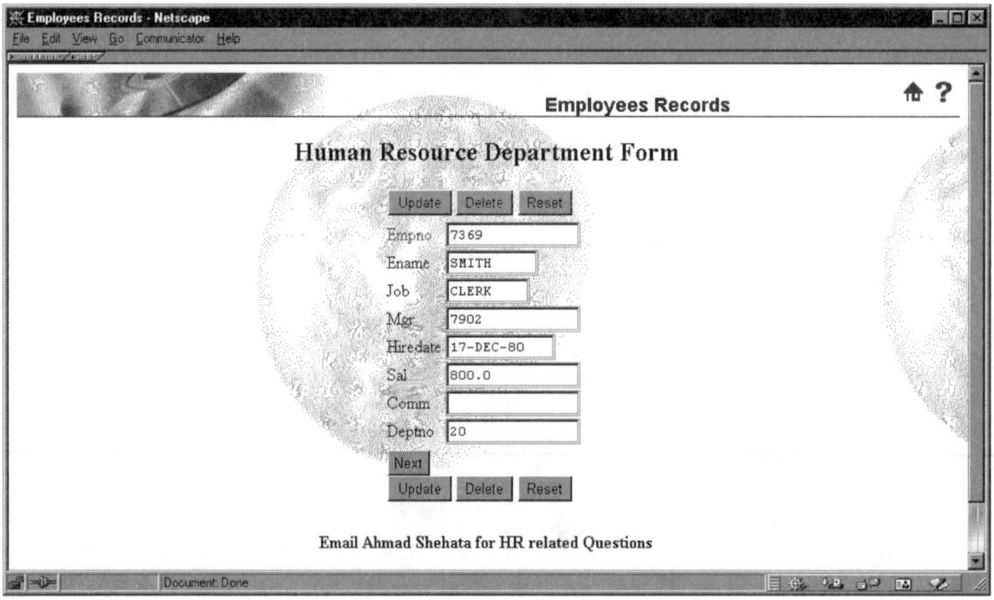

Figure 5.20 Run a Form: Query.

You can go back to the Manage Component window for further operations. The Manage Component page has three tabs. The default tab displayed is the Develop tab, where we ran the form. The other two tabs are the Manage tab (Figure 5.21), and the Access tab (Figure 5.22). For a description of each task you can perform on a component, refer to Table 5.1. To be able to add the form component to a portal page, you need to select the "Publish to Portal" check box in the Access tab, and then click "Apply" (Figure 5.22).

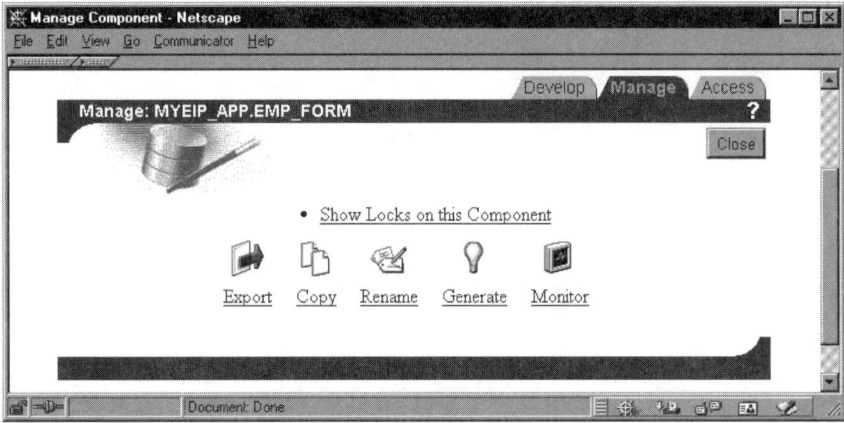

Figure 5.21 Manage a Form: Manage Tab.

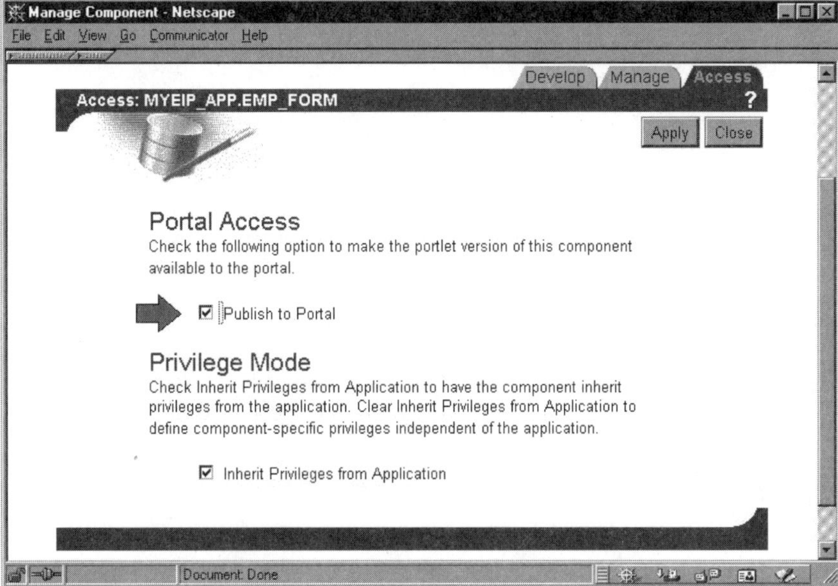

Figure 5.22 Manage a Form: Access Tab.

Table 5.1 Component Operations

Operation	Icon	Description
Edit		Edits the most recent version of the component.
Run		Runs the latest version (i.e., production) of the component in standalone (i.e., full page) mode (using the template).
Run as portlet		Runs the latest version of the component, like it would be displayed if added as a portlet to page.
Customize	 XY	Displays the component customization form to provide values for the component parameters. The default parameter that can be customized is the Form Display Name.
Add to Favorites		Adds a link to the component to the Favorites portlet.
About		Displays the component information (e.g., internal ID, name, type, version numbers, etc.).
Delete		Deletes the component. You will be asked to confirm the deletion before it occurs.
Export		Exports component from the database.
Copy		Copies a component to another Oracle Portal application, or copies it to the same application with a new name.
Rename		Renames an existing component.
Generate		Recompiles the component database packages. This is helpful if the database object, which the component uses, got changed.

Table 5.1 (*continued*)

Operation	Icon	Description
Monitor		If the Oracle Portal administrator has set up logging on a component, you can monitor it to get a list of activities performed on it.
Show locks		Sometimes you need to show the locks on a component and also unlock these locks. For example, if you are modifying a component and then you closed your Web browser before finishing, the component package is still being locked, and you need to unlock it using the show locks icon before you can update.

Note

Both the individual component and its application have to be "published" to be able to add the component as a portlet.

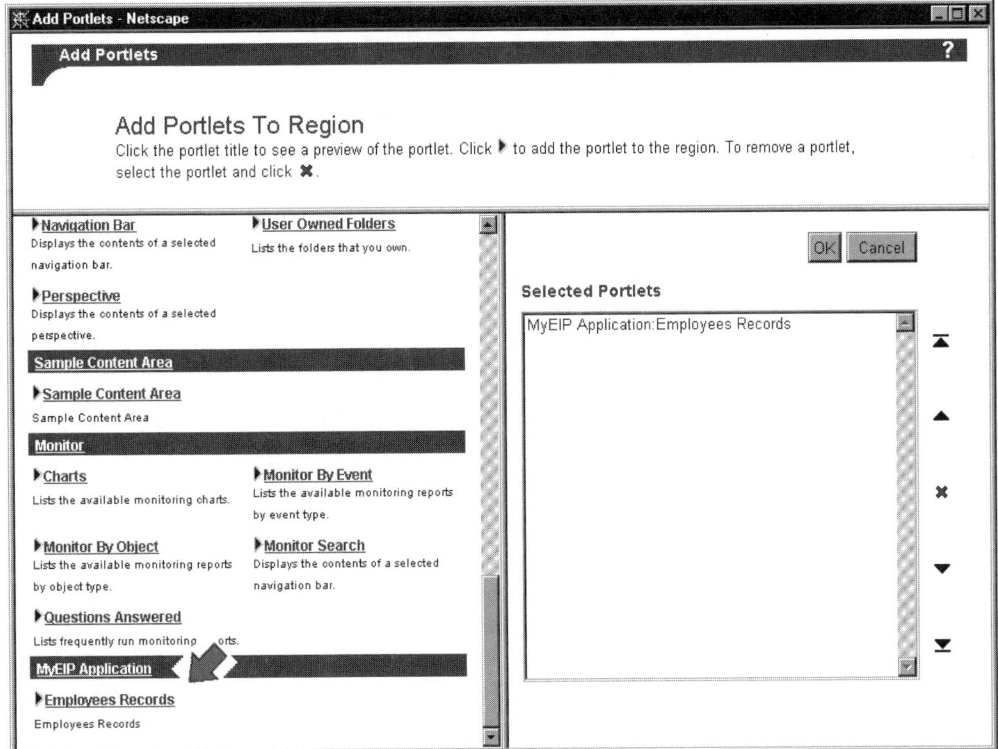

Figure 5.23 Edit a Page: Portlet Repository.

Now that you have successfully created your form component, you can add the form to your page by navigating to the page and editing it. Click on the add portlet icon in the Employees Salaries tab to display the Portlet Repository. The form component is displayed at the end of the list. The provider of the form is the MYEIP_APP application (Figure 5.23 and Figure 5.24). In Oracle9*i*AS Portal version 3.0.9, the MYEIP_APP provider is displayed in the Portlet Repository under "Other Providers", so it is easier to find, because you do not need to scroll.

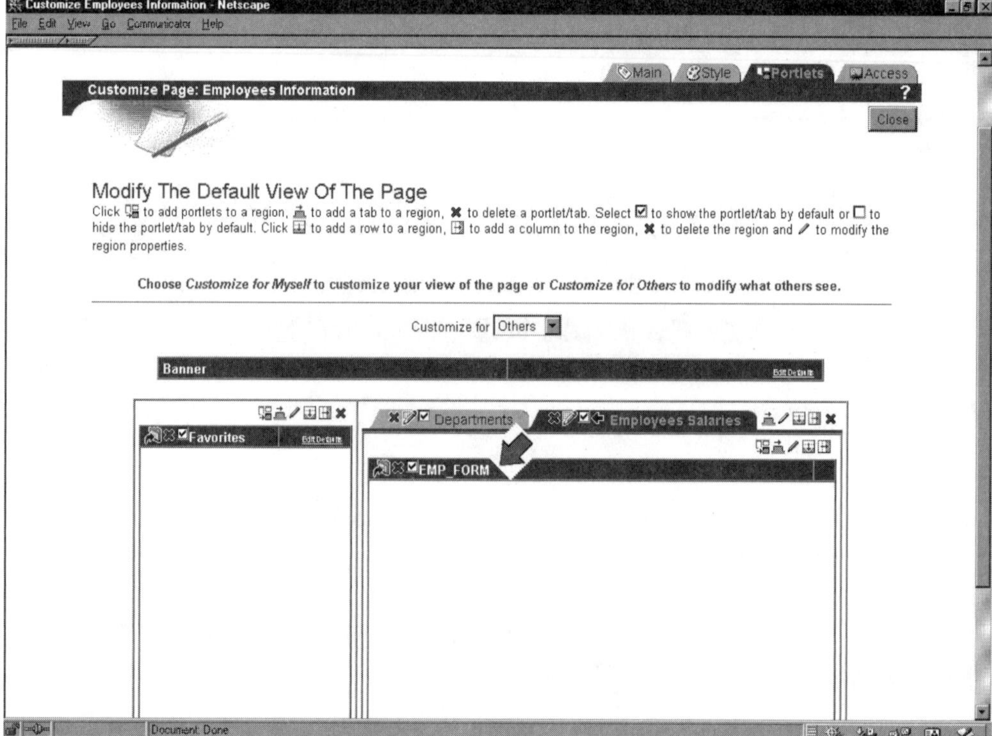

Figure 5.24 Edit a Form: Modify the Page View.

You can order the selected portlets in the right frame by using the icons in Table 5.2. You can delete a selected portlet by clicking on the delete icon.

Close and display the page (Figure 5.25). The form component is displayed in the page as a portlet. It has two links in its header, "Customize" and "Help". The help link is displayed because you have added a help text in Form Text (step 6 of 7).

Table 5.2 Sorting Icons

Icon	Description
	Move up
	Move down
	Move top
	Move bottom

Note

The portlets of the right region might stretch to fill the width of the portal page displayed in the browser.

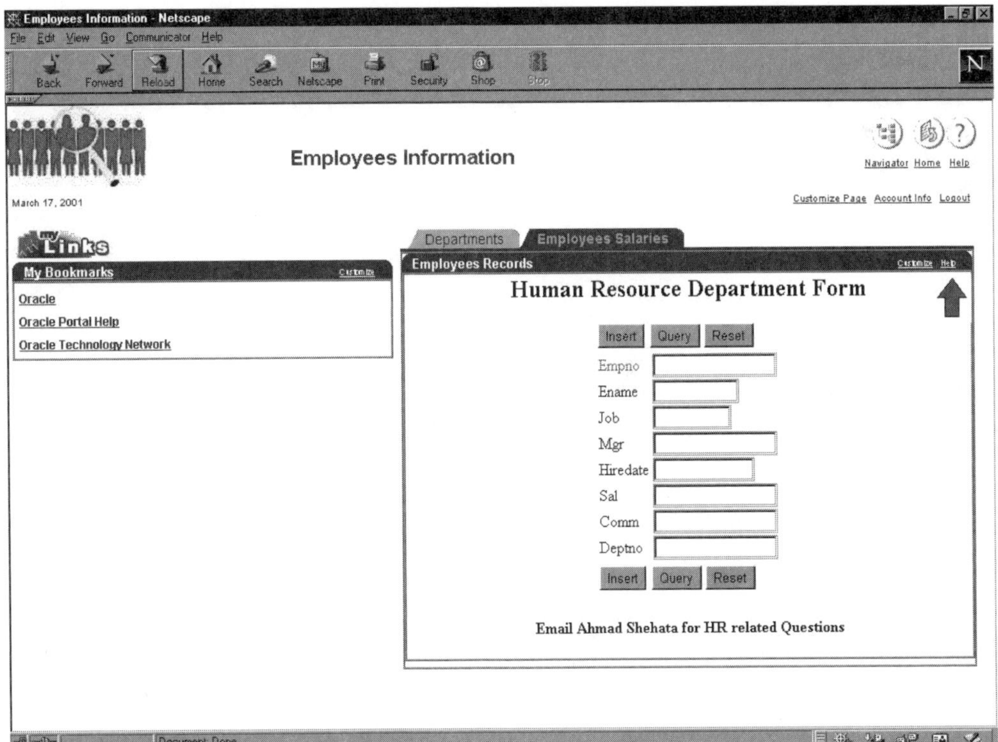

Figure 5.25 Employees Information Page.

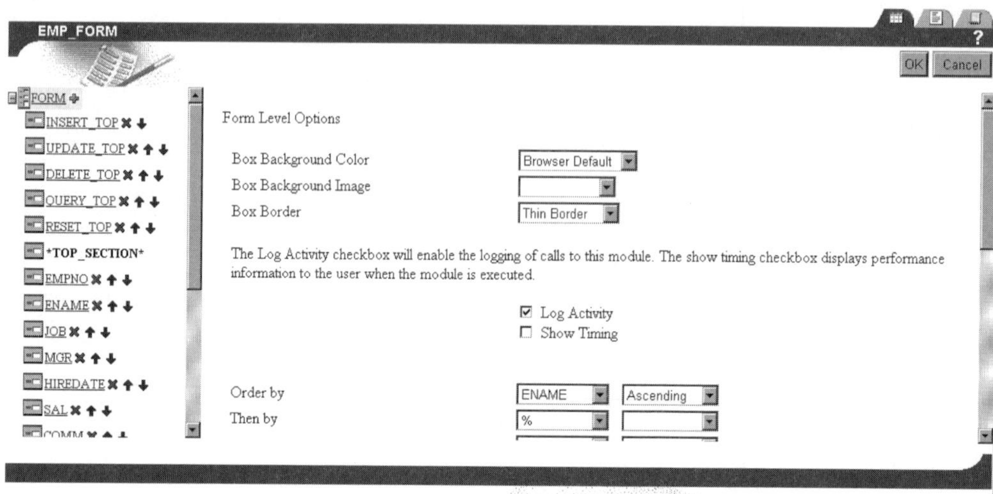

Figure 5.26 Edit Form: Formatting and Validation Options Tab: Form Options.

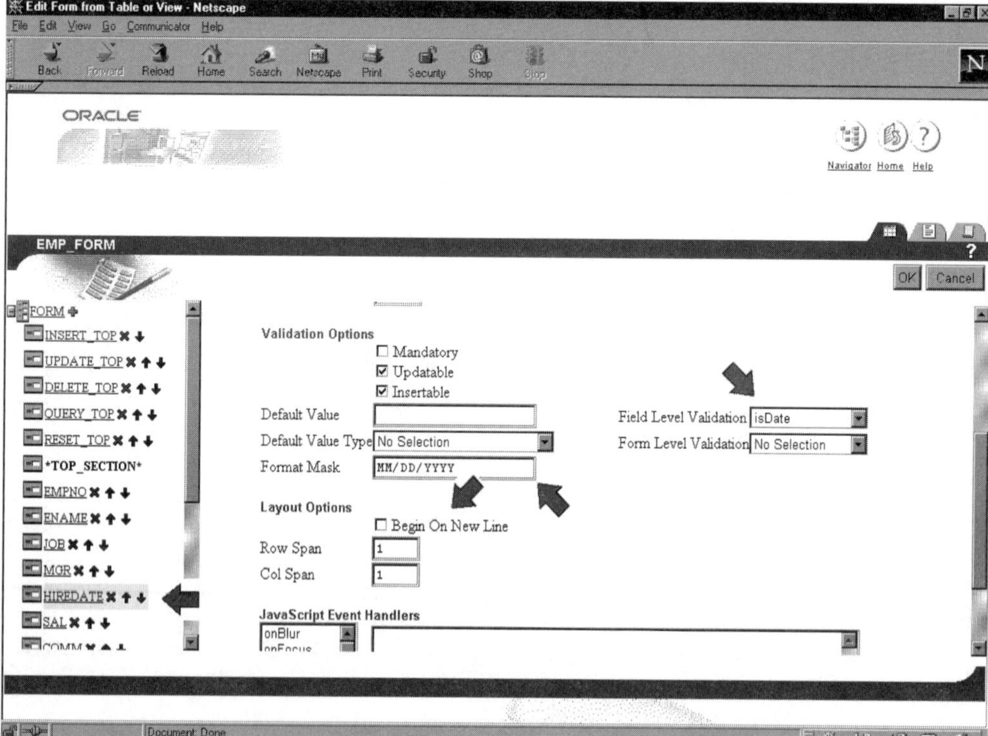

Figure 5.27 Edit Form: Formatting and Validation Options Tab: HIREDATE Field Options.

For practice, edit the form component by going to the Portal Navigator and clicking on its edit action. The editing form screen has three tabs: Formatting and Validation Options, Form Text, and Additional PL/SQL tabs. You cannot modify the table name or the form layout (from tabular to custom, or vice versa). Add a thin box border around the component and change the "Order by" of the form to be ordered by the ENAME column (Figure 5.26).

You can change a field's properties (such as its label) by clicking on the field name link on the navigation frame and then changing the field's label in the options frame. Click on the HIRE-DATE field and change its default format mask to "MM/DD/YYYY". Also, you can choose one of the built-in Javascripts to ensure the validity of the date value entered by the user into the field. By default each field is displayed in a new line. If you need a field to be displayed adjacent to its predecessor, unselect the "Begin On New Line" check box (Figure 5.27).

By default the form fields are displayed in a table format (columns and cells). If you stretched the width of one column (e.g., from 10 characters to 20), the whole form is stretched to make space for the expansion. You can set the field's column span to stretch the field across other fields without expanding the whole form (Figure 5.28).

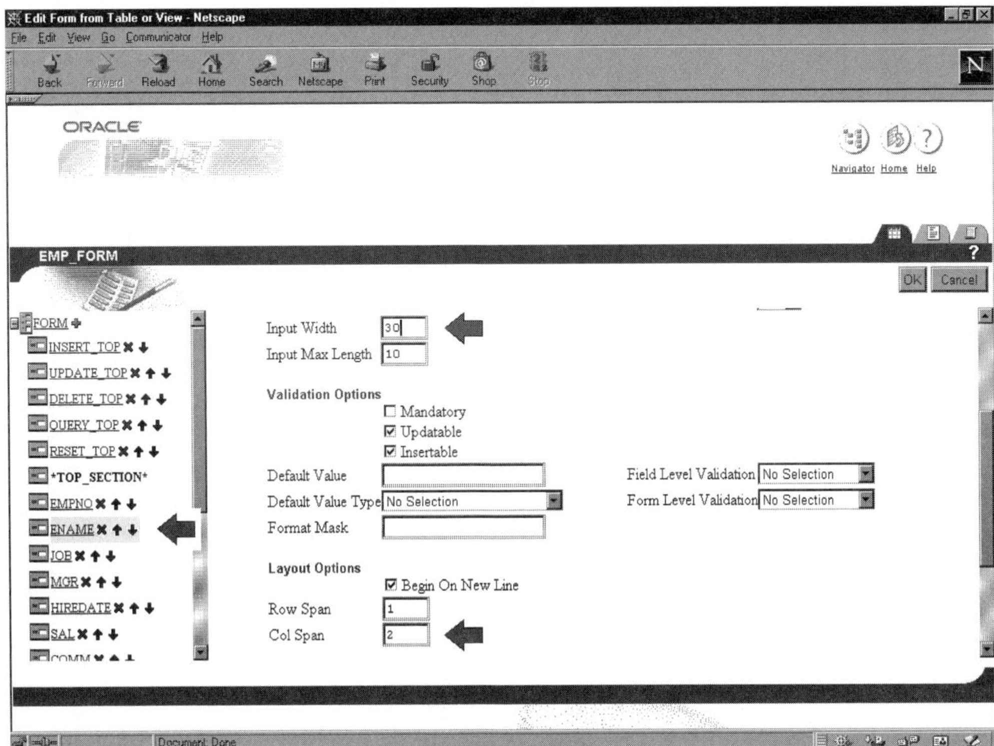

Figure 5.28 Edit Form: Formatting and Validation Options Tab: EMAIL Field Options.

The input max length property defines how many characters can be entered in the field. The input width property defines how many characters are displayed. The input max length should be equal to or greater than input width.

Click on the Additional PL/SQL tab to enter the following sample PL/SQL code to be executed before displaying the component (Figure 5.29):

```
declare
      cnt number;
begin
      select count(*) into cnt
      from scott.emp;
      htp.p('Total number of Employees: '||to_char(cnt));
end;
```

This code displays the total number of employee records in the SCOTT.EMP table. Database object names referenced in your PL/SQL have to be qualified with their owner name for the

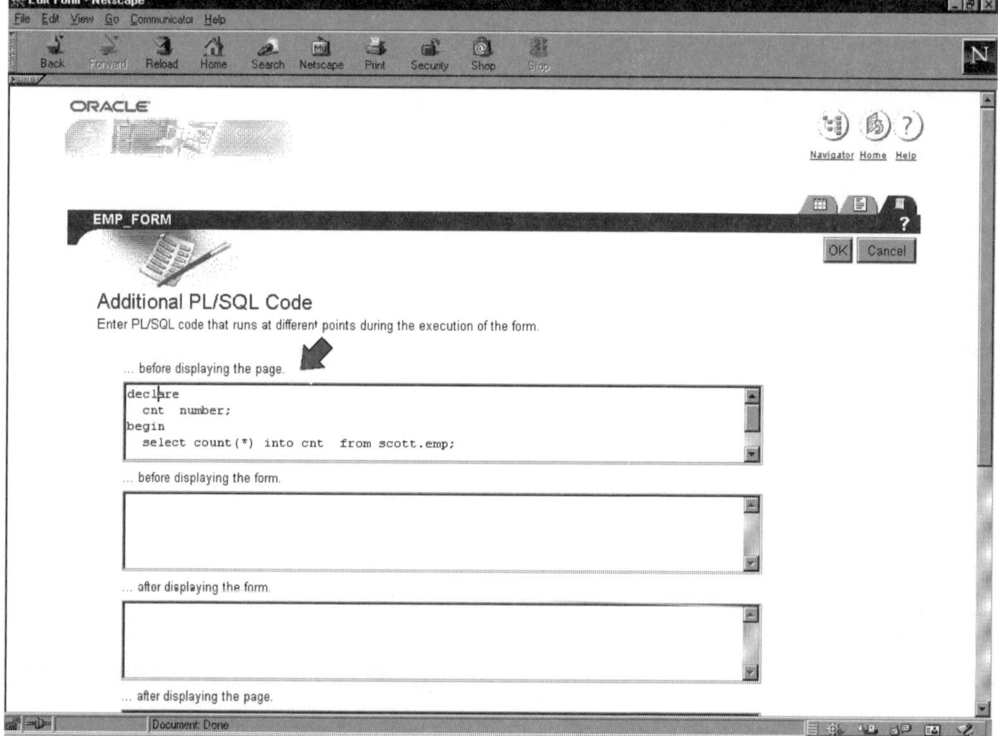

Figure 5.29 Edit Form: Additional PL/SQL Tab.

Oracle Portal to be able to access it correctly, because the component is run by the user connecting to the Oracle Portal (i.e., PORTAL30_PUBLIC).

When you are done modifying the properties, click the "OK" button to save the changes. The Manage Components screen is displayed, where you can rerun the form (Figure 5.30).

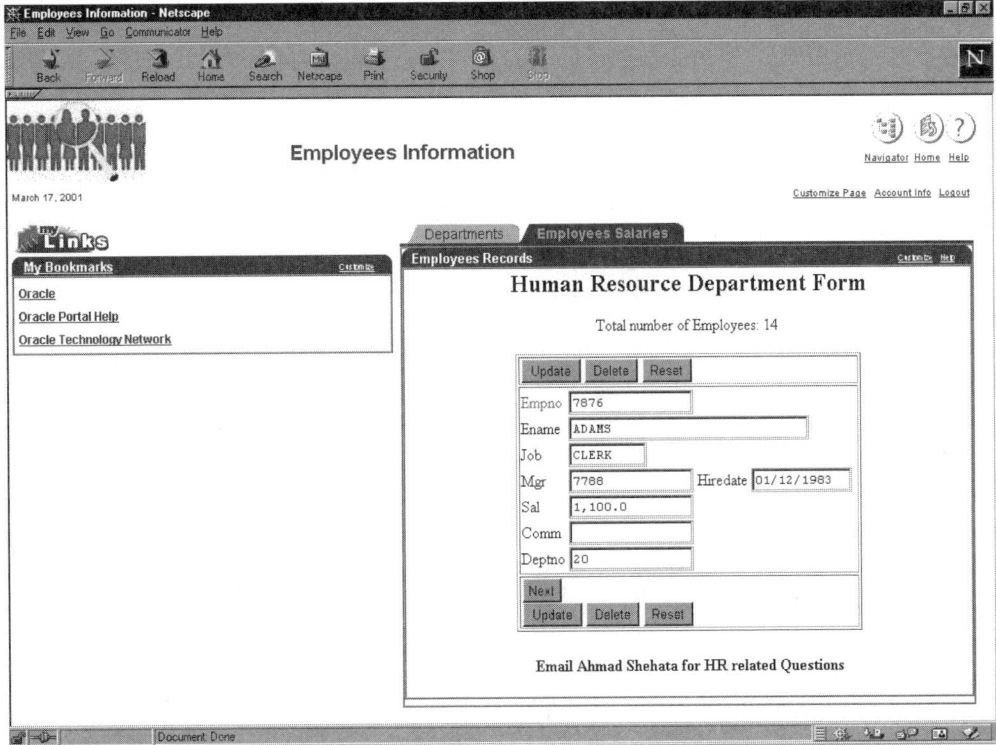

Figure 5.30 Employees Information Page.

Master-Detail Form

This section explores creating Master-Detail Form components. Go to the Oracle Portal Navigator and start the Form wizard, just as you have done to create the Form on a Table. Name this form EMP_PER_DEPT_FORM (Figure 5.31). The next step is to specify the name of the master table/view and detail table/view (Figure 5.32). You can use the List of Values icon to search for the tables.

In step 3 you specify how these two tables or views are going to be joined together. If there is a database foreign key constraint defined on the Detail table, Oracle Portal populates the join conditions with the foreign constraint column(s) (Figure 5.33). If there is no foreign key database constraint defined, you will need to specify the join columns.

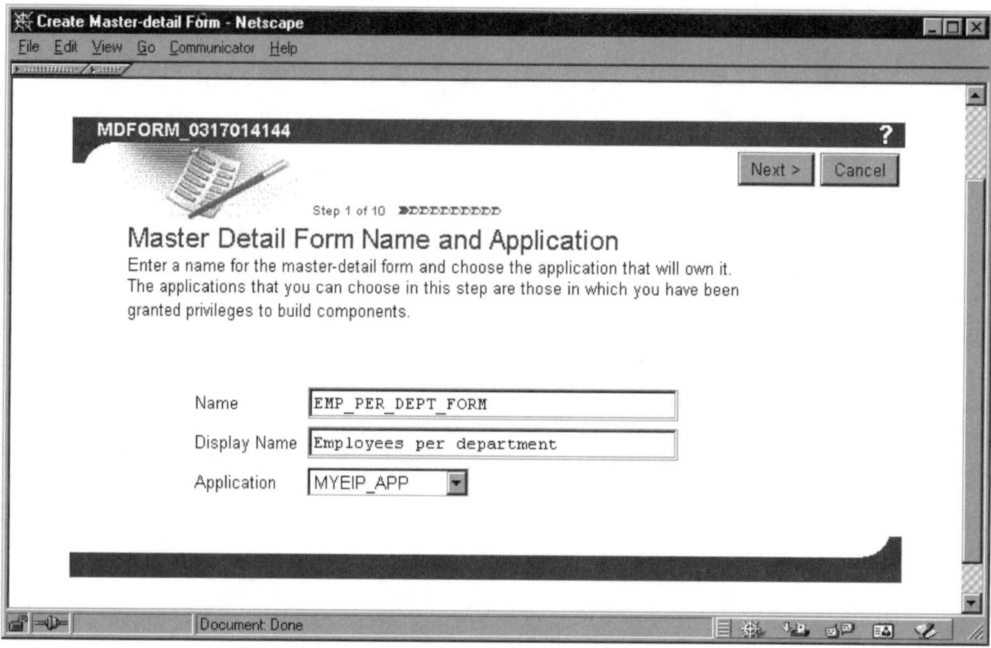

Figure 5.31 Create a Master-Detail Form: Name and Application (Step 1 of 10).

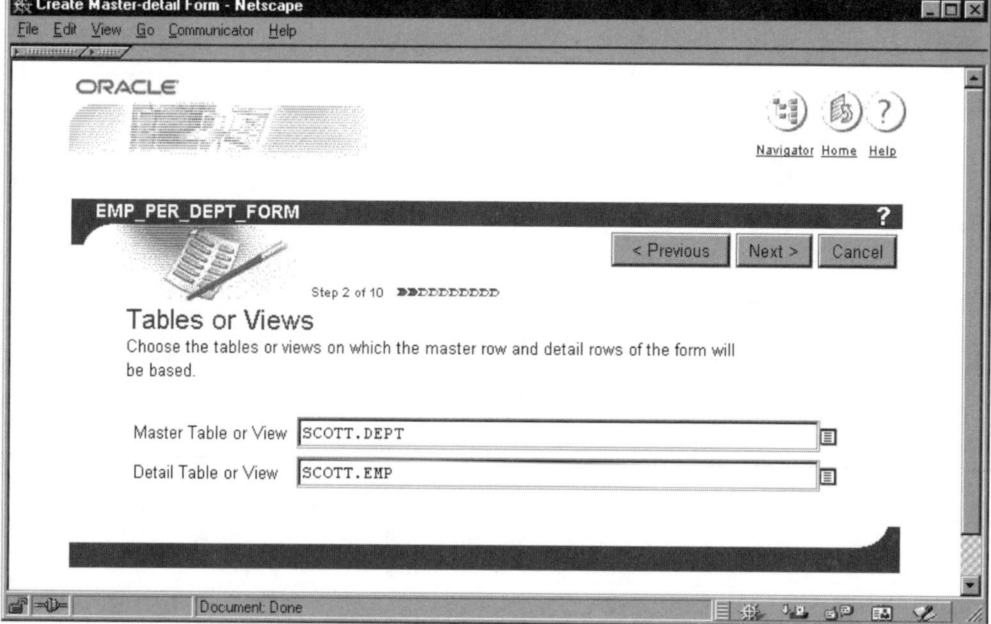

Figure 5.32 Create a Master-Detail Form: Tables or Views (Step 2 of 10).

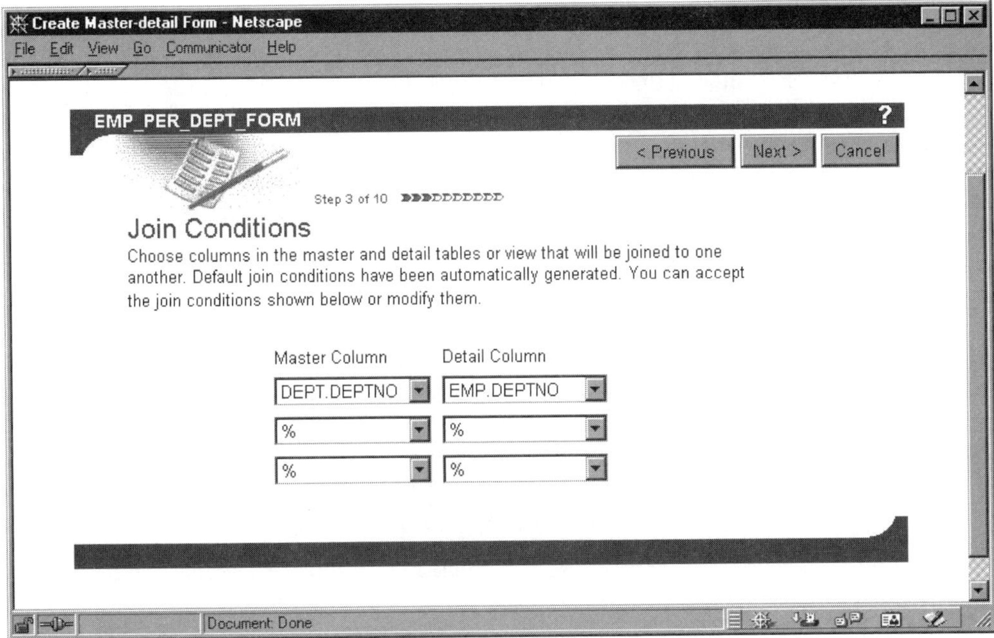

Figure 5.33 Create a Master-Detail Form: Join Conditions (Step 3 of 10).

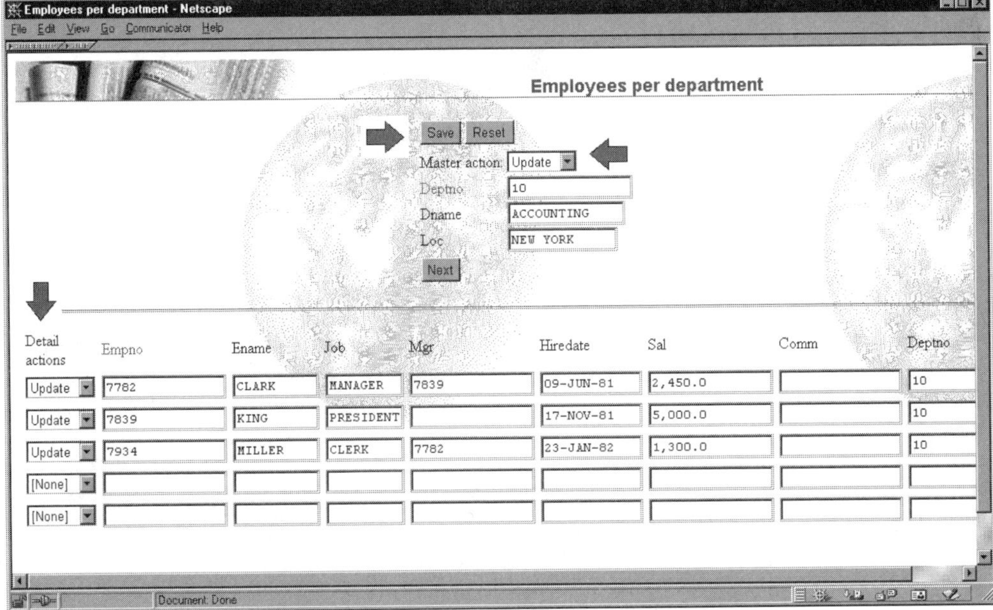

Figure 5.34 Run Master-Detail Form.

The remaining steps in the form creation are similar to the steps covered earlier with the Form on Table. The difference is that in the case of Master-Detail Form, you need to specify the formatting and validation options for both tables. When you click the "Finish" button and run the form, you can click on the "Query" button to retrieve data from the database. Records are retrieved from the Master table (e.g., Dept) and their matching records from the Detail table (e.g., EMP). Then you can specify the action needed on any or all of the records and then finally click on the "Save" button to commit the changes (Figure 5.34).

Form Based on Procedure

This section explores creating a form component that is based on database PL/SQL procedure. The form created in this section is based on the GIVE_RAISE procedure owned by the demo database schema SCOTT (Figure 5.35). The form acts as an interface to the procedure, accepting values for the procedure parameters. Start by specifying the name and the display name of the new form (Figure 5.36). The second step is to specify the procedure name, prefixed with its schema owner (i.e., SCOTT.GIVE_RAISE; Figure 5.37).

In step 3 you choose the form layout (e.g., tabular by default). The fourth step is the Formatting and Validation Options. The Form Based on Procedure has two buttons (i.e., "submit" and "reset"). The fields of the form are the parameters of the stored procedure. You can choose

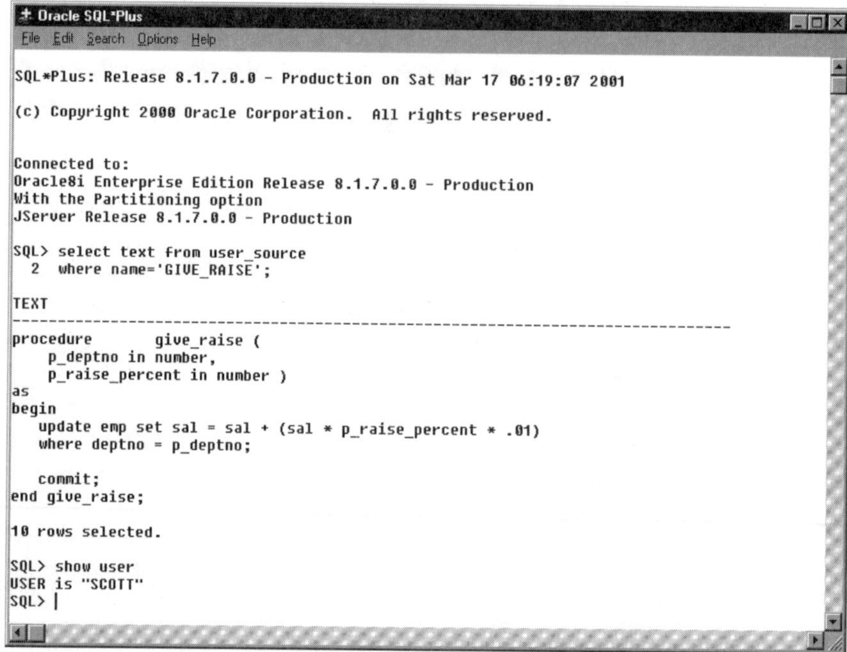

Figure 5.35 GIVE_RAISE PL/SQL Procedure Code.

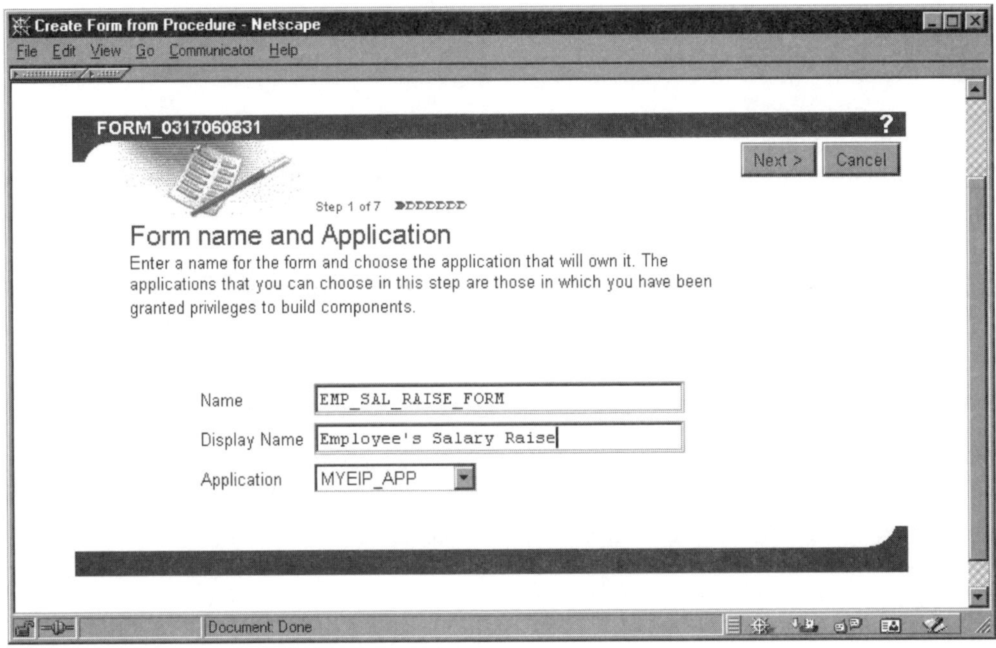

Figure 5.36 Create a Form Based on Procedure: Form Name and Application (Step 1 of 7).

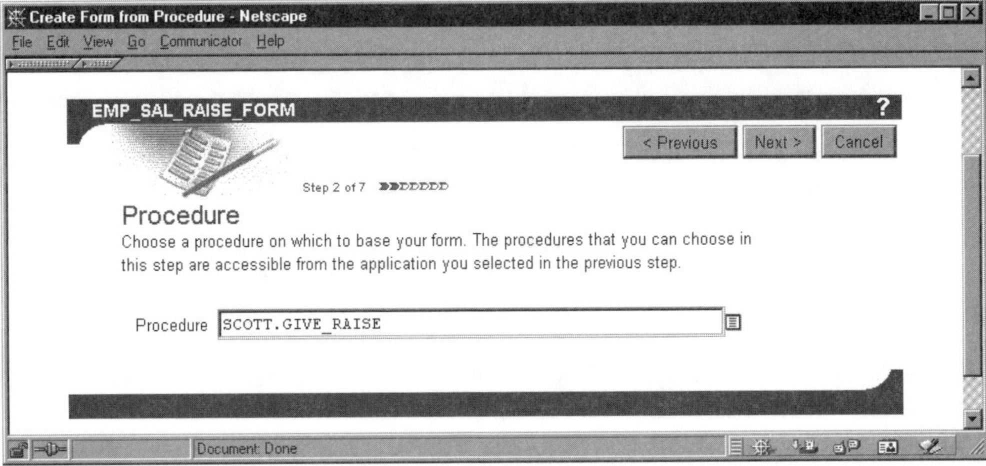

Figure 5.37 Create a Form Based on Procedure: Procedure (Step 2 of 7).

default values for your fields. To specify a default value, you need to pick a type for the default value. The simplest default value type is the "Constant", where you specify a constant value as your default (e.g., 10 for the P_DEPT_NO, which is a number field; Figure 5.38). For a primary key in a form, you might want to assign to it a sequence so a new unique value is automatically generated for each record. The default value type for using the sequence is "Expression returns number", and the default value is "<Sequence Owner>.<Sequence Name>.nextval".

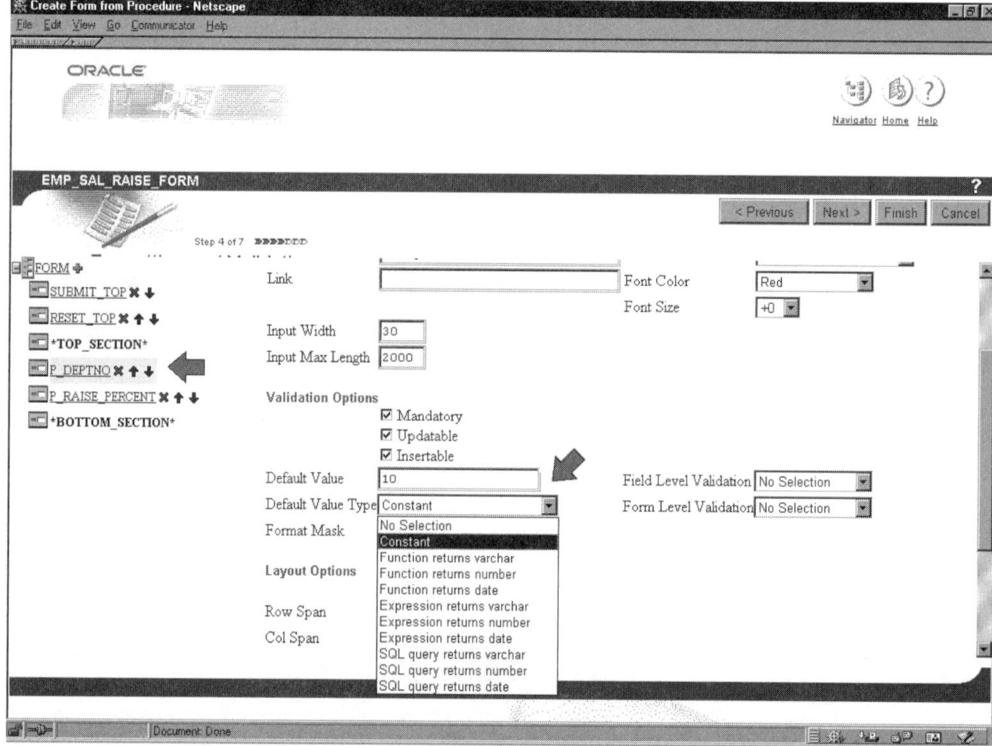

Figure 5.38 Create a Form Based on Procedure: Formatting and Validation Options (Step 4 of 7).

The remaining steps in the form creation are similar to the steps covered earlier with the other form type. Click the "Finish" button and run the form (Figure 5.39). When you specify values for the fields and click "Submit", Oracle Portal executes the PL/SQL procedure.

Create a Report Component

As you go through the rest of this chapter, the rhythm is starting to speed up, because you are becoming more familiar with different steps of application component creation, which are common

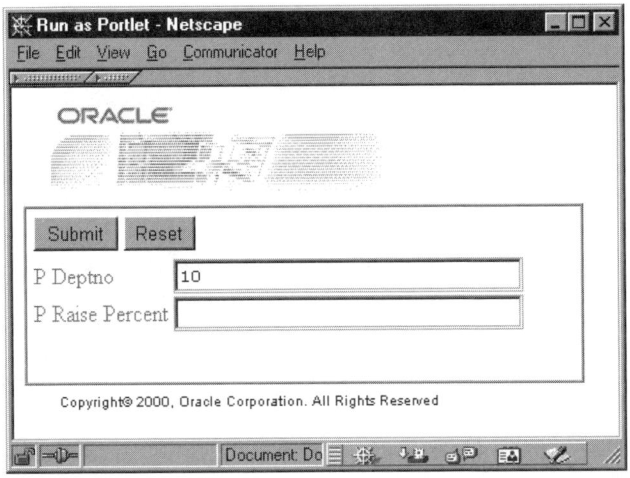

Figure 5.39 Run a Form Based on Procedure.

between different component types. The next component type covered is the report. When you click on the "Report" link in the Application page in the Oracle Portal Navigator, you get three different types of reports (Figure 5.40). In a Query By Example (QBE) report, you specify one and only one table (or view name), upon which the report is based. A report created by the Query wizard can be based on more than one table joined together, through specifying their join conditions using the GUI wizard. The third report type is based on an SQL SELECT statement.

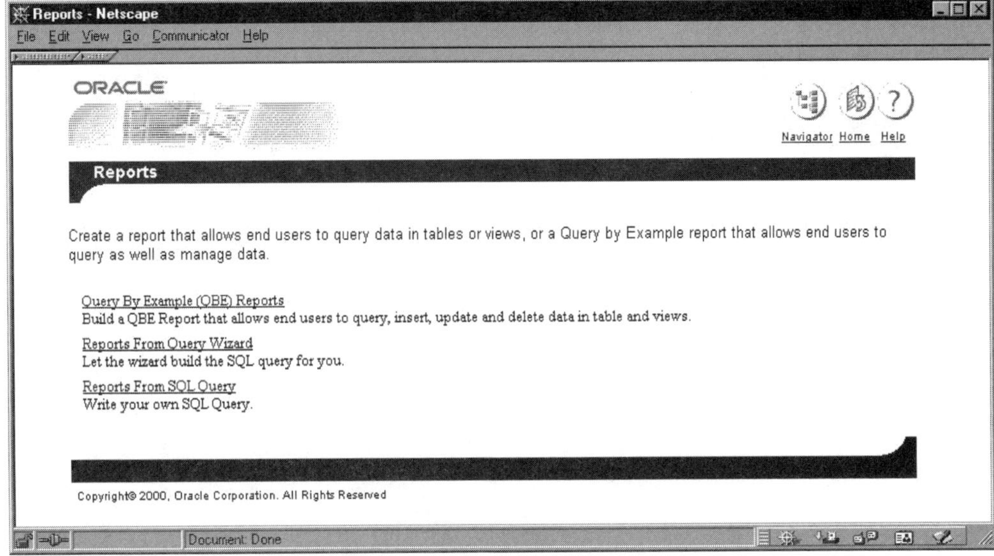

Figure 5.40 Oracle Portal Navigator: Create a Report Component.

Create a Query By Example (QBE) Report

Start by specifying the report internal name and its display name (Figure 5.41). Then you need to specify the table upon which the report is based (Figure 5.42). The next step is the selection of the columns that are to be included in the report (Figure 5.43). This is step 3. Depending

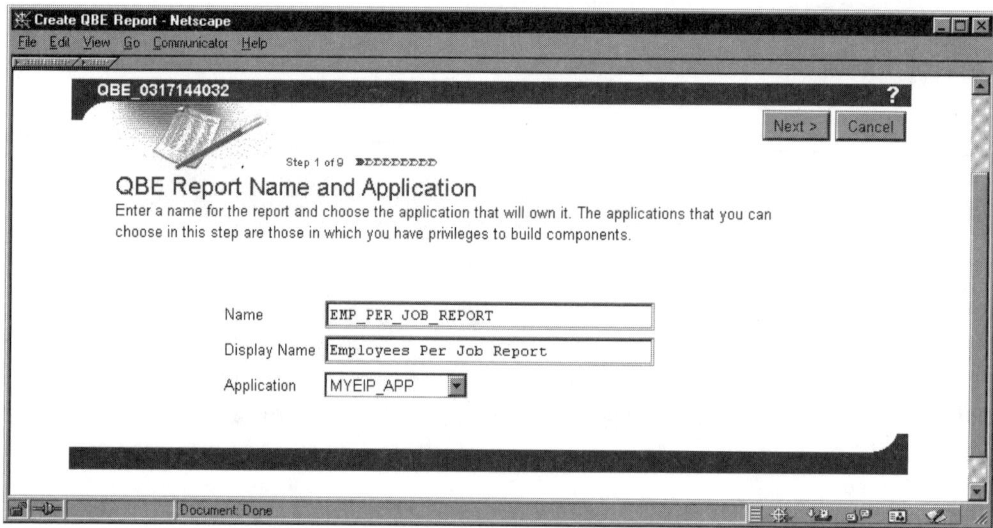

Figure 5.41 Create a QBE Report: Report Name and Application (Step 1 of 9).

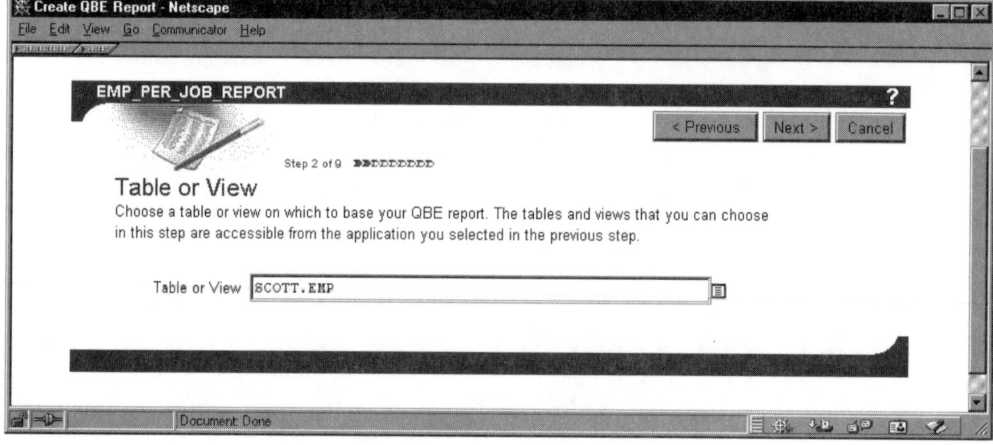

Figure 5.42 Create a QBE Report: Table or View (Step 2 of 9).

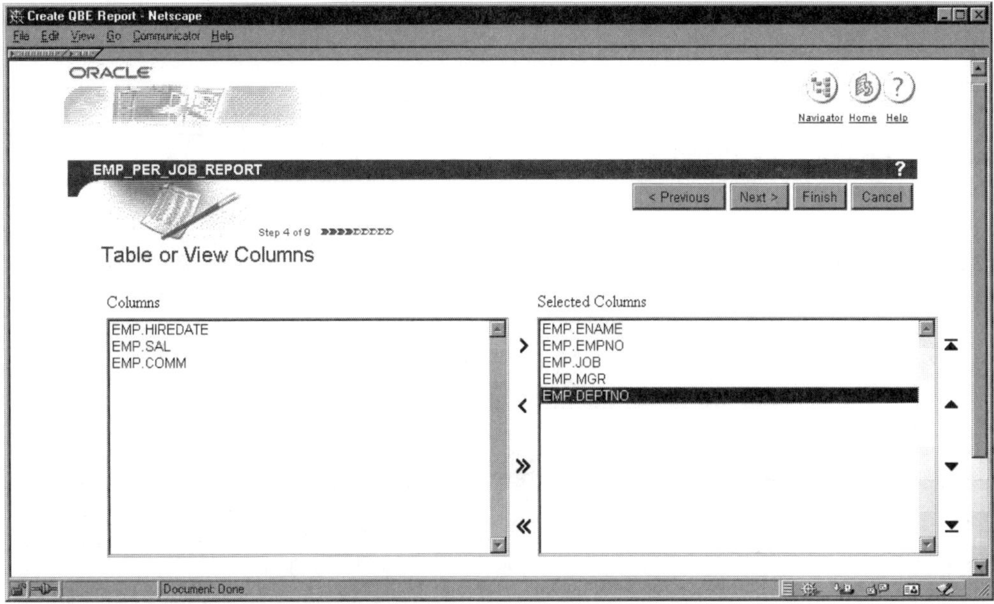

Figure 5.43 Create a QBE Report: Table or View Columns (Step 3 of 9).

Table 5.3 Movement Icons

Icon	Description
>	Select
<	Deselect
»	Select all
«	Deselect all

on the Oracle Portal version number, the wizard status bar might say step 4 instead of step 3 because of a bug. You can select and deselect columns by using the icons in Table 5.3.

The fourth step is setting column formatting, such as column heading, alignment, format mask, width, and so on (Figure 5.44). Setting the "Display as" property to "HTML" allows the Oracle Portal to render HTML tags retrieved from the report table as HTML (e.g., the HREF tag is displayed as a hyperlink).

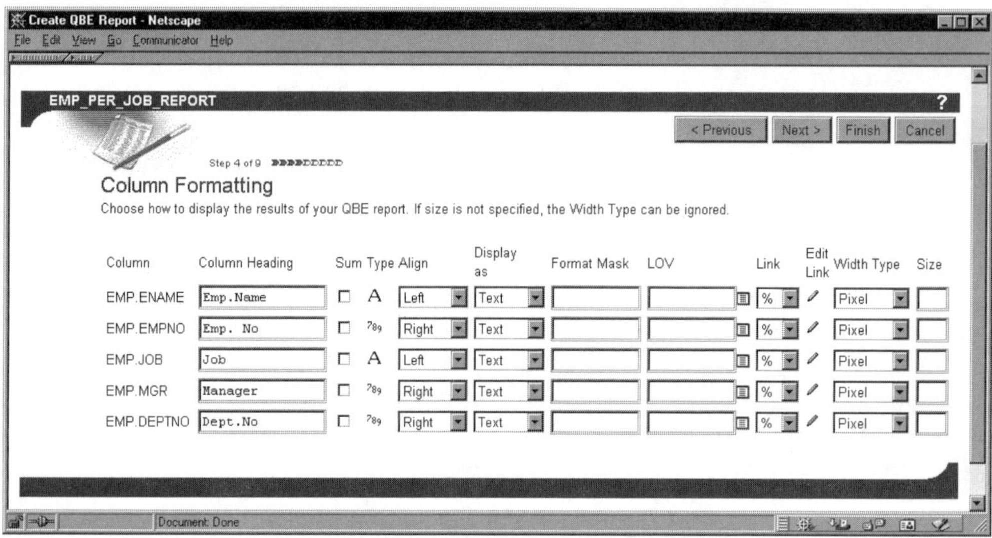

Figure 5.44 Create a QBE Report: Column Formatting (Step 4 of 9).

In step 5 you have the ability to define how certain records are to be displayed if they satisfy a certain condition. You can make the whole record or just a certain column look different (e.g., boldface, different color, etc.). In Figure 5.45 the employee records with JOB = 'MANAGER' will be displayed in boldface.

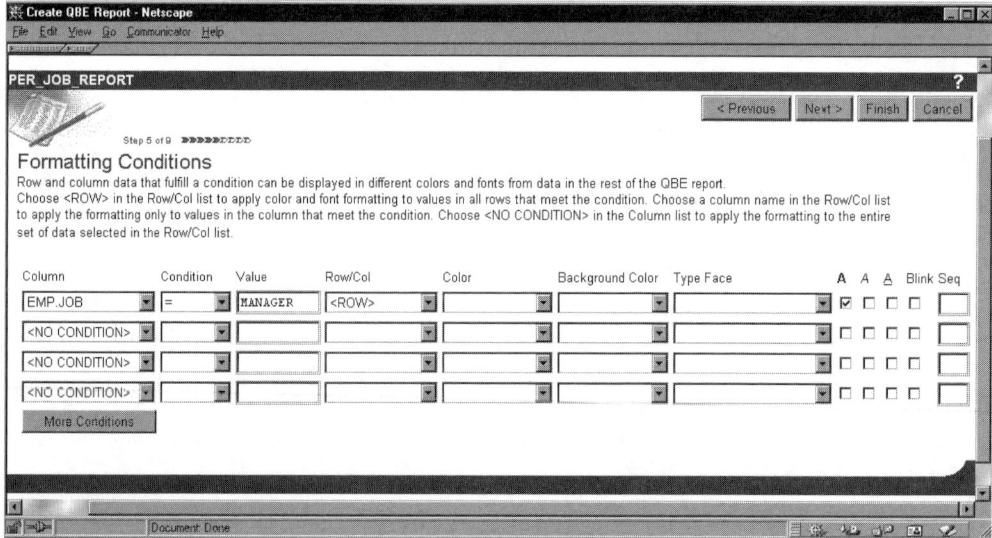

Figure 5.45 Create a QBE Report: Formatting Conditions (Step 5 of 9).

Step 6 in creating the QBE report defines the display options. The display options are categorized into three groups: common options, full page options (when you run the component individually), and portlet options (when you run the component as a portlet in a page). Because there are a lot of options in this page, you can start with simple changes such as changing the number of rows per page in the full page options from the default value (i.e., 20) to just 10 (Figure 5.46).

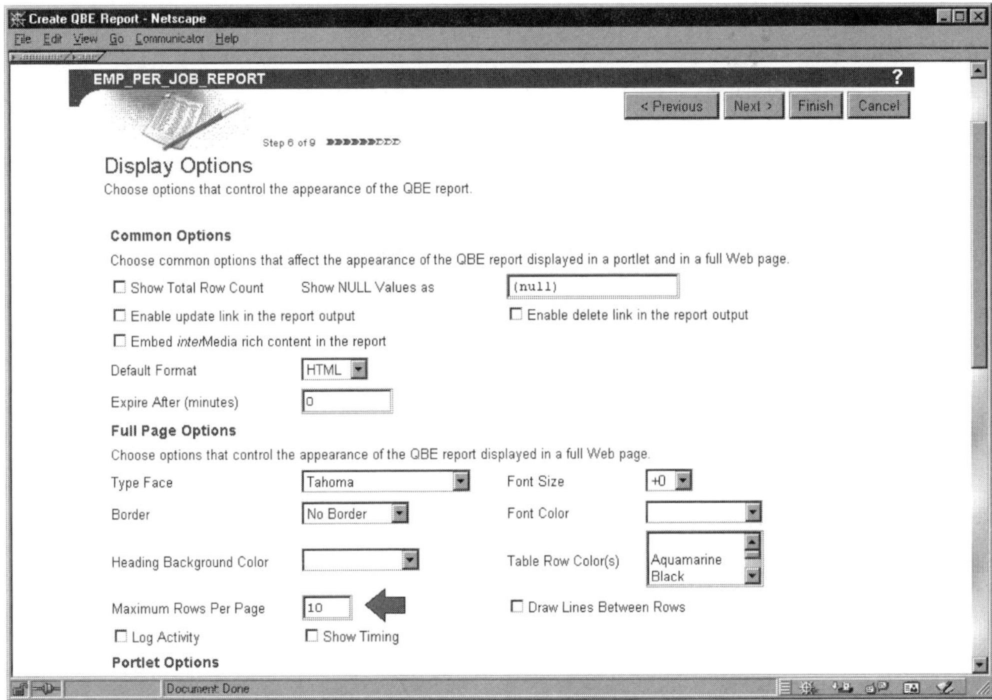

Figure 5.46 Create a QBE Report: Display Options (Step 6 of 9): Top.

Also, you can set the following in the portlet options: the border to thin border, the maximum number of rows per page to 7 instead of the default value (e.g., 20), and the order by columns (Figure 5.47). In addition, you can change the background color of the report data by choosing a color in the "Table Row Color(s)" list. You can choose two colors to alternate by pressing the mouse button while holding the Control key.

Step 7 allows you to define how the component Customize Form looks. The end-user accesses the Customize Form by clicking on the "Customize" link in the portlet header. By default all the options are selected (Figure 5.48). You can deselect any of the options if you do not want the end-user to have access to that option.

Step 8 allows you to add your HTML code for both the QBE report and its customization

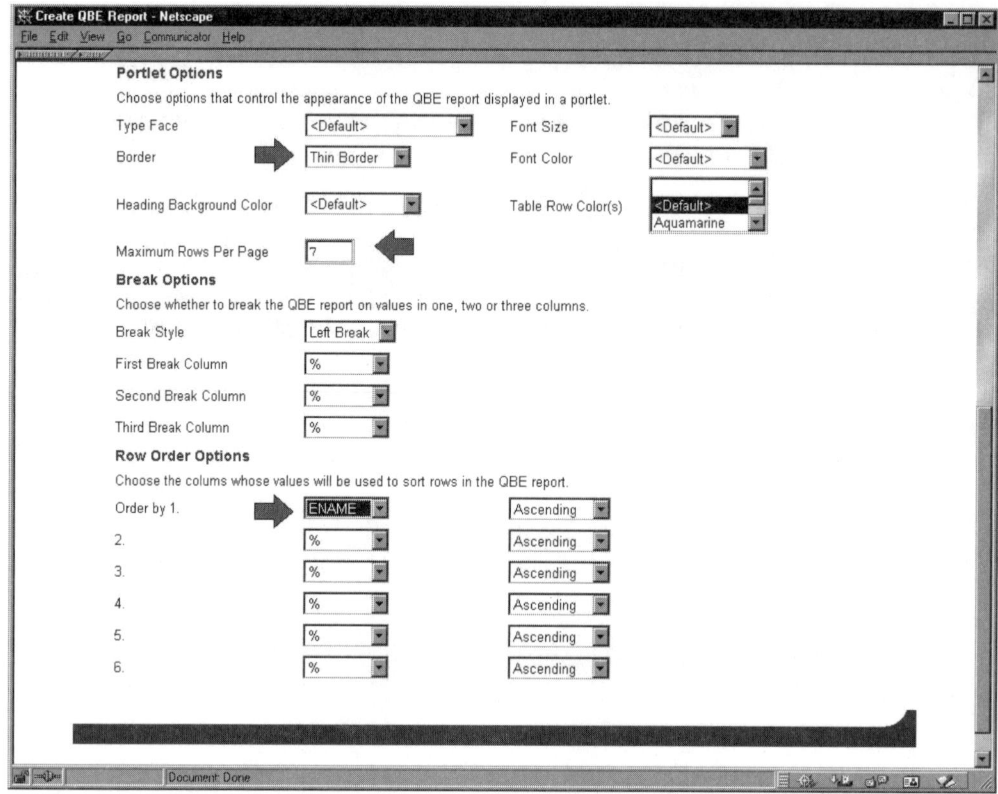

Figure 5.47 Create a QBE Report: Display Options (Step 6 of 9): Bottom.

form. Step 9 allows you to add your own PL/SQL code for both the report component and the customization form. Click "Finish" to create the report and then run the report component in a full page (Figure 5.49).

Create a Report from Query Wizard

Creating a report using the Query wizard allows you to choose more than one table joined together. Start as usual by giving the report an internal name and a display name (Figure 5.50). The second step is choosing your report tables. Type or select your table from the list of values, and then click the "Add" button to add the table to the selected tables/views list (Figure 5.51). You can remove a table from the selected list by clicking on the delete icon on its left side.

In the third step, the Report creation wizard populates the join conditions from the database foreign key constraints to join the selected tables (Figure 5.52). Step 4 shows a complete list of the columns of all the tables selected, so you can choose the columns you want to include in your report (Figure 5.53).

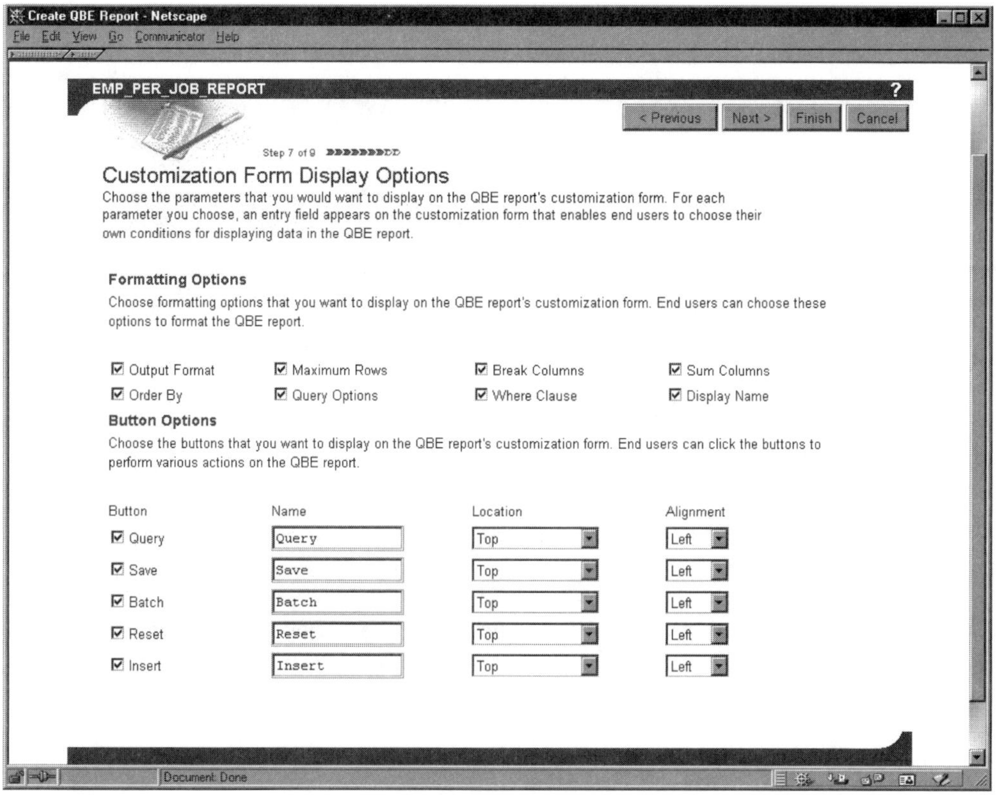

Create QBE Report - Netscape

File Edit View Go Communicator Help

EMP_PER_JOB_REPORT ?

< Previous | Next > | Finish | Cancel

Step 7 of 9

Customization Form Display Options

Choose the parameters that you would want to display on the QBE report's customization form. For each parameter you choose, an entry field appears on the customization form that enables end users to choose their own conditions for displaying data in the QBE report.

Formatting Options

Choose formatting options that you want to display on the QBE report's customization form. End users can choose these options to format the QBE report.

☑ Output Format	☑ Maximum Rows	☑ Break Columns	☑ Sum Columns
☑ Order By	☑ Query Options	☑ Where Clause	☑ Display Name

Button Options

Choose the buttons that you want to display on the QBE report's customization form. End users can click the buttons to perform various actions on the QBE report.

Button	Name	Location	Alignment
☑ Query	Query	Top	Left
☑ Save	Save	Top	Left
☑ Batch	Batch	Top	Left
☑ Reset	Reset	Top	Left
☑ Insert	Insert	Top	Left

Document: Done

Figure 5.48 Create a QBE Report: Customization Form Display Options (Step 7 of 9).

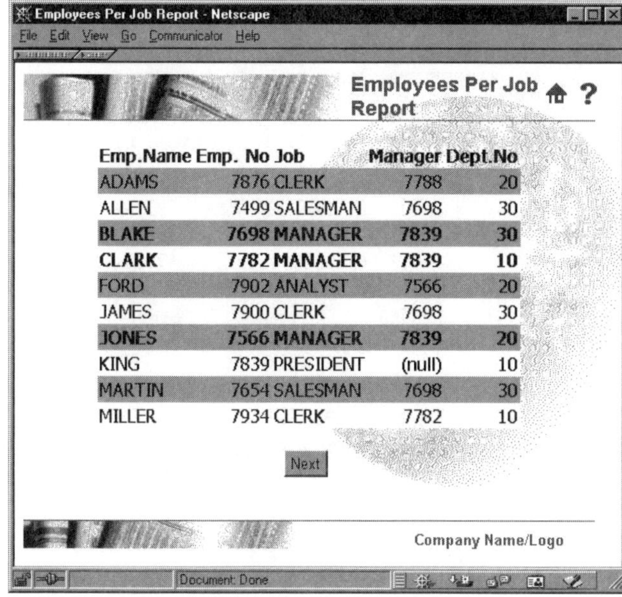

Emp.Name	Emp. No	Job	Manager	Dept.No
ADAMS	7876	CLERK	7788	20
ALLEN	7499	SALESMAN	7698	30
BLAKE	7698	MANAGER	7839	30
CLARK	7782	MANAGER	7839	10
FORD	7902	ANALYST	7566	20
JAMES	7900	CLERK	7698	30
JONES	7566	MANAGER	7839	20
KING	7839	PRESIDENT	(null)	10
MARTIN	7654	SALESMAN	7698	30
MILLER	7934	CLERK	7782	10

Figure 5.49
Run a QBE Report in Full Page.

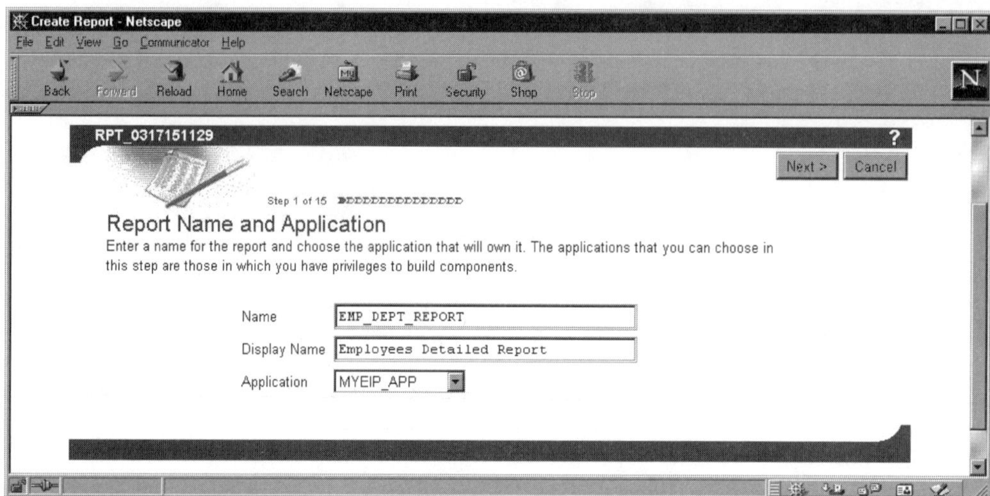

Figure 5.50 Create a Report from Query Wizard: Report Name and Application (Step 1 of 15).

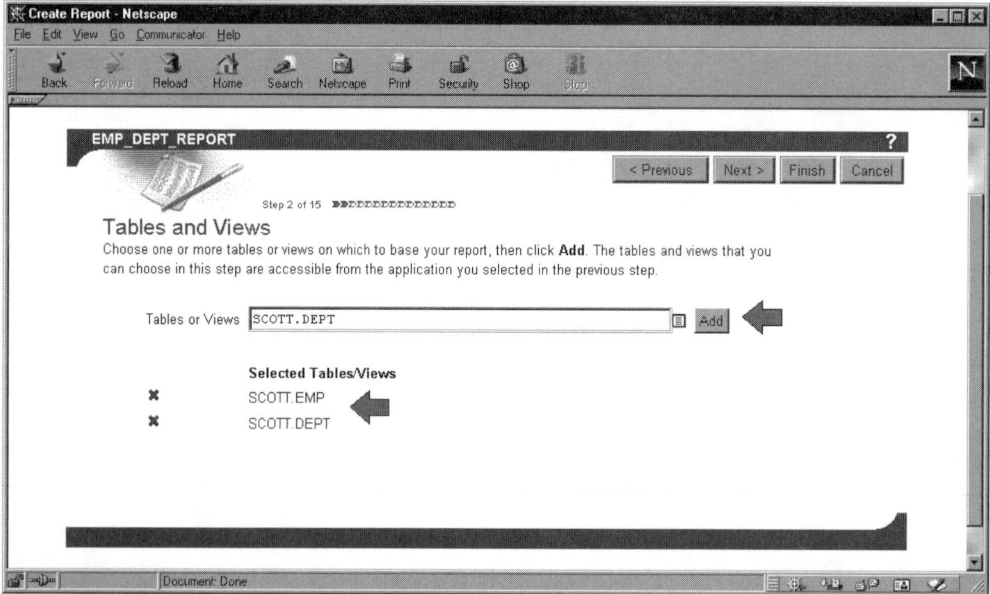

Figure 5.51 Create a Report from Query Wizard: Tables and Views (Step 2 of 15).

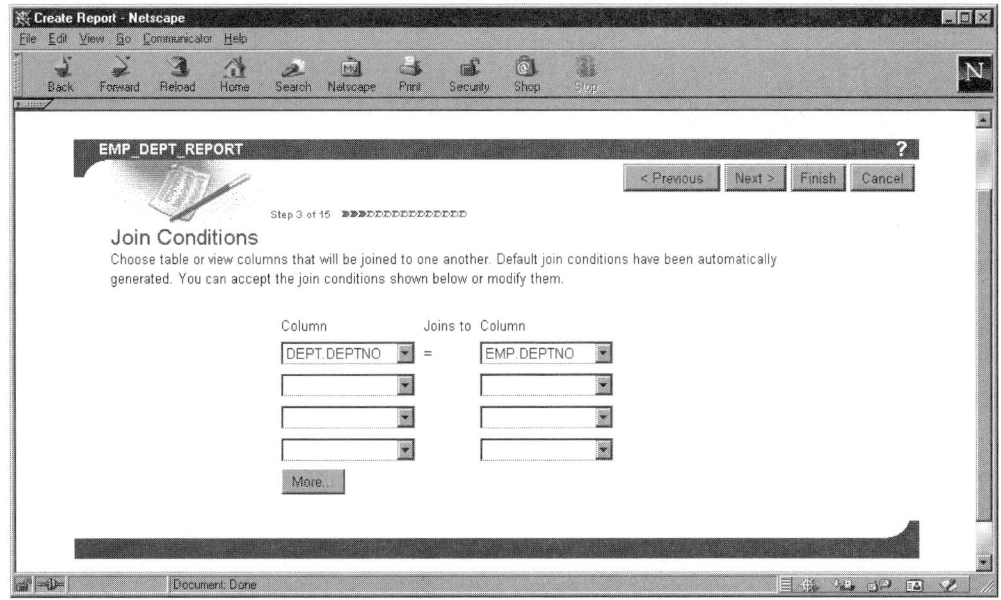

Figure 5.52 Create a Report from Query Wizard: Join Conditions (Step 3 of 15).

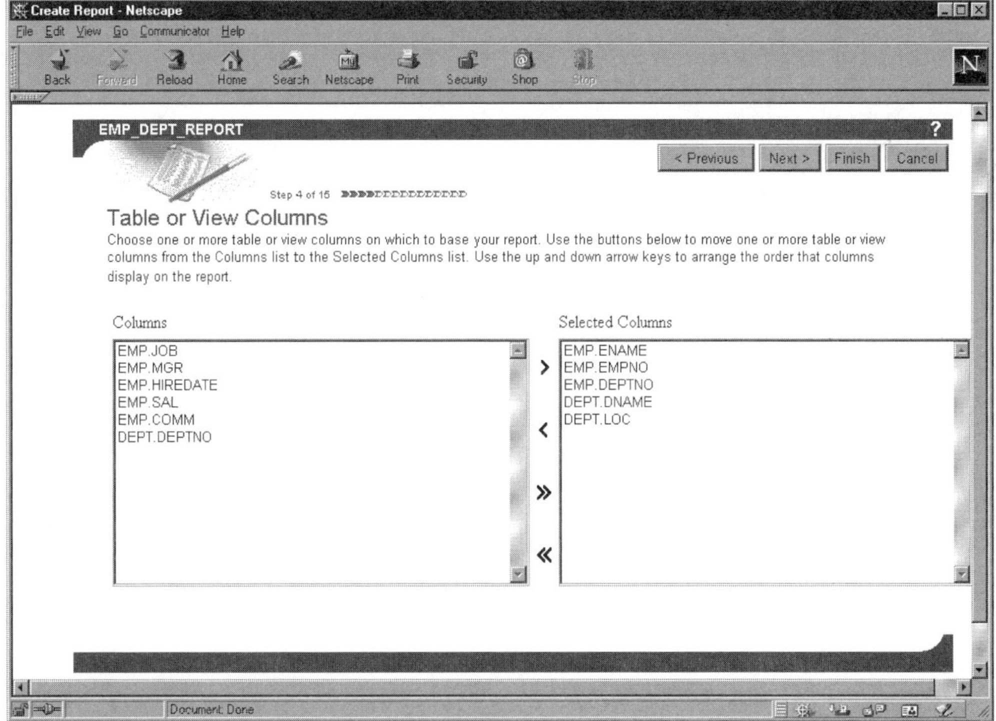

Figure 5.53 Create a Report from Query Wizard: Table or View Columns (Step 4 of 15).

Step 5 allows you to specify conditions to restrict the rows retrieved in the report (Figure 5.54). You can select any of the columns of the tables, an operator (e.g., NOT NULL), and a value to compose the WHERE clause condition(s).

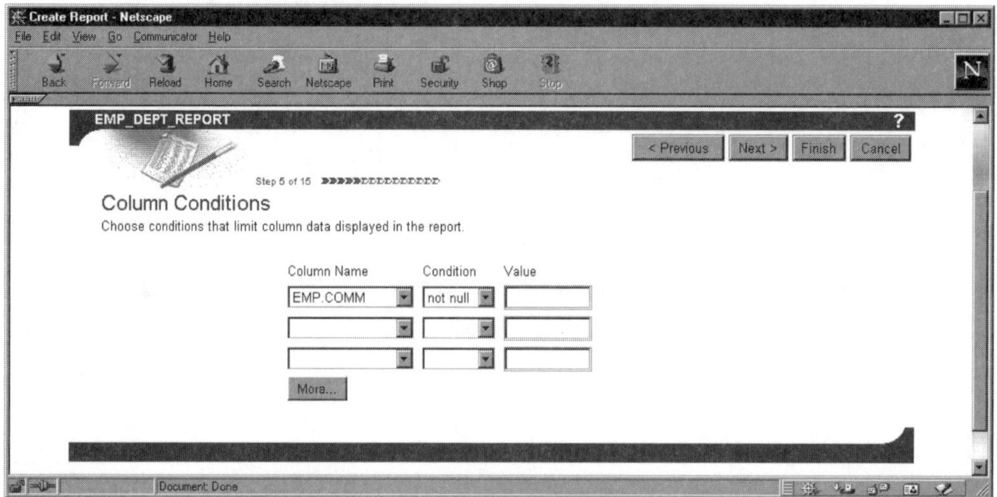

Figure 5.54 Create a Report from Query Wizard: Column Conditions (Step 5 of 15).

There are three types of report layout:

- Tabular: The data is displayed in tabular format, rows and columns.
- Form: Each column value is displayed in a line by itself.
- Custom: You specify the HTML code to define the report layout.

You choose the report layout in step 6 (Figure 5.55). Step 7 (Column Formatting), step 8 (Formatting Conditions), and step 9 (Display Options) are similar to the QBE report steps. In step 13 (Customization Form Display Options), you can choose columns to be included in the component customization form. The end-user can specify operators and values for these columns in the run time and hence retrieve only the rows that satisfy these customized conditions (Figure 5.56).

Note

In Oracle9*i*AS Portal verson 3.0.9, you need to specify an Order by column (or columns) to avoid getting an SQL parse error when running the report.

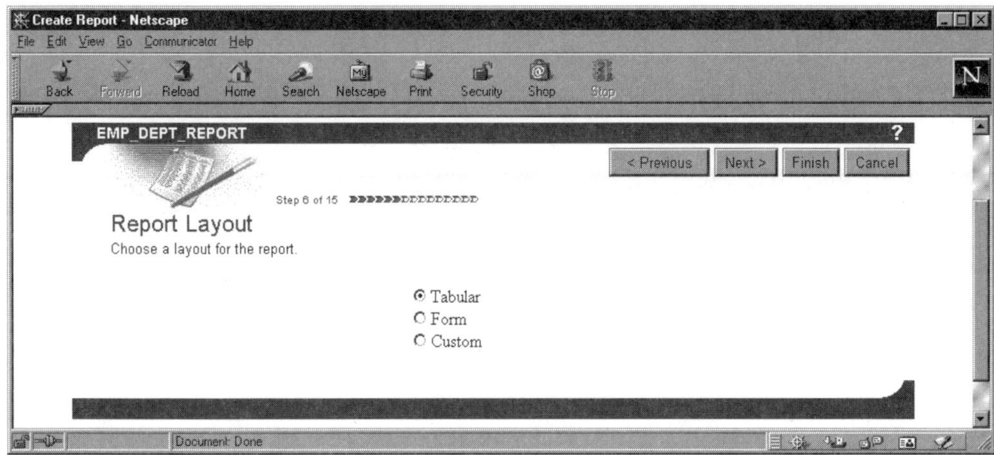

Figure 5.55 Create a Report from Query Wizard: Column Conditions (Step 6 of 15).

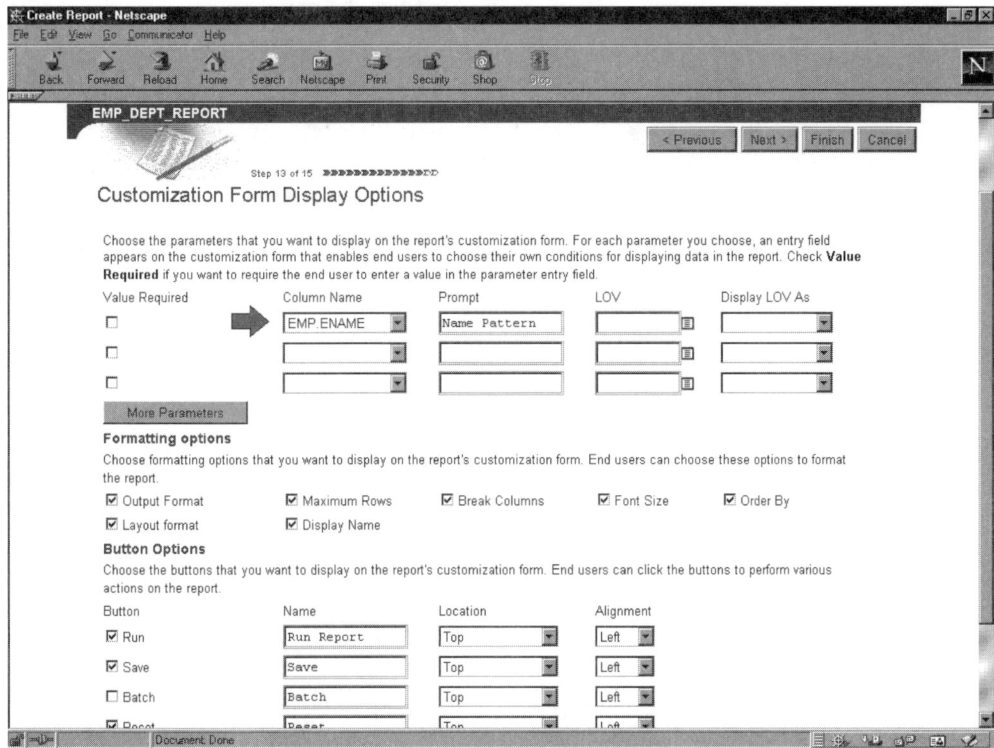

Figure 5.56 Create a Report from Query Wizard: Customization Form Display Options (Step 13 of 15).

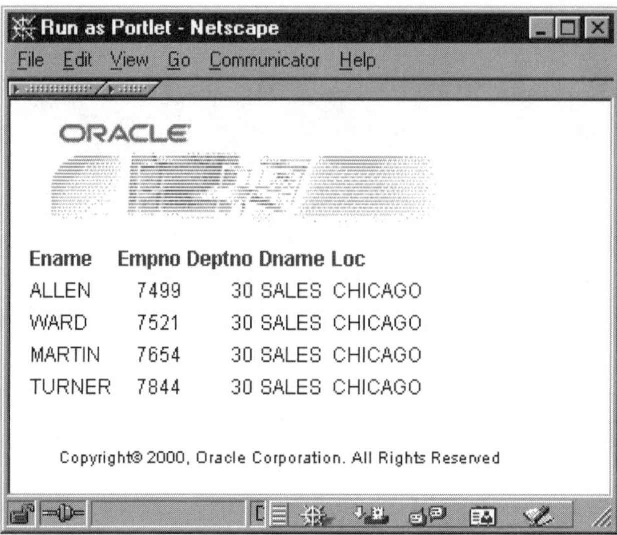

Figure 5.57 Run a Report as a Portlet.

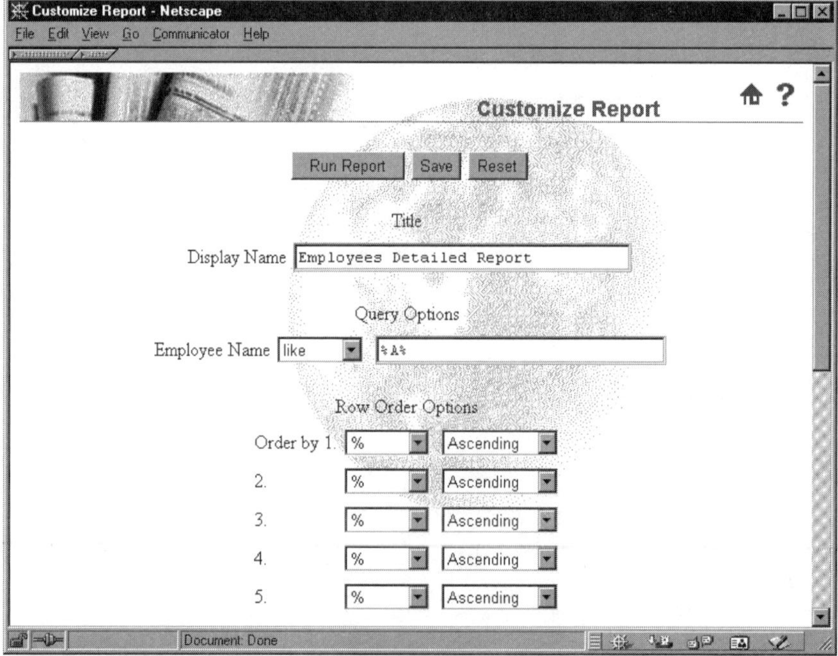

Figure 5.58 Reports Customization Form: Top.

Customize Report - Netscape

File Edit View Go Communicator Help

5. % Ascending

Break Options

First Break Column %

Second Break Column %

Third Break Column %

General Options

Output Format HTML

Layout Style TABULAR

Maximum Rows/Page 20

Font Size +0

Company Name/Logo

Document: Done

Figure 5.59 Reports Customization Form: Bottom.

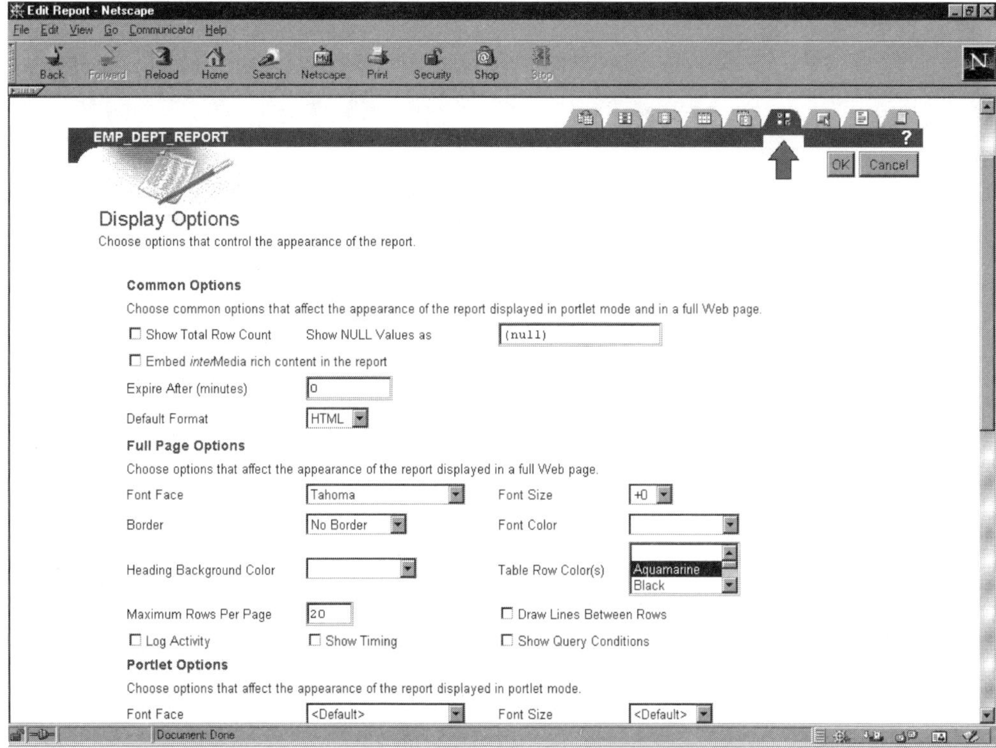

Figure 5.60 Edit a Report.

Step 14 (Report and Customization Form Text), and step 15 (Additional PL/SQL Code) are similar to the QBE report's steps. Click "Finish" to create the report. Run the report as a portlet (Figure 5.57).

Click on the "Customize" button in the Manage Report screen to display the customization form (Figure 5.58 and Figure 5.59). When you run the report, you get only the employees with a letter "A" in their name. You can also edit the report and change its properties (Figure 5.60).

Create a Report from SQL Query

In this report type you get to specify the SQL statement yourself. The QBE report is good enough if you have one table or view. The Query wizard is good enough if the join condition(s) between the tables are equijoin (that use the equal sign operator). For more complex reports you need the third type where you type the SELECT statement. The example in this section uses the SCOTT.SALGRADE table. This table is not granted to the public like the other two tables, SCOTT.DEPT and SCOTT.EMP. You need to grant the SELECT object privilege on the SALGRADE table to the MYEIP_OWNER user, because MYEIP_OWNER is the owner of the report components package. There are two ways to perform the grant. The first is to log on to SQL*Plus as SCOTT/TIGER and grant select on salgrade to myeip_owner. The other way is to edit the

Figure 5.61 Edit Schema: Grants Tab.

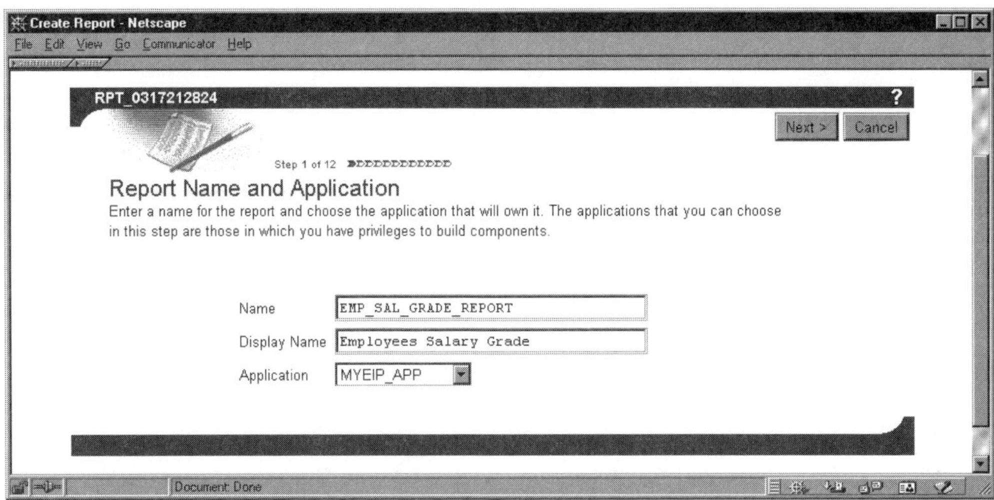

Figure 5.62 Create a Report from SQL Query: Report Name and Application (Step 1 of 12).

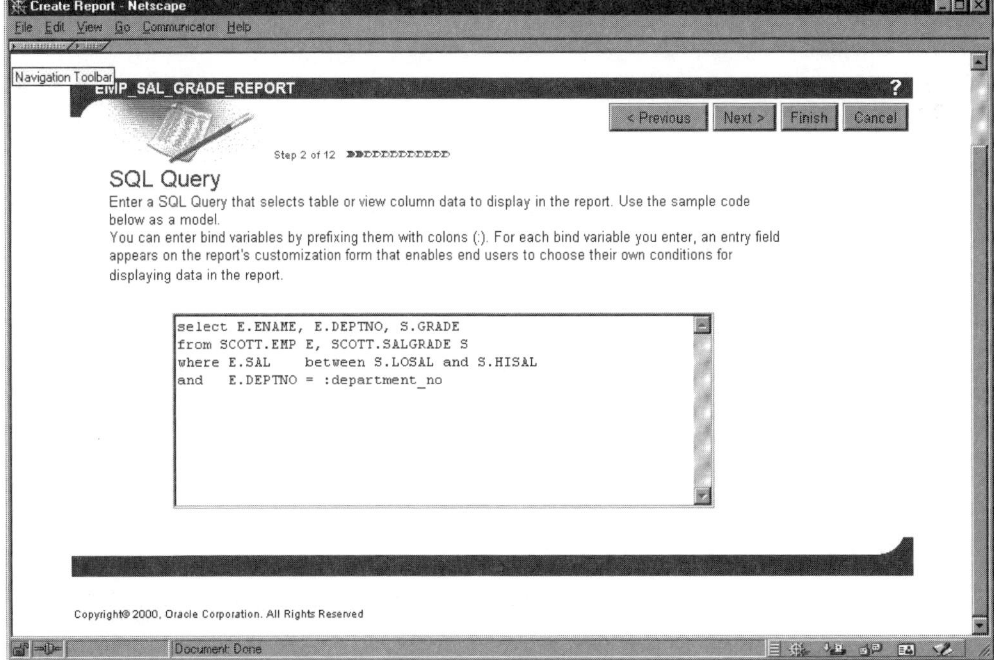

Figure 5.63 Create a Report from SQL Query: SQL Query (Step 2 of 12).

MYEIP_OWNER schema using the schema portlet in the Oracle Portal home page. Then go to the Grants tab in the Edit Schema screen. Type the object name (e.g., SCOTT.SALGRADE) and then click the "Add" button. When the table is displayed in the selected list, check its "SELECT" privilege check box. Finally, apply your changes (Figure 5.61).

Now you are ready to do the example. The first step in the creation is to specify the report name (Figure 5.62). In the second step, you specify the SELECT statement. In the example in Figure 5.63, a bind variable is used (i.e., :department_no) to be a parameter in the customization form of the report.

Step 3 (Report Layout), step 4 (Column Formatting), step 5 (Formatting Conditions), and step 6 (Display Options) are similar to the corresponding steps of creating a report from the Query wizard.

In step 10 you can change the prompt of the bind variable entered earlier in the SELECT statement. It is very important to enter a valid default value (e.g., 10) for the bind variable; otherwise the report component will not retrieve any rows when it is run without customization (Figure 5.64).

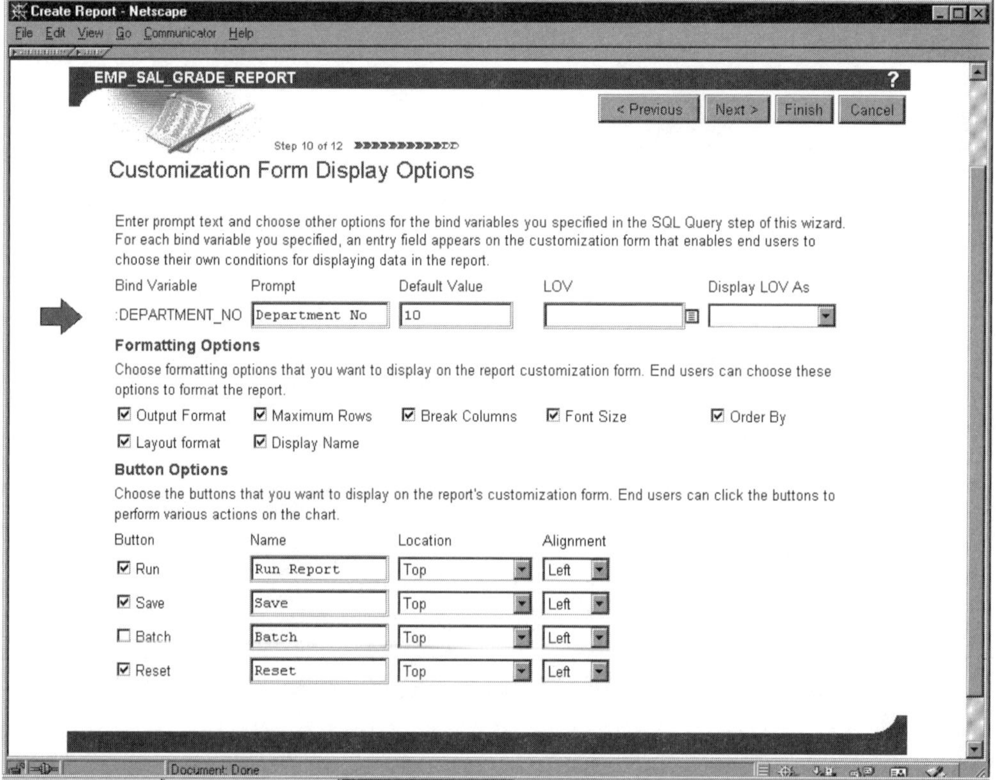

Figure 5.64 Create a Report from SQL Query: SQL Query (Step 10 of 12).

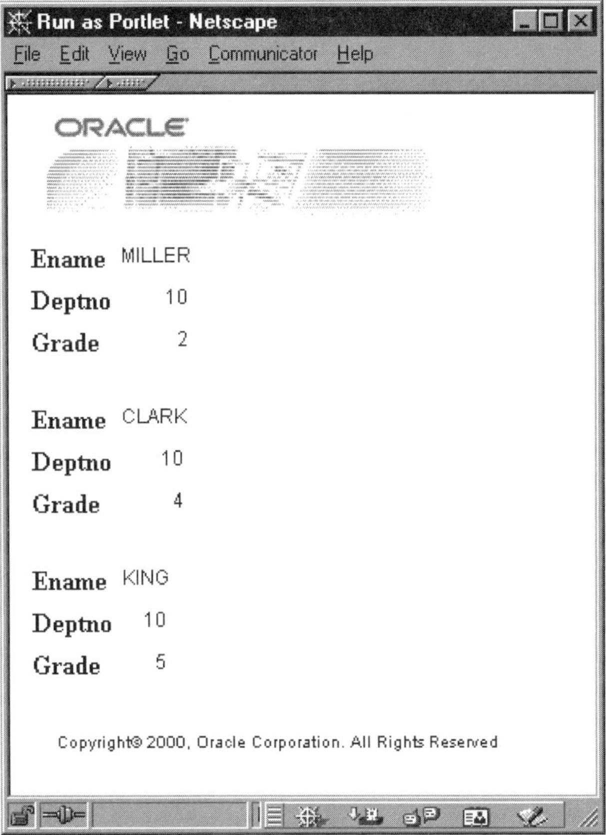

Figure 5.65 Run a Report from the Query Wizard.

Note

In Oracle9*i*AS Portal version 3.0.9, you might need to choose an Order by column or columns in the display options.

Step 11 (Report and Customization Form Text) and step 12 (Additional PL/SQL Code) are similar to the steps of creating a report from the Query wizard. Click "Finish" to create the report. Run the report as a portlet (Figure 5.65).

You can add the components created in this chapter to any Oracle Portal page, as long as you select their "Publish to Portal" check box in the Access properties. Chapter 6 continues our exploration of creating the other types of application components.

CHAPTER 6

Charts, Calendars, Dynamic Pages, Hierarchies, Menus, and Frame Drivers

Introduction

This chapter continues the explanation of the different Oracle Portal components. In this chapter I cover the following component types: charts, calendars, dynamic pages, hierarchies, menus, and frame drivers.

Create a Chart Component

They say an image is worth a thousand words. You can use charts to convey information to your end-users quickly and in an easy-to-understand format. There are three types of charts in Oracle Portal: charts from Query wizard, charts from SQL query, and image charts from Query wizard. Similar to creating other components, to create a chart go to the Applications tab in the Oracle Portal Navigator, and then drill down to the components under the MYEIP_APP application. When you click on the "Chart" link to create a new chart, you are asked to choose from the three chart types (Figure 6.1).

Note

Depending on the version of your Oracle 9*i*AS Portal, the image charts might not be displayed. To add image charts, refer to the "Image Chart from Query Wizard" section in this chapter.

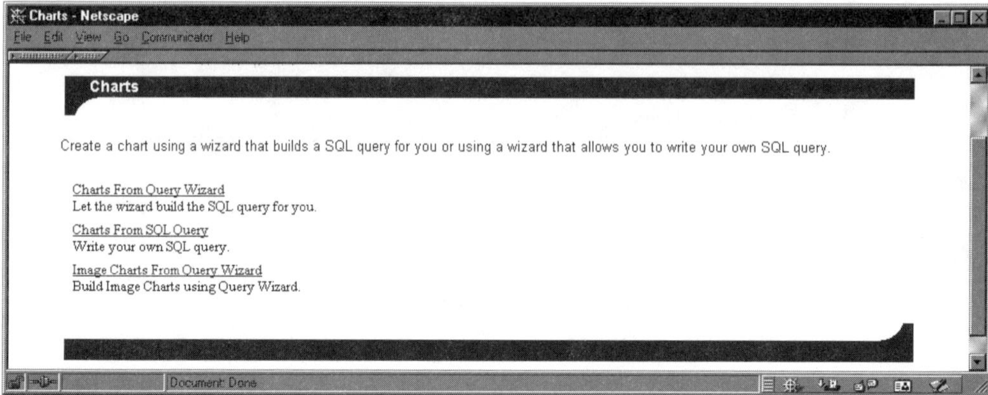

Figure 6.1 Create a Chart.

Chart from Query Wizard

This chart type is based on one table or view. To build a chart you will need to specify the source of the x-axis (i.e., LABEL) and the source of the y-axis (i.e., VALUE). Start by specifying the chart internal and display names (Figure 6.2). The second step is to specify the table name or view name upon which the chart is based (Figure 6.3).

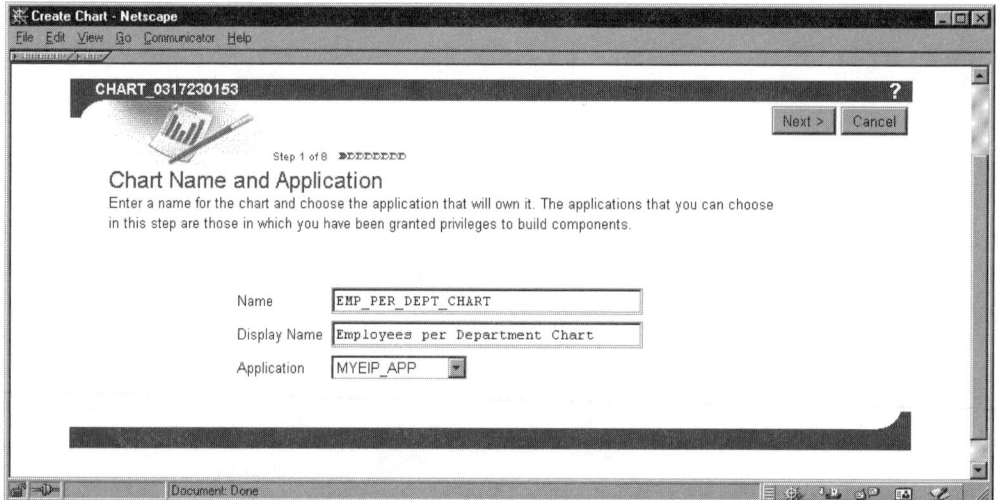

Figure 6.2 Create a Chart from Query Wizard: Chart Name and Application (Step 1 of 8).

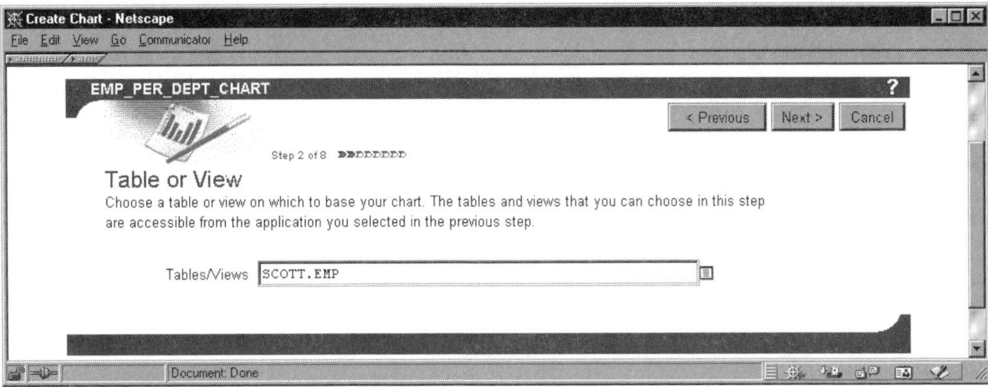

Figure 6.3 Create a Chart from Query Wizard: Table or View (Step 2 of 8).

In step 3 you choose the source of the chart label (i.e., one of the table columns). Also, you need to choose the source column for the chart value and its group function (Figure 6.4). You can think of the Chart Value as a group function column in a SELECT statement that is grouped by the Chart Label column. If you need to display the number of employees in each department rather than the sum of their salaries, choose "1" in the value.

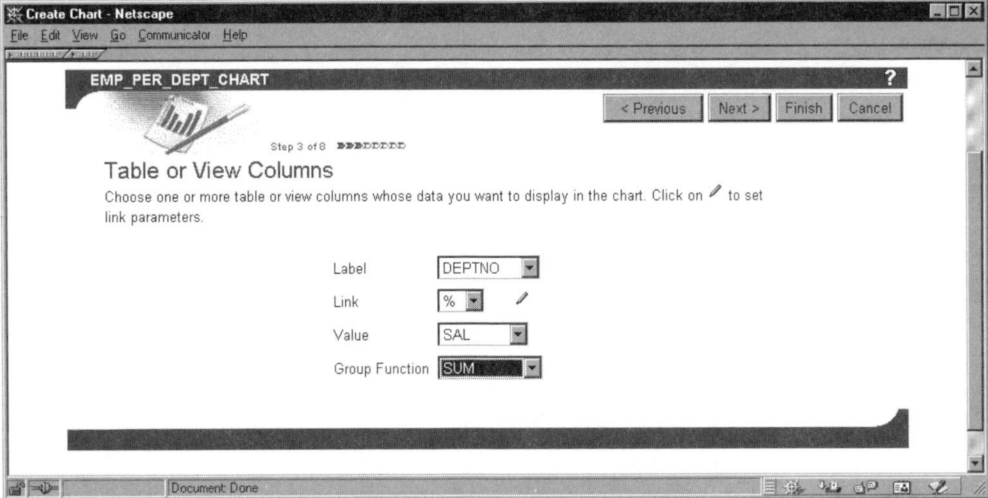

Figure 6.4 Create a Chart from Query Wizard: Table or View Columns (Step 3 of 8).

Create Chart - Netscape

File Edit View Go Communicator Help

EMP_PER_DEPT_CHART ?

< Previous Next > Finish Cancel

Step 4 of 8

Column Conditions

Choose any conditions that you want to use to limit column data displayed in the chart.

Column Name	Condition	Value
%		
%		
%		

More Conditions

Document: Done

Figure 6.5 Create a Chart from Query Wizard: Column Conditions (Step 4 of 8).

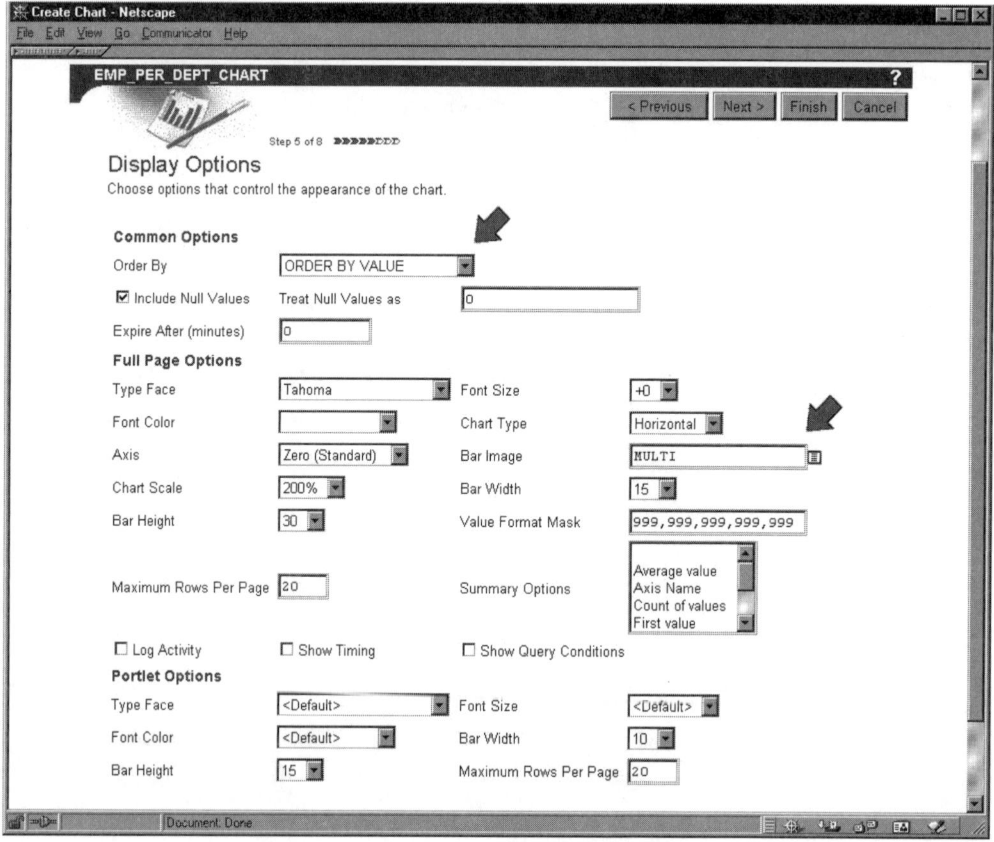

Figure 6.6 Create a Chart from Query Wizard: Display Options (Step 5 of 8).

The next step is to specify the column conditions to decide which records to retrieve and hence include in the chart data (Figure 6.5). In the Display Options step, you can control how the chart looks (Figure 6.6). For example, you can decide how data is ordered in the chart, either by the value [e.g., SUM(SAL)] or by the label (e.g., DEPTNO). This order can be ascending or descending. Also, you can choose the color of the bars in the charts. The default choice is multiple colored bars.

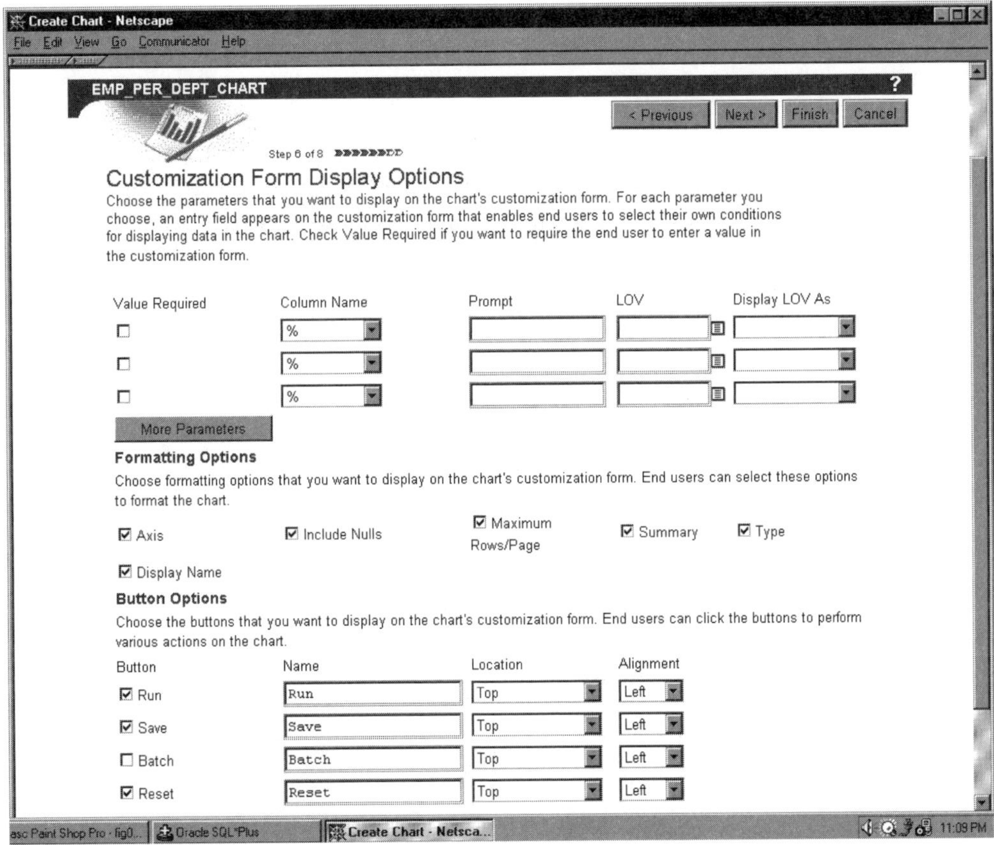

Figure 6.7 Create a Chart from Query Wizard: Customization Form Display Options (Step 6 of 8).

In step 6 you specify the customization form options of your chart (Figure 6.7). When you are ready to create the chart, click on the "Finish" button. Run the chart as a portlet (Figure 6.8). The default chart orientation is horizontal, so you find the x-axis values (e.g., department numbers) are displayed on the left side. The bars are scaled to be able to fit into a portlet and the values of the y-axis [e.g., SUM(SAL)] are displayed on the top of the bars.

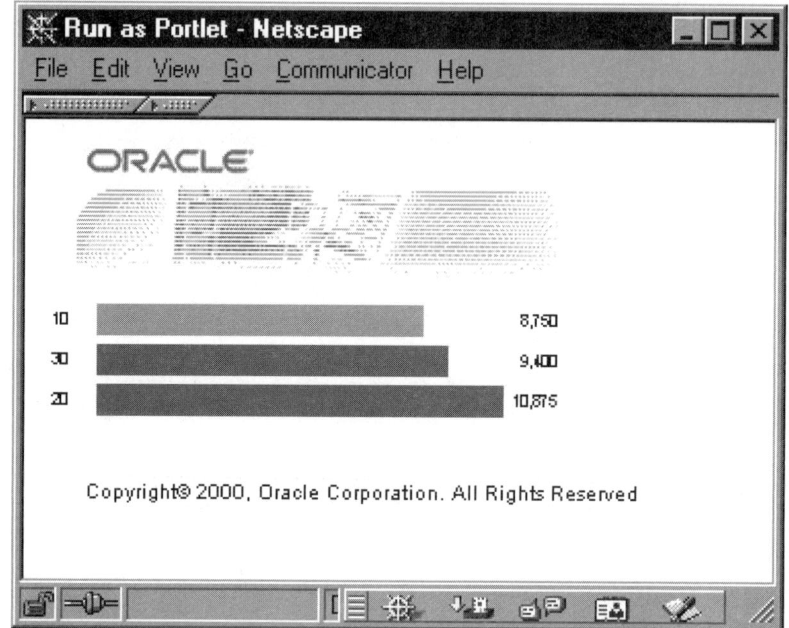

Figure 6.8 A Chart from Query Wizard: Run as Portlet.

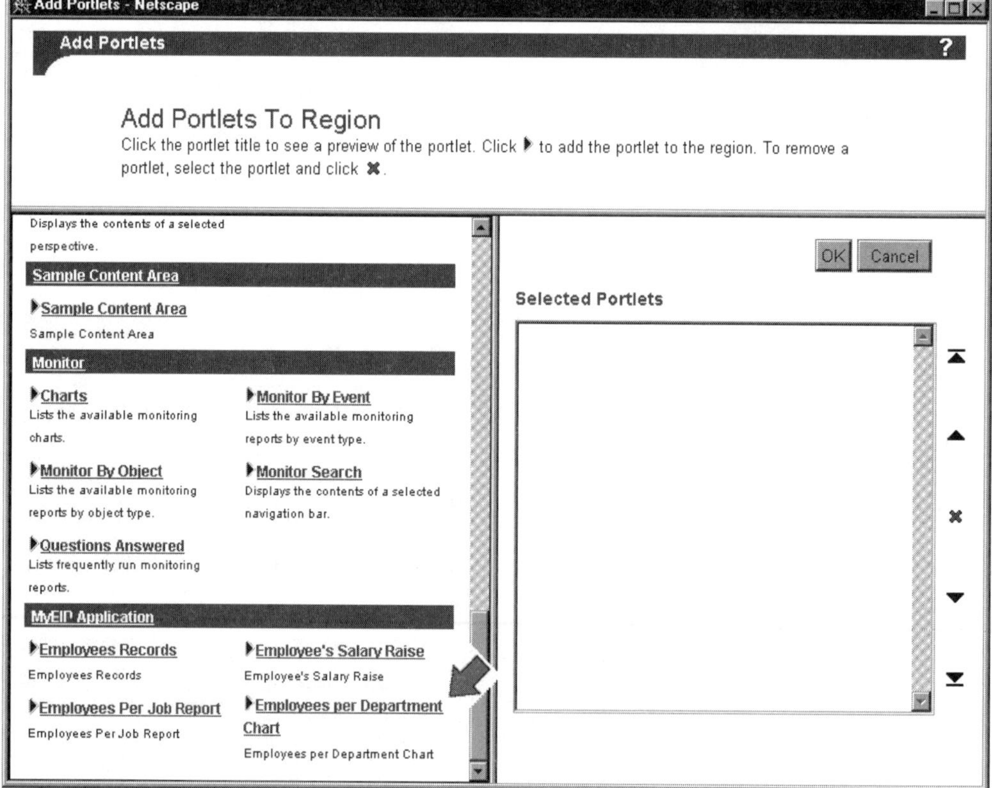

Figure 6.9 Portlet Repository.

Select the "Publish to Portal" check box in the Access tab. You can refer to Chapter 5 for an illustration. To add the chart to the Employees Salaries tab in the EMPLOYEE_PAGE, edit the page and click on the Add Portlets icon to display the Portlet Repository (Figure 6.9). You can click on the chart name link (e.g., "Employees per Department Chart") to preview the chart before you add it to the selected portlets (Figure 6.10).

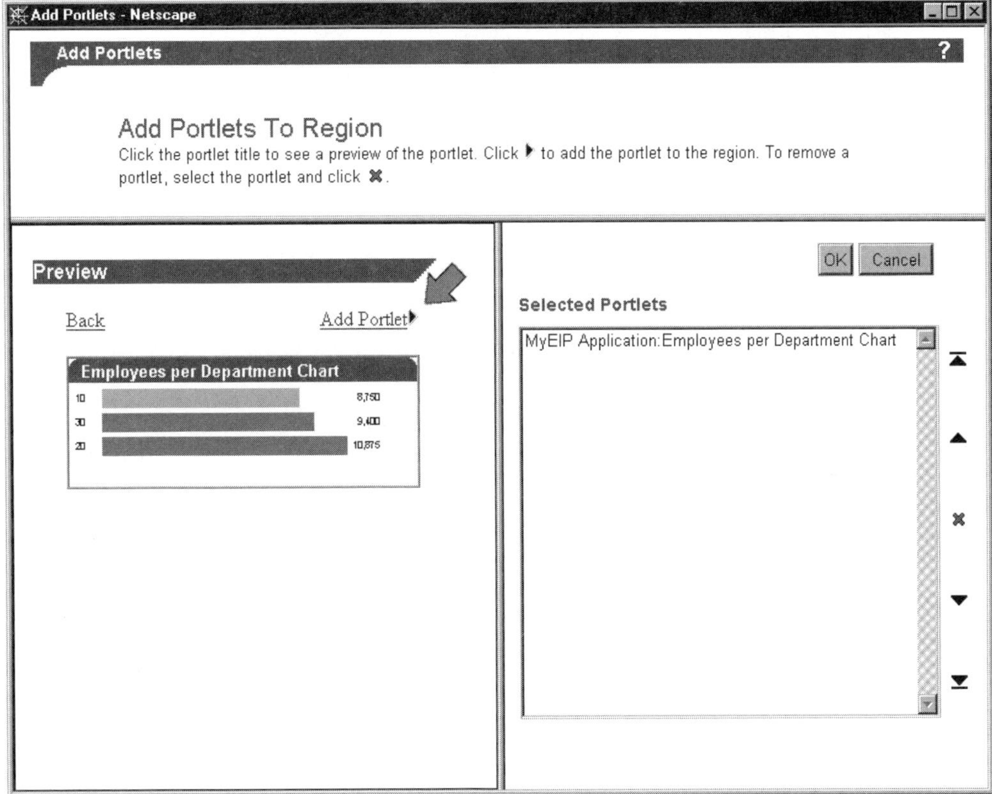

Figure 6.10 Portlet Repository: Preview Chart Portlet.

Note

As I mentioned in Chapter 3, for Portlet Repository in O9*i*AS Portal 3.0.9, clicking on a portlet will not preview the portlet, rather it will add it to the selected portlet list. In Portal 3.0.9, there is a preview icon on the right side of all the portlet names, which opens a separate window for portlet review.

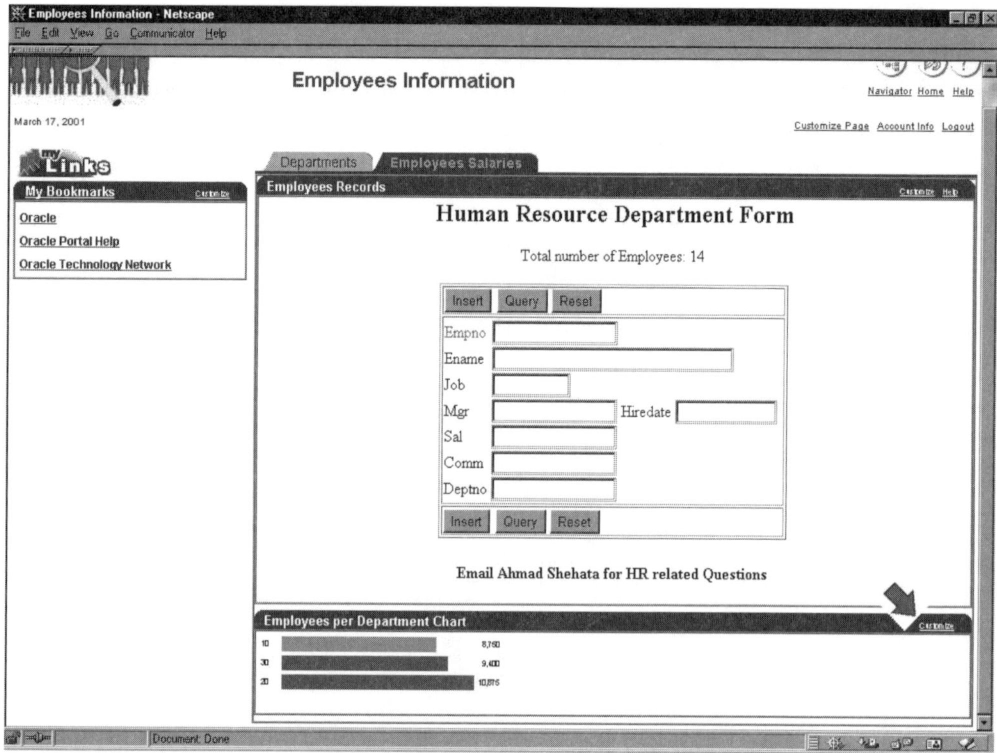

Figure 6.11 Employees Information Page.

The Employees Page should look similar to Figure 6.11.

You can customize the chart from the page by clicking on its "Customize" link. The Chart Customization Form is displayed. You can change the chart title, orientation (i.e., horizontal or vertical), and order by options (Figure 6.12).

Chart from SQL Query

Creating a chart using the Query wizard is limited to one table only. Charts based on SQL statements give you the ability to populate the chart from tables joined together. Specify the chart name in the first step (Figure 6.13).

The SELECT statement has to have three columns. The first column is the hyperlink for the chart label, which can hold a URL value for each label. So the end-user can click on the label to navigate to another Web page. If you do not have a link, you can leave the column as NULL. The second column is the chart label or x-axis name. The third column is the chart value or the y-axis data (Figure 6.14).

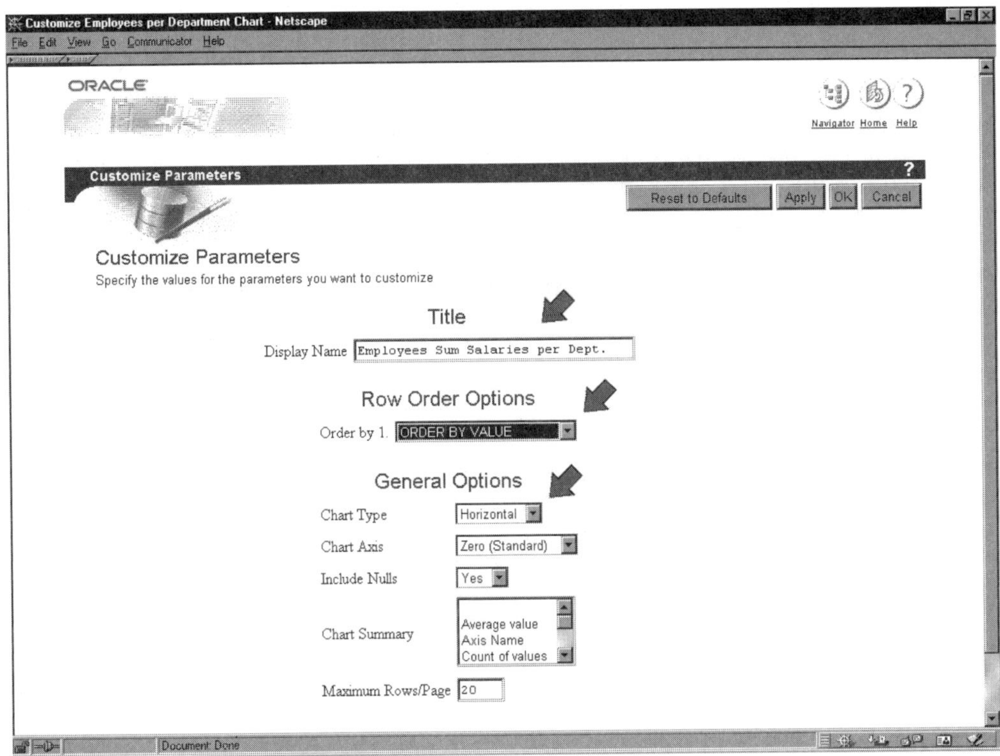

Figure 6.12 Chart Customization Form.

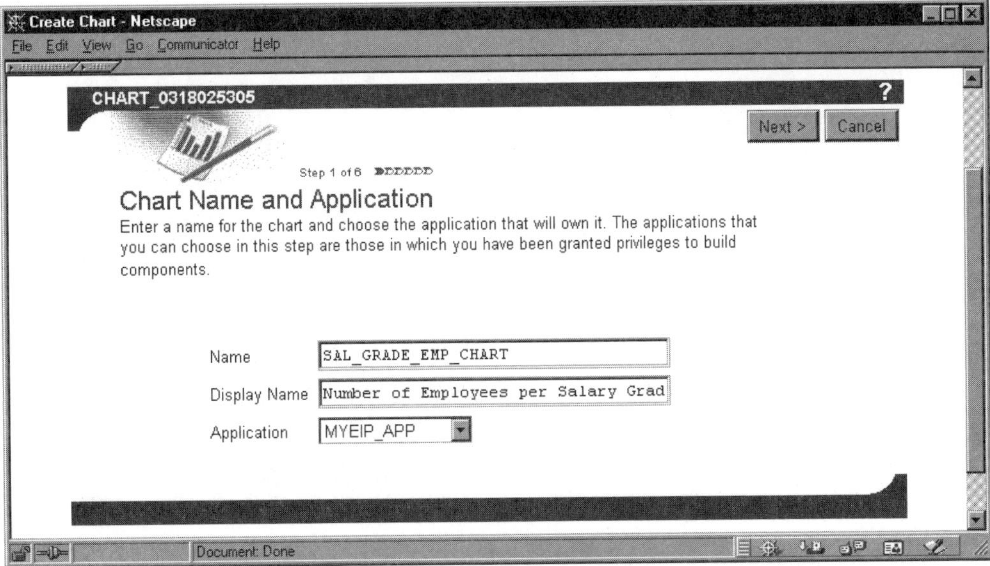

Figure 6.13 Create a Chart from SQL: Chart Name and Application (Step 1 of 6).

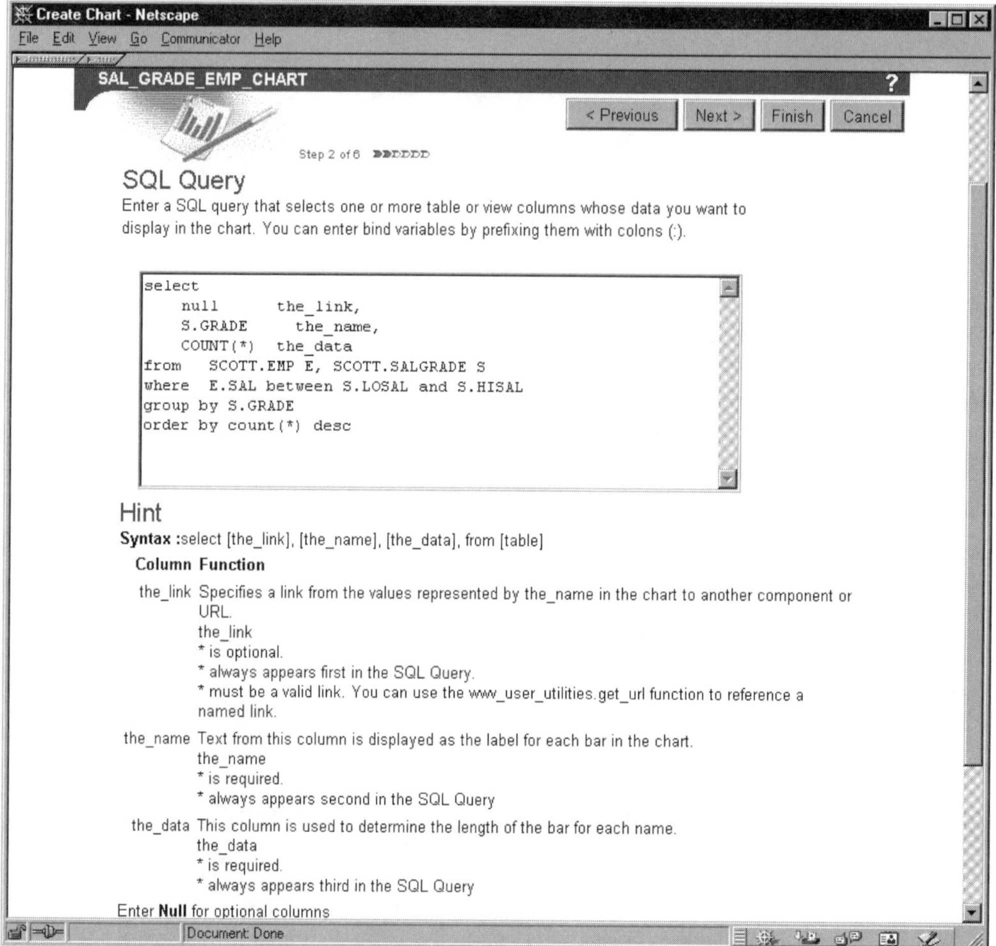

Figure 6.14 Create a Chart from SQL: SQL Query (Step 2 of 6).

The third step is the Display Options. Change the chart type to vertical, reduce the maximum number of rows per page, and change the summary option to display the count of values (Figure 6.15).

You can accept the default values for the remaining steps, finish, and run the chart (Figure 6.16). The first line of numbers under the chart shows the salary grade numbers, and the second line shows the number of employees in each grade.

You can edit the chart to change the SELECT statement to include a DECODE function as well as a sample link (Figure 6.17). Run the modified chart as a portlet (Figure 6.18).

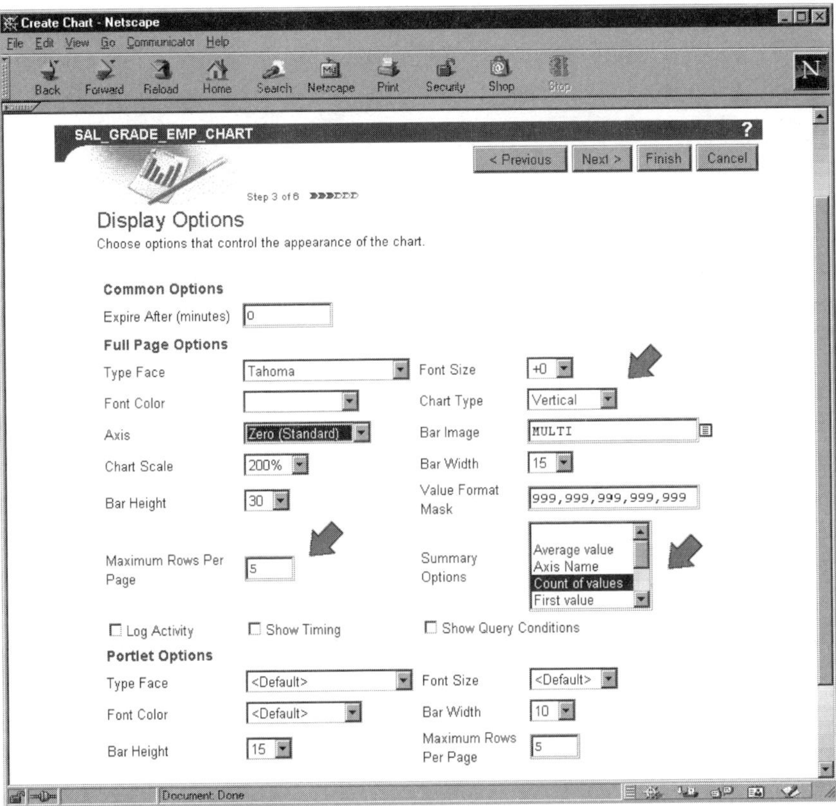

Figure 6.15 Create a Chart from SQL: Display Options (Step 3 of 6).

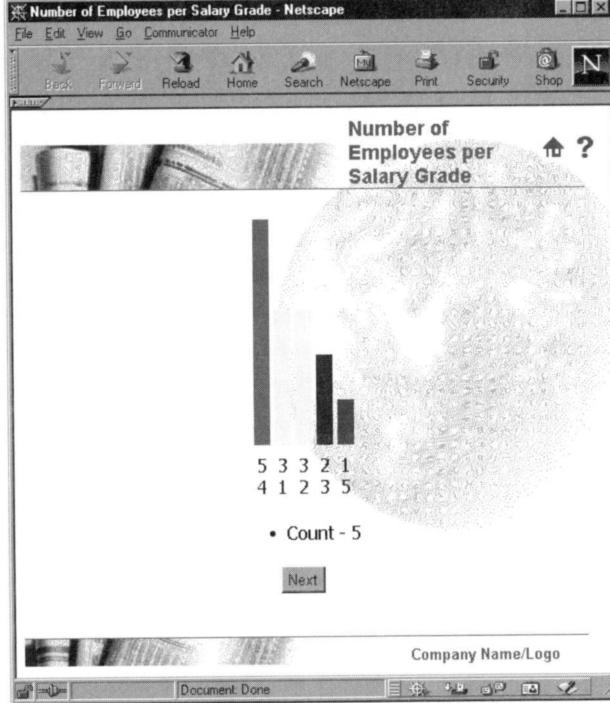

Figure 6.16 Run a Chart from SQL.

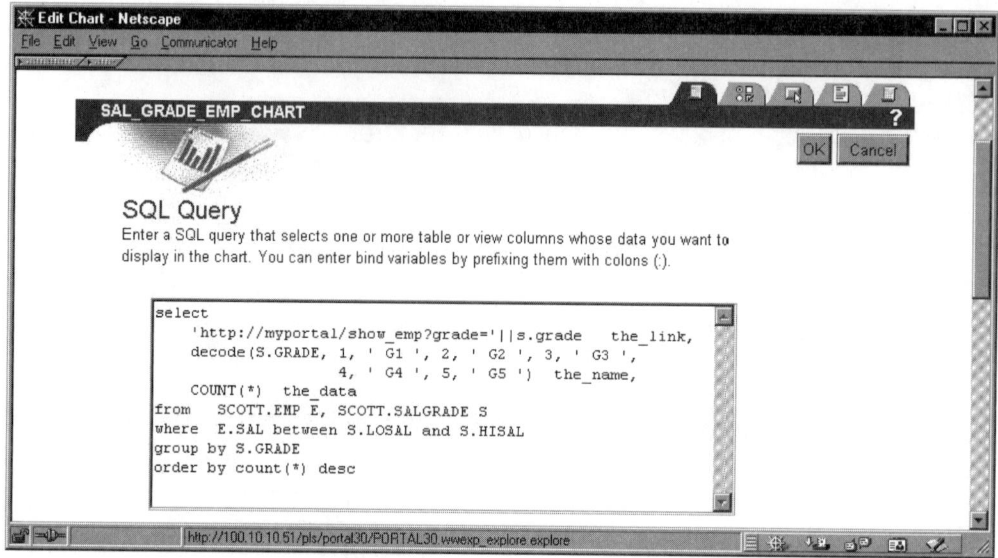

Figure 6.17 Edit a Chart from SQL.

Figure 6.18
Run a Chart from SQL as a Portlet.

Image Chart from Query Wizard

The earlier two chart types are limited in their graphical abilities. You cannot build a pie chart or 3D chart using them. The image charts are provided in Oracle Portal 3.0 as a beta feature and are not enabled by default. To be able to use this feature in Oracle Portal 3.0, you need to enable it. Go to Oracle Portal home page and click on the Administer tab. Click on the "Global Settings" link in the Services portlet (Figure 6.19).

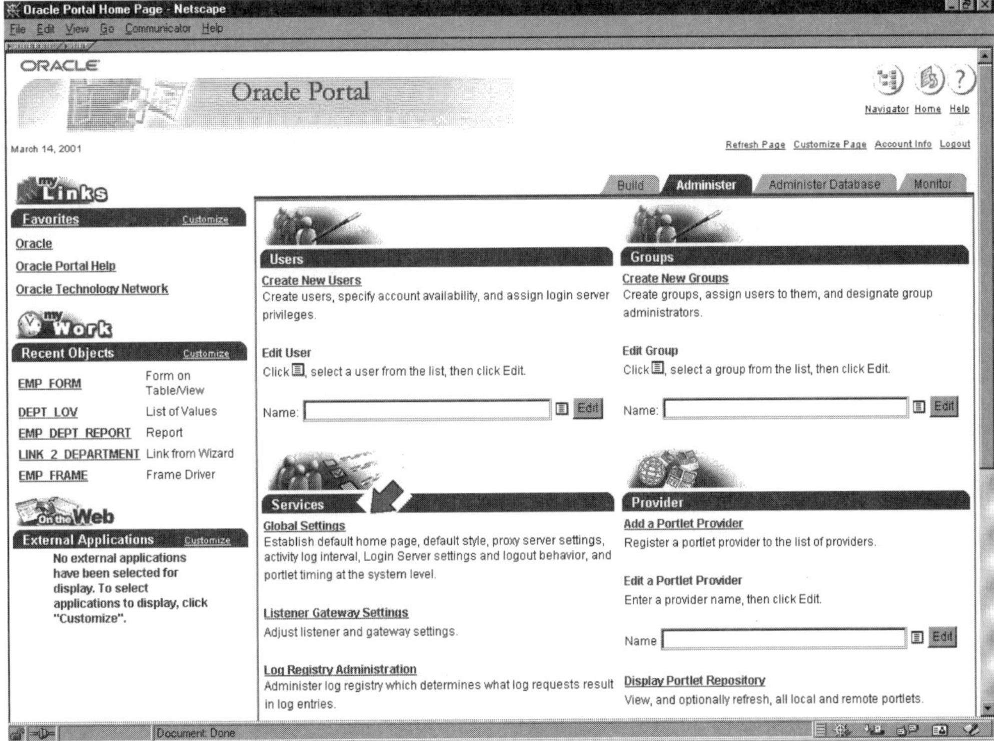

Figure 6.19 Oracle Portal Home Page: Administer Tab.

In the Global Settings page, you can change Oracle Portal-level settings, such as Default Style for all the Oracle Portal pages and the Proxy Server settings. The proxy settings are needed if you are using Oracle Portal from inside a firewall, and you need to connect to the outside network from within your portal (Figure 6.20).

Select the "Image Charts From Query Wizard" check box (Figure 6.21). The Global Settings is one place to check the version of your Oracle Portal. When you click "OK", you are ready to create image charts.

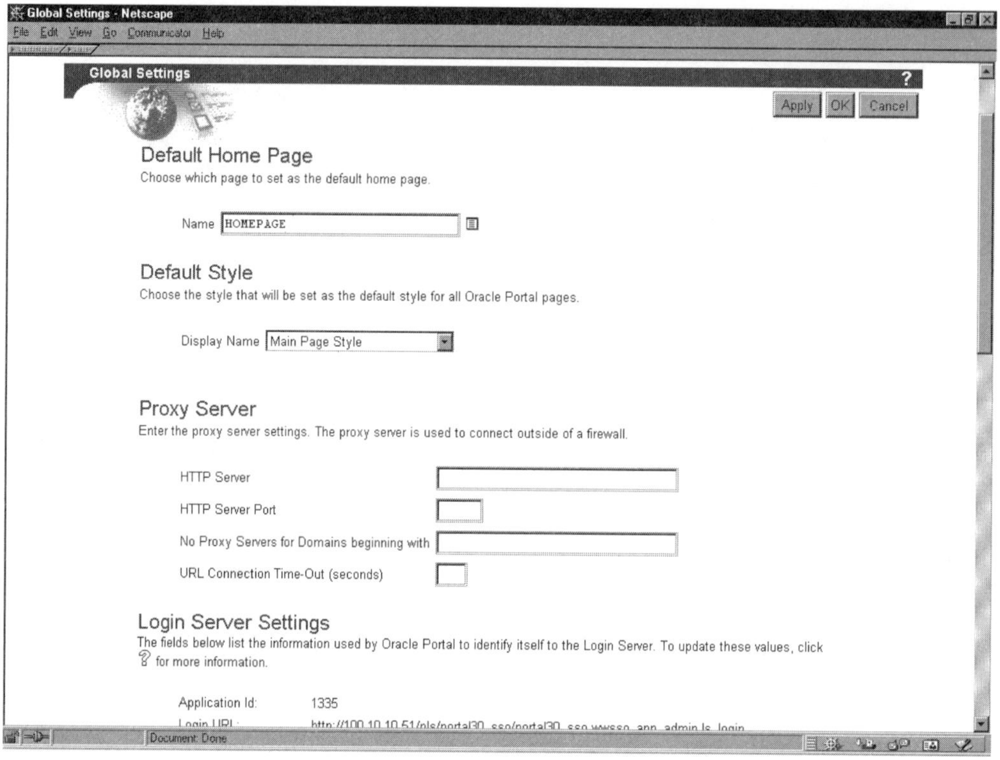

Figure 6.20 Global Settings: Top.

The image chart example created in this section will show each employee's number along with his or her salary. Specify the name of the image chart (Figure 6.22).

In the second step you specify the chart type. There are five different chart types and each has its own subtypes. When you choose a chart type, illustrations of the subtypes will be displayed. For your first image chart, leave the chart type as PIE_CHART with the default subtype (Figure 6.23).

Next, specify the table or view upon which the image chart is based (Figure 6.24).

In step 4 you need to specify the series (i.e., chart label). Think of the series as your x-axis column. Also, you need to select the group column (i.e., chart values or the y-axis column; Figure 6.25). Because this is a pie chart, the actual salaries will not be displayed in the chart run time, only their percentages out of the total salaries for all the employees selected.

Step 5 is the Column Conditions. By not providing any conditions, all EMP table rows are retrieved. Step 6 is the Display Options step where you specify the chart width and height for both the full page and portlet run time (Figure 6.26).

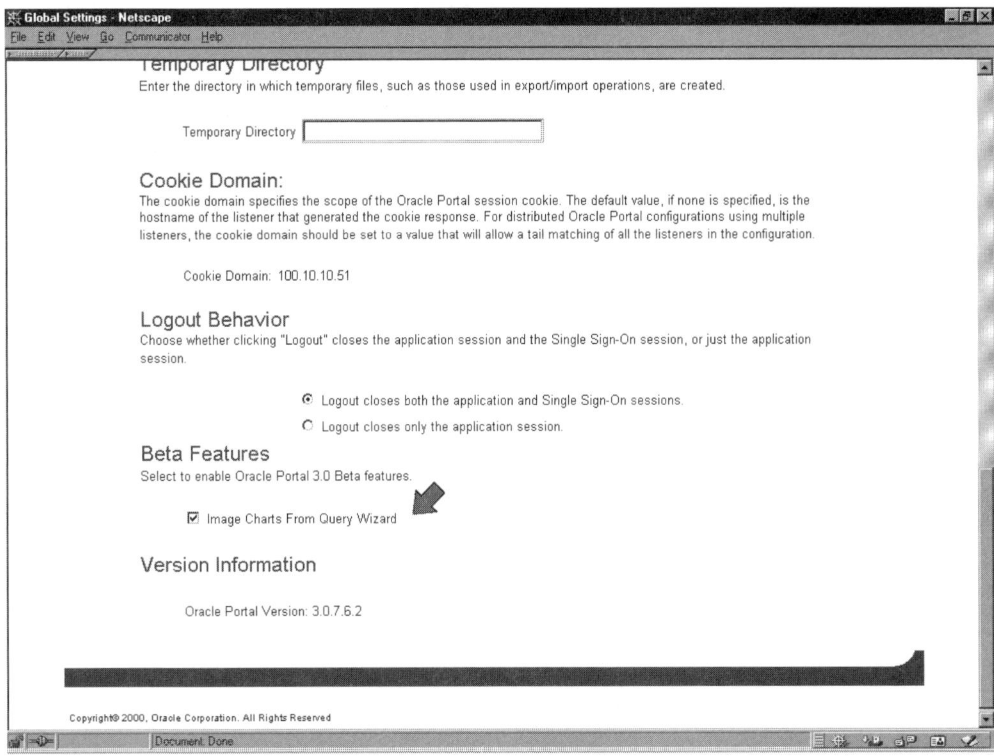

Figure 6.21 Global Settings: Bottom.

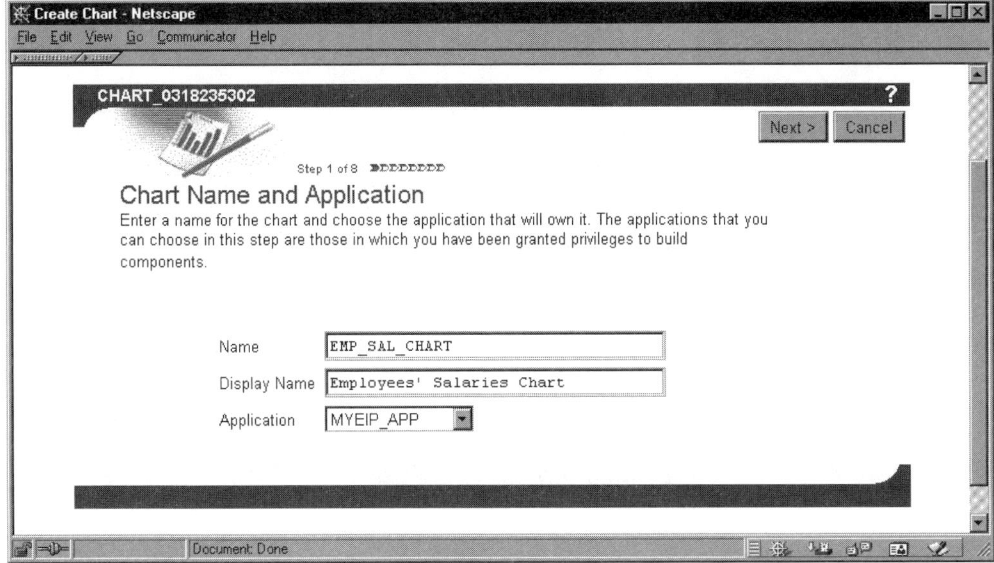

Figure 6.22 Create an Image Chart: Chart Name and Application (Step 1 of 8).

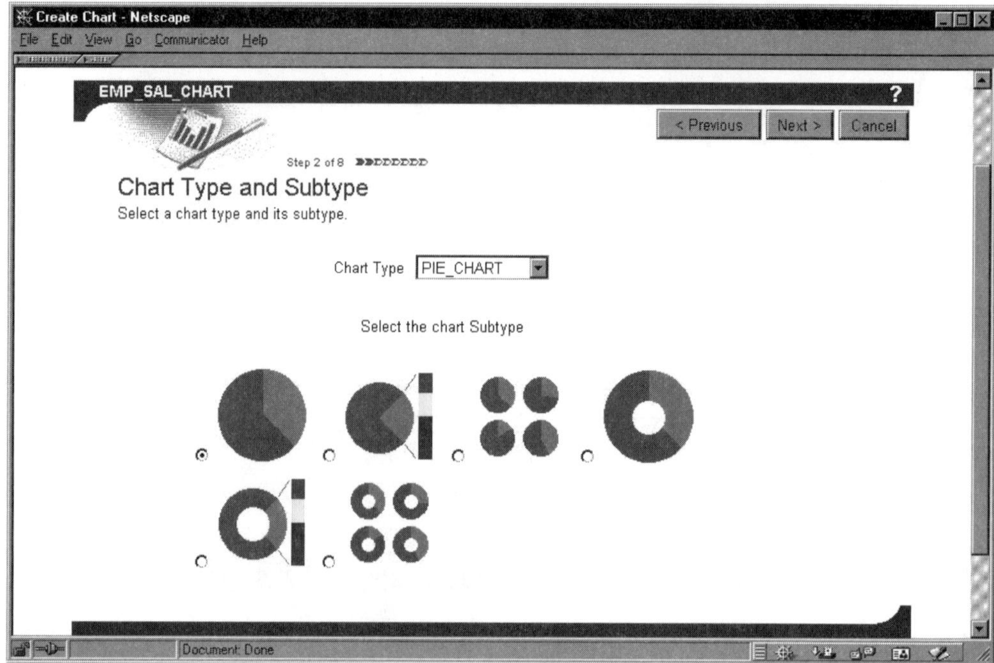

Figure 6.23 Create an Image Chart: Chart Type and Subtype (Step 2 of 8).

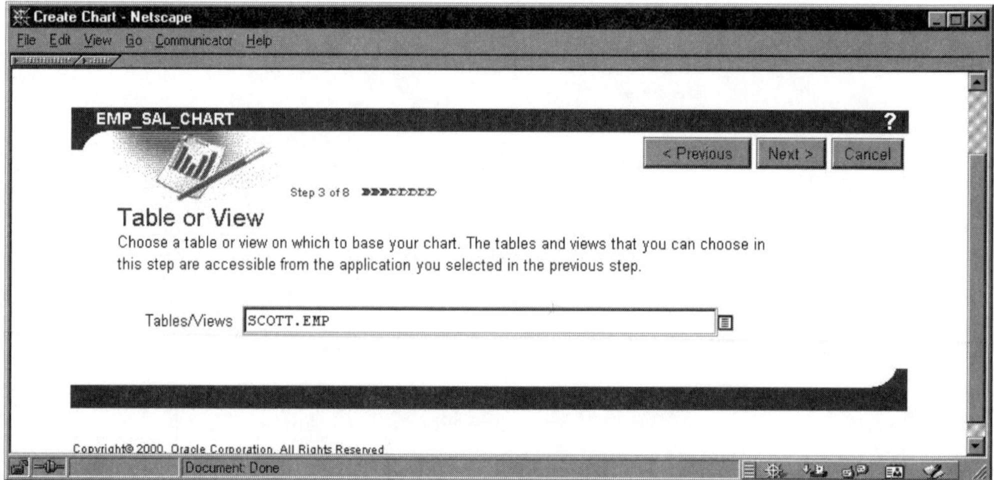

Figure 6.24 Create an Image Chart: Table or View (Step 3 of 8).

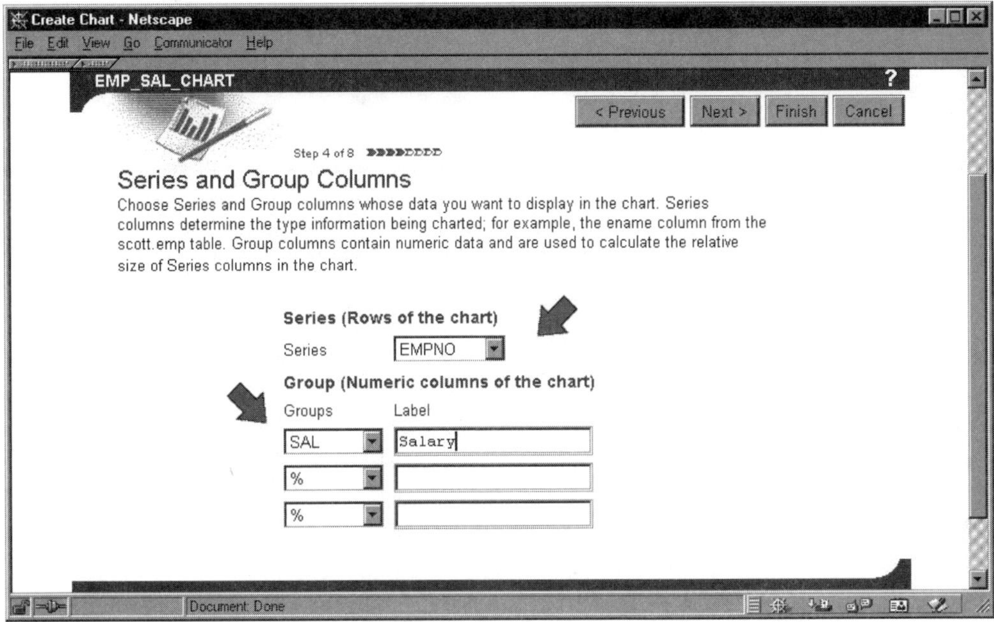

Figure 6.25 Create an Image Chart: Series and Group Columns (Step 4 of 8).

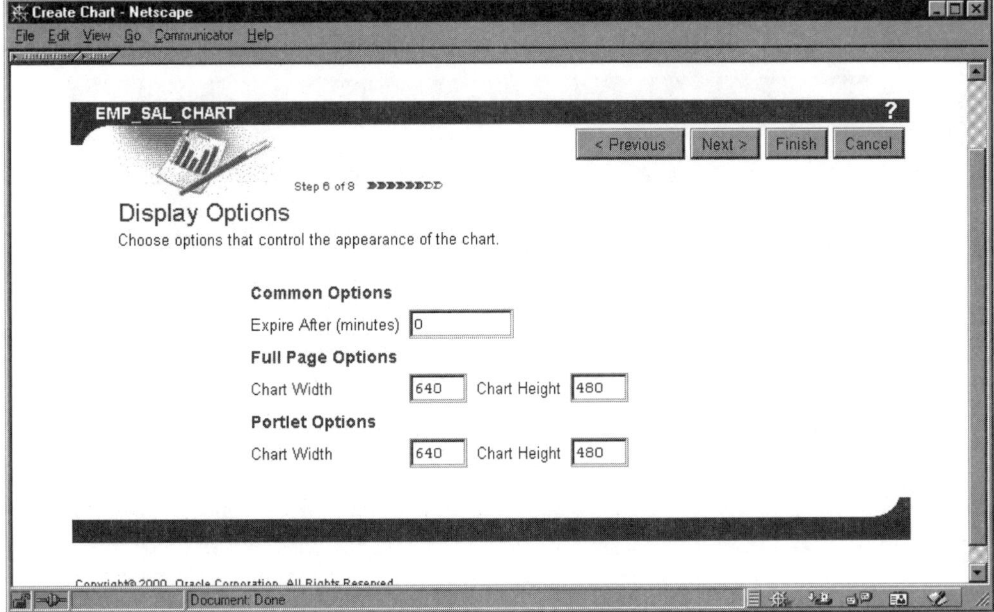

Figure 6.26 Create an Image Chart: Display Options (Step 6 of 8).

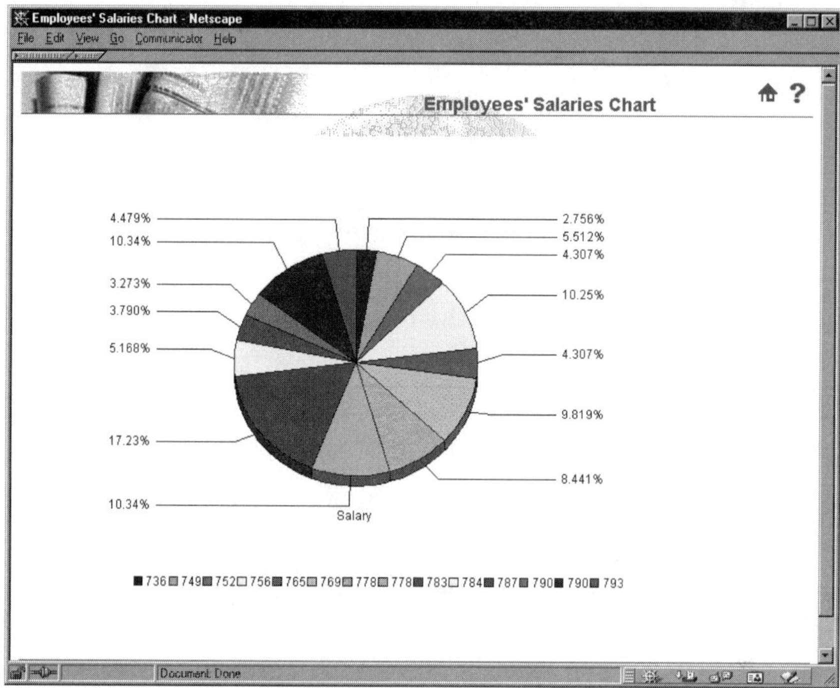

Figure 6.27 Run an Image Chart.

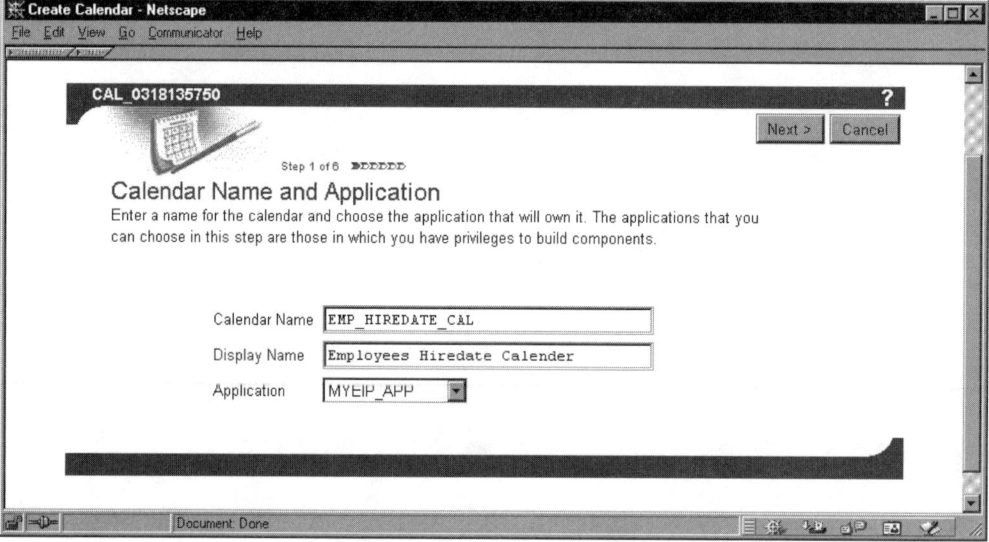

Figure 6.28 Create a Calendar: Calendar Name and Application (Step 1 of 6).

There is no customization form supported for image charts. The remaining two steps are the Chart Text Options and Additional PL/SQL code. Run the chart (Figure 6.27). Because these types of images cannot be built with just HTML code, the image chart is built by the Java Virtual Machine (JVM) in the O9*i*AS and sent as an image in the HTML page to the browser. If you decide to edit the chart and rerun it, you might need to delete the browser cache for the Oracle Portal to refresh the chart output. If the Oracle Portal version you are using has the image charting as a beta feature, you should not rely on it for your production portal.

Note

Due to the chart width limit, the employees' numbers are truncated to three digits only to be able to fit the legend in the page.

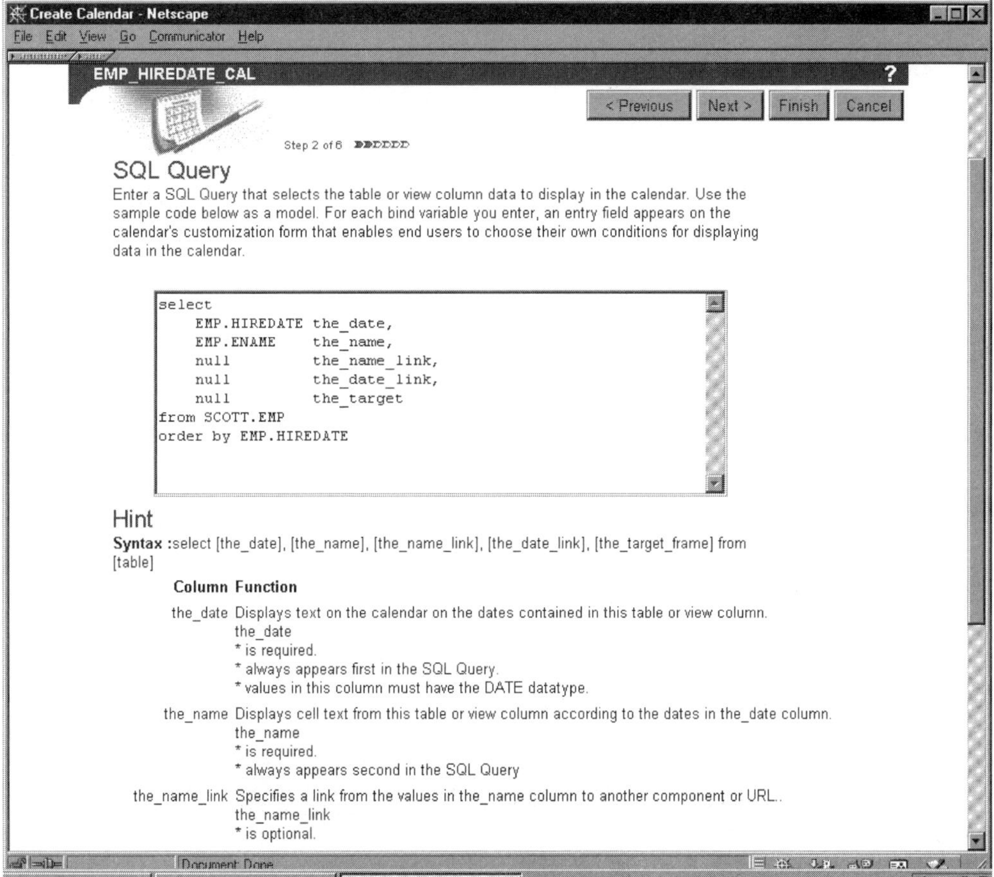

Figure 6.29 Create a Calendar: SQL Query (Step 2 of 6).

Create a Calendar

A calendar component is based on a sorted date column. The calendar is displayed in a monthly format where you can include other columns or values to be displayed in each day's cell. Specify a name for your calendar (Figure 6.28).

You need to specify an SQL SELECT statement that feeds the data to the calendar. This SELECT statement has to have five columns with the names: the_date, the_name, the_name_link, the_date_link, and the_target (Figure 6.29). The first two columns of the SELECT statement are mandatory, and you have to order by the date column. Even though you can sort in descending

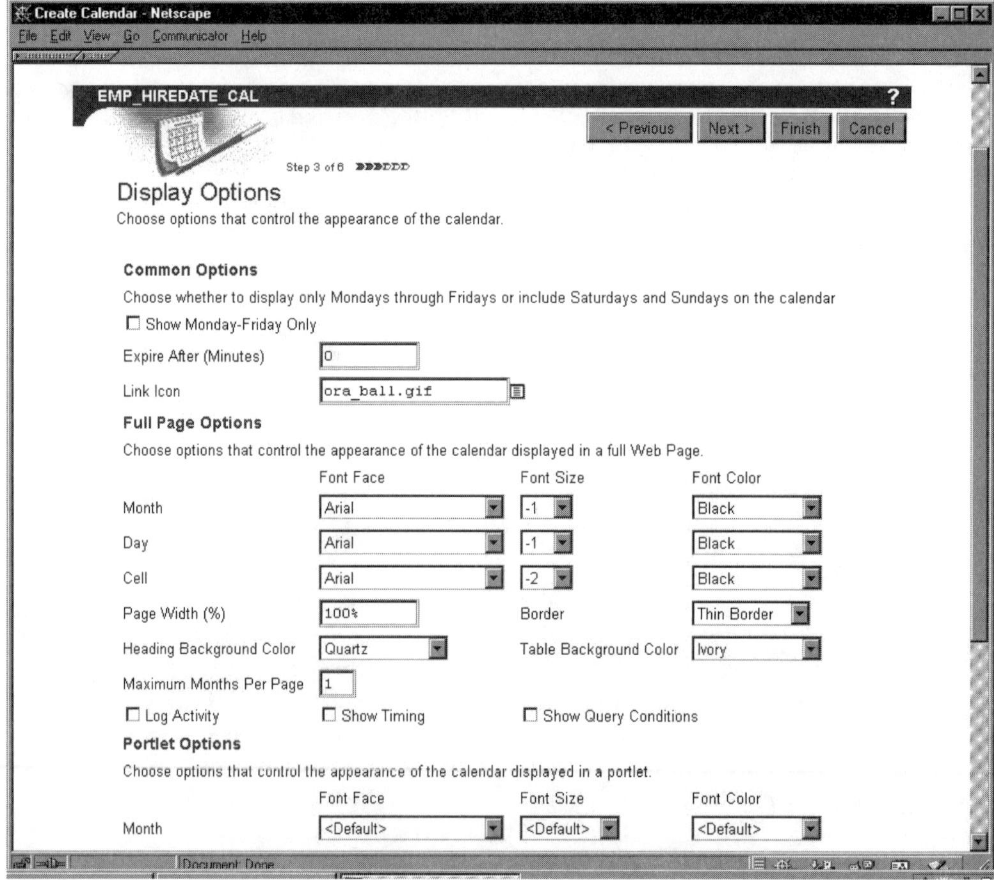

Figure 6.30 Create a Calendar: Display Options (Step 3 of 6).

order, sorting it in ascending order has more calendar-nature to it. When you order by descending, the "Next" button takes you earlier in time. The date and the name are displayed in the calendar as normal text if you do not specify their links in the SELECT statement. If you need to link the calendar to frames, the target column should hold the URL value of the linked frames.

Like most of the components, calendar items have display options that are categorized into three groups: common, full page, and portlet. You can change how the calendar looks in run time by changing these properties (Figure 6.30).

When you are done specifying the rest of the creation step options, finish the creation and run the calendar (Figure 6.31). The calendar starts from the minimum date value, assuming ascending order by clause.

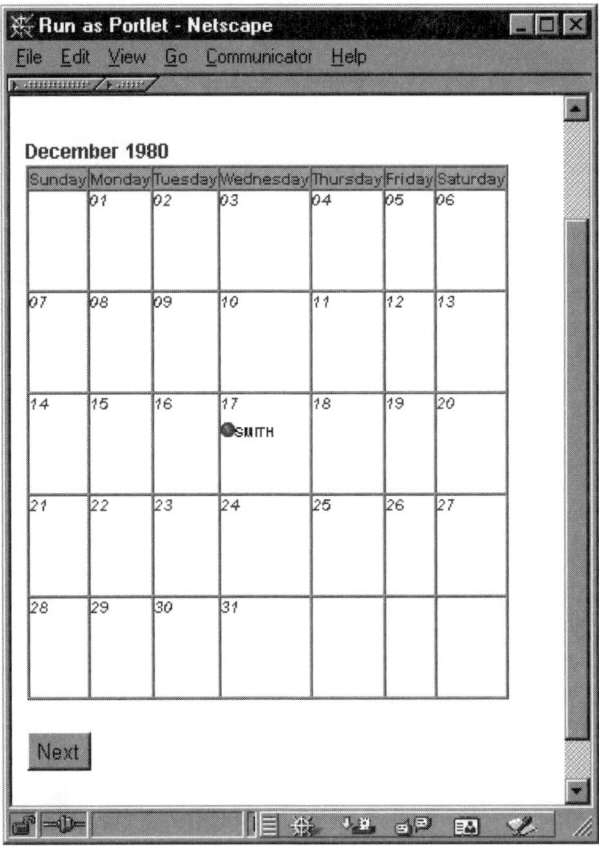

Figure 6.31 Run a Calendar.

Create a Dynamic Page

Dynamic pages are HTML pages with the <ORACLE> tag. You can write SQL and PL/SQL code between the <ORACLE> and </ORACLE> tags. Oracle9*i* Application Server sends the code between the Oracle tags to the database to be executed. O9*i*AS merges the output with its enclosing HTML code and sends it to the browser. In this section you create a dynamic page that prints each department name along with its employees. Start by naming your dynamic page (Figure 6.32).

The HTML code gives the component page a title, displays a header, and then executes PL/SQL block (Figure 6.33). The code defines two PL/SQL cursors to fetch the data into PL/SQL records. The outer cursor is DEPT_CUR, which retrieves all the DEPT rows. The inner cursor is EMP_CUR, which retrieves all the EMP rows that work for the matching department number in the outer join. The code uses the HTP.PRINT procedure to display the output in HTML format.

```
<HTML>
<HEAD>
<TITLE>Employee Per Department</TITLE>
</HEAD>
<BODY> <H2>Employees Per Department</H2>
<ORACLE>
declare
   cursor dept_cur is select DEPTNO, DNAME from SCOTT.DEPT;
   cursor emp_cur(deptno_p number) is
          select ENAME from SCOTT.EMP where DEPTNO = deptno_p;
begin
   for dept_rec in dept_cur loop
       htp.print('<B><BR>Department: '||dept_rec.dname||'</B>');
       for emp_rec in emp_cur(dept_rec.deptno) loop
           htp.print('<BR>'||emp_rec.ename);
       end loop;
   end loop;
end;
</ORACLE>
</BODY>
</HTML>
```

The code uses the <B> tag to display the department name in boldface and the <BR> tag to put a carriage return between rows. The third step in the creation displays the PL/SQL code by itself (Figure 6.34).

Create Dynamic Page - Netscape

File Edit View Go Communicator Help

DYN_0318140432

Next > Cancel

Step 1 of 7

Dynamic Page Name

Enter a name for the dynamic page and choose the application that will own it. The applications that you can choose in this step are those in which you have been granted privileges to build components.

Name DEPT_EMP_DYN

Display Name Employees per Departments

Application MYEIP_APP

Document: Done

Figure 6.32 Create a Dynamic Page: Dynamic Page Name (Step 1 of 7).

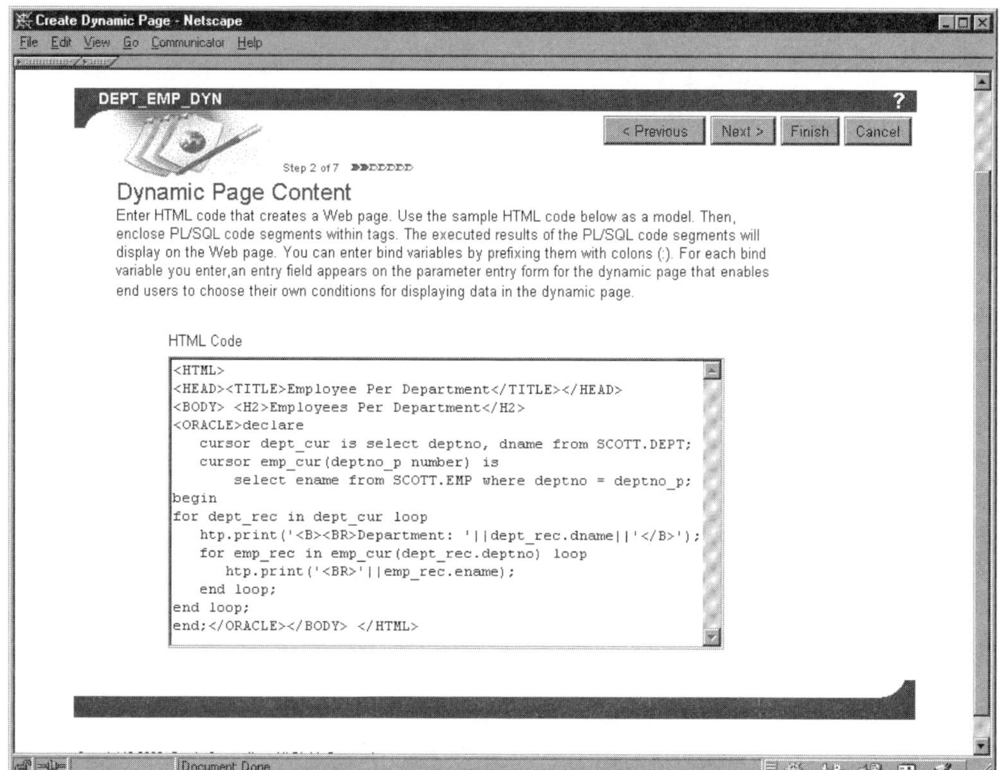

Figure 6.33 Create a Dynamic Page: Dynamic Page Content (Step 2 of 7).

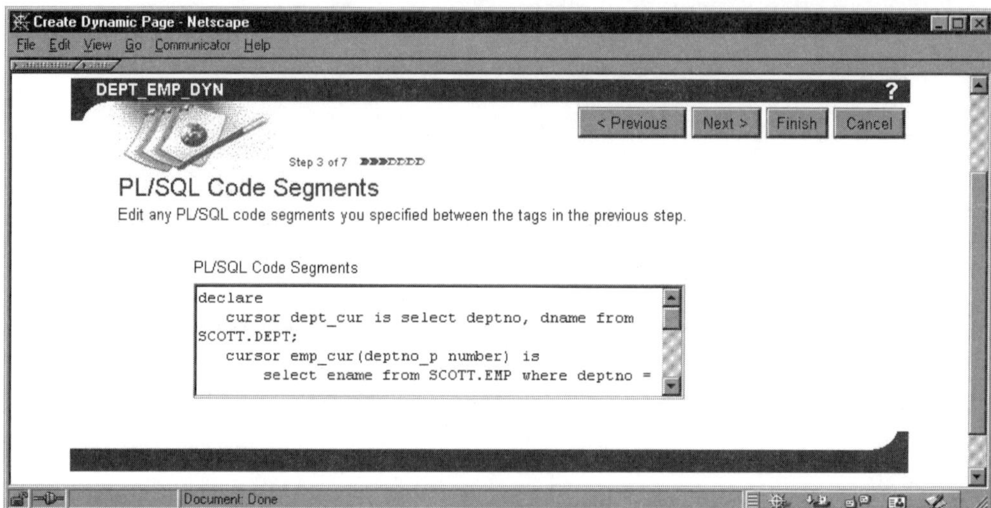

Figure 6.34 Create a Dynamic Page: PL/SQL Code Segments (Step 3 of 7).

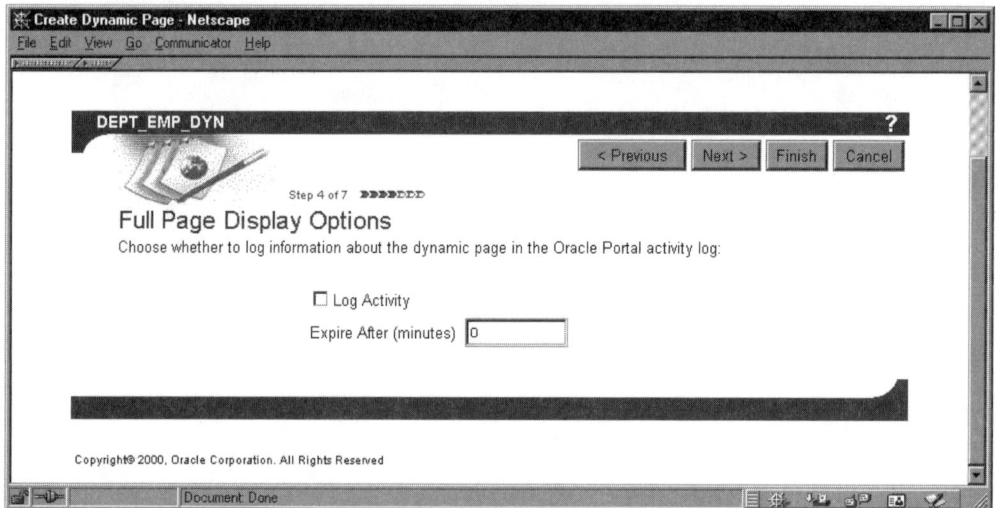

Figure 6.35 Create a Dynamic Page: Full Page Display Option (Step 4 of 7).

The fourth step is the Display Options. There are two options: You can log the activity on the component and you can expire the component-cached version after a certain number of minutes. By default there is no activity logging, and each time you run the component, it executes against the database to retrieve its data (Figure 6.35).

Go through the creation steps. When you run the component, you should see the output of the dynamic page (Figure 6.36).

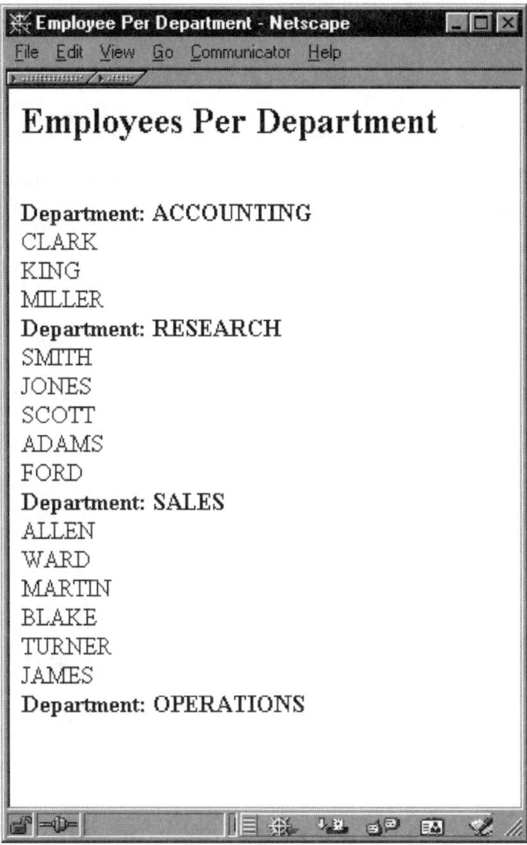

Figure 6.36 Run a Dynamic Page.

Create a Hierarchy

A hierarchy is a GUI presentation of a self-relationship (e.g., EMPLOYEE-EMPLOYEE, because an employee's manager is an employee). Start by specifying a name for the new hierarchy component (Figure 6.37). The second step is to specify the table upon which the hierarchy component is created (Figure 6.38).

The third step defines how the table is linked to itself (Figure 6.39). You choose the Primary Key (i.e., EMPNO) and the Foreign Key (i.e., MGR). Also, for the hierarchy to run, it needs to start with a certain record. To specify the record, you need to specify the Start With Column and the Start With Value (i.e., EMP.ENAME = 'KING'). The Start with LOV (List of Values) provides the end-user with a list of start values in the customization form of the hierarchy. Then, you choose a column to display inside an organization cell. You can also use an expression such as EMP.ENAME||, ||EMP.EMPNO, or UPPER(EMP.ENAME). Finally, in this step you can specify a link for your displayed column, so the end-user can click on the displayed column to be routed to a related URL. Links are covered in Chapter 7.

For practice, specify column conditions to retrieve only the employees who are working in (DEPTNO 10 or 20) and who were hired before 1 March 2001 (Figure 6.40).

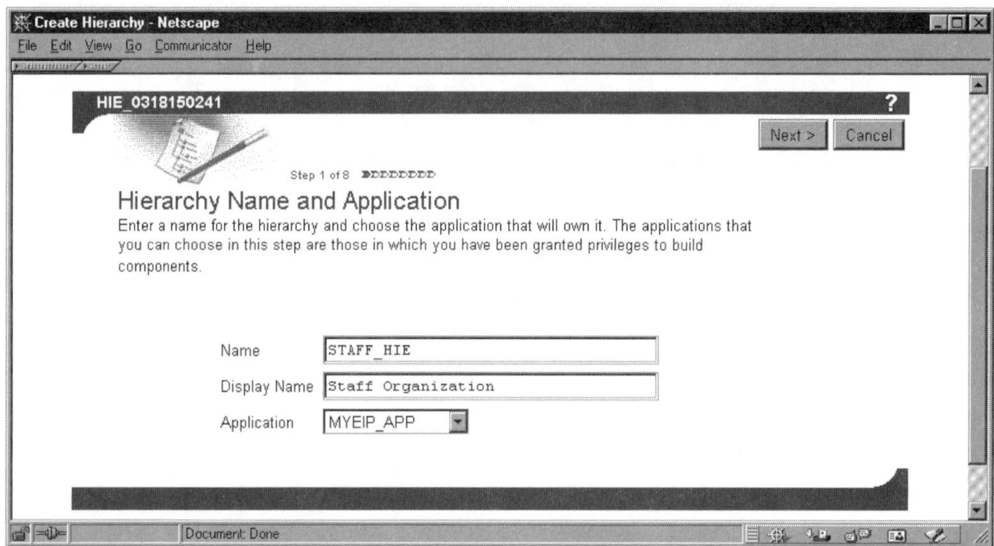

Figure 6.37 Create a Hierarchy: Hierarchy Name and Application (Step 1 of 8).

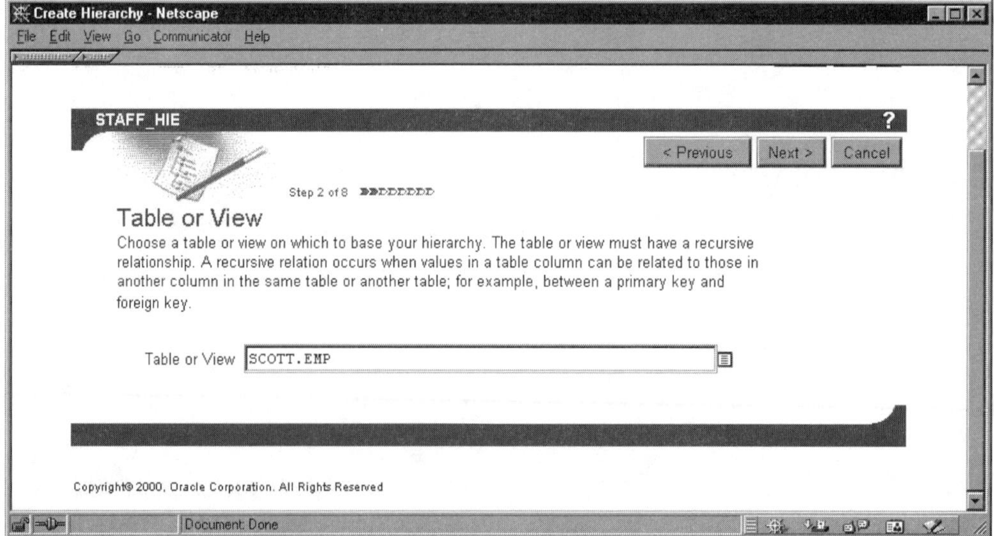

Figure 6.38 Create a Hierarchy: Table or View Name (Step 2 of 8).

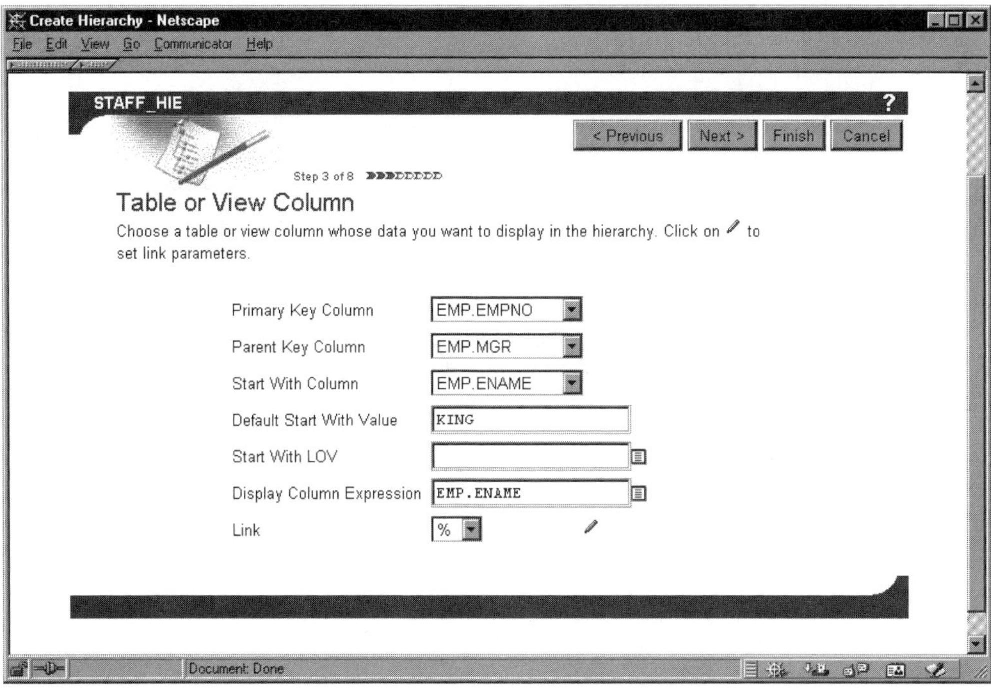

Figure 6.39 Create a Hierarchy: Table or View Column (Step 3 of 8).

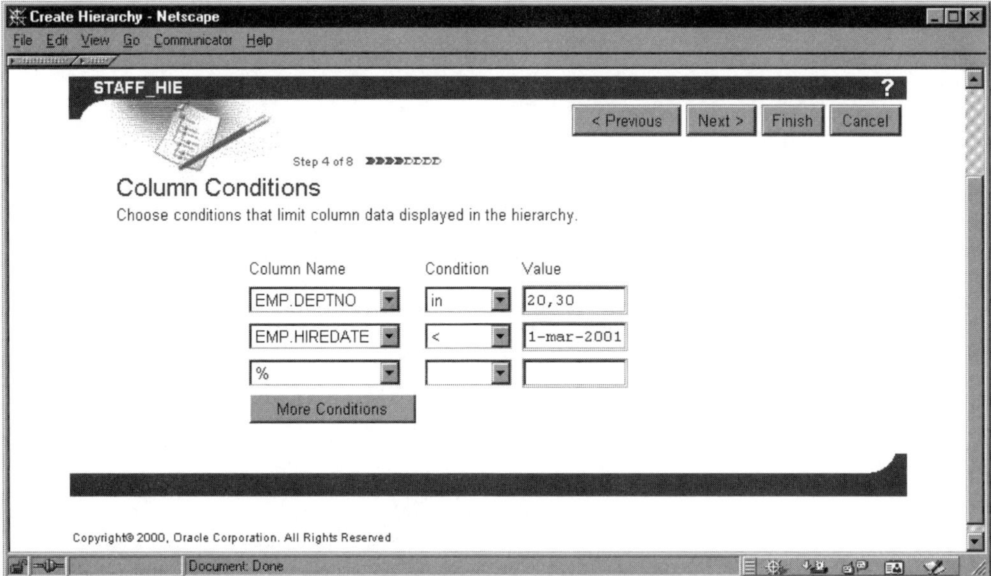

Figure 6.40 Create a Hierarchy: Column Conditions (Step 4 of 8).

In step 5 you can change how the component is displayed. For example, you can set the maximum number of children to be displayed for the level under the root node of the hierarchy (i.e., Level 1; Figure 6.41).

When you finish creating the hierarchy component, run and test it (Figure 6.42). Then you can edit the hierarchy to change its type from an HTML table to breakdown. The breakdown hierarchy type displays the nodes of the hierarchy as a bulleted list where lower levels are indented to the right.

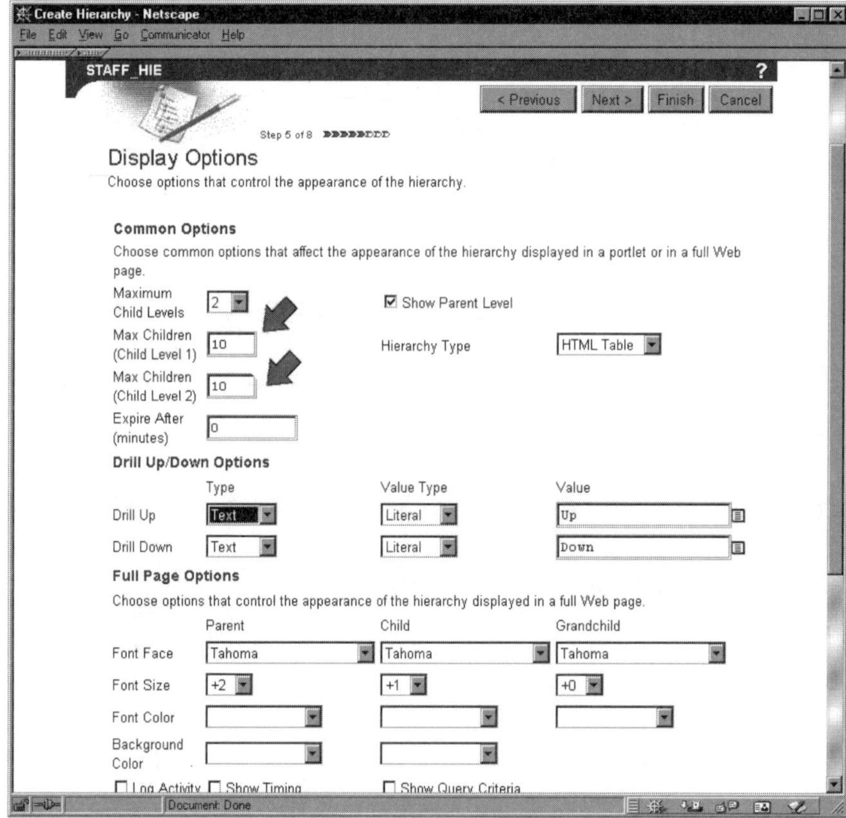

Figure 6.41 Create a Hierarchy: Display Options (Step 5 of 8).

Create a Menu

A menu provides end-users with an easy-to-use and organized means to access other modules or URLs. The menu can be composed of submenus, and both the main menu and its submenus can have items. Start by specifying a name for your menu (Figure 6.43).

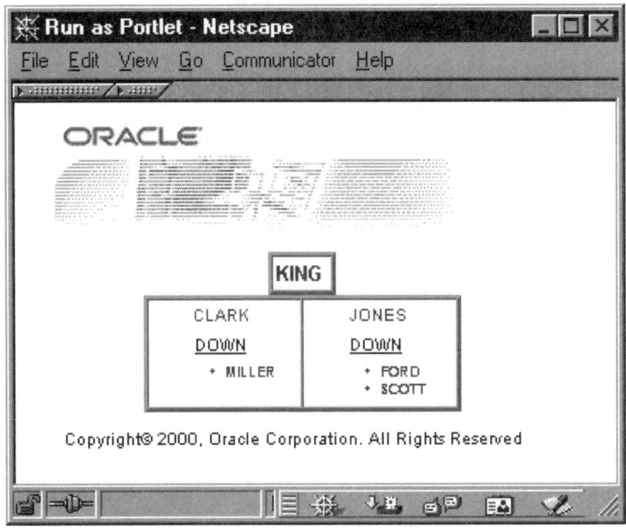

Figure 6.42 Run a Hierarchy.

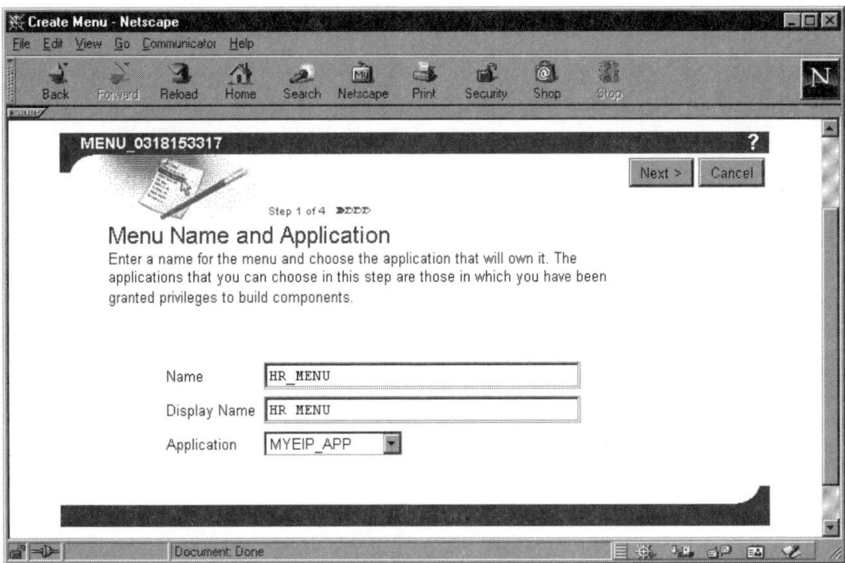

Figure 6.43 Create a Menu: Menu Name and Application (Step 1 of 4).

In the second step start by giving the main menu a name. You can also change its template. Change the number of sublevels to 2 in both the Full Page Options and the Portlet Options (Figure 6.44). In the same step you can add submenus and items by clicking on the Add Submenu icon and the Add Item icon, respectively. Add two submenus, one for the reports components and the other for the forms components (Figure 6.45). Add two items under each submenu. When you add an item, specify its name, description, and its component (Figure 6.46). To select a component for a menu item, click on the List of Values icon to search for the component by its name. You can use wildcards (Figure 6.47).

When you finish adding all your submenus and items, go to the third step, which is the Customization Form Display Options (Figure 6.48). Create and run the menu in full page mode (Figure 6.49). Publish the component to the portal and then add it to the EMPLOYEE_PAGE portal page (Figure 6.50 and Figure 6.51).

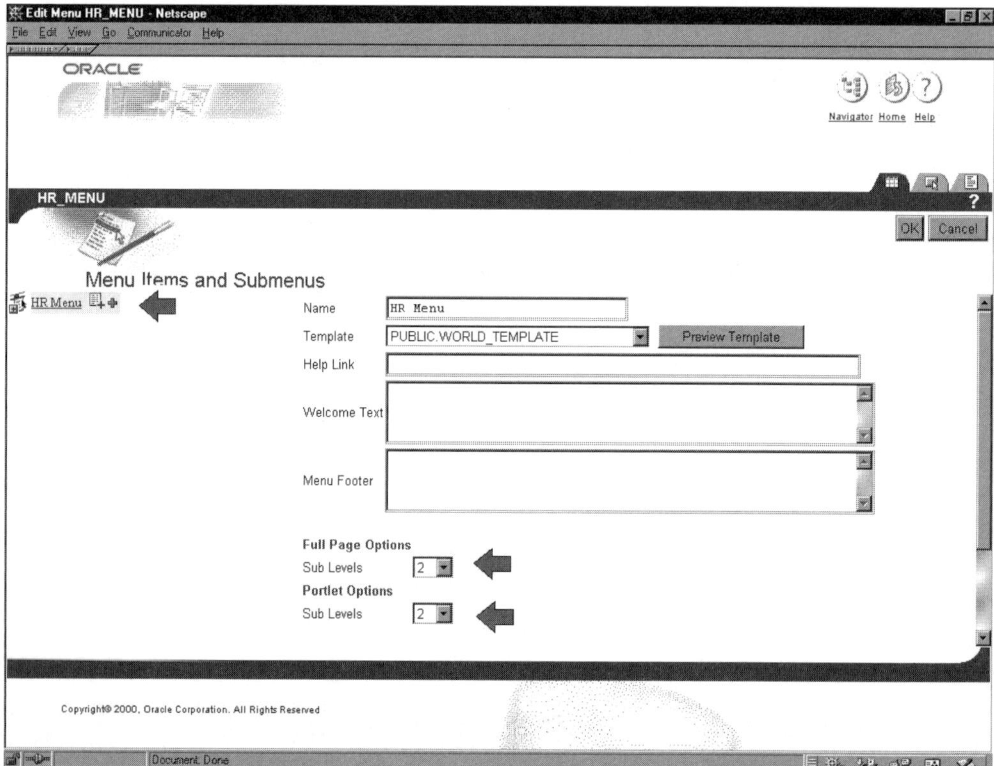

Figure 6.44 Create a Menu: Menu Items and Submenus (Step 2 of 4): Main Menu Properties.

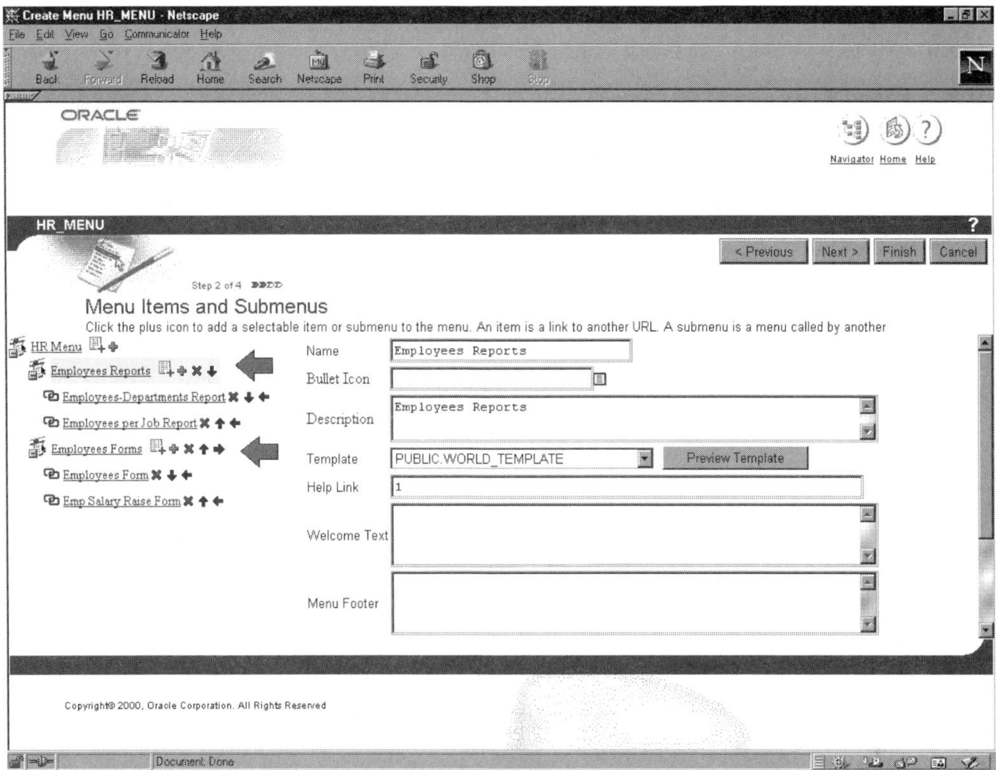

Figure 6.45 Create a Menu: Menu Items and Submenus (Step 2 of 4): Submenu Properties.

Create a Frame Driver

The frame driver component is split into two frames, a driver frame and a driven frame. Start by specifying a name for the frame component (Figure 6.52).

In step 2 write your SELECT statement. The SELECT statement has to have two columns, the first column is what is displayed in the driver frame, and the second column is the target (i.e., what is displayed in the driven frame). When the end-user selects a different value from the list in the driver frame and clicks submit, the driven frame is updated to show the related column. There are three different types of the target: HTML/Text, URL, and PL/SQL. The Target Link Type defines the data of the second column. For practice, choose PL/SQL Target Link Type. Also, choose Radio Group type for the driver List of Values (Figure 6.53).

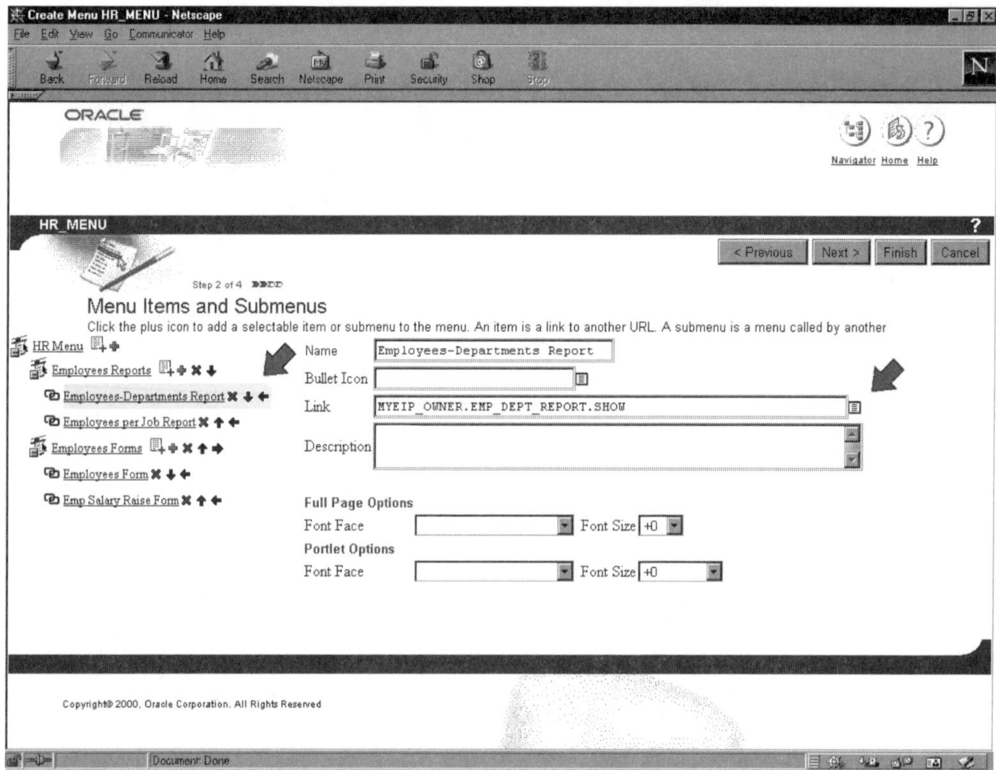

Figure 6.46 Create a Menu: Menu Items and Submenus (Step 2 of 4): Menu Item Properties.

The PL/SQL code is

```
select dname,
       'declare '||chr(10)||
       'cursor emp_cur(deptno_p number) is '||chr(10)||
       'select ENAME from SCOTT.EMP '||chr(10)||
       'where DEPTNO=deptno_p; '||chr(10)||
       'begin '||chr(10)||
       'for emp_rec in emp_cur('||to_char(deptno)||') '||chr(10)||
       'loop'||chr(10)||
       'htp.print(emp_rec.ename||"<BR>"); '||chr(10)||
       'end loop; '||chr(10)||
       'end; ' plsql_code
from scott.dept
```

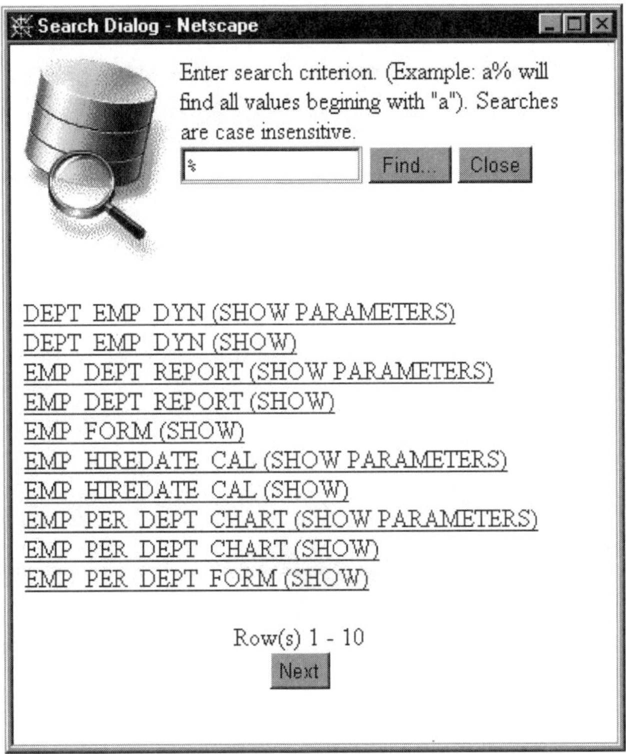

Figure 6.47 Create a Menu: Menu Items and Submenus (Step 2 of 4): Components List of Values.

The first column is the department name. The second column is a PL/SQL block that defines an employee cursor to retrieve the employees' names for each department. CHR(10) is an SQL function that returns the character with ASCII code 10, which is the carriage return. The HTP.PRINT procedure is used to output the employees' names.

The third step is the Customization Form Display Options. The fourth step is the Initial Target Frame Content where you specify the contents of the target (i.e., driven frame) content before the end-user selects a value in the driver frame (Figure 6.54).

In the fifth step specify how you want to divide the frames: COLS (i.e., vertically) or ROWS (i.e., horizontally). For practice, divide the frames by columns and change the width percentages of the driver and target frames to 20% and 80%, respectively (Figure 6.55).

Finish and run the frame driver (Figure 6.56). The frame driver cannot be run or added as a portlet due to the fact that the portlets in a portal page are implemented using HTML tables, and HTML table cells do not support frames.

Chapter 7 continues our exploration of components where we will create the remaining types of application components.

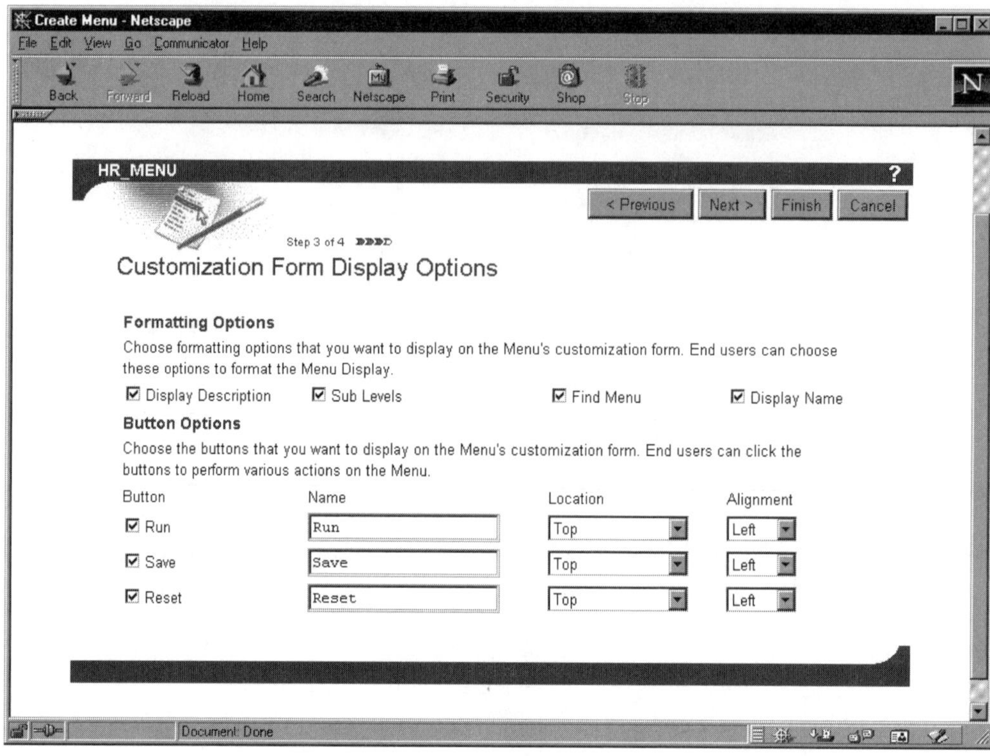

Figure 6.48 Create a Menu: Customization Form Display Options (Step 3 of 4).

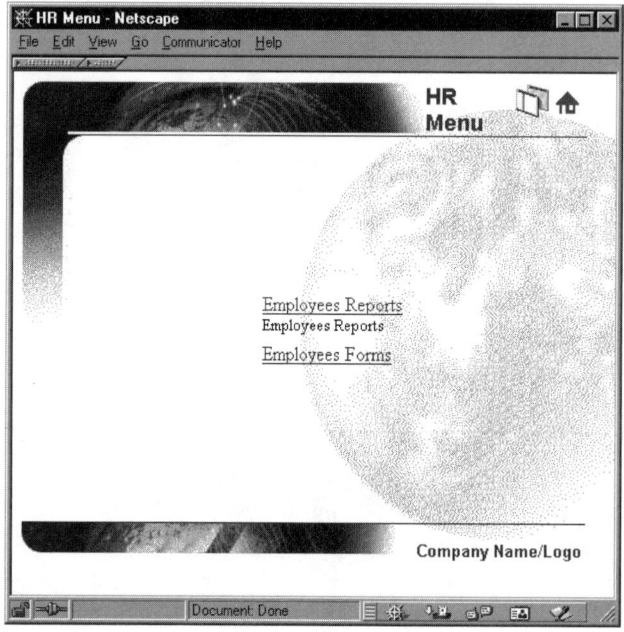

Figure 6.49
Run a Menu: Full Page.

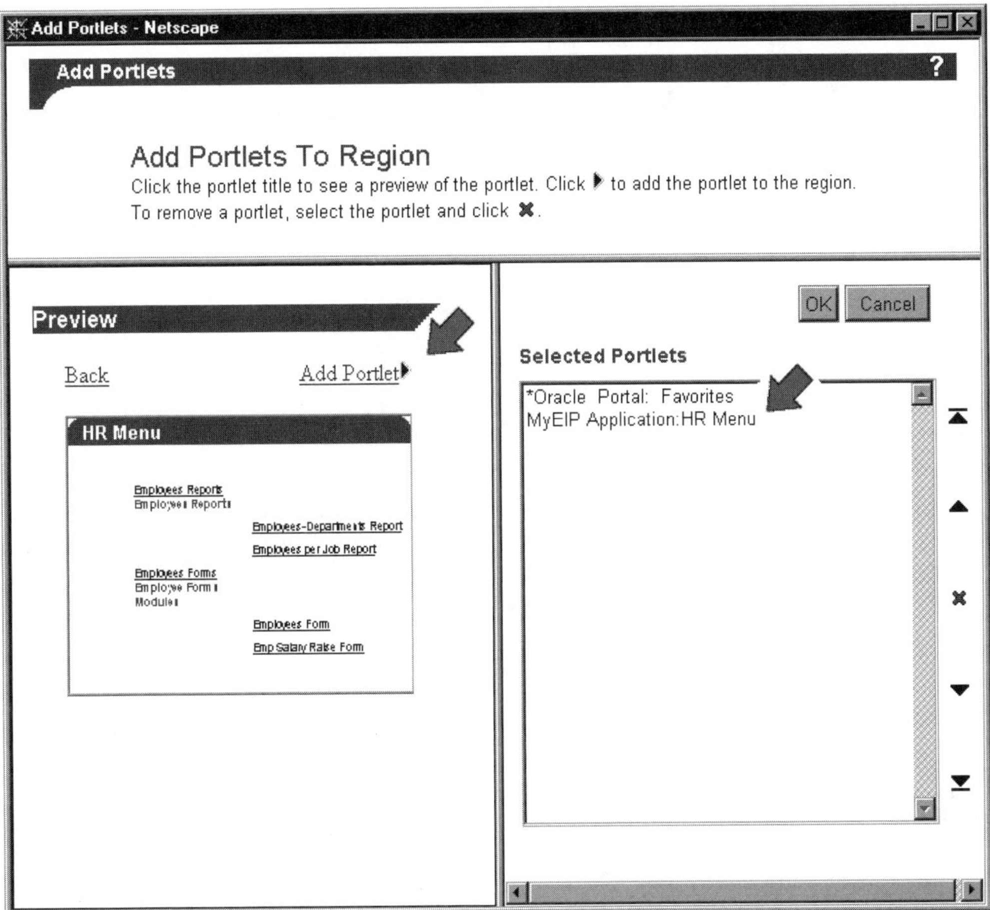

Figure 6.50 Portlet Repository.

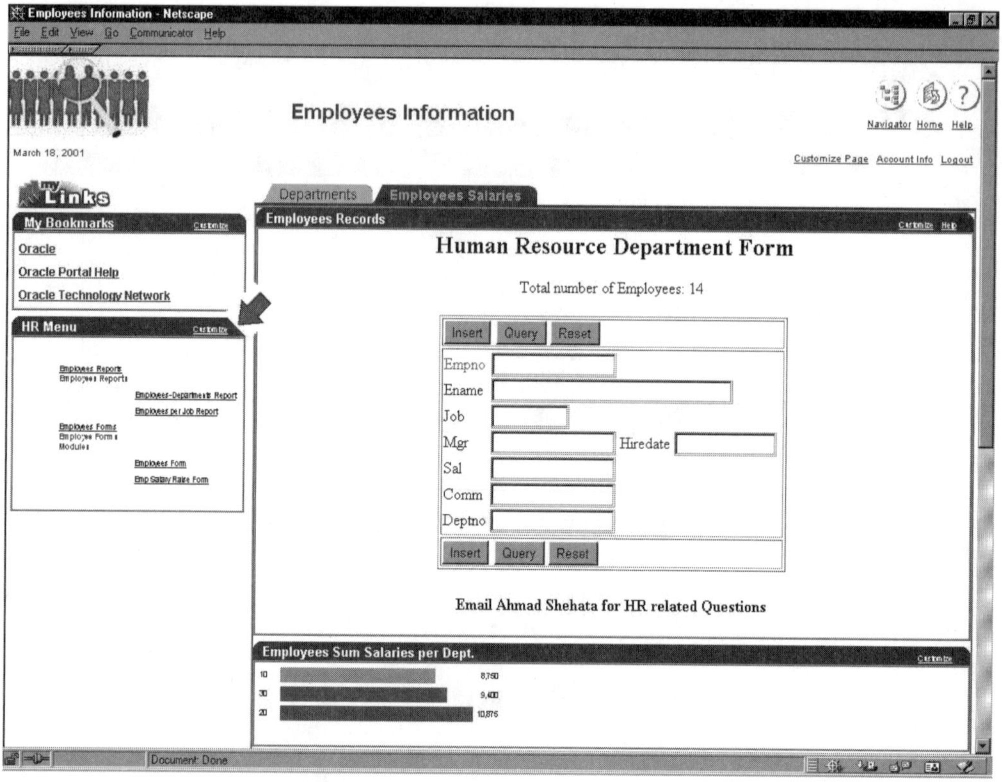

Figure 6.51 Add the Menu to the Page.

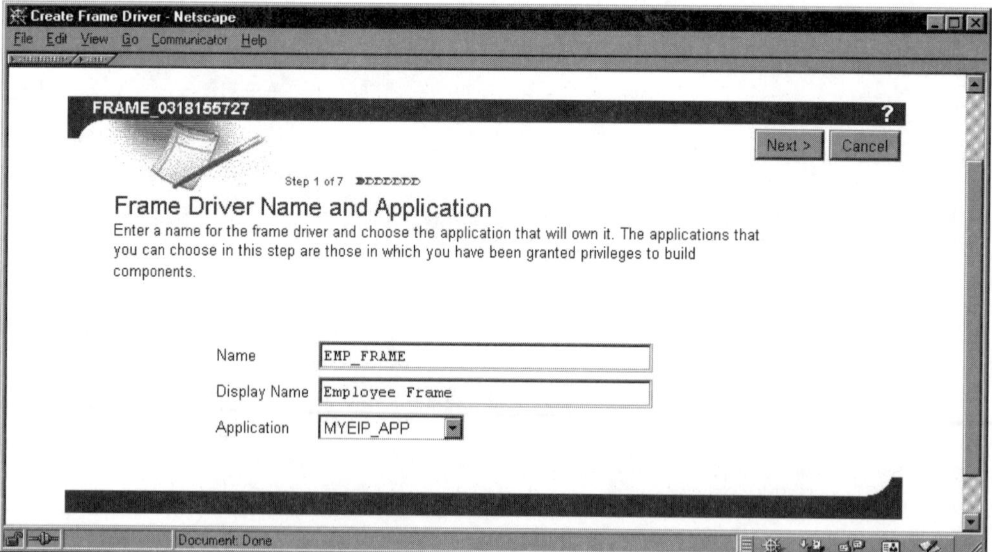

Figure 6.52 Create a Frame Component: Frame Driver Name and Application (Step 1 of 7).

Create Frame Driver - Netscape

EMP_FRAME

Step 2 of 7

SQL Query

Enter a SQL Query whose results will populate the frame driver.

```
select dname,
'declare '||chr(10)||
'cursor emp_cur(deptno_p number) is '||chr(10)||
'select ename from scott.emp '||chr(10)||
'where deptno=deptno_p; '||chr(10)||
'begin '||chr(10)||
'for emp_rec in emp_cur('||to_char(deptno)||') '||chr(10)||
'loop'||chr(10)||
'htp.print(emp_rec.ename||''<BR>''); '||chr(10)||
'end loop; '||chr(10)||
```

Target Link Type PL/SQL

LOV Type Radio Group

Show NULL

NULL Text

NULL Value

Hint

Example:

select [displayed_value], [returned_url] from [table]

where

Figure 6.53 Create a Frame Component: SQL Query (Step 2 of 7).

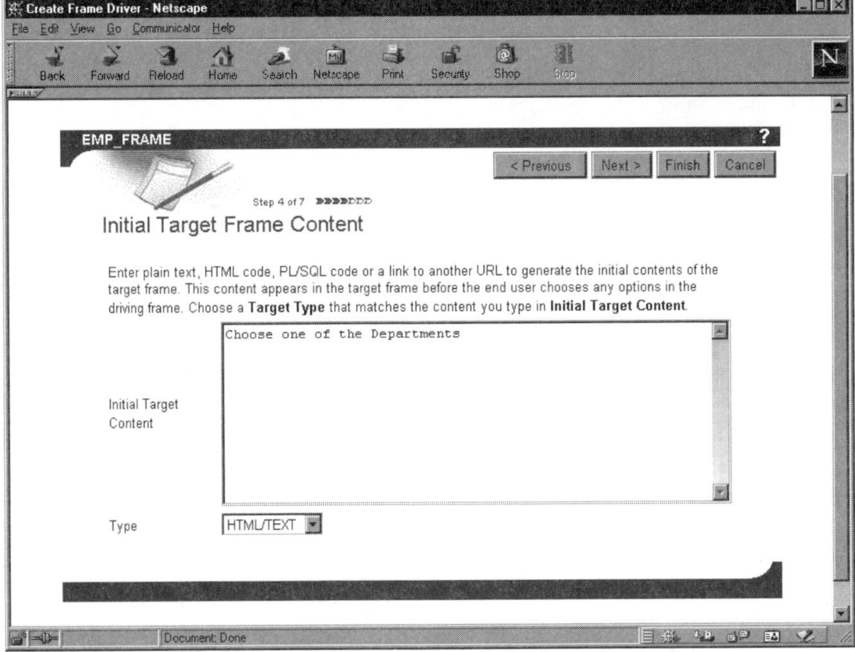

Figure 6.54 Create a Frame Component: Initial Target Frame Content (Step 4 of 7).

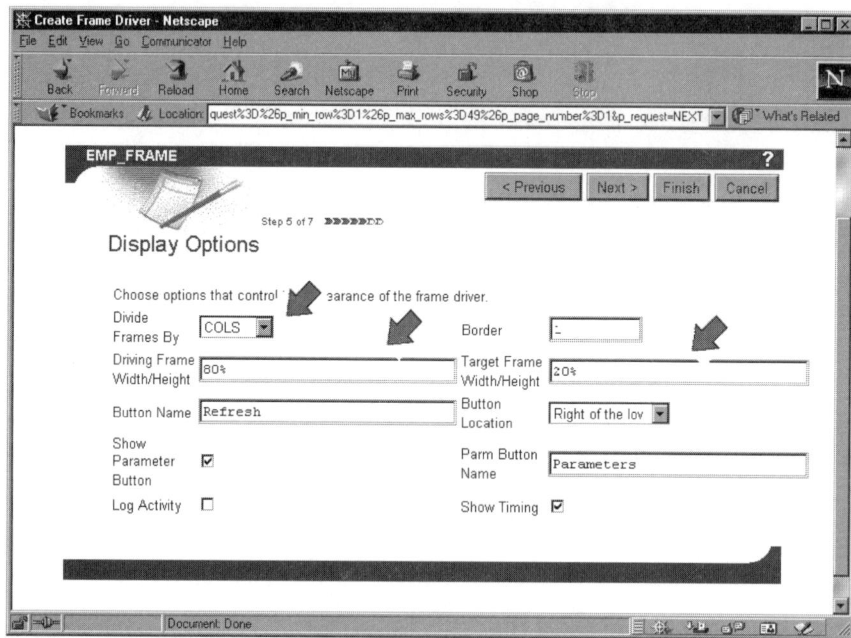

Figure 6.55 Create a Frame Component: Display Options (Step 5 of 7).

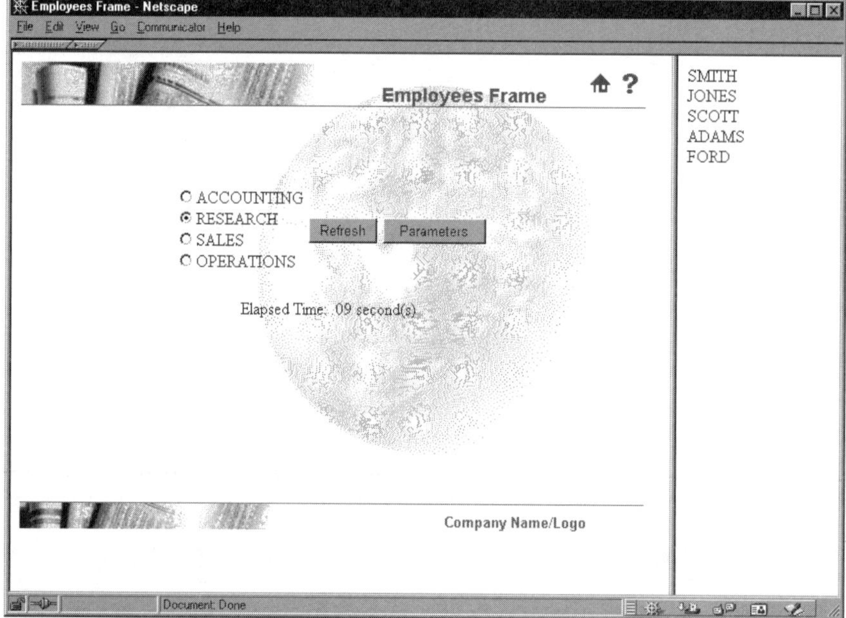

Figure 6.56 Run a Frame Component.

CHAPTER 7

Links, List of Values, and Shared Components

Introduction

This chapter continues the explanation of the different Oracle Portal component types. First I will cover links and lists of values. Then I will discuss the shared components such as colors, fonts, images, and templates.

Create a Link

In Chapter 5 you created a report (i.e., EMP_DEPT_REPORT) that displays the employee's information. Using links, you can give your end-user the ability to drill down from this report to another report (i.e., EMP_SAL_GRADE_REPORT) to display salary grade information. Start by creating a link that will point to the destination report (Figure 7.1). The next step is to specify the target component (Figure 7.2 and Figure 7.3).

The Link creation wizard checks the target component and displays its user parameters (e.g., department_no) along with the system parameters (e.g., max_rows), so you can specify default values for them (Figure 7.4). These default values will be used if you call the Link destination component without specifying values for the parameters.

Create the link. Now you need to assign this link to one or more columns of the source component (i.e., EMP_DEPT_REPORT). Edit the source report, then go to the Column Formatting tab. Select the link name (i.e., LINK_2_DEPARTMENT) in the DNAME column properties (Figure 7.5).

Even though the destination report has the Department Number as a parameter, you can assign the link to any of the columns in the source report because, through editing the link, you can choose which column of your source (i.e., calling) report is passed as the department number value to the target (i.e., called) report. Click on the Edit Link icon (Figure 7.6).

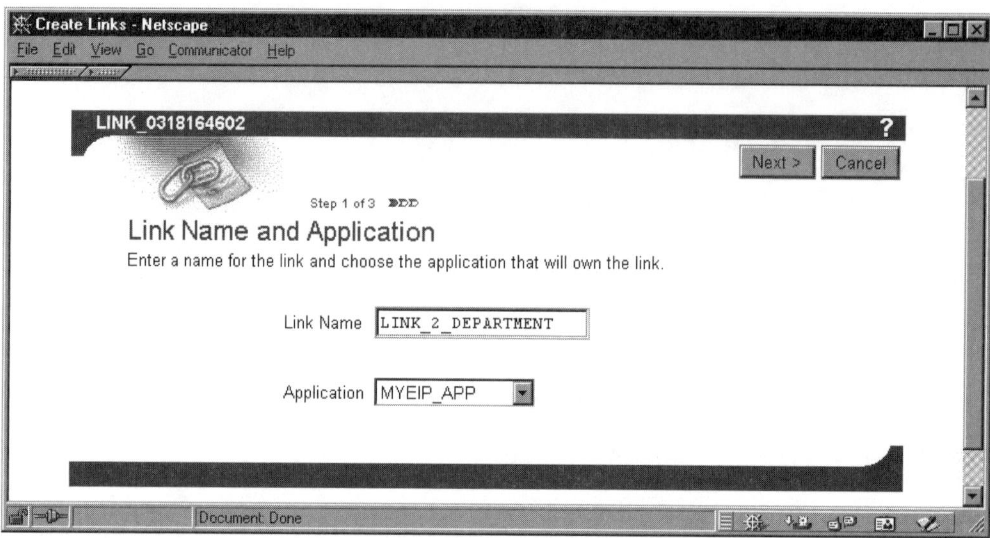

Figure 7.1 Create a Link: Link Name and Application (Step 1 of 3).

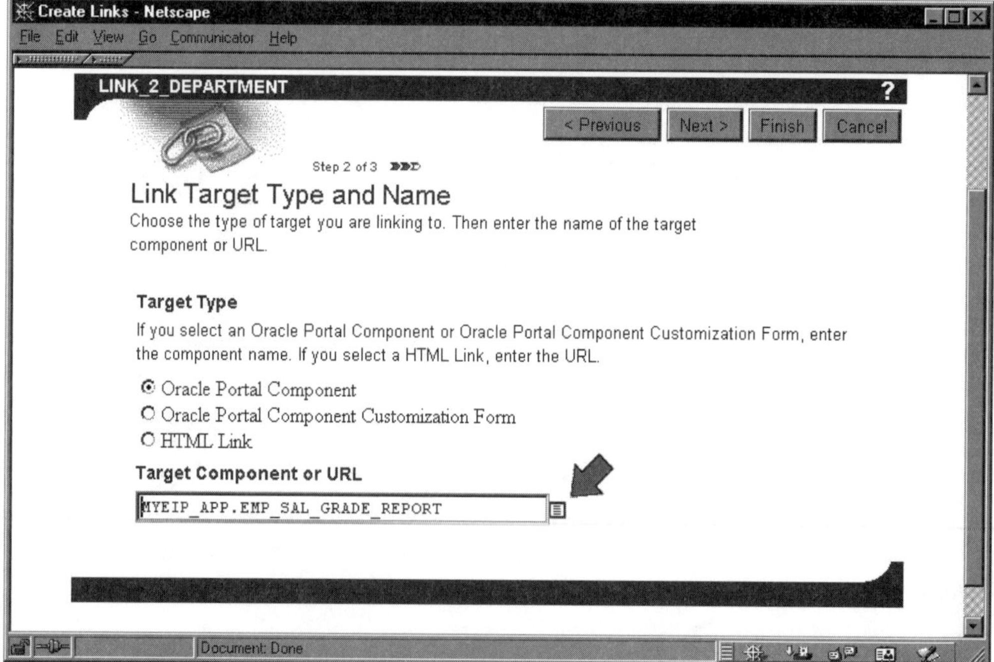

Figure 7.2 Create a Link: Link Target Type and Name (Step 2 of 3).

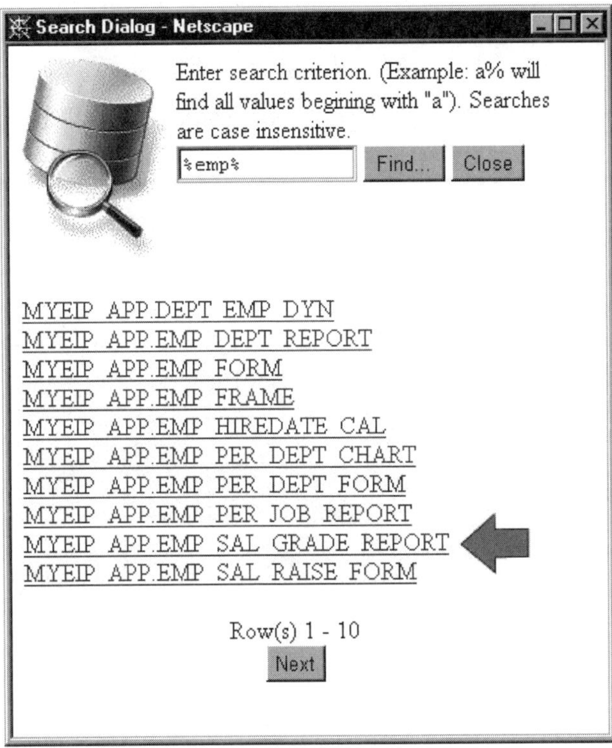

Figure 7.3 Create a Link: Link Target Type and Name (Step 2 of 3): List of Values.

Save your changes and run the report. The department name column becomes a hyperlink (Figure 7.7).

Click on an employee department name (e.g., SALES); the destination report is displayed for department number 30 (Figure 7.8). Notice the URL generated when you click on the department name (i.e., SALES). The URL is calling the report component and passing to it the name and value of the department number report parameter. The URL should have the following format:

```
http://<Hostname>:<portno>/pls/<DADname>/
      <ApplicationSchema>.<ReportName>.SHOW?
      p_arg_names=<ParameterName>&
      p_arg_values=<ParameterValue>
```

For example,

```
http://myportal/pls/portal30/MYEIP_OWNER.EMP_SAL_GRADE_
      REPORT.SHOW?
```

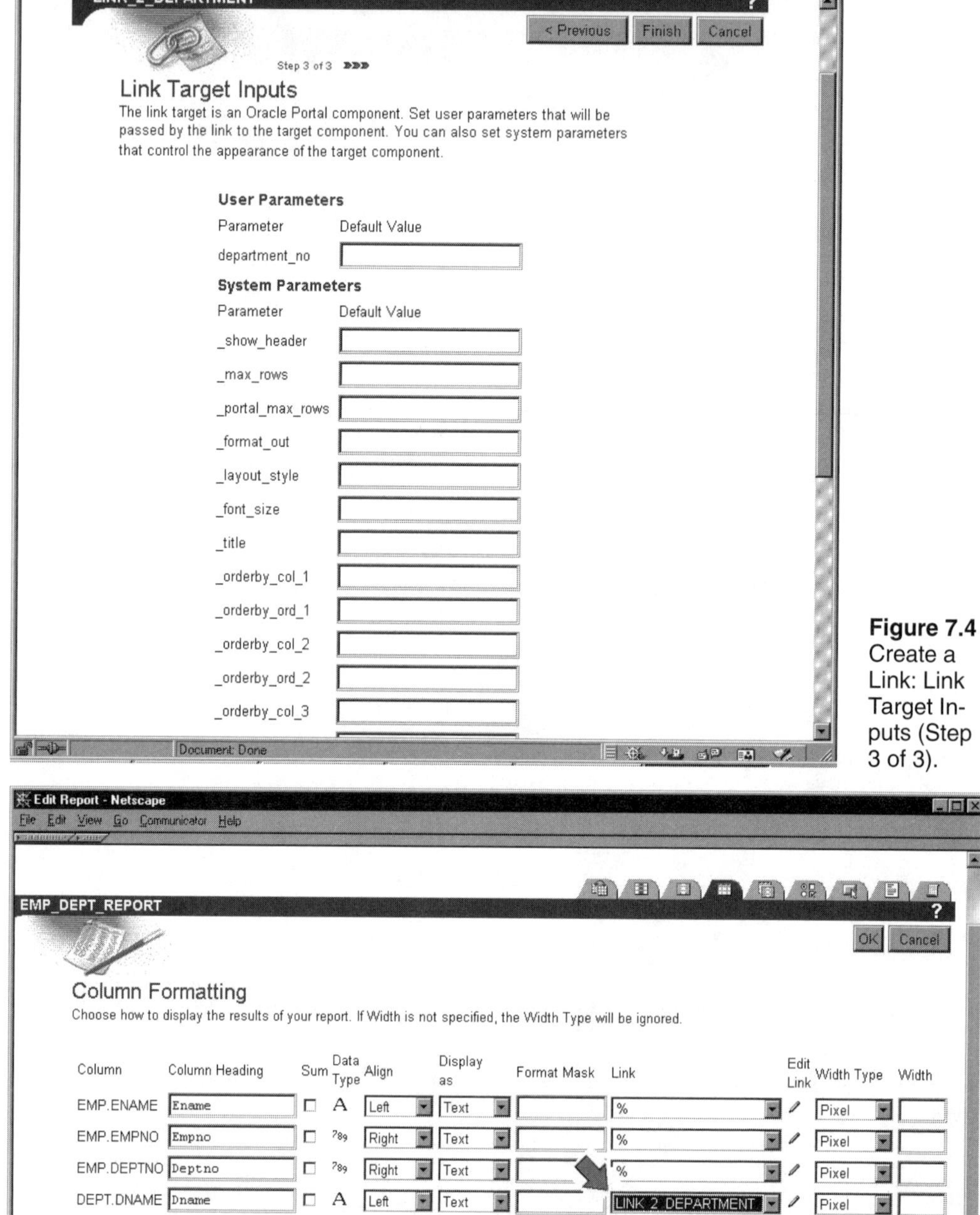

Figure 7.4 Create a Link: Link Target Inputs (Step 3 of 3).

Figure 7.5 Source Report: Column Formatting: Link Assignment.

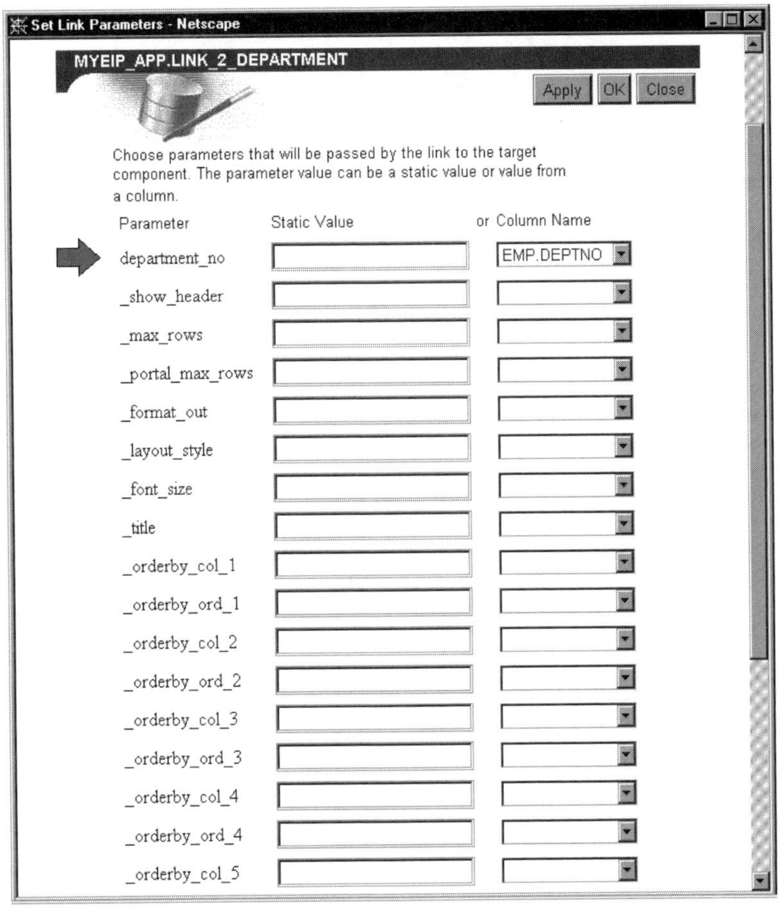

Figure 7.6 Source Report: Column Formatting: Link Assignment: Edit Link.

```
p_arg_names=department_no&
p_arg_values=30
```

Create a List of Values

List of Values (LOVs) are very convenient GUI tools that are used to simplify the data entry process. For example, by using LOVs, the end-user does not have to navigate out of the employee data entry form to get the department number for the Sales department. LOVs also relieve the end-user from memorizing codes such as 1 for single, 2 for married, and so on, because the LOV displays these descriptions. When the user selects a value, its code is sent to the database.

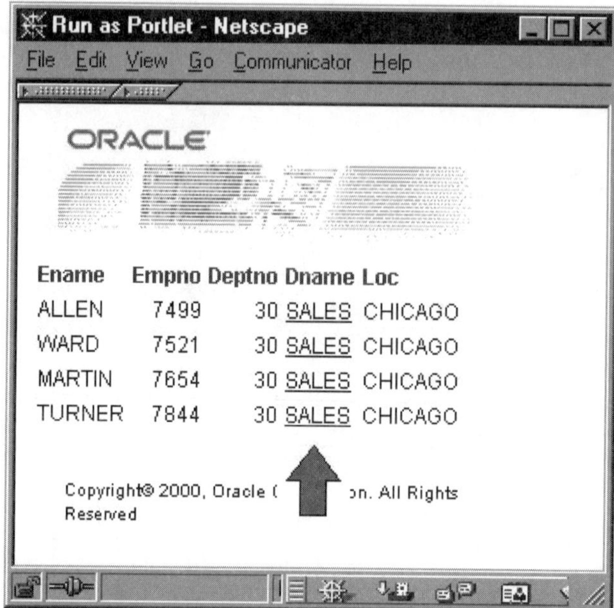

Figure 7.7
Run Source Report.

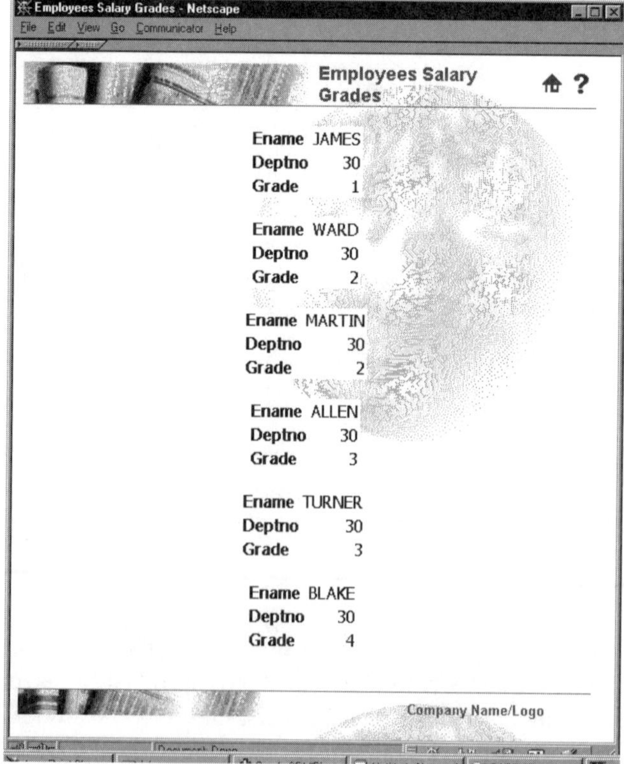

Figure 7.8
Call Target Report.

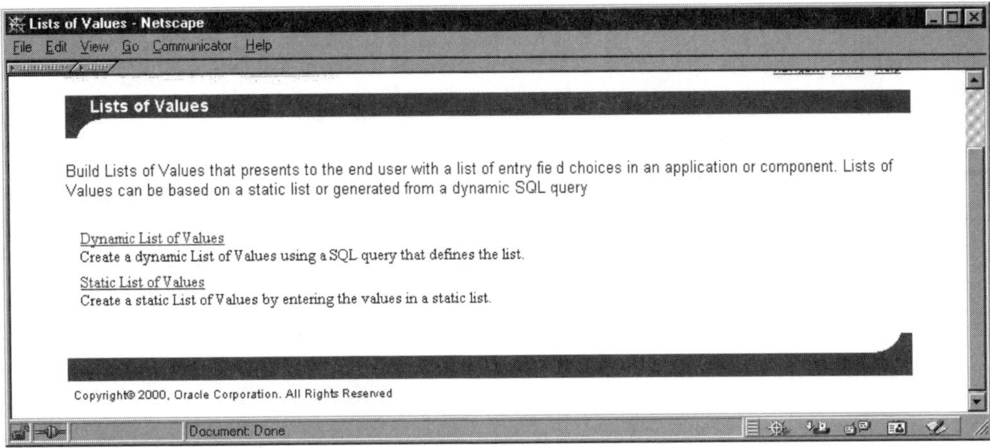

Figure 7.9 Create a List of Values: LOV Type.

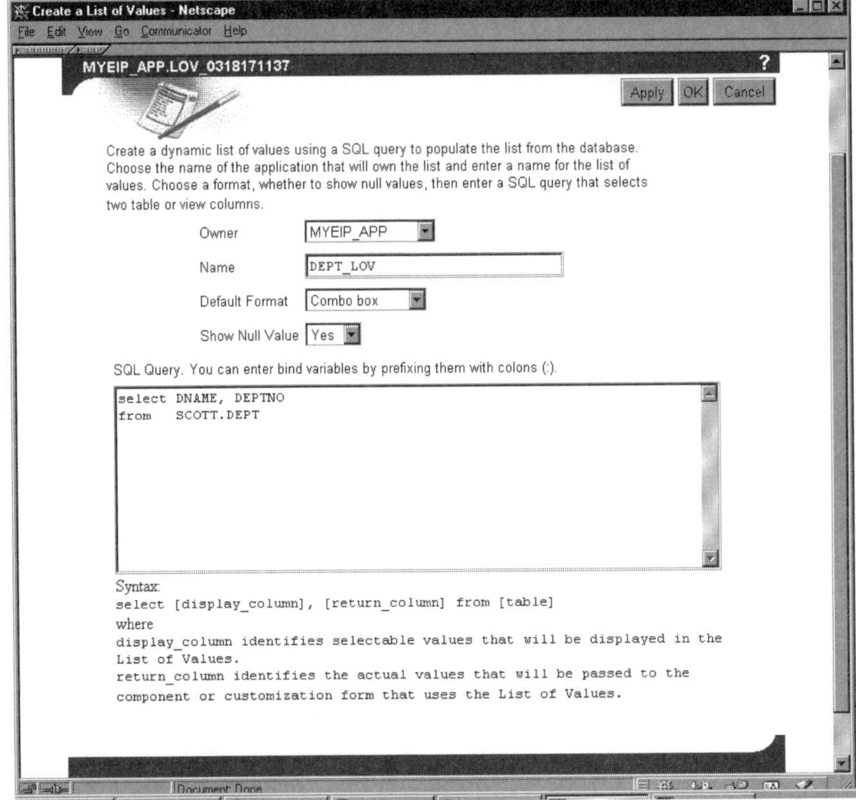

Figure 7.10 Create a Dynamic List of Values.

There are two types of LOVs in Oracle Portal: dynamic and static (Figure 7.9). With static LOVs, you provide the list of choices in the LOV definition. To change the static LOV choices, you need to edit the LOV component. The dynamic LOV reads its values from a table, so to change its choices, all you need to do is change its underlying table data. No changes are needed to the component definition itself.

To create a dynamic LOV, you need to give it a name and write down its select statement. Also, you need to decide on what LOV type you need (Figure 7.10). Create the LOV and run it to display the different LOV types. The LOV displays the values retrieved from the first column of the LOV select statement. When the user selects a certain record from the LOV, the second column value will be returned to the field that has the LOV attached to it. There are five different

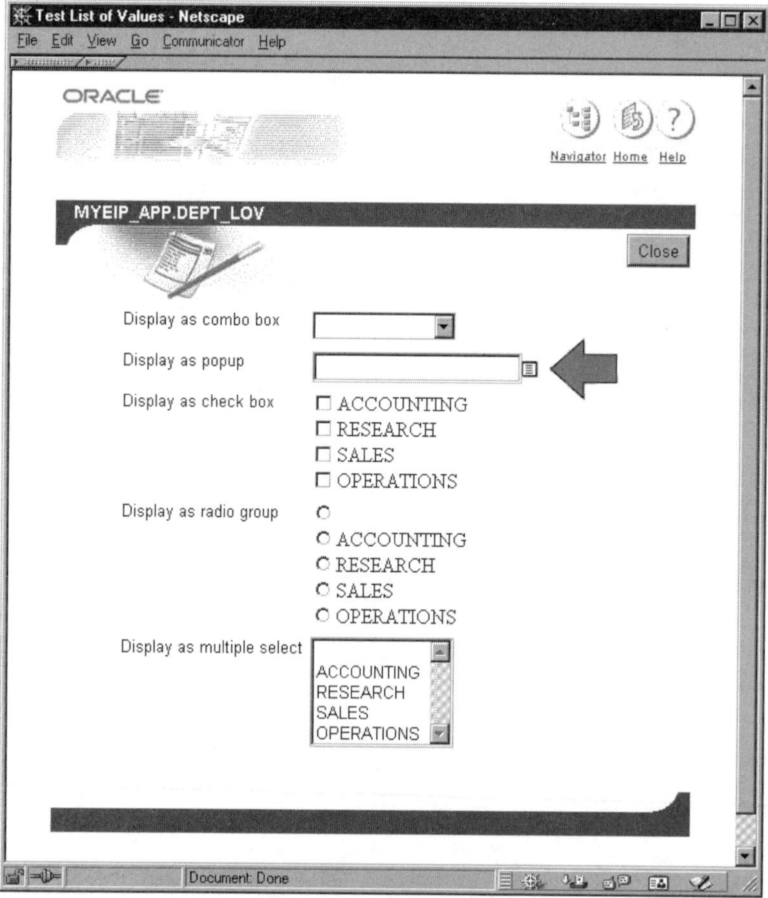

Figure 7.11 Create a List of Values: LOV Types.

LOV types available: check box, combo box, popup, radio group, and multiple select. For practice, choose combo box for the DEPT_LOV (Figure 7.11). The combo box is a good choice if there are not many values in the LOV. A popup LOV is more suitable for large selections, because it has a Find feature that allows the end-user to search the LOV values using wildcard characters (Figure 7.12). Radio groups and check boxes are good choices for very few numbers of values (i.e., five or less).

To see how the popup LOV looks, click on the LOV icon (Figure 7.12).

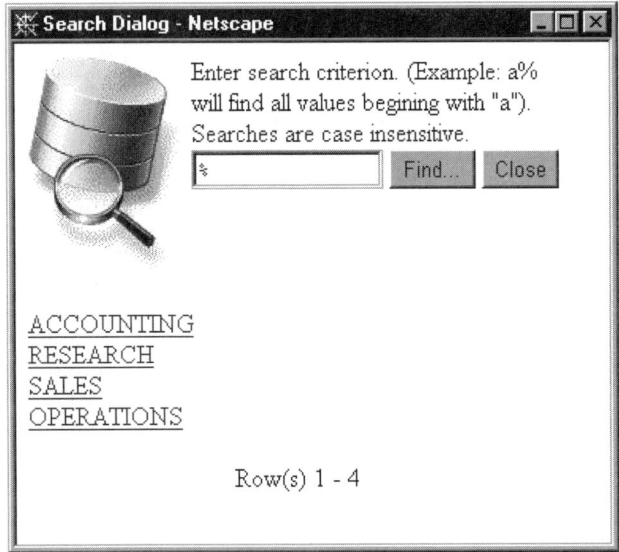

Figure 7.12 Create a List of Values: LOV Types: Popup LOV.

When you finish creating the DEPT_LOV, you can assign it to different fields and parameters. You can assign the LOV to the DEPTNO field in the EMP_FORM data entry form, created in Chapter 5. Edit the form and in the Formatting and Validation Options tab, click on the DEPTNO field in the navigation frame to display the field's display options. Change the item type from "Textbox" (the default) to "Combobox" and choose DEPT_LOV as the List of Values for DEPTNO (Figure 7.13).

Run the EMP_FORM to test the DEPT_LOV functionality (Figure 7.14). You can change the item type of the DEPTNO to "Popup" or "Radio Group" and test the LOV functionality in each.

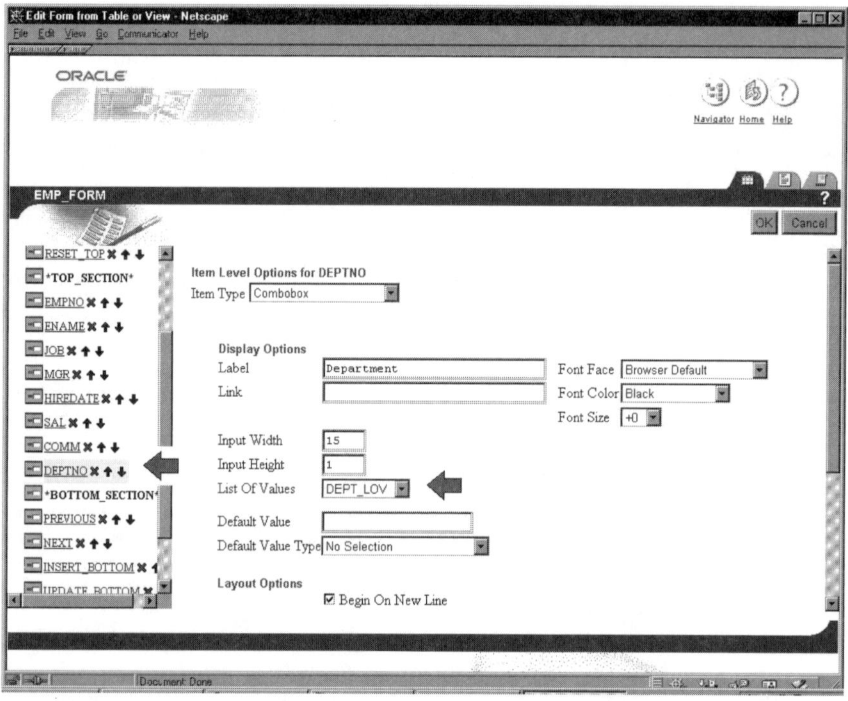

Figure 7.13 Edit EMP_FORM Form: Formatting and Validation Options: DEPTNO Field.

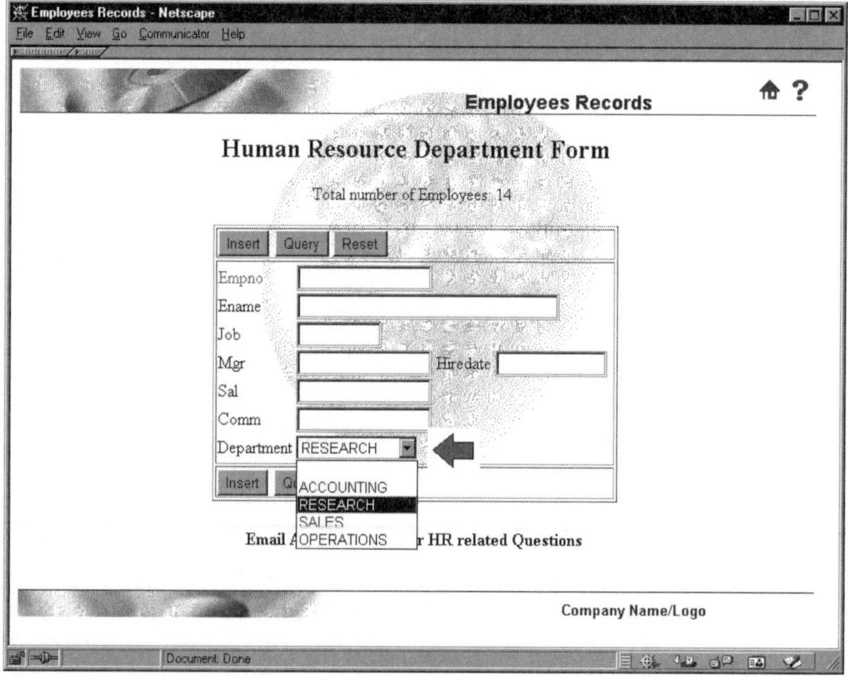

Figure 7.14 Run Form and Test DEPT_LOV.

Shared Components

Oracle Portal comes with a group of shared application components for all the portal developers to use in their own applications. Also, the portal administrators (e.g., portal30) can create more shared components. To access the existing shared components and to create your own, go to the Application tab in the Oracle Portal Navigator (Figure 7.15). This section discusses the following shared components: colors, fonts, images, and templates. JavaScripts are covered in Chapter 10.

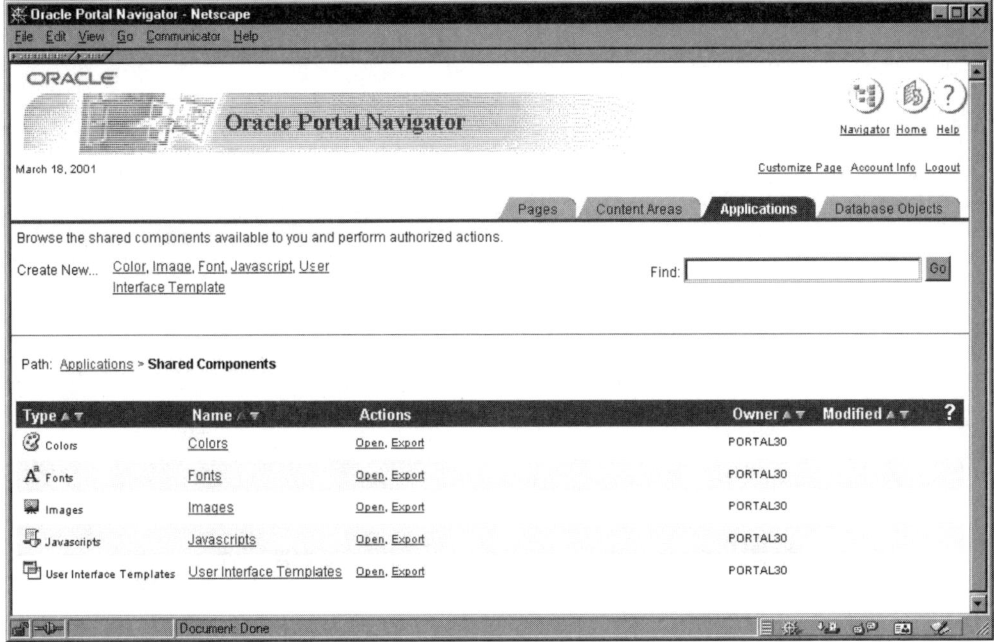

Figure 7.15 Oracle Portal Navigator: Applications Tab: Shared Components.

Create a Color

Oracle Portal comes with a predefined set of colors. Most of these colors are system colors; the system colors cannot be edited or deleted but can be viewed and copied. The rest of the colors are user colors, which you can delete, copy, and export (Figure 7.16).

Create a new color and give it a name. This new name can be a real color name or it can be a business name, such as EmployeeColor. The business name makes it easier to remember when assigning colors to Employee Portal components. You can choose the color value for the new color by clicking on a color from the list (Figure 7.17). Also, you can use the RGB (red, green, blue) color values. Combining different values of R, G, and B can create all the colors. Each R,

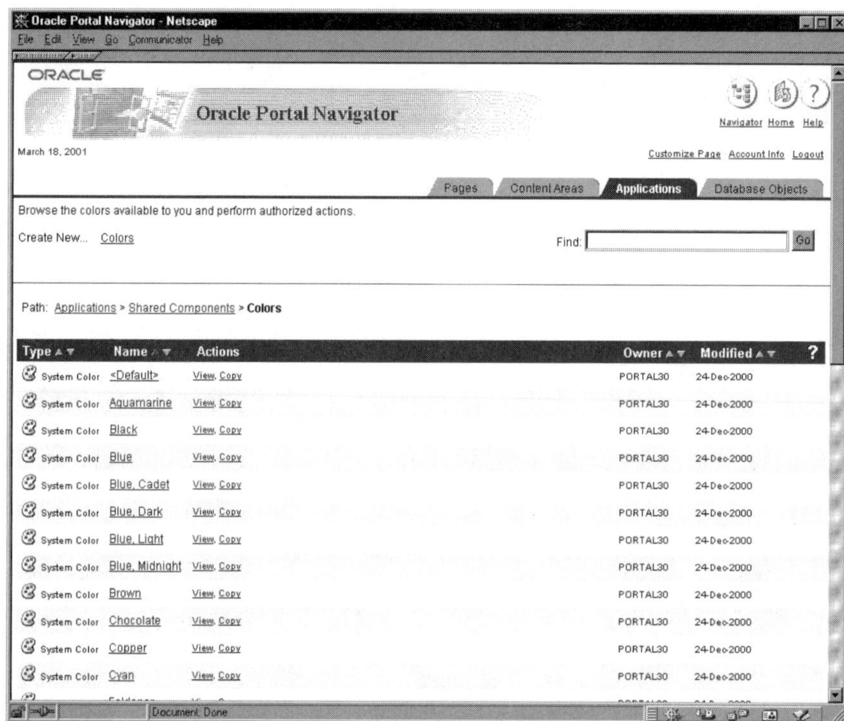

Figure 7.16 Oracle Portal Navigator: Applications Tab: Shared Components: Colors.

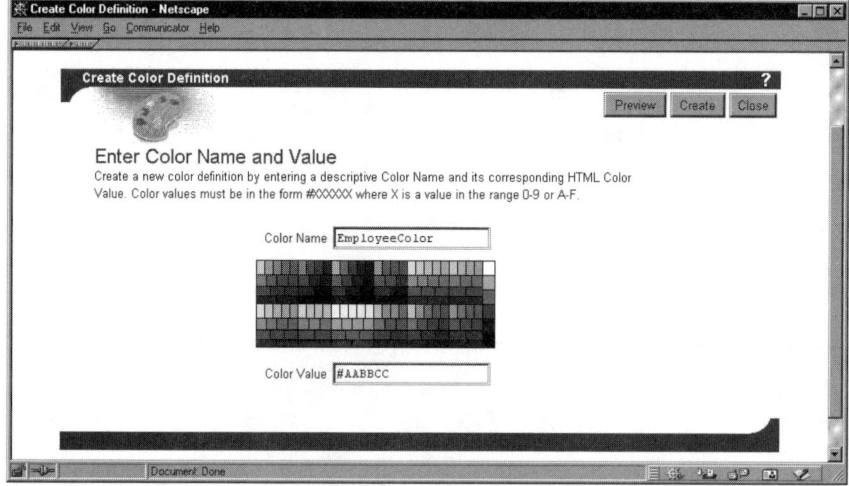

Figure 7.17 Oracle Portal Navigator: Applications Tab: Shared Components: Create a Color.

G, and B value is specified in a range from 0 to 255. To specify the color value, you should use the hexadecimal numeric system where the numeric digits you can use are 0 to 9, A, B, C, D, E, and F. A equals 10, B equals 11, 10 equals 16, and FF equals 255. So white is FFFFFF in RGB and black is 000000. Note that the RGB value has to be prefixed with a "#".

Preview the new color and click the "Create" button. Now the new color is ready for use.

Create a Font

Oracle Portal comes with a set of system fonts, which cannot be edited or deleted (Figure 7.18). Create a new font by giving it a name and a value. In the font value, you can specify a list of font names separated by commas (Figure 7.19). When you use the new font, Oracle Portal tries to use the first font in the list (e.g., Times New Roman), if supported by the Web browser. Otherwise, if the first font is not available in the browser and you specified another font in the font definition, Oracle Portal uses the second font in the list (e.g., Courier).

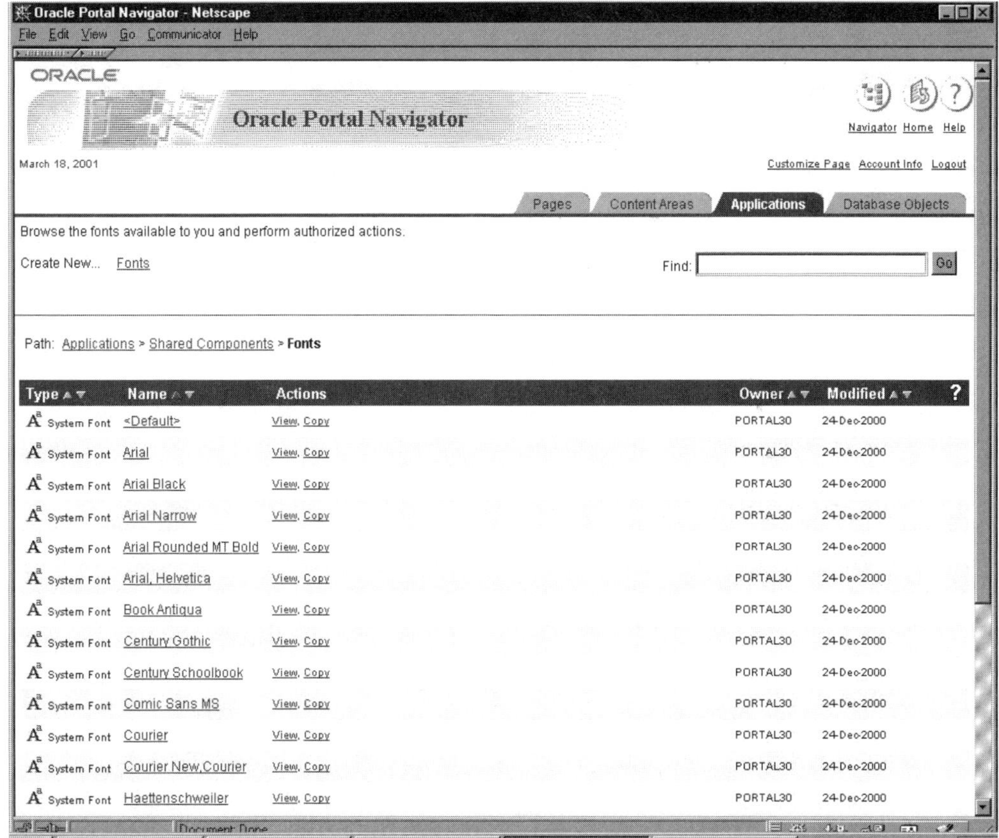

Figure 7.18 Oracle Portal Navigator: Applications Tab: Shared Components: Fonts.

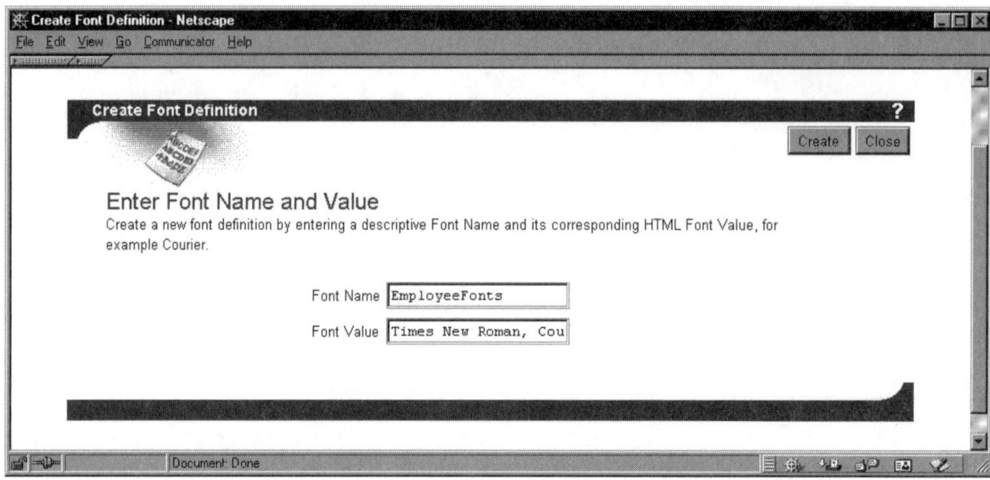

Figure 7.19 Oracle Portal Navigator: Applications Tab: Shared Components: Create a Font.

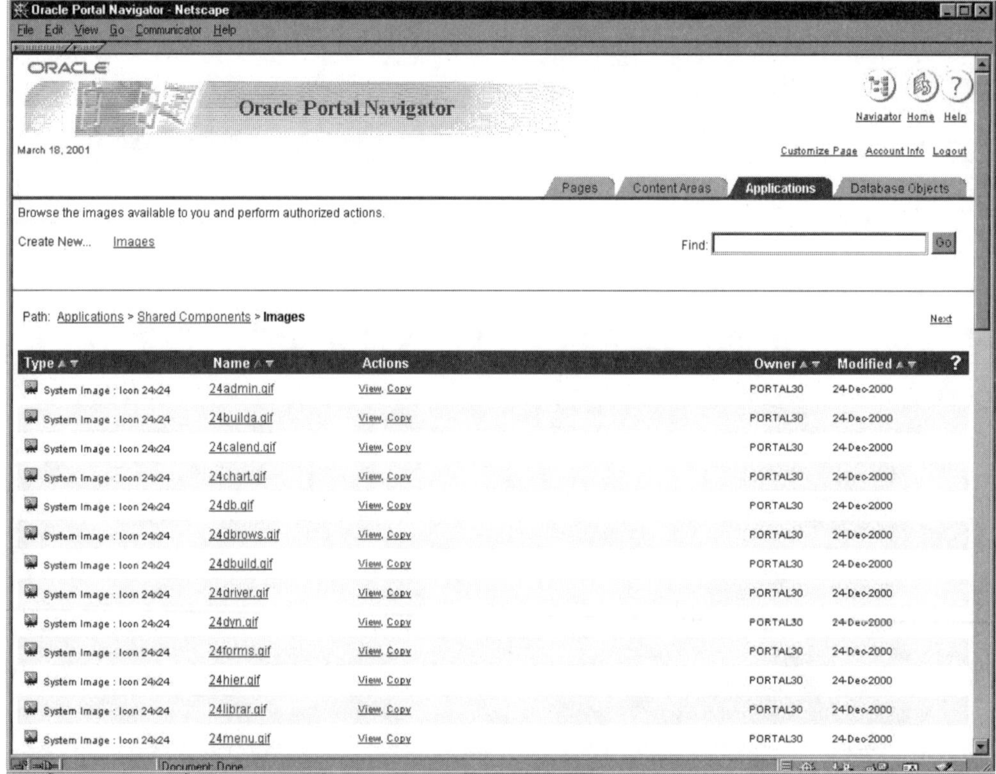

Figure 7.20 Oracle Portal Navigator: Applications Tab: Shared Components: Images.

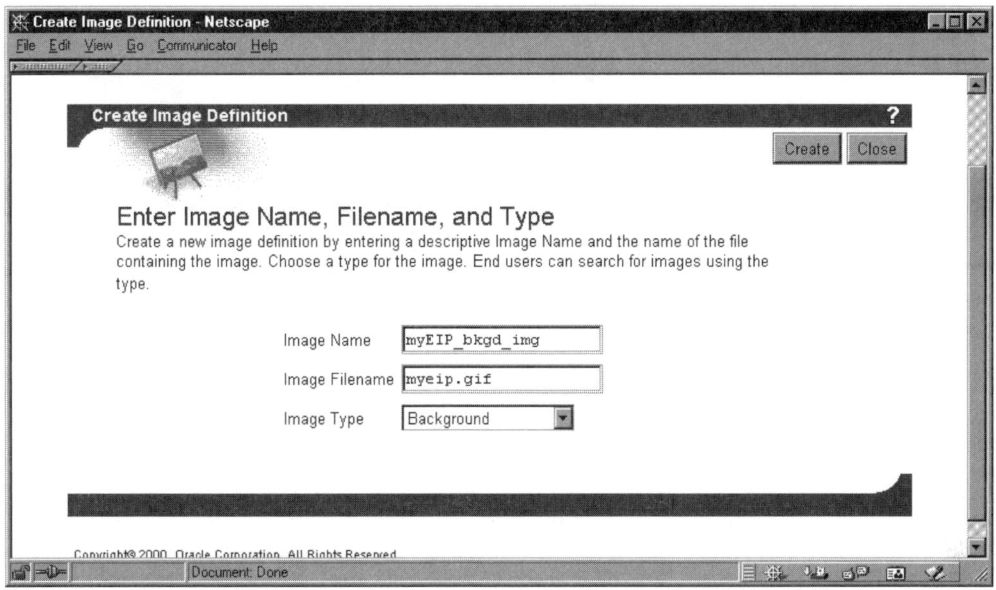

Figure 7.21 Oracle Portal Navigator: Applications Tab: Shared Components: Create an Image.

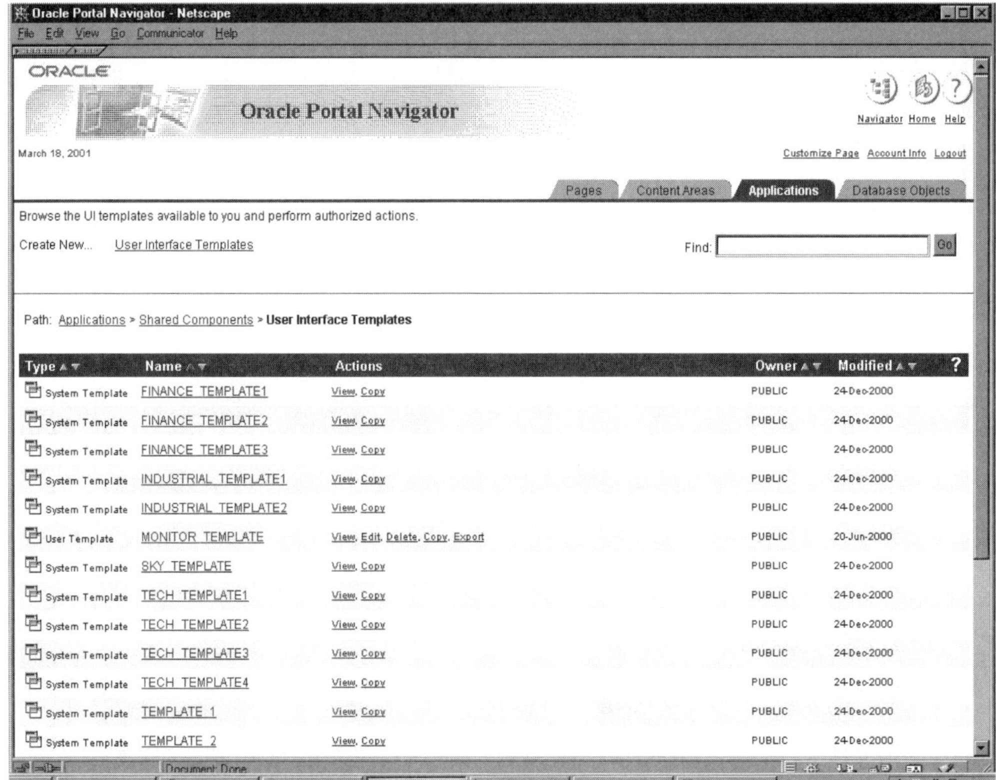

Figure 7.22 Oracle Portal Navigator: Applications Tab: Shared Components: User Templates.

Create an Image

Oracle Portal uses a set of preinstalled images that come with the product. These images are available for you to use in your components (e.g., background images, logos, etc.; Figure 7.20). These images are saved in the file system and not inside the database. They are kept in the */image* virtual path (on Microsoft Windows NT/2000, it is by default under <iAS_ORACLE_HOME>\portal30\images). Other images that you load separately and not as shared component images are saved inside the database.

Before you create your own image, you need to copy the image file to the */image* directory. Then you need to specify the new image name, the image file name (with no path), and the image type (Figure 7.21). The image type determines where you will see the new image in Oracle Portal. For example, if you add the new image as a background image, you will be able to select it for any background image property, such as the template heading background image (see Figure 7.24).

Create a Template

You have been using the system templates with the components created so far to run these components in full page mode. You can access the existing system templates from the Oracle Portal Navigator (Figure 7.22). Because system templates cannot be edited or deleted, you can copy a system template to a user template (e.g., owned by PORTAL30), and then you can edit this new user template.

You can create a new template in one of two ways (Figure 7.23). Structured templates are where you just specify the properties of the templates. Unstructured templates are where you specify the HTML code of your template.

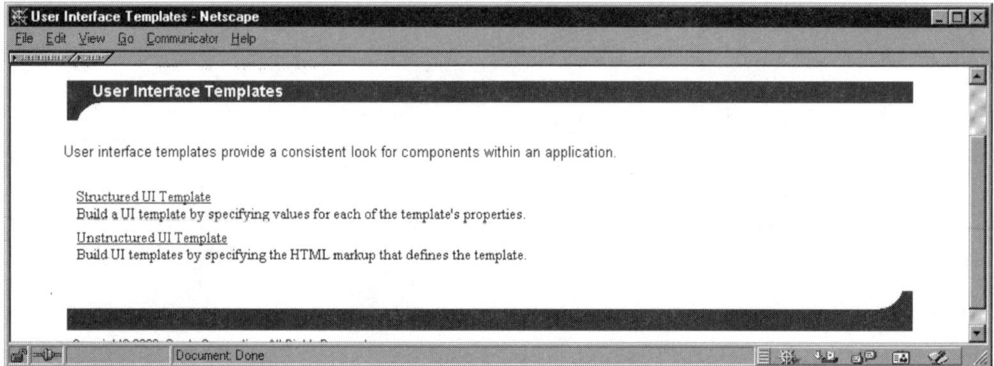

Figure 7.23 Oracle Portal Navigator: Applications Tab: Shared Components: Template Type.

Figure 7.24 shows an example of how to create a structured template by specifying its properties. You can use the shared components you have created earlier, such as EmployeeColor and EmployeeFont. Also, you can use the LOV icon to choose the background image you created earlier (Figure 7.25).

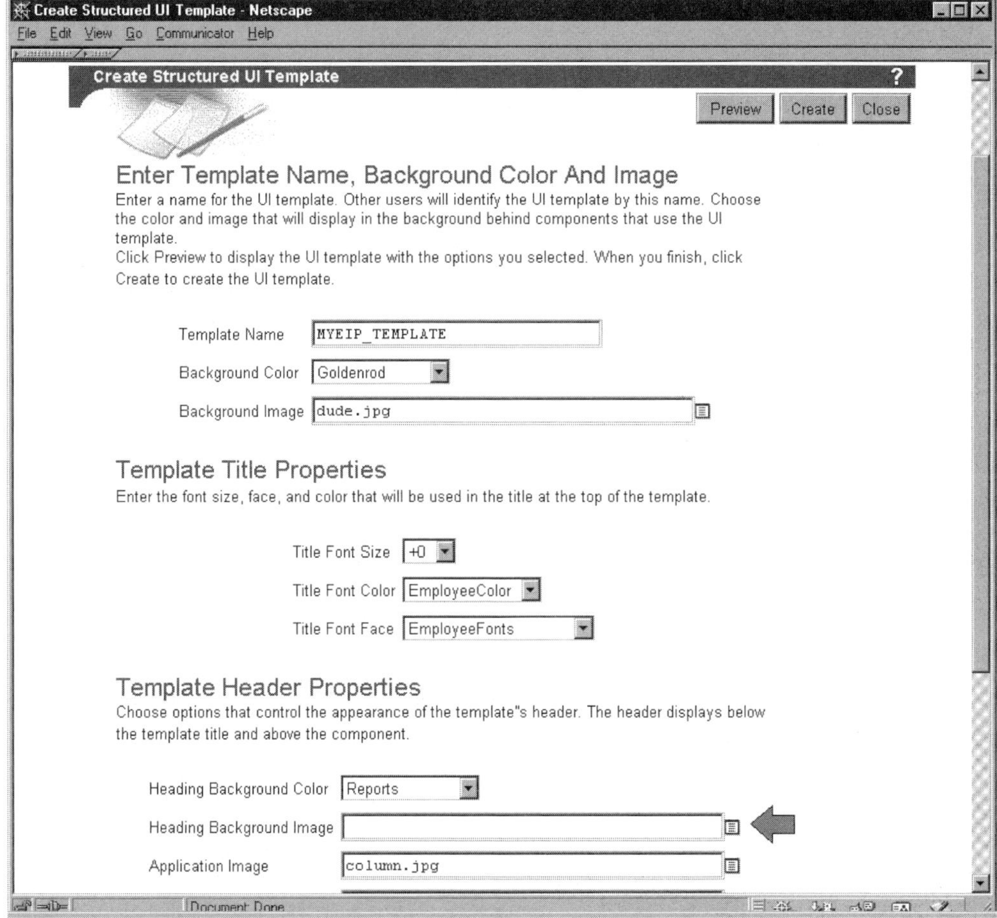

Figure 7.24 Oracle Portal Navigator: Applications Tab: Shared Components: Create a Structured Template.

Now that you have created your new template, you can edit any of your forms and apply the new template by selecting it in the Form Text tab (Figure 7.26). You can preview the selected template before you save your component (Figure 7.27). Then you can run your form with the new edited template (Figure 7.28).

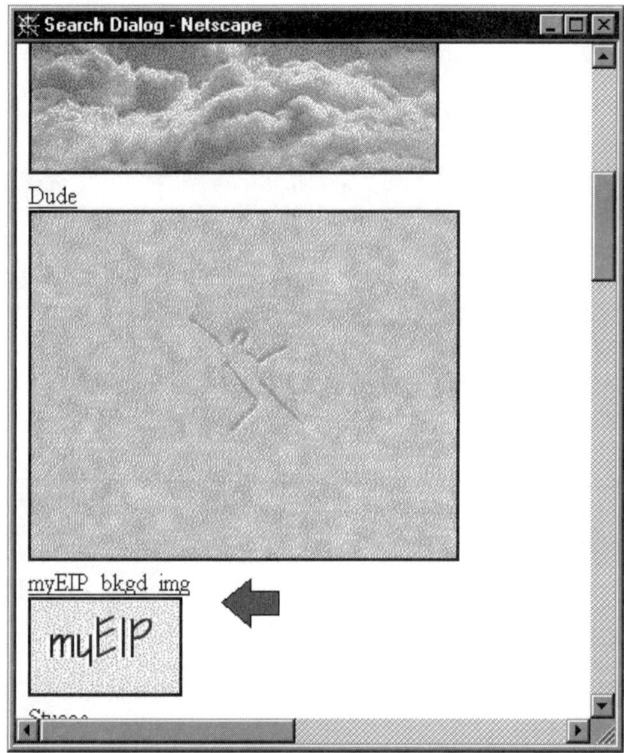

Figure 7.25
Create a Template: Heading Background Image LOV.

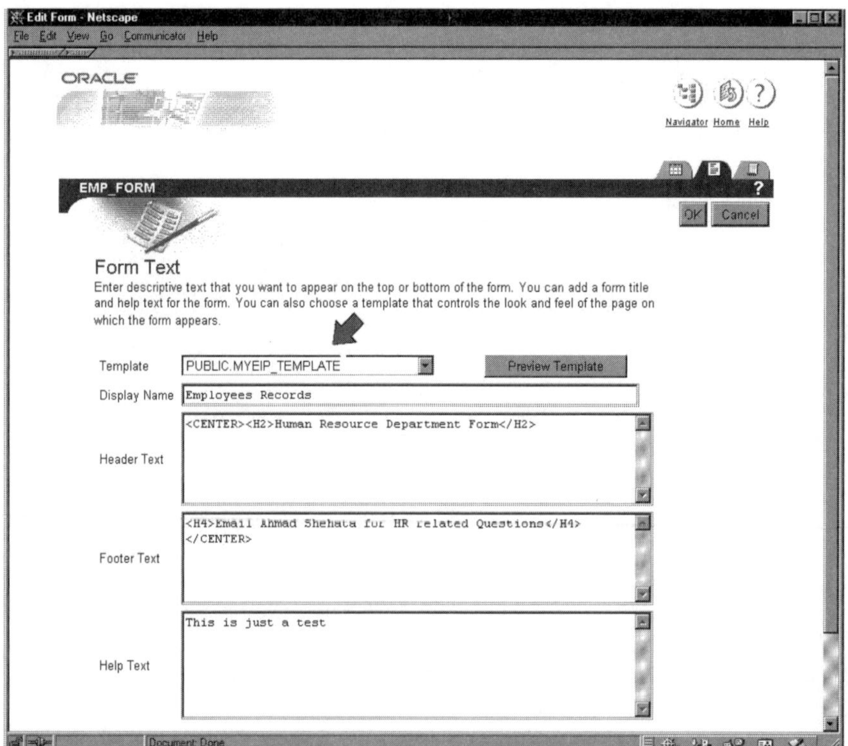

Figure 7.26
Edit Form: Apply the New Template.

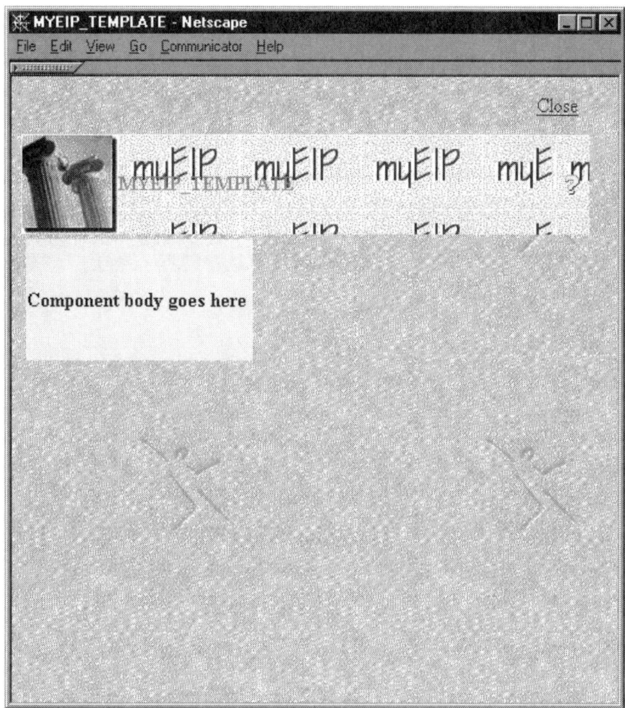

Figure 7.27 Edit Form: Preview the New Template.

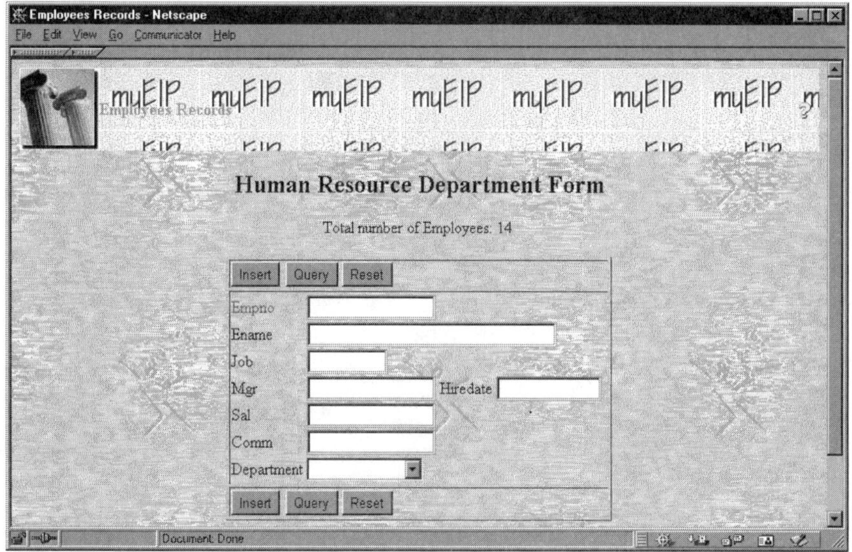

Figure 7.28 Run Form with the New Template.

If you decide to create an unstructured template, you need to specify the HTML code of your template (Figure 7.29). Inside the template HTML code, you can refer to component properties such as the title (e.g., Form Display Name), by enclosing the property name between hashes (e.g., #TITLE#).

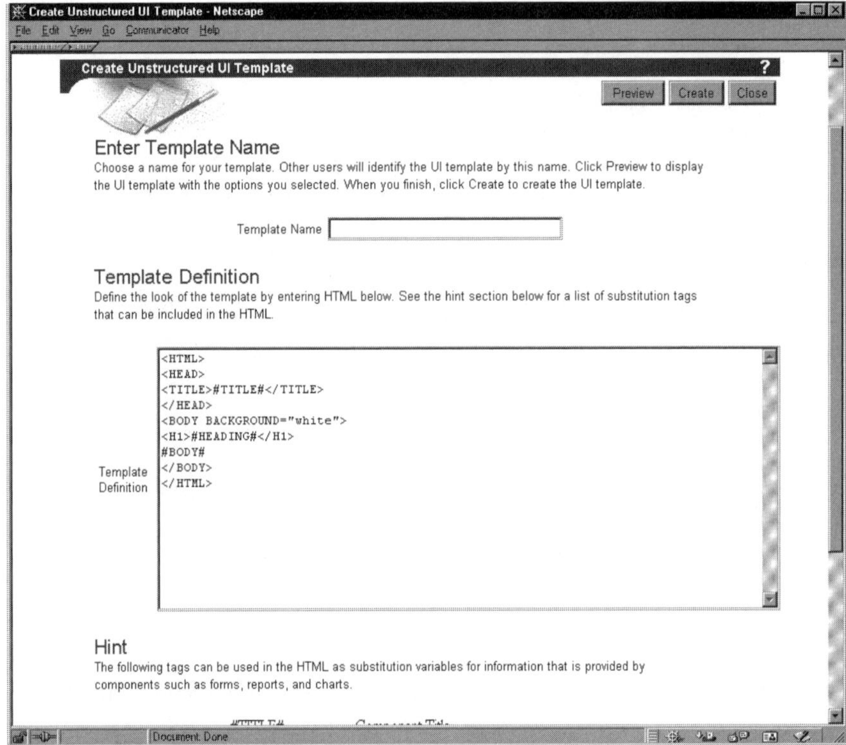

Figure 7.29 Create an Unstructured UI Template.

Note

In Oracle9*i*AS Portal version 3.0.9, there are two other application components. The first is the XML component, where you can embed SQL and PL/SQL code inside an XML document. It is similar to the dynamic page component, but the difference is that an XML document uses XML rather than HTML code. The XML component also supports XML style sheets (XSL) and XML Document Type Definition (DTD) code. The second component is the URL component, which holds the URL to an Internet site or intranet Web page. The URL component can be published as a portlet and added to a portal page.

In Chapter 8 we start exploring content areas and how they differ from portal pages.

CHAPTER 8

Introduction to Content Areas

Introduction

This chapter explores content areas and explains the differences between content areas and portal pages. I provide examples of creating folders and different items inside the content areas. I will also explain the default item types and their properties. Finally, this chapter explores the ability of extending the default item types by creating custom item types.

What Is a Content Area?

The content areas are the publishing services in Oracle Portal. They are the Oracle Portal answer to content and document management systems (e.g., Live Link). The question that usually comes to mind is Why do I need to use content areas when I have Oracle pages? The answer is simply three points, organization, security, and self-service publishing. To understand the difference, ask yourself the following questions: Can you easily categorize your portlets into a hierarchy based on their information type and who is accessing them? Can you easily define who can modify or delete documents inside one or more of your portlets? Can you easily give your users the ability to administer their own documents inside their portlets?

The answer to these three questions is typically no. They can be done but not easily. You have to do significant coding and customization to implement such features. This is where content areas come into the picture to provide a built-in solution. Content areas can act as portlet providers, as demonstrated in this chapter.

Note

Content areas are named sites in Oracle WebDB 2.x.

Create Your First Content Area

There are two ways to create a content area. One way is to navigate back to the Oracle Portal home page , and click on the "Create a New Content Area" link (Figure 8.1). Another way is to go to the Oracle Portal Navigator . Click on the Content Areas tab, then click on the "Create New . . . Content Area" link (Figure 8.2).

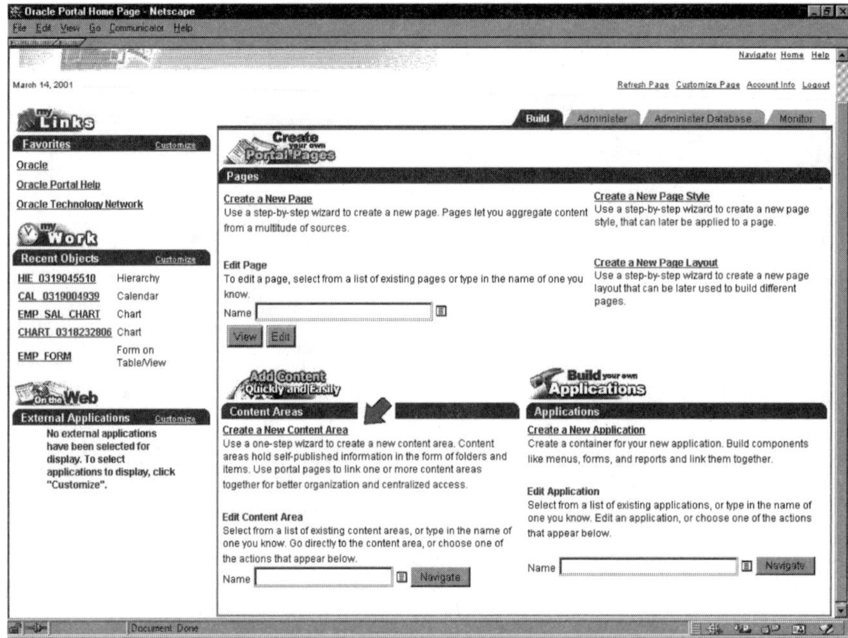

Figure 8.1 Oracle Portal Home Page: Content Areas Portlet.

To create a new content area, you need to specify its internal name and display name. The default language of the content area is English and the default content area administrator is the current logged-on user (e.g., PORTAL30; Figure 8.3).

When the content area is created, the screen is reset to allow you to create another content area. By clicking on the name of the content area on the top middle of the screen, you can edit the properties of the newly created content area (Figure 8.4).

The Edit Content Area page has six tabs: Main, Items, Labels, Translations, Page, and Access. In the Main tab you can change the internal name or the display name. Also, you can add a contact email address that is displayed in the content area home page. By default the content area has no limit on its space. You can establish a limit by specifying a value—in megabytes—in the limit property (Figure 8.5).

Figure 8.2 Oracle Portal Navigator: Content Areas Tab.

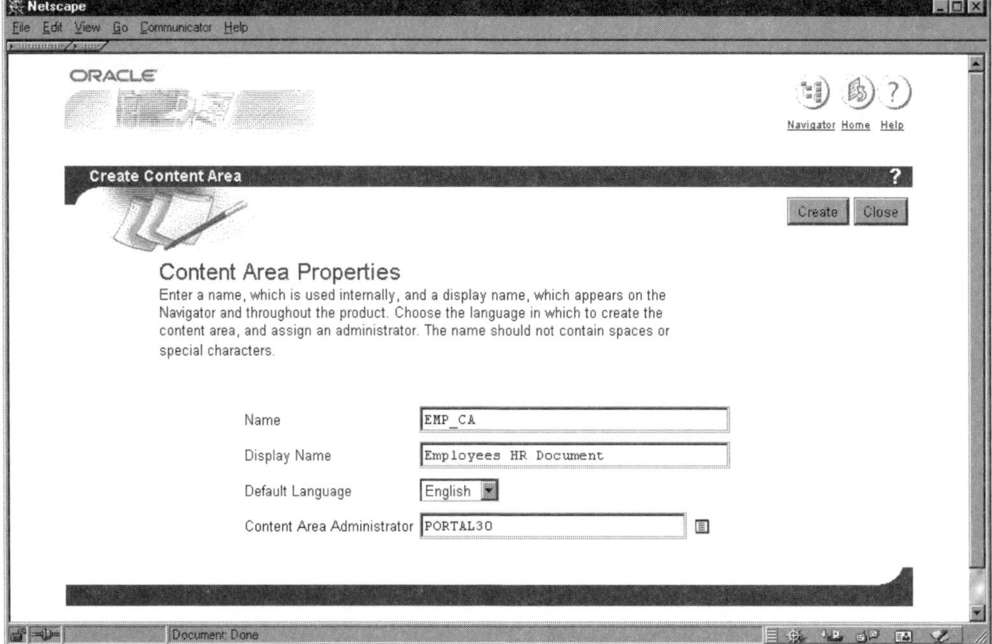

Figure 8.3 Create Content Area.

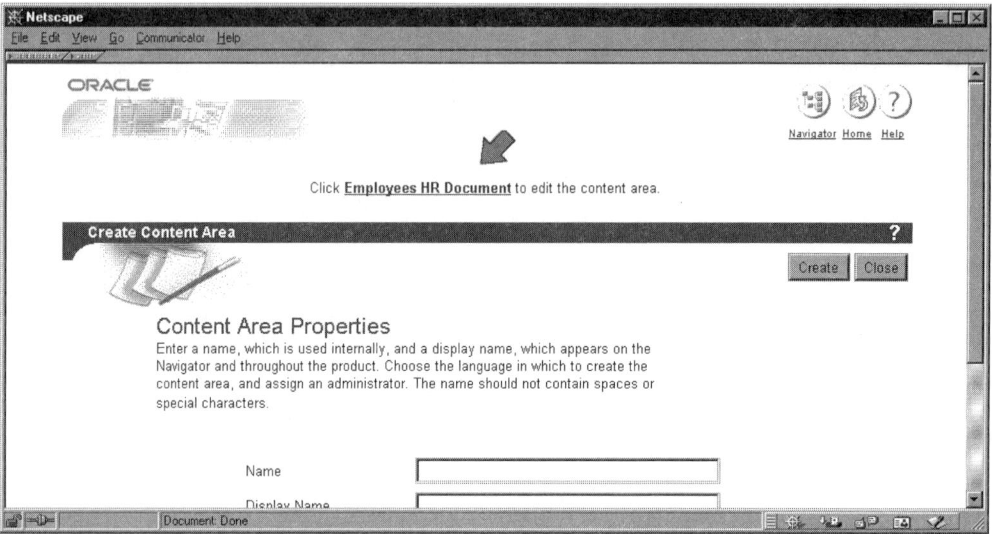

Figure 8.4 Create Content Area: Edit Link.

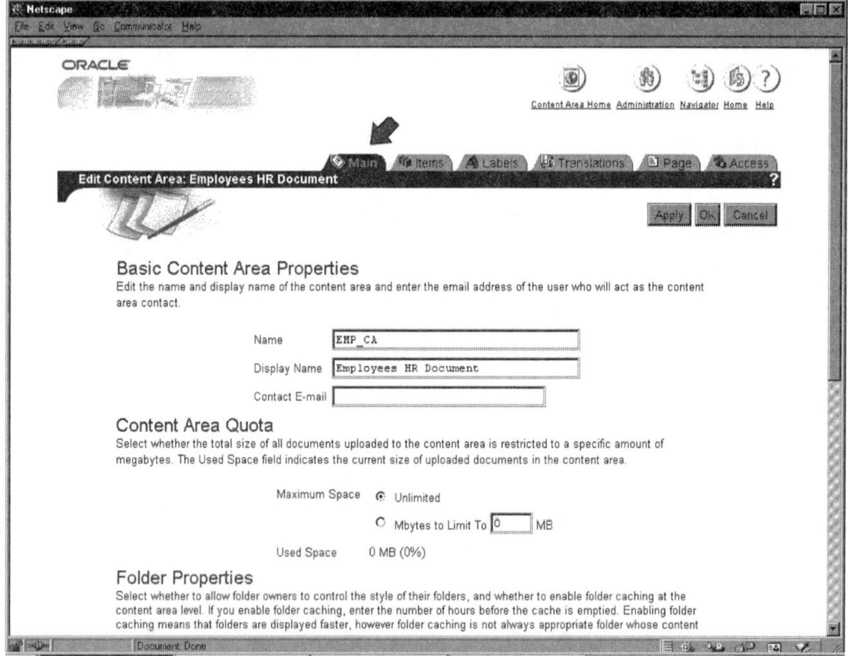

Figure 8.5 Edit Content Area: Main Tab (Top).

In the rest of the Main tab properties, you can specify two folder properties that affect the behavior of all the folders inside this content area. These properties are "Enable Folder Owners To Control Style" and "Enable Folder Caching". These two check boxes are selected by default. The first check box allows the folder owners—under a content area—to change the default style picked by the content area owner. The second check box allows the folder owner to enable caching their folders. This chapter discusses the styles in more details. Also, you can replace the default content area logo with a new logo (GIF or JPG; Figure 8.6). You need to click on the "Apply" button to be able to see the new logo in the content area properties.

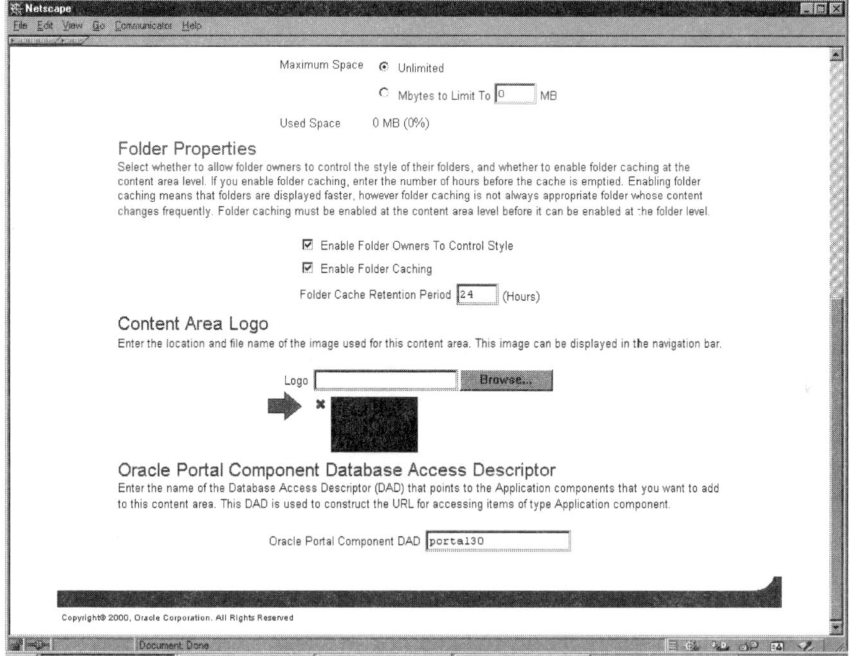

Figure 8.6 Edit Content Area: Main Tab (Bottom).

Click on the "OK" button to finish editing the content area. Display the Content Area home page (Figure 8.7) by either clicking on its name from the navigator or by typing its name and clicking on the "View" button from the Oracle Portal home page. Each content area can contain a hierarchy of folders (similar to subdirectories in a hard disk). Each new content area created has a root folder, which has the same name as the content area and is displayed by default when you click on the content area name in the Oracle Portal Navigator. On the top right side of Figure 8.7, you find the following icons: Edit folder, show properties, add folder to my interest list, and help.

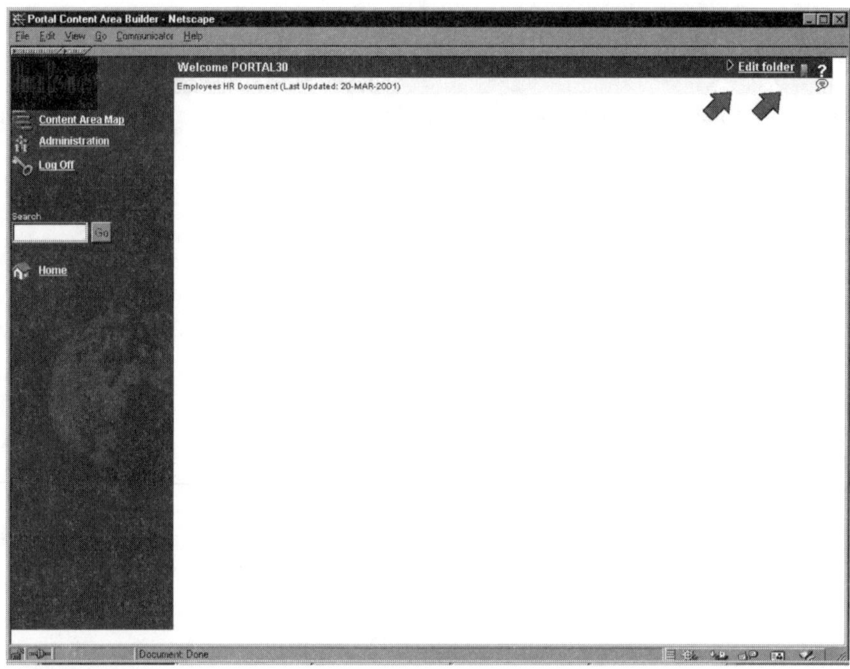

Figure 8.7 Content Area Home Page: Display Mode.

Figure 8.8 Content Area Display: Show Folder Properties.

Click on the show properties icon to display the root folder properties of your content area (Figure 8.8). The URL for the content area format is

```
http://<Hostname>:<portno>/pls/<DADname>/url/FOLDER/
        <FolderName>
```

Clicking on the add folder to my interest list icon adds a link to the content area to the Favorites portlet. So, from the Oracle Portal home page you can directly navigate to the Content Area home page.

Click on the Edit folder icon to display the folder Edit Tools. These edit tools allow you to add folders and items to your content area. The tools also allow you to manipulate the navigation bar (Figure 8.9).

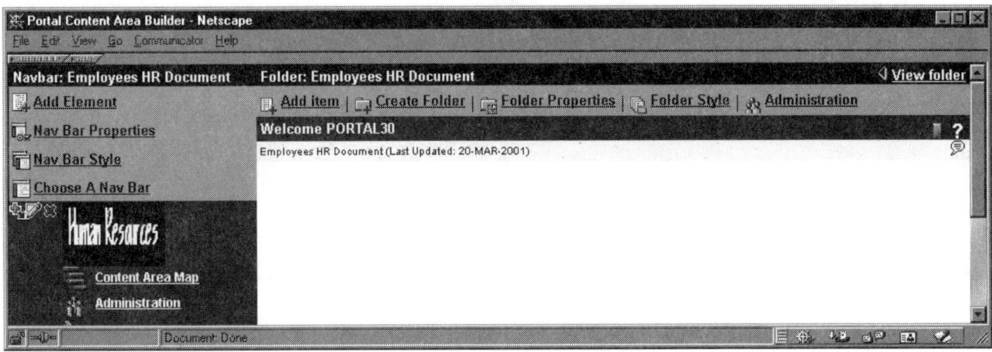

Figure 8.9 Edit the Content Area Root Folder and Navigation Bar.

Create Your First Item

Click on the "Add item" link to add a new URL item under the root folder. There are three steps involved in creating a new item. The first step is to choose the item type (e.g., URL; Figure 8.10).

Table 8.1 describes the different item types that you can create in your content areas. A content area is split into five regions and a navigation bar. The region default names are Quickpicks, Announcements, Sub-folders, News, and Regular Items. You do not have to have items in all of these regions in your content area. These regions offer a means of locating the items of a content area across the content area page. The regions' locations depend on the content area layout. The default layout has the navigation bar on the left side and the five regions on top of each other on the right side of the page. Changing the folder layout in the content area style properties is covered in Chapter 9.

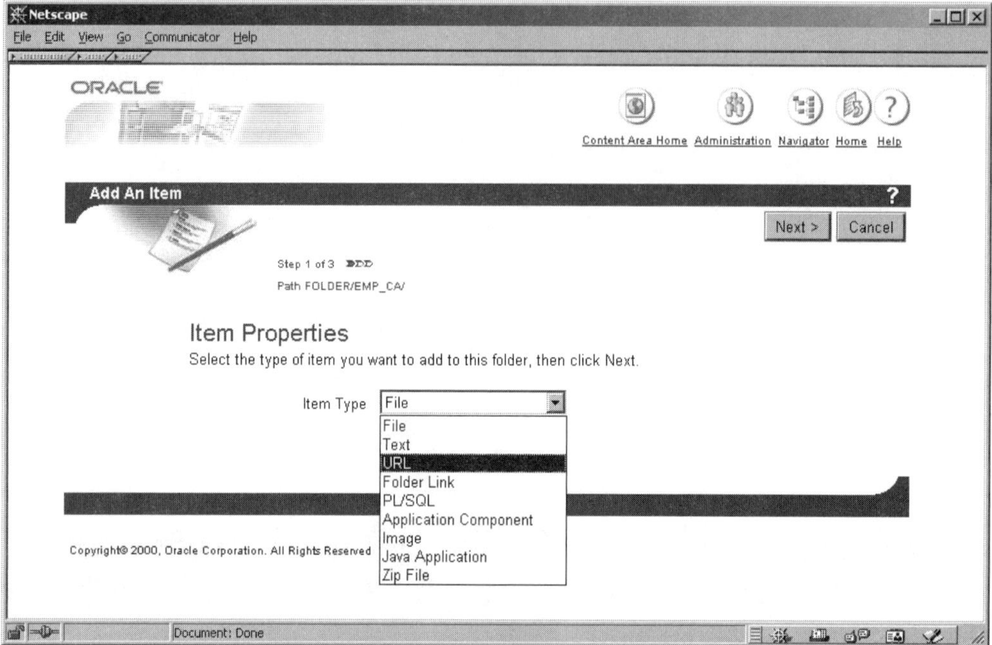

Figure 8.10 Add a URL Item (Step 1 of 3).

Table 8.1 Content Areas Item Types

Item Type	Item Description
File	A file loaded and stored inside the content area
Folder link	A link that is pointing to another folder in the content area
Image/Imagemap	An image loaded and stored inside the content area. This image can be an imagemap, which performs a different action when the user clicks on separate areas of the map.
PL/SQL	PL/SQL code that is executed when the user clicks on the item and the output is displayed
Text	Text content (up to 32KB) to be displayed in the content area
URL	A link to a Web page pointing to either inside or outside the content area
Java application	A Java Server Pages (JSP) application
Zip file	A Zip file is loaded and stored in the content area. This simplifies the operation of loading multiple files.
Application component	An application component (e.g., form, report, chart, etc.) is displayed inside the content area

In the second step, choose the folder region where you want the item to reside (e.g., News; Figure 8.11). Type the URL value of the item. When the end-user clicks on the item, he or she is routed to this URL. Specify a display name for the new item. Also, all the items added to a content area have to be categorized. Because you have not created any categories yet, the only category displayed is "General", which is the default precreated category. Categories are ways to classify the items based on their contents. They answer the question, What is the item? An item belongs to one and only one category. Optionally, you can specify a description for the item that will be displayed under the item when the content area is displayed.

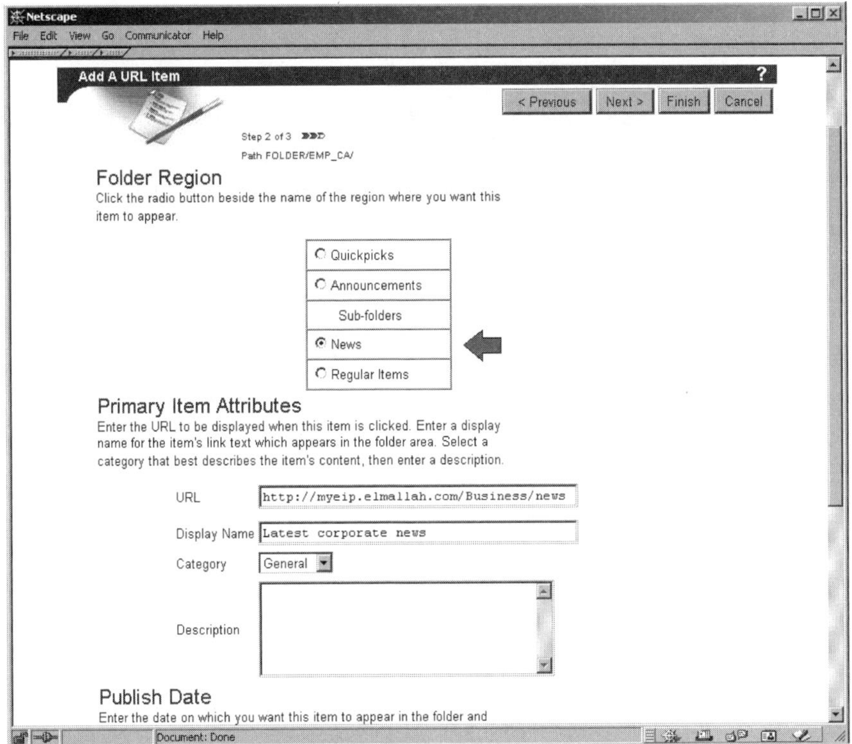

Figure 8.11 Add a URL Item (Step 2 of 3, Top).

You can also change the publish date and expiration settings for an item (Figure 8.12). The publish date is defaulted to the system date, so the item is available to the users once created. The item or folder owner (e.g., PORTAL30) or the users who are granted the Manage Items privilege can access the item immediately in edit mode, regardless of the publish date. Chapter 12 explains content area security and privileges.

Publish Date

Enter the date on which you want this item to appear in the folder and become available in View mode.

Publish Date 27-MAR-2001 (DD-MON-YYYY)

Expiration Period

Choose whether this item is always available, available only for a specified number of days, or if it expires on a certain date.

Never Expires

Expires In Days

Expires On (DD-MON-YYYY)

Apply OK Cancel

Document: Done

Figure 8.12 Add a URL Item (Step 2 of 3, Bottom).

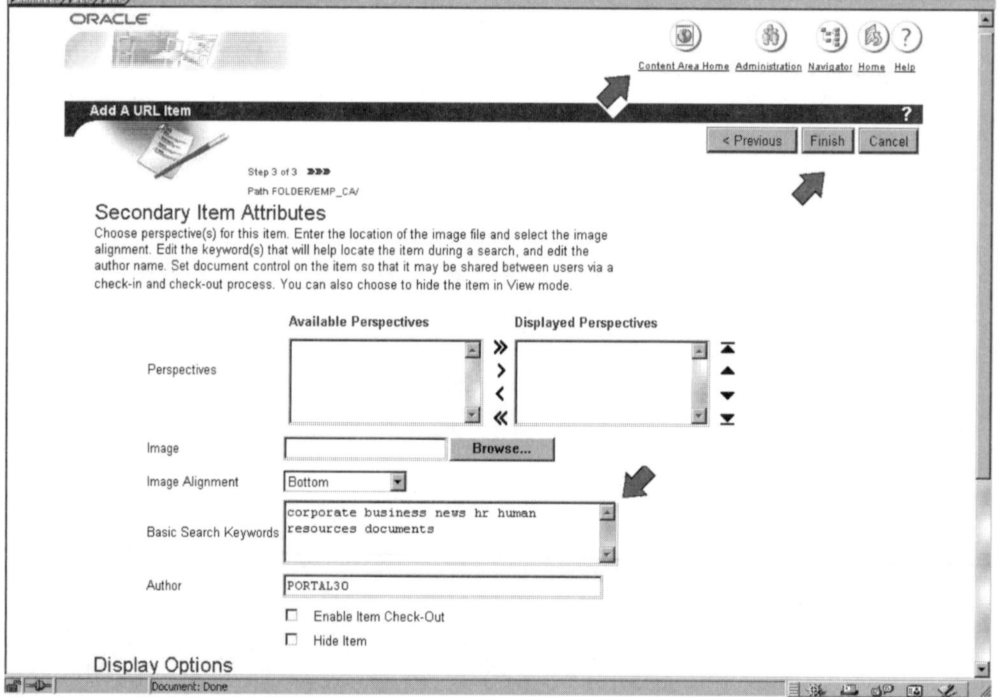

Figure 8.13 Add a URL Item (Step 3 of 3, Top).

You can also set the expiration period for the item. There are three choices: The default value is "Never Expires", which means that the item is permanently displayed until it is explicitly removed. The second choice is to set the number of days before the item expires. The number of days is calculated from the item's publish date. The third choice is to specify the day on which this item expires. When an item expires, it is viewable only by the folder owner and content area administrator (e.g., PORTAL30). If you are the folder owner or the content area administrator, you can redisplay the expired item by editing it and extending its expiration period.

In the third step (Figure 8.13) you can associate the item with one or more perspectives. Perspectives are cross-category classifications. They answer the question, Who will be interested in accessing the item? Initially, there are no available perspectives to choose. Later on you can create perspectives in the Oracle Portal Navigator and then edit the item to associate it with one or more perspectives. You can choose an image to be associated with the new URL item. Also, you can enter search key words to be associated with the item, so when a search is performed, using one or more of these search key words, the item will show up. The search key words are separated by spaces. You can enclose multiple key words in single quotation marks (e.g., 'Human Resources').

You can also decide to create the item but not display it. This is can be done by selecting the "Hide Item" check box. This is useful if the item is still under construction and not ready for user access.

While working on content areas, there is a new icon displayed at the top of the pages. This new icon is Content Area Home. By clicking on this icon, you are routed to the Content Area home page.

Next you need to specify how you want to display the item. There are four display options (Figure 8.14). The options are self-explanatory, and the easiest way to understand the differences between these options is to try each on the same item. Now the content area includes the URL item displayed as a link (Figure 8.15).

Table 8.2 describes the item icons.

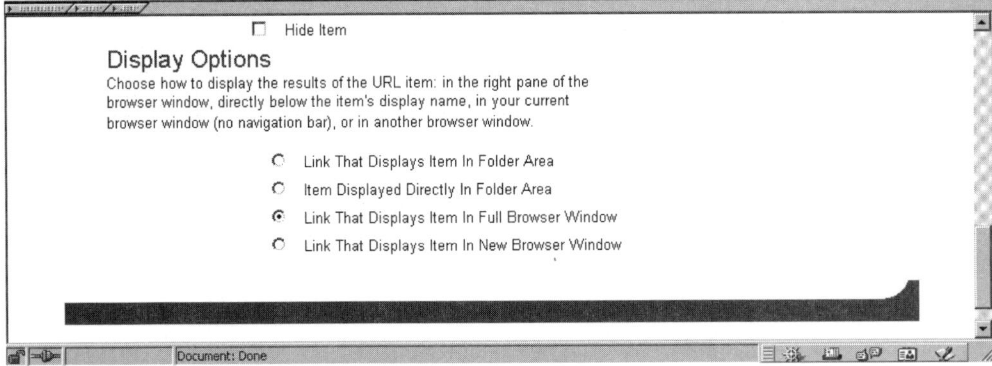

Figure 8.14 Add a URL Item (Step 3 of 3, Bottom).

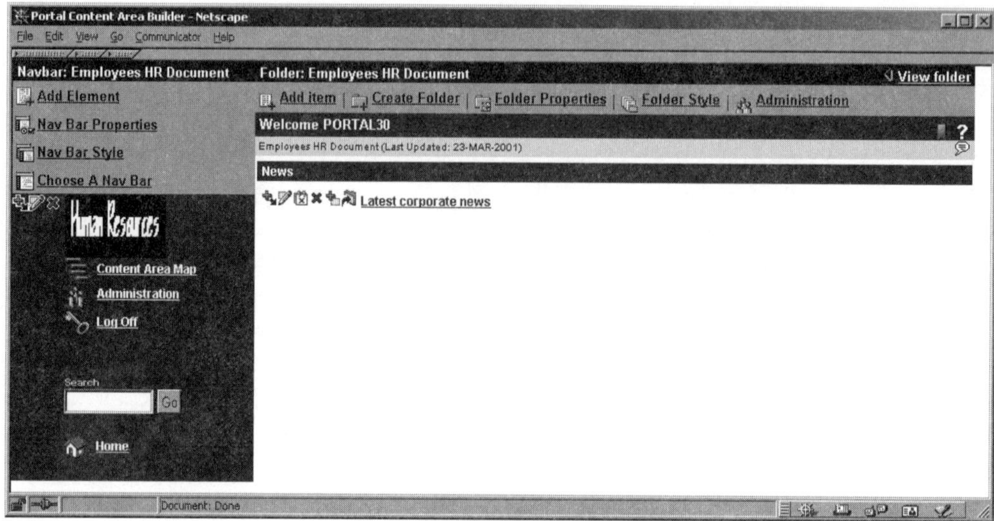

Figure 8.15 Content Area Home Page: Editing Mode.

Table 8.2 Item Icons

Icon	Description
	Adds another item after this item
	Edits item properties
	Expires item
	Deletes item
	Adds a subitem
	Moves item to another folder
	Moves item up
	Undeletes
NEW	Displays new items

Note

In Oracle9*i*AS Portal version 3.0.9, there is another icon, the copy item icon, which you can use to copy an item to another content area or to another folder in the same content area.

You can delete an item by clicking on the delete icon on the item's left side. You need to confirm the deletion (Figure 8.16). The deleted item is still displayed in the editing mode of the content area but not in the display mode. As the content area administrator (i.e., PORTAL30), you can permanently remove deleted and also expired items from the content area by performing a system purge. To perform a system purge, click on the "Administration" link in the folder dashboard (i.e., Editing Toolbar; Figure 8.17).

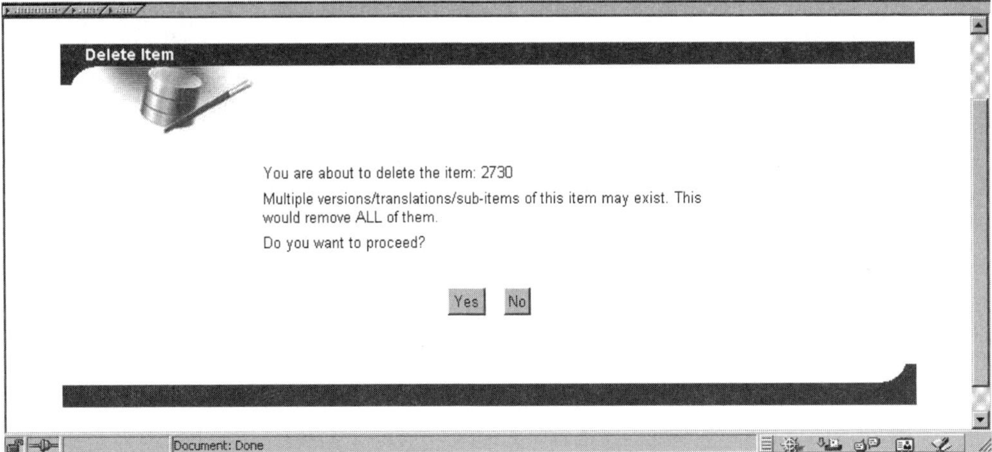

Figure 8.16 Delete Item Confirmation.

Next, under the Content Area Managers section, click on the "Content Area" link (Figure 8.18). The content area properties are displayed. To purge the deleted and expired items in the content area, click on the Items tab (Figure 8.19). At the bottom of the page, click on the "Purge" button (Figure 8.20).

By unselecting the "Purge Deleted Items" check box or the "Purge Expired Items" check box, you can purge only the deleted items or the expired items, respectively. By default the deleted items are retained and displayed to content area administrators and folder owners; you can change that by unselecting the corresponding check boxes. Also, you can change the number of days that the item is considered to be new or changed. By default after seven days the new icon is not displayed any more on the right side of the item.

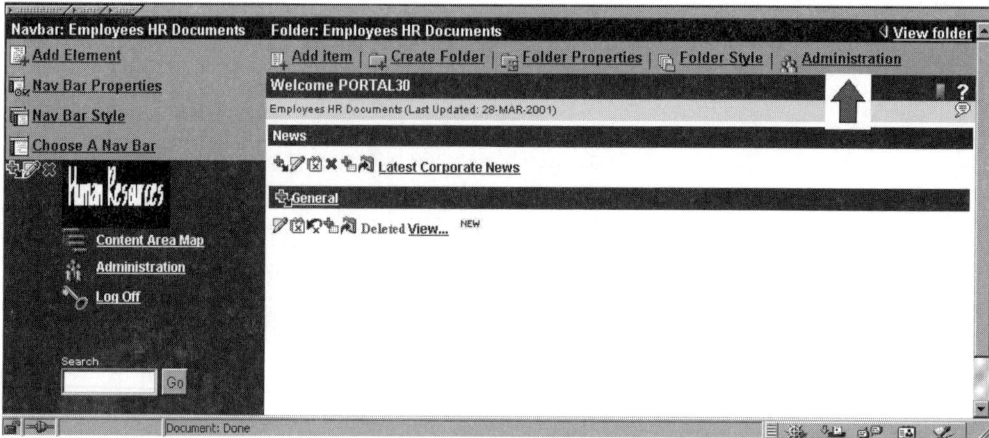

Figure 8.17 Content Area Home Page: Editing Mode.

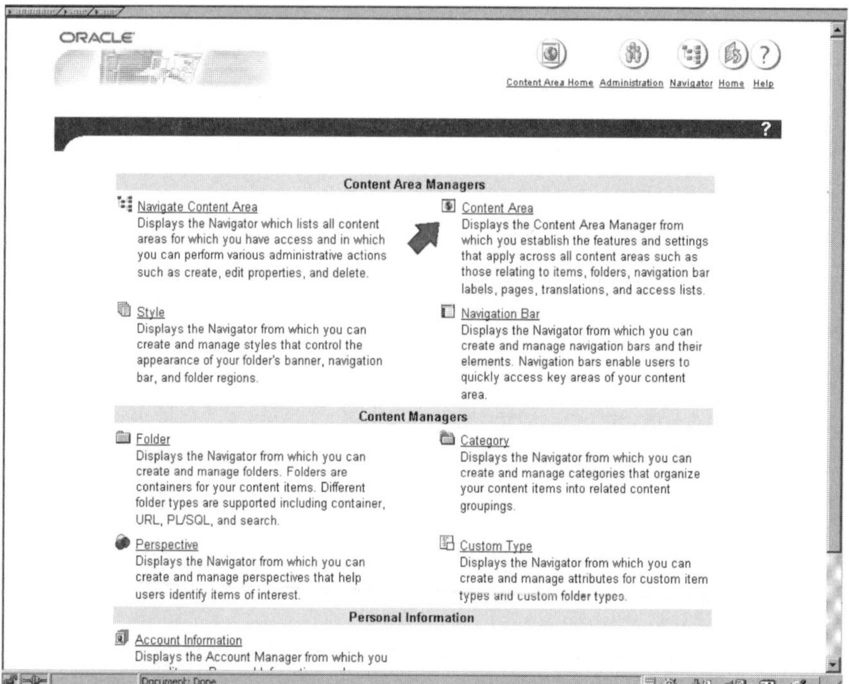

Figure 8.18 Content Area Managers (Administration).

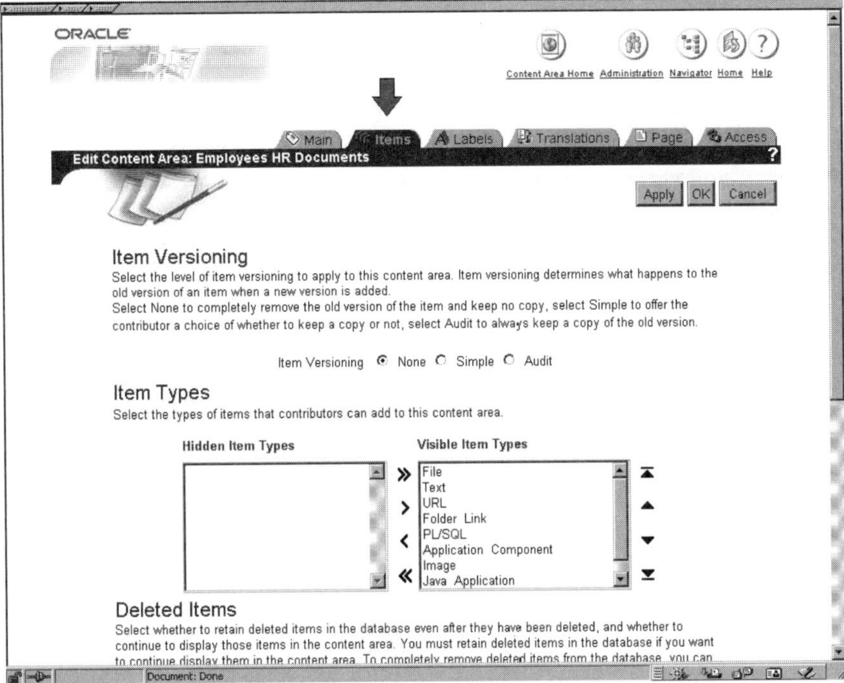

Figure 8.19 Content Area Editing: Items Tab (Top).

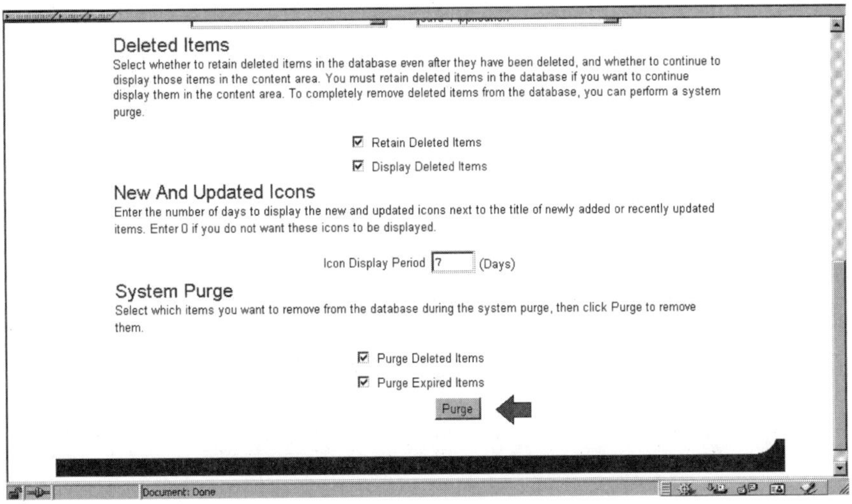

Deleted Items

Select whether to retain deleted items in the database even after they have been deleted, and whether to continue to display those items in the content area. You must retain deleted items in the database if you want to continue display them in the content area. To completely remove deleted items from the database, you can perform a system purge.

☑ Retain Deleted Items

☑ Display Deleted Items

New And Updated Icons

Enter the number of days to display the new and updated icons next to the title of newly added or recently updated items. Enter 0 if you do not want these icons to be displayed.

Icon Display Period 7 (Days)

System Purge

Select which items you want to remove from the database during the system purge, then click Purge to remove them.

☑ Purge Deleted Items

☑ Purge Expired Items

Purge

Document: Done

Figure 8.20 Content Area Editing: Items Tab (Bottom).

Create Your First Folder

Click on the "Create Folder" link in the folder dashboard to add folders under the current folder (i.e., root folder; Figure 8.21). Leave the default folder type (i.e., Container) and click "Next" (Figure 8.22). In Chapter 9 there is an explanation of the different folder types.

The new folder is created to contain the New Hire Orientation documents and training material. You need to provide its name and title accordingly (Figure 8.23). Once you click the "Finish" button, you are taken back to the Content Area home page where you see the new folder

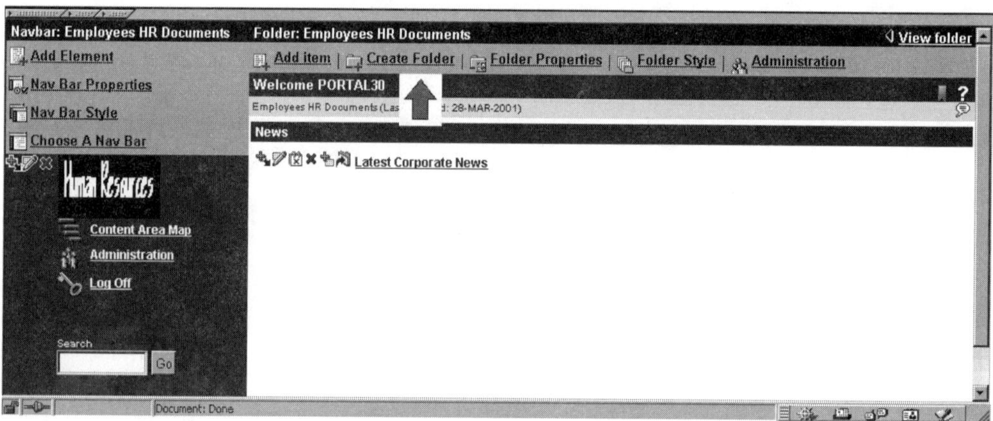

Figure 8.21 Content Area Home Page: Editing Mode.

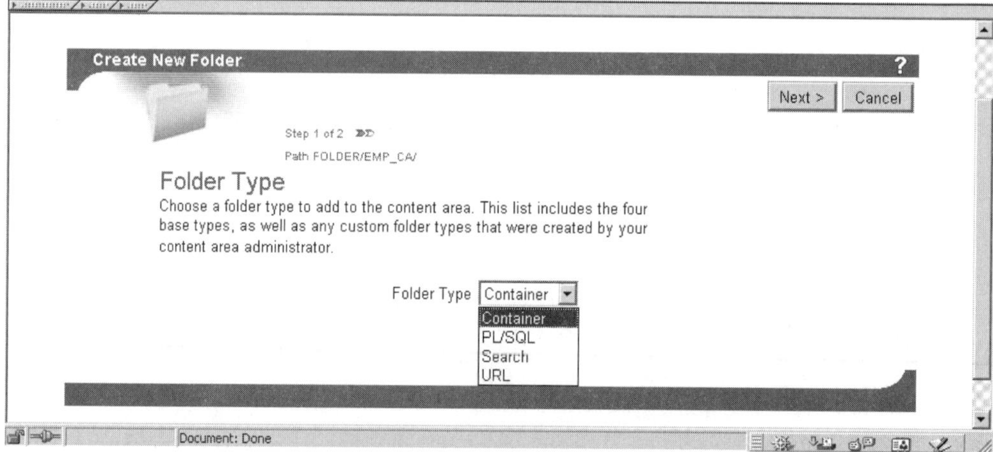

Figure 8.22 Create Folder: Folder Type (Step 1 of 2).

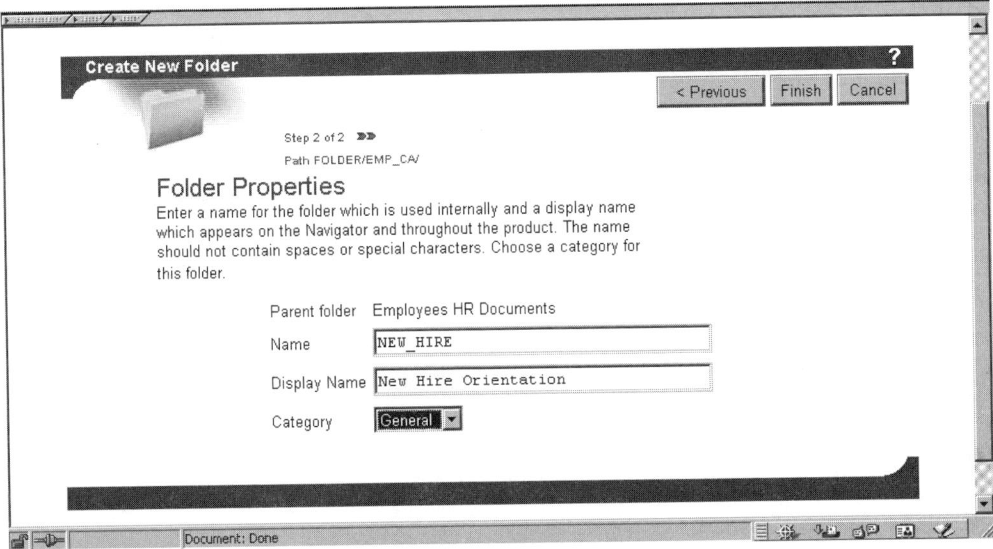

Figure 8.23 Adding Folder: Folder Properties (Step 2 of 2).

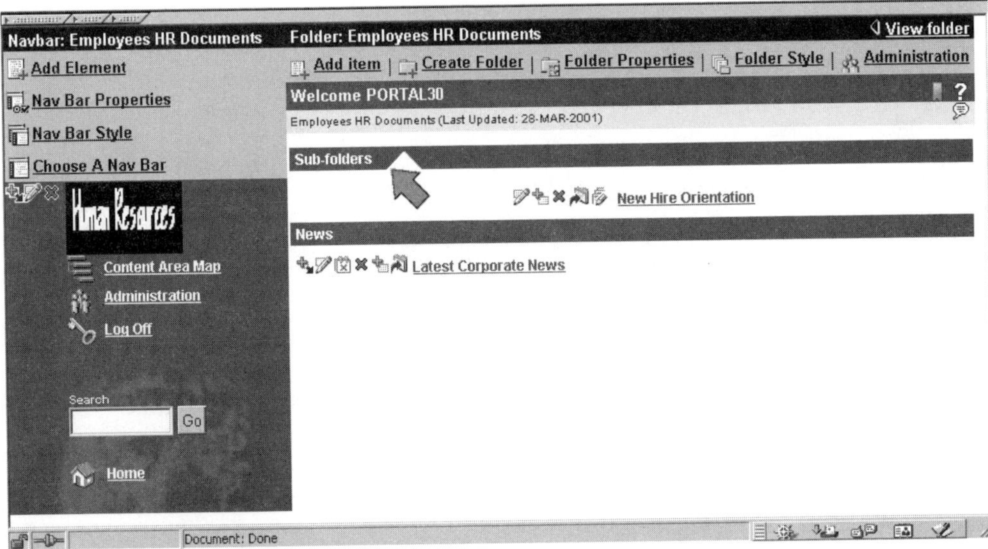

Figure 8.24 Content Area Home Page.

(Figure 8.24). Table 8.3 describes the folder icons, and Table 8.4 describes the icons in the folder dashboard. You can create other folders under your root folder by repeating steps in Figure 8.22 and Figure 8.23.

Table 8.3 Folder Icons

Icon	Description
	Edits folder properties
	Deletes folder
	Adds a subfolder
	Moves folder to another folder
	Copies folder

Table 8.4 Folder Dashboard Icons

Icon	Description
	Views folder
	Adds item under the current folder
	Creates a new folder under the current folder
	Shows current folder properties
	Show/Edits current folder style
	Content Area administration

Note

In Oracle9*i*AS Portal version 3.0.9, there is another link in the folder dashboard, "Item Bulk Action", where you can manipulate multiple items at the same time.

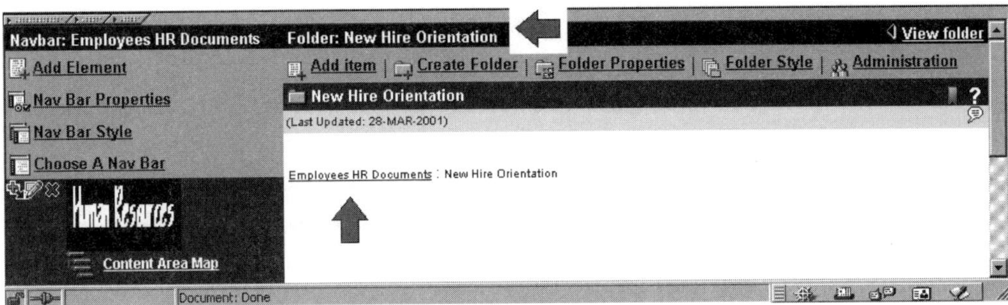

Figure 8.25 Content Area: Subfolder.

The name of the current folder is displayed in the top banner. The root folder name is the same name as the content area (i.e., Employees HR Documents). You can navigate to a subfolder by clicking on the folder name link in the subfolders region (Figure 8.24). You can navigate back to the root folder by clicking on its name link at the bottom of the folder area (Figure 8.25).

Create a PL/SQL item under the New Hire Orientation folder. Navigate first to the folder (Figure 8.25). Choose the PL/SQL item type (Figure 8.26). In the second step you need to specify the PL/SQL code to be executed when this item is clicked. You can use the procedures in the PL/SQL Web Toolkit such as the OWA_UTIL.TABLEPRINT to print the contents of a table (Figure 8.27).

In the third step specify the search key words. For practice, choose to display the item in the folder area (Figure 8.28). The table print is displayed in place within the folder area (Figure 8.29).

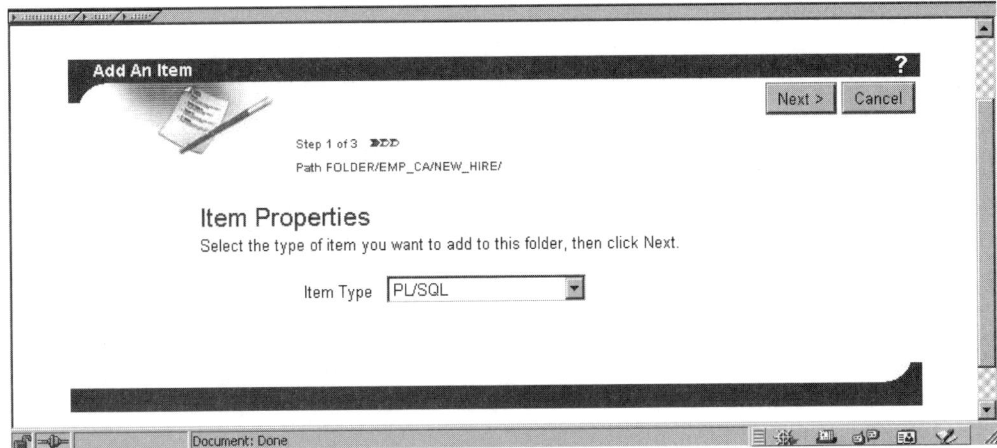

Figure 8.26 Create Item: PL/SQL Item Type (Step 1 of 3).

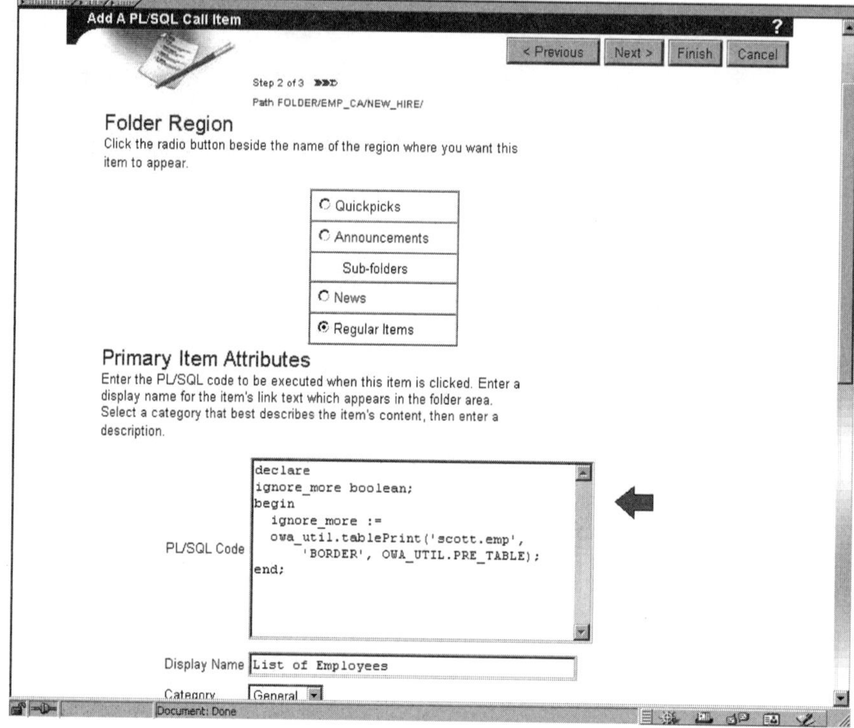

Figure 8.27 Create Item: PL/SQL Item Type (Step 2 of 3).

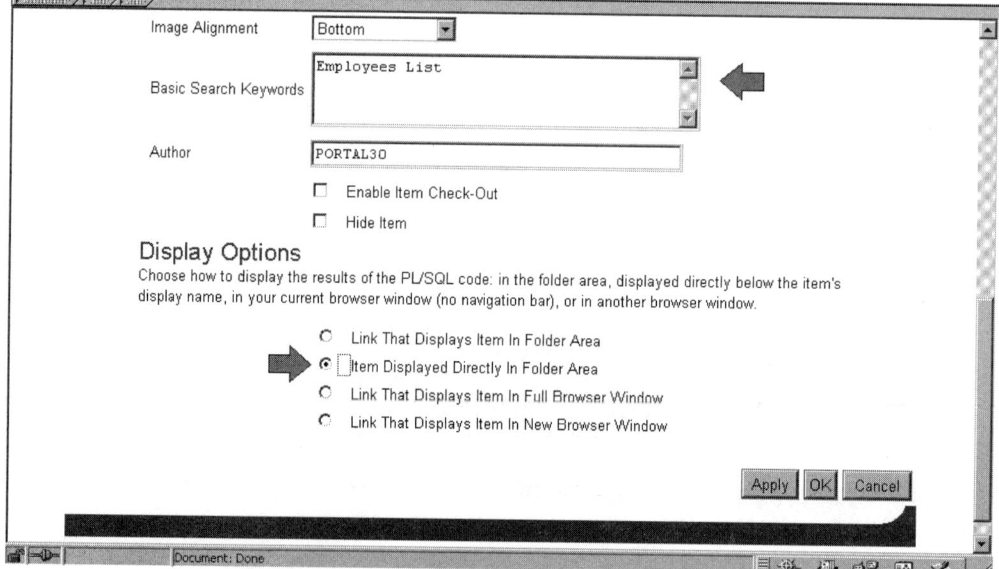

Figure 8.28 Create Item: PL/SQL Item Type (Step 3 of 3).

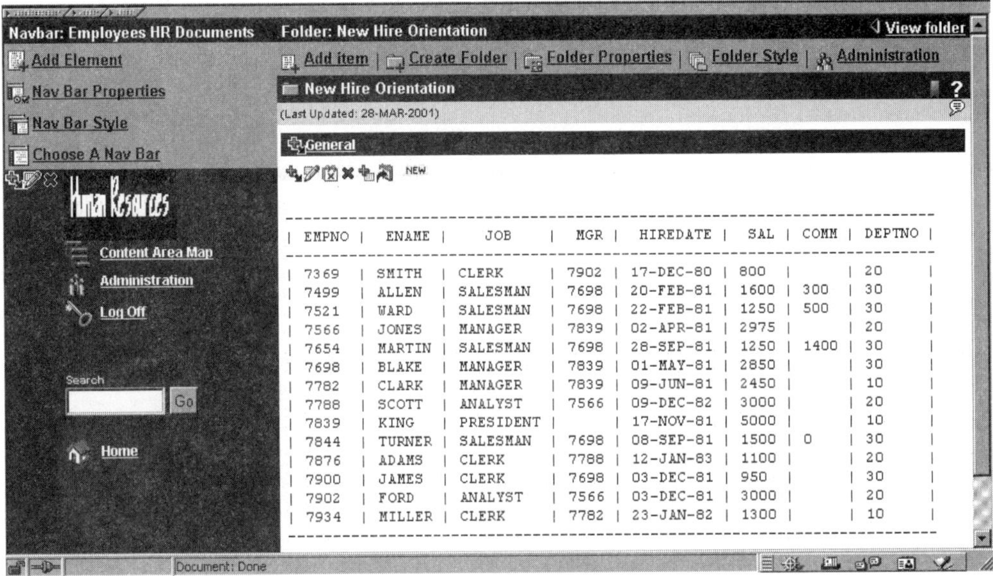

EMPNO	ENAME	JOB	MGR	HIREDATE	SAL	COMM	DEPTNO
7369	SMITH	CLERK	7902	17-DEC-80	800		20
7499	ALLEN	SALESMAN	7698	20-FEB-81	1600	300	30
7521	WARD	SALESMAN	7698	22-FEB-81	1250	500	30
7566	JONES	MANAGER	7839	02-APR-81	2975		20
7654	MARTIN	SALESMAN	7698	28-SEP-81	1250	1400	30
7698	BLAKE	MANAGER	7839	01-MAY-81	2850		30
7782	CLARK	MANAGER	7839	09-JUN-81	2450		10
7788	SCOTT	ANALYST	7566	09-DEC-82	3000		20
7839	KING	PRESIDENT		17-NOV-81	5000		10
7844	TURNER	SALESMAN	7698	08-SEP-81	1500	0	30
7876	ADAMS	CLERK	7788	12-JAN-83	1100		20
7900	JAMES	CLERK	7698	03-DEC-81	950		30
7902	FORD	ANALYST	7566	03-DEC-81	3000		20
7934	MILLER	CLERK	7782	23-JAN-82	1300		10

Figure 8.29 Content Area: Subfolder.

Navigate back to the root folder and create a Folder Link item pointing to the New Hire Orientation subfolder (Figure 8.30). Keep the region setting as Quickpicks to place the link item in the topmost area of your site page. Specify the display name and description of the item. Then, to specify the path of the Folder Link, click on the Path List Of Values (LOV) icon on the right side of the Path Field (Figure 8.31). The Path LOV window shows a list of available content areas.

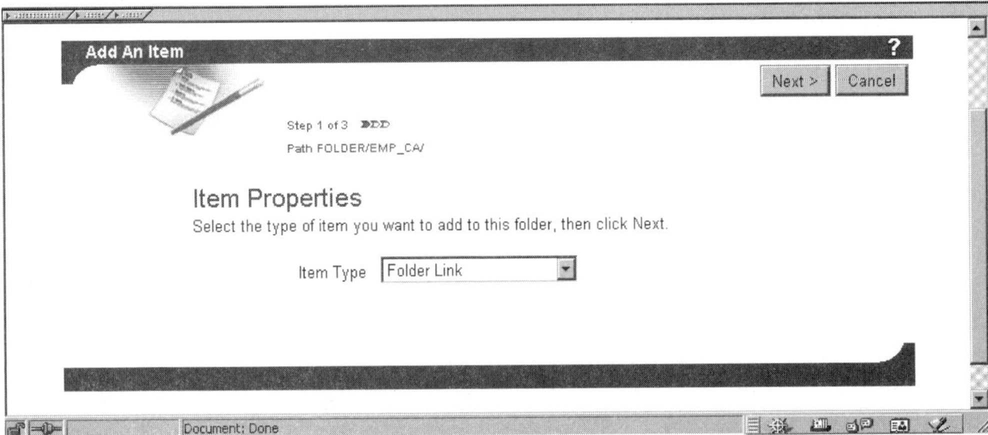

Figure 8.30 Add a Folder Link Item (Step 1 of 3).

Add A Folder Link Item

< Previous | Next > | Finish | Cancel

Step 2 of 3

Path FOLDER/EMP_CA/

Folder Region

Click the radio button beside the name of the region where you want this item to appear.

- Quickpicks
- Announcements
- Sub-folders
- News
- Regular Items

Primary Item Attributes

In the Display Name field, enter the link text for the item that users can click. This text may or may not correspond to the actual folder name. Click to identify the actual folder to display when the link text is clicked. Select a category that best describes the item's content, then enter a description.

Path: Employees HR Documents

Display Name:

Category: General

Description:

Document: Done

Figure 8.31 Adding a Folder Link Item (Step 2 of 3).

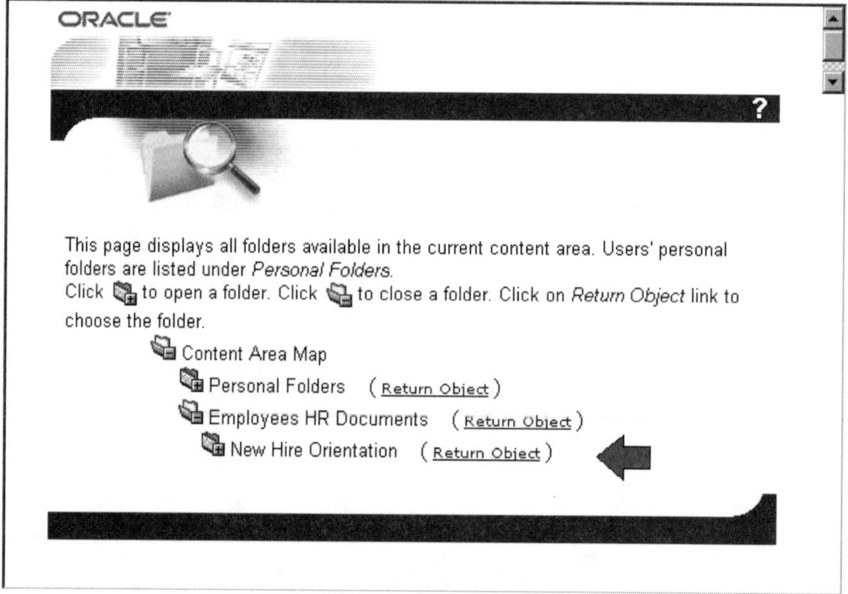

Figure 8.32 Add a Folder Link Item: Folder Selection.

Click on the Employees HR Documents node to expand it and show its subfolders. Click on the "Return Object" link on the right side of the New Hire Orientation folder (Figure 8.32).

Click on the "Next" push button to specify the Optional Item attributes, click on the "Browse" push button to choose an image to be attached to the item. Click "Finish" to go back to the Content Area home page where you can see the newly added folder link item (Figure 8.33).

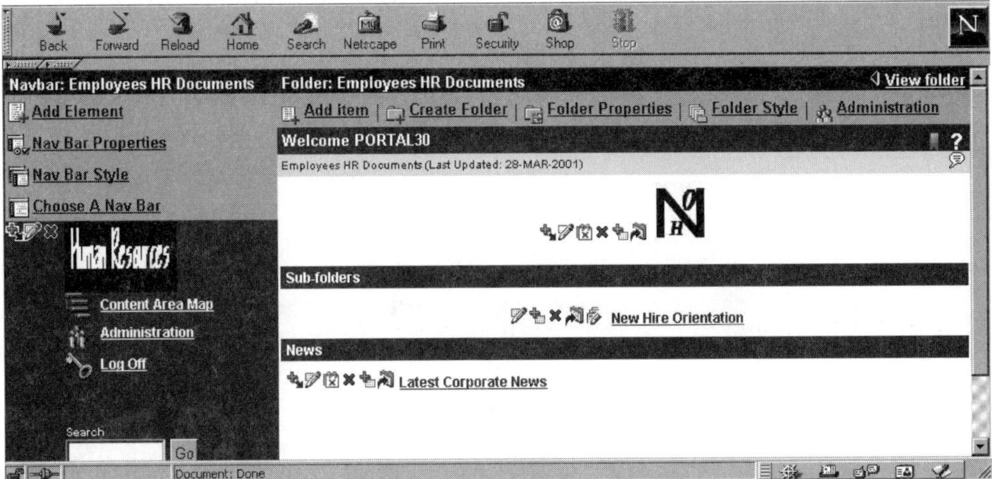

Figure 8.33 Content Area Home Page.

Publishing Folders

Now, you have built your first simple content area. You can set your content area folders to act as portlet providers. Navigate to the subfolder and click on the "Folder Properties" link in the folder dashboard. Select the "Publish As Portlet" check box under the Required tab (Figure 8.34).

To add a portlet based on your folder, you need to edit the Oracle Page. There is more than one way to navigate to your Oracle Page from the content area. One way is by clicking on the Home icon in the Content Area navigation bar to go to the Oracle Portal home page. From there you can edit the page. The second way is to click on the "Administration" link and click on the "Navigate Content Area" link in the Content Area Managers section, which takes you to the Oracle Portal Navigator.

When you display the Portlet Repository, the content area is displayed as a provider. Under the content area, the folders that are published are included (Figure 8.35).

Note

In Oracle9*i*AS Portal version 3.0.9, the Portlet Repository displays the published folder link under an entry with the content area name under the "other providers" link.

Edit Folder: New Hire Orientation

Required | Optional | Style | Image | Nav Bar | Access

Apply | OK | Cancel

Path FOLDER/EMP_CA/NEW_HIRE/

Folder Properties

Enter a name for the folder which is used internally and a display name which appears on the Navigator and throughout the product. Edit the description, and choose a category that better describes the contents of this folder.

Folder Type Container

Name NEW_HIRE

Display Name New Hire Orientation

Description

Category General

Portlet Properties

Select Publish As Portlet to be able to include this folder as a portlet on a page. Choose to use the page style instead of the folder style when displaying the portlet. If you want the folder to display a different name when used as a portlet, enter the Portlet Display Name.

☑ Publish As Portlet

☐ Use Page Style

Portlet Display Name New Hire Orientation

Document: Done

Figure 8.34 Content Area Folder Properties: Required Tab.

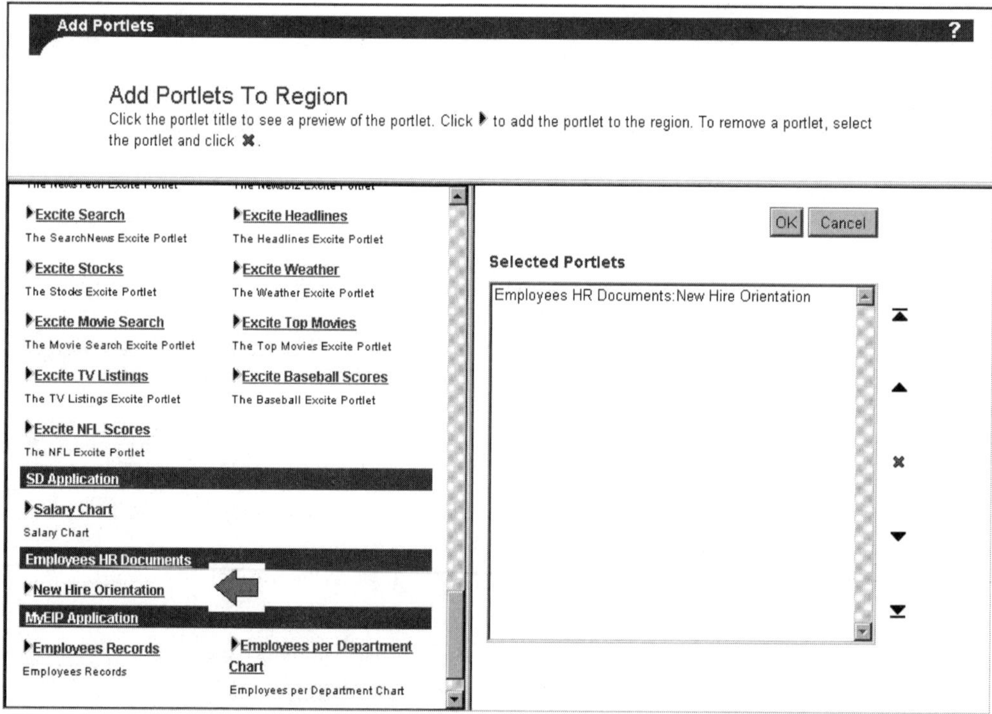

Figure 8.35 Portlet Repository.

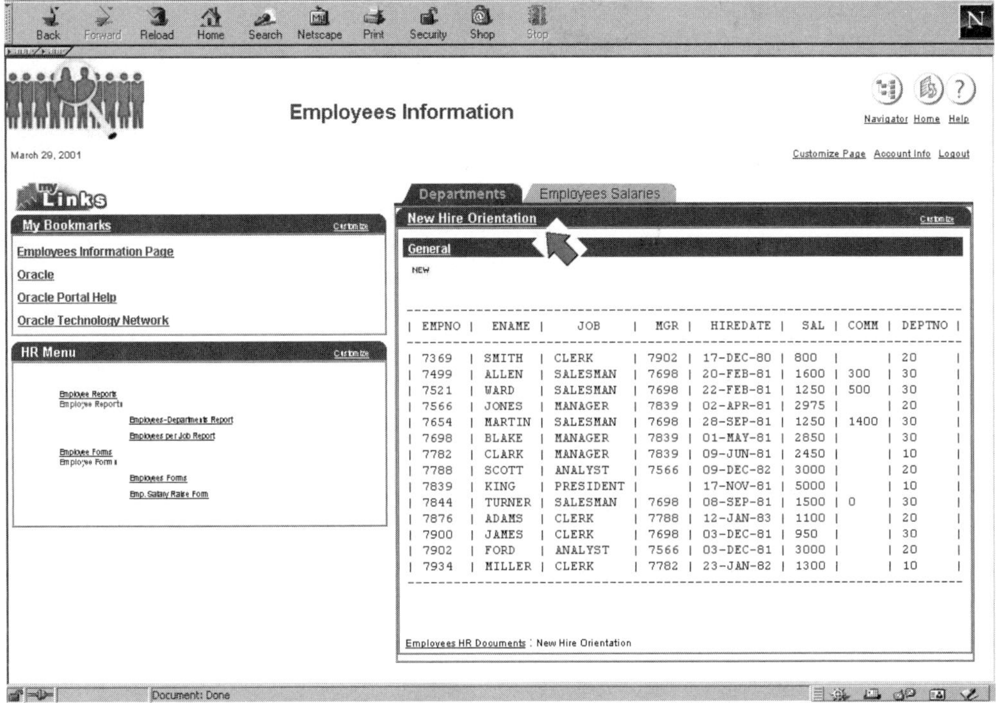

Figure 8.36 Page Display: Content Area Folder Included as a Portlet.

The folder is displayed as a portlet inside the page (Figure 8.36). To navigate to the Content Area home page, click on the folder name (i.e., New Hire Orientation). By clicking on the category name (i.e., General), a list of all the items classified under this category in the content area is displayed.

The customization of the Content Area folder portlet includes changing the portlet display name and choosing which regions of the content area are to be displayed in the page (Figure 8.37).

Note

In Oracle9*i*AS Portal version 3.0.9, an "Edit" link is displayed in the folder portlet that allows you to add item, delete item, create folder, and display item and folder properties.

You can also add Oracle Portal application components as items to your content areas (Figure 8.38). Next, select one of the application components from the drop-down list (Figure 8.39). The list displays the components on which you have the right privileges, and they are published as portlets. Also, do not forget to specify the item display name.

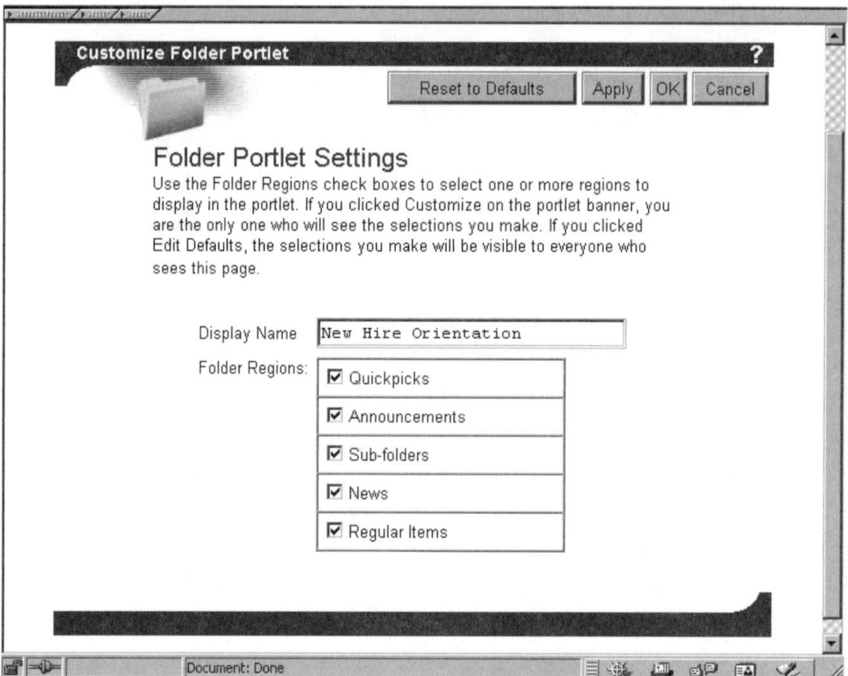

Figure 8.37 Content Area Folder Portlet Customization.

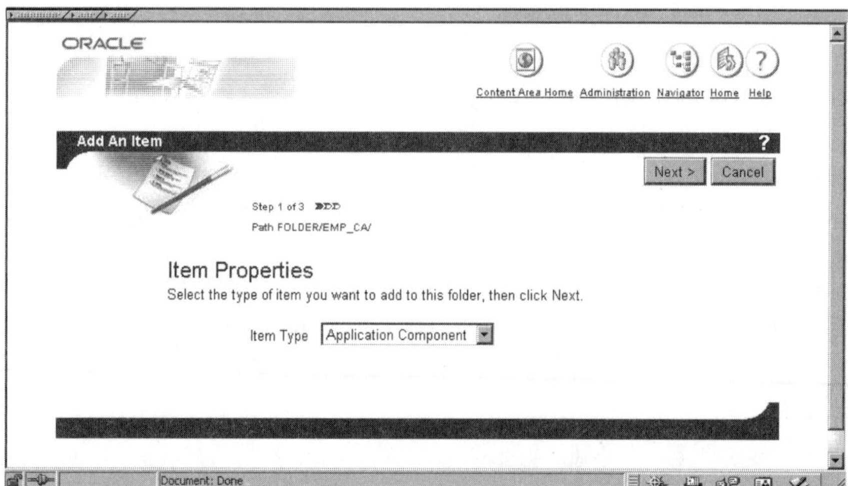

Figure 8.38 Add an Application Component Item (Step 1 of 3).

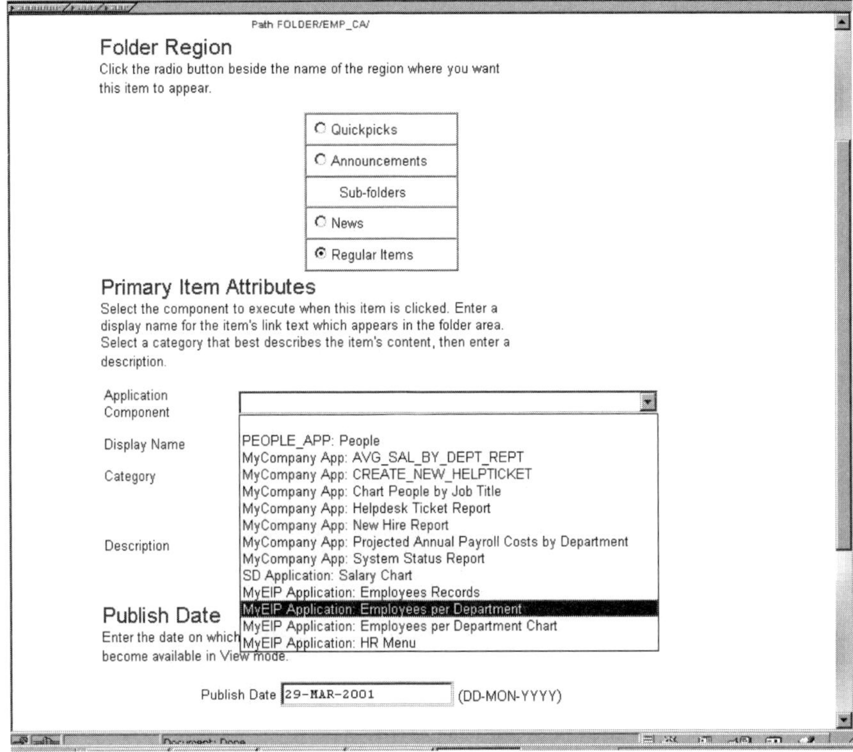

Figure 8.39 Add an Application Component Item (Step 2 of 3).

Click on "Finish". The content area is displayed with the new application component item added to the folder.

Content Area Page

When you create a new content area, a page is created automatically and attached to the new content area. You can edit this page, choose another page, or create a new page and attach it to the content area. Click on the "Administration" link in the folder dashboard to display the Content Area Administration page; under the Content Area Managers section, click on the Content Area icon to display the Content Area properties. You can also click on the Administration icon on the top of the page (Figure 8.40). Click on the Page tab in the Content Area properties to display the page name of the content area (Figure 8.41). By clicking on the "Edit" button, you can reconfigure the content area regions (Figure 8.42).

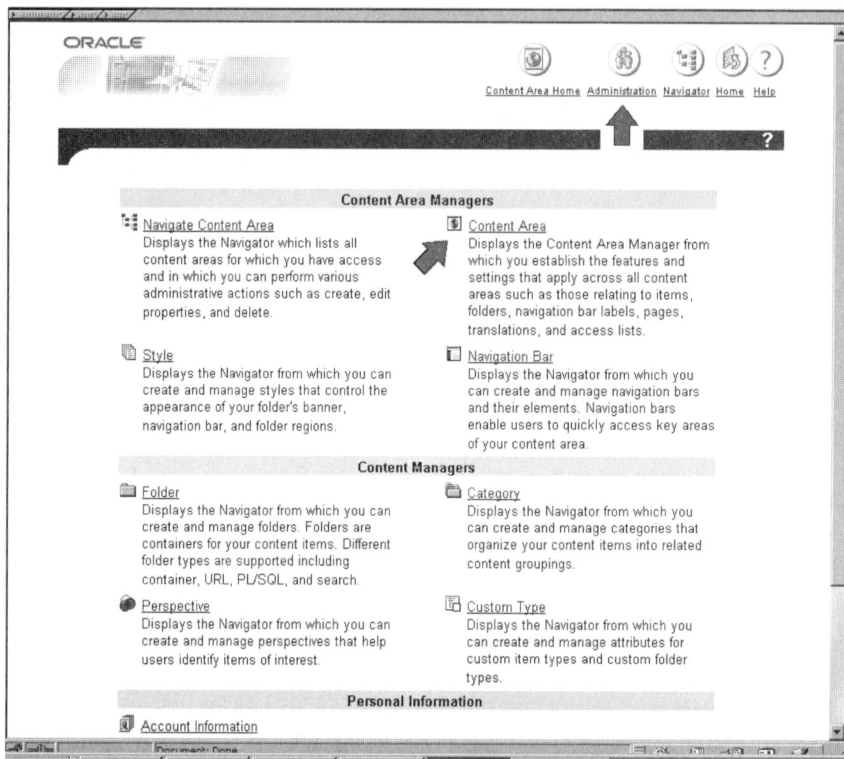

Figure 8.40 Content Area Managers.

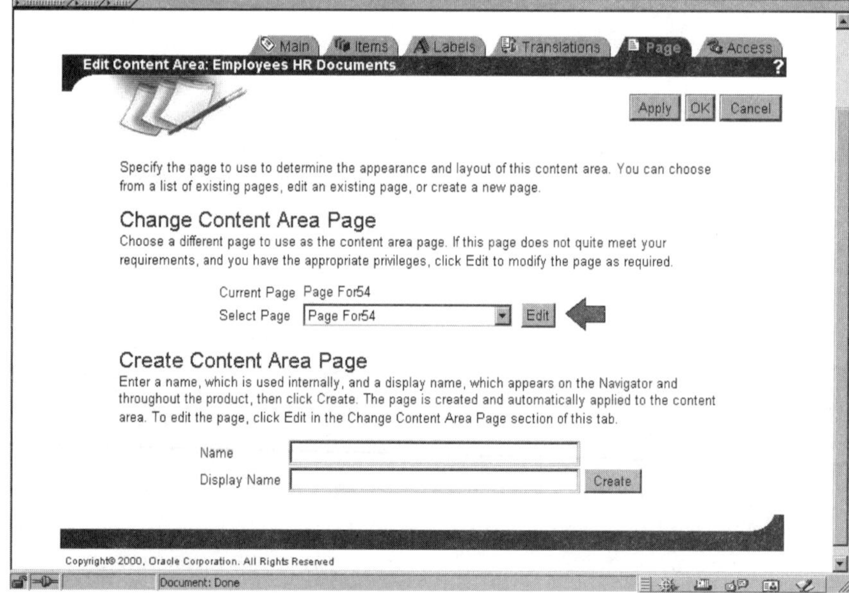

Figure 8.41 Edit Content Area: Page Tab.

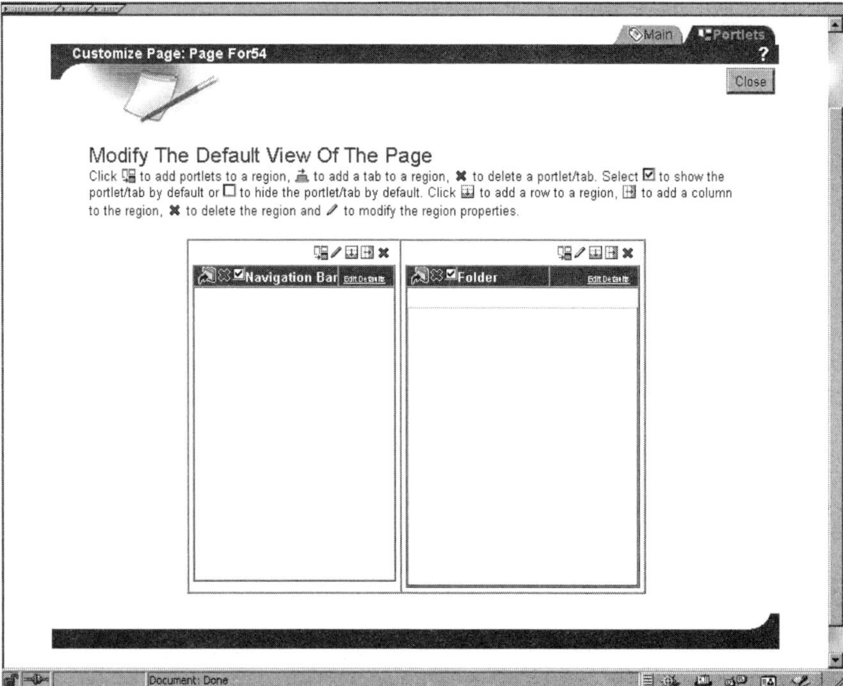

Figure 8.42 Edit Content Area: Page Tab: Edit Page.

Default Item Types and Attributes

To add an item to an Oracle Portal content area folder, the first step is choosing the item type. Based on the item type, the Item creation wizard prompts you with the related properties. The default preinstalled item types in Oracle Portal are File, Text, URL, Folder Link, Image/Imagemap, Zip File, PL/SQL, Java Application, and Application Component. Table 8.5 describes attributes that are available for the default Oracle Portal item types.

Extending Item Types

Oracle default item types are limited to the default attributes assigned to them, which means that you cannot add another attribute to a default item type. If you wish to append additional attributes to a default item type, you can create your own custom (i.e., extended) item types. These new attributes can represent business-related data items, as illustrated in the example described in this section.

Table 8.5 Oracle Portal Default Item Types and Their Attributes

Attribute	File	Text	URL	Folder Link	PL/ SQL	App. Com.[1]	Image/ Map	Java App.[2]	Zip File
Folder Region	X	X	X	X	X	X	X	X	X
File Name(s)	X						X	X	X
Display Name	X	X	X	X	X	X	X	X	X
Category	X	X	X	X	X	X	X	X	X
Description	X	X	X	X	X	X	X	X	X
Initial Page Name/Type								X	
Publish Date	X	X	X	X	X	X	X	X	X
Expiration Period	X	X	X	X	X	X	X	X	X
PL/SQL Execute Options					X				
Perspectives	X	X	X	X	X	X	X	X	X
Image	X	X	X	X	X	X		X	X
Image Alignment	X	X	X	X	X	X		X	X
Basic Search Keywords	X	X	X	X	X	X	X	X	X
Author	X	X	X	X	X	X	X	X	X
Check-Out	X	X	X	X	X	X	X	X	X
Hide Item	X	X	X	X	X	X	X	X	X
Link that displays item in folder area		X	X		X	X			
Item displayed directly in folder area		X	X		X	X			
Link that displays item in full browser		X	X		X	X			
Link that displays item in new browser window		X	X		X	X			
Display Parameter Form						X			

[1]Application Component
[2]Java Application t

You can create custom item types in two ways:

1. Create a new item type based on a default item type where the default is copied along with its related attributes. Then you can extend the copied item type by creating additional attributes.
2. Create an item type that is not based on any default item type. In this case, the item type begins with just basic attributes, such as title, category, and perspectives. Then you can assign additional attributes to it.

Creating Attributes

To be able to extend the default item types provided by Oracle Portal, you need to create new attributes first. Attributes are custom fields that the site administrator creates to capture more data about an item. These attributes can be displayed when an item or folder is displayed. These attributes can also be passed to external procedures to integrate your Web site with other applications. You can reuse attributes that you create across multiple item types.

You can create custom objects either under shared objects to be accessed by other portal developers, or you can create them under the content area to be accessed by these content area administrators. This section uses the first method.

To create a new attribute, go to the Oracle Portal Navigator. Click on the Content Areas tab, click on the Shared Objects "Contents" action link, and then click on the "Custom Types" link. Click on the "Create" action link on the right side of the "Attributes" entry (Figure 8.43).

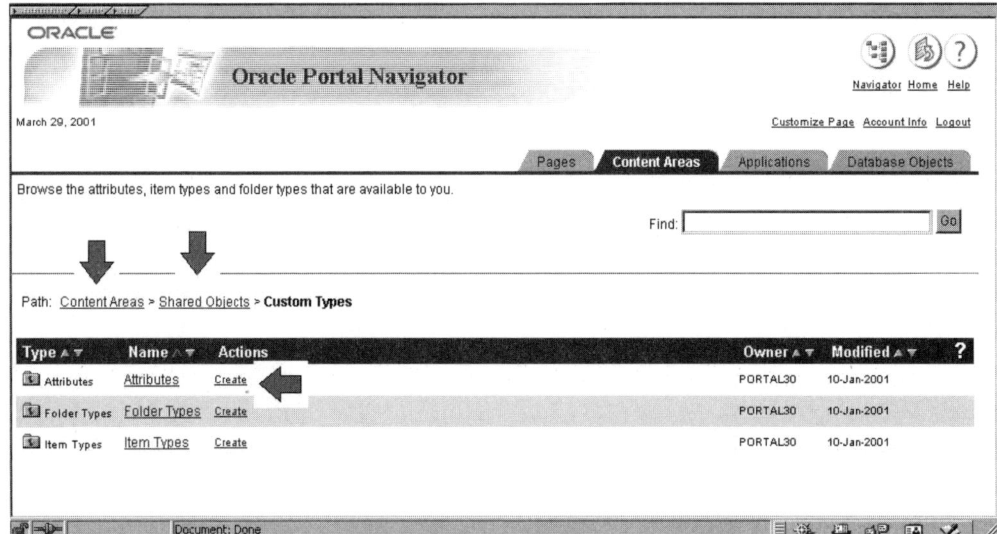

Figure 8.43 Oracle Portal Navigator: Content Areas: Shared Objects.

For the exercise, specify the name "EMPNO" as the name of the new attribute. You can choose one of the following attribute types as the basis of your new attribute: text, URL, file, date, number, boolean, PL/SQL, and Oracle Portal component. Choose the "Number" attribute type (Figure 8.44). Click on the "Create" button to create the attribute. When the attribute is created, you can click on the name of the attribute to edit it. You can specify a List of Values for the attribute.

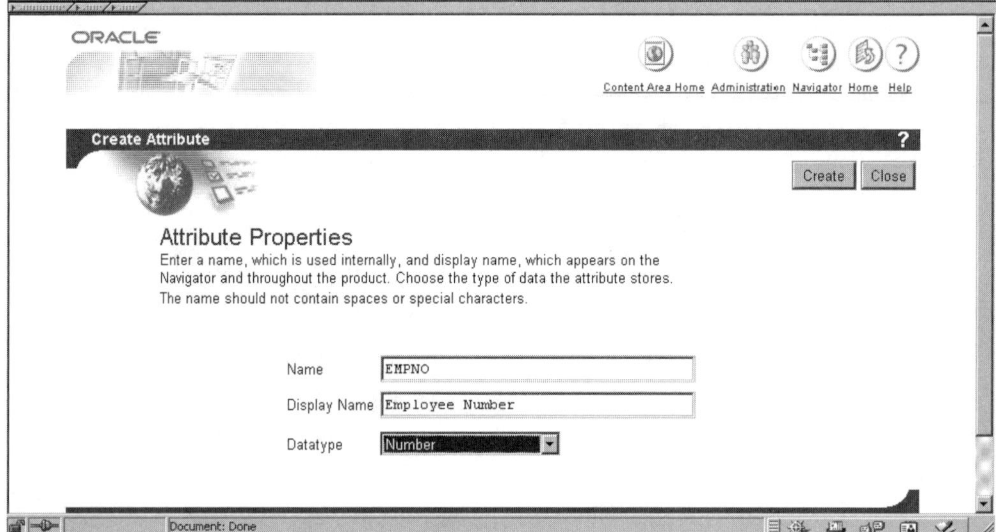

Figure 8.44 Creating an Attribute.

Creating Custom Item Types

After creating custom attributes, you can create custom item types that include these custom attributes. To create a custom item type, click on the "Create" link on the right side of the "Item Types" entry in the Oracle Navigator. You need to specify a name, display name, and a base item type (Figure 8.45). Click the "Create" button to submit the new item type properties. Then you can click on the new item type name link to edit it (Figure 8.46).

Important

The name of an item type must have no spaces and no special characters, with a maximum of 30 characters.

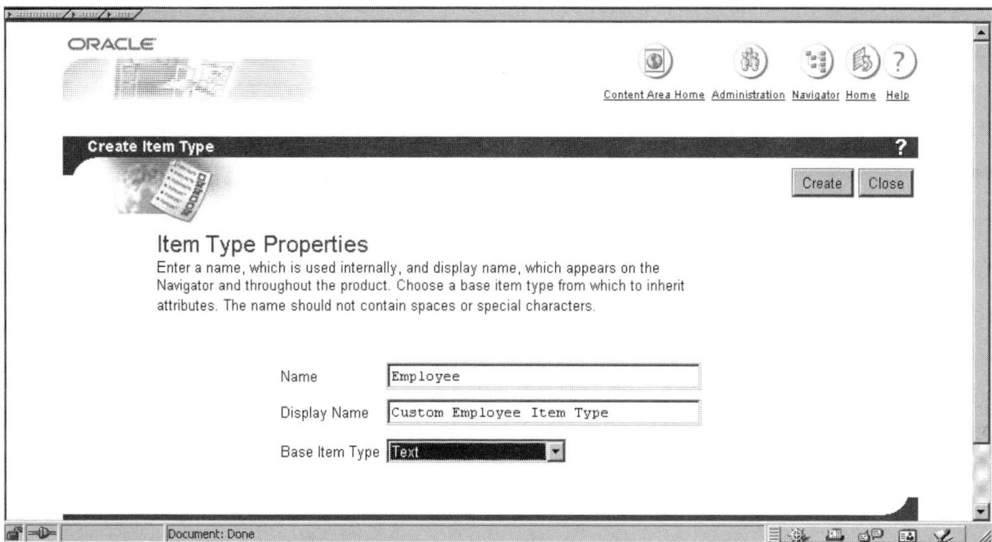

Figure 8.45 Creating an Oracle Portal Custom Item Type.

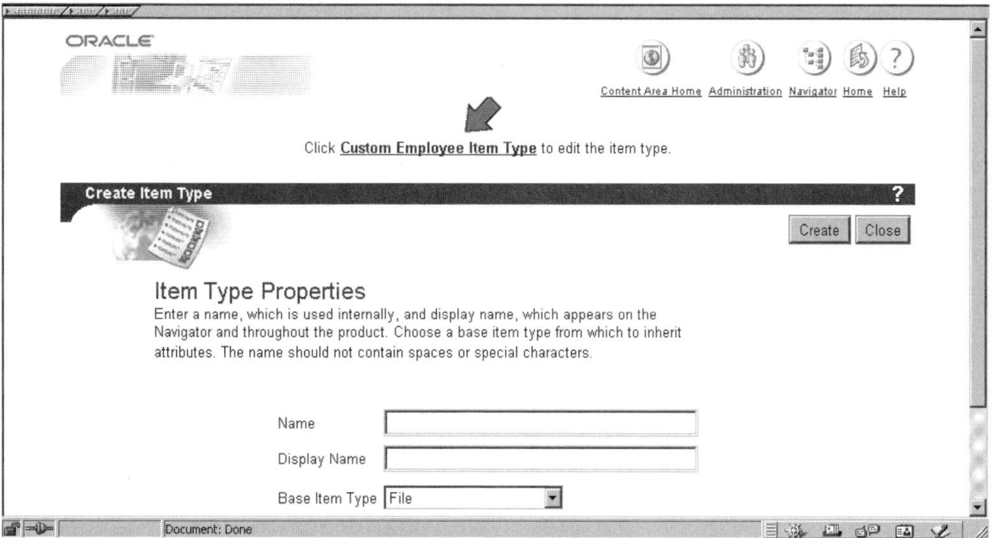

Figure 8.46 Editing Oracle Portal Custom Item Type.

Click on the Attributes tab to add the EMPNO custom attribute to the new custom EMPLOYEE item type (Figure 8.47). When you click on the "Apply" button, you will be able to specify a default value for the custom attribute.

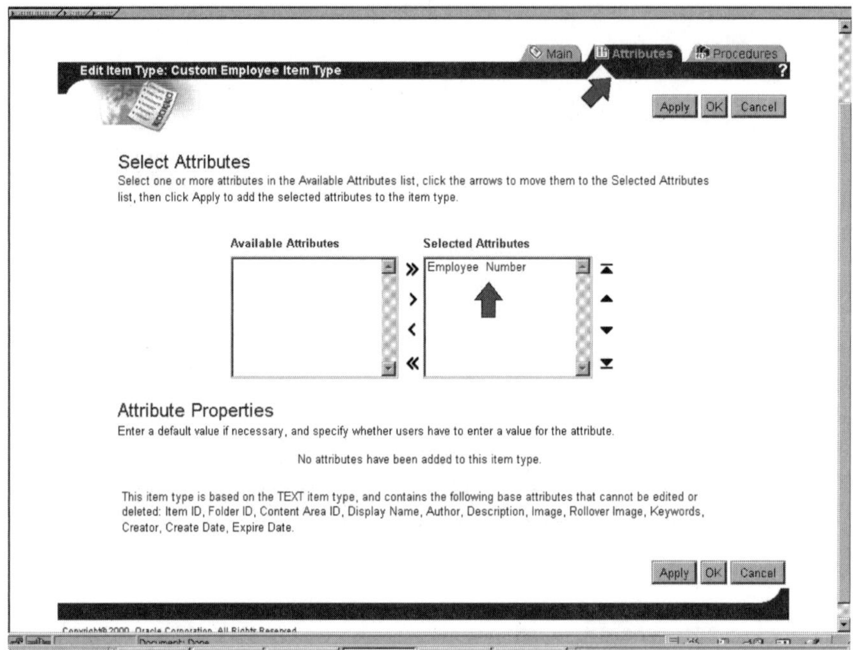

Figure 8.47 Editing an Oracle Portal Custom Item Type: Attributes Tab.

For the practice, you need to create a small procedure that retrieves the name and job of a certain employee. Run SQL*Plus, connect as myeip_owner schema, and run the following PL/SQL code:

```
Create or replace procedure myeip_emp(empno_p in number) is
      name_v varchar2(100);
begin
      select ename||', '||job into name_v
      from scott.emp
      where empno = empno_p;
      htp.bold(name_v);
end;
/
grant execute on myeip_emp to public;
```

Then connect as portal30 schema and run the following PL/SQL code:

```
create public synonym myeip_emp for myeip_owner.myeip_emp;
```

After adding the custom attribute to the Item Type Attributes, click on the Procedures tab to attach the created procedure to the new custom item type (Figure 8.48). You need to specify the procedure name (or its synonym), the link text, and you need to select the "Display Procedure Results with Item" check box. Finally, before pushing the "Apply" button, you need to select the employee number and its matching procedure parameter in the attributes. When you click on the "Apply" button, this procedure call is added to the existing procedure calls (Figure 8.49). Click on the "OK" button to finish creating the custom item type. Now you can create new items based on it.

Navigate to your content area, and add a new item into your News region. If you have an existing item in the News region, click on the add an item after this item icon. Choose the Custom Item Type (i.e., EMPLOYEE; Figure 8.50). In the third step you need to specify a value for the custom attribute (i.e., EMPNO=7839; Figure 8.51). Click the "OK" button to finish creating the item. Then view your content area to display the new added custom item (Figure 8.52).

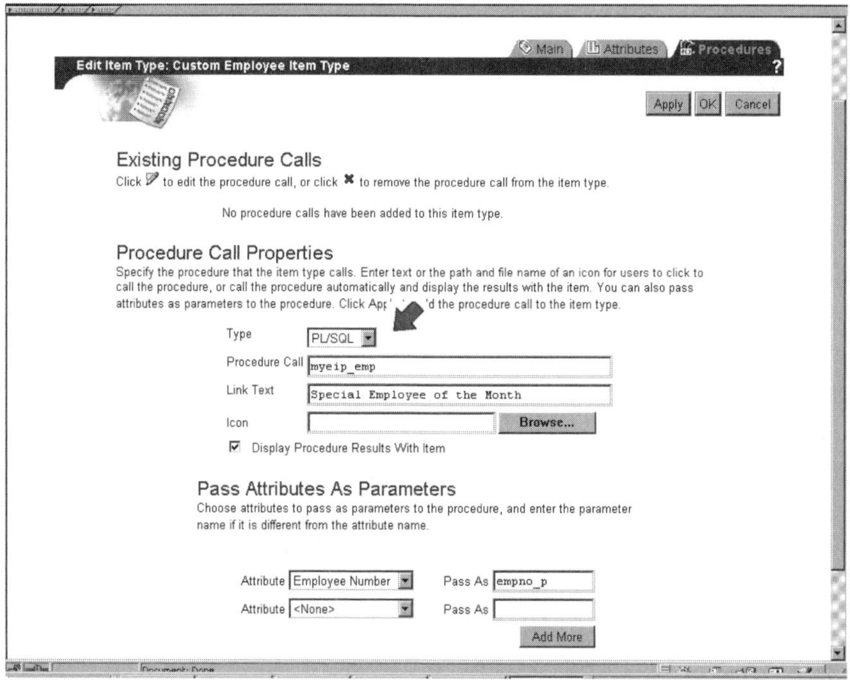

Figure 8.48 Editing an Oracle Portal Custom Item Type: Procedures Tab.

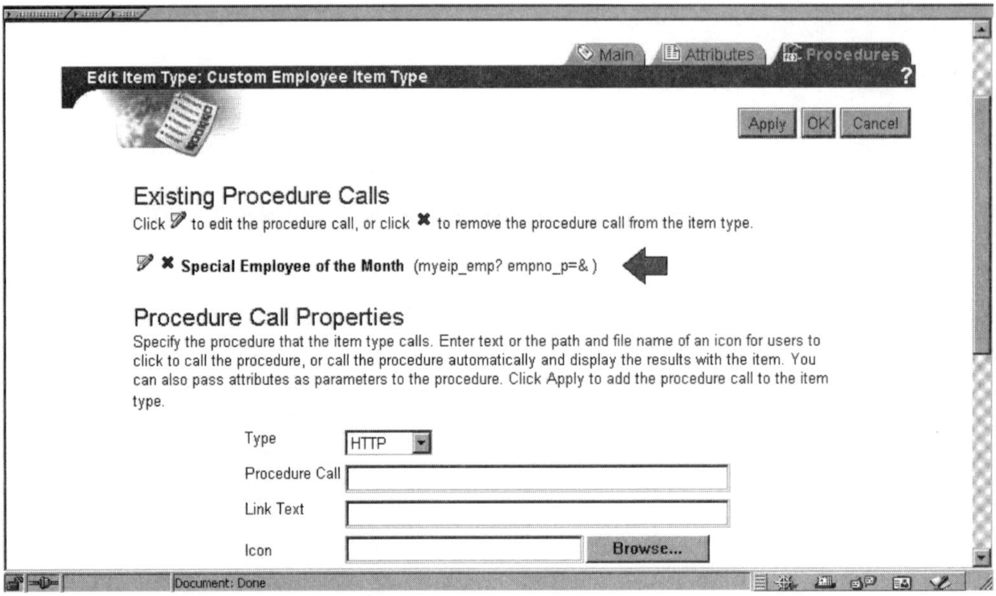

Figure 8.49 Editing an Oracle Portal Custom Item Type: Procedures Tab (Apply).

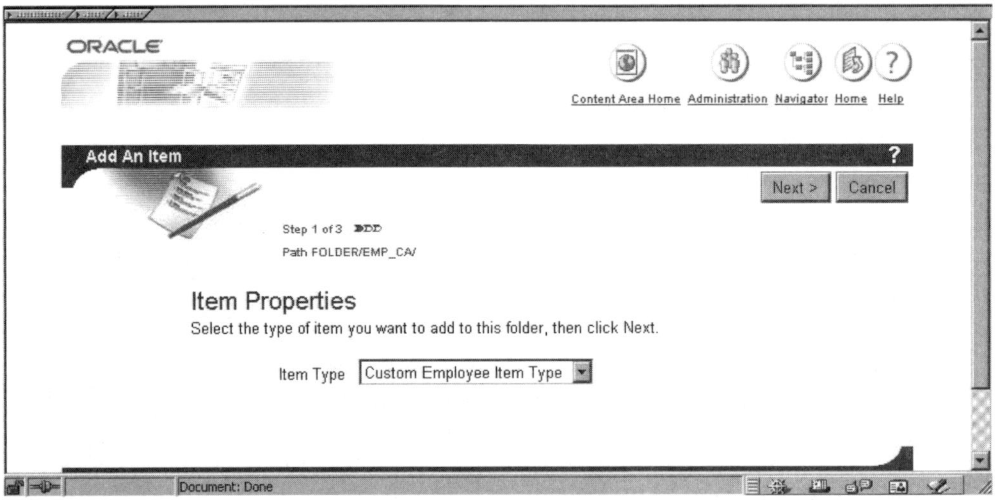

Figure 8.50 Add an Item (Step 1 of 3).

You can easily add more items of the same type by changing the EMPNO attribute for each. The Display Options in Figure 8.51 is ignored because in Figure 8.48 the check box "Display Procedure Results with Item" is selected.

Chapter 9 discusses more advanced topics on how to customize your folders and navigation bars inside content areas.

Secondary Item Attributes

Choose perspective(s) for this item. Enter the location of the image file and select the image alignment. Edit the keyword(s) that will help locate the item during a search, and edit the author name. Set document control on the item so that it may be shared between users via a check-in and check-out process. You can also choose to hide the item in View mode.

Perspectives — Available Perspectives / Displayed Perspectives

Image — Browse...

Image Alignment — Bottom

Basic Search Keywords

Author — PORTAL30

Enable Item Check-Out

Hide Item

Employee Number — 7839

Display Options

Choose how the text item displays when the item is clicked: in the right pane of the browser window, directly below the item's display name, in your current browser window (no navigation bar), or in another browser window.

- Link That Displays Item In Folder Area
- Item Displayed Directly In Folder Area
- Link That Displays Item In Full Browser Window
- Link That Displays Item In New Browser Window

Document: Done

Figure 8.51 Add an Item (Step 3 of 3).

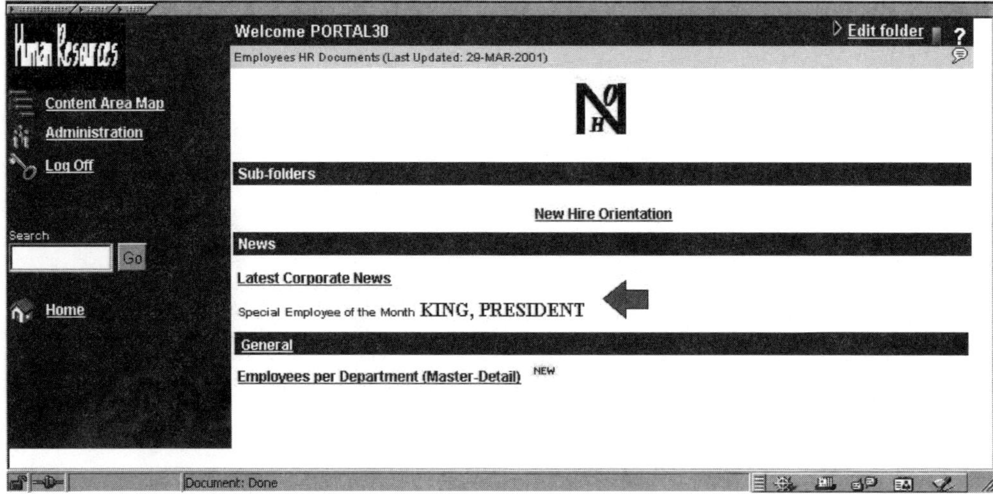

Figure 8.52 Content Area Home Page.

CHAPTER 9

Content Area Administration

Introduction

This chapter explains the default folder types available in Oracle Portal content areas. It also explains how you can create custom folder types. Content area categories and perspectives are covered as well as the basic and advanced search capabilities in Oracle Portal. We will explore navigation bars and how they can be customized and displayed in portal pages, and, lastly, we will explore Oracle Portal styles and how they can be used to change the interface of your content areas.

Default Folder Types

As seen in Chapter 8, when adding a folder to an Oracle Portal content area, you need to select the folder type. In each Oracle Portal content area, you can create one or more folders of the following types:

- Container folders: They hold content area items. You can build a tree hierarchy of folders to organize the items in the content area just as you would organize your files in your hard disk.
- PL/SQL folders: Here you can specify associated PL/SQL code. This PL/SQL code can generate HTML, which is rendered when the folder is selected for viewing.
- Search folders: They are based on an Oracle Portal search. The search criterion is saved and executed each time the folder is rendered.
- URL folders: These folders provide the user with a method of linking external URLs into the Oracle Portal folder hierarchy.

Chapter 8 explained creating a container folder; this chapter explains creating a PL/SQL folder.

PL/SQL Folder

To create a new PL/SQL folder, you need to edit your content area. Click on the "Create Folder" link in the folder dashboard. Choose PL/SQL as the Folder Type. In the next step you need to enter the PL/SQL code of your folder along with other folder properties (e.g., Name, Display Name, etc.; Figure 9.1). The following PL/SQL code displays an HTML table that lists different jobs and the number of employees in each job.

```
begin
  htp.p('<CENTER>');
  htp.p('<TABLE BORDER>');
  htp.p('<TR><TD><B><CENTER>Job</B>'||
        '</CENTER></TD><TD><B>'||
        'Num.Of Emp.'||
        '</B></TD></TR>');
  for job_rec in (
      select    job, count(*) emp_cnt
      from      scott.emp
      group by  job)
```

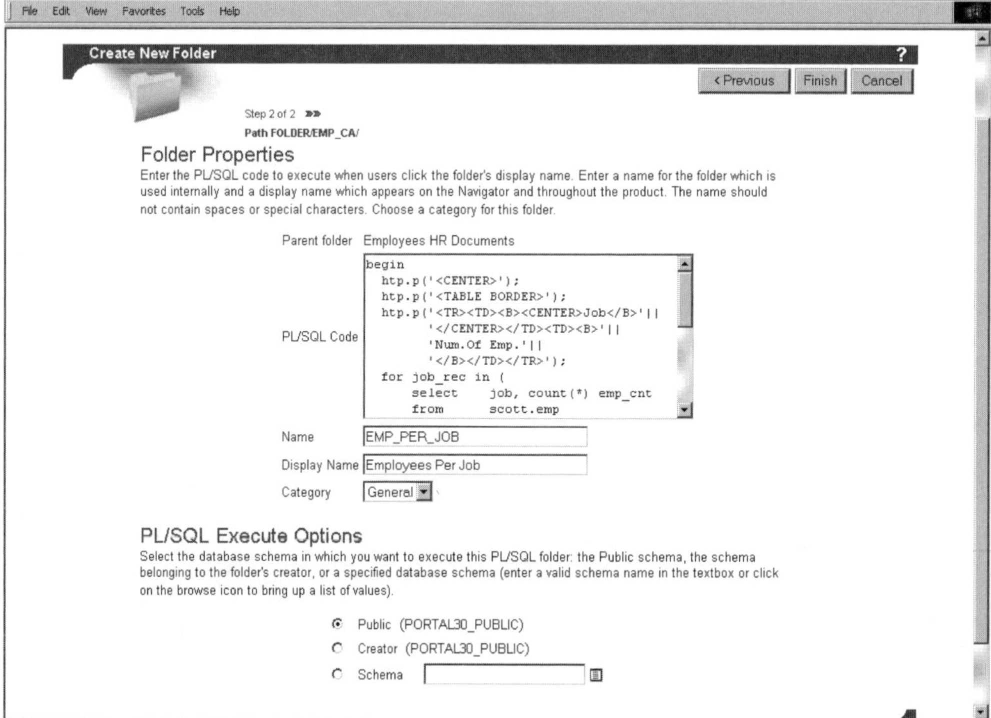

Figure 9.1 Content Area: Create New PL/SQL Folder (Step 2 of 2).

```
loop
    htp.p('<TR>');
    htp.p('<TD> '||job_rec.job||
          '</TD><TD><CENTER> '||
          to_char(job_rec.emp_cnt)||
          '</CENTER></TD>');
    htp.p('</TR>');
end loop;
```

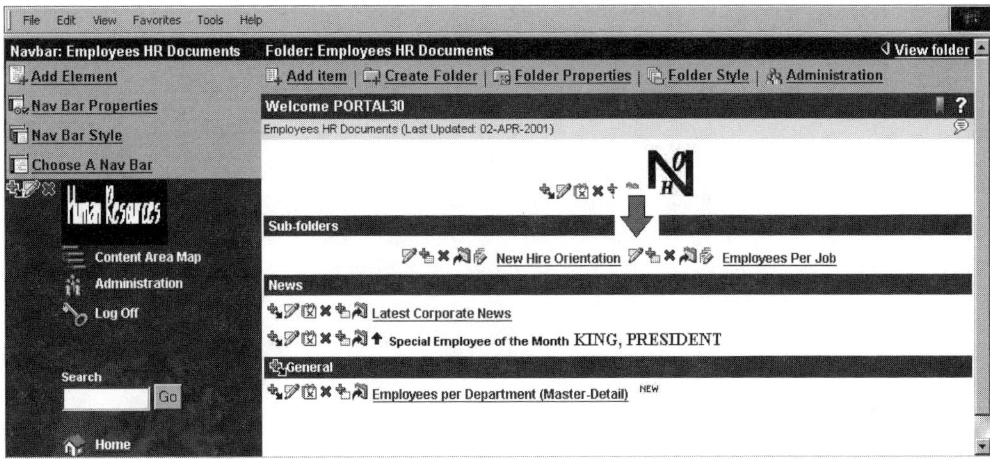

Figure 9.2 Content Area: Edit Folder Properties.

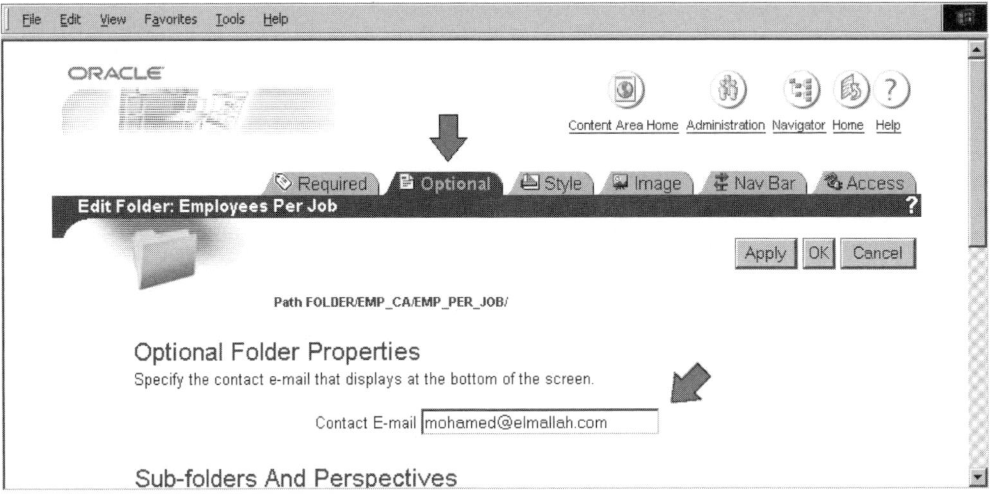

Figure 9.3 Edit Folder Properties: Optional Tab.

```
    htp.p('</TABLE>');
    htp.p('</CENTER>');
  end;
```

Click on the "Finish" button to create the folder. Then the folder link is displayed in the Content Area subfolders region (Figure 9.2) where you can edit the folder properties by clicking on its edit icon. Click on the Optional tab to enter a contact email address (Figure 9.3). This email is displayed at the bottom of the new PL/SQL folder output.

Creating Custom Folder Types

All folder types share most of the attributes. You can add your own folder attributes to represent your business data. The objective of this section's practice is to create folders that are based on a customized folder type. These folders look up the value of the folder attributes on the Internet using the Yahoo search engine.

Start by creating a new custom attribute; you can refer to Chapter 8 for details. The new attribute name is "p" (Figure 9.4). The next step is to create a new custom folder type (Figure 9.5). You can go to the Custom Types either by drilling down the Portal Navigator or by clicking on the Dashboard Administration icon, then the Custom Type icon.

The next step is to add the Search Parameter custom attribute to the new custom folder type in the Attributes tab of the Edit Folder Type screen (Figure 9.6). Then you define how the folder

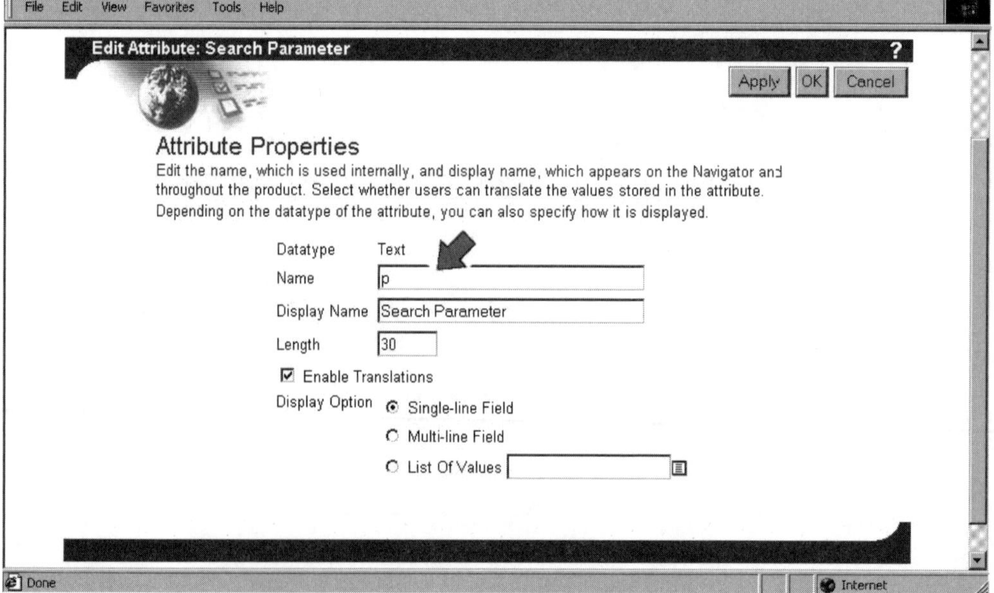

Figure 9.4 Custom Attribute Properties.

File Edit View Favorites Tools Help

Main | Attributes | Procedures

Edit Folder Type: Web Folder ?

Apply | OK | Cancel

Folder Type Properties

Edit the name, which is used internally, and display name, which appears on the Navigator and throughout the product. Enter a description to provide additional information about the folder type, and the path and file name of an image to use as the folder type's icon. The description is visible only when you edit the folder type.

Base Folder Type	Container
Name	WebFolder
Display Name	Web Folder
Description	
Icon	Browse...

Figure 9.5 Custom Folder Type: Main Tab.

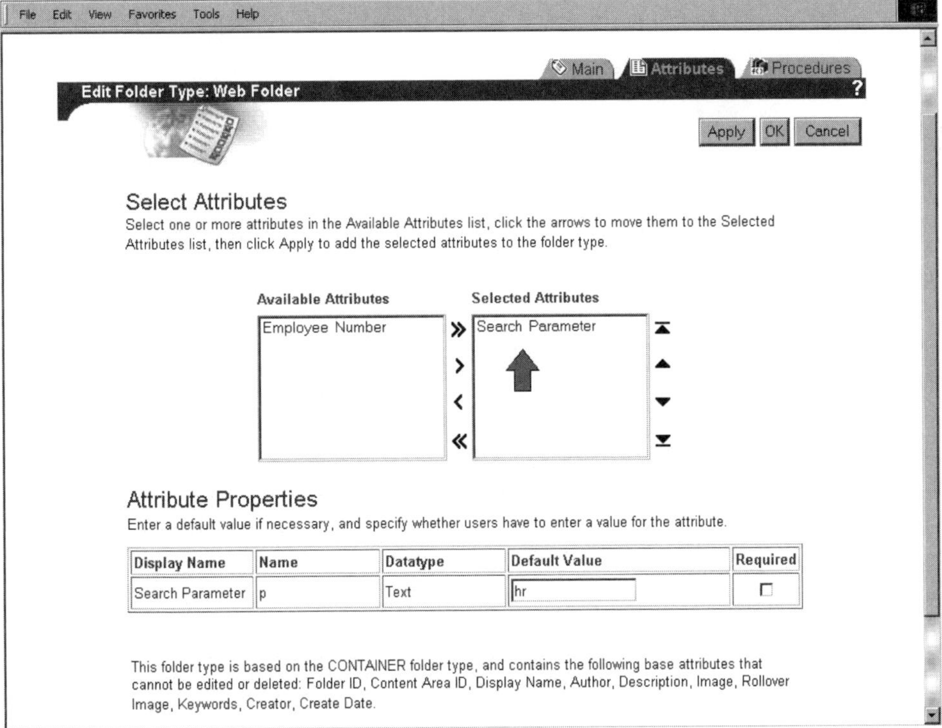

Figure 9.6 Custom Folder Type: Attributes Tab.

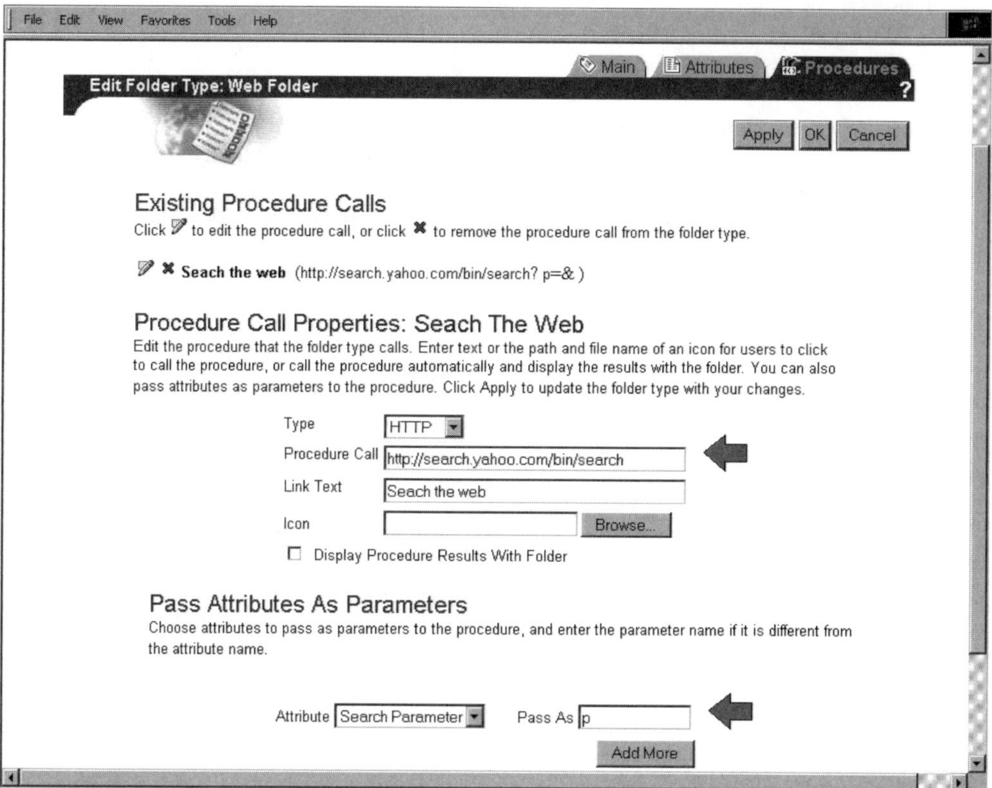

Figure 9.7 Custom Folder Type: Procedures Tab.

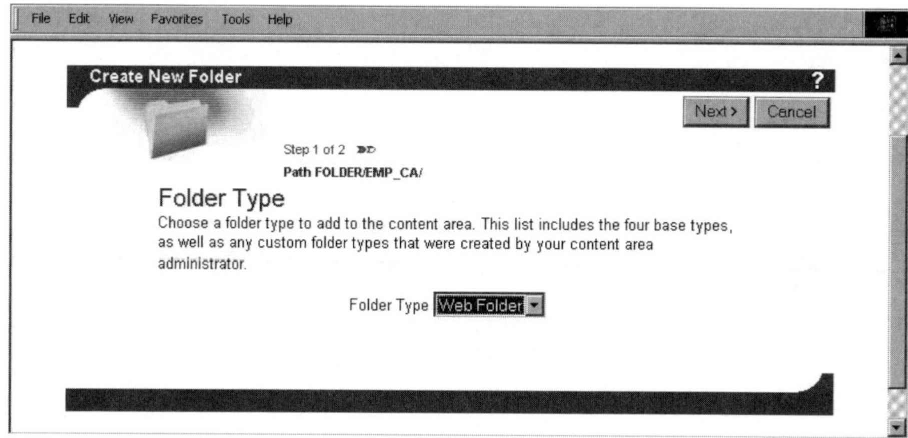

Figure 9.8 Content Area: Create New Folder.

uses the custom attribute value. You can attach PL/SQL and HTTP calls to your custom folder types, so when the folder is displayed these calls are executed with the attributes' values. Add an HTTP call to search for the Search Parameter attribute value on the Web using the Yahoo Internet search engine (Figure 9.7).

Now your custom folder type is ready to be used. You can add new folders of this type into your content area (Figure 9.8). In step 2, specify a name and display name for your new folder (e.g., Lookup Folder), and then click the "Finish" button.

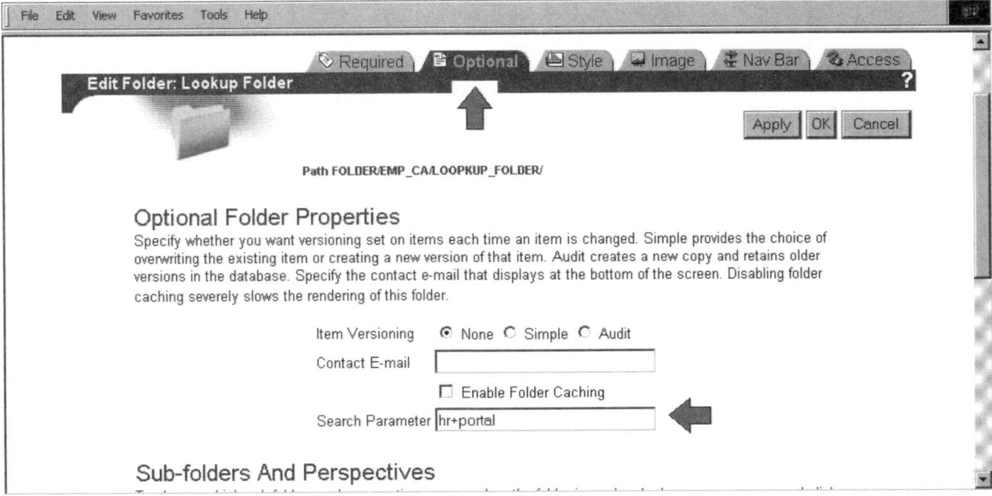

Figure 9.9 Edit Folder: Optional Tab.

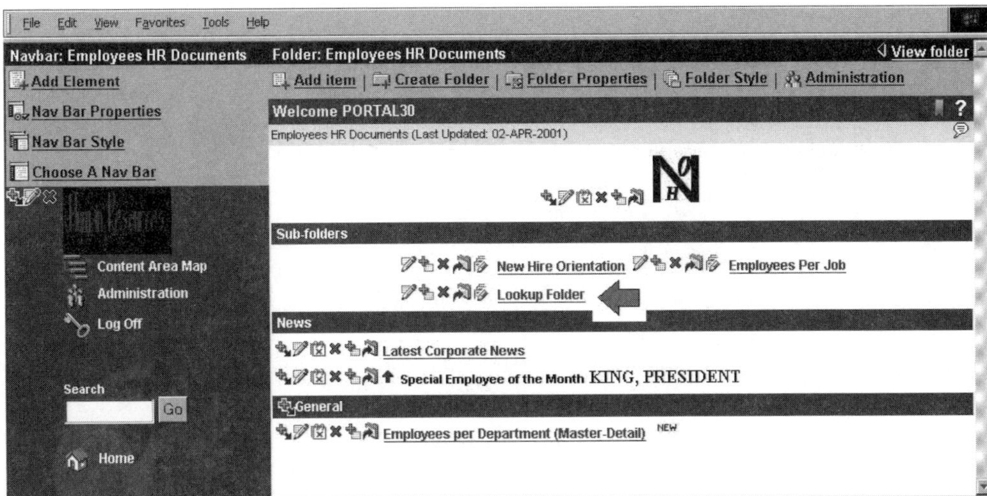

Figure 9.10 Content Area Display.

Edit your new folder to specify a value for your search parameter attribute. These are the words that the folder is going to look for on the Web (Figure 9.9 in the Optional tab). Separate the words by "+" so they can be passed to the HTTP search URL specified earlier in the customer folder type. When you are finished editing the new folder, click the "OK" button to test the new folder in your content area (Figure 9.10). Click on the new folder name (e.g., Lookup Folder) to drill down to the new folder. Click on the "Search the Web" link to search for the two words "hr" and "portal" on the Web (Figure 9.11).

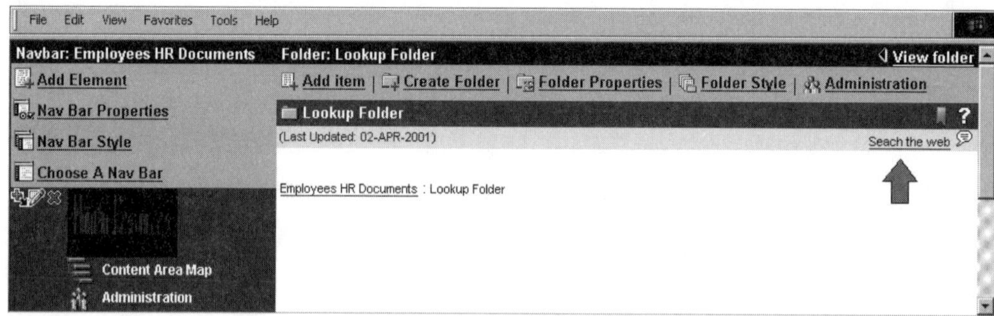

Figure 9.11 Content Area: Folder Display.

Oracle Portal Search

You can allow your portal end-users to search the portal contents. There are three levels of searches provided with Oracle Portal: basic search, advanced search, and *inter*Media Text search. This section describes the basic and advanced searches. The Oracle Portal integration with *inter*Media Text is covered later in Chapter 16.

To understand the search capability in Oracle Portal, let's start by explaining two components of content areas that are used to organize and search the portal contents. These two components are categories and perspectives.

Categories

By default, your new content area does not contain any categories except the predefined general category. All the folders and items created so far in the content area are categorized under the general category. Create a new category by clicking on the "Create" link on the right of the Categories node in the Oracle Portal Navigator, under your content area's contents. Click on the "Create" button to create the category (Figure 9.12). Then click on the category name to edit the category (Figure 9.13). You can continue to create more categories if you do not need to edit the category.

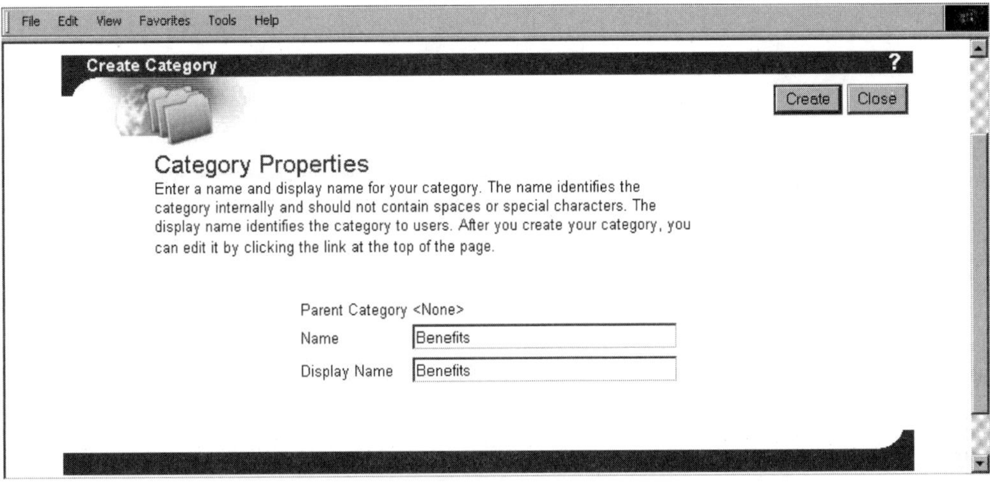

Figure 9.12 Create Category.

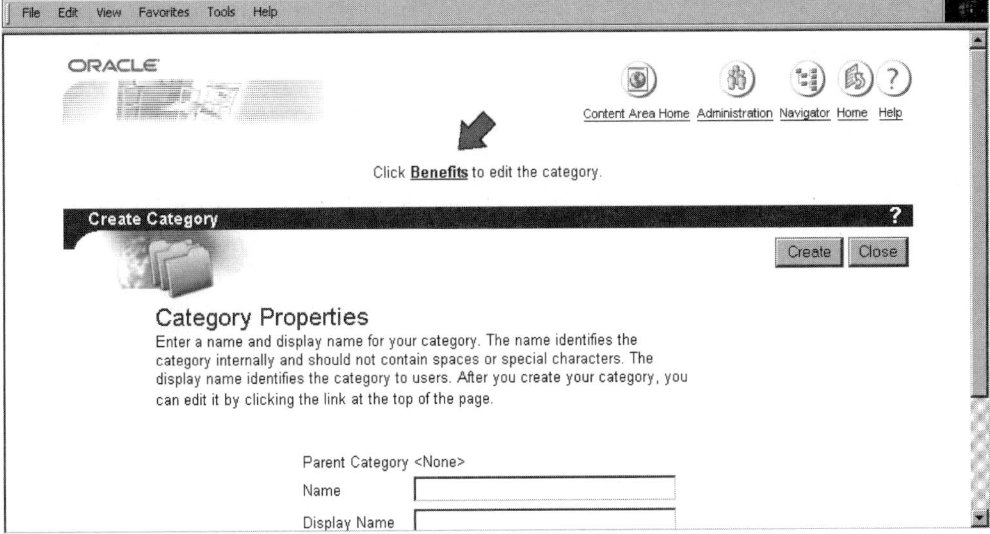

Figure 9.13 Category Created.

One powerful feature of categories is the ability to display the items of a certain category in a portlet. You can enable the category publishing option by selecting the "Publish As Portlet" check box. By default, when a category is published as a portlet, the portlet's style is the same as the content area's style. By selecting the "Use Page Style" check box, the category's portlet inherits the style of the page to which the portlet is being added (Figure 9.14).

File Edit View Favorites Tools Help

Main Image

Edit Category: Benefits

Apply OK Cancel

Path CATEGORY/EMP_CA/BENEFITS/

Category Properties

Enter a name and display name for your category. The name identifies the category internally and should not contain spaces or special characters. The display name identifies the category to users. Enter an optional description of the category, which only appears in the Category Manager.

Name BENEFITS

Display Name Benefits

Description

Portlet Properties

Select Publish As Portlet to include this category as a portlet on a page. To use the page style instead of the folder style when rendering the page, select Use Page Style. If you want the category to display a different name when used as a portlet, enter the Portlet Display Name.

Publish As Portlet

Use Page Style

Portlet Display Name Benefits

Figure 9.14 Edit Category: Main Tab.

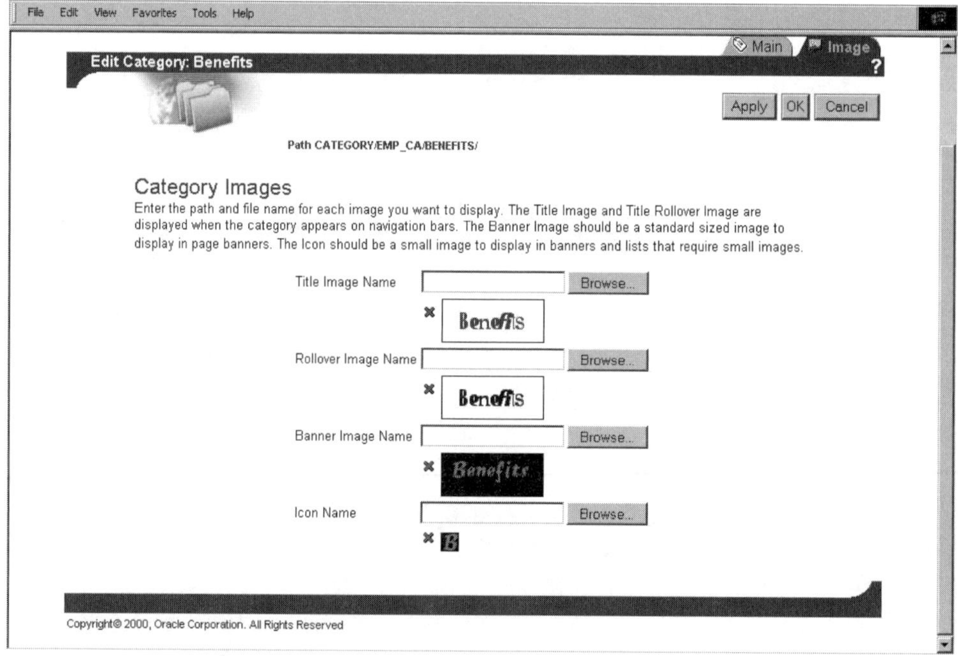

Figure 9.15 Edit Category: Image Tab.

Another powerful feature of categories is the ability to add a link for the category in the navigation bar. If the end-user wants to get all the information under a certain category, he or she clicks on that link. In the Image tab you can specify images to go with your category (Figure 9.15).

You can display the category items in the content area by clicking on the category name in the Oracle Portal Navigator (Figure 9.16). The Category Title image is displayed in the content area navigation bar when the category is added to the navigation bar (refer to the navigation bar section in this chapter). The Rollover image is displayed when the end-user moves the mouse arrow over the category Title image. The banner image is displayed in the category folder area, and the category icon is displayed in the category folder banner.

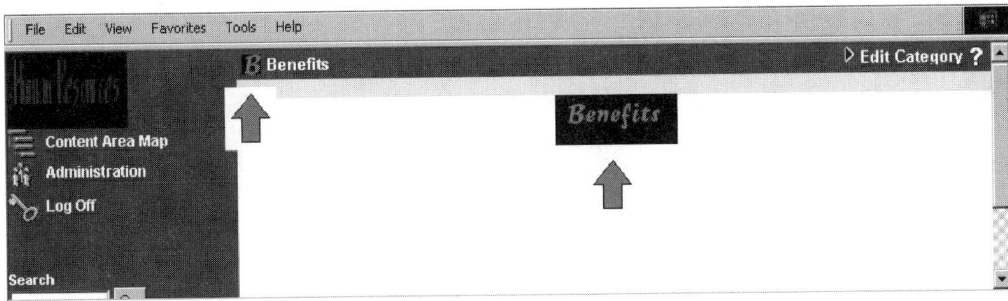

Figure 9.16 Content Area: Category Display.

Create another category named "New Hires", which we will use in the following section. You also need to edit its properties to publish it as a portlet.

Figure 9.17 Create Perspective.

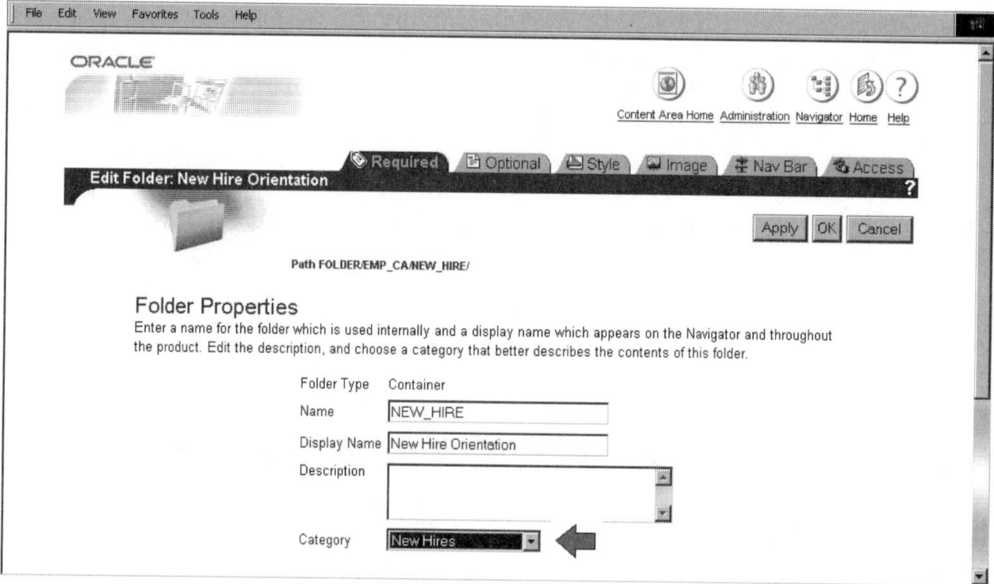

Figure 9.18 Edit Container Folder: Required Tab.

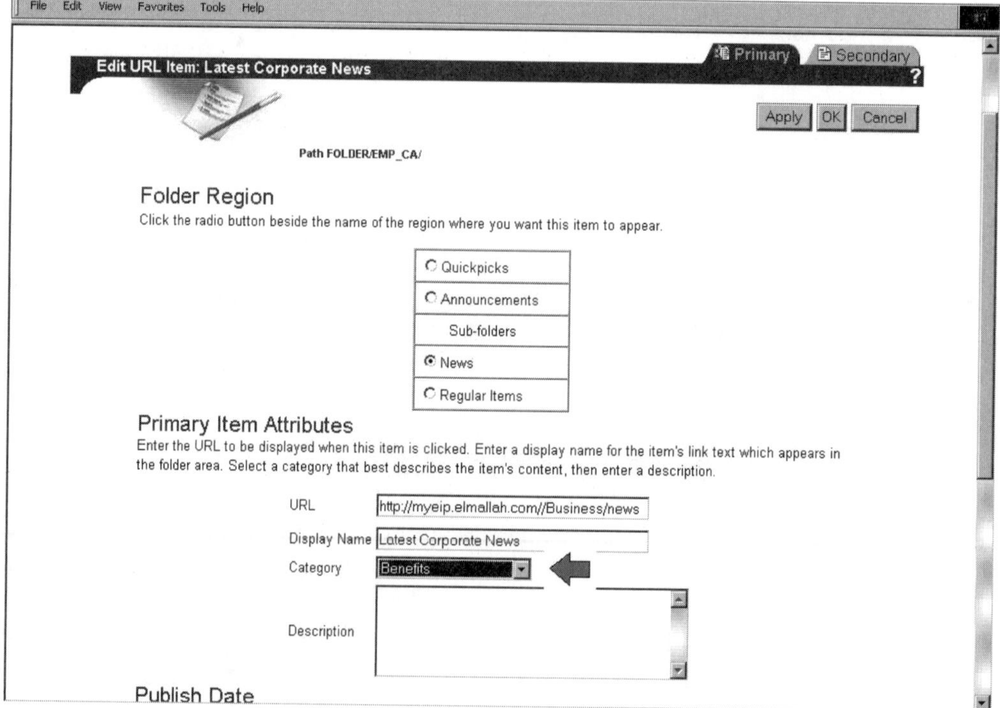

Figure 9.19 Edit URL Item: Primary Tab.

Perspectives

Now that you have created your categories that define the different types of information in your content area, you can create perspectives that classify information in your content area based on who accesses the information. Create perspectives (HR Employees, Managers, Top Guns) under your content area in the Oracle Portal Navigator (Figure 9.17).

Classifying Content Area Items

When your categories and perspectives are in place, you can start assigning existing and new content area items to them. You can assign a category to a folder by editing the folder properties (Figure 9.18). You can also assign the content area items to categories by editing the item properties (Figure 9.19). You can assign one or more perspectives to a folder by editing the folder's Optional tab properties (Figure 9.20). You can assign one or more perspectives to an item by editing the item's Secondary tab properties (Figure 9.21).

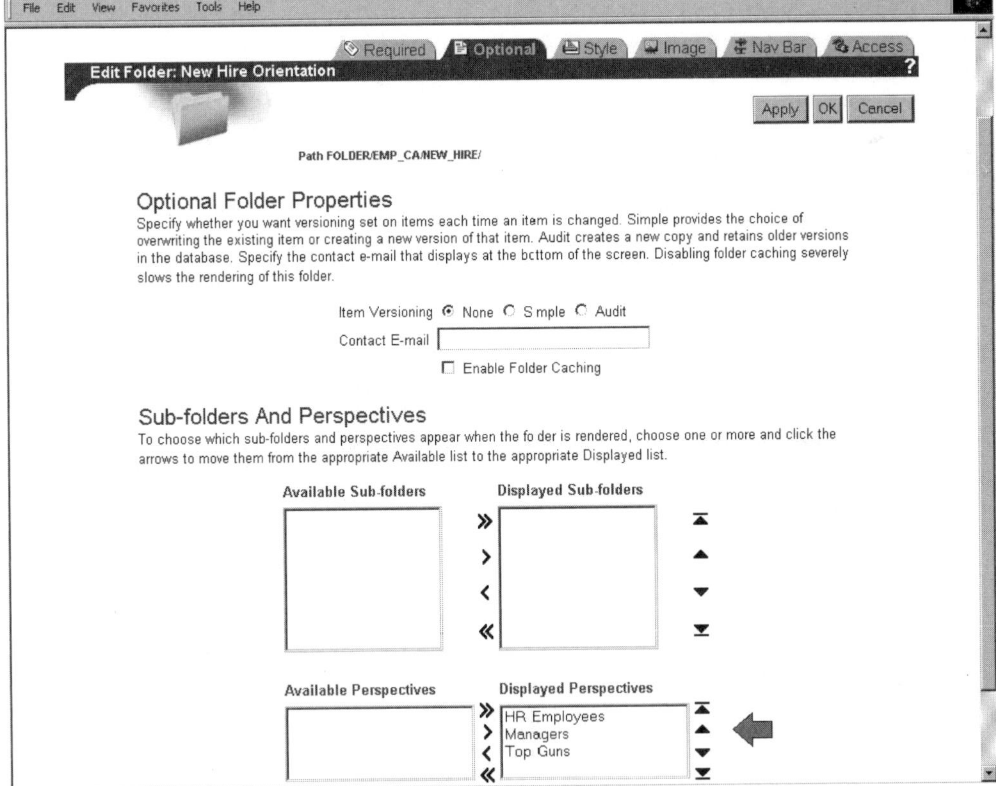

Figure 9.20 Edit Container Folder: Optional Tab.

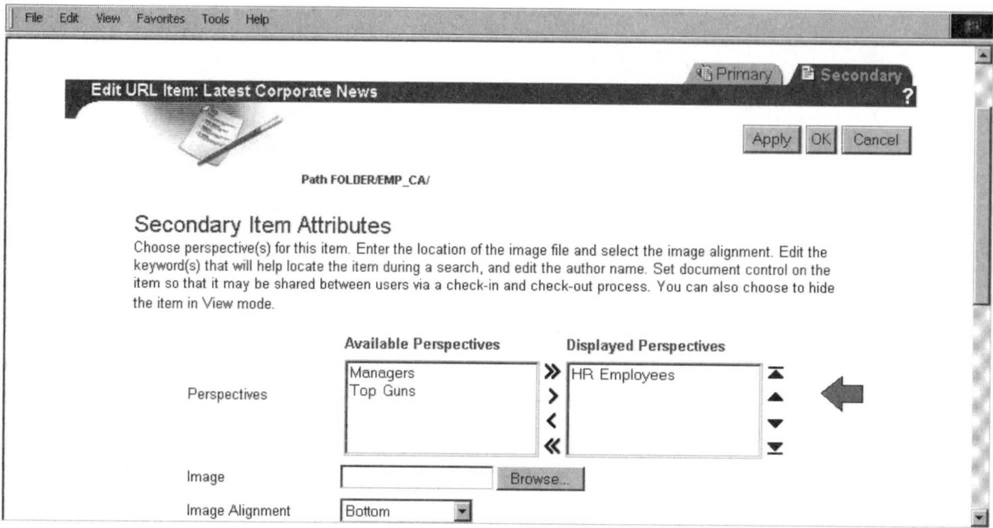

Figure 9.21 Edit URL Item: Secondary Tab.

Publishing Categories

When you click on the category name in the Oracle Portal Navigator, the folders and items classified under the category are displayed (Figure 9.22). Now you can add the category to your portal page. You should see the published categories and perspectives in the Portlet Repository under the content area name, because you have selected their "Publish As Portlet" check boxes (Figure 9.23).

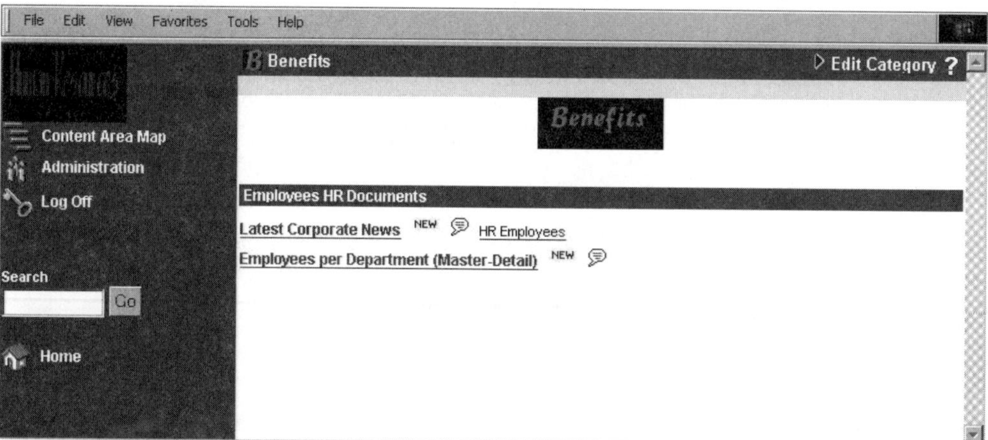

Figure 9.22 Edit URL Item: Secondary Tab.

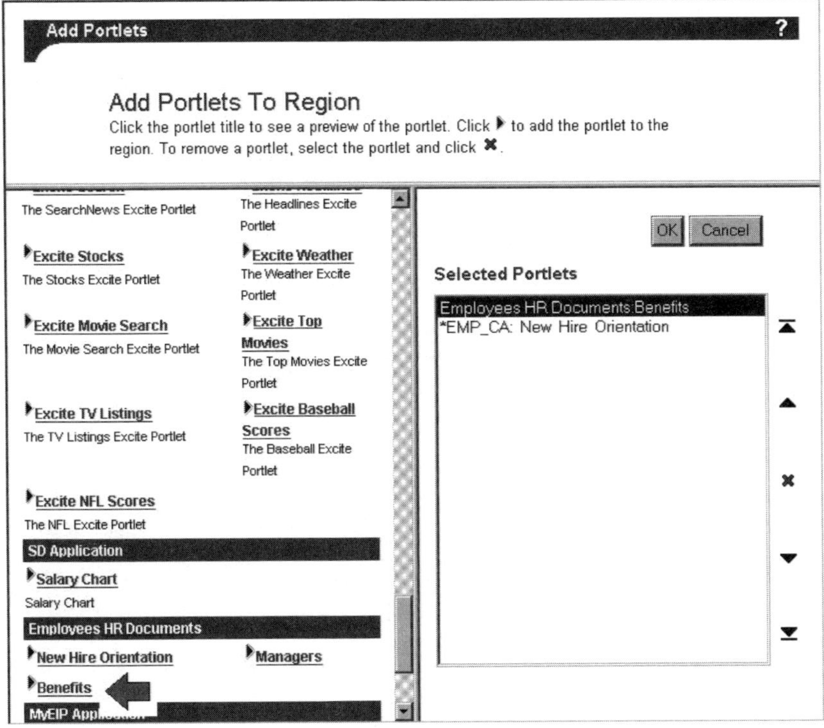

Figure 9.23 Edit Page: Add Portlet: Portlet Repository.

Note

The items displayed in your category may vary from the figure, depending on which items you have edited to categorize them under the Benefits category.

After adding the category portlet to your page, you can click on any of the items of the category to display it. Also, you can click on the content area name to display the content area (Figure 9.24).

Publishing Perspectives

You can publish a perspective by selecting its "Publish As Portlet" check box. Then, the perspective is available under the content area in the Portlet Repository. Another method of publishing both categories and perspectives is to add a generic portlet for each. This portlet has a category and perspective name parameter. The end-user can set this parameter value to display certain

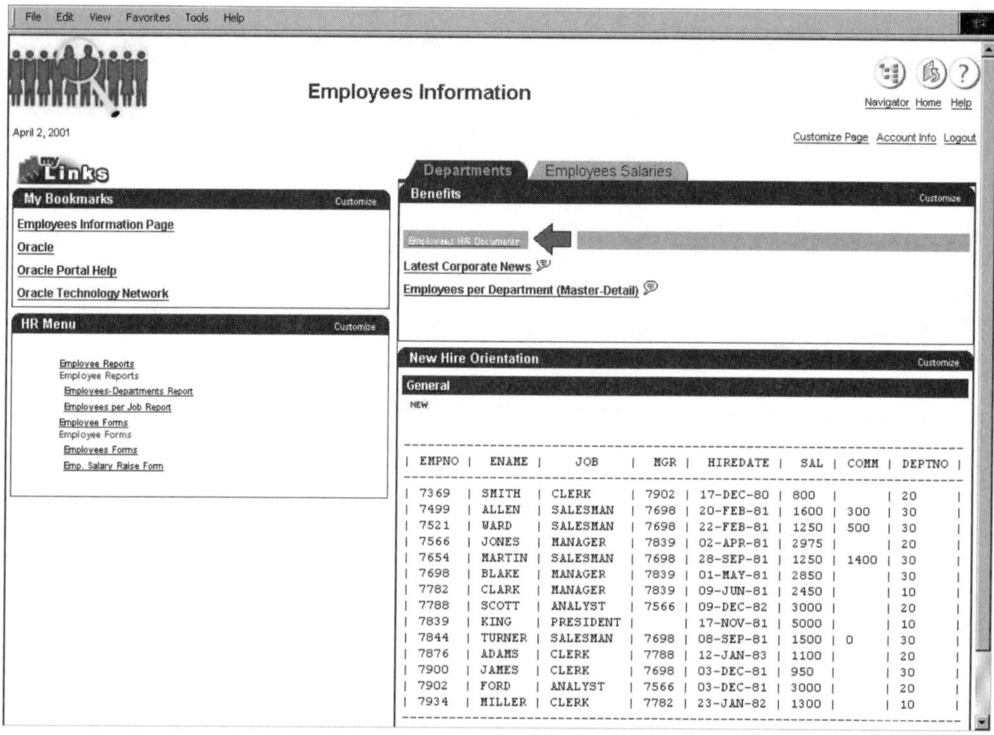

Figure 9.24 Display Page with a Category Portlet.

category or perspective contents. The following example demonstrates this feature for perspectives; similar steps can be followed for categories.

Start by editing your page, and then click on the add portlet icon to display the Portlet Repository (Figure 9.25). Add the perspective portlet to your page (Figure 9.26). Initially, the new perspective portlet does not have any contents. Click on the "Customize" link to assign a perspective to the portlet (Figure 9.27). You can type the perspective name in the Selected Perspective field, or you can click on the List of Values icon to display a list of available perspectives (Figure 9.28). Choose one of the perspectives from the list by clicking on its "Return Object" link. When you accept the portlet customization changes, the perspective portlet displays all the items under the selected perspective (Figure 9.29).

Note

In Oracle9*i*AS Portal version 3.0.9, the perspective portlet is available in the Portlet Repository under Available Portlets → Seeded Providers → Portal Content Area.

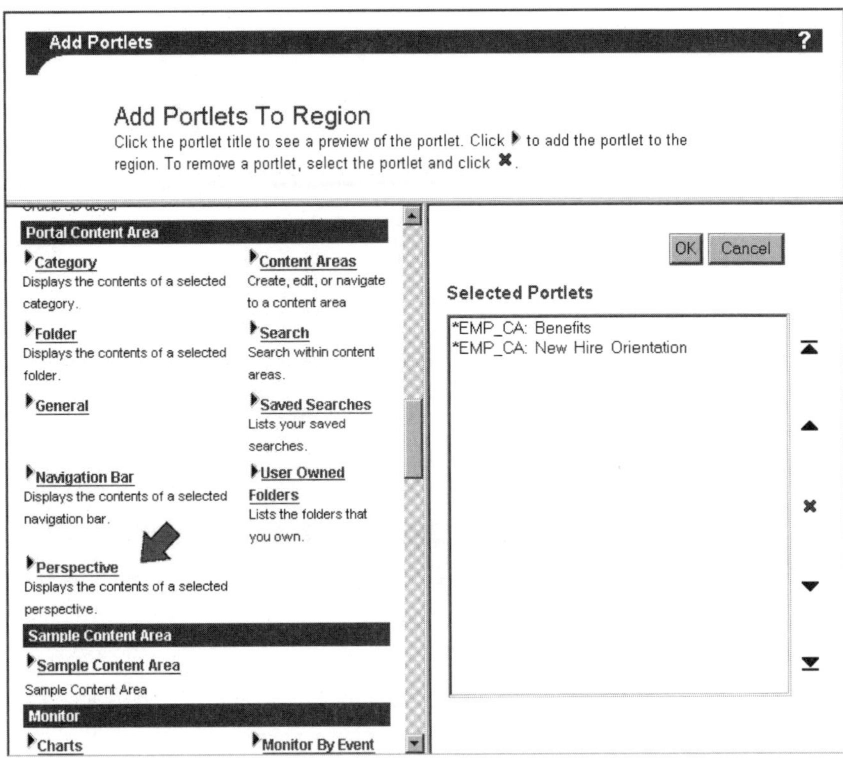

Figure 9.25 Portlet Repository: Add Perspective Portlet.

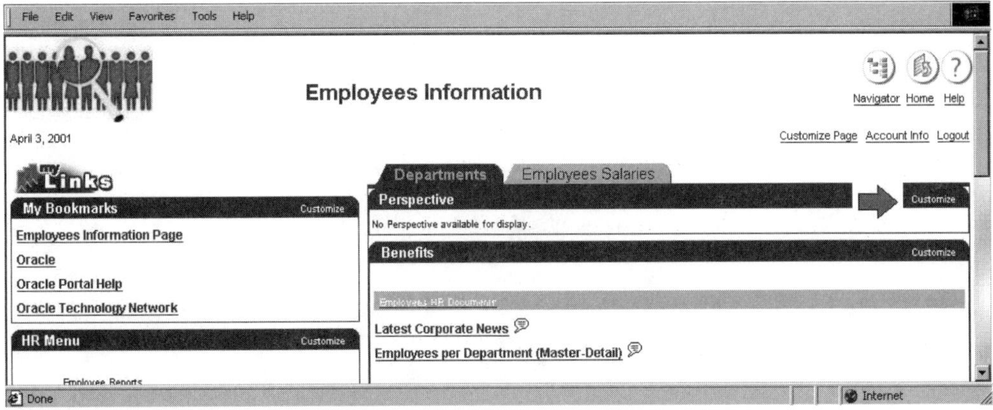

Figure 9.26 Page Display: Perspective Portlet.

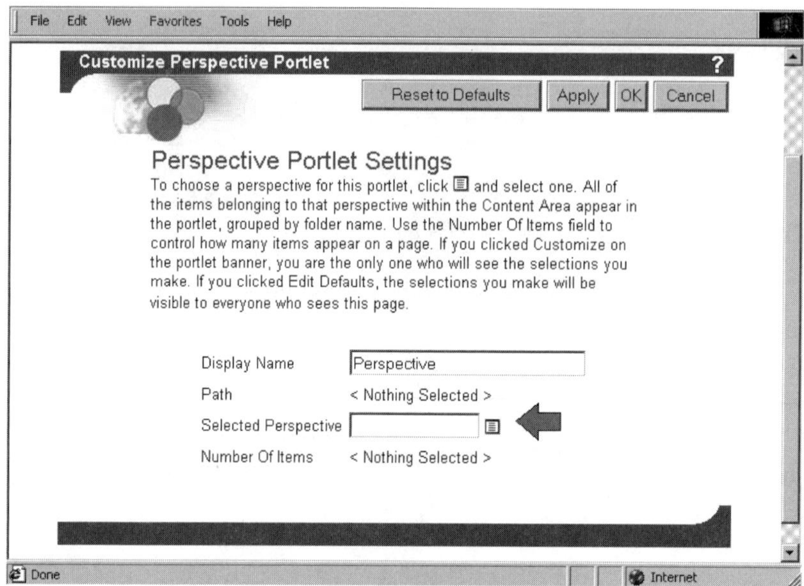

Figure 9.27 Customize Perspective Portlet.

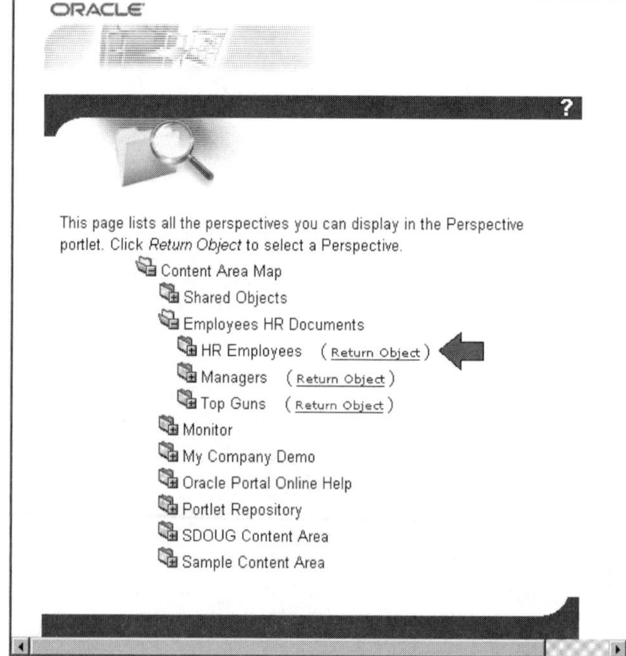

Figure 9.28 Perspective List of Values.

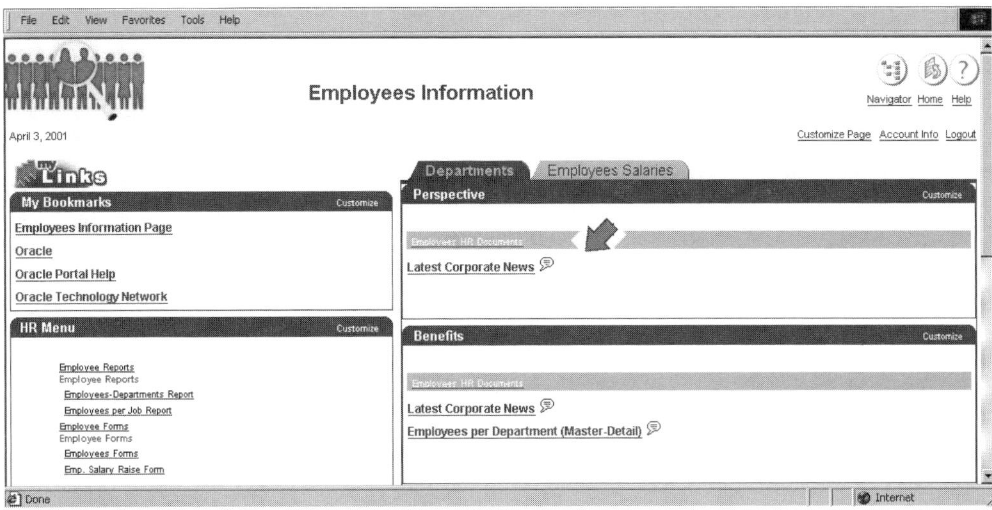

Figure 9.29 Page Display.

Basic Search

A search is performed on item attributes such as display name, description, and key words of items, as well as the display name and description of folders, categories, and perspectives. You can use a basic search to search the current content area for items, folders, categories, and perspectives that contain specific words.

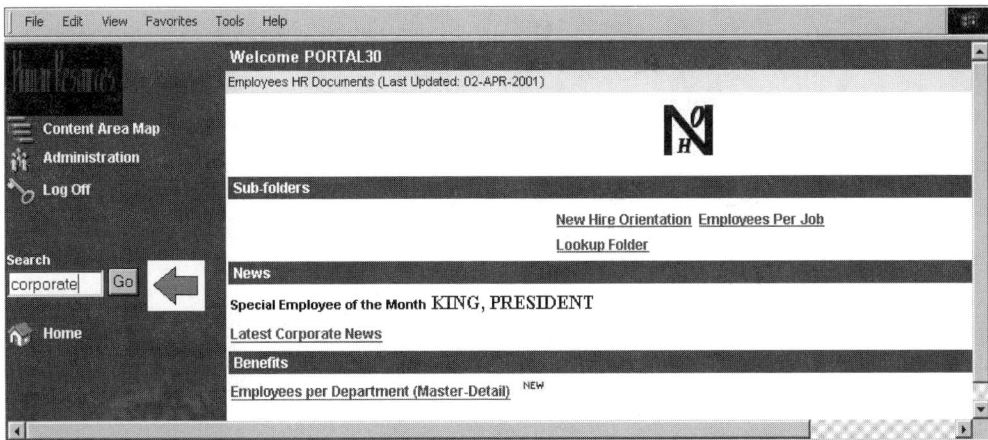

Figure 9.30 Basic Search.

Performing a Basic Search

In the Search field on the navigation bar, enter the words that you want to search for, then click the "Go" button, or press the Enter or Return key (Figure 9.30). Basic search finds contents that contain all the specified words. For example, if you enter "corporate documents," basic search finds contents that contain the words *corporate* and *documents.*

Basic Search Rules

- Search is not case-sensitive.
- To search for multiple words, separate them with spaces.
- To search for a phrase, enclose the phrase in single quotes, for example,

  `'corporate documents'.`

- The search results page displays only content that you are authorized to view.
- If *inter*Media is installed and enabled, search automatically uses the stem operator. It searches for words that have the same linguistic root as the specified word. For example, if you specified the word *invest,* the search feature returns contents that contain the words *invest, investing, invested,* and so on. The *inter*Media Text will be covered in detail in Chapter 16.

Advanced Search

Advanced search capabilities allow you to perform the following in addition to the basic search features:

- Find contents that contain any of the specified words.
- Search in a different content area other than the current content area, or across all content areas.
- Restrict the search to a particular folder, category, perspective, item type, or attribute.
- If you have *inter*Media Text installed and enabled, you can also use advanced search to perform near, soundex, and fuzzy searches. This is covered in detail in Chapter 16.

How to Perform an Advanced Search

1. Click on the "Advanced Search" link in the basic search results page (Figure 9.31). The Advanced Search page is displayed (Figure 9.32).

Note

By default the "Advanced Search" link does not appear on the navigation bar. To display it, enter any word in the basic search field and click the "Go" button to display the search results page, where you can click the "Advanced Search" link.

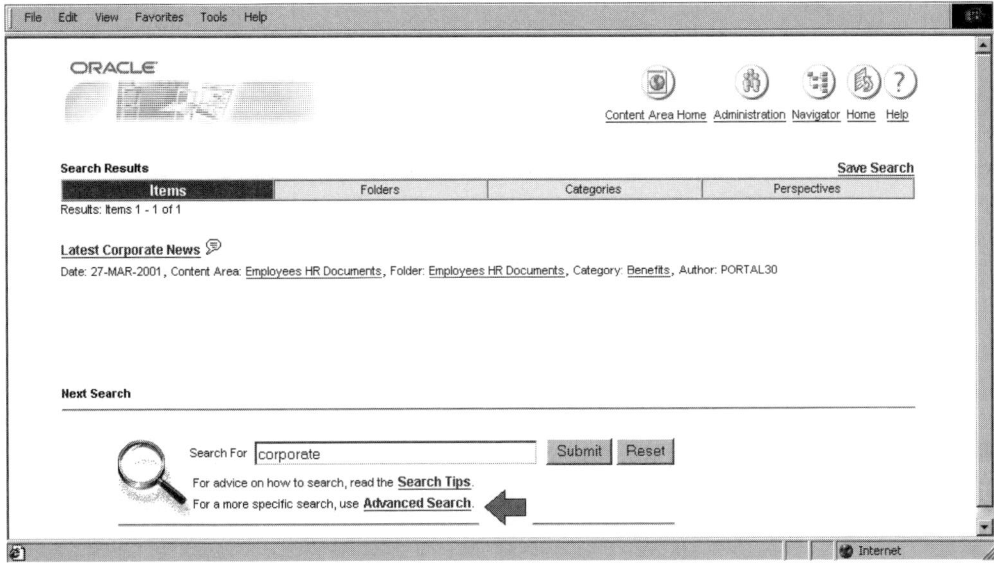

Figure 9.31 Basic Search Results: "Advanced Search" Link.

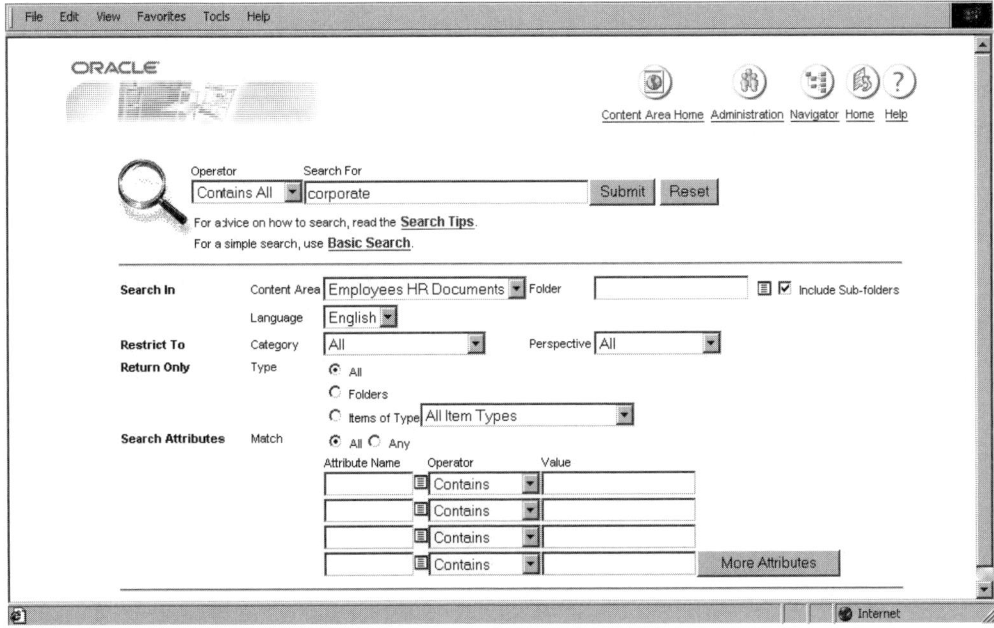

Figure 9.32 Advanced Search.

Table 9.1 Advanced Search Operators

Operator	Description
Contains All	Searches for contents that contain all of the specified words
Contains Any	Searches for contents that contain any of the specified words

Note

You can save the search result and give it a name, and then you will be able to add a built-in portlet called "Saved Searches" to any of your pages. This portlet contains links to your saved searches results.

2. In the Operator list choose the search operator. The search operator can be one of the values in Table 9.1. Other values for the operator need the *inter*Media Text to be installed.
3. In the Search For field, enter the words that you want to search for.
4. In the Content Area list, choose the content area in which you want to search. Or you can choose "All" Content Areas.

Note

When you choose a content area, the page is refreshed and the remaining fields (folders, categories, and perspectives) are updated with values appropriate to the chosen content area. For example, if you choose the "Employees HR Documents", only that content area's folders are listed in the folder List of Values (i.e., Employees Per Job, Lookup Folder, New Hire Orientation).

5. In the Language list choose the language in which you want to search. By default only English is available in Oracle Portal. You can add more language support. For example, if the content area is available in English and French, you can search only the French translation of the content area for the specified words. The installation steps needed to load other languages are covered in Chapter 18.
6. Click on the List of Values icon next to the Folder field to select the folder in which you want to search (Figure 9.33). Check "Include Sub-folders" if you also want to search in folders beneath the folder you specified.
7. In the Category and Perspective lists, choose the category and perspective in which you want to search. By default "All" Categories and "All" Perspectives are selected.
8. In the Type radio group, you can click any of the radio buttons in Table 9.2.
9. You can also restrict your search to specific attributes of folders and items. For example, if you know that the item you want to find contains the word *corporate* in its display name or that it was added some time after 1 January 2001, you can search those particular attributes.

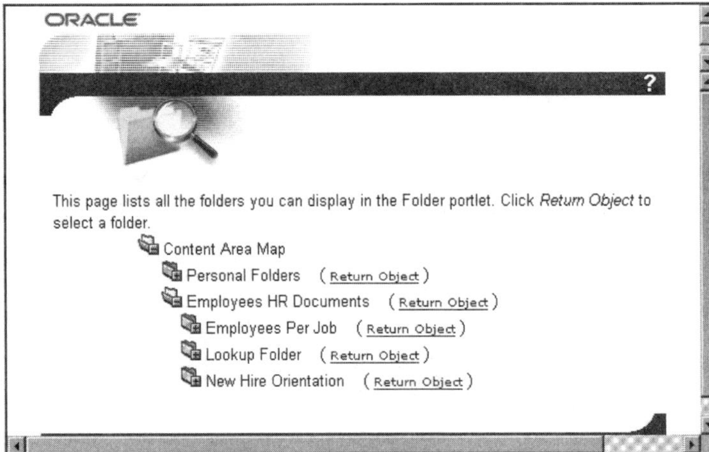

Figure 9.33 Folder Selection.

Table 9.2 Advanced Search Types

Radio Button	Function
All	To search for folders, items, categories, and perspectives that match the search criteria
Folders	To search for folders that match the search criteria
Items of Type	To search for items that match the search criteria. You can also specify what type of items to search for by choosing the item type in the list. This list shows only the item types relevant to the content area chosen in the Content Area list.

In the Match radio group, you can choose one of the two radio buttons "All" or "Any", which specify how the property conditions are evaluated, either logically ANDed or ORed, respectively.

10. In the first Attribute Name field, enter the attribute name, for example Display Name or Create Date. You can also click on the attribute List of Values icon; you need to click on the "Find" button to display the attributes list (Figure 9.34).
11. In the Operator list, choose the search operator, for example Contains or Greater Than.

Note

The Equals to, Greater than, and Less than search operators should be used only with numeric and date attributes.

12. In the Value field enter the attribute values you want to search for, for example "corporate" or "01-JAN–01".
13. Click "More Attributes" if you want to specify more attribute search criteria.
14. Click the "Submit" button.

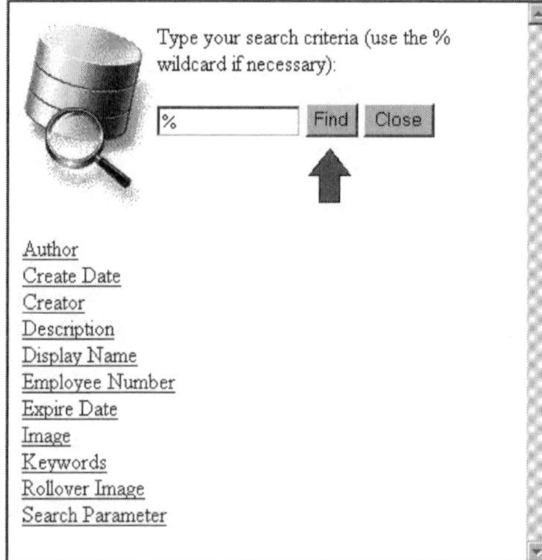

Figure 9.34
Attributes List of Values.

Publishing a Search Portlet

If you need to provide your portal end-users with search capabilities, you can add a built-in search portlet to your page. Customize your page and click on the add portlet icon to display the Portlet Repository (Figure 9.35). You can add the search portlet under the Portal Content Area provider to your page (Figure 9.36).

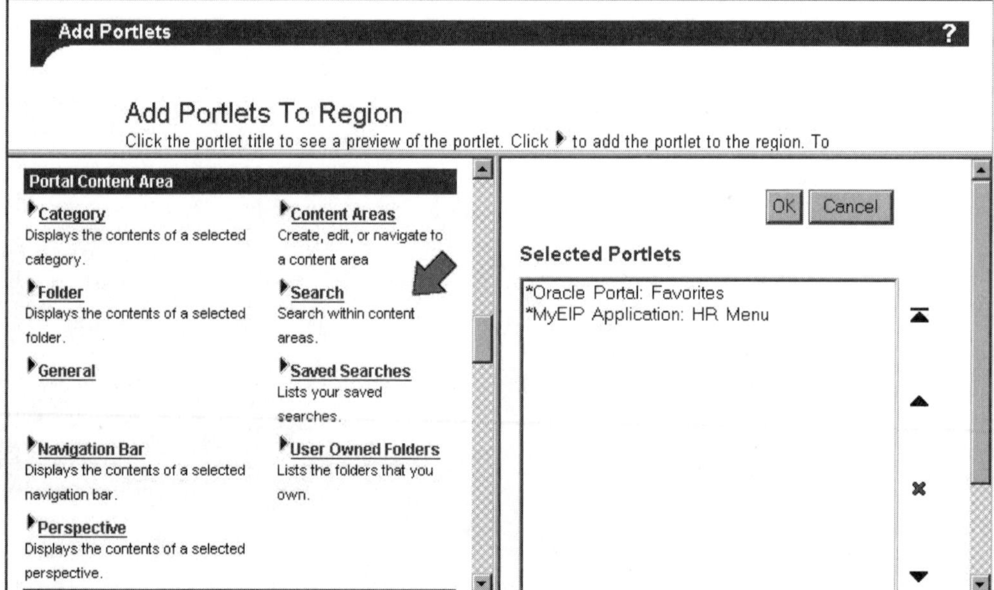

Figure 9.35 Portlet Repository.

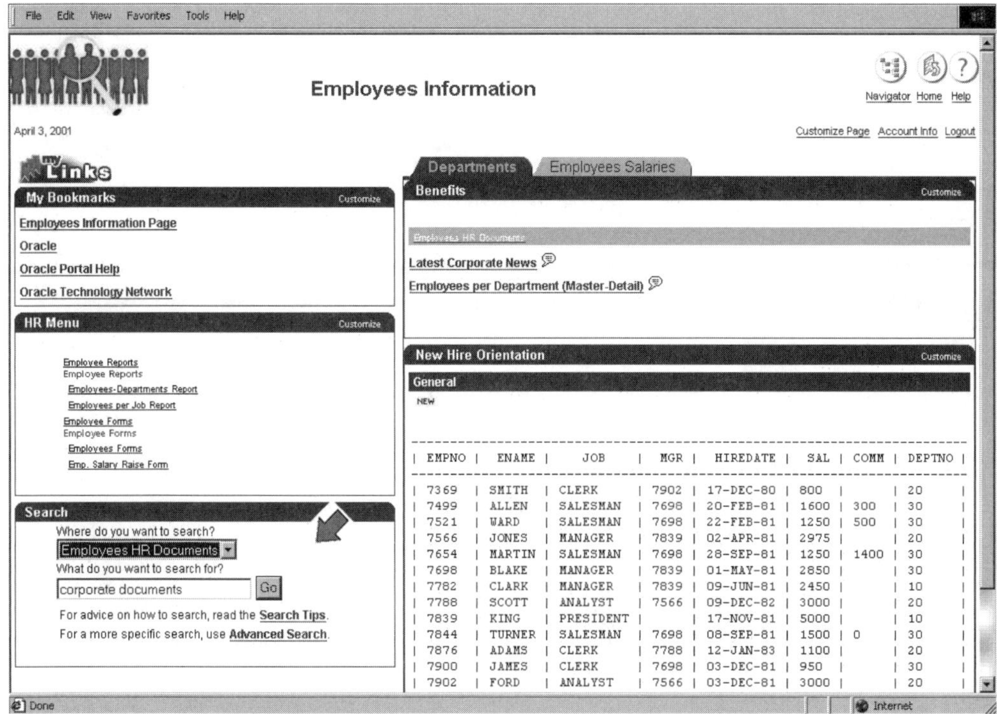

EMPNO	ENAME	JOB	MGR	HIREDATE	SAL	COMM	DEPTNO
7369	SMITH	CLERK	7902	17-DEC-80	800		20
7499	ALLEN	SALESMAN	7698	20-FEB-81	1600	300	30
7521	WARD	SALESMAN	7698	22-FEB-81	1250	500	30
7566	JONES	MANAGER	7839	02-APR-81	2975		20
7654	MARTIN	SALESMAN	7698	28-SEP-81	1250	1400	30
7698	BLAKE	MANAGER	7839	01-MAY-81	2850		30
7782	CLARK	MANAGER	7839	09-JUN-81	2450		10
7788	SCOTT	ANALYST	7566	09-DEC-82	3000		20
7839	KING	PRESIDENT		17-NOV-81	5000		10
7844	TURNER	SALESMAN	7698	08-SEP-81	1500	0	30
7876	ADAMS	CLERK	7788	12-JAN-83	1100		20
7900	JAMES	CLERK	7698	03-DEC-81	950		30
7902	FORD	ANALYST	7566	03-DEC-81	3000		20

Figure 9.36 Oracle Portal Display.

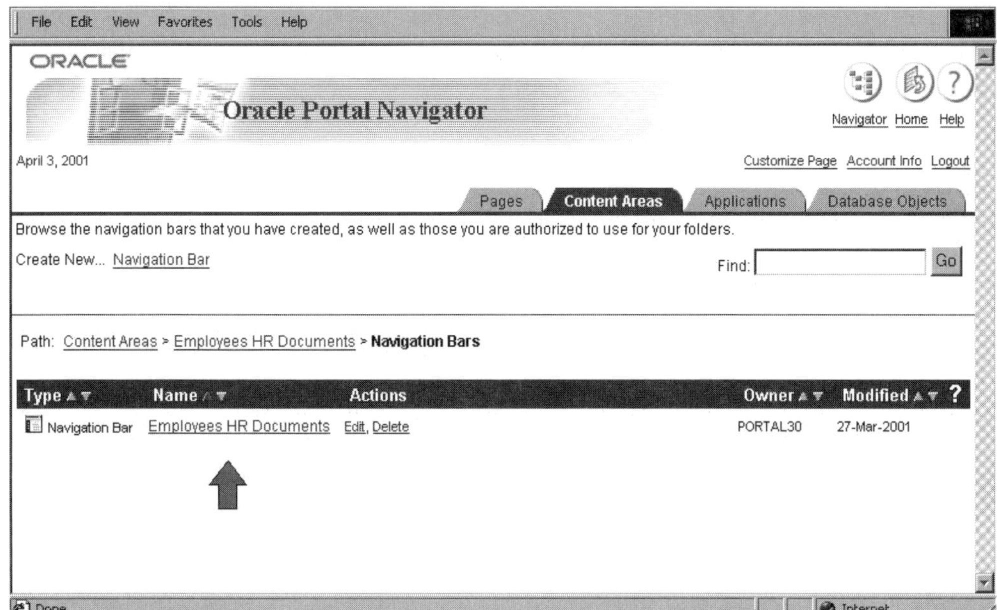

Figure 9.37 Oracle Portal Navigator: Employees HR Documents Content Area: Navigation Bars.

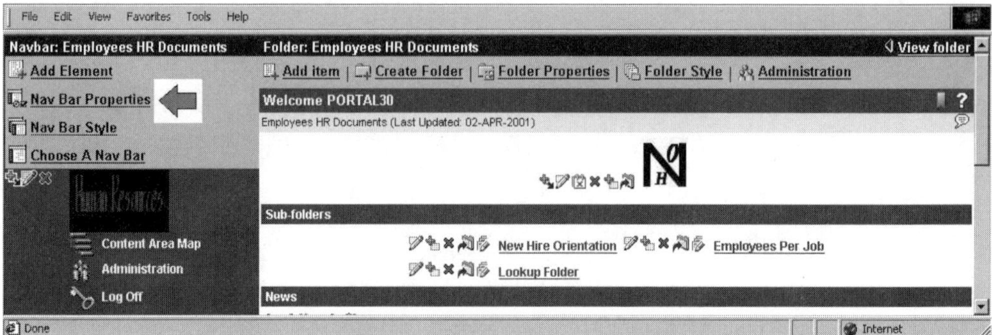

Figure 9.38 Content Area Home Page: Edit.

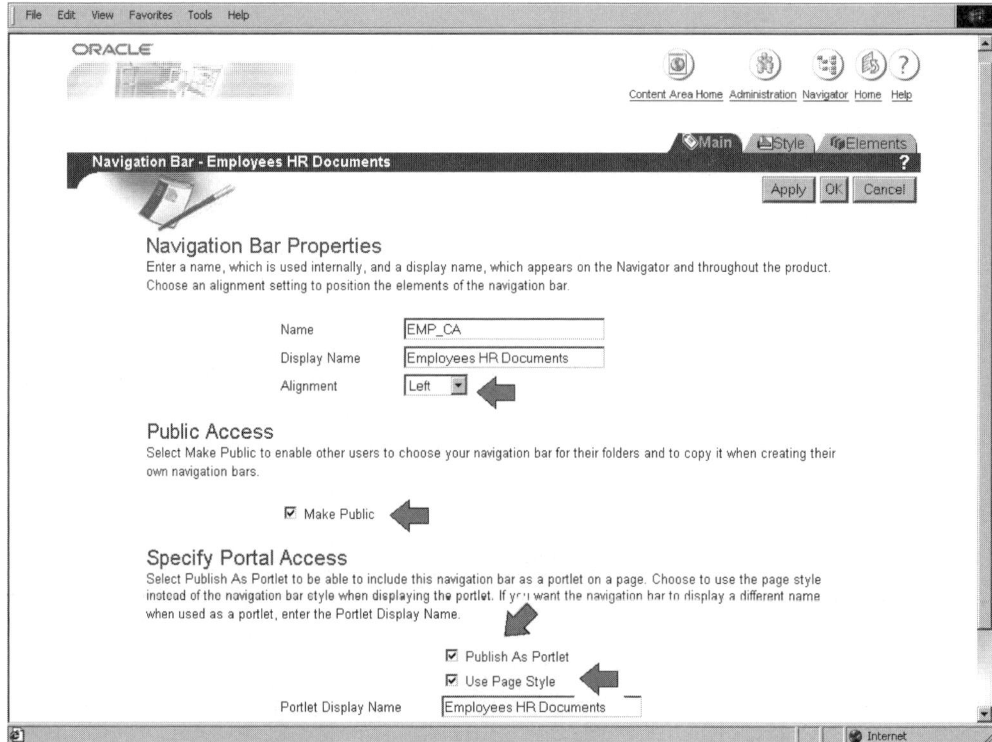

Figure 9.39 Edit Navigation Bar: Main Tab.

Navigation Bar

This section explores navigation bar properties. Each time a new content area is created (e.g., EMP_CA), a navigation bar with the same name is created. To edit the navigation bar, go to the Oracle Portal Navigator and drill down to Navigation Bars node under your particular content area (Figure 9.37). You can also edit the navigation bar properties from the Content Area home page while in the editing session (Figure 9.38).

Click on the "Edit" action link to edit the navigation bar properties (Figure 9.39). By default the alignment of the navigation bar is left, and it is accessible by the public. You can select the "Publish As Portlet" check box to be able to add this navigation bar to your portal pages. Selecting the "Use Page Style" check box is considered a good idea if your navigation bar style is much different than your page style. Styles are covered in more detail later in this chapter.

You can change the style properties of your navigation bar in the Style tab (Figure 9.40). When a new content area is created, two styles are automatically created: one for the content area itself and the other for its navigation bar. You can select another style for the navigation bar, edit the navigation bar style properties, or create a new style from another existing style.

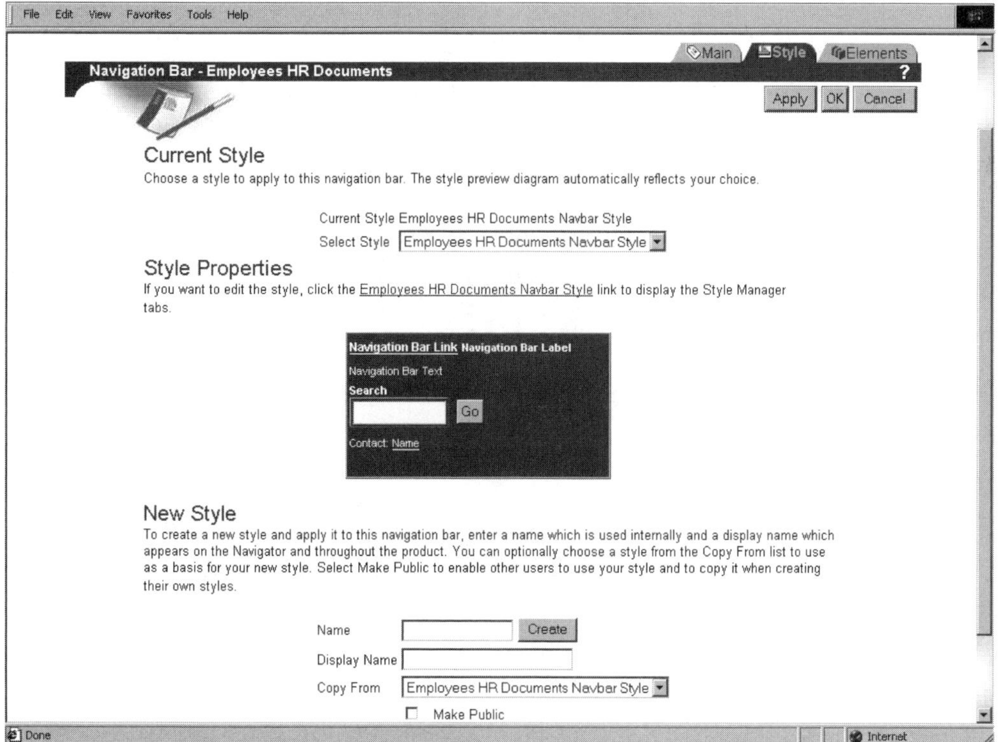

Figure 9.40 Edit Navigation Bar: Style Tab.

In the Elements tab you can manipulate your navigation bar (Figure 9.41). Notice that the elements are placed in your navigation bar in groups. The delete icon deletes the basic elements group and all of its elements (which were created by default).

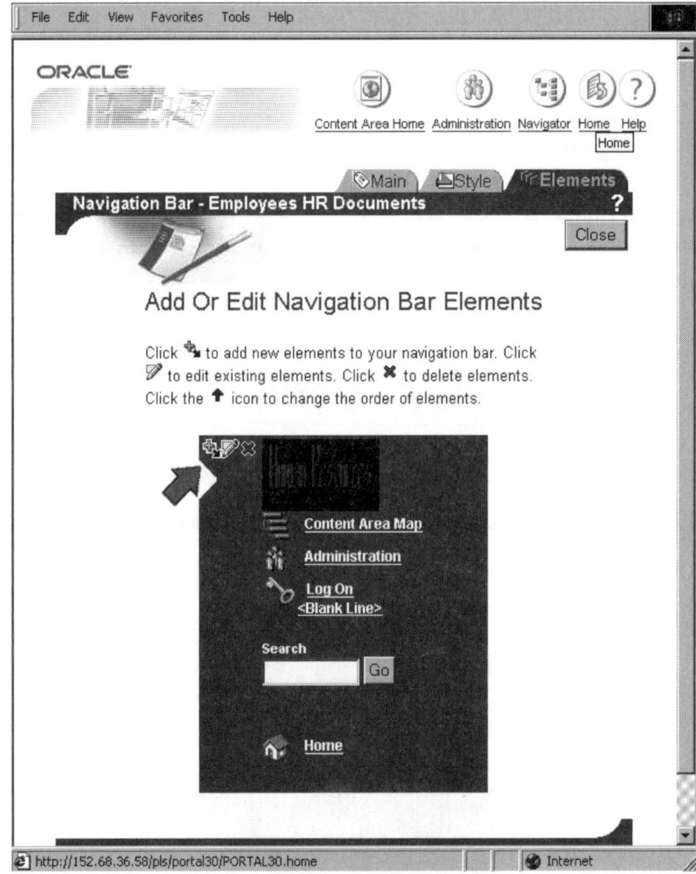

Figure 9.41 Edit Navigation Bar: Elements Tab.

You can edit the existing elements group by clicking on the edit icon (Figure 9.42). Then you can select from the list of basic elements on the left side. Notice that you can select one element more than one time.

You can add new element groups to the navigation bar by clicking on the add icon . The first step is to select the element type from the element type list (Figure 9.43). Choose Perspectives if you want to add links to your perspectives in your navigation bar. This makes it easier for different types of end-users to access their job-related information just by clicking on the perspective name in the navigation bar.

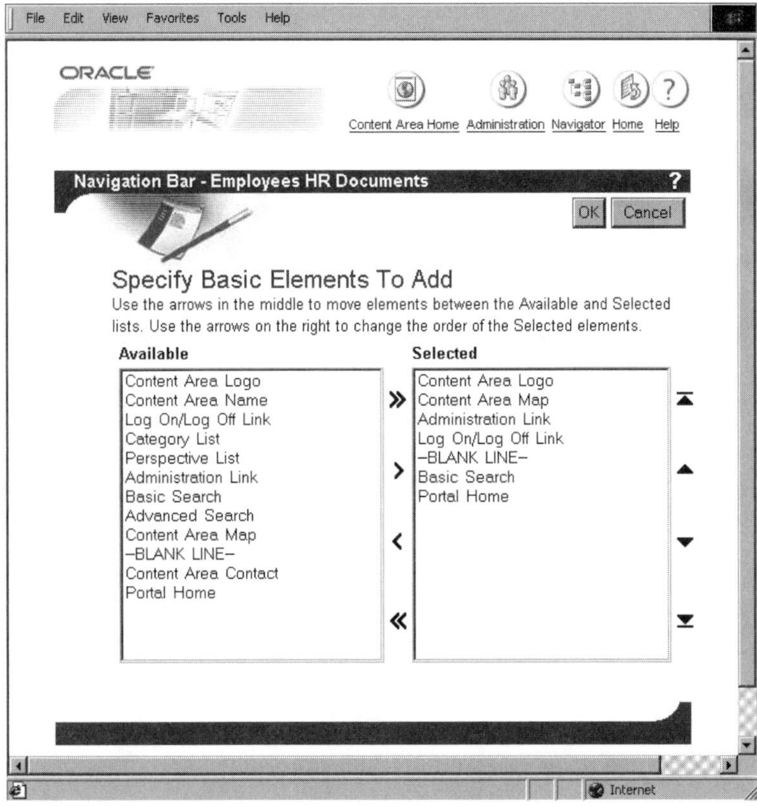

Figure 9.42 Edit Navigation Bar: Elements Tab: Edit Elements.

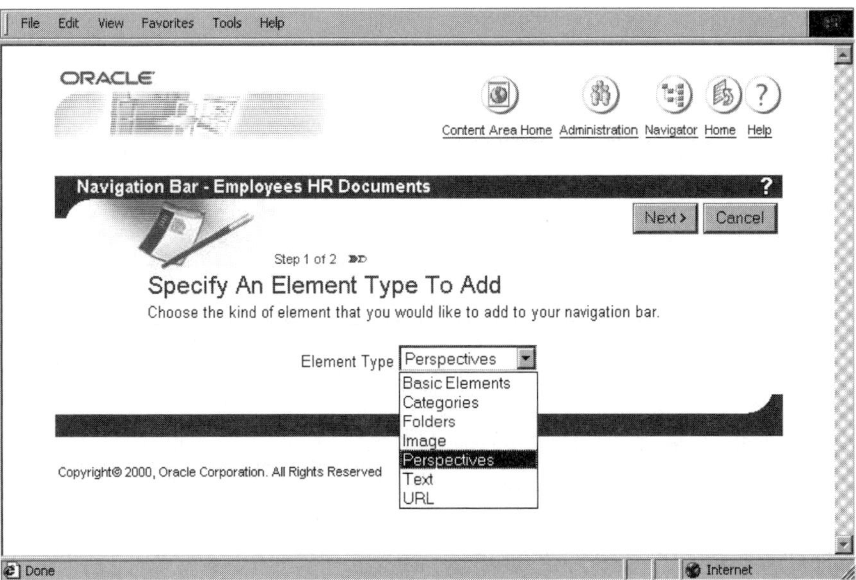

Figure 9.43 Edit Navigation Bar: Elements Tab: Add an Element (Step 1 of 2).

The next step is based on the element type you chose in the first step. For a perspective element type, you can select one or more perspectives from the available perspective list (Figure 9.44).

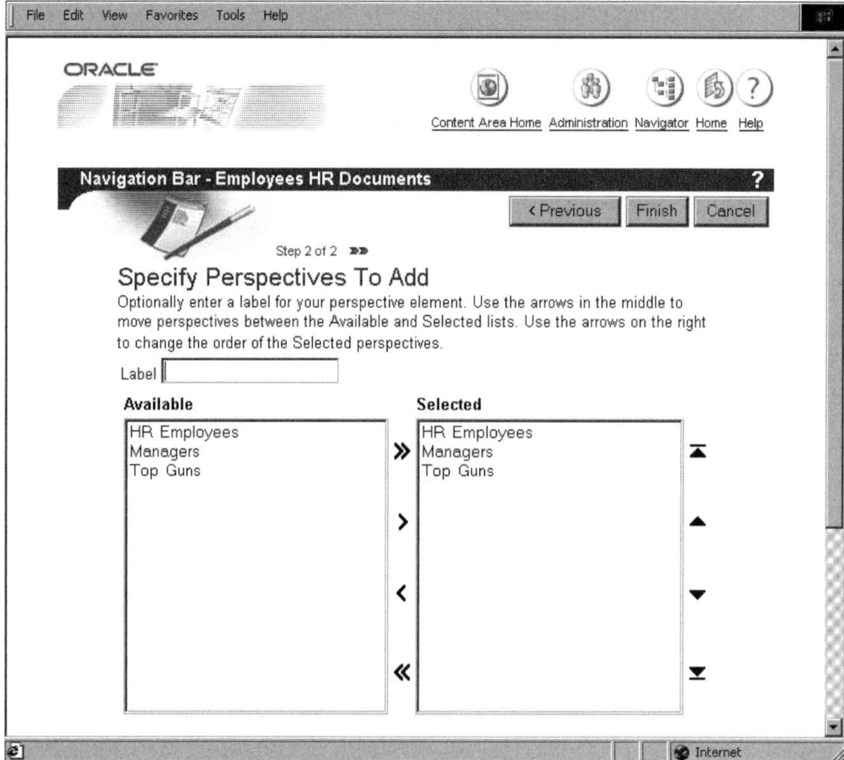

Figure 9.44 Edit Navigation Bar: Elements Tab: Add an Element (Step 2 of 2).

Remove the basic search and the portal home elements from the first group. Then, add another basic element group after the perspectives group. This new element group contains the basic search element, the content area name (i.e., link), and the Oracle Portal Home link. Click "Finish" to end your navigation bar editing. Now your navigation bar should look like Figure 9.45.

Publish your navigation bar to your portal page as a portlet. When you customize the page, the navigation bar will be available in the Portlet Repository under the content area (Figure 9.46). If you are running out of space in your portal page, you can add another tab or create a new page (Figure 9.47).

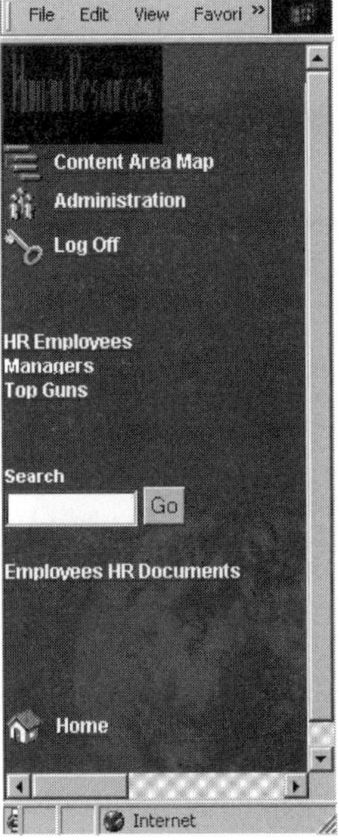

Figure 9.45 Navigation Bar.

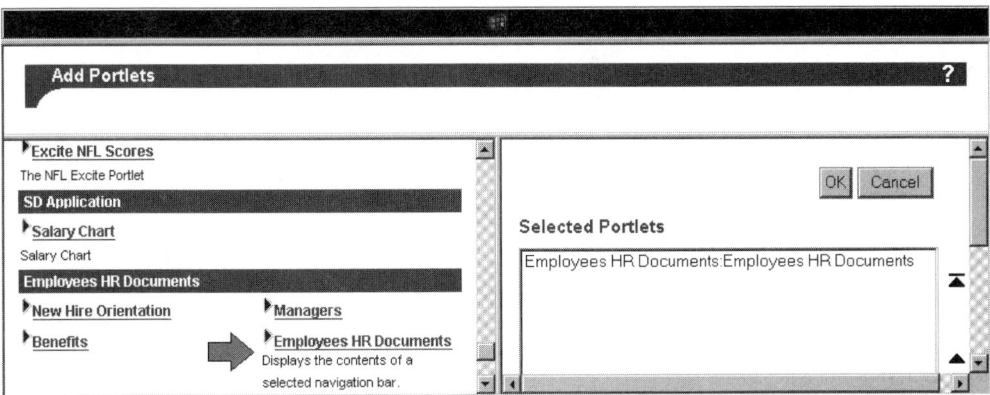

Figure 9.46 Portlet Repository.

You can shrink the navigation bar to only include the basic search element. Also, you can add URL elements to point to different components of your portal content areas. For example, you can add the following URL to your content to navigate to the Employees content area:

```
http://myportal/pls/portal30/url/FOLDER/EMP_CA/
```

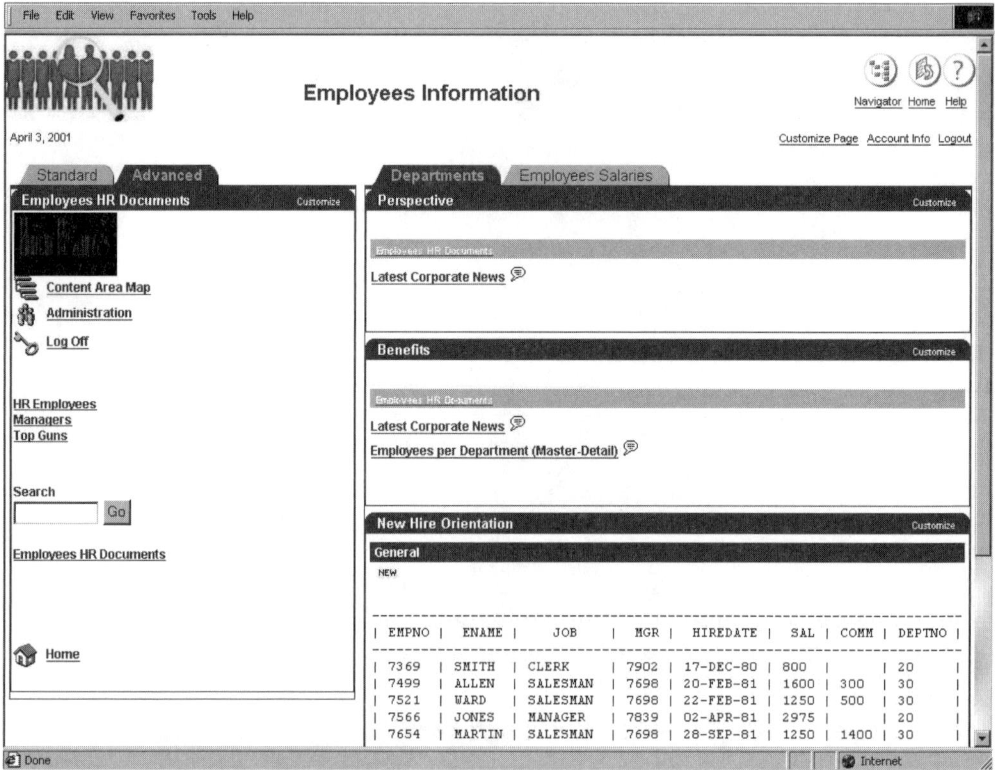

Figure 9.47 Page Display with Navigation Bar.

Note

If you choose to use the page style for your navigation bar, check all the elements to make sure you like them in the new style, otherwise you will need to unselect the navigation bar check box property and create your own navigation bar style.

Content Area Styles

The content area style is a group of display properties. These properties define how the content area's different components are displayed. To create a new style for your content area, drill down to your content area in the Oracle Portal Navigator. Click on the "Create" link on the right side of the Styles node (Figure 9.48).

To create a new style, you need to specify its name, display name, and the style source (i.e., from which the new style is copied). You can choose the content area style as the source of the new style. Finally, you need to specify if the new style is public, which means that other Oracle

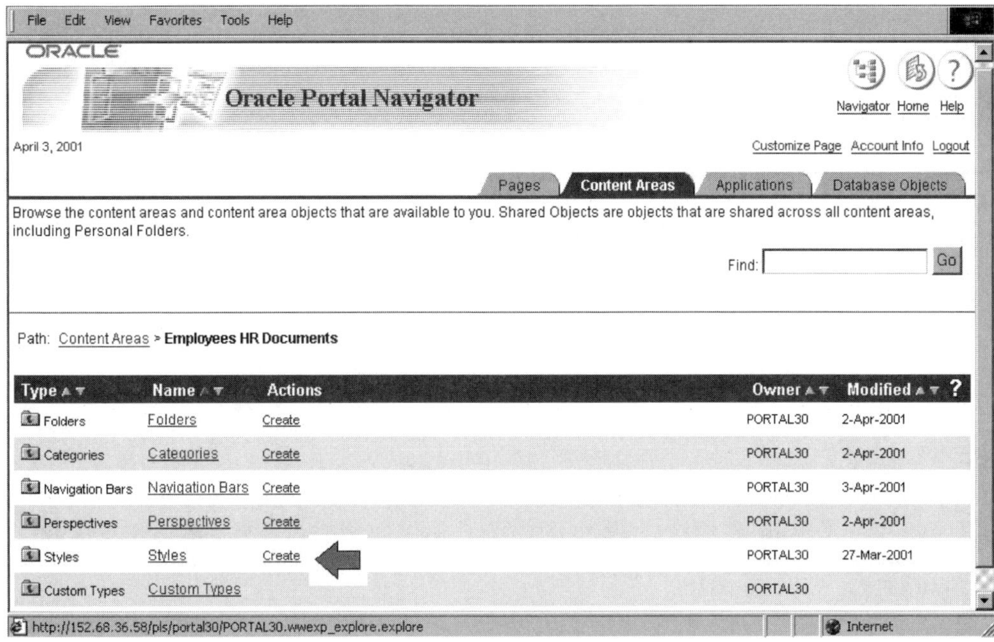

Figure 9.48 Oracle Portal Navigator: Create a Style.

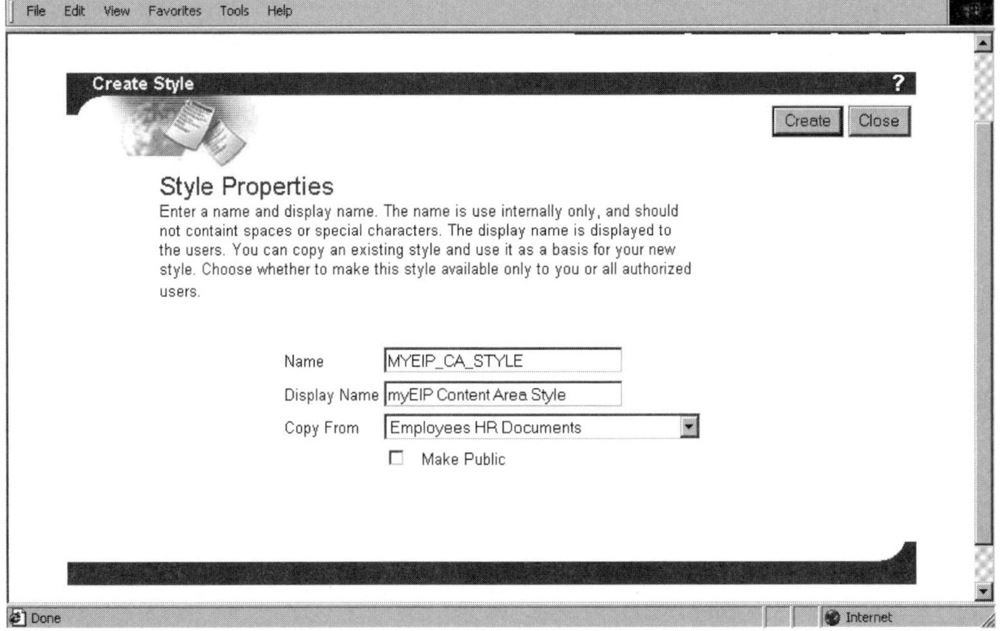

Figure 9.49 Create a Style: Style Properties.

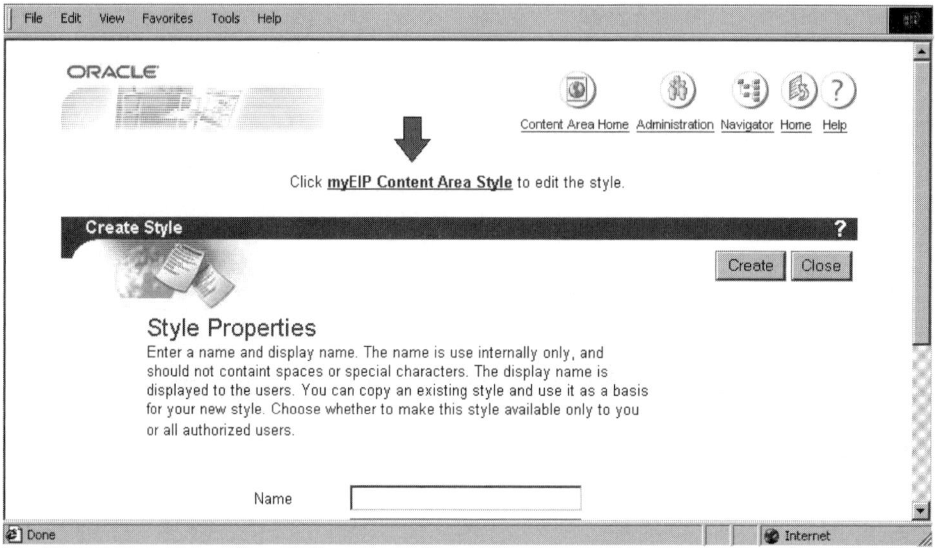

Figure 9.50 Style Created.

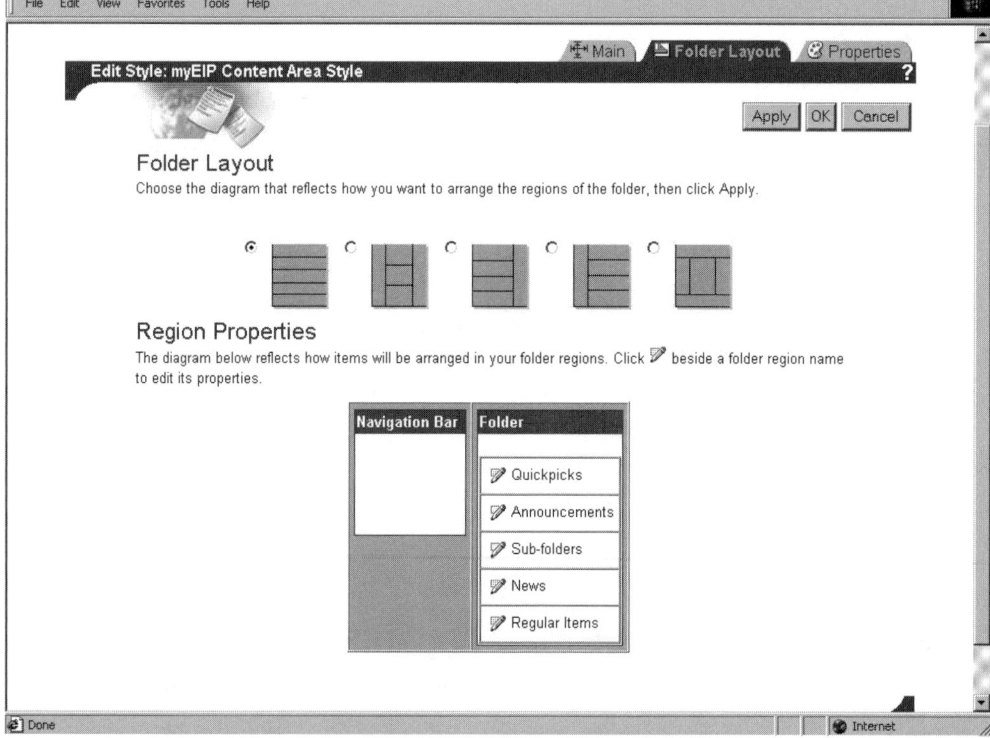

Figure 9.51 Edit Style: Folder Layout Tab.

Portal users can use it for their content area (Figure 9.49). When the style is created, you can edit its properties by clicking on its name (Figure 9.50).

The Folder Layout tab contains the folder layout choices along with their region properties (Figure 9.51). You can change the Folder Region Layout, and by clicking the "Apply" button, the region properties diagram is changed to reflect the new layout. You can edit each region of your layout by clicking on its edit icon. There are a lot of properties to change for each region, such as the region display name, the list of attributes to be displayed in the content area, and so forth (Figure 9.52).

Important

Remember to click on the "Apply" button after you change any properties under any tab and before you navigate out to another tab. Even though your changes are kept while navigating from one tab to the other, you still can lose your changes if you do not click on the "Apply" or "OK" buttons before navigating to another component of Oracle Portal.

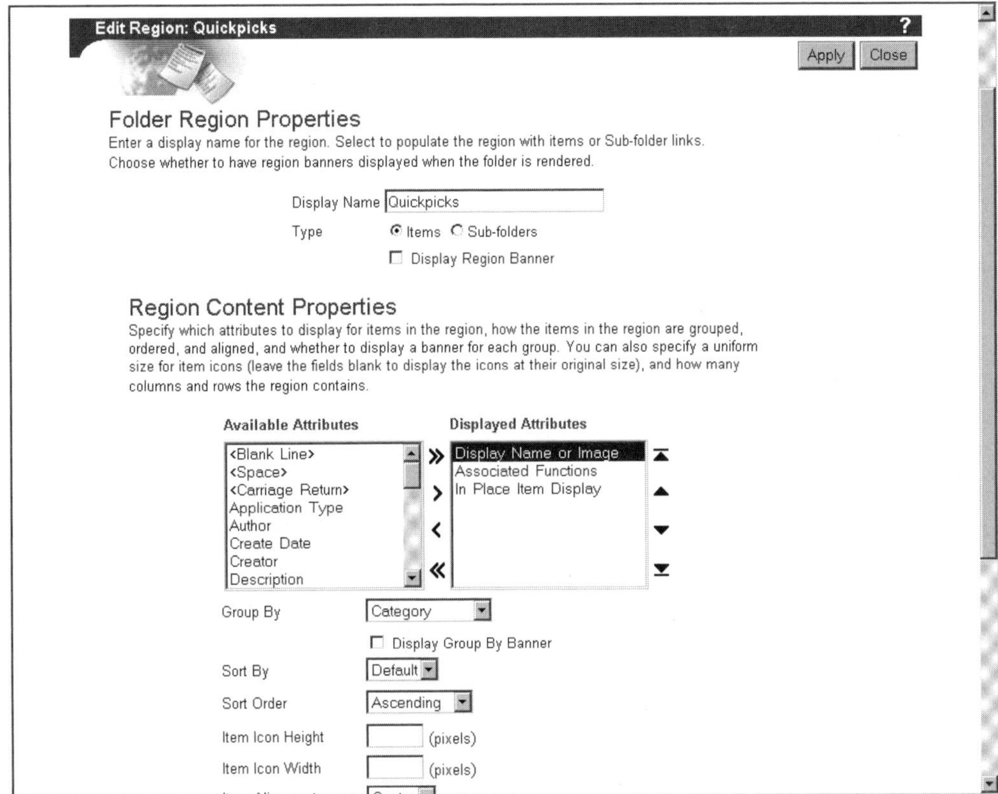

Figure 9.52 Edit Style: Folder Layout Tab: Edit Quickpicks Region.

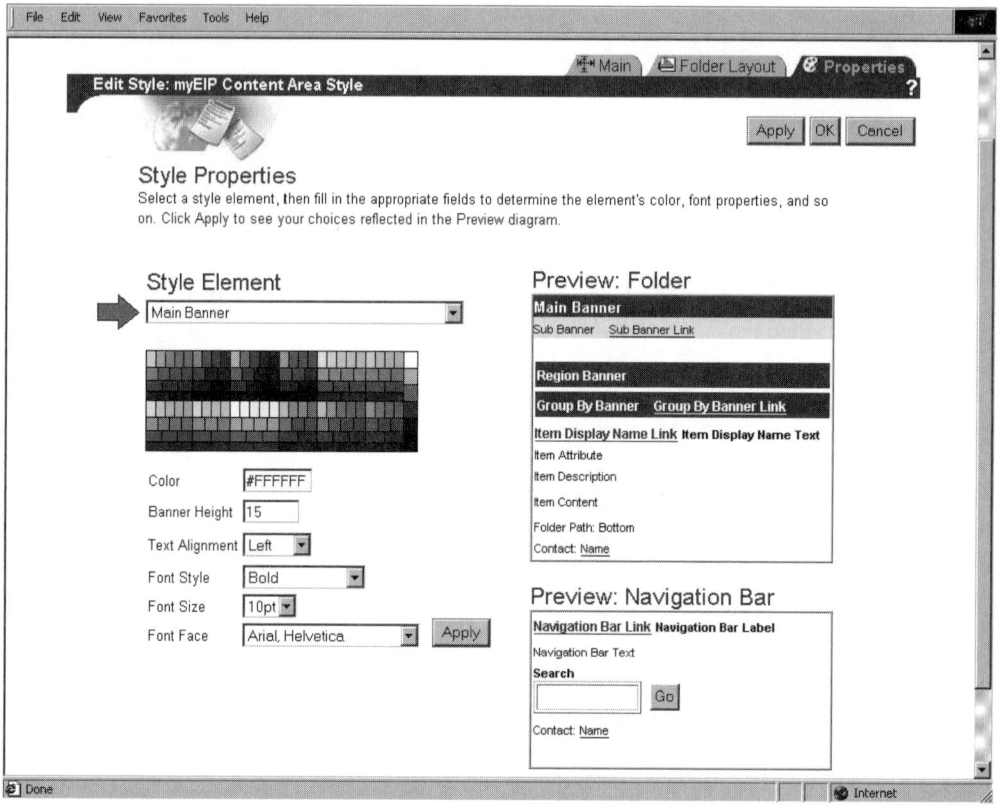

File Edit View Favorites Tools Help
Main
Folder Layout
Properties
Edit Style: myEIP Content Area Style
Apply
OK
Cancel
Style Properties
Select a style element, then fill in the appropriate fields to determine the element's color, font properties, and so on. Click Apply to see your choices reflected in the Preview diagram.
Style Element
Main Banner
Color
#FFFFFF
Banner Height
15
Text Alignment
Left
Font Style
Bold
Font Size
10pt
Font Face
Arial, Helvetica
Apply
Preview: Folder
Main Banner
Sub Banner
Sub Banner Link
Region Banner
Group By Banner
Group By Banner Link
Item Display Name Link
Item Display Name Text
Item Attribute
Item Description
Item Content
Folder Path: Bottom
Contact: Name
Preview: Navigation Bar
Navigation Bar Link
Navigation Bar Label
Navigation Bar Text
Search
Go
Contact: Name
Done
Internet

Figure 9.53 Edit Style: Properties Tab: Main Banner Element.

File Edit View Favorites Tools Help
Main
Folder Layout
Properties
Edit Style: myEIP Content Area Style
Apply
OK
Cancel
Style Properties
Select a style element, then fill in the appropriate fields to determine the element's color, font properties, and so on. Click Apply to see your choices reflected in the Preview diagram.
Style Element
Background Image
Background Image
Browse...
Apply
Preview: Folder
Main Banner
Sub Banner
Sub Banner Link
Region Banner
Group By Banner
Group By Banner Link
Item Display Name Link
Item Display Name Text
Item Attribute
Done
Internet

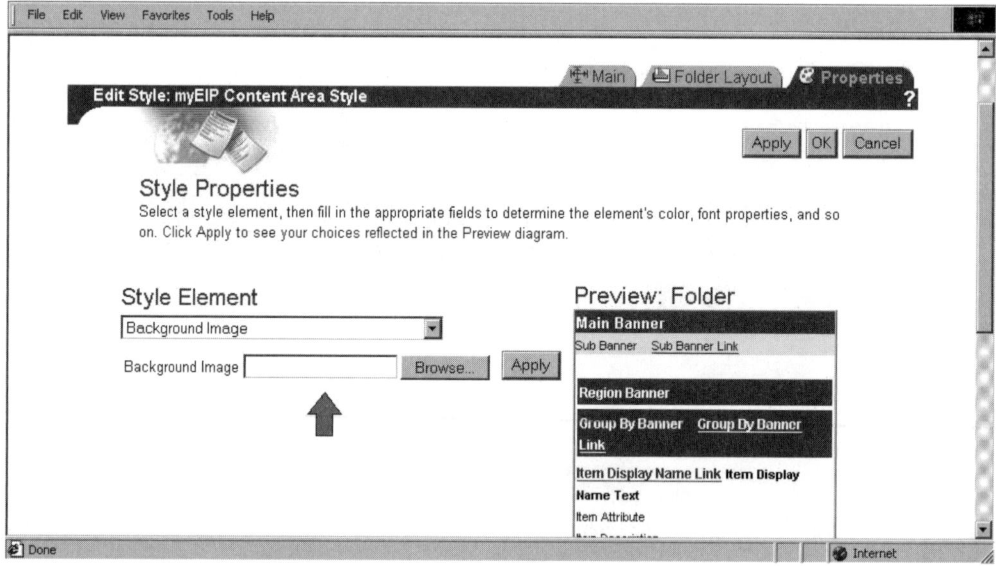

Figure 9.54 Edit Style: Properties Tab: Background Image Element.

When you finish changing the region properties, you can click on the Properties tab of your Edit Style window to change different style elements. By default, the main banner element is chosen and the color palette is displayed. The right side of your Properties tab window contains a preview of your folder and navigation bar, so when you apply a change to one of the style elements, you can check how it will look in your content area (Figure 9.53). You can choose a color either by clicking on a specific color so the hexadecimal color number (i.e., #CCFFCC) is put in the color field, or you can type the color value directly in the color field.

Note

The default element displayed in the properties might change based on the portal version.

Each style element has its own set of properties. For example, choose a background image for your content area (e.g., root folder). Select the Background Image element in the Style Element list. The image file name field is displayed, so you can specify the file name (Figure 9.54).

When you are done modifying the style elements, you need to apply the new style to one or more folders in your content area. You can click on the to go to the Content Area home page. Then, click on the "Edit Folder" link to display the root folder dashboard. Click on the Folder Style icon in the folder dashboard to jump to the Style tab of the root folder properties (Figure 9.55).

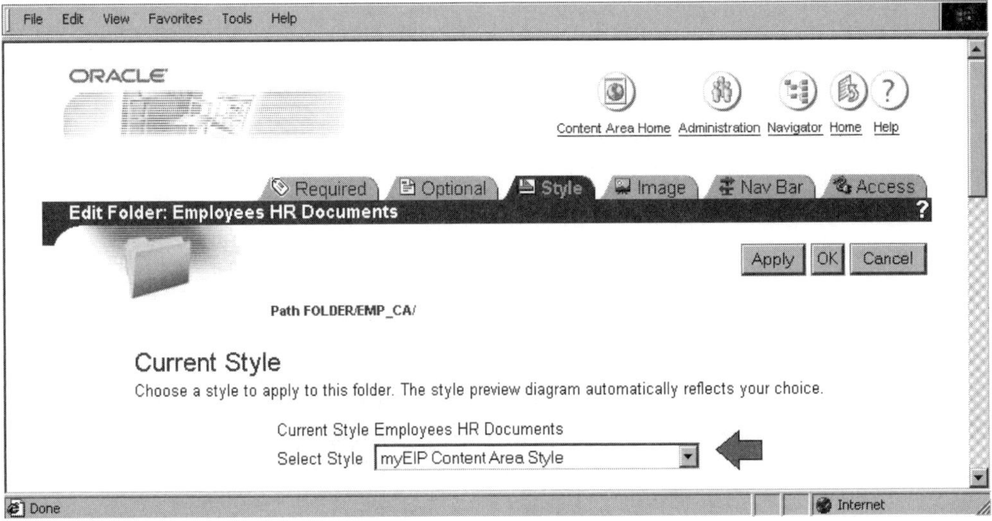

Figure 9.55 Edit Folder: Style Tab.

When you click the "Apply" button, the folder picks up the new properties from the new selected style. Notice that this style will only apply to the root folder; all the subfolders are still assigned to the original content area style.

Chapter 10 explains the event handling and JavaScript capabilities of Oracle Portal.

PART III

Advanced Features of Oracle Portal

CHAPTER 10

Event Handling

Introduction

This chapter introduces you to adding validation and event handling capabilities to your Oracle Portal pages. Oracle Portal supports JavaScript in more than one location. You can create JavaScript shared components to be attached to data entry items to perform validation. You can add JavaScript event handling code to any item in your Oracle Portal forms. You can also add JavaScript to your application components' HTML code or through the additional PL/SQL code. This chapter covers how you can use PL/SQL to augment the event handling in Oracle Portal. At the end of the chapter, there is a brief introduction to JavaScript language.

JavaScript in Oracle Portal

JavaScript is a lightweight, interpreted scripting language developed by Netscape. The core (i.e., interpreter) of the JavaScript language is embedded in most of the Internet browsers (e.g., Netscape and Internet Explorer), and this core is what is called Client-Side Java.

You can write JavaScript functions and store them inside Oracle Portal as shared components. To create a shared component, go to the Oracle Portal Navigator by clicking on , then go to the Applications tab. Click on "Shared Components", then click on "Javascripts" (Figure 10.1). Initially, the only scripts under JavaScripts are the System JavaScripts (Figure 10.2). A good start for learning JavaScript programming in Oracle Portal is to look at the existing System JavaScripts. Click on the JavaScript named "inRange0_100" and the script is displayed (Figure 10.3).

If you are not familiar with writing JavaScript code, later in this chapter I provide an introduction to JavaScript language. As a start, you can get a feel for the language by reading the code of the System JavaScript components (e.g., inRange0_100).

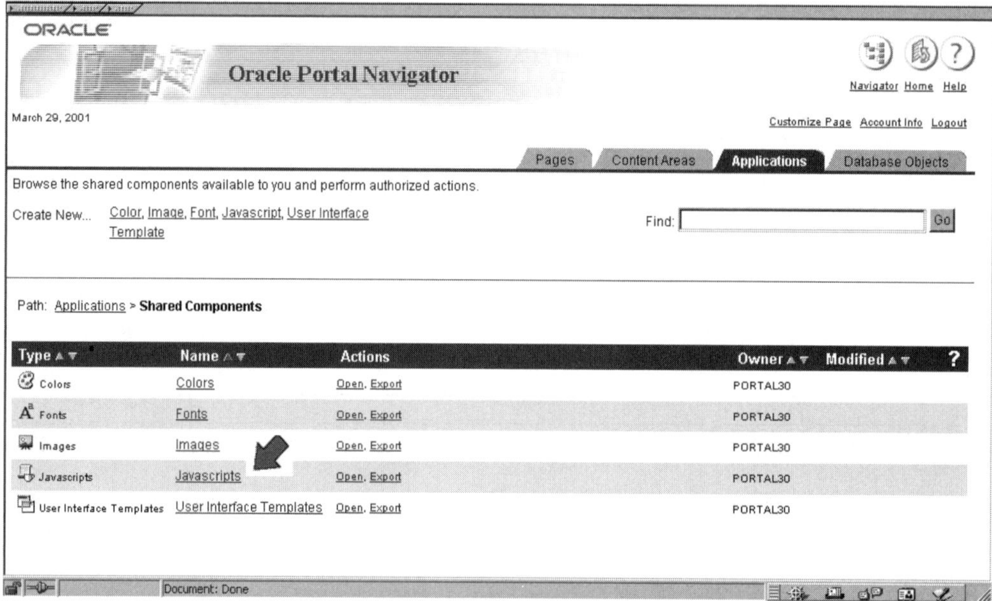

Figure 10.1 Oracle Portal Navigator: Applications: Shared Components.

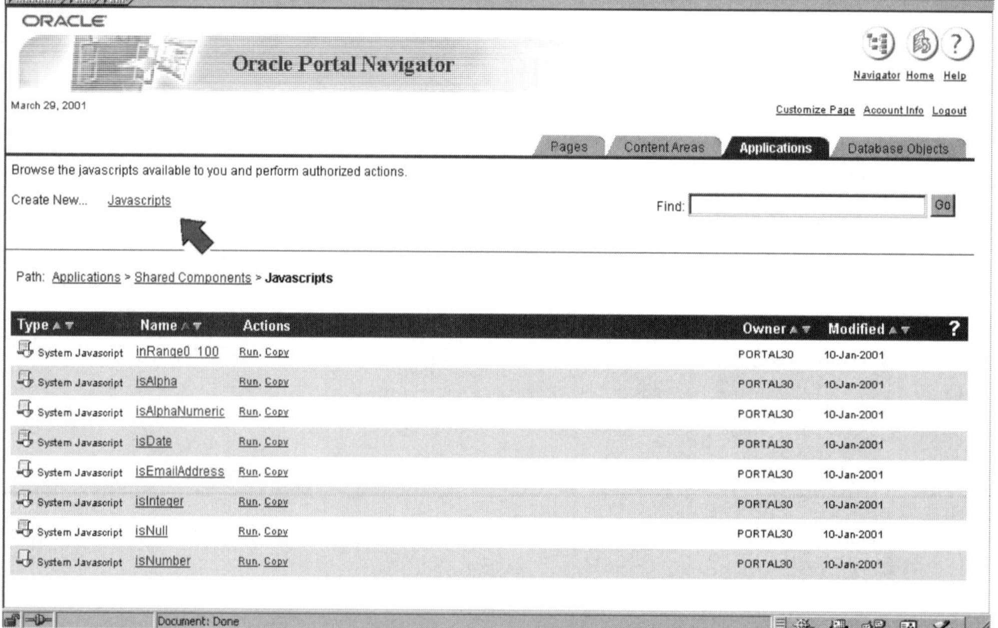

Figure 10.2 Oracle Portal Navigator: Applications: Shared Components: JavaScripts.

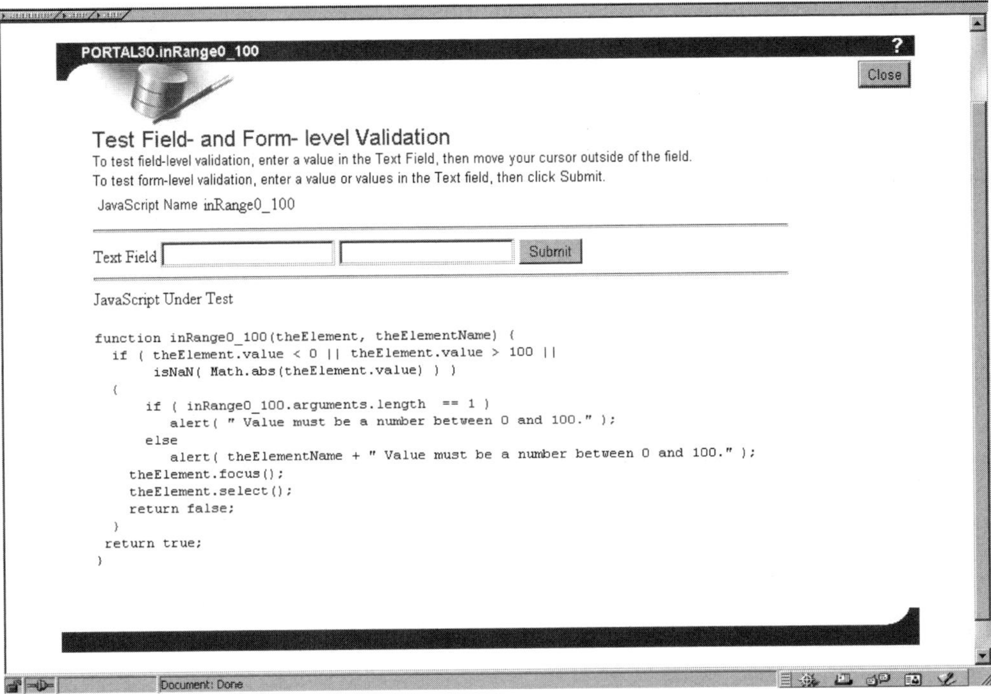

Figure 10.3 JavaScript: inRange0_100.

The inRange0_100 is a function with two parameters (i.e., theElement and theElementName). When you attach this JavaScript code to an Oracle Portal component item (e.g., a TextBox item in a form component), "theElement.value" returns the value of the text item. The first statement in the function is an "if" statement that checks if the value entered in the item is less than zero, greater than zero, or not a number. The function uses the Math.abs function to get the absolute value, just in case the number entered is a negative number. If the value does not satisfy any of these conditions, the function displays an error message using the "alert" function. Then, it returns the focus (i.e., text cursor) to the element, and selects the value so you can change it.

Testing a JavaScript Component

You can test any of the existing JavaScript routines by clicking on the "Run" action on the right side of the routine name under the shared components in the Oracle Portal Navigator. You perform the tests by entering test values into the leftmost text field. And then if you want to test the field-level validation, move the cursor out from the first field to the second field (e.g., using the Tab key or by clicking on the second field; Figure 10.4).

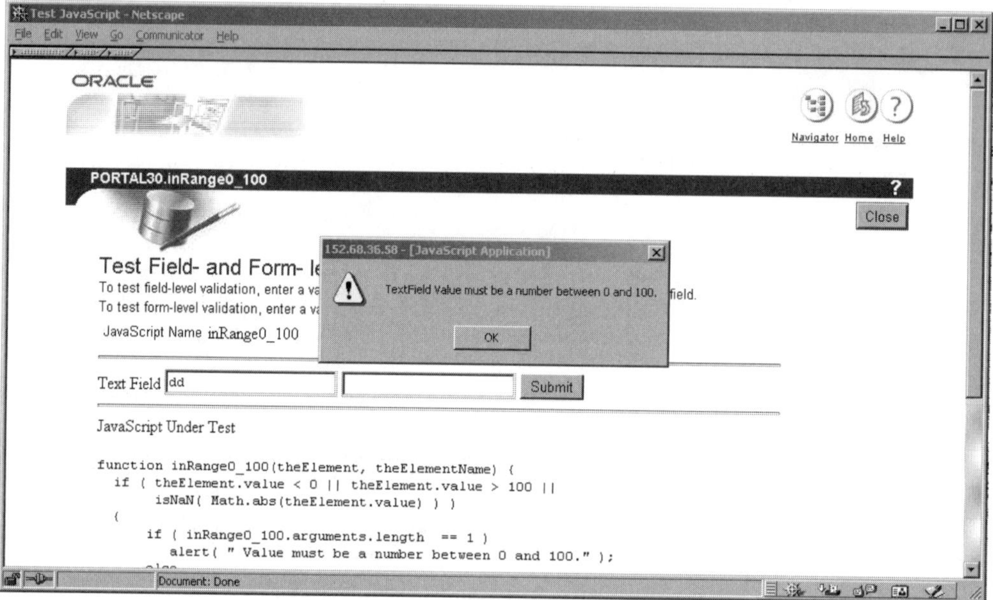

Figure 10.4 Test a JavaScript Component: Field-Level Validation.

If you want to test the form-level validation, click on the "Submit" button. For example, if you enter the value 12 and click "Submit", the JavaScript returns "true", and you get the screen shown in Figure 10.5. The difference between field validation and form validation is explained in the following sections.

Figure 10.5 Test a JavaScript Component: Form-Level Validation.

JavaScript for Validation

You can apply the JavaScript routines to data entry items in your application components. For example, to attach the inRange0_100 JavaScript function to the Commission (e.g., COMM) field of your EMP_FORM (e.g., Employee data entry Form), you need to edit the form component. Then, in the item's Formatting and Validation Options tab, choose the inRange0_100 routine in the Field Level Validation drop list (Figure 10.6). Finish editing the form and test the JavaScript function by trying to insert or update values in the commission field. The Form Level Validation routine by default is set to "isNumber" for all the numeric database fields (e.g., SAL, COMM, etc.).

Field-level validation routines are implemented in JavaScript and run when the OnBlur Event occurs; for example, when the end-user presses the Return key after typing a value in the field.

Form-level validation routines run when the end-user submits the information on the page, for example, after clicking an "Insert" button on the form. The "Insert" button sends the data of the new record to be inserted inside the database. The explanation of the OnBlur event along with other events is covered in the following sections.

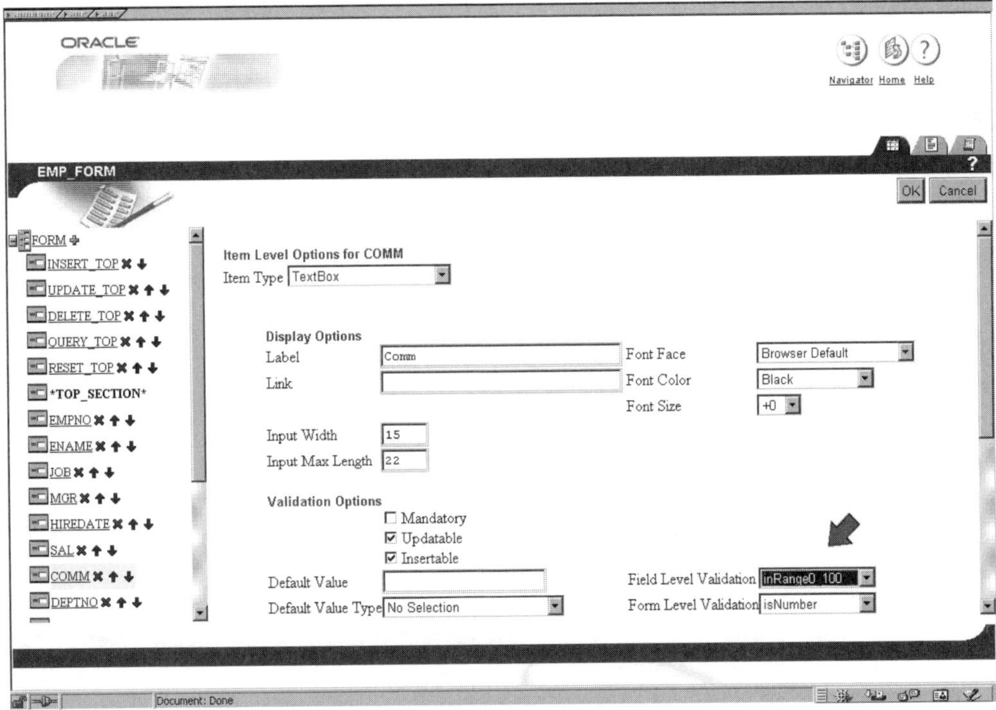

Figure 10.6 Apply JavaScript Routine to an Application Component Item.

Creating a New JavaScript Component

You can create a new JavaScript shared component from scratch by clicking on the "Create New . . . Javascripts" link. You need to specify the script name, which acts as the function name, and the JavaScript language version (e.g., JavaScript 1.1, JavaScript 1.2, or JavaScript 1.3; Figure 10.7). Your browser must support the version of JavaScript that you use.

You cannot edit a System JavaScript component, but you can copy an existing script and give it a new name by clicking on the "Copy" action link in the Oracle Portal Navigator (Fig-

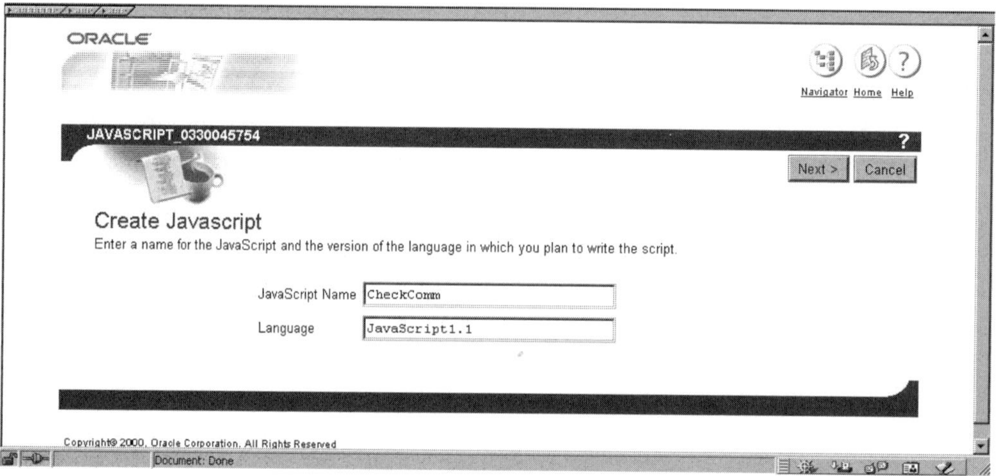

Figure 10.7 Create a new JavaScript Component.

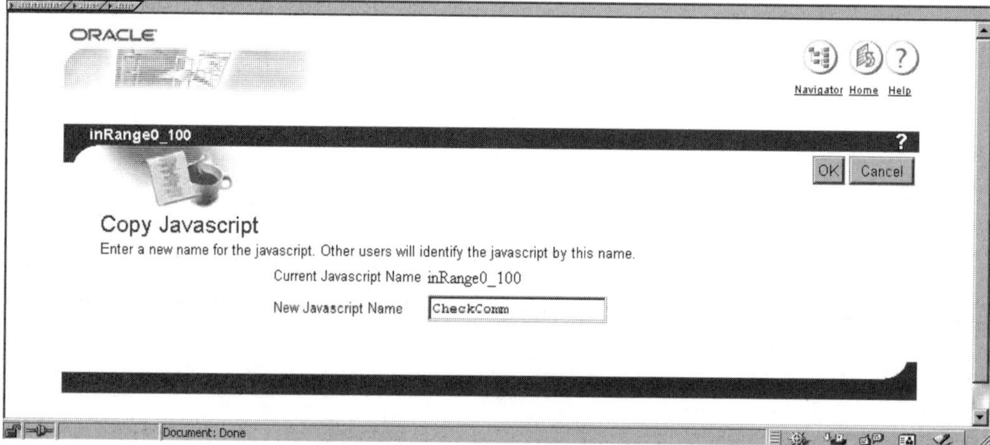

Figure 10.8 Copy JavaScript Component.

ure 10.8). You can start with the code in the inRange0_100 body to write the code for a new JavaScript component that checks that the employee's commission cannot be more than 40%. Also, you can check for each error, to provide the user with more meaningful error messages (Figure 10.9).

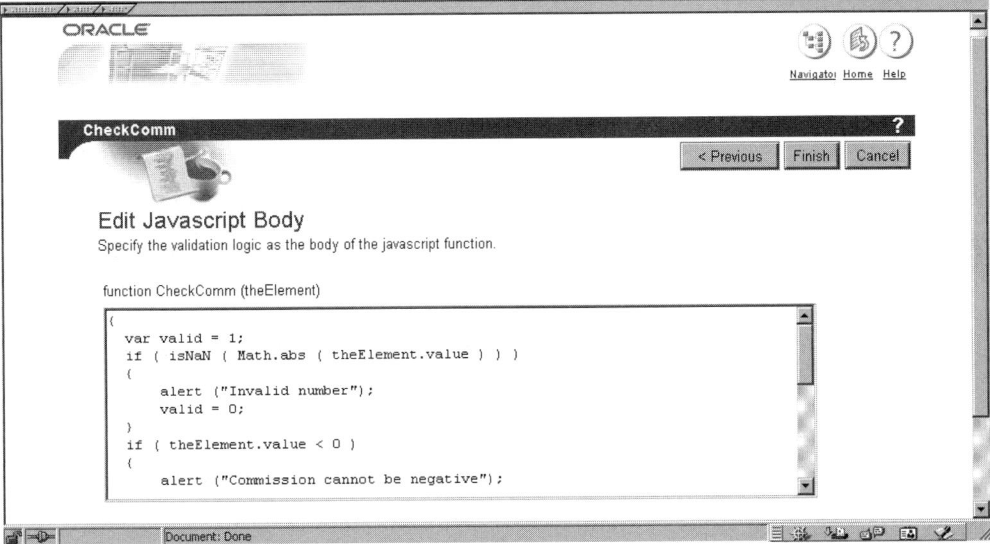

Figure 10.9 Edit JavaScript Body.

The following is the complete code listing for the new JavaScript:

```
{
  (theElement, theElementName)
  var valid = 1;
  if ( isNaN ( Math.abs ( theElement.value ) ) )
  {
      alert ("Invalid number");
      valid = 0;
  }
  if ( theElement.value < 0 )
  {
      alert ("Commission cannot be negative");
      valid = 0;
  }
```

```
        if ( theElement.value > 40 )
        {
            alert ("Commission cannot be more than 40%");
            valid = 0;
        }
        if ( valid == 0 )
        {
           theElement.focus();
           theElement.select();
           return false;
        }
    }
```

Table 10.1 Event Handlers

Event Handler	Triggered When	Elements
onBlur	Element loses input focus	Windows and all form elements
onChange	User changes the value of an element (including selection or deselection of list)	Text field (e.g., textbox), text area, and select list elements
onClick	User clicks once	Link, button, radio button, and check box elements
onFocus	Element given input focus	Windows and all form elements
onKeyDown	User presses a key	Document, image, link, and text area elements
onKeyPress	User presses a key or holds a key down; a combination of onKeyDown and onKeyUp	Document, image, link, text area elements
onKeyUp	User releases a key	Document, image, link, and text area elements
onMouseDown	User presses mouse button	Document, button, and link elements
onMouseOut	Mouse moves off an element	Link and image elements
onMouseOver	Mouse moves over an element	Link elements
onMouseUp	User releases a mouse button	Document, link, and button elements
onReset	A form reset is requested	Forms
onResize	A window is resized	Windows
onSubmit	A form submission is requested	Form

When the new JavaScript component is created, test it using different sample data. Then, attach it to the COMM item in the EMP_FORM. Finally, test the whole form.

JavaScript Item Event Handlers

Besides using the JavaScript components for validation, you can utilize the JavaScript event-driven programming features in writing event handler code. These handlers are executed when their events occur. Table 10.1 lists the most frequently used JavaScript event handlers. Also, the table lists the events' triggering reason(s) along with event-applicable elements. You can add the JavaScript code to perform your event handling in the Formatting and Validation Options tab (Figure 10.10).

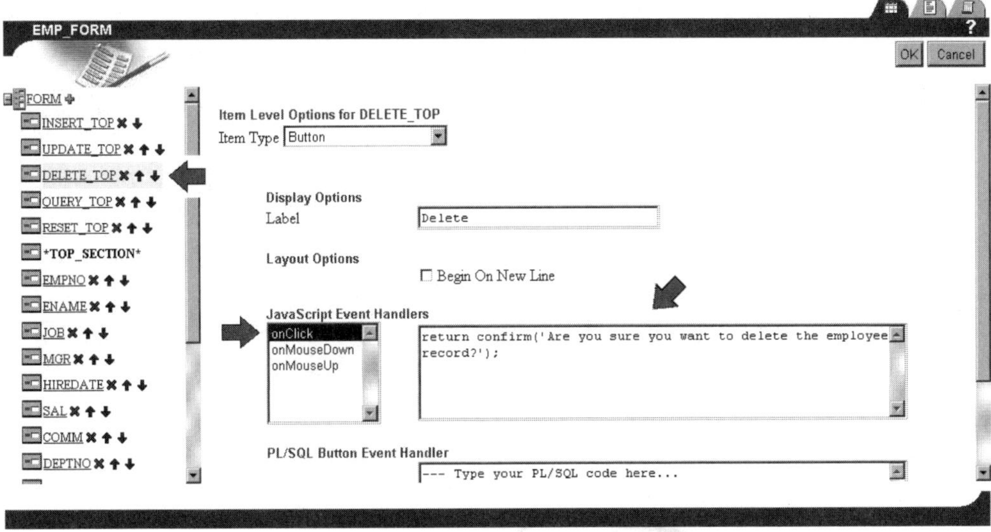

Figure 10.10 JavaScript Item Event Handlers.

When the end-user clicks on the "Delete" button to delete a queried record, he or she is prompted to confirm the deletion. The confirm function returns "true" if the end-user selected the alert "OK" button, otherwise it returns "false" (Figure 10.11).

Note

Remember there are two delete buttons, one on the top and one on the bottom. Most likely you will need to add the JavaScript code in both.

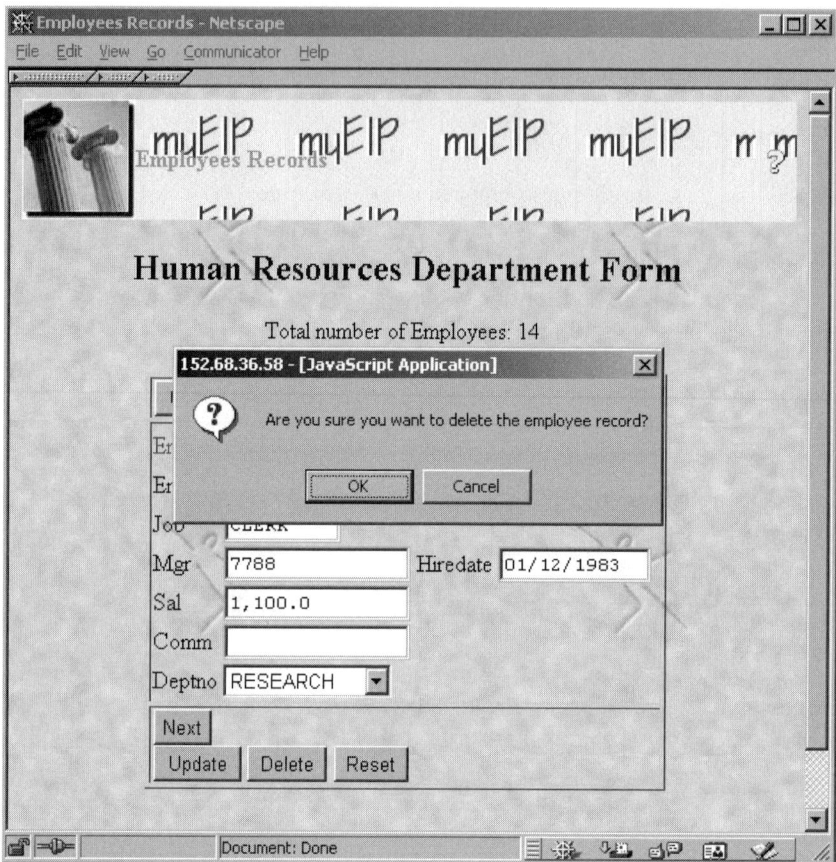

Figure 10.11 Running a Form with the "Delete" Button "onClick" JavaScript Event Handler.

PL/SQL Event Handling

You can add your own PL/SQL event handling to the buttons in the application components. You can augment the PL/SQL event handlers of buttons such as Query, Insert, Update, Delete, Reset, Pagination Next, Pagination Previous, and Custom. You can also augment the code through JavaScript by using the HTP.P procedure. For example, you can display a confirmation alert after the user clicks the "Update" button of a form (Figure 10.12).

While the browser executes the JavaScript code in Oracle Portal, the PL/SQL code is routed to the Oracle HTTP server and then to the Oracle Portal database. So, the PL/SQL event handling is usually preferred when a database access is required (e.g., maintain and audit logs of inserts and updates). And the JavaScript is preferred for client-side event handling and data validation.

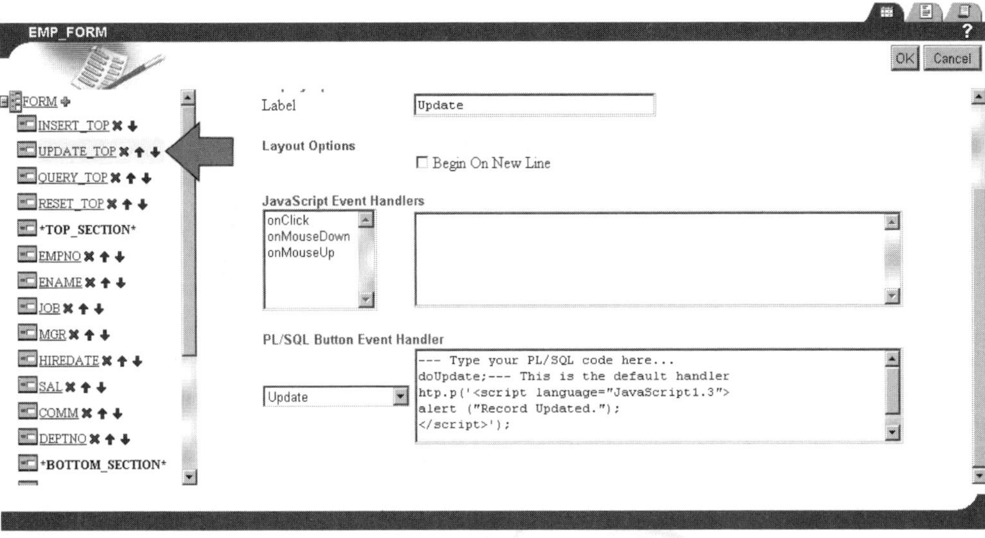

Figure 10.12 Form Edit: UPDATE_TOP: PL/SQL Button Event Handler.

Accessing Form Items in JavaScript

In an Oracle Portal form component, the items are named initially based on the underlying database column names (i.e., names displayed on the navigation frame in the Formatting and Validation Options tab). Internally, Oracle Portal does not use these item names to generate the HTML for the form; therefore, you cannot reference the items by these names inside your JavaScript programs.

The internal item names have the following format:

```
<FormName>.<FormBlockName><ItemName><InstanceNumber>

Examples:

EMP_FORM.DEFAULT.COMM.01
EMP_PER_DEPARTMENT_FORM.MASTER_BLOCK.DNAME.01
EMP_PER_DEPARTMENT_FORM.DETAIL_BLOCK.SAL.01
```

- FormName is the name of the portal form component.
- FormBlockName is the block name where the item is located.
- ItemName is the item name defined in the Formatting and Validation Options tab.
- InstanceNumber is a sequence number starting with "01". It is used if you have more than one item based on the same column.

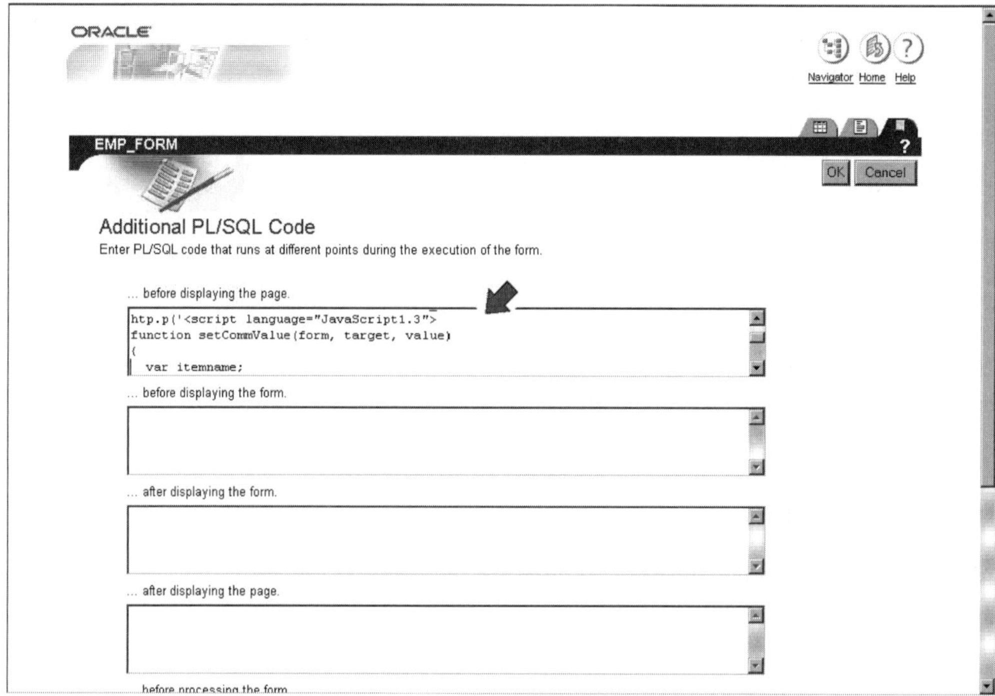

Figure 10.13 Adding a JavaScript Function in the Form Additional PL/SQL.

To be able to locate an item, you need to write a JavaScript function to loop through all the items of the form. This function looks for the ItemName (i.e., third section of the internal item name). For example, the following code is used to look up the commission item in the employee form; when found it sets its value to 10% of the salary item. Add this code to the Additional PL/SQL tab in the "before displaying the page" section (Figure 10.13).

```
htp.p('<script language="JavaScript1.3">
function setCommValue(form, target, value)
{
  var itemname;
  //Loop through all elements in the form
  for(var i = 0; i < form.length; i++)
  {
    itemname = form.elements[i].name.split(".");
    //Compare the 3rd section of the internal name with the
          target
    if (itemname[2] == target)
```

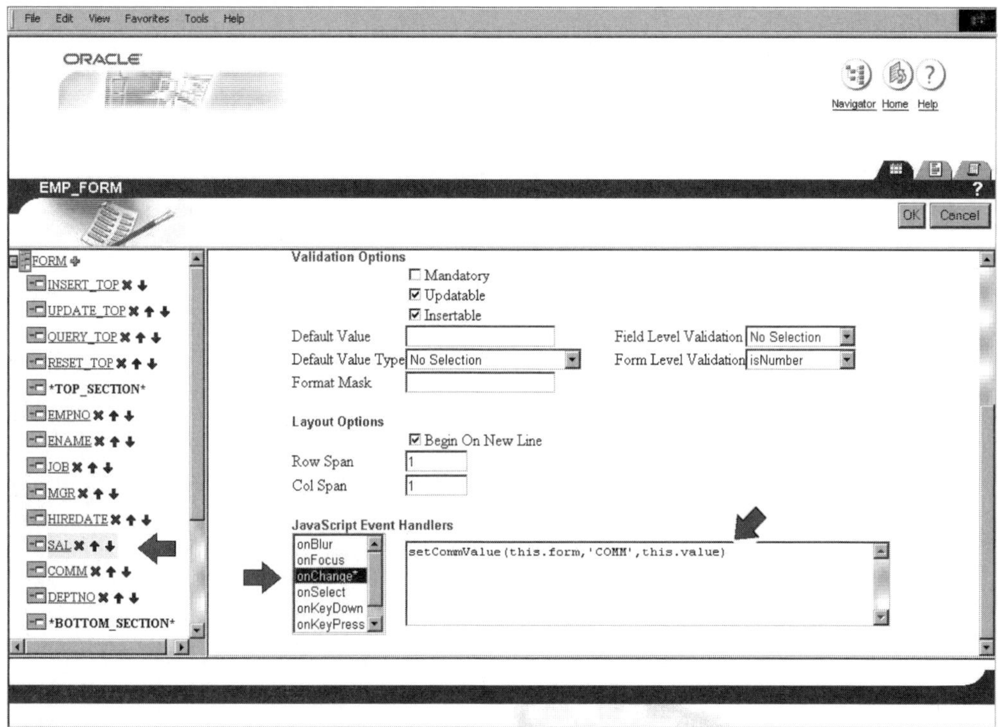

Figure 10.14 Calling a JavaScript Function from the Form Item OnChange Event.

```
            //Set the item value
            form.elements[i].value = value * 0.1;
        }
    }
    </script>');
```

By adding the setCommValue function in the "Before Display Page" PL/SQL, this function becomes available throughout your form. You can call this form from the onChange JavaScript event of the salary item (Figure 10.14). So, whenever the end-user changes the salary of an employee, the employee's commission will change automatically to 10% of the new salary.

Introduction to JavaScript

Even though this book is not a JavaScript tutorial, this section introduces the basics of JavaScript programming to help you understand the preinstalled JavaScript components and start writing your own simple JavaScript routines. JavaScript has a lot of capabilities, but this chapter mainly concentrates on the basics of the language.

JavaScript Lexical Structure

The lexical structure of any programming language is the set of rules that defines how to write programs in this language. This includes the language syntax rules, identifier names, and so on.

- JavaScript is a case-sensitive language.

Note

Whereas JavaScript is a case-sensitive language, HTML is not case-sensitive.

- Spaces, tabs, and newlines are used to separate JavaScript tokens, allowing you to format your JavaScript programs to be easier to read and understand.
- Statements in JavaScript are followed by semicolons. If a statement is placed on a line by itself, you can omit its semicolon. Some JavaScript programmers choose to use a semicolon to terminate all of their statements, so they do not have to think about whether it is required.
- You can use a double slash "//" to comment the text between the two slashes and the end of the line. Also, you can use "/*" and "*/" to comment the text between them. You cannot nest /* */ comments in JavaScript.
- Character literals can be enclosed between single quotations or double quotations. You can use "true", "false", and "null" literals (without quotations).

Note

The null keyword used in JavaScript is similar to the Oracle database (e.g., no value is assigned).

- Identifier names must start with an alphabetic letter, an underscore, or dollar sign. Numbers can be used in identifier names except as the first character. Also, identifier names cannot be the same as any JavaScript keyword.

JavaScript Data Types

JavaScript has three primitive data types: numbers, strings, and boolean. JavaScript also supports two composite data types: objects and arrays. Composite data types are composed of other data types.

Numbers

You can use JavaScript arithmetic operators with numeric literals and variables. These operators are: "+", "–", "*", and "/".

Table 10.2 Built-in Numeric Constants

Constant	Description
Number.MAX_VALUE	Largest absolute number that can be represented in JavaScript
Number.MIN_VALUE	Smallest absolute number that can be represented in JavaScript
Number.NaN	Not-a-number
Number.POSITIVE_INFINITY	Positive infinity presentation
Number.NEGATIVE_INFINITY	Negative infinity presentation

Here is an example of a numeric variable declaration:

```
var  x = 12;
```

Numeric Constants As of JavaScript 1.1, there is a set of constants defined as properties of the number object that you can use in your JavaScript programs (Table 10.2).

Strings

A string is a sequence of zero or more characters enclosed within single or double quotes. Double-quote characters may be enclosed within single quotes and vice versa. For example,

```
'Hello World'
"123.45"
"My name is: 'Mohamed' "
'My name is: "Mohamed" '
```

Note

JavaScript does not have a one-character data type such as "char" in C.

You can concatenate strings using the "+" operator.

Important

JavaScript strings are indexed starting with zero like C and Java languages.

Strings have methods that you can use to manipulate the strings. Table 10.3 lists some of these methods.

Boolean

The only possible values of a boolean variable are "true", "false", and "null".

Table 10.3 String Properties (i.e., Methods)

Property	Description	Example
Length	Returns the number of characters in a string	*s.length*
CharAt	Returns a character at a certain position in the string	*s.charAt(2)* Returns the third character in string *s*
Substring	Returns a substring of a string by specifying the substring start and end character positions	*s.substring(1,2)* Returns the second and the third characters from the string *s*
IndexOf	Returns the position of a character inside a string	*s.indexOf('c')* Returns the position of the character *c* in the string *s*

Objects

You can think of an object as a container of properties (i.e., attributes) and functions (i.e., methods).

Creating Objects Objects are created by means of invoking a special function called the constructor. For example, contractor is a new object created by calling the Employee constructor:

```
var  contractor = new Employee();
```

Once the object is created, you can access its attributes using the dot notation:

```
contractor.firstname = 'Noah';
contractor.lastname = 'Adams';
```

Dealing with Objects You can refer to the current object (e.g., interface element such as textbox) using the "this" construct. "this.value" returns the value entered in the textbox. Then you apply methods on the value. For example:

```
this.value = this.value.toUpperCase();
```

This line of code converts the current value in the text item to uppercase.

Arrays

An array is a collection of data values. You can refer to individual array elements using an index.

Creating Arrays You can use the *Array( )* constructor to create a new array. Once the array is created, it expands automatically to hold new values assigned to it. The JavaScript array can hold values from different data types:

```
var test = new Array();
test[0] = "Oracle Portal"
test[1] = 3.0;
test[2] = true;
```

JavaScript Functions

A function is a named group of statements. A function can have parameters that are used to pass values to the function. A JavaScript function can return a value similar to the following example:

```
function calculate_salary(salary, bonus)
{
      return salary + bonus;
}
```

You can invoke the function in the example using the following statement:

```
tot_sal = calculate_salary(60000, 5000);
```

JavaScript Operators

Most of the JavaScript operators exist in C, C++, and Java. Table 10.4 lists the most commonly used operators.

Table 10.4 JavaScript Operators (Sample List)

Operator	Description
++, --	Pre- or post-increment and decrement
-, +, *, /, %	Subtraction (unary minus), addition, multiplication, division, remainder
!	Logical complement
<, <=, >, >=	Less than, less than or equal, greater than, greater than or equal
==, !=	Equal, not equal
&&, ||	Logical AND, logical OR

JavaScript Flow Control Statements

Within a JavaScript function, the code is executed statement by statement sequentially from top to bottom and each statement is executed once. You can use flow control statements to alter this default program flow.

"If" Statement

The "if" statement allows the program to add conditional flow control to the program. There are two syntaxes for the "if" statement, for example:

```
username = 'Non Administrator';
if ( userid == 'PORTAL30' )
      username = 'Administrator';
```

and,

```
if ( userid == 'PORTAL30')
          username = 'Administrator';
else
          username = 'Non Administrator';
```

You can use one statement to be executed when the "if" condition is true and one statement to be executed when it is false. But also you can use compound statements instead of single statements. A compound statement in JavaScript is a group of single statements enclosed by curly braces.

Important

The condition of the "if" statement has to be enclosed in parentheses.

"Switch" Statement

Instead of using multiple "if" statements to perform multiway branches, you can use the "switch" statement to reduce the number of condition evaluations and make the program more readable.

```
switch ( title ) {
      case 'OPERATOR':
            salary = 1000;
            break;
      case 'SALES':
            salary = 1500;
            break;
```

```
        case 'MANAGER':
                salary = 5000;
                break;
        default:
                salary = 500;
                break;
}
```

The "break" statement causes the program to jump directly to the end of the "switch" statement instead of testing the remaining cases.

"While" Statement

The "while" statement is used to keep executing one or more statements, as long as the while condition is true. The following example prints numbers from 0 to 9:

```
i = 0;
while ( i < 10 ) {
        document.write( i + "<br>" );
        i++;
}
```

"For" Statement

The "For" loop is another looping construct in JavaScript. Usually, it is more convenient to use if you know up front how many times you need to loop. The following example performs the same functionality as the earlier example, but using the "For" loop:

```
for ( i = 0 ; i < 10 ; i++ )
        document.write( i + "<br>" );
```

Pattern Matching with Regular Expressions

A regular expression describes a pattern of characters that can be used to validate the format of data entered by users.

Defining Regular Expressions

Just as string literals are specified as characters within quotation marks, regular expression literals are specified as characters within a pair of slash "/" characters. All alphabetic characters and digits match themselves in regular expressions, so if you included the letter "m" in your expression, JavaScript will look for the letter "m" in the data verified by the expression. The following example creates a new regular expression that matches any string that ends with the letter "m":

```
var filter = /m$/;
```

The following example creates a new regular expression that matches "ab", "cd", or "ef":

```
var filter = /ab|cd|ef/;
```

JavaScript regular expression syntax also supports certain nonalphabetic characters through escape sequences that begin with a backslash "\", such as "\n" for newline and "*" for literal "*".

Also, "\s", in a regular expression, is any white character; "\S" is any nonwhite character; "\w" is any alphanumeric; "\W" is any nonalphanumeric; "\d" is any digit; and "\D" is any nondigit.

Character Classes

A character class is a combination of literal characters placed within square brackets. Thus, the regular expression /[xyz]/ matches any one of the letters x, y, and z. An opposite of a character class can be defined by placing a caret "^" as the first character inside the square brackets. So /[^xyz]/ matches any character except x, y, or z. You can use a hyphen to indicate ranges, thus /[a-z]/ matches all the lowercase alphabetic characters, and /[a-zA-Z0-9]/ matches all alphanumeric characters.

The following example expression matches five digits or six lowercase letters:

```
var filter = /\d{5}|[a-z]{6}/;
```

Working with Regular Expressions

You can use the "test" and "search" regular expression methods to discover whether a pattern exists in a string. Also, you can use the "split" method to break a string into an array of substrings.

The following example validates that a form item has letters:

```
var letters_found = form.ename.value.search(/[a-z]|[A-Z]/);
if ( letters_found == -1) alert("Emp.Name has no characters");
```

JavaScript in HTML

You can embed JavaScript in HTML using the <SCRIPT> tag, which is an extension to HTML. An HTML document can have multiple <SCRIPT> tags, and each can enclose any number of JavaScript statements. Because each version of the Web browsers supports a different version of JavaScript, you need to specify the JavaScript version in your HTML document. The

LANGUAGE attribute of the <SCRIPT> tag is used for that purpose. For example, to use JavaScript 1.3 syntax, you specify the following:

```
<SCRIPT LANGUAGE="JavaScript1.3">
      JavaScript statements...
</SCRIPT>
```

Chapter 11 discusses advanced page customization topics in Oracle Portal.

CHAPTER 11

Advanced Page Customization

Introduction

Previous chapters have taken you through creating pages and adding different components as portlets to these pages. This chapter explores page customization through creating and modifying page layouts and styles.

Create a Page Layout

When you create a new page, you can use one of the precreated page layouts. These precreated layouts can be found under the Page Layouts node in the Pages tab of the Oracle Portal Navigator (Figure 11.1). Create a new page layout by clicking on the "Page Layout" link. You need to specify the layout display name, the layout description, and if the layout is to be made public (Figure 11.2).

Click on the "Next" push button to define the regions of the new page layout. You can start adding vertical and horizontal regions to your layout by clicking on the Add Column icon and the Add Row icon (Figure 11.3). You can edit each region's properties by clicking on its edit icon. You can set the following properties for each region: width percentage of the whole page, portlets display (rows or columns), space between portlets in pixels, show portlet headers flag, and show portlet borders flag.

Note

In Oracle 9*i*AS Portal version 3.0.9, you can also specify the number of pixels around portlets for each region.

Click "Finish" to create the layout. In the next section you will create a new page style. Then you can use the new layout and style when creating new pages.

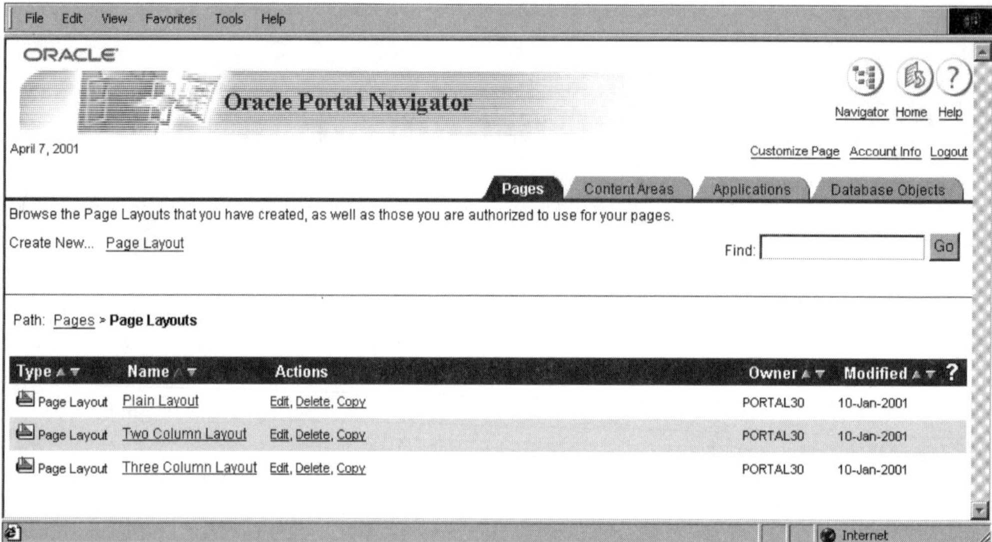

Figure 11.1 Oracle Portal Navigator: Pages: Page Layouts.

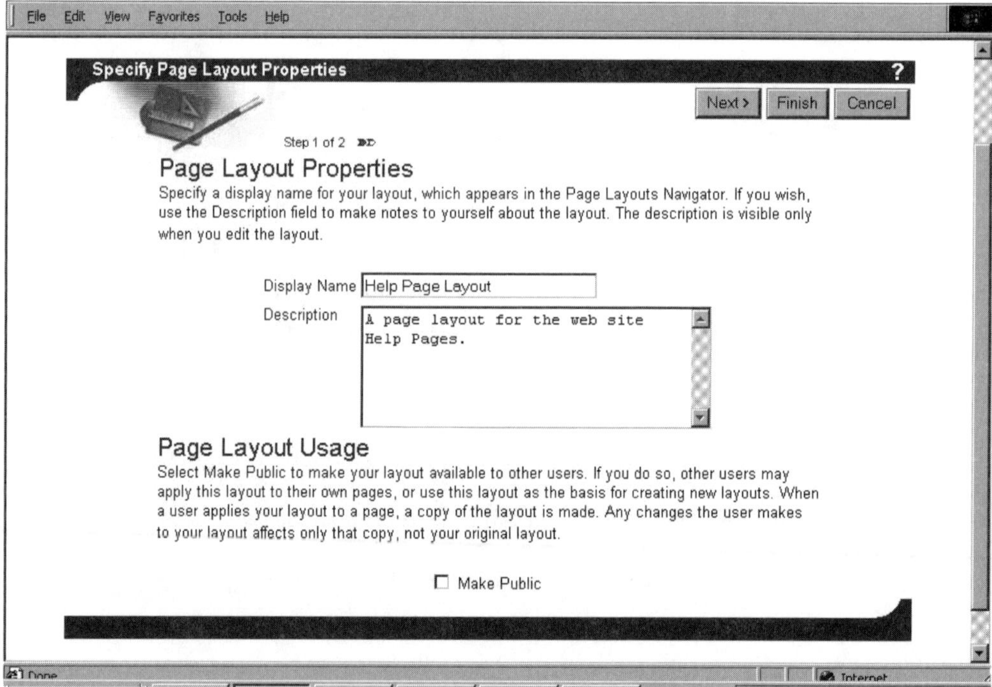

Figure 11.2 Create Page Layout: Page Layout Properties: Step 1 of 2.

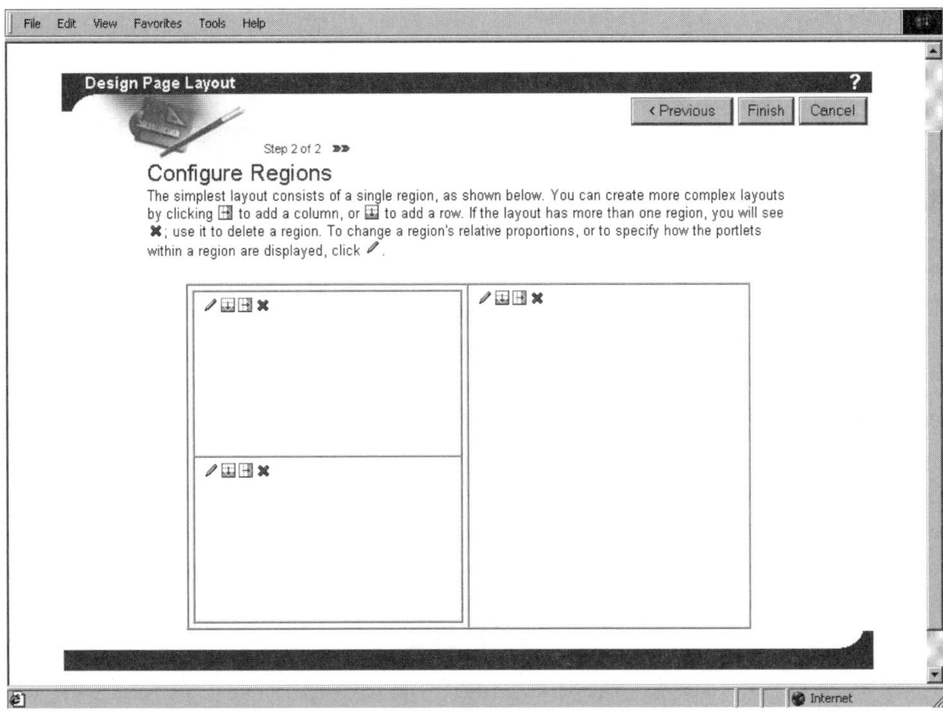

Figure 11.3 Create Page Layout: Configure Regions: Step 2 of 2.

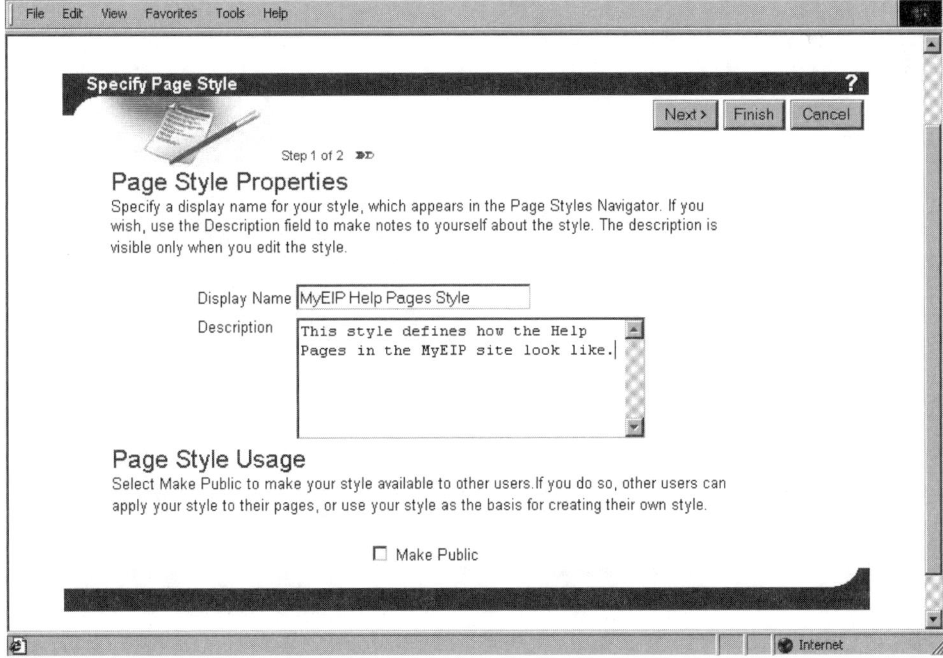

Figure 11.4 Create Page Style: Style Properties: Step 1 of 2.

Create a Page Style

To create a new page style, click on the "Create" link on the right side of the Styles node under the Pages tab of Oracle Portal Navigator. You need to specify the new page style name, description, and if the page style is to be made public (Figure 11.4).

Note

In Oracle 9*i*AS Portal version 3.0.9, you can also select the caching mode of the page style. Chapter 19 explains the different caching modes.

In step 2 the page style element list allows you to choose a style element so you can change its value. Because the default element displayed in the list is the page color, the color palette is displayed (Figure 11.5).

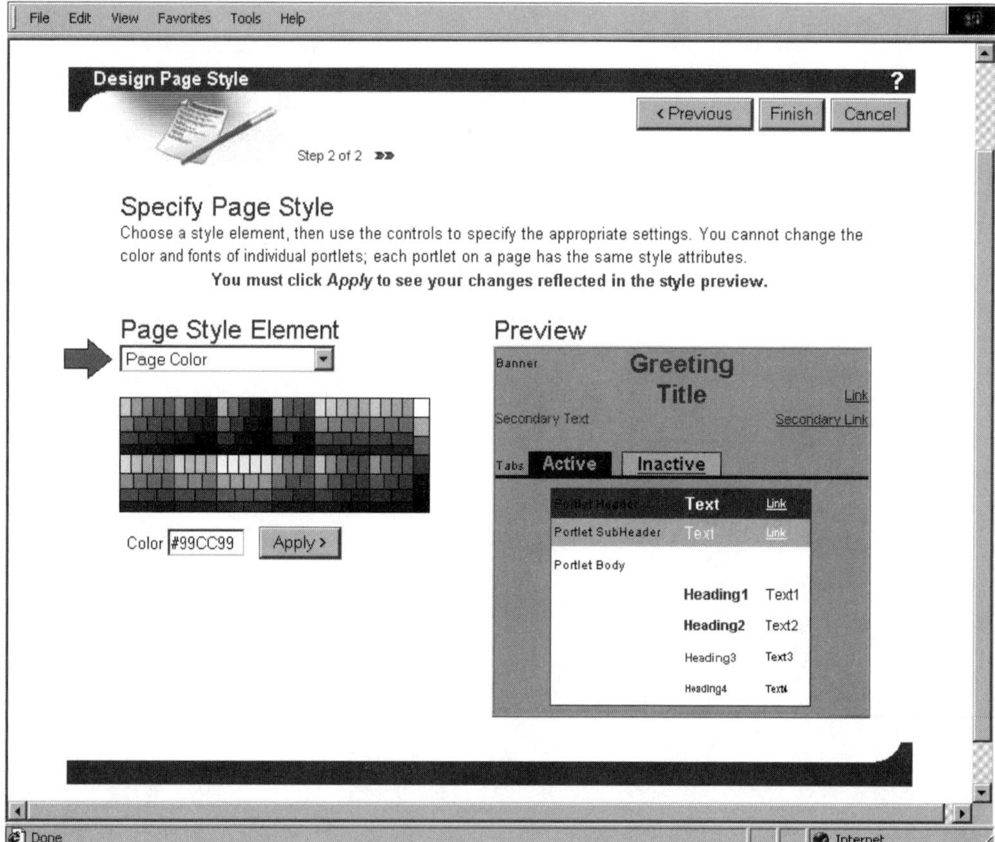

Figure 11.5 Create Page Style: Design: Step 2 of 2.

The preview of a page is displayed on the right side. The preview contains the names of the different page elements. When you change an element and click the "Apply" button, the preview reflects the change. For color elements, you can choose a color by clicking on the color box in the palette or by typing the Hex decimal RGB value. For practice, you can change the page color and the banner background color. Otherwise, you can choose an image as the page background image.

When you click the "Finish" button, the style is created. Now that you have created a new page layout and a new page style, you are ready to create a new page based on them.

Creating Pages

You can create new pages under the My Pages node, which is under the Pages node in the Pages tab of the Oracle Portal Navigator. Under the Pages tab is Top-Level Pages, which contains the pages designated by the Oracle Portal administrators as targets of a large audience. By putting a page under top-level node, you're making it easier to be found, because there shouldn't be many of those in general. Looking for a page that is not yours under User Pages might not be as fast as

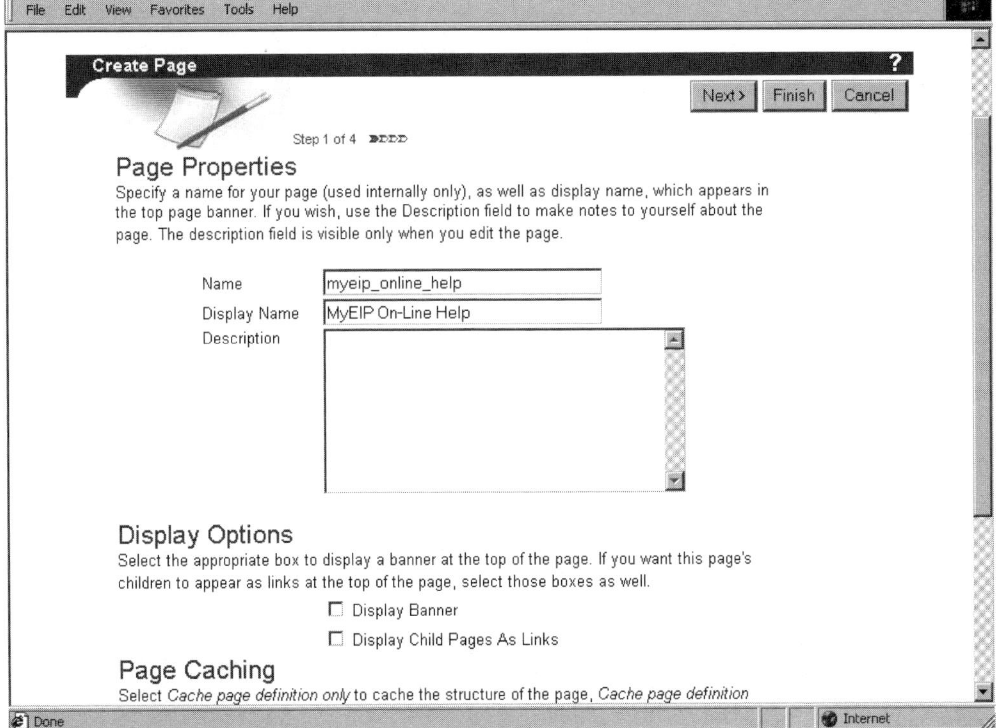

Figure 11.6 Create Page: Page Properties: Step 1 of 4.

you wish. The second node is My Pages, which contains all the pages that the current logged-in user has created. The third node is User Pages, which lists all the pages made accessible to the current user. This list is grouped by the owners of the pages. For practice, create a new page to hold your online help (Figure 11.6). You might not want to display the banner page, because this page is intended for displaying help, and keeping the page small might be more efficient.

In the next step choose the created page layout and page style (Figure 11.7). You can click the "Next" button to add portlets to your page. You can add your help text and links to the help page using the HTML Portlet, which is available under the Oracle Portal provider in the Portlet Repository. When you click the "Finish" button, the page is created. If you decided not to include a banner in the new page (Figure 11.6), you need to go to the portal navigator to edit the page, because the "Customize" link is not displayed in the page.

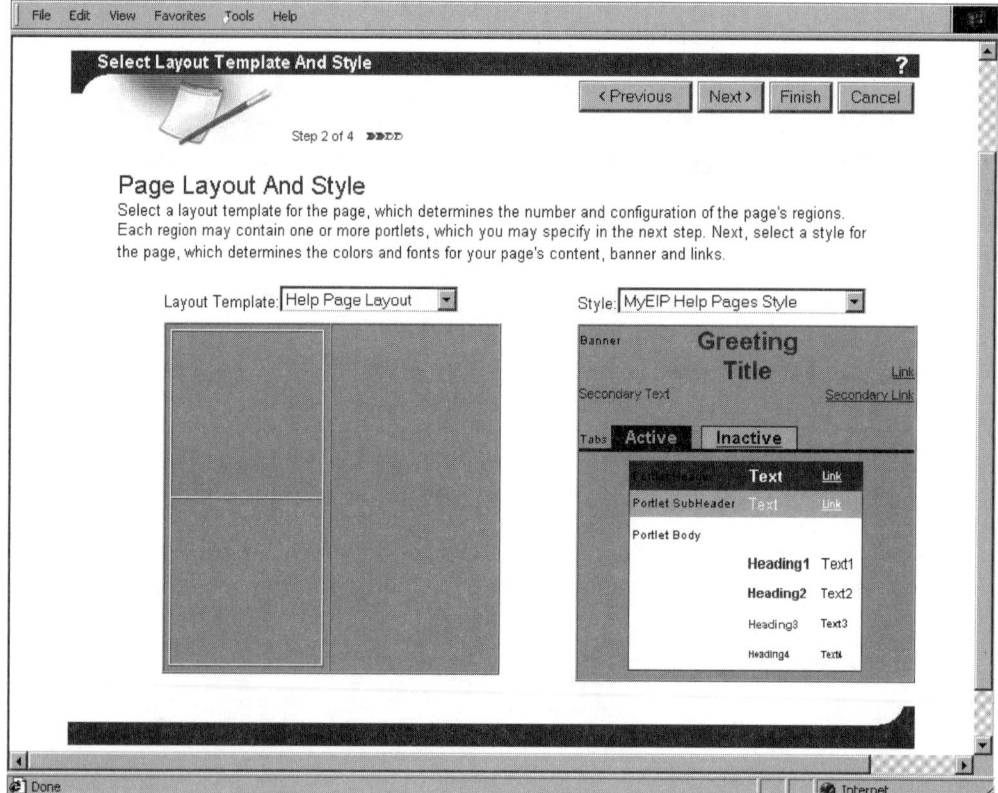

Figure 11.7 Create a Page: Page Layout and Style: Step 2 of 4.

Important

To display the page without going to the portal navigator, use the following URL: http://<Hostname>:<portno>/pls/<schemaDAD>/url/page/<pagename> (i.e., http://myportal/pls/portal30/url/page/myeip_online_help).

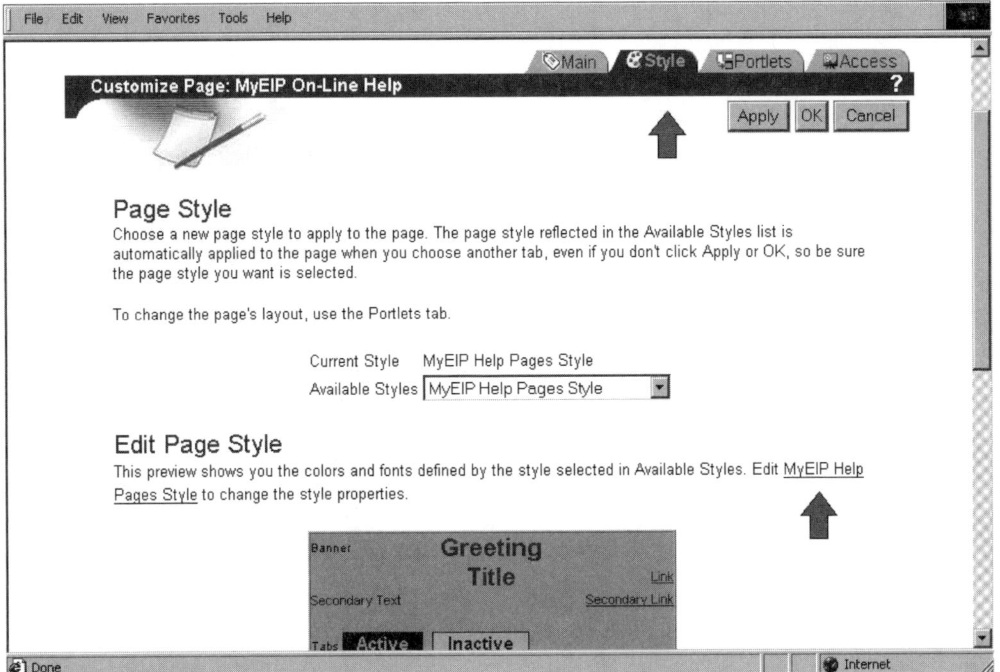

Figure 11.8 Edit Page: Style Tab.

You can edit the page style by clicking on the Style tab while editing the page. Once there you can choose another page style for the page; you can click on the "Edit Style" link and edit the current style; and, finally, you can create a new page style from scratch or copy one from another page style (Figure 11.8). You cannot choose a different page layout while editing the page, similar to choosing a different page style, but you can edit the layout regions in the Portlets tab. When you are done editing the page, click on the "OK" button; the page should be displayed with the new modifications.

Chapter 12 discusses security topics in Oracle Portal.

CHAPTER 12

Security in Oracle Portal

Introduction

One of the most important requirements in any information system, especially systems designed for the Internet, is security. This chapter explores the security capabilities of Oracle Portal and describes the different levels of security that can be defined on different objects in your Oracle Portal Web sites.

User Account Information

When you log in to Oracle Portal, you can change your account information by clicking on the "Account Info" link in the Oracle Portal home page (Figure 12.1). You can enter the account user's first name, middle name, last name, email address, and photograph image file (Figure 12.2). You can change the account password by clicking on the "Change Password" link, which takes you to the change password page under the login server administration site (i.e., http://<Hostname>:<portno>/pls/portal30_sso; Figure 12.3).

The default requirements for a password are dependent on the portal version. For example, in Portal 3.0.7.2, passwords are case-sensitive and need to be at least four characters long, and in Portal 3.0.9.8, the passwords are case-insensitive. So, if you try providing a new password that is less than four characters, you get the error message: "You have entered a password that does not meet the password requirements. Please try again. (WWC-41627)".

As mentioned in Chapter 5, each Oracle Portal user is associated with a database user. By changing the password of the portal user PORTAL30, you are not changing the password of the PORTAL30 database schema. If you need to change the password of a database user (i.e., schema), you need to edit the schema. You can edit the schema from the Administer Database tab or from the Database Objects tab in the Oracle Portal Home Navigator.

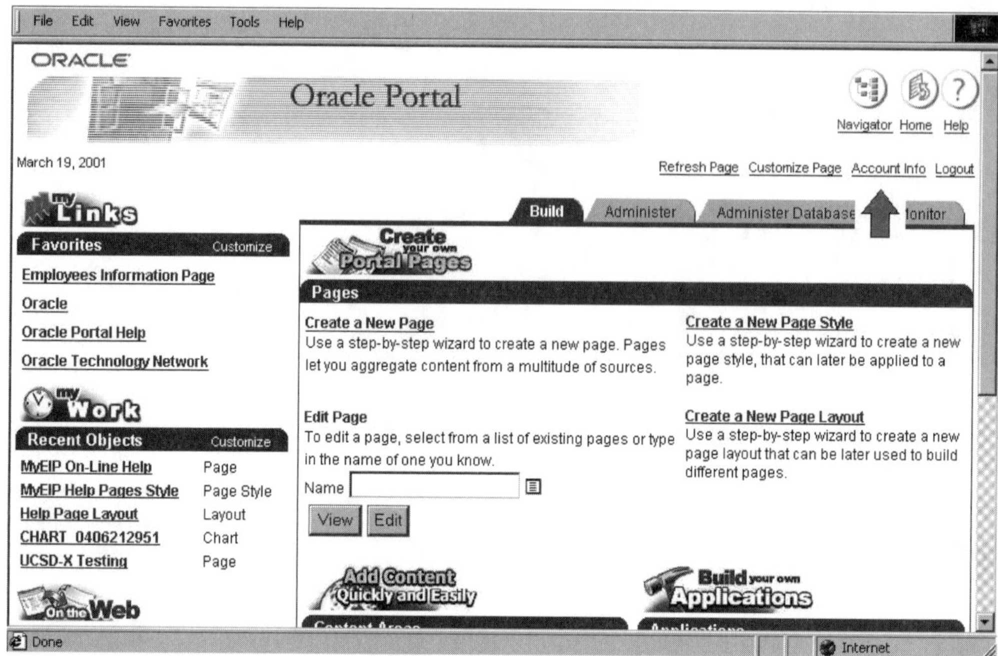

Figure 12.1 Oracle Portal Home Page: Account Info Link.

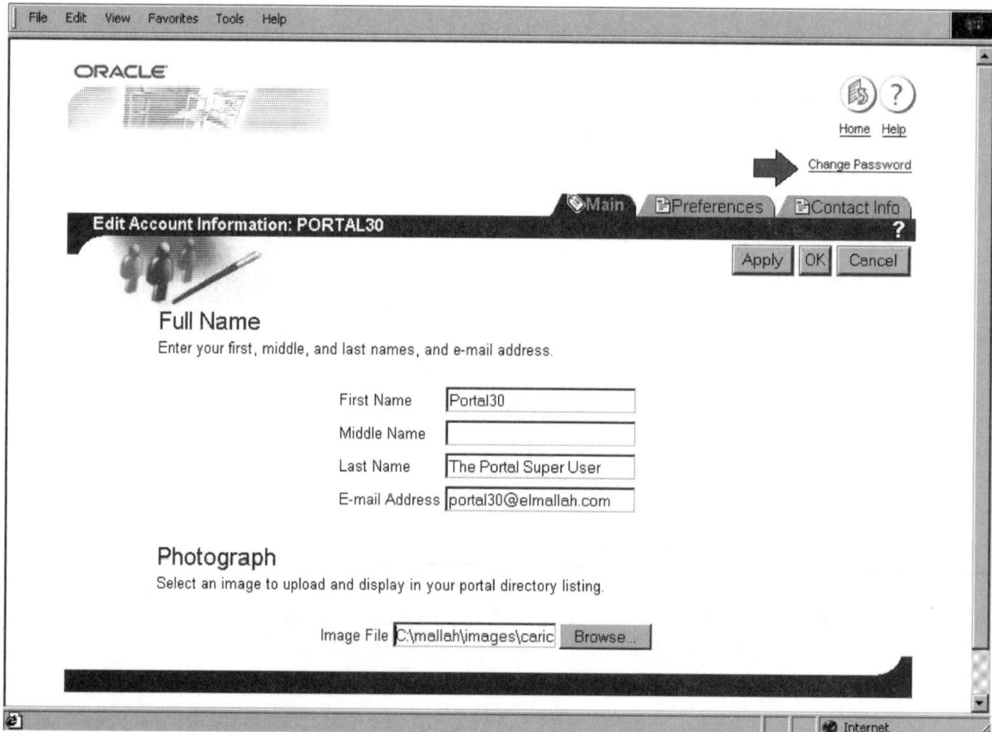

Figure 12.2 Account Info: Main Tab.

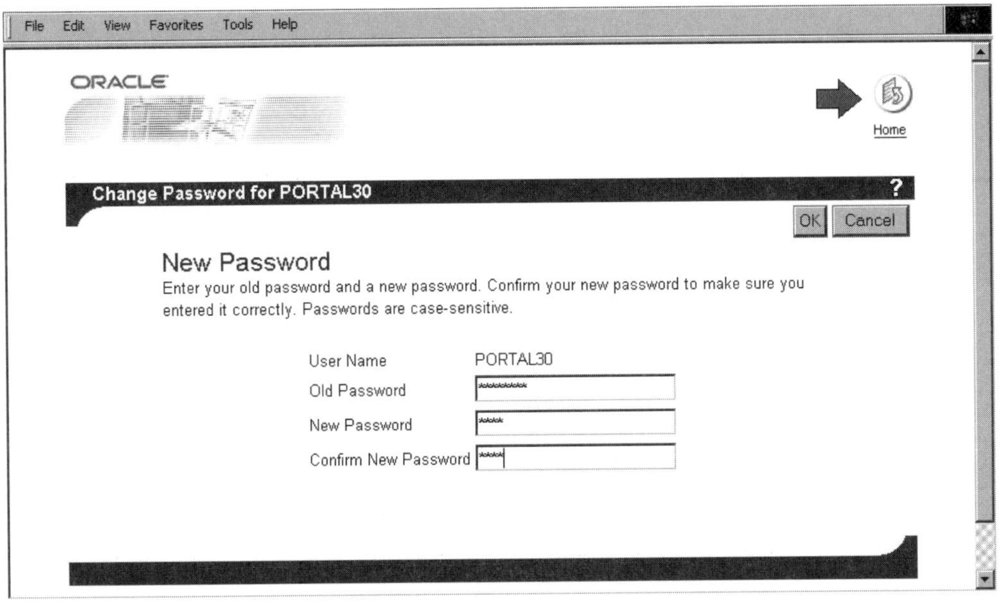

Figure 12.3 Change Password.

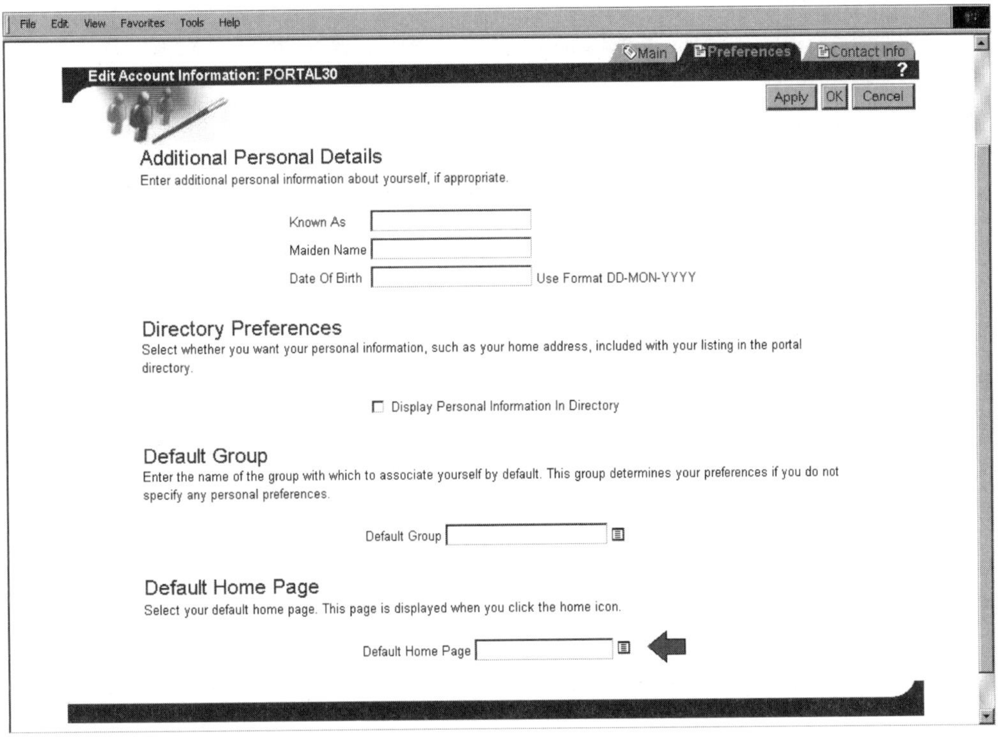

Figure 12.4 Account Info: Preferences Tab.

Important

If you changed your portal database schema (i.e., PORTAL30), you need to change the password in the PORTAL30 DAD definition before you try logging on to the portal. You can access the DAD information by going to http://<Hostname>:<portno>/pls/portal30/admin_/dadentries.htm.

You can specify other personal information for the account as well as the default home page in the Preferences tab of the Edit Account page (Figure 12.4). The default home page is the first page displayed when the user logs on to Oracle Portal. You can specify extra account contact information in the Contact Info tab (Figure 12.5).

Portal Security Architecture

Now we turn our attention to the different pieces of the security framework in Oracle Portal.

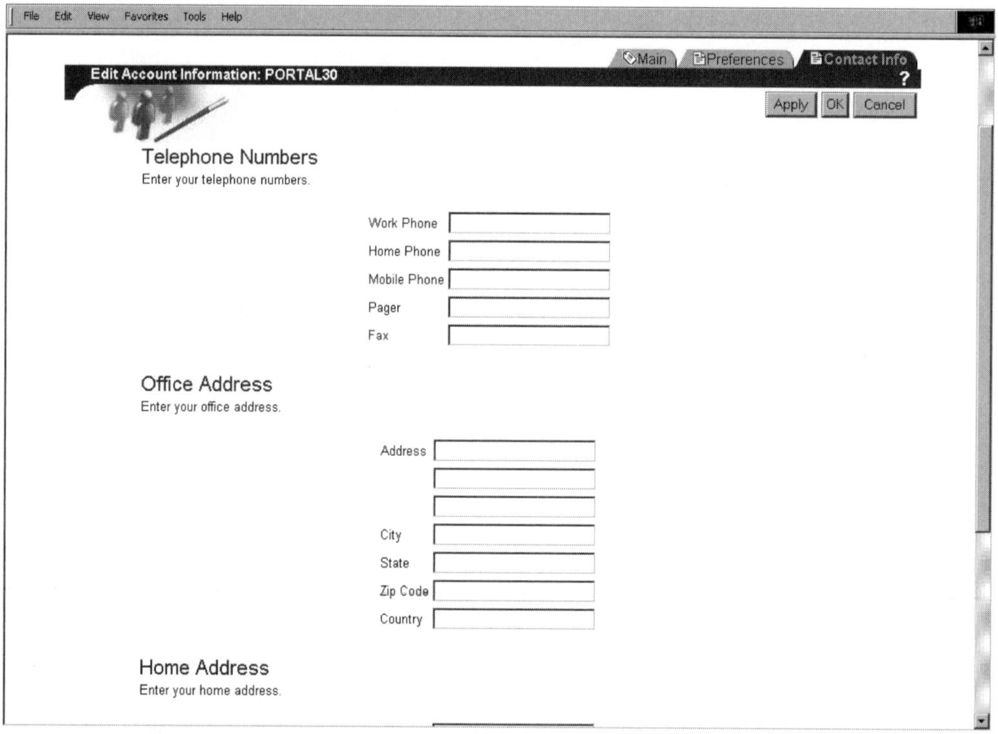

Figure 12.5 Account Info: Contact Info Tab.

Authentication

Oracle Portal users are called lightweight users because by default the portal user does not have a unique database user assigned to it. This feature is very important for enterprise-wide portals, which can be accessed by thousands and thousands of users. In such large Web applications, creating a large number of database users increases the administration overhead. Administering end-users' accounts at the portal level and mapping them into a few database accounts simplifies the administration.

Local lightweight user authentication is used to grant users access to the Oracle Portal product. This authentication mechanism relies on a table of user accounts, which contains users' names, passwords, and access information. Optionally, this table can contain other users' demographics. The login server in the O9*i*AS authenticates the user by validating the user's name and password against the information in the user's table and sets an encrypted login cookie on the client browser to save the user information for future portal page access.

After you log on, you have access to all the pages, sites, and applications available to public users, as well as those that you've created and that have been made available to you by others. A public user is a user who has not logged on to the Oracle Portal Web site yet.

The other type of authentication mode is external, where the login server accesses an external security directory to get the user information (e.g., LDAP-compliant Oracle Internet Directory). Chapter 16 discusses the usage of OiD with Oracle Portal in more detail.

Users

Users are required to authenticate to the Oracle Portal product. The login server performs the administration of portal users. To go to the Login Server Administration page, navigate to the Single Sign-On DAD URL:

```
http://<Hostname>:<portno>/pls/portal30_sso
```

You can also get to the Login Server home page by clicking on the home icon in the Change Password page (Figure 12.3).

The Login Server home page contains the link to the administration of the login server (Figure 12.6). To start creating a new user account and editing existing user accounts, click on the "Administer Users" link (Figure 12.7 and Figure 12.8). Click on the "Create New Users" link to create a new Oracle Portal account (Figure 12.9).

So far, you have seen two different methods to edit the portal user account information. One method is from the "Account Info" link and the other is from the Login Server Administration page. The two methods are not the same, because you can set the user Login Server Privilege in the second. The third method to edit more information of a portal user account is through the User portlet in the Administer tab of the Oracle Portal home page (Figure 12.10). You can disallow a certain user from logging on to Oracle Portal by unselecting its "Allow User To Log On" check box.

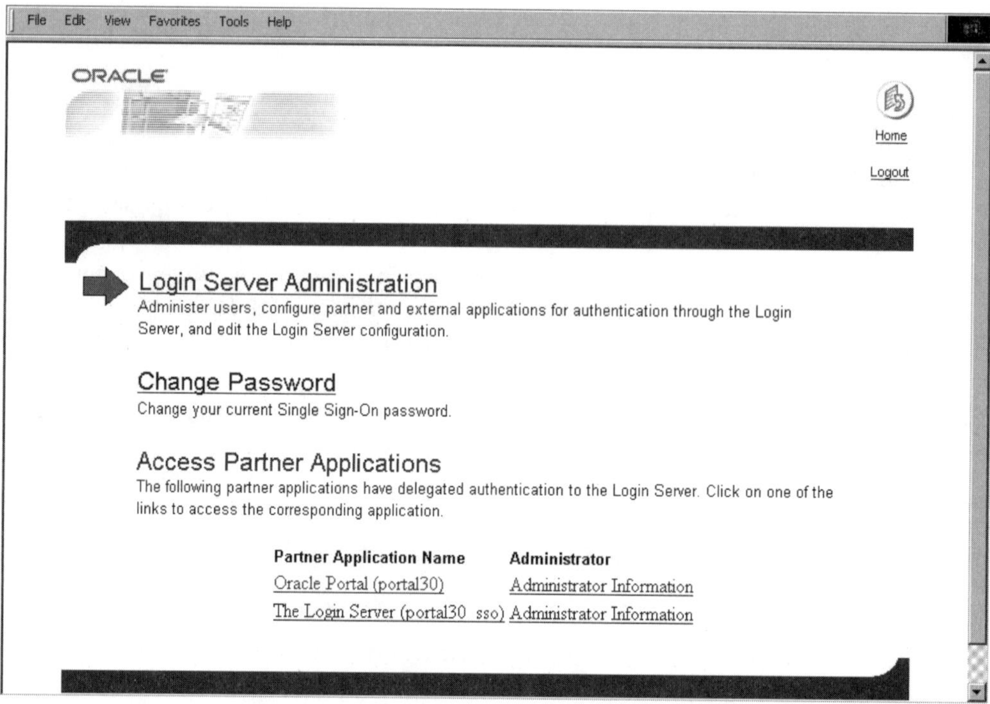

Figure 12.6 The Login Server Home Page.

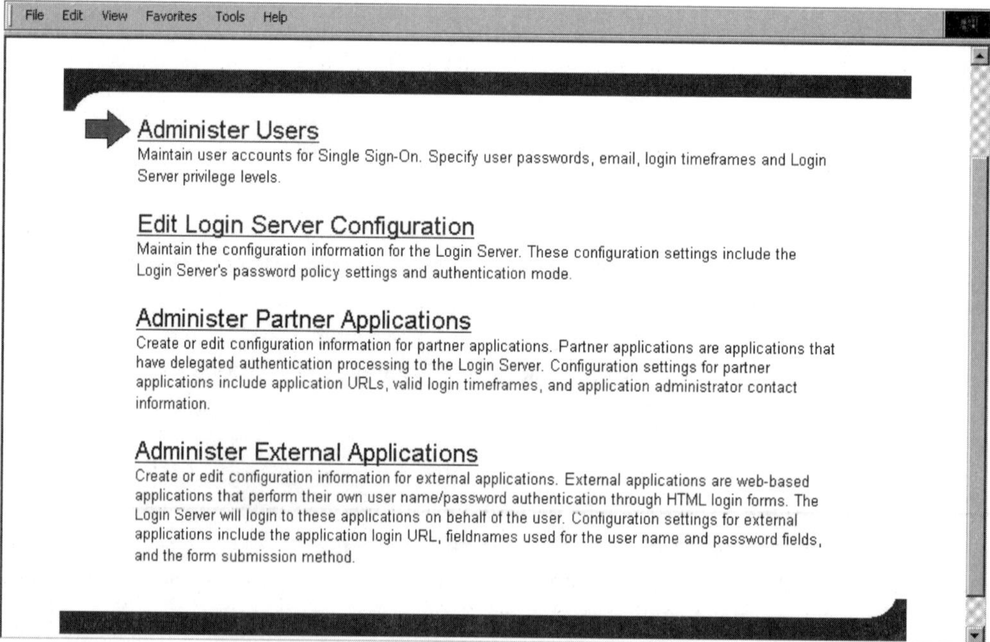

Figure 12.7 The Login Server Home Page: Login Server Administration.

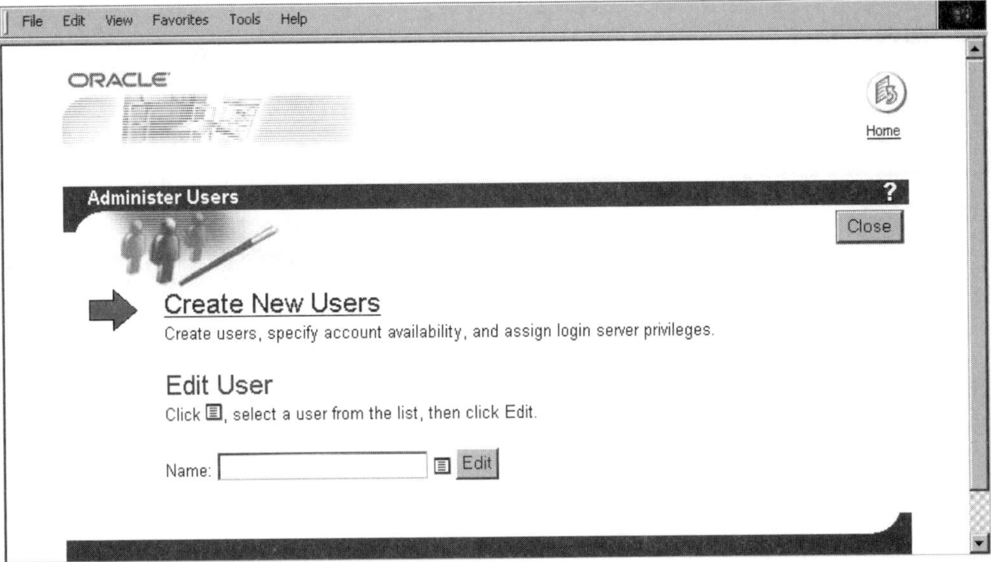

Figure 12.8 Login Server Administration: Administer Users.

Note

In Oracle Portal version 3.0.9, the user information in Figure 12.10 is accessed from a new portlet in the Administer tab called Portal User Profiles.

By default, the only database schema that can be associated to portal users for connection is the PORTAL30_PUBLIC (Figure 12.11). To use another database schema, you need to create a new schema or edit an existing schema, making sure that the "Use This Schema For Portal Users" check box is selected.

The Privileges tab allows the portal administrator to grant individual users object privileges that are applicable to all objects of a certain type. These privileges are covered in detail later in this chapter. To delete an existing user, edit the user account. Click on the "Delete" button in the Edit User page.

User's Login Server Privileges

When you create a new user and when you edit an existing user, you can grant the user the Login Server privilege level desired (Table 12.1). Most of the users do not need these administrative privileges. You can restrict the Full Administrator privilege to the Oracle Portal administrators and the database administrators. You must be an Oracle Portal administrator to change a user's Login Server privileges.

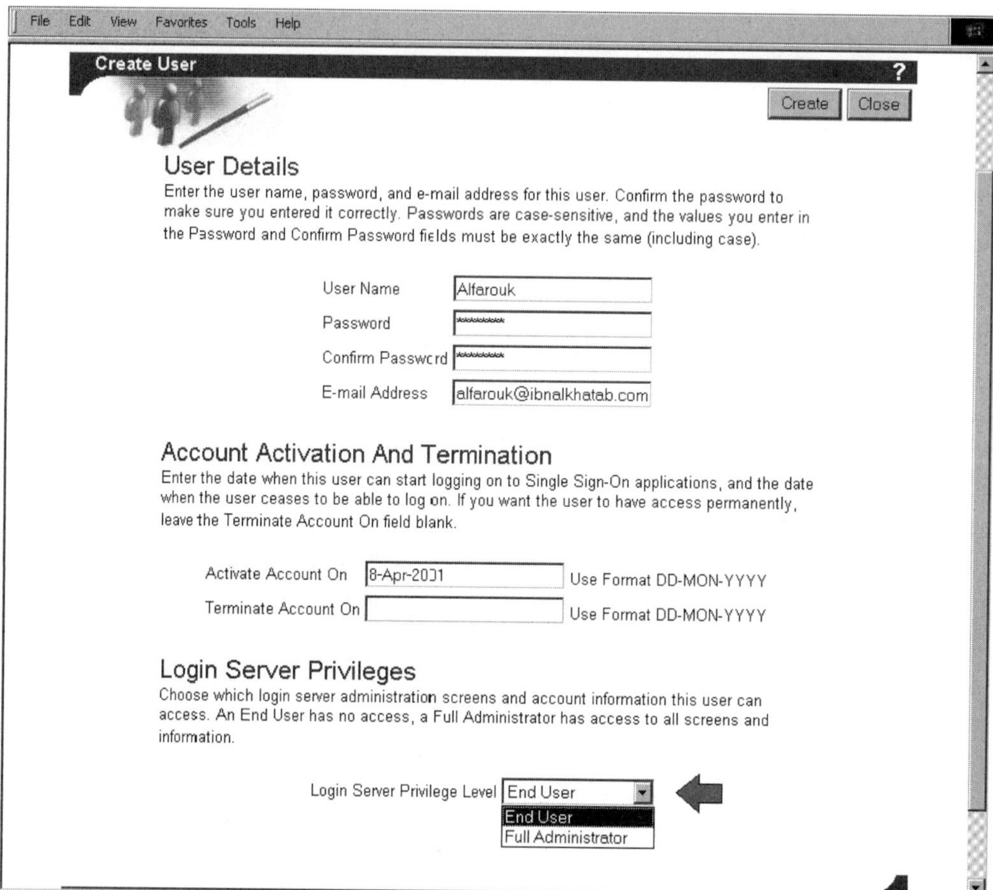

Figure 12.9 Login Server Administration: Create User.

Table 12.1 Login Server Privilege Level

Privilege	Description
End User	It has no administrative privileges on the login server.
Full Administrator	It has full administrative privileges on the login server.

Groups

A group consists of both users and other groups. Groups are used to simplify the privilege grants management. Instead of granting individual privileges to individual users, privileges are granted to groups, and hence, these privileges are granted to the groups' users. Any user may cre-

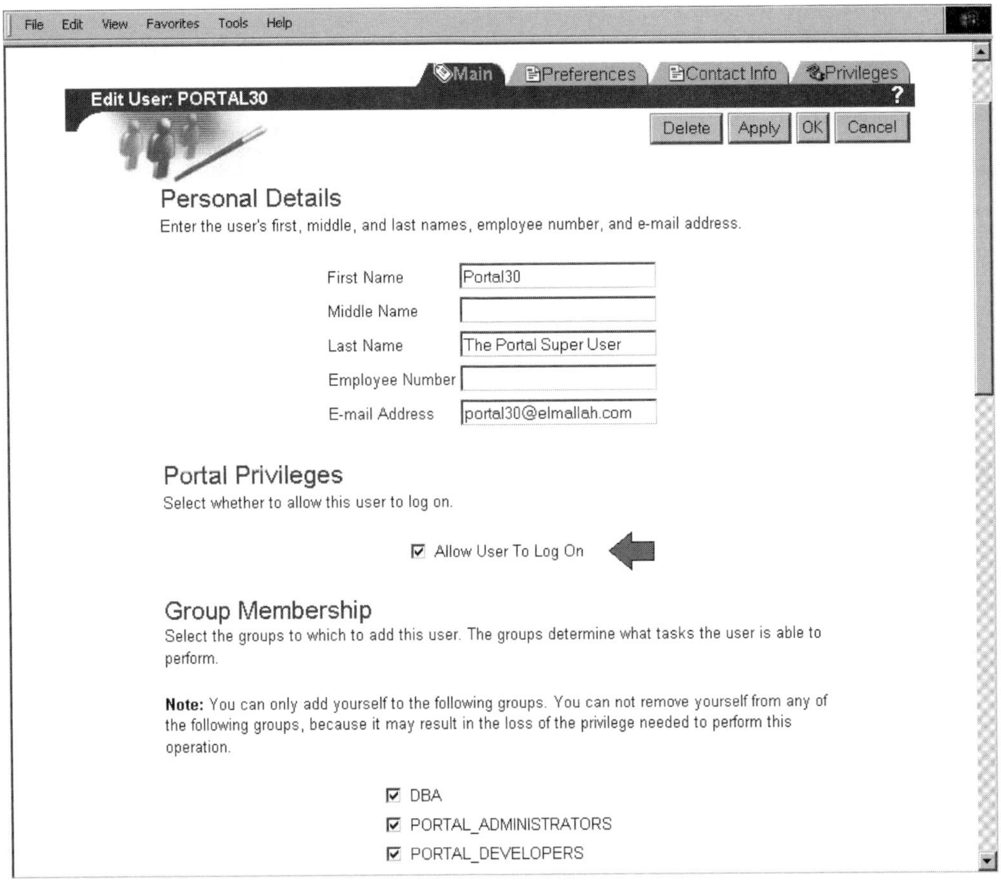

Figure 12.10 Edit User: Main Tab (Top).

ate a group. Any user may be designated as a group administrator. A group administrator may modify the attributes, membership, and administrators of a group. All group administrators have the same level of privileges as any other administrator of the same group. Groups may be defined for a content area or shared across all content areas in a single instance of Oracle Portal. If a user is a member of two groups, the user is granted the union of both groups' privileges.

Oracle Portal comes with a list of predefined groups. To display the predefined groups information, use the Groups Portlet in the Administer tab in the Oracle Portal home page (Figure 12.12).

The predefined groups in Oracle Portal are

- AUTHENTICATED_USERS: This group represents all users that are logged on to the system. You cannot edit this group membership.

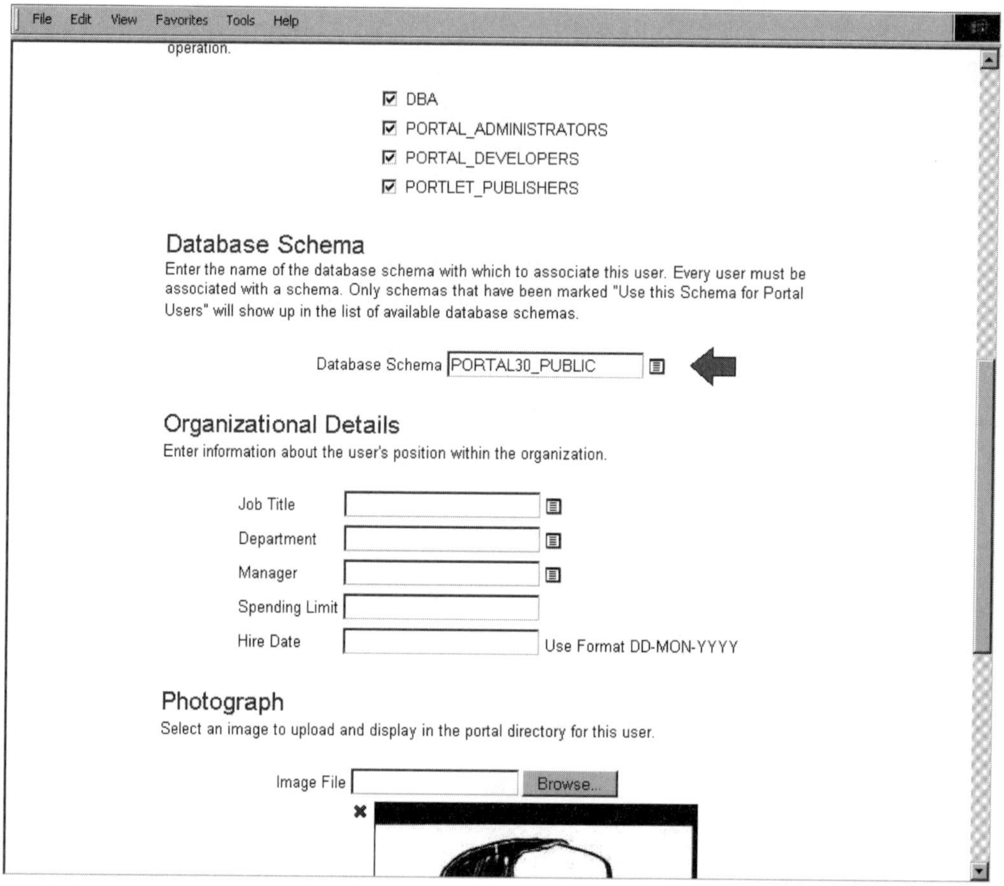

File Edit View Favorites Tools Help

operation.

- [x] DBA
- [x] PORTAL_ADMINISTRATORS
- [x] PORTAL_DEVELOPERS
- [x] PORTLET_PUBLISHERS

Database Schema

Enter the name of the database schema with which to associate this user. Every user must be associated with a schema. Only schemas that have been marked "Use this Schema for Portal Users" will show up in the list of available database schemas.

Database Schema PORTAL30_PUBLIC

Organizational Details

Enter information about the user's position within the organization.

Job Title

Department

Manager

Spending Limit

Hire Date Use Format DD-MON-YYYY

Photograph

Select an image to upload and display in the portal directory for this user.

Image File Browse...

Figure 12.11 Edit User: Main Tab (Bottom).

- DBA: Members of this group can perform DBA actions on the Portal Node database (e.g., ORCL). PORTAL30 is a member of this group.
- PORTAL_ADMINISTRATORS: This group represents the non-DBA privileged administrators (e.g., PORTAL30_ADMIN, PORTAL_HELP_ADMIN). Its members can administer Oracle Portal but not the Portal Node database. They have most of the DBA portal group's privileges except a few, such as creating and managing database schemas.
- PORTAL_DEVELOPERS: This group is oriented toward the portal users who are responsible for creating and managing application components.
- PORTLET_PUBLISHERS: The members of this group are responsible for publishing portlets to portal pages.

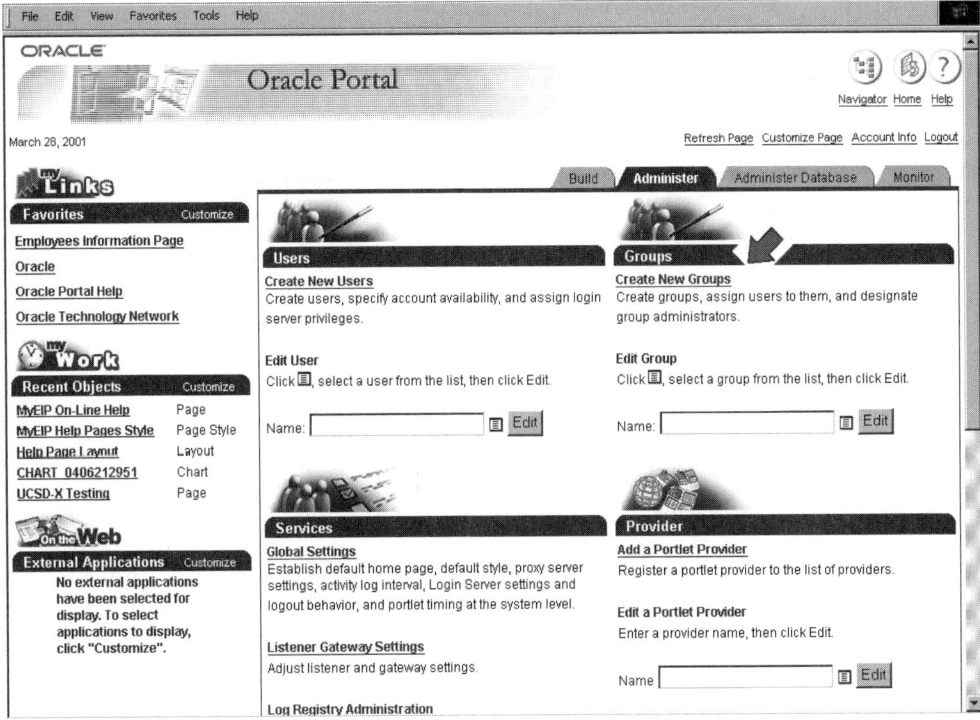

Figure 12.12 Oracle Portal Home Page: Administer Tab: Groups Portlet.

You can get the list of these predefined groups by clicking on the List of Values icon in the groups' portlet.

For the Employees Information in the myEIP portal site, there are certain portions of the portal that should be viewable only by human resource employees. If you create an HR group, you could set the privileges for all the HR-related and sensitive material, so that only users who belong to the HR group would have view privileges. As new employees are hired in the HR department, give them access to the human resource information by adding them to the HR group.

Click on the "Create New Groups" link in the groups portlet to create a new group. To create the group, you need to specify the following group information in the first step: name, application level, description, visibility, group home page, and default style (Figure 12.13). If the "Hide Group" check box is selected, then the group is only available to the group owners for use in the assignment of privileges and also to the users with the Manage All Groups privilege. Group Home Page specifies the name of the page to be used as the default home page for users that select this as their default group. Users may override this setting by choosing their own personal home page.

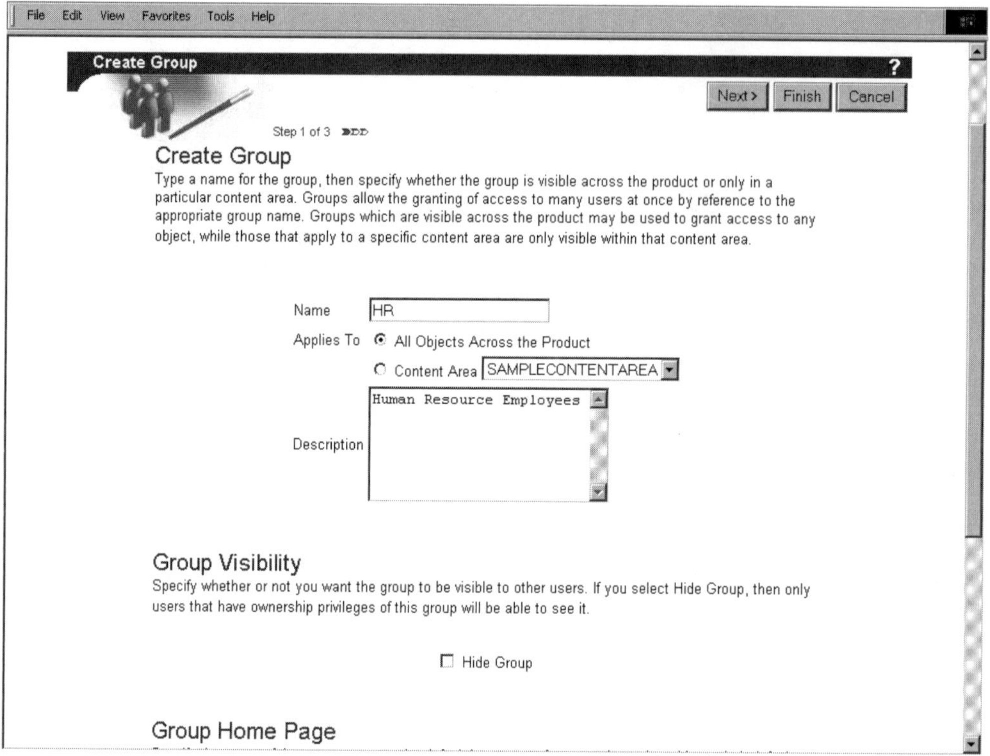

Figure 12.13 Create a Group: Step 1 of 3.

In the next step you can add users and groups to the group (Figure 12.14). Click on the Add User icon to display the list of users available in Oracle Portal (Figure 12.15). You can add other groups to your group by clicking on the Add Group icon (Figure 12.16).

Similar to the object privileges granted to individual users, in the last step you specify the object privileges granted to this group and hence to each of its members. The privileges that are set are applicable to all the objects of a certain type (Figure 12.17). For example, setting the View privilege in the All Pages grants the group members the right to view all the pages in Oracle Portal. The privileges list displayed for each object depends on the object type.

Each privilege in each list includes all other privileges below it. For example, the Manage content area privilege includes Manage Styles, View, Make Public, and Create privileges. It also includes granting the Manage privilege to other users or groups. These privileges are covered in the next sections of this chapter, organized by their object type.

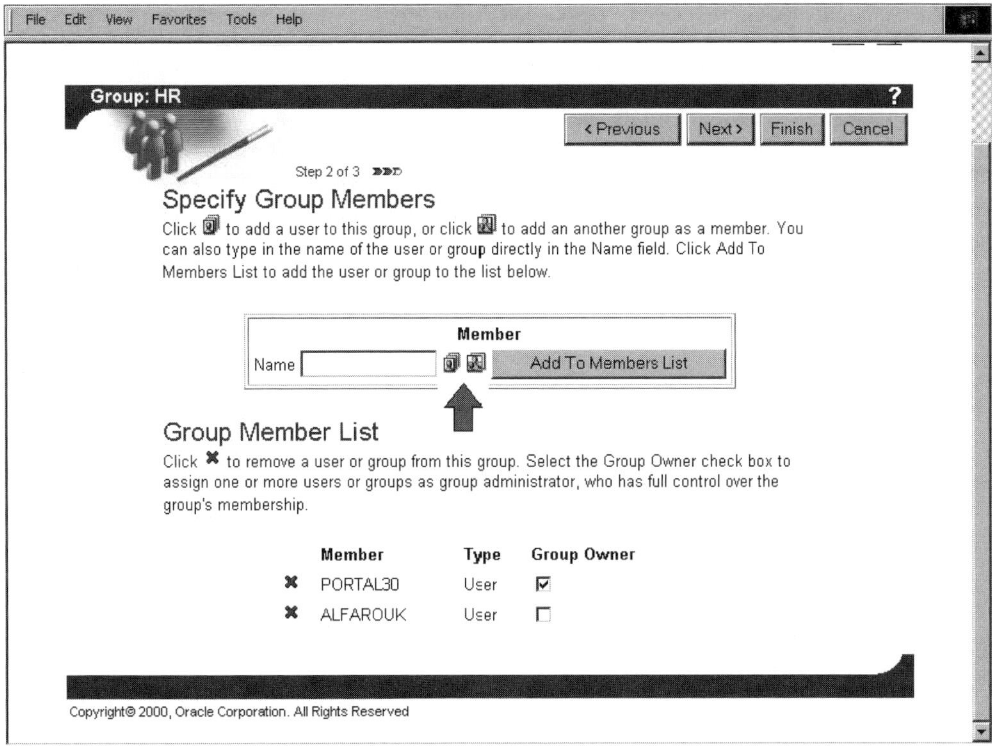

Figure 12.14 Create a Group: Group Members: Step 2 of 3.

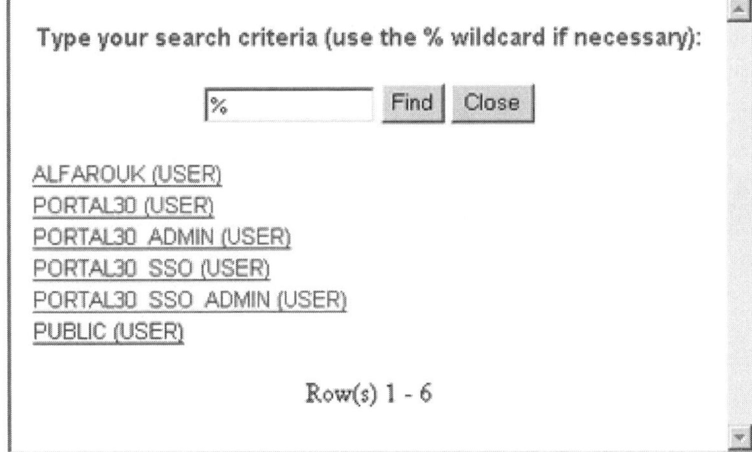

Figure 12.15 Users List of Values.

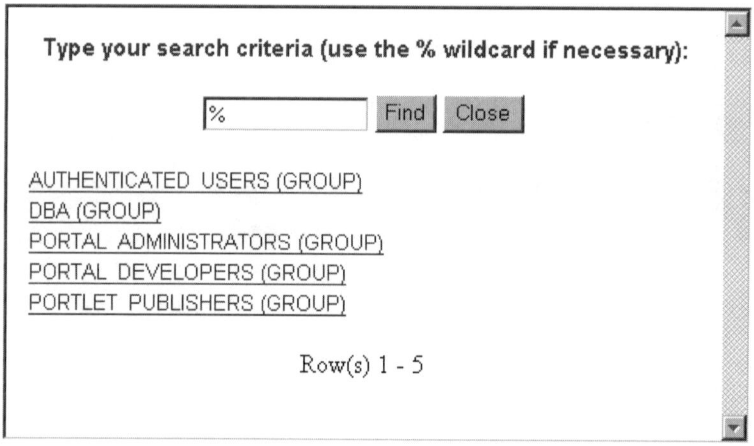

Type your search criteria (use the % wildcard if necessary):

% | Find | Close

AUTHENTICATED_USERS (GROUP)
DBA (GROUP)
PORTAL_ADMINISTRATORS (GROUP)
PORTAL_DEVELOPERS (GROUP)
PORTLET_PUBLISHERS (GROUP)

Row(s) 1 - 5

Figure 12.16 Groups List of Values.

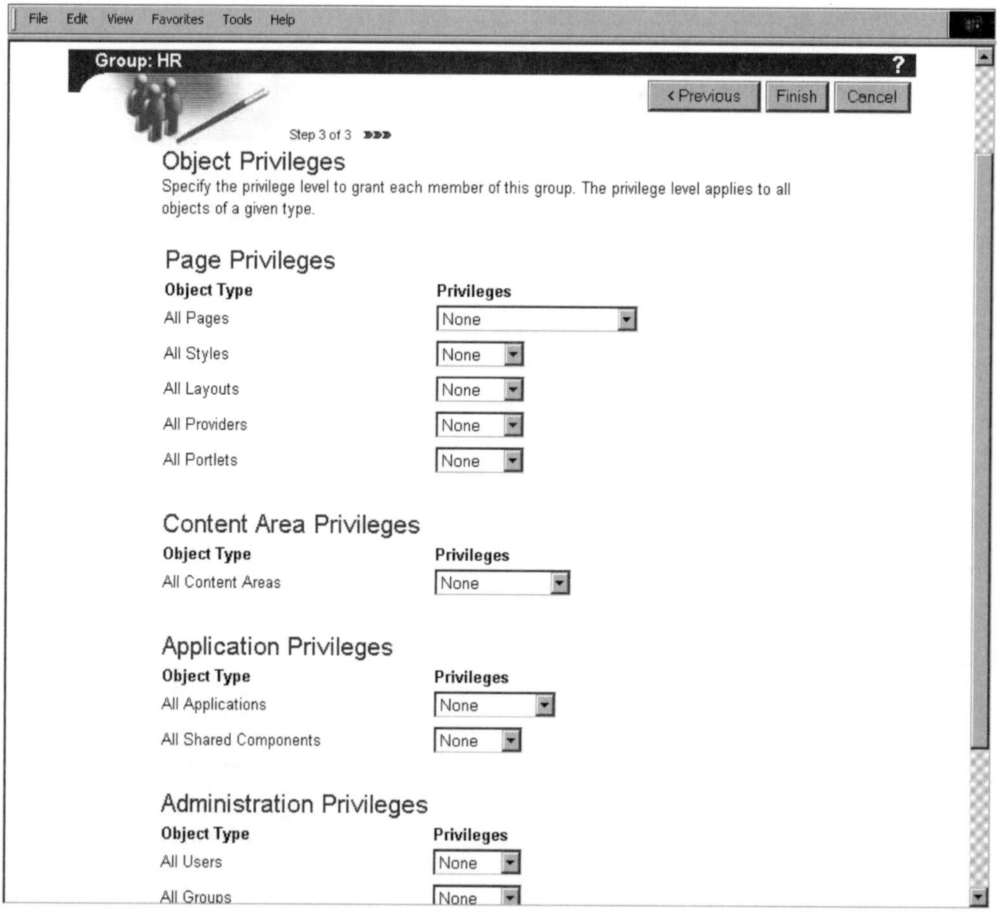

File Edit View Favorites Tools Help

Group: HR

< Previous | Finish | Cancel

Step 3 of 3

Object Privileges

Specify the privilege level to grant each member of this group. The privilege level applies to all objects of a given type.

Page Privileges

Object Type	Privileges
All Pages	None
All Styles	None
All Layouts	None
All Providers	None
All Portlets	None

Content Area Privileges

Object Type	Privileges
All Content Areas	None

Application Privileges

Object Type	Privileges
All Applications	None
All Shared Components	None

Administration Privileges

Object Type	Privileges
All Users	None
All Groups	None

Figure 12.17 Create a Group: Object Privileges: Step 3 of 3.

Content Area Security

When you edit a content area, you can grant or revoke privileges on the content area from the Access tab (Figure 12.18). When a new content area is created, the user who created the content area (e.g., PORTAL30) is granted the Administer privilege on the content area.

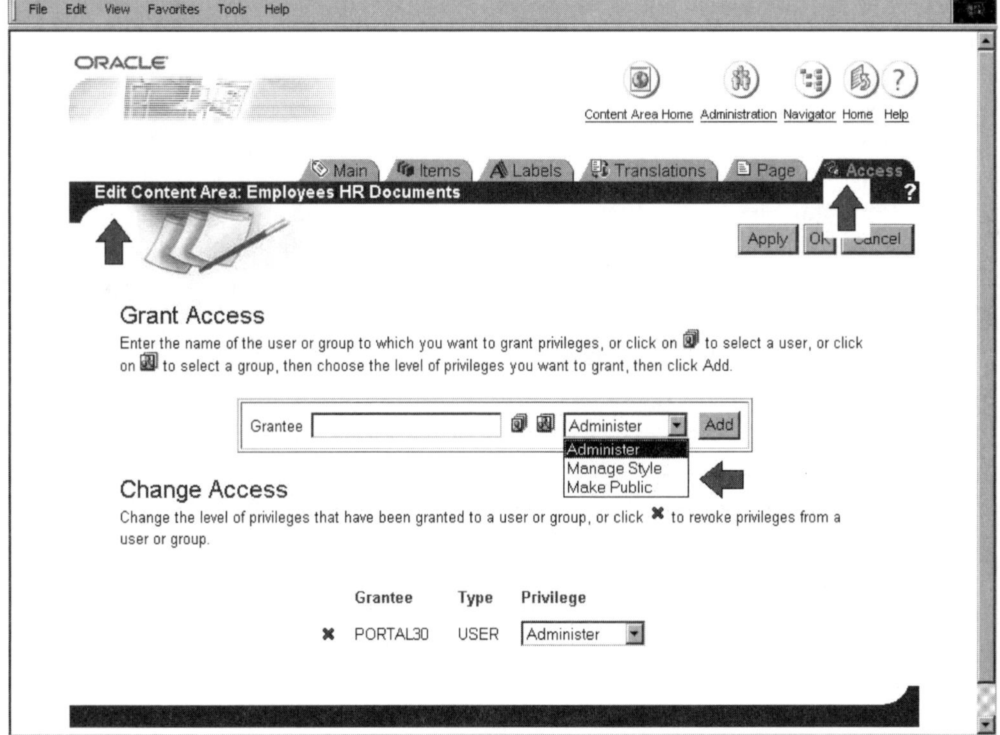

Figure 12.18 Edit Content Area: Access Tab.

When you grant a user the Administer privilege, this user becomes a content area administrator. A content area administrator has full privileges on the style and contents of the content area. He or she can view, edit, and delete any content area object. A content area administrator can assign content area privileges to other users. A content area administrator cannot create new content areas or users. The portal administrators (i.e., members of the DBA group and members of PORTAL30_ADMINISTRATORS group) perform these tasks.

When you grant a user the Manage Style privilege, this user becomes a style administrator for the content area. A style administrator can create, edit, and delete styles in the content area. Also, he or she can assign a style to any folder or navigation bar.

Folder Security

The folder owner and the content area administrators can grant access privileges on the folder contents to other Oracle Portal users and groups. To grant privileges on the folder, edit the Access tab in the folder properties (Figure 12.19 and Figure 12.20). The content area owner (i.e., PORTAL30) is included by default in the Access List, and cannot be removed. You can grant privileges on the folder to a user by adding him or her to the Access List. The default granted privilege is View Content. Table 12.2 lists the available folder access privileges with the tasks that can be performed by the grantees. In addition to these explicit privileges, the folder owner has the ability to display this folder to public users (i.e., all users, even those who are not logged on).

The folder owner also has the option to increase the granularity of security within the folder by enabling item level security (ILS). With item level security enabled, folder owners or item managers may choose to specify ILS settings to restrict access to specific items within a folder. By default, all items inherit folder level security settings.

Folder pages are stored in the cache only when the user is viewing a folder that has item level security disabled. If the user is editing the folder, or the folder has item level security enabled, the folder page is always reloaded from the server when it is displayed.

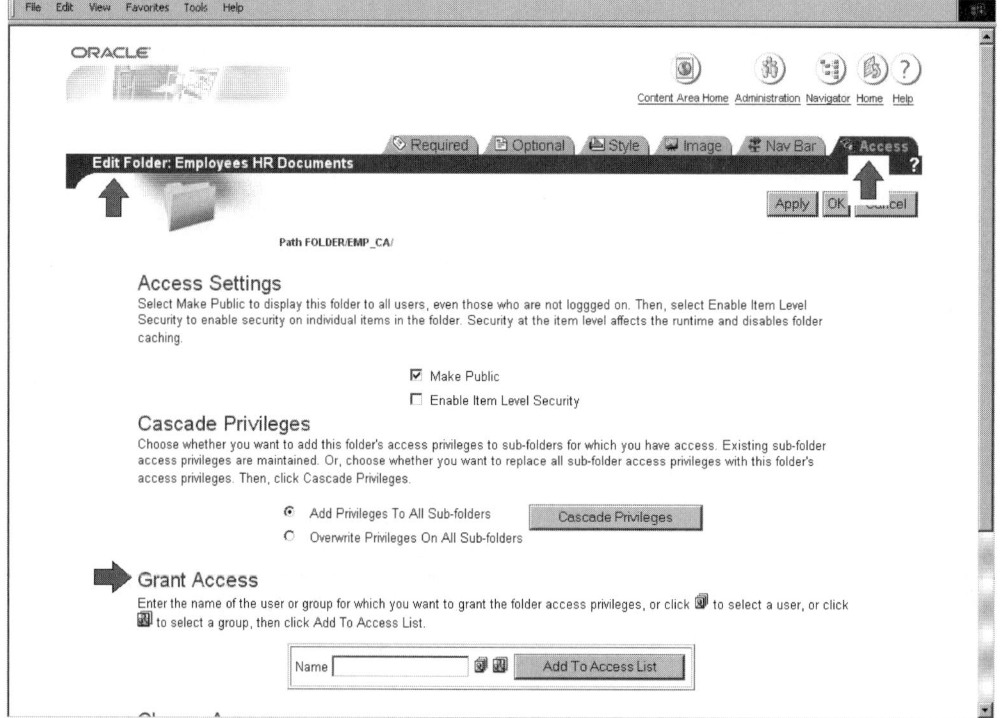

Figure 12.19 Edit Folder: Access Tab (Top).

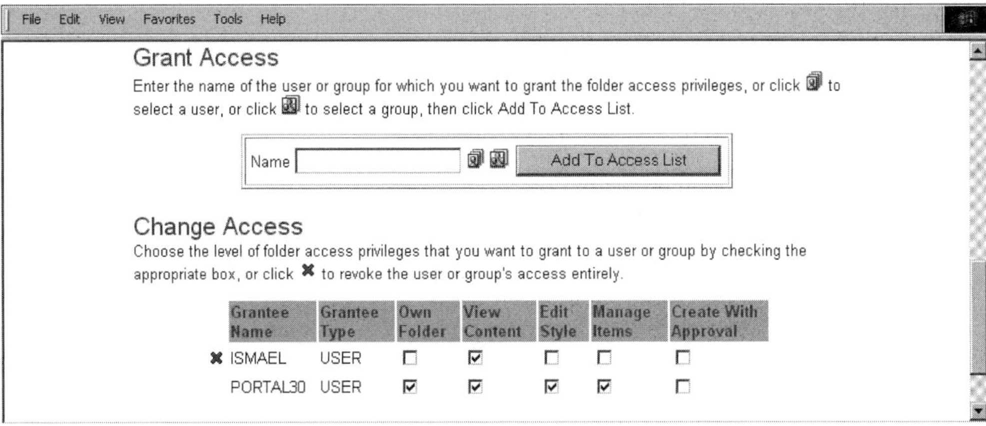

Figure 12.20 Edit Folder: Access Tab (Bottom).

Table 12.2 Folder Privileges

Folder Privilege	Description
Own Folders	Highest level of folder privilege • Add/modify/delete folder items. • Change the folder style and navigation bar selection. • Create subfolders and edit folder privileges.
View Content	Lowest level of folder privilege • View items in the folder (any "expired" or "marked for delete" items are not viewed).
Edit Style	Change the folder style.
Manage Items	Add/modify/delete items.
Create with Approval	Add new items (All items created with this privilege must be approved by a folder owner before being available for view in the folder).

Item Level Security

A major functionality of Oracle Portal is the option to turn on the item level security. ILS permits you to set access privileges at the item level, in addition to the folder level. If ILS is turned on for a folder, all items placed in the folder initially use the security of the folder itself. For practice, change the root folder properties of the EMP_CA content area to enable the item level security (Figure 12.21).

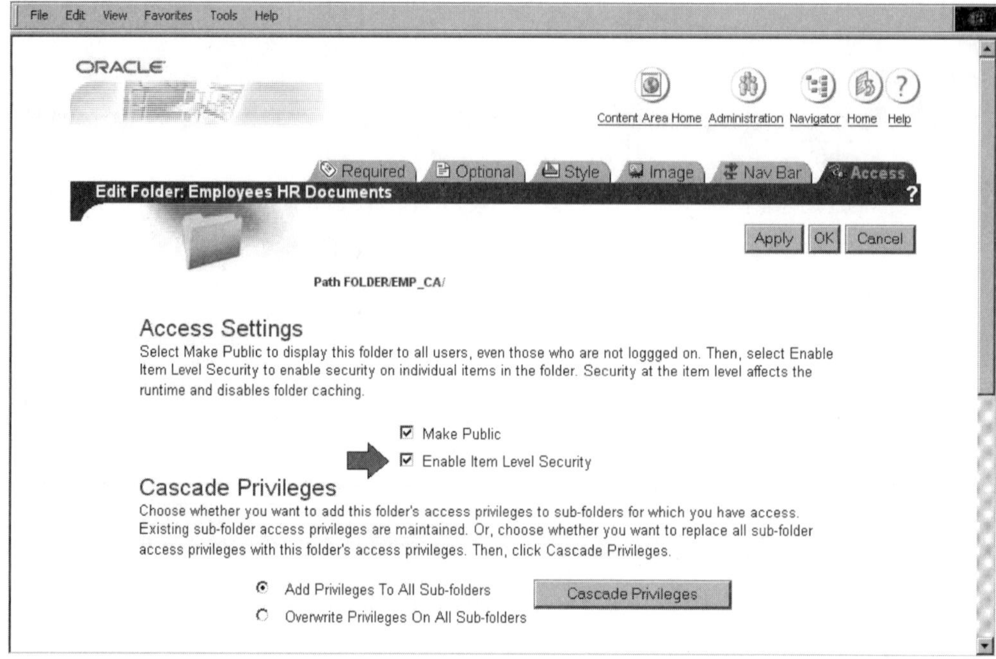

Figure 12.21 Folder Properties: Access Tab: Enable Item Level Security.

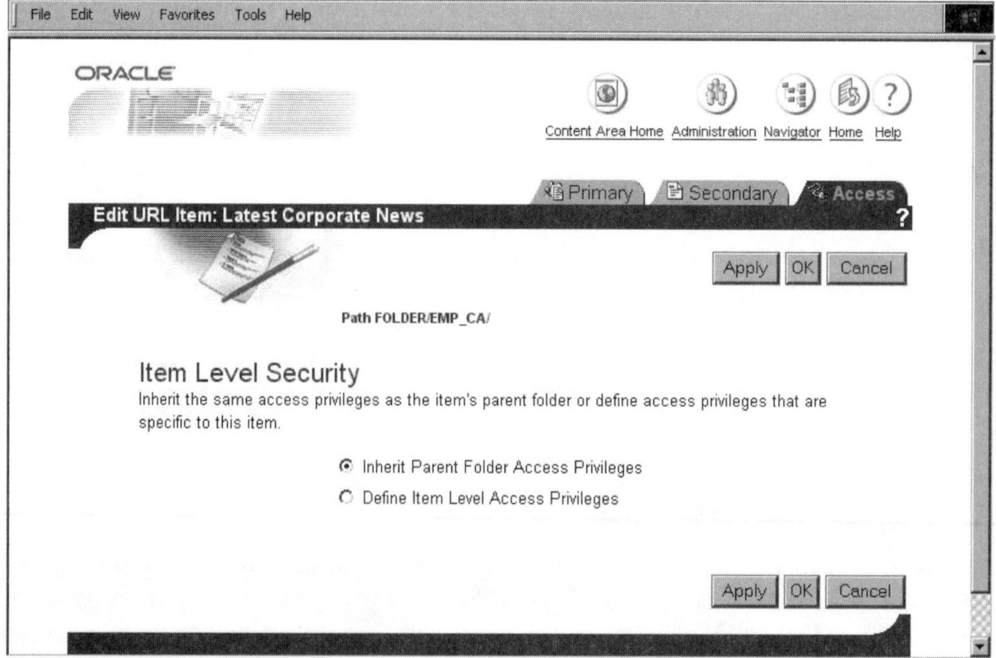

Figure 12.22 Item Properties: Access Tab.

There are two Item Level Security Access Control options. These options are controlled from the Access tab in the Edit Item page for each item:

1. Inherit Parent Folder Access Privileges: If this option is selected, the item uses the access privileges granted at the folder level. This is the default option.
2. Define Item Level Access Privileges: If this option is selected, then portal administrators, folder owners, and item managers may grant the following access privileges on the item to users and groups of users:
   - Item Owner is permitted to update the item and to modify its access privileges.
   - Item Manager is permitted all update privileges on the item.
   - Item Viewer is permitted to view item.

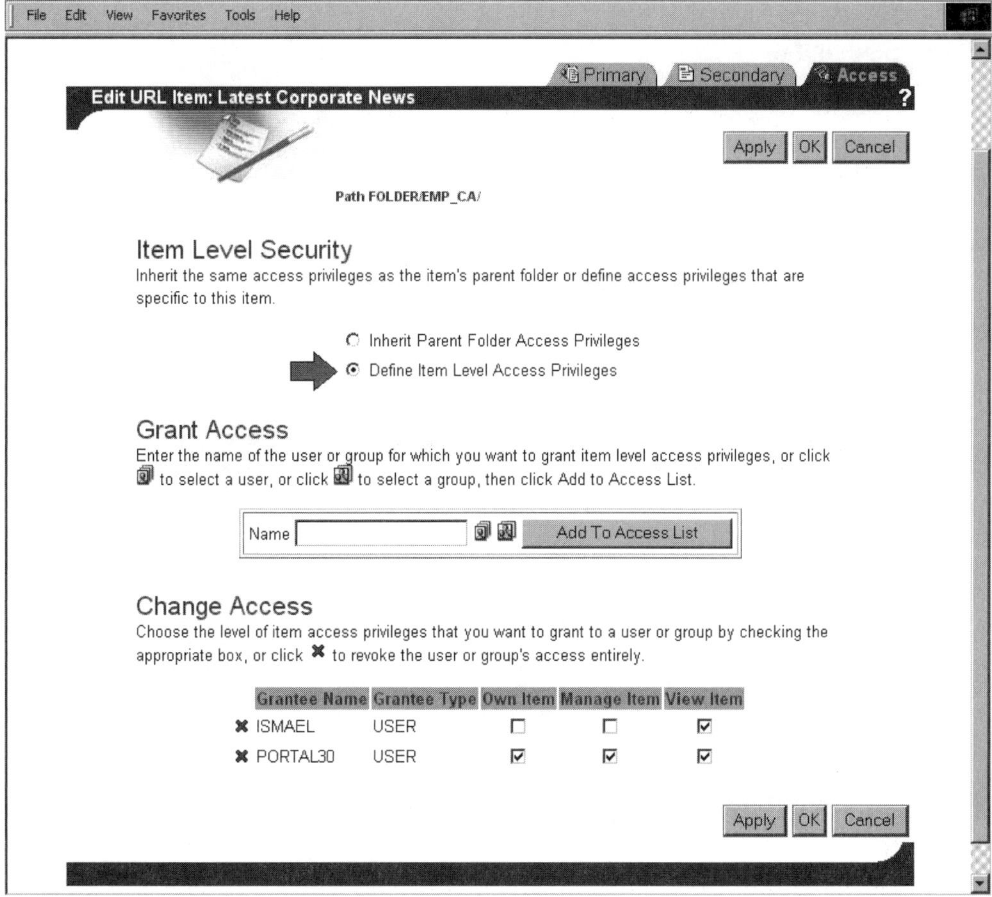

Figure 12.23 Edit Item: Access Tab.

Note

Privileges designated at the item level override the privileges set at the folder level.

After enabling the ILS, the Access tab is added to the Items properties under the root folder (Figure 12.22). When you change the radio button to "Define Item Level Access Privileges" and click "Apply", the access list is displayed (Figure 12.23).

Navigation Bar Security

Any Oracle Portal user can create a navigation bar, and then he or she can edit and delete it. If a navigation bar is made public by its creator (Figure 12.24), other folder owners can associate the navigation bar to their folders.

Page Security

When you edit a portal page, you can edit its security properties by going to the Access tab (Figure 12.25). There are two types of page customizations. The first is the private customization where the end-user customizes for him- or herself only (i.e., personalization). The second is pub-

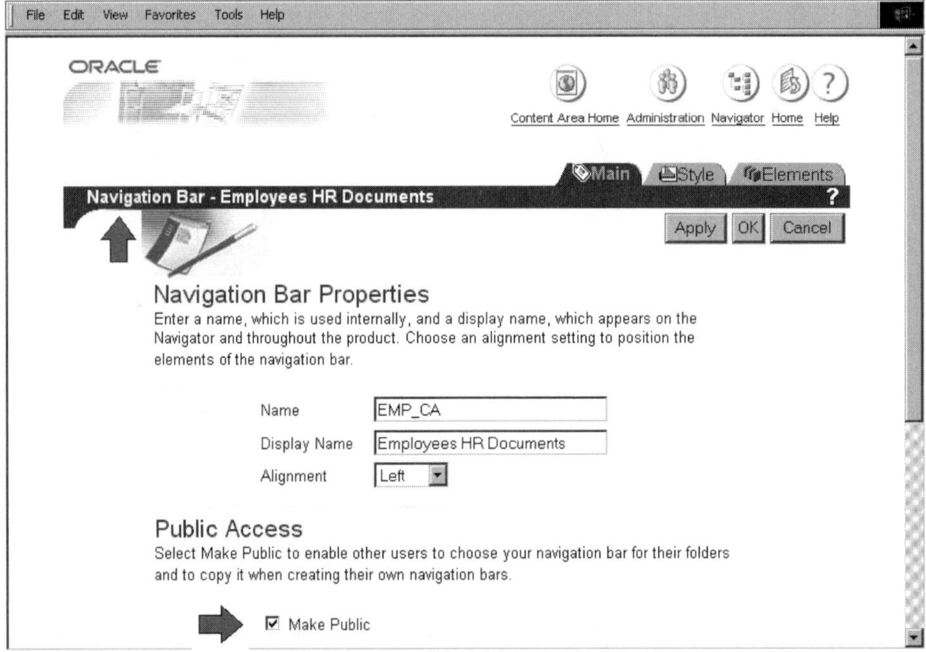

Figure 12.24 Edit Navigation Bar: Main Properties.

lic customization (i.e., page editing) where the portal page administrator customizes for everyone. Page privileges are listed in Table 12.3.

A user has Manage privileges over all the pages (public and private customizations) that he or she creates. Also, the Oracle Portal administrators and DBAs have full control over all pages available in Oracle Portal.

Portal Applications Security

When you edit an application, you can edit its security properties by clicking on the "Grant Access" action link in the Oracle Portal Navigator (Figure 12.26 and Figure 12.27). The applications simplify the security model of Oracle Portal, because by granting application privileges to users, you are—by default—granting the same privileges on all the application components to the users. Applications privileges are listed in Table 12.4.

Table 12.3 Page Privileges

Privilege	Allows the Grantees to Do the Following
Manage	• Edit the properties of the page (name, display name, and description). • Add, delete, hide, and show portlets/tabs. • Add or delete page regions. • Choose a different page style. • Change the page access privileges. It is the highest page privilege. It allows the grantee to customize the page for him- or herself and others.
Edit Contents	• Add other portlets to existing regions on the page. • Add, delete, hide, and show portlets/tabs. A user with the Edit Contents privilege cannot create or delete regions.
Manage Style	Select a new style for the public or private version of the page.
Customization (Full)	• Hide Public portlets added by the page's creator. • Add Portlets to existing regions on the page (that they alone can access). • Remove portlets that you have added It only allows the grantee to customize the private version of the page. A user with the Customizations (Full) privilege may not create or delete regions.
Customization (Add-Only)	• Add Portlets to existing regions on the page. • Remove portlets that you have added. It only allows you to customize the private version of the page. A user with the Add-Only Customization privilege may not create or delete regions or hide public portlets.
View Only	• View the page. • Set it as the default home page (from the Preferences tab in the Edit Account page). • Copy the page.

Table 12.4 Applications Privileges

Privilege	Description
Manage	It is the highest application privilege. It includes all the other application privileges plus the Delete privilege.
Edit	The grantee can change the application name and display name. The grantee cannot delete the application. The grantee can create new components, and edit and delete existing components. The grantee cannot grant access on the application or its components to others.
View Source	The grantee cannot edit the application or its components. Grantee can run the components and can view the component package source (i.e., from the Manage action).
Customize	The grantee can only run the components and access the components' customization forms.
Execute	The grantee can only run the application components.

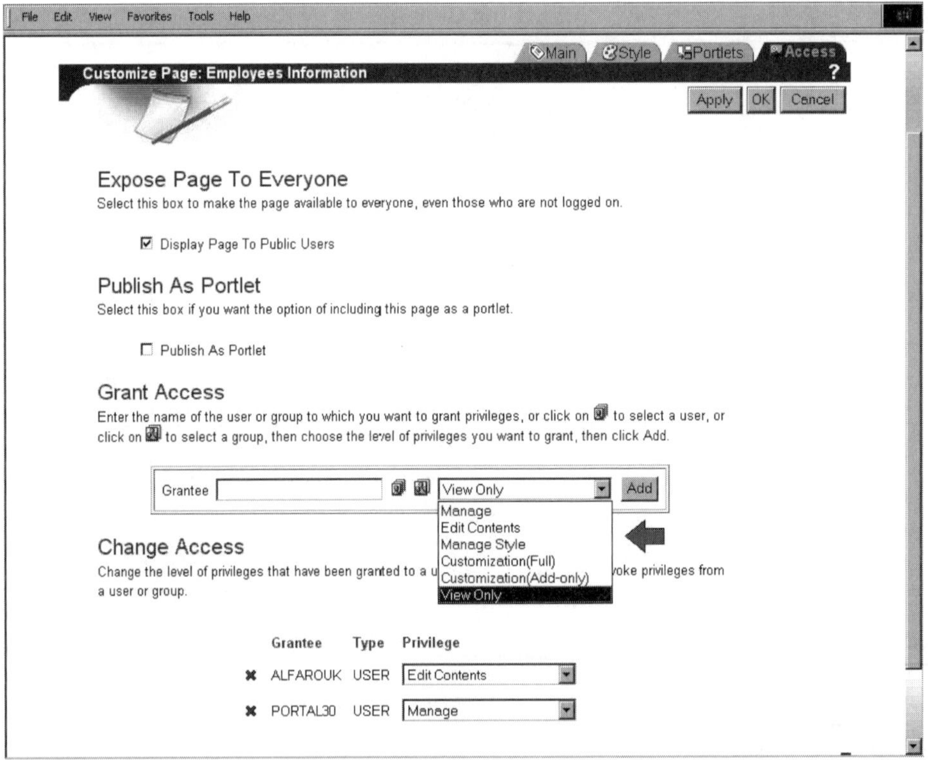

Figure 12.25 Customize Page: Access Tab.

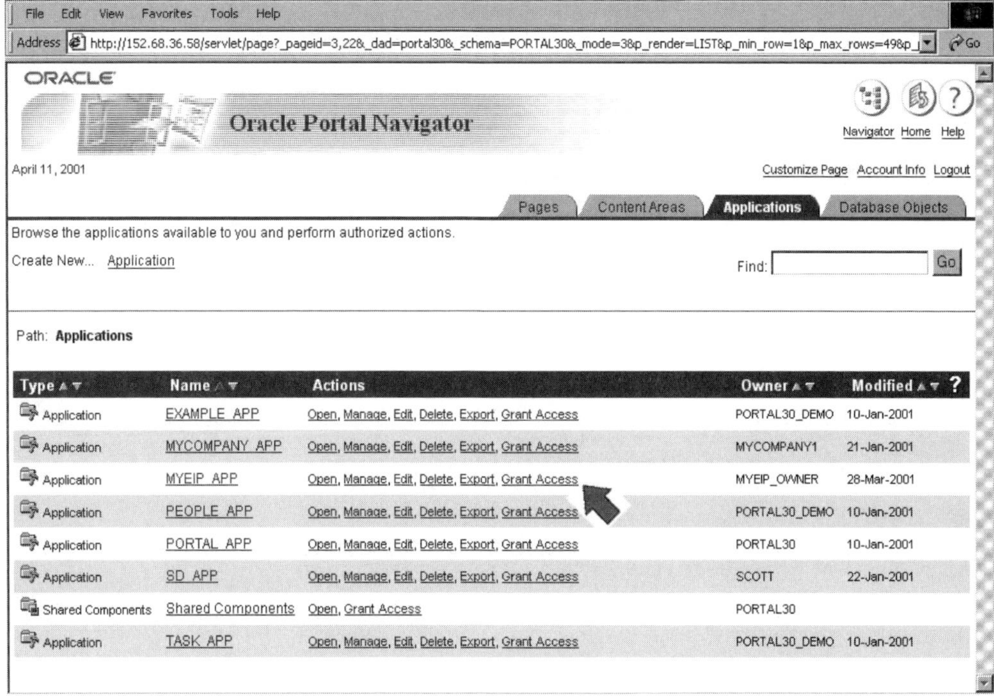

Figure 12.26 Oracle Portal Navigator: Applications.

Application Components Security

When you edit a component, you can edit its security properties by clicking on the "Grant Access" action link under Applications in the Oracle Portal Navigator (Figure 12.28). By default all the components under the application inherit the same access privileges from the application. If you need to specify different privileges for a specific component, unselect the "Inherit Privileges from Application" check box and click the "Apply" button to display the Access List (Figure 12.29).

Portlets Security

Portlet access is inherited from the portlet source access. For example, in the case of a portlet that is based on an application component, the end user is only able to run the portlet if he or she has the Execute privilege (or higher) on the component or if the component/application is made public.

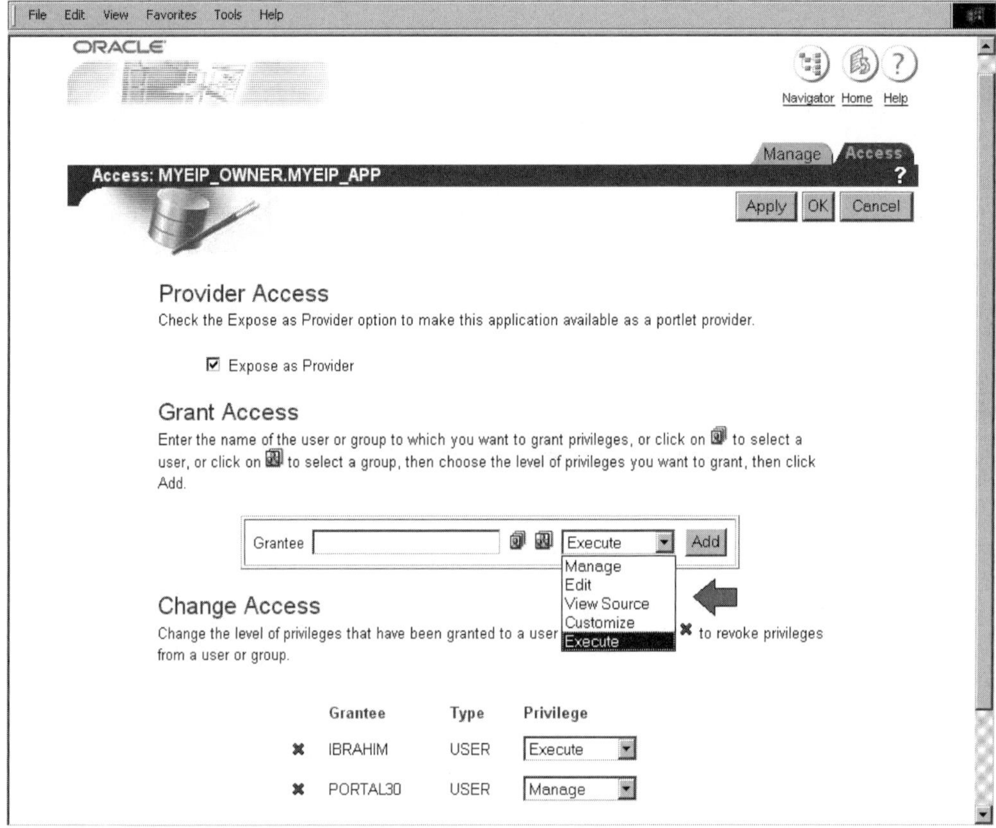

Figure 12.27 Oracle Portal Navigator: Applications: Grant Access.

Other security topics in Oracle Portal, such as LDAP authentication and SSL (Secured Socket Layer), are covered in Chapters 16 and 20.

Chapter 13 begins explaining how to build PL/SQL database providers.

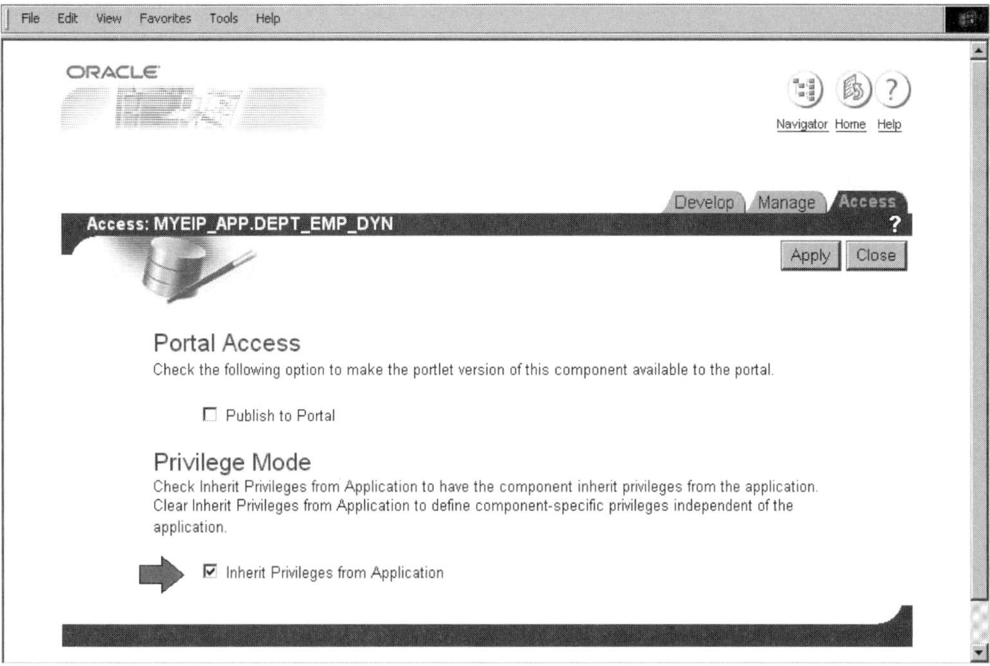

Figure 12.28 Oracle Portal Navigator: Applications: Component: Grant Access: Inheritance On.

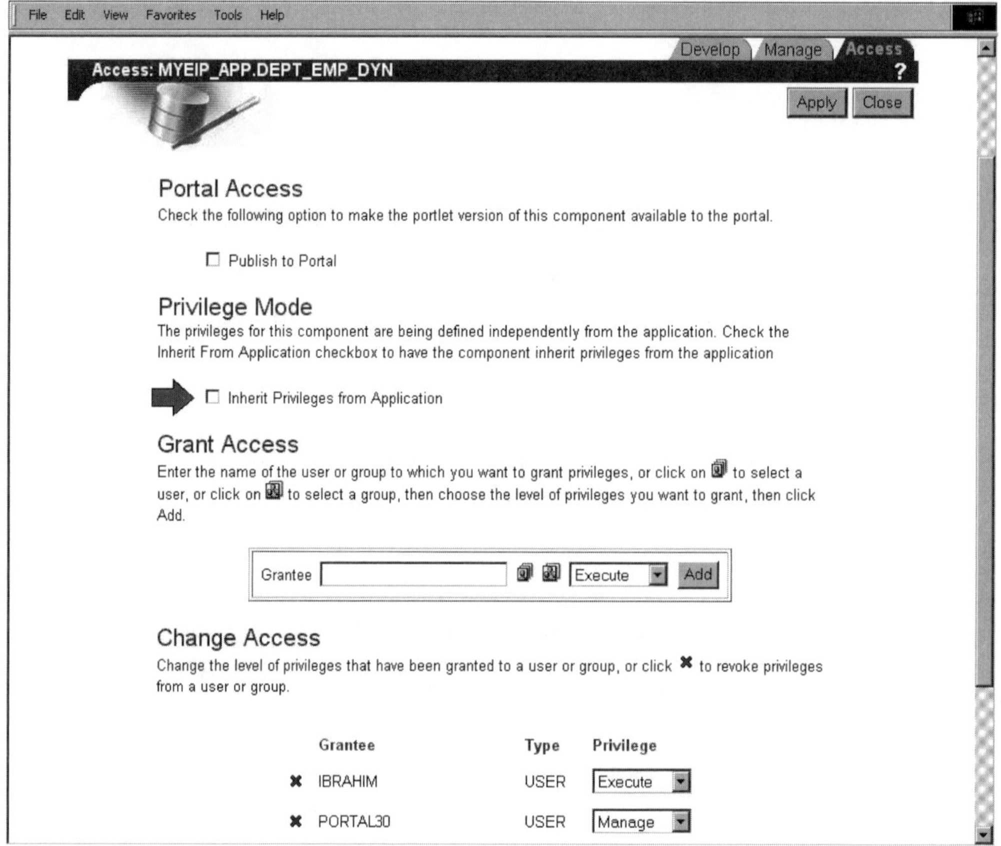

Figure 12.29 Oracle Portal Navigator: Applications: Component: Grant Access: Inheritance Off.

CHAPTER 13

Building PL/SQL Database Providers

Introduction

You have seen how you can build Oracle Portal pages and add to them built-in portlets such as the Favorites portlet and the application components portlets. This chapter introduces you to building your own Oracle Portal portlets. First we explore the different portlet implementations, then we demonstrate how to create your own PL/SQL database portlet providers. These providers reside in the database and access different enterprise data sources, and then they provide display data to the portlets. Some sample applications of database providers are showing a customized chart based on data queried from the database and showing data retrieved from a legacy system.

Portlet Implementations

Portlets can be categorized as follows:

1. Built-in Portlets: These portlets are available out of the box and you can add them to your pages.
2. Application Components Portlets: These are constructed declaratively by using the Creation wizards. They can be published as portlets to be added to the portal pages. You can customize these portlets by adding your own HTML, PL/SQL, and JavaScript code.
3. Content Areas Portlets: This is where you can publish unstructured data (e.g., text documents) into portal pages.
4. Programmable Portlets: Here you extend the Oracle Portal by building your own portlets. Instead of Oracle Portal communicating with each portlet separately, you can write portlet providers. Each provider displays one or more portlets. The provider program calls the Oracle Portal Application Programming Interface (API) calls. There are two types of providers:

   a. Database Providers: The provider code resides inside an Oracle database. You can use PL/SQL or Java to write these providers. Database providers are covered in this chapter.
   b. Web Providers: The provider code resides outside the Oracle database and can be accessed through a URL. Web providers are covered in Chapter 15.
5. Partners' Portlets: These portlets are developed by companies other than Oracle and then installed into the Oracle Portal. A sample of these portlets can be found in the Portal Development Kit. Also, you can obtain a list of these companies at *http://www.oracle.com/portals/partners.*

Each portlet in Oracle Portal is managed by a provider. The provider is a program that runs either inside a database or outside the database. It is responsible for providing the portlet display data to the Oracle Portal Framework (Figure 13.1).

The Oracle Portal Framework manages communication and registration of all providers, which provide portlets contents. Providers may be defined within the local portal instance (node), a remote portal node, or within an external Web application.

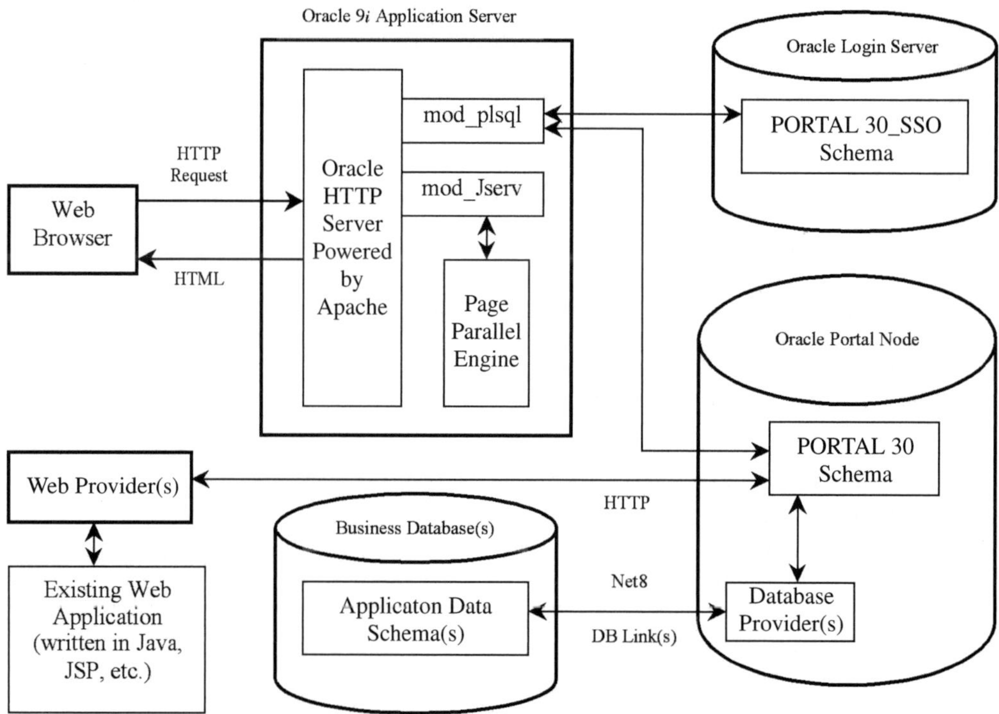

Figure 13.1 Oracle Portal Architecture.

The Parallel Page Engine is responsible for assembling the portal pages. If the portlet is based on an application component, the engine communicates with the portal schema (i.e., PORTAL30) and the application schema (i.e., myeip_owner) to generate its display code. If the portlet is a programmed portlet, the engine communicates with its provider: The engine receives all the output of its portlets and then assembles it into a page and delivers the completed page to the browser.

The framework stores and retrieves user page preferences (customization settings) and applies them to the rendered pages. The framework exposes, through public APIs, services that are used within Oracle Portal for use by provider portlets. These services are discussed in more detail in Chapter 14. Table 13.1 compares database and Web providers to help you decide when it is more suitable to use one over the other.

Table 13.1 Comparison Between Database Portlet Providers and Web Portlet Providers

	Database Provider	Web Provider
Information Source	Existing business data stored in Oracle database(s)	External/remote information sources
Development Required Skills	Familiarity with stored procedures technology (PL/SQL or Java)	Familiarity with writing applications using specific Web technologies (e.g., JSP, Perl, CGI, etc.)

Portlet Provider Tasks

From what was mentioned in the previous section, you can see that the portlet provider is the primary mechanism through which the portal accesses the portlets. One provider can service one or more portlets. The portlet provider performs the following tasks:

1. Communication between the Oracle Portal and the portlets: When the portal renders a page, it calls the provider of each portlet on the page, which in turn executes the portlet display methods (i.e., program subroutines) and returns the results.
2. Session startup/login: Each provider may include a method that authenticates the user and initializes any provider-specific session requirements. This method is called once by the portal for a given user session.
3. Portlet list management: The provider is also called to find the list of the portlets it "provides."
4. Provider registration: Each provider needs to be registered with Oracle Portal for the Oracle Portal to know the name and location of the provider code.

Provider Development Life Cycle

This section introduces the life cycle of developing portlets. I describe each phase starting from analysis and collection of the requirements through interface design to implementation.

Portlet Analysis

As with any development effort, understanding the requirements is a crucial first step. During this step, developers analyze the source application or information and identify the appropriate portlets. The main goal of a portlet should be to provide summary or navigational information that is pertinent to the target user and to reduce the user's effort in getting the information he or she needs. For example, a summary of all active orders for a given customer shows the customer that he or she will be notified whenever anything is changed. If nothing has changed, the customer does not have to navigate to the order tracking Web site.

The portlet specification should include a detailed description of the intended functionality. It should also include the definition of what customizations are appropriate for the portlet. For example, the orders tracking portlet may allow the user to choose a date range for orders displayed or decide how the orders are sorted in the portlet.

Once the portlet requirements are well understood, the developer can choose the appropriate implementation method. Depending on the complexity of the portlet and the functional requirements, he or she may choose to implement using built-in portal capabilities (content areas or applications) or to code/program the portlet.

Provider/Portlet Design

Decisions in portlet design center around the information source and the logic required. Depending on where the information is located, the developer may choose from a variety of design options including straight database calls, URL calls, or through JavaScript calls from the browser. This is the point where the decision between database and Web provider is made.

Provider Coding

Once design is complete, coding can begin. If the decision to use coded (i.e., programmable) portlets is made, because other portlet implementations cannot satisfy the portlet requirements, the portlet developer writes the portlet provider(s) using API calls.

The final step in the process is to install the new provider and register it with the Portal Framework. Installation depends on the implementation style. For a database provider it involves creating a schema and storing the provider/portlet code in the schema. The Web provider installation requirements are specific to the deployment architecture of the chosen environment, and it is covered in Chapter 15. Once the portlet code is installed and ready to run, it is registered with the framework using the Provider portlet or a script. Details of the installation/registration process are explained later in this chapter.

PL/SQL Database Providers

This section describes how to code your own providers using PL/SQL, assuming that you are already familiar with basic PL/SQL programming concepts. To create your own provider, you need to use the Oracle Portal PL/SQL API packages. To understand the provider internal structure, start by looking at the specification of the PORTAL30.WWPRO_API_PROVIDER_REGISTRY package. You can get the source of the package specification by logging on to SQL*Plus using your portal schema username and password (i.e., PORTAL30/PORTAL30) and selecting the source from the USER_SOURCE data dictionary view (Figure 13.2). Displaying the source gives you the chance to read the comments included. You can describe WWPRO_API_PROVIDER_REGISTRY to get the functions' and procedures' names and parameters in SQL*Plus, but without comments.

```
Oracle SQL*Plus
File Edit Search Options Help
SQL> show user
USER is "PORTAL30"
SQL> set pages 0
SQL> l
  1  SELECT    text
  2  FROM      user_source
  3  WHERE     name = 'WWPRO_API_PROVIDER_REGISTRY'
  4  AND       type = 'PACKAGE'
  5* ORDER BY  line
SQL> /
package            wwpro_api_provider_registry
is

    /**
    * Providers need to be registered with the system before they can
    * provide Portlets for general use.  Providers are registered on
    * the local node.  The installation of a Provider
    * consists of a number of steps.  Please refer to the Portlet
    * Developer's Kit documentation for further information.
    *
    * Note: Register and Edit functions are secure.  Users must have
    * All Provider Manage or All Provider Publish rights to use them.
    *
    * @scope External
    */

    -- PROVIDER REGISTRY CONSTANTS
    -- Implementation Type
    DATABASE_IMPL               constant    integer := 2  ;
    WEB_IMPL                    constant    integer := 3  ;
    -- -- The following implementation types are the same as Database and
    -- -- Web respectively.
    PLSQL_IMPL                  constant    integer := 2  ; --same as Database
    HTTP_IMPL                   constant    integer := 3  ; --same as Web

    -- Portlet Login Frequency
    LOGIN_FREQUENCY_ALWAYS      constant    char(1) := 'A';
    LOGIN_FREQUENCY_ONCE        constant    char(1) := 'O';
    LOGIN_FREQUENCY_NEVER       constant    char(1) := 'N';

    -- Distribution Flag
    ENABLE_DISTRIBUTION_YES     constant    number  := 1  ;
    ENABLE_DISTRIBUTION_NO      constant    number  := 0  ;

    -- Require Proxy Flag
```

Figure 13.2 Using SQL*Plus to View the Source of an Oracle Portal PL/SQL API Package.

Also, you can use a GUI PL/SQL editor for better scrolling capabilities. Oracle Forms and Oracle DBA Studio are two tools you can use. Figure 13.3 shows the WWPRO_API_PROVIDER_REGISTRY package specifications in the DBA Studio. The package specification has a lot of comments describing each line of code. You can use this code as a reference for the provider PL/SQL constants declarations, types declarations, functions headers, and procedures headers.

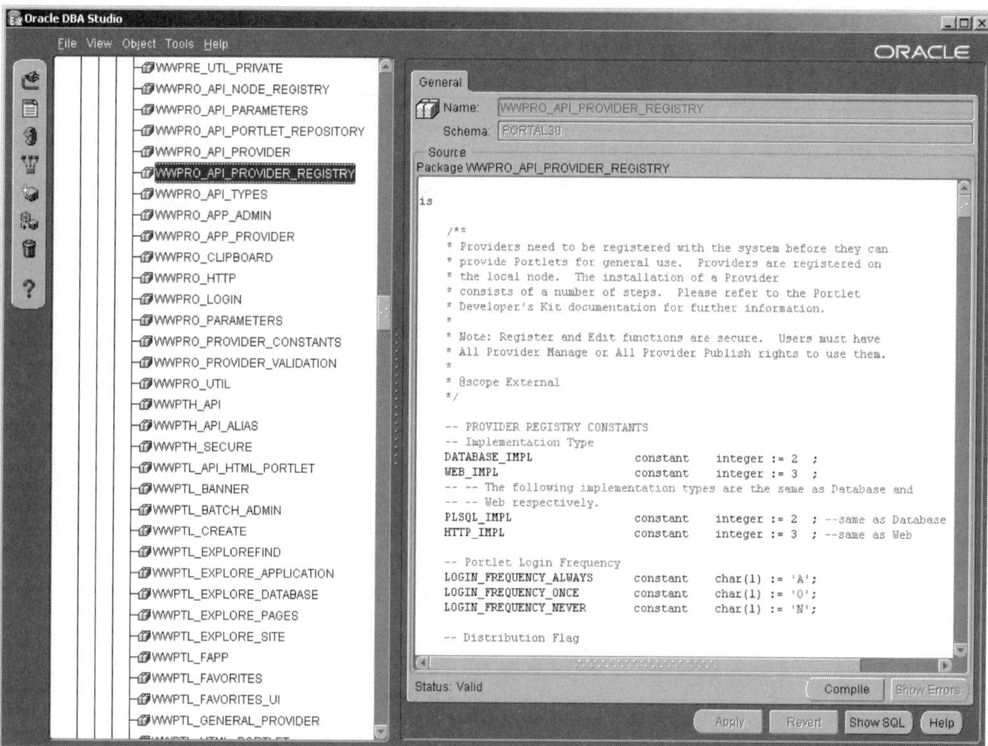

Figure 13.3 Using DBA Studio to View the Source of an Oracle Portal PL/SQL API Package.

Important

When you log on as PORTAL30, you are the owner of the PL/SQL package specifications and package bodies. Be careful not to edit or drop these packages, because this might affect your Oracle Portal node.

Provider Record

The provider record is a data structure that contains a set of fields; these fields store information about the provider. Because you will be creating and registering your own providers programmatically, you need to know the fields' description of the provider record (Table 13.2). The provider record is declared in the PORTAL30_SSO.WWPRO_API_PROVIDER_REGISTRY package specification.

Note

The PL/SQL record structures described in this chapter are based on Oracle Portal version 3.0.7. Please refer to the package's source and the corresponding Portal Development Kit for later version changes.

For more details on the provider record fields descriptions, you can refer to the Portal Development Kit (PDK) documentation. The PDK is a group of documentation materials and code examples that you can download from the Oracle Technology Network (*http://technet.oracle.com*). PDK is a utility separate from the O9*i*AS Portal product, so Oracle Corporation can update it more frequently than the product. For example, you can find a new PDK every month, while it takes more than that to get a new version of Oracle 9*i* Application Server. The PDK is downloaded as a zipped file; when you unzip it, it is uncompressed under a directory named "pdk". So, assuming that you have uncompressed the PDK under c:\portal directory, the page that describes the Portal Provider Record structure—in the April 2001 PDK—can be found in the following Windows file system URL:

```
file:///C|/portal/pdk/plsql/doc/sdk1rec.htm
```

You can also get there by clicking on the following links in sequence from c:\portal\pdk\index.html:

1. PDK Services for PL/SQL
2. PL/SQL API Reference
3. wwpro_api_provider_registry package
4. provider_record record structure

Provider Procedures/Methods

Once a database provider is created inside the Oracle Portal node database, it needs to be registered with Oracle Portal. Once a provider is registered with the Oracle Portal, Oracle Portal calls the provider procedures/methods as needed.

Table 13.2 Provider Record Fields

Field	Description
id	Unique identifier for each provider
name	Internal name for the provider
display_name	The provider display name
node_id	A unique identifier for the portal node
timeout	The default number of seconds that the Oracle Portal should try to connect to this provider before displaying the timeout message
timeout_msg_id	The NLS message ID for the provider's timeout message
timeout_msg	The message to be displayed when timeout occurs
implementation_style	Can be one of the following values: • DATABASE_IMPL • WEB_IMPL
implementation_owner	The database user account that contains the database provider's implementation package; only applicable for database providers
implementation_name	The name of the database provider's implementation package
language	The language used
enable_distribution	If TRUE, it indicates that the provider installed on the local node can be registered on remote nodes.
login_frequency	• LOGIN_FREQUENCY_ALWAYS: The portal performs a login operation every time a portlet is requested to be viewed from this provider. • LOGIN_FREQUENCY_ONCE: The portal performs a login operation only the first time a portlet is requested to be viewed from this provider in the same user session. • LOGIN_FREQUENCY_NEVER: Oracle Portal does not log in to the provider. In case of a database provider, this flag determines the frequency of calls made to the wwwpro.api_provider.do_login API procedure. In the case of a Web provider, this flag determines the frequency of calls made to the initSession method.
http_url	The URL that portal uses to make calls to the Web provider (The Web providers are explained in Chapter 15).
same_cookie_domain	Indicates whether the Web provider is in the same cookie domain as the portal
require_proxy	Proxy servers are used to provide access to servers outside a firewall. This flag indicates that a proxy server is required to make a URL connection. If a proxy server is required, specify the proxy server name in the Services portlet under Global Settings (Figure 13.4 and Figure 13.5).
http_app_type	• EXTERNAL_SECURED: The Web provider requires its own ID for the user. • PORTAL: The Web provider accepts the portal's ID for the user.

Table 13.2 *(continued)*

Field	Description
http_app_id	If the http_app_type is EXTERNAL_SECURED, this field stores the external application ID, otherwise this field is null.
existing_provider_id	Used with the PORTAL30_SSO.WWPRO_API_PROVIDER_REGISTRY .EDIT_PROVIDER procedure to identify the provider that will have its ID changed.
provider_key	A key passed to the Web provider; the provider uses it to look up and track the Oracle Portal's use of the Web provider.
encryption_key	This key is used to encrypt and decrypt data communicated to the provider.
created_on	The date of the provider registration with portal
created_by	The user who registered this provider with portal
last_updated_on	The date of the last provider update operation
last_updated_by	The user who last updated the provider

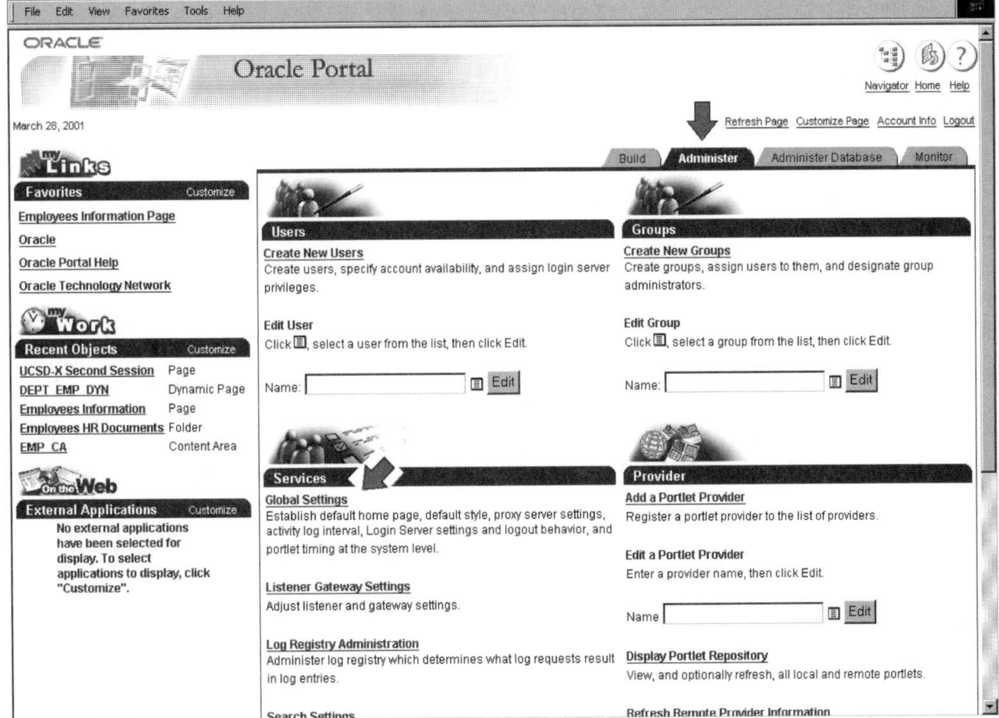

Figure 13.4 Oracle Portal Home Page: Administer Tab.

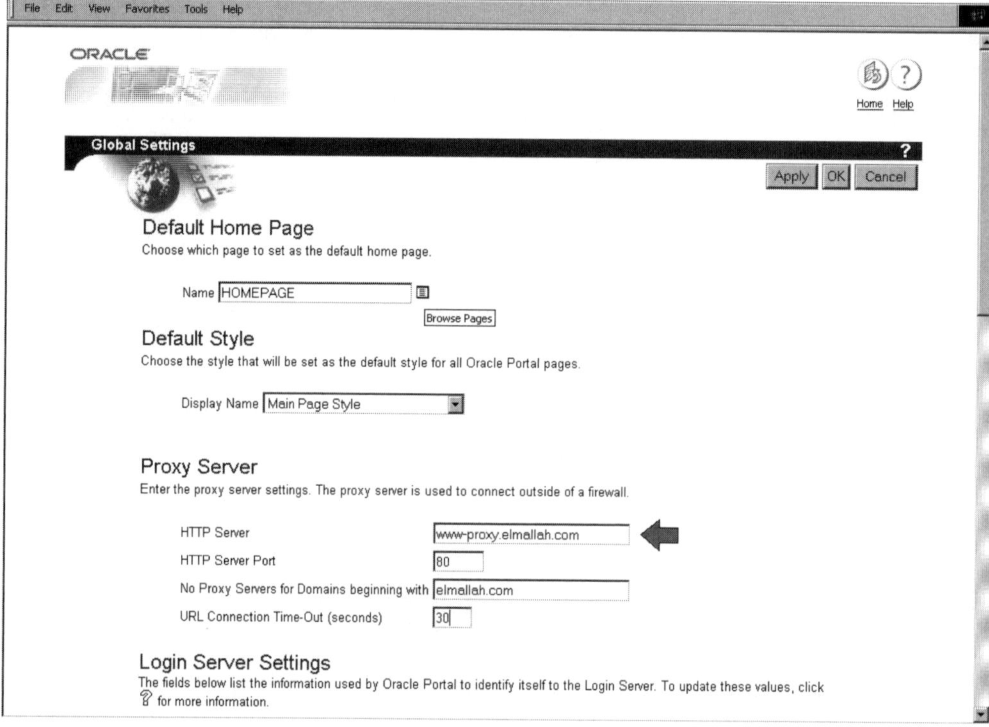

Figure 13.5 Oracle Portal Home Page: Administer Tab: Global Settings.

Note

The term "procedures" is used in the title to refer to both PL/SQL procedures and functions.

Important

The provider and portlet code examples have been written and tested on Oracle Portal 3.0.7.x on Windows NT/2000.

Here are the PL/SQL database provider procedures (or the Java database provider methods).

1. get_portlet function is used to return the portlet information in a portlet record. The portlet record structure is explained later in this chapter. Its specification is

```
function get_portlet (
      p_provider_id in integer,
      p_portlet_id in integer,
      p_language in varchar2 )
return wwpro_api_provider.portlet_record;
```

2. get_portlet_list function is used to return a list of the portlets implemented by a certain provider. Its specification is

```
function get_portlet_list (
      p_provider_id in integer
      p_start_row in integer,
      p_row_count in integer,
      p_language in varchar2,
      p_security_level in boolean default TRUE,
      p_type in integer default LIST_PORTLET )
return wwpro_api_provider.portlet_table;
```

- p_start_row is the number for the first row of the requested data table.
- p_row_count is the maximum number of rows to be returned.
- p_security_level is an indicator for the presence of user-level security. This function may be called in two modes. These two modes are determined by the value of the p_security_level parameter. If p_security_level is false, this method should generate a list of portlets implemented by this provider without performing any portlet security checks. Oracle Portal calls this method with p_security_level set to false when it performs a refresh of the Portlet Repository in order to get the complete list of portlets for this provider that will be made available in the portal. If p_security_level is true, this method should generate a list of portlets in which a security check is performed for the portlets. Such a call may be performed by the Oracle Portal to retrieve the list of portlets to display on the Add Portlets screen, so that only the portlets that the user can access are returned.
- p_type is an indicator for the type of list to be returned (LIST_PORTLET or LIST_COMPONENT).
- The portlet_table is a PL/SQL table of portlet records:

```
type portlet_table is table of portlet_record
     index by binary_integer;
```

3. is_portlet_runnable function performs a security check on the portlet. When the reference_path field in the portlet_instance_record is null, this means that the user is trying to see the

portlet in the Portlet Repository. When the reference_path field in the portlet_instance_record is not null, then the is_portlet_runnable method is called for a portlet instance. This is the case when a portlet is displayed in a page. Its specification is

```
function is_portlet_runnable (
      p_portlet_instance in
            wwpro_api_provider.portlet_instance_record )
return boolean;
```

A portlet instance refers to a portlet after adding it to a portal page. The same portlet may be displayed multiple times on the same page. Each time a portlet is added to a page, the portal generates a unique portlet instance ID that is the instance's reference path. The portlet_instance_record structure is explained later in this chapter.

4. register_portlet function is called by the Oracle Portal to register the use of a portlet every time the portlet is added to a page. Its specification is

```
procedure register_portlet (
      p_portlet_instance in
            wwpro_api_provider.portlet_instance_record );
```

5. deregister_portlet function is called by the Oracle Portal when a portlet is removed from a page. Its specification is

```
procedure deregister_portlet (
      p_portlet_instance in
            wwpro_api_provider.portlet_instance_record );
```

6. show_portlet: This procedure is called by the Oracle Portal to render a portlet on a page. It generates the necessary HTML or XML/XSL to display its portlet on the portal page. Its specification is

```
procedure show_portlet (
      p_portlet_record in out
            wwpro_api_provider.portlet_runtime_record );
```

The structure of the PORTLET_RUNTIME_RECORD PL/SQL record can be found in the WWPRO_API_PROVIDER package specification and is explained later in this chapter in Table 13.6. This method may be called in one of seven different modes; these modes are listed in Table 13.3. You can specify the portlet show mode by setting the PORTLET.RUNTIME_RECORD.EXEC_MODE field to one of the seven mode constants.

7. copy_portlet: This procedure is called for each portlet on a page when this page is being copied. This procedure copies the portlet customizations from the current portlet instance (in the original page) to another portlet instance (in the new page). Its specification is

Table 13.3 Portlet Show Modes

Mode Constant	Constant Value	Description
MODE_SHOW	1	Displays the portlet output. This is the most commonly used mode, because this is what is used when the portlet page is rendered.
MODE_SHOW_ABOUT	2	Displays the portlet internal information, such as version number, source, and so on. Its common use is to be called by an "About" link in the portlet banner.
MODE_SHOW_EDIT	3	Displays the portlet customization page. It is typically called by a "Customize" link on the portlet banner to customize setting for the current authenticated user.
MODE_SHOW_HELP	4	Displays the portlet help page. It is typically called by a "Help" link on the portlet banner.
MODE_SHOW_EDIT_ DEFAULTS	5	Displays the "Edit Defaults" page where the portlet can be customized for all the users. It is called by the "Edit Defaults" link while the page is being edited.
MODE_SHOW_DETAILS	6	Displays the full portlet. It is typically called by a link in the portlet banner.
MODE_PREVIEW	7	Displays the portlet in the Portlet Repository, giving the end-user the ability to preview the portlet before adding it.

```
procedure copy_portlet ( p_copy_portlet_info in
                  wwpro_api_provider.copy_portlet_record );
```

8. describe_portlet_parameters: This function returns a table of all the portlet parameters. It specification is

```
function describe_portlet_parameters (
      p_provider in integer,
      p_portlet_id in integer,
      p_language in varchar2 )
return wwpro_api_provider.portlet_parameter_table;
```

9. get_api_version: Oracle Portal calls this function to get the version of the Oracle Portal API used to implement the provider. For Oracle Portal 3.0 the function should return wwpro_api_provider.API_VERSION_1. Its specification is

```
function get_api_version( provider_id in integer )
return integer;
```

10. do_login: Oracle Portal calls this procedure to allow the provider to perform any needed initialization, such as generating an HTML cookie. Its specification is

```
procedure do_login (
      p_provider_id in integer,
      p_browser_cookies in wwpro_api_provider.cookie_table,
      p_provider_cookies out
            wwpro_api_provider.cookie_table );
```

11. register_provider: Oracle Portal calls this procedure when the provider is registered. Its specification is

```
procedure register_provider ( p_provider_id in integer );
```

A provider can be registered within the Oracle Portal GUI or using the wwpro_api_provider_registry.register_provider function.

12. deregister_provider: Oracle Portal calls this procedure when the provider is deregistered (i.e., removed from Oracle Portal). Its specification is

```
procedure deregister_provider ( p_provider_id in integer );
```

Create Your First PL/SQL Database Provider

In this exercise you walk through all the steps needed to create a very basic portlet using the PL/SQL Database API.

Prepare the Database Schema

Instead of using the Oracle Portal schema (i.e., PORTAL30) to be the owner schema of your PL/SQL database provider code, you can create a new database user to hold the provider code. To create a new provider schema, log in to SQL*Plus using a DBA account (e.g., SYSTEM) and execute the following commands:

```
SQL> CREATE USER PDK04 IDENTIFIED BY PDK04;
SQL> GRANT CONNECT, RESOURCE TO PDK04;
```

Note

It is a good idea to specify the default tablespace and the temporary tablespace in the "Create User" SQL statement, otherwise they are assigned to the SYTEM tablespace, which might lead to fragmentation and increases the chances of input/output contention. You can perform this using the following SQL command:

```
SQL>ALTER USER PDK04 DEFAULT TABLESPACE USERS TEMPORARY
      TABLESPACE TEMP;
```

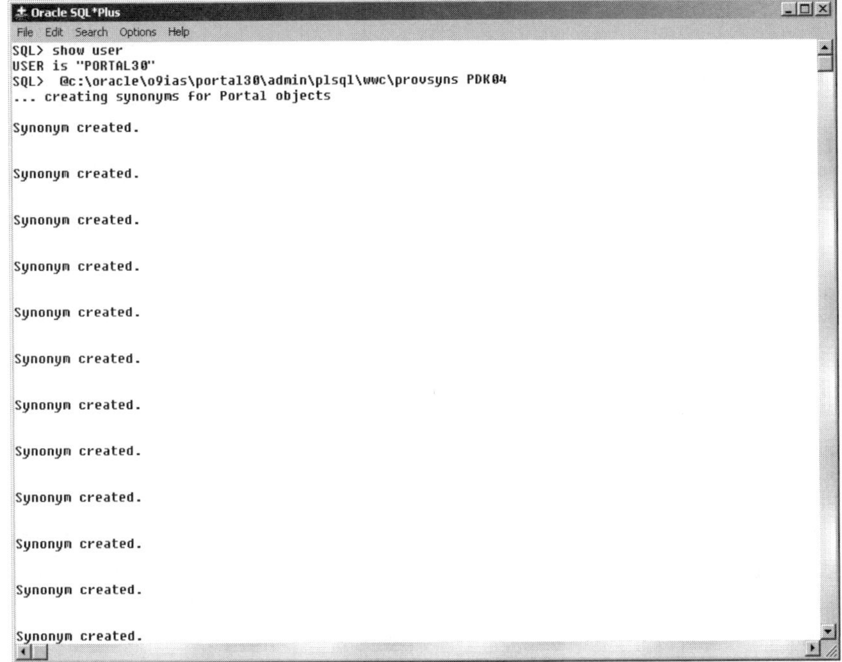

Figure 13.6 Running the provsyns.sql Script.

Because this new schema will own the provider code, it needs to access the PL/SQL API procedures. To grant access to the new provider schema (e.g., PDK04) to the PL/SQL API, run the script "provsyns.sql" as the PORTAL30 user. You need to specify the provider schema name as the first parameter for the script (Figure 13.6). This script is located under

```
<iAS_ORACLE_HOME>\portal30\admin\plsql\wwc
```

Note

Make sure you do not put a space after the username, because the username is concatenated to table names in the script.

The script runs under the portal schema owner creating private synonyms (i.e., owned by the schema provider PDK04 rather than public synonyms that are accessible by all the users) for PL/SQL API procedures. Then, the script grants the Execute privilege on these API PL/SQL procedures to the provider schema.

Create the Provider Package

The provider name created in this section is emp_provider. The emp_provider provides the information for a group of portlets that display employee-related information. Rather than putting all the provider code and each portlet code into the same provider package, we will create a separate package for each portlet. The emp_provider creates the list of available portlets and then makes calls to the portlet's package when the portlet is selected. The portlet package is covered in the next section.

Create the package specification in a file called emp_provider.pks and the package body in the emp_provider.pkb. The code adds all the API functions and procedures to the package. Even though you will not need or use all of them, they are available to you as a skeleton for later changes.

Note

Do not give the portlet packages (i.e., dept_portlet and salary_portlet) the same names as the portlets' constant names (i.e., PORTLET_DEPT and PORTLET_SALARY) in the provider package specifications.

The following is the printout of the Employee Provider package specification (i.e., emp_provider.pks) with line numbers. When you write this code, do not include the line numbers, they are included in the printout for illustration purposes. Although no comments are added to the code printout in order to fit it in a small number of pages, I recommend you add comments to each variable, function, and procedure. The packages' source code is available on the CD-ROM for this book.

```
create or replace package emp_provider
is

    PORTLET_SALARY constant integer := 1;
    PORTLET_DEPT constant integer := 2;

    function get_api_version (
        p_provider_id in integer )
    return integer;

    procedure register_provider (
        p_provider_id in integer );

    procedure deregister_provider (
        p_provider_id in integer );

    procedure do_login (
        p_provider_id in integer,
        p_browser_cookies in wwpro_api_provider.cookie_table,
        p_provider_cookies out wwpro_api_provider.cookie_table );

    function get_portlet (
        p_provider_id in integer,
        p_portlet_id in integer,
        p_language in varchar2 )
    return wwpro_api_provider.portlet_record;

```

```
28       function get_portlet_list (
29           p_provider_id in integer,
30           p_start_row in integer,
31           p_rowcount in integer,
32           p_language in varchar2,
33           p_security_level in boolean,
34           p_type in integer )
35       return wwpro_api_provider.portlet_table;
36
37       function is_portlet_runnable (
38           p_portlet_instance in wwpro_api_provider.portlet_instance_record )
39       return boolean;
40
41       procedure register_portlet (
42           p_portlet_instance in wwpro_api_provider.portlet_instance_record );
43
44       procedure deregister_portlet (
45           p_portlet_instance in wwpro_api_provider.portlet_instance_record );
46
47       procedure show_portlet (
48           p_portlet_record in out wwpro_api_provider.portlet_runtime_record );
49
50       procedure copy_portlet (
51           p_copy_portlet_info in wwpro_api_provider.copy_portlet_record );
52
53       function describe_portlet_parameters (
54           p_provider_id in integer,
55           p_portlet_id in integer,
56           p_language in varchar2 )
57       return wwpro_api_provider.portlet_parameter_table;
58
59   end emp_provider;
60   /
```

emp_provider.pks

The emp_provider initially has two portlets: the salary portlet and the department portlet. The emp_provider package specification declares two constants to refer to these two portlets in lines 4 and 5.

The following is the printout of the Employee Provider package body, which includes all the bodies of the procedures and functions mentioned in the specification.

```
create or replace package body emp_provider
is

    function get_api_version ( p_provider_id in integer )
    return integer
    is
    Begin
        return wwpro_api_provider.API_VERSION_1;
    end get_api_version;
```

```

    procedure register_provider ( p_provider_id in integer )
    is
    Begin
        null;
    end register_provider;

    procedure deregister_provider ( p_provider_id in integer )
    is
    Begin
        null;
    end deregister_provider;


    procedure do_login (
         p_provider_id in integer,
         p_browser_cookies in wwpro_api_provider.cookie_table,
         p_provider_cookies out wwpro_api_provider.cookie_table )
    is
    begin
        null;
    end do_login;

    function get_portlet (
         p_provider_id in integer,
         p_portlet_id in integer,
         p_language in varchar2 )
    return wwpro_api_provider.portlet_record
    is
    begin
        if ( p_portlet_id = PORTLET_SALARY )
        then
            return salary_portlet.get_portlet_info (
                 p_provider_id  => p_provider_id,
                 p_language     => p_language );
        elsif ( p_portlet_id = PORTLET_DEPT )
        then
            return dept_portlet.get_portlet_info (
                 p_provider_id => p_provider_id,
                 p_language    => p_language );
        else
            raise wwpro_api_provider.PORTLET_NOT_FOUND_EXCEPTION;
        end if;
    end get_portlet;

    function get_portlet_list (
         p_provider_id in integer,
         p_start_row in integer,
         p_rowcount in integer,
         p_language in varchar2,
         p_security_level in boolean,
         p_type in integer )
    return wwpro_api_provider.portlet_table
```

```
      is
           portlet_list_tab wwpro_api_provider.portlet_table;
           cnt   number;
      begin
           cnt := 0;
           if ( p_security_level = false )
           then
                  cnt := cnt + 1;
                  portlet_list_tab ( cnt ) := get_portlet (
                       p_provider_id  => p_provider_id,
                       p_portlet_id   => PORTLET_SALARY,
                       p_language     => p_language );
                  cnt := cnt + 1;
                  portlet_list_tab ( cnt ) := get_portlet (
                       p_provider_id => p_provider_id,
                       p_portlet_id => PORTLET_DEPT,
                       p_language => p_language );
          else
              if ( salary_portlet.is_runnable (
                   p_provider_id      => p_provider_id,
                   p_reference_path   => null ) )
              then
                  cnt := cnt + 1;
                  portlet_list_tab ( cnt ) := get_portlet (
                       p_provider_id  => p_provider_id,
                       p_portlet_id   => PORTLET_SALARY,
                       p_language     => p_language );
              end if;
              if ( dept_portlet.is_runnable (
                   p_provider_id      =>  p_provider_id,
                   p_reference_path   =>  null ) )
              then
                  cnt := cnt + 1;
                  portlet_list_tab ( cnt ) := get_portlet (
                       p_provider_id  => p_provider_id,
                       p_portlet_id   => PORTLET_DEPT,
                       p_language     => p_language );
              end if;
          end if;
          return portlet_list_tab;
      end get_portlet_list;

      Function is_portlet_runnable (
          p_portlet_instance in wwpro_api_provider.portlet_instance_record )
      Return boolean
      is
      Begin
          If ( p_portlet_instance.portlet_id = PORTLET_SALARY )
          Then
              return salary_portlet.is_runnable (
                   p_provider_id      => p_portlet_instance.provider_id,
                   p_reference_path   => p_portlet_instance.reference_path);
          elsif (p_portlet_instance.portlet_id = PORTLET_DEPT )
```

```
        Then
            return dept_portlet.is_runnable(
                p_provider_id => p_portlet_instance.provider_id,
                p_reference_path => p_portlet_instance.reference_path);
        Else
            raise wwpro_api_provider.PORTLET_NOT_FOUND_EXCEPTION;
        end if;
    end is_portlet_runnable;


    procedure register_portlet (
        p_portlet_instance in wwpro_api_provider.portlet_instance_record )
    is
    Begin
        if ( p_portlet_instance.portlet_id = PORTLET_SALARY )
        Then
            salary_portlet.register( p_portlet_instance );
        elsif ( p_portlet_instance.portlet_id = PORTLET_DEPT )
        Then
            dept_portlet.register( p_portlet_instance );
        Else
            raise wwpro_api_provider.PORTLET_NOT_FOUND_EXCEPTION;
        end if;
    end register_portlet;

    procedure deregister_portlet (
        p_portlet_instance in wwpro_api_provider.portlet_instance_record )
    is
    Begin
        if ( p_portlet_instance.portlet_id = PORTLET_SALARY )
        Then
            salary_portlet.deregister( p_portlet_instance );
        elsif ( p_portlet_instance.portlet_id = PORTLET_DEPT )
        Then
            dept_portlet.deregister ( p_portlet_instance );
        Else
            raise wwpro_api_provider.PORTLET_NOT_FOUND_EXCEPTION;
        end if;
    end deregister_portlet;

    procedure show_portlet (
        p_portlet_record in out wwpro_api_provider.portlet_runtime_record)
    is
    Begin
        if ( p_portlet_record.portlet_id = PORTLET_SALARY ) then
            salary_portlet.show( p_portlet_record );
        elsif ( p_portlet_record.portlet_id = PORTLET_DEPT ) then
            dept_portlet.show( p_portlet_record );
        Else
            raise wwpro_api_provider.PORTLET_NOT_FOUND_EXCEPTION;
        end if;
    end show_portlet;

```

```
    procedure copy_portlet (
         p_copy_portlet_info in wwpro_api_provider.copy_portlet_record )
    is
    Begin
        if ( p_copy_portlet_info.portlet_id = PORTLET_SALARY ) then
            salary_portlet.copy( p_copy_portlet_info );
        elsif ( p_copy_portlet_info.portlet_id = PORTLET_DEPT ) then
            dept_portlet.copy( p_copy_portlet_info );
        Else
            raise wwpro_api_provider.PORTLET_NOT_FOUND_EXCEPTION;
        end if;
    end copy_portlet;

    Function describe_portlet_parameters (
         p_provider_id in integer,
         p_portlet_id in integer,
         p_language in varchar2 )
    return wwpro_api_provider.portlet_parameter_table
    is
    Begin
        if ( p_portlet_id = PORTLET_SALARY )
        Then
            return salary_portlet.describe_parameters (
                 p_provider_id     =>  p_provider_id,
                 p_language        =>  p_language );
        elsif ( p_portlet_id = PORTLET_DEPT )
        Then
            return dept_portlet.describe_parameters (
                 p_provider_id     =>  p_provider_id,
                 p_language        =>  p_language );
        Else
            raise wwpro_api_provider.PORTLET_NOT_FOUND_EXCEPTION;
        end if;
    end describe_portlet_parameters;

end emp_provider;
/
```

emp_provider.pkb

You can add more portlets to your provider by adding the necessary checks to the procedures and functions. For example if you need to add a new portlet named PAYROLL_PORTLET to the EMP_PROVIDER, start by adding a new constant to the emp_provider.pks and then add an "elsif" statement to each of the functions and procedures of the emp_provider.pkb to check if the portlet processed is the PAYROLL_PORTLET. If you get a match, call the related procedure or function from the new portlet package. The next section covers the portlet record structure and the portlet methods needed to build this portlet package.

Theoretically, you can include the portlets' procedures and functions in the provider package. But separating each portlet code in its own package achieves better modularization and makes your code easier to maintain.

Table 13.4 Portlet Record Fields

Field	Description
id	Unique identifier for each portlet within the provider
provider_id	The ID of the portlet provider
name	The internal name of the portlet
title	The title of the portlet
description	The description of the portlet
timeout	The time period in seconds that the Oracle Portal keeps trying to execute the portlet before it times out; if a null value is specified, the provider record timeout value is used.
timeout_msg	The message to be displayed when timeout occurs
content_type	• CONTENT_TYPE_HTML • CONTENT_TYPE_XML
api_version	The version of the API to which the portlet conforms; for Oracle Portal 3.0, this value must be wwpro_api_provider.API_VERSION_1.
has_show_edit	If TRUE, it indicates that the portlet has a customization page/form. This page is accessed by clicking on the portlet "Customize" link in the page display mode (Figure 13.7). That gives the user the ability to customize the portlet for her- or himself only.
has_show_edit_defaults	If TRUE, it indicates that the portlet has an "Edit Defaults" link in the Page Edit mode (Figure 13.8). Portal administrators can edit the defaults for all the page users.
has_show_preview	If TRUE, it indicates that the portlet can be showed in the preview mode before it is added to a page (Figure 13.9).
language	The language of the portlet text
created_on	The date of the portlet record creation
created_by	The user who created the portlet record
last_updated_on	The date of the last portlet record update operation
last_updated_by	The user who last updated the portlet record
preference_store_path	The base preference store path where the provider has stored the portlet customization information. Session storage and customization services are covered in Chapter 14.

In line 70 in the function get_portlet_list, the code is incrementing a local variable by one to use as the index of the PL/SQL table of portlet records. If you have a large number of portlets, you can use a FOR loop to reduce the redundant code.

Note

You should create all the packages' specifications (provider and portlet) before their bodies. If you try creating the provider package body first, you will get compilation errors because it is calling portlet package procedures and functions.

Portlet Record

The portlet record is a data structure that contains a set of fields; these fields store information about the portlet. Because you will be creating your own portlets programmatically, you need to know the fields' descriptions of the portlet record (Table 13.4). The portlet record is declared in the PORTAL30.WWPRO_API_PROVIDER package specification.

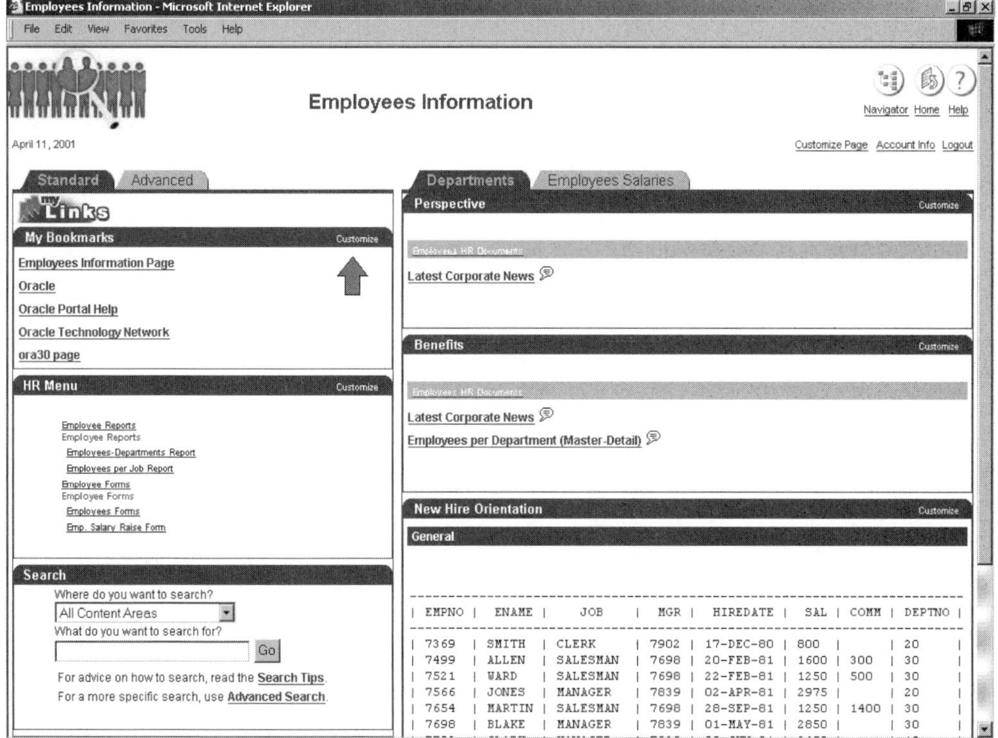

Figure 13.7 Page Display: Portlet Customize Link.

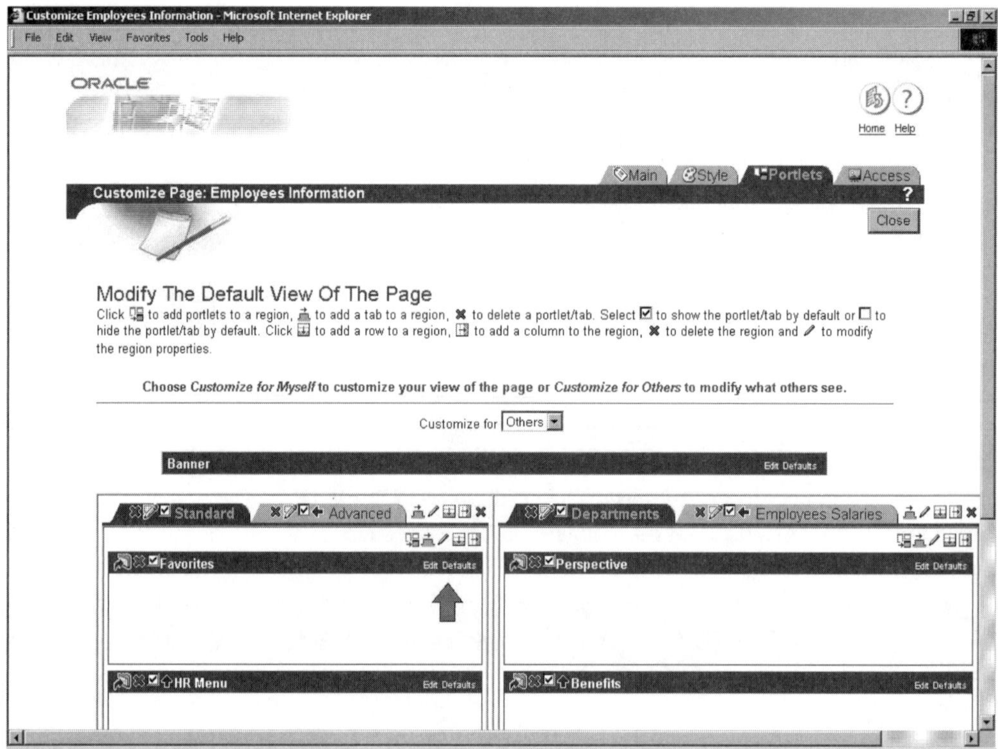

Figure 13.8 Page Edit: Portlet Edit Defaults Link.

Portlet_Instance_Record

These fields of the portlet instance record store information about a portlet placement in a page (Table 13.5). A portlet_instance_record structure is passed into the following provider methods: is_portlet_runnable, register_portlet, and deregister_portlet.

Portlet_Runtime_Record

These portlet_runtime_record fields store run-time information of a portlet (Table 13.6). A portlet_runtime_record structure is passed into the show_portlet provider methods.

Portlet Procedures/Methods

As you see in the provider package body, the provider methods are calling the portlet methods. This section explains the different methods of a portlet package.

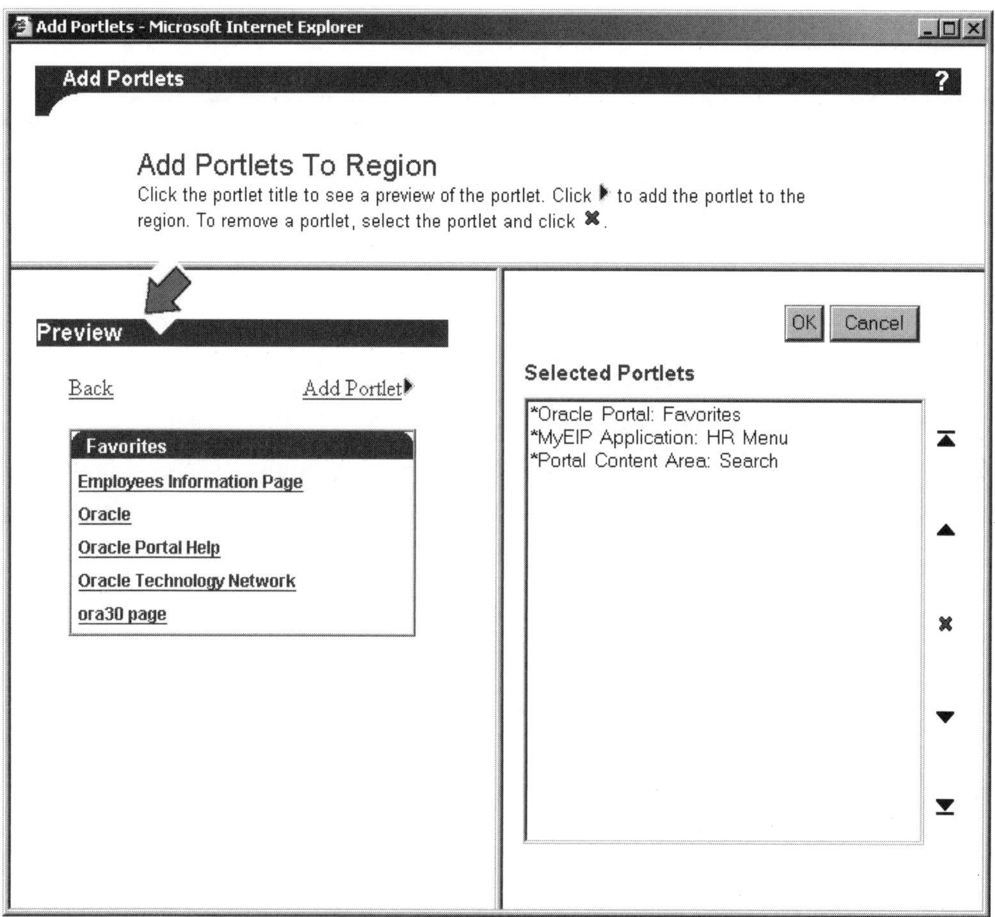

Figure 13.9 Portlet Repository: Portlet Review.

Table 13.5 Portlet Instance Record Fields

Field	Description
provider_id	The ID of the portlet provider
portlet_id	The ID of the portlet added to the page
reference_path	Used to store and retrieve portlet instance-specific information
page_type	To be used by the Oracle Portal product internally

Table 13.6 Portlet Runtime Record Fields

Field	Description
provider_id	The ID of the portlet provider
portlet_id	The ID of the portlet added to the page
node_id	The provider's host node
reference_path	The unique portlet instance ID; used to save portlet instance-specific information
language	The language of the portlet instance
exec_mode	The mode of the portlet call
back_page_url	The URL of the calling page; can be NULL if there is no calling page
page_url	The URL of the portlet instance page
page_type	For Oracle Portal product internal use
has_title_region	If TRUE, it indicates that the portlet has a title bar.
has_border	If TRUE, it indicates that the portlet has a border.
caching_key	Used to indicate that the portlet contents have changed and hence the portlet provider needs to be called
caching_level	• SYSTEM: Where Oracle Portal looks for the portlet in the cache by its URL and language • USER: Where Oracle Portal looks for the portlet in the cache by its URL, language, and the user_id
caching_period	The cache expiration time (in minutes). If the caching_period is specified, the caching_key is ignored. If the expiration time is zero, the portlet is never cached.

1. get_portlet_info: This function returns a WWPRO_API_PROVIDER.PORTLET_RECORD that contains the portlet information. Its specification is

```
function get_portlet_info (
     p_provider_id in integer,
     p_language in varchar2 )
return wwpro_api_provider.portlet_record;
```

2. is_runnable: This function returns TRUE if the portlet can be viewed by the current user. Its specification is

```
function is_runnable (
     p_provider_id in integer,
     p_reference_path in varchar2 )
return boolean;
```

A security check should be performed on each portlet instance before displaying it in any of the show modes (Table 13.3) to make sure that the user has the right privilege to display it. In this case the reference_path parameter is not null because it contains the portlet instance record. On the other side, while a user is displaying the Portlet Repository to pick a portlet, the "is_portlet_runnable" function is called for each portlet with a null p_reference_path parameter value to check if the portlet name should be displayed in the portlet list.

The portlet may use the context package wwctx_api procedure and functions (e.g., wwctx_api.get_user) in the implementation of the portlet security. This package is covered in Chapter 14.

3. register: Oracle Portal calls this procedure when a portlet is added to a page. It can be used to set the initial values of user customization fields. Its specification is

```
procedure register (
    p_portlet_instance in wwpro_api_provider.portlet_instance_record
);
```

4. deregister: Oracle Portal calls this function when a portlet is removed from a page. This provides the portlet an opportunity to perform instance-level cleanup such as the removal of end-user customizations. Its specification is

```
procedure deregister (
    p_portlet_instance in wwpro_api_provider.portlet_instance_record
);
```

5. show_portlet: This code generated the HTML/XML to be displayed in the portlet. The generated HTML must not contain any tags that cannot be included in an HTML table cell. For example, it cannot contain a 'BODY' tag.
6. copy: This procedure copies a portlet customization and defaults from one portlet to another. The register_portlet API procedure is called prior to calling this procedure.

```
procedure copy (
    p_copy_portlet_info in wwpro_api_provider.copy_portlet_record
);
```

7. describe_parameters: This function is called by Oracle Portal to get the description of the portlet parameters. Its specification is

```
function describe_parameters (
     p_provider_id in integer,
     p_language in varchar2 )
return wwpro_api_provider.portlet_parameter_table;
```

Create the Portlet Package

Start by creating the package specification for your first portlet (i.e., SALARY_PORTLET).

```
create or replace package salary_portlet is

    function get_portlet_info (
         p_provider_id in integer,
         p_language in varchar2 )
    return wwpro_api_provider.portlet_record;

    function is_runnable (
         p_provider_id in integer,
         p_reference_path in varchar2 )
    return boolean;

    procedure register (
        p_portlet_instance in wwpro_api_provider.portlet_instance_record );

    procedure deregister (
        p_portlet_instance in wwpro_api_provider.portlet_instance_record );

    procedure show (
        p_portlet_record        wwpro_api_provider.portlet_runtime_record);

    procedure copy (
         p_copy_portlet_info in wwpro_api_provider.copy_portlet_record );

    function describe_parameters (
         p_provider_id in integer,
         p_language in varchar2 )
    return wwpro_api_provider.portlet_parameter_table;

end salary_portlet;
/
```

salary_portlet.pks

```
create or replace package body salary_portlet is

    function get_portlet_info (
         p_provider_id in integer,
         p_language in varchar2 )
    return wwpro_api_provider.portlet_record
    is
```

```
     portlet_rec wwpro_api_provider.portlet_record;
Begin

     portlet_rec.id := emp_provider.PORTLET_SALARY;
     portlet_rec.provider_id := p_provider_id;
     portlet_rec.title := 'Employee Salaries';
     portlet_rec.name := 'SALARY_PORTLET';
     portlet_rec.description :=
        'This portlet displays the Employees Salaries';
     portlet_rec.timeout := null;
     portlet_rec.timeout_msg := null;
     portlet_rec.language := 'us';
     portlet_rec.has_show_edit  := true;
     portlet_rec.has_show_edit_defaults := true;
     portlet_rec.has_show_preview := true;
     portlet_rec.content_type :=
        wwpro_api_provider.CONTENT_TYPE_HTML;
     portlet_rec.preference_store_path := null;
     portlet_rec.created_on := sysdate;
     portlet_rec.created_by := wwctx_api.get_user;
     portlet_rec.last_updated_on := sysdate;
     portlet_rec.last_updated_by := wwctx_api.get_user;

    return portlet_rec;
end get_portlet_info;

function is_runnable (
     p_provider_id in integer,
     p_reference_path in varchar2 )
return boolean
is
begin

    if (p_reference_path is null) then

        if (wwctx_api.is_logged_on) then
            return true;
        else
            return false;
        end if;
    else
        return true;
    end if;
end is_runnable;

procedure register (
  p_portlet_instance in wwpro_api_provider.portlet_instance_record )
is
Begin
    null;
end register;
```

```
    procedure deregister (
       p_portlet_instance in wwpro_api_provider.portlet_instance_record)
    Is
    Begin
        null;
    end deregister;

    procedure show (
      p_portlet_record wwpro_api_provider.portlet_runtime_record )
    Is
        portlet_rec wwpro_api_provider.portlet_record;
    begin
        if ( not is_runnable (
             p_provider_id => p_portlet_record.provider_id,
             p_reference_path => p_portlet_record.reference_path ) )
        then
            raise wwpro_api_provider.PORTLET_SECURITY_EXCEPTION;
        end if;

        portlet_rec := get_portlet_info(
             p_provider_id => p_portlet_record.provider_id,
             p_language => p_portlet_record.language );

        if ( p_portlet_record.exec_mode = wwpro_api_provider.MODE_SHOW )
        then
            if ( p_portlet_record.has_title_region) then
                wwui_api_portlet.draw_portlet_header (
                     p_provider_id       => p_portlet_record.provider_id,
                     p_portlet_id        => p_portlet_record.portlet_id,
                     p_title             => portlet_rec.title,
                     p_has_details       => true,
                     p_has_edit          => true,
                     p_has_help          => true,
                     p_has_about         => true,
                     p_referencepath     =>
                          P_portlet_record.reference_path,
                     p_back_url          => p_portlet_record.page_url
                );
            end if;

            wwui_api_portlet.open_portlet(p_portlet_record.has_border);

            htp.p(wwui_api_portlet.portlet_text(
                 p_string   => 'Emp. Salaries - Mode Show',
                 p_level    => 1 ) );

            if (p_portlet_record.has_border) then
                wwui_api_portlet.close_portlet;
            end if;
        elsif (p_portlet_record.exec_mode =
                     wwpro_api_provider.MODE_SHOW_ABOUT)
        Then
            htp.p('Emp. Salaries - Mode Show About');
```

```
113          elsif (p_portlet_record.exec_mode =
114              wwpro_api_provider.MODE_SHOW_EDIT)
115          Then
116              htp.p('Emp. Salaries - Mode Show Edit');
117          elsif (p_portlet_record.exec_mode =
118                      wwpro_api_provider.MODE_SHOW_HELP)
119          Then
120              htp.p('Emp.Salaries - Mode Show Help');
121          elsif (p_portlet_record.exec_mode =
122                      wwpro_api_provider.MODE_SHOW_EDIT_DEFAULTS)
123          Then
124              htp.p('Emp.Salaries - Mode Edit Defaults');
125          elsif (p_portlet_record.exec_mode =
126                      wwpro_api_provider.MODE_SHOW_DETAILS)
127          Then
128              htp.p('Emp.Salaries - Mode Show Details');
129          elsif (p_portlet_record.exec_mode =
130                      wwpro_api_provider.MODE_PREVIEW)
131          Then
132              htp.p('Emp.Salaries - Mode Show Preview');
133          end if;
134
135      end show;
136
137      procedure copy (
138         p_copy_portlet_info in wwpro_api_provider.copy_portlet_record ) is
139      Begin
140          null;
141      end copy;
142
143      function describe_parameters (
144           p_provider_id in integer,
145           p_language in varchar2 )
146      return wwpro_api_provider.portlet_parameter_table is
147           params_tab wwpro_api_provider.portlet_parameter_table;
148      Begin
149          return params_tab;
150      end describe_parameters;
151
152  end salary_portlet;
153   /
```

salary_portlet.pkb

In the "show" procedure the HTP.P procedure is called to generate the portlet HTML output in each mode. In the SHOW_MODE the function wwui_api_portlet.portlet_text is used—in line 102—to return the text in the p_string parameter with the cascading style sheet (CSS) font settings of the portal page. So the SALARY_PORTLET will have the same style properties as the portal page to which the portlet is added. The guidelines for rendering the portlets are covered in more detail in Chapter 14.

As a start, you can build the second portlet (i.e., DEPT_PORTLET) package similar to the SALARY_PORTLET except for the names and the display text. These changes are in lines 11, 13, 14, 16, 103, 112, 116, 120, 124, 128, and 132. To simplify applying the changes to the packages, you can create an SQL script that just calls the other packages' creation scripts. You can call this script emp_provider.sql. It should look like the following:

```
@@emp_provider.pks
@@salary_portlet.pks
@@dept_portlet.pks
@@emp_provider.pkb
@@salary_portlet.pkb
@@dept_portlet.pkb
```

The double @s tell SQL*Plus to look for these files in the same directory of the emp_provider.sql. You should execute the package specification first so the package bodies, which depend on the components of these packages, do not generate compilation errors.

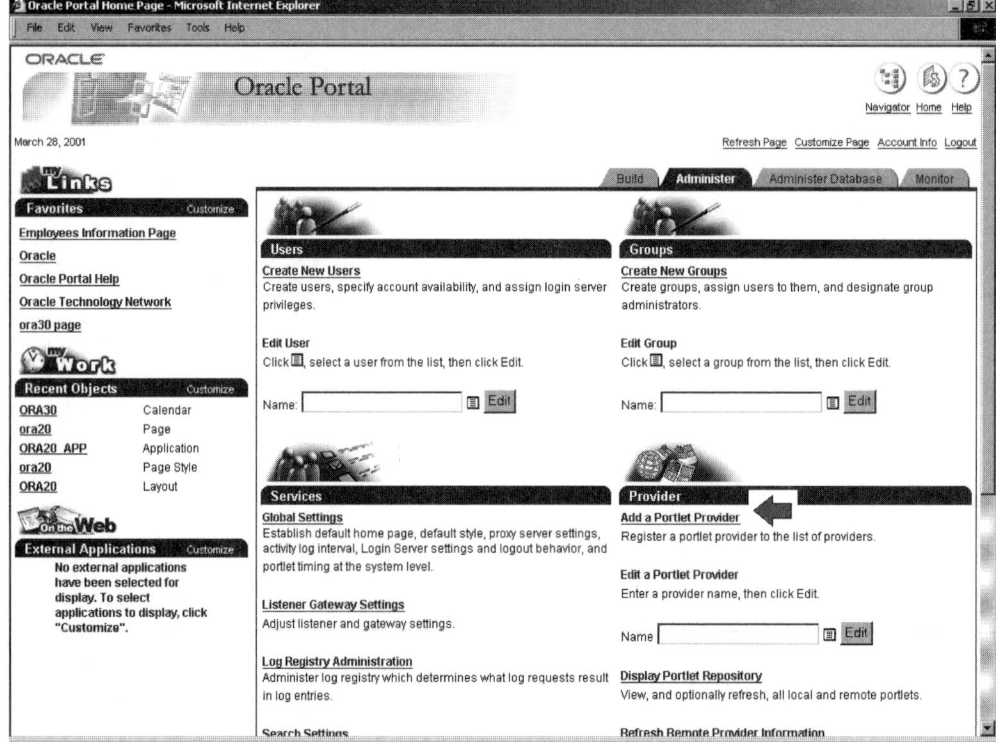

Figure 13.10 Oracle Portal Home Page: Administer Tab.

Register the Portlet Provider

When all the packages are created successfully without any compilation errors (e.g., due to syntax errors), you are ready to register the employees provider. Click on the "Add a Portlet Provider" link from the Oracle Portal home page Administer tab (Figure 13.10).

Note

In Oracle9*i*AS Portal version 3.0.9, the provider portlet is the third portlet from the top on the left side of the page because a new portlet is added for portal user profiles.

You need to specify a name, a display name, the owning schema, and the package name of the employees provider (Figure 13.11). In Oracle9*i*AS Portal version 3.0.9, you need to specify your provider's user/session information by choosing whether the provider requires logging on to the database and choosing the logging-on frequency.

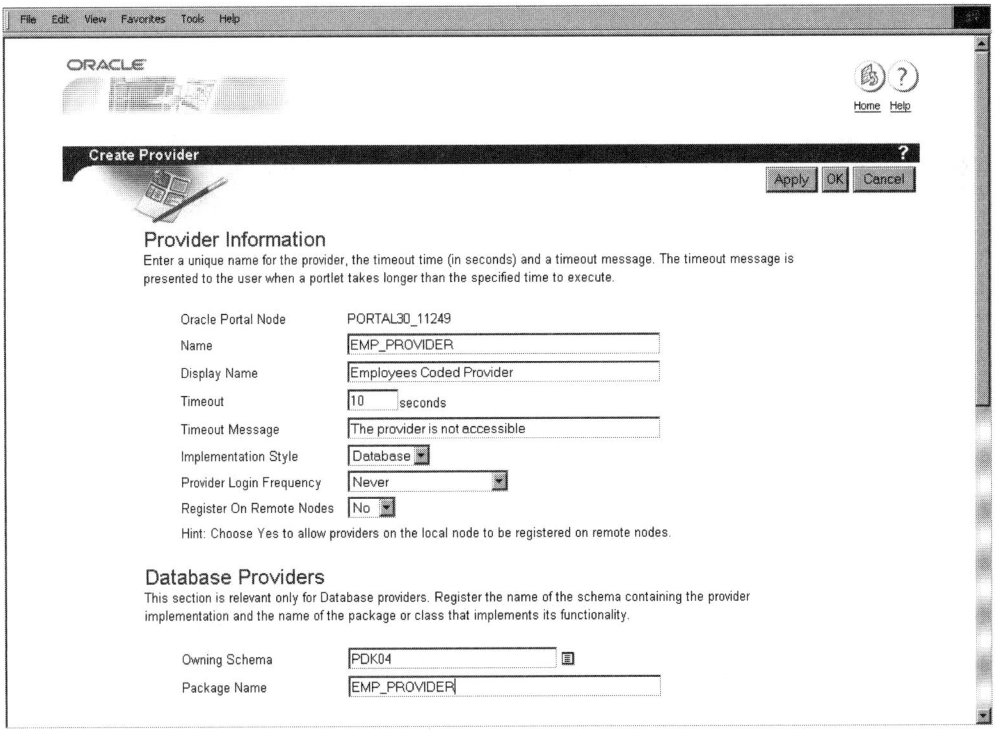

Figure 13.11 Add a Database Portlet Provider.

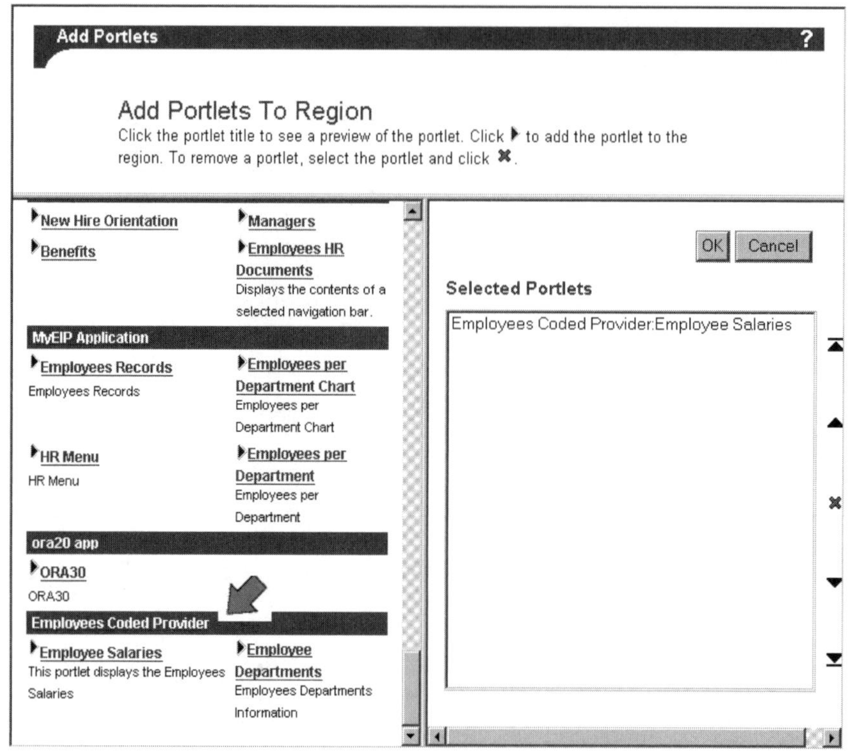

Figure 13.12 Portlet Repository: The New Database Portlet Provider.

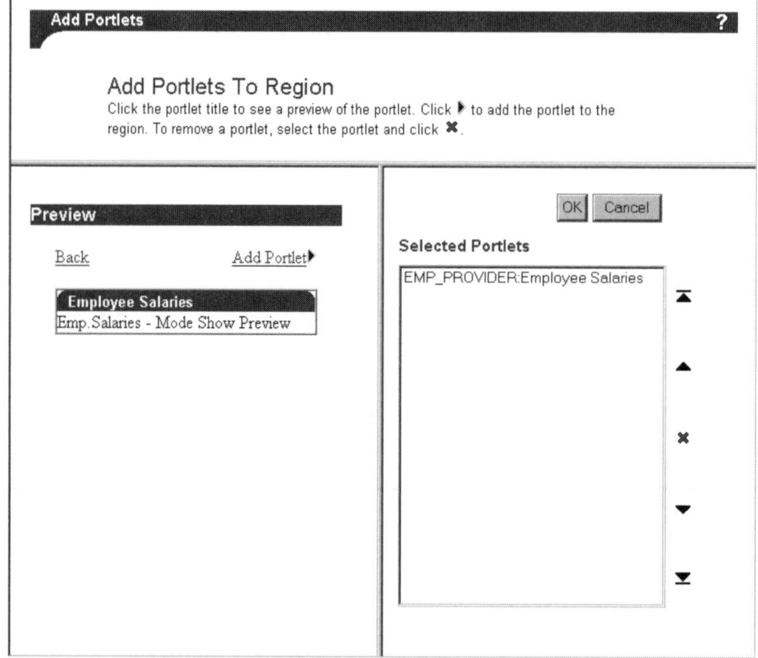

Figure 13.13 Portlet Repository: Employees' Salary Portlet Preview Mode.

Note

You can deregister the provider by first editing it and then clicking on the "Delete" push button.

Once the portlet is registered, you can add its portlets to your existing page (Figure 13.12). The name of the provider in the Portlet Repository is the display name specified in the provider registration. The names of the portlets are specified in the portlet_record in the get_portlet_info function of the portlet package body (i.e., line 13 in salary_portlet.pkg). If one of the portlet names is missing from the Portlets Repository, check the provider package body (e.g., lines 40, 42, 47, 73, 81, etc., in emp_provider.pkb).

Note

In Oracle9*i*AS Portal version 3.0.9, the database provider portlets can be found in the Portlet Repository under the Other Providers node.

Click on the portlet name in the Portlet Repository to display the portlet in the preview mode (Figure 13.13). You can change the preview of a portlet by adding your own code in line 132 of the portlet package body. When you display your page, you should find the new portlet in the show mode (Figure 13.14). You can change your portlet by changing the code in lines 102, 103, and 104 in the portlet package body. Now you can use the PL/SQL features to pull data from different Oracle databases (e.g., PL/SQL cursor using database links or views).

Chapter 14 discusses the guidelines for rendering HTML/XML in the portlets as well as the Oracle Portal services API available for providers.

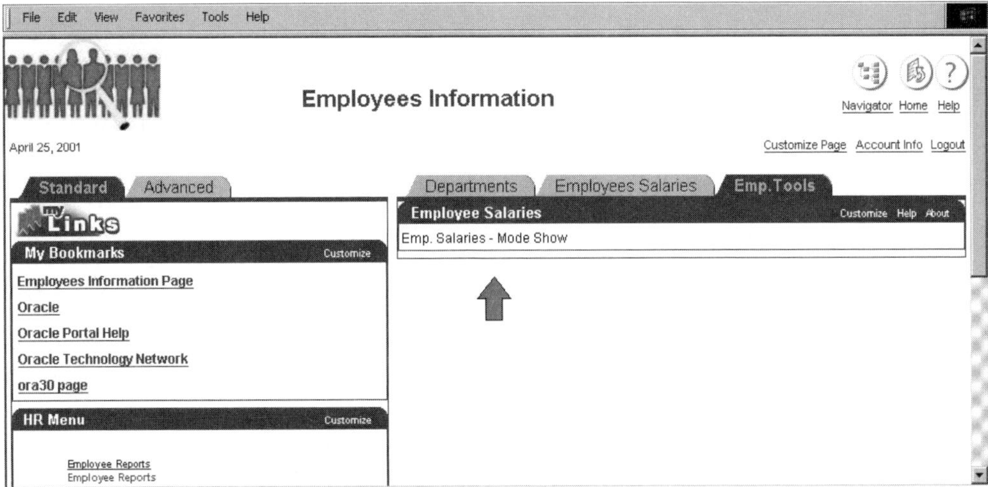

Figure 13.14 Page Display: Employees' Salaries Portlet Added.

CHAPTER 14

Advanced Portlet Programming

Introduction

This chapter has two main parts. The first part explains the HTML display guidelines that you need to consider when you are writing your own providers. The second part introduces the different Oracle Portal framework services (i.e., PL/SQL API packages) that you can utilize in your code.

Portlet HTML Display Guidelines

As you have seen in Chapter 13, the portlet package "show" procedure uses the HTP package to generate HTML text that browsers use to draw the portlet. The generation of the HTML and also the XML text to be displayed in a browser is called portlet rendering.

Portlets in an Oracle Page are implemented as cells in an HTML table. Most of the HTML constructs (e.g., links, forms, images, tables, etc.) can be displayed inside the portlets. Some constructs cannot be used inside a portlet because they cannot be inserted inside an HTML cell, such as frames.

You should use standard HTML in building your portlets. Nonstandard and improperly written HTML may appear inconsistently across different browsers and could cause parts of your portlet not to appear. Unterminated and misplaced tags are frequent syntax errors that cause inconsistent behavior.

Note

The official w3c HTML specification is available at *http://w3c.org.* Also, you can use tools to check the HTML before adding it to your portlets. HTML Tidy, for example, can be downloaded from *http://www.w3.org/People/Raggett/tidy/.*

Cascading Style Sheets (CSS)

Cascading style sheets (CSS) is a simple mechanism for adding style (e.g., fonts, colors, spacing, etc.) to Web documents. The style sheet is inserted into an HTML document by putting the style sheet inside a style element at the top of the HTML document.

```
<HTML>
    <TITLE>Web Development With Oracle Portal</TITLE>
    <STYLE type="text/css">
       BODY { color: yellow; background: black; }
       H1, H2 { color: red }
    </STYLE>
    <BODY>
       <H1>Oracle9i Application Server</H1>
       <P> Oracle9i AS is Deployment Middleware software
       suite
       <H2>O9i AS Services</H2>
       <UL>
           <LI>Oracle Forms
           <LI>Oracle Reports
           <LI>Oracle Portal
           <LI>....
       </UL>
    </BODY>
</HTML>
```

ch14.html

The notation used between the STYLE tags defines the style rules. Each rule starts with a tag name (e.g., BODY) followed by a list of style properties enclosed between braces. In this example the style properties of the BODY rule state that the text color of the document body is yellow and its background color is black. The second style rule states that the text color of Header 1 and Header 2 is red (Figure 14.1).

Note

The official w3c CCS specification is available at *http://www.w3.org.*

Typically, the fonts and colors of every portlet on a page should have the same style settings. This page style is initially set up by the page developer (or the portal administrator) then

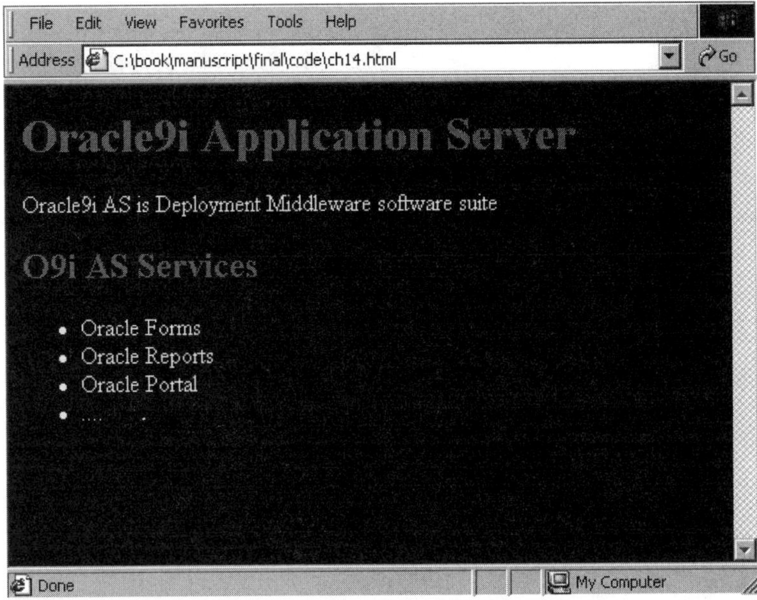

Figure 14.1 HTML Document with CCS.

optionally edited by the end-user. These style settings are embedded using a CSS on each Oracle Portal page. The portlets can then access these settings for their fonts and colors.

If you do not use the page style and instead use your own fonts and colors, your portlet may look out of place when the user changes the page style settings. It is also possible that your hard-coded portlet may use the same text color as the background, and thus its text will be impossible to see.

You can look at your page style rules by viewing the source of your Oracle Portal page (from the view menu item, choose source; Figure 14.2). The cascading style sheet is linked through the following URL:

```
<HTML>
<HEAD>
<TITLE>Employees Information</TITLE>
<LINK REL=Stylesheet TYPE="text/css"
 HREF="http://myportal/pls/portal30/PORTAL30.wwpob_app_style.render_css?p_style_id=-1">
<base href="http://myportal/pls/portal30/"></HEAD>
<BODY leftMargin="0" rightMargin="0" topMargin="0" marginheight="0" marginwidth="0" class="PageBg" >
<SCRIPT LANGUAGE="JavaScript">
function show_context_help(h) {
    newwindow = window.open(h,"ContextHelp","menubar=1,scrollbars=1,resizable=1,width=600,height=400");
}
</SCRIPT>
<SCRIPT LANGUAGE="JavaScript">
function show_task_help() {
   newwindow = window.open("http://myportal/pls/portal30/PORTAL30.site?p_siteid=5", "Help", "menubar=1,to
}
</SCRIPT>
```

Figure 14.2 HTML Source of an Oracle Portal Page.

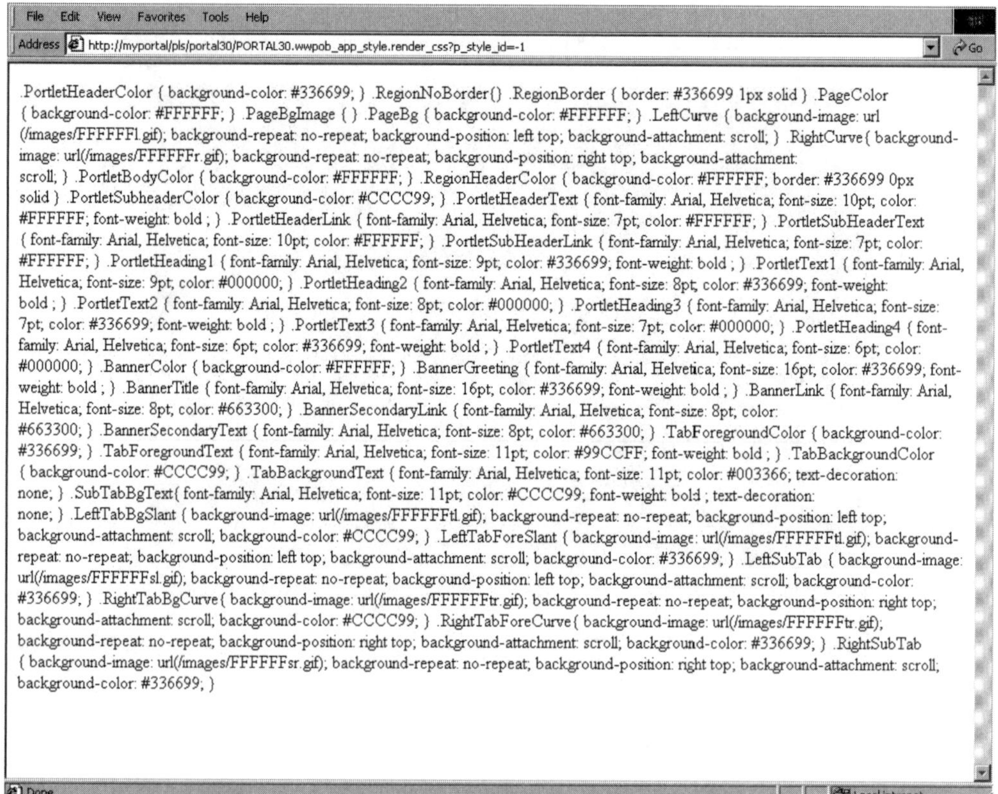

Figure 14.3 Oracle Portal CCS Source.

```
http://myportal/pls/portal30/PORTAL30.wwpob_app_style.
render_css?p_style_id=-1
```

where −1 refers to the default style of the user. If the user customizes the page and chooses another page style, the number changes to reflect the new style chosen. You can look at the page style CCS text by typing this URL in the browser (Figure 14.3).

The following is a sample of the CCS text:

```
.PortletBodyColor
{
background-color: #FFFFFF;
}
.PortletText1
{
font-family: Arial, Helvetica;
```

```
font-size: 10pt;
color: #000000;
}
```

You can access the style sheet definitions in HTML tags using the class property.

```
<font class="PortletText1">Emp. Salaries - Mode Show</font>
```

In Chapter 13 the salary_portlet.pkb code calls the portlet_text procedure—in line 102—to generate text using the portal page style. So, you can use the following code to produce the same output following the page style, without using the portlet_text:

```
htp.p( '<font class="PortletText1">Emp.Salaries -
Show</font>' ) ;
```

Tips for Displaying Portlets in Show Mode

The actual size of the portlet depends on the user settings, the browser width, and the amount and style of content placed in the portlet.

1. Try to keep the portlet contents concise. Putting too much data in a small portlet makes it harder on the users to view it all, especially on small screen resolutions.
2. Try to avoid using fixed-width HTML tables in portlets, because generally you do not have control on the portlet width.
3. Try to avoid long continuous lines of text.
4. Test resizing the page to ensure that the portlets work in different browser window sizes.
5. Test changing the browser default font to make sure that the portal page is displayed normally if the end-user decides to change the browser default font.

Portlet Header (Banner or Title Bar)

Because users can decide whether they want the portlet banners displayed or not, when you build your portlets you must check the has_title_region flag in the portlet_runtime_record to see whether you should display the title bar. Refer to line 85 in the salary_portlet.pkb in Chapter 13. The users can hide the banner by editing the properties of the region (Figure 14.4).

Note

You can use JavaScript inside your portlet. Because it is needed for Oracle Portal, the browser has to enable the JavaScript support. Also, Java applets and the browser plug-ins can be used inside the portlets.

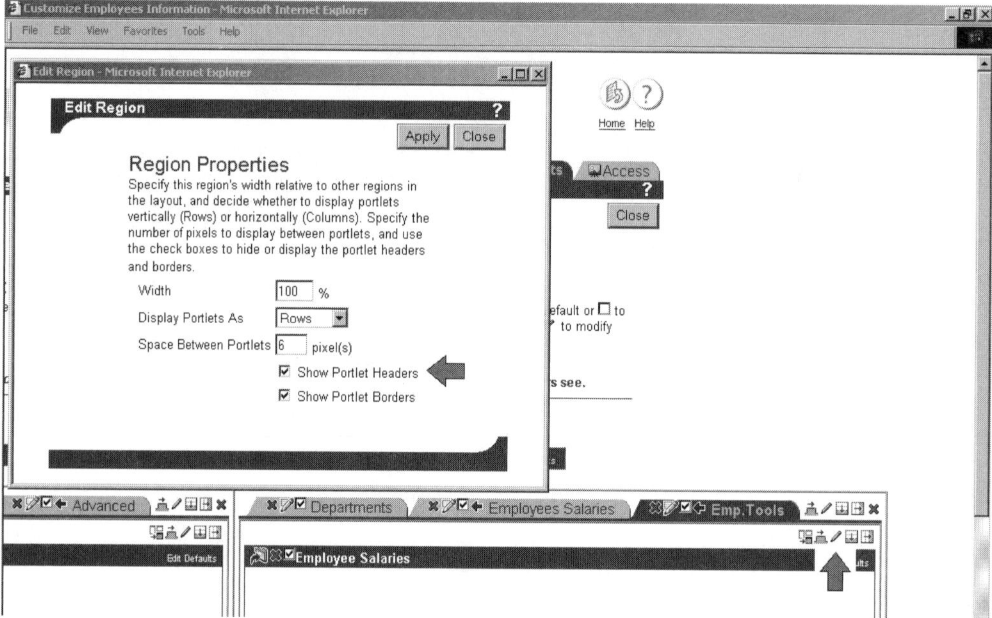

Figure 14.4 Customizing the Page to Hide the Portlets' Headers for a Region.

Tips for Displaying Portlets in Edit Mode

The edit mode allows the portlet users to customize the portlet. Edit mode provides a list of customizable settings that may include the portlet title, formatting options, and so on. For example, it is always a good idea to allow users to customize the title of the portlet. Because the same portlet may be added to the same portal page more than one time, the end-user can give each portlet instance a different title.

Typically, portal users access the portlet's edit mode by clicking on the "Customize" link on the portlet banner (Figure 14.5). The customize link takes the user to a new Web page in the same browser window. The Edit Portlet page allows end-users to change the customizable portlet settings. Once the settings are either applied or dismissed, the user is then automatically taken back to the Oracle Portal page containing the portlet.

Also, end-users can access the portlet's edit mode by clicking on the "Customize" link on the page (Figure 14.6). In Oracle 9*i*AS Portal 3.0.7 and 3.0.8, the end-user can choose "Myself" in the "Customize for" list item, then the "Edit Defaults" links are changed to "Customize" (Figure 14.7).

For the edit mode of your coded portlets to be consistent with the other edit modes of the built-in portlets, it should implement the following buttons in order (Figure 14.8):

1. "OK" button: The end-user clicks on this button to save his or her customizations and return to the calling portal page.

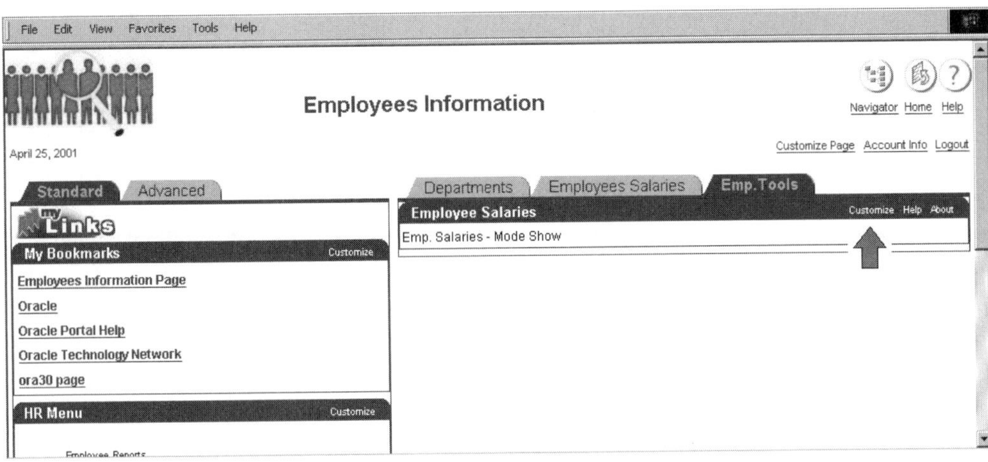

Figure 14.5 Portlet Customize Link.

2. "Apply" button: The end-user clicks on this button to save his or her customizations and reload the current page.
3. "Revert to Defaults" button: The end-user clicks on this button to remove all the user customization changes and revert to the portlet defaults (set up by the portlet developer). This button then redirects the browser to the calling portal page. I recommend you provide default values for all the portlets, so end-users do not have to customize the portlets before displaying them.
4. "Cancel" button: The end-user clicks on this button to cancel the settings changes he or she entered in this edit session. The button then takes the user back to the calling portal page.

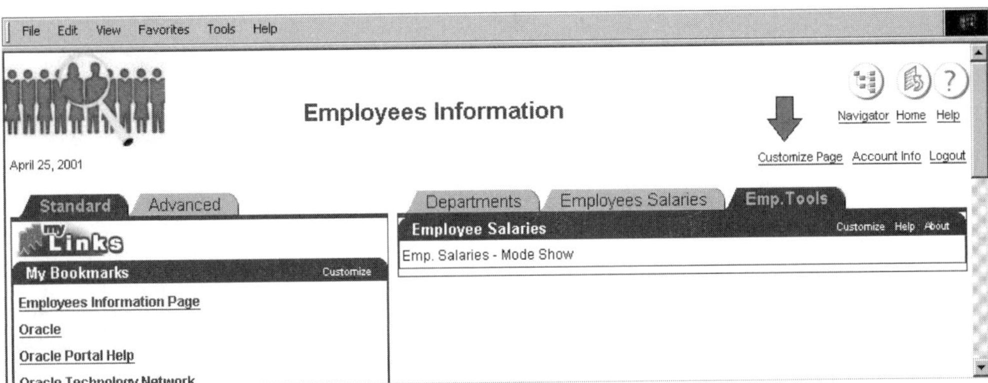

Figure 14.6 Portal Page Customize Link.

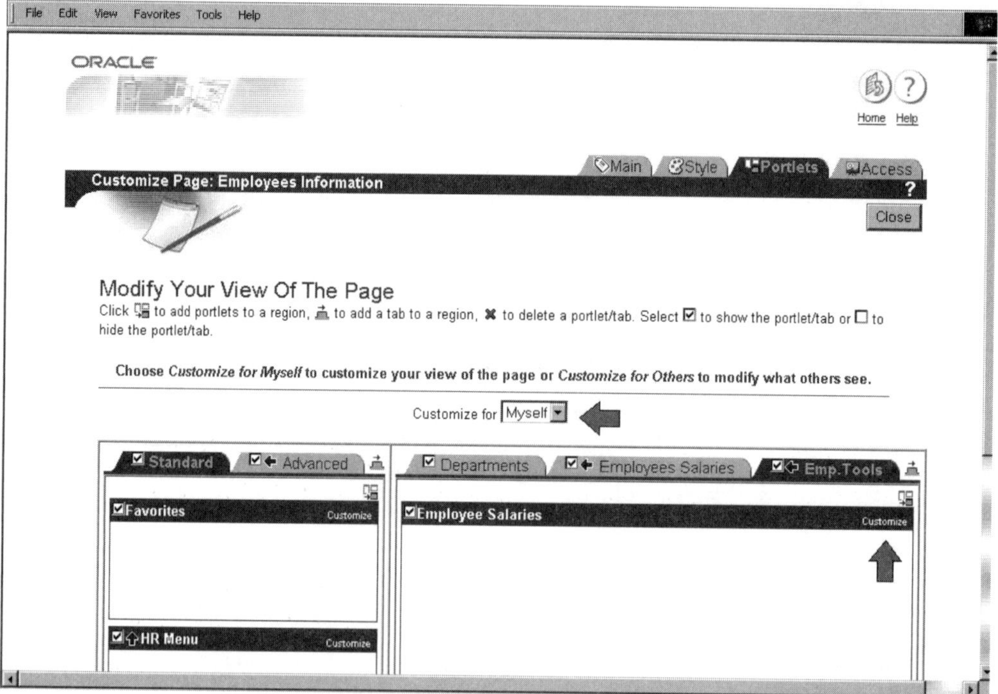

Figure 14.7 Customize Page: Customize for Myself.

Note

You cannot access the style CSS of the portlet instance page in the MODE_SHOW_EDIT mode.

How Can You Enable the MODE_SHOW_EDIT Mode?

Providers indicate whether they support the MODE_SHOW_EDIT in two ways:

1. Values returned from the get_portlet_info method (line 20 of salary_portlet.pkb). When the provider is queried for information about a portlet, one of the values that it returns is the has_show_edit flag, which indicates whether it supports MODE_SHOW_EDIT. This flag controls the appearance of the "Customize" link in "Customize Page—Customize for Myself" portlet title banner.
2. When a database provider draws the portlet header, it does so by calling wwui_api_portlet.draw_portlet_header. One of the parameters for this procedure is p_has_edit. p_has_edit is a flag that indicates whether to render the "Customize" link in the portlet header (line 91). Because the default value for this flag is false, the "Customize" link will not appear in the portlet header if the parameter is omitted from the call to wwui_api_

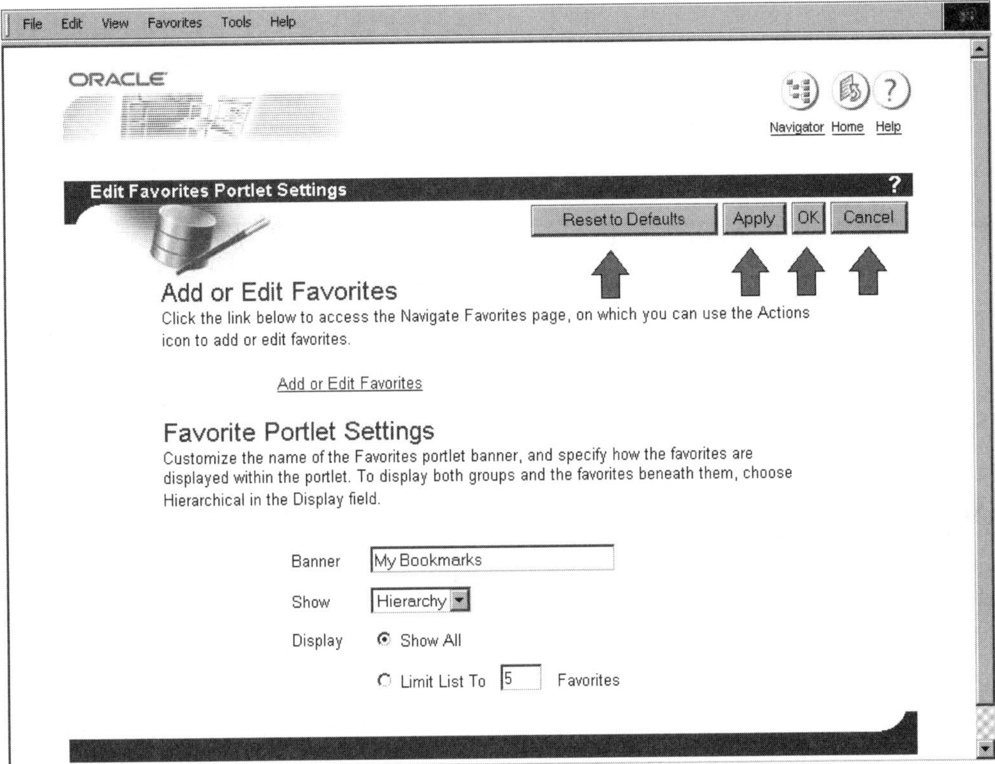

Figure 14.8 Edit Favorites Portlet Settings.

portlet.draw_portlet_header. When calling draw_portlet_header, this flag will override the value of the has_show_edit flag returned by the provider's get_portlet method.

How Can You Store Customizations?

You can use the Preferences Storage API package to store customization of a portlet, because it is tightly integrated with the provider architecture. Another advantage of using the Preferences Storage API is that it allows customizations to be imported and exported along with the database portlets. Exporting and importing portlets are covered in Chapter 18. You can use other mechanisms to store customizations, but you need to perform the customizations export and import separately.

Page Navigation in the MODE_SHOW_EDIT Mode

When a portlet's show method is called, it is passed a portlet run-time record (refer to Table 13.6 for more information on the record structure). This portlet run-time record contains the page URL and the back page URL. When the show procedure is called in the edit mode, the page URL is the URL for the MODE_SHOW_EDIT page. You can use this URL to redraw the page after the end-user clicks on the "Apply" action. The back page URL represents the URL for the page that actually called MODE_SHOW_EDIT. This back page can be either the portal page that contains the portlet or the "Customize Page—Customize for Myself" page. You can use this URL to navigate back to the calling page after the end-user clicks on the "OK", "Revert to Default", or "Cancel" button.

Tips for Displaying Portlets in "Edit Defaults" Mode

The page administrators use the edit defaults mode to customize the default settings for all the other users who access the portlet page. The edit defaults mode can be called the system-level portlet defaults. For example, you can log in as PORTAL30 user and change the title of a portlet, and this title is what all the other users see by default, unless they customize the portlet with their own title.

The Edit Defaults page can be accessed from the Customize Page screen when the "Customize for" list is set to "Others". Typically, when the user clicks on the "Edit Defaults" link of a portlet, he or she is taken to a new page where the portlet settings can be customized. Once the settings are applied, the user is then automatically returned to the portal page. The buttons of the "Edit Defaults" page have the same guidelines as the guidelines of the buttons in the Edit mode.

Note

You cannot access the style CSS of the portlet instance page in the MODE_SHOW_EDIT_DEFAULTS mode.

How Can You Enable the MODE_SHOW_EDIT_DEFAULTS Mode?

To enable the "edit defaults" mode of a coded portlet, the get_portlet method of the provider should return a portlet record with the "has_show_edit_defaults" flag set to TRUE (refer to line 21 in the salary_portlet.pkb in Chapter 13). The same points made earlier in the customization storage and navigation in the Mode_Show_Edit mode are valid in the Mode_Show_Edit_Defaults mode.

Tips for Displaying Portlets in Preview Mode

The end-users access the preview mode of the portlets to see what the portlet looks like before adding it to a page. Clicking on the portlet's title from the Portlet Repository window displays the portlet's preview. Because the display area of the portlet preview is small, the show procedure in the portlet package, line 132 of the salary_portlet.pkb, should generate as few lines as possible, enough for the user to get an idea about the portlet interface and functionality.

Using active hyperlinks in the preview mode might cause navigation outside the Portlet Repository (i.e., Add Portlet dialog). You can simulate the hyperlinks by displaying the fonts underlined. Also, the push buttons displayed in the preview mode should not have any actions attached to them.

How Can You Enable the MODE_PREVIEW Mode?

The "has_show_preview" field of the portlet record, which is returned by the get_portlet provider function, should be set to TRUE to enable the preview mode. Refer to line 22 of the salary_portlet.pkb.

Tips for Displaying Portlets in Full Screen Mode

A portlet can be displayed in a full screen mode in a page by itself. Because a portal page displays its portlets sharing the same Web page, the space allocated to each portlet is limited. The portal users access a portlet's full screen mode by clicking on the title of the portlet. A link should be included in the full screen page to take the user back to the portal page.

How Can You Enable the MODE_SHOW_DETAILS Mode?

To enable the MODE_SHOW_DETAILS mode, set the p_has_details parameter of the draw_portlet_header procedure to TRUE. The draw_portlet_header is used by the portlet in the SHOW_MODE to display the banner of the portlet (refer to line 90 in the salary_portlet.pkb). When the end-user clicks on the banner link, it calls the show procedure within the MODE_SHOW_DETAILS mode (refer to line 128 in the salary_portlet.pkb).

Tips for Displaying Portlets in Help Mode

When the end-user clicks on the help link in the portlet banner, a help page in the same browser window is displayed. The portlet help should tell the user how to use the portlet and describe all the features of the portlet. The portlet help screen should provide a link back to the portlet page.

How Can You Enable the MODE_SHOW_HELP Mode?

To display the help link in the portlet banner, the p_has_help parameter is set to TRUE in the call to the draw_portlet_header procedure (refer to line 92 of the salary_portlet).

Tips for Displaying Portlets in About Mode

The about mode is used to display information about the portlet, such as copyright, version, author contact information, and so on.

How Can You Enable the MODE_SHOW_ABOUT Mode?

To display the about link in the portlet banner, the p_has_about parameter is set to TRUE in the call to the draw_portlet_header procedure (refer to line 93 of the salary_portlet).

Portal Framework Services

The portal framework provides a set of standard services available to provider/portlet developers. You do not have to use these services, but doing so reduces the effort required to create portlets.

This part of the chapter starts with a brief description of these services, and then some of these services are described in more detail later.

1. Session Context is used to provide information about the current user and session, such as Who is the current user? Which database schema does the portal lightweight user use to connect to the portal database? What time did the user log on? What is the IP address of the user's client?
2. Session Storage is used to preserve user selections because it allows developers to store and retrieve session level information. The lifetime of the data in the session store is the lifetime of the portal session itself. When the session ends, by logging out or closing the browser, the data stored in the session store is lost.
3. End-User Personalization (i.e., Preference Storage) allows portlet developers to define a set of preferences and then provide the end-users with the ability to set and retrieve those preferences. This service can be used to implement the Edit and Edit Defaults show modes of portlets.
4. National Language Support (NLS) is used to support the development of portlets with multiple languages. It allows developers to define and store string translations and access the translations based on the browser's language(s). The other alternative would be hard-coding the translated strings inside the portlet/provider code.
5. Event Logging is used to allow developers to define logging events and log occurrences of those events at run time. The Oracle Portal developers can call the service API to log actions performed on Oracle Portal objects and store these logs in the database, then make them available through standard SQL calls and reporting tools.
6. Error Handling is used to generate customized error messages from the coded portlets and present them to the end-users.
7. Security allows developers to implement the access control to the portlet programmatically and then check for the appropriate users' privileges at run time. It can provide answers to security questions, such as Of which groups is the current user a member? Does the user (or his or her group) have the required privileges to access the portlet?
8. Caching is used to allow developers to build portlets that utilize the O9*i*AS Portal caching capabilities.

We will discuss the first three API service packages in more detail. Full documentation of all the services API offers can be found in the PDK.

Session Context API

The package name is wwctx_api package. Table 14.1 lists most of the functions of the package with their descriptions. For a complete list of methods, you can either describe the package name from SQL*Plus or read the package specification.

Some of the session context functions are used in the emp_provider in Chapter 13. For example, in salary_portlet.pkb, line 26, the wwctx_api.get_user is used to initialize the

Table 14.1 wwctx_api Package Methods

Method	Description
get_user	This function returns the name of the user currently logged on the Oracle Portal.
get_user_id	This function returns the user ID.
get_db_user	This function returns the database user (i.e., schema) name that the lightweight user uses to connect to the database.
get_product_version	This function returns the version of Oracle Portal.
get_product_schema	This function returns the name of the Oracle Portal schema (PORTAL30).
is_logged_on	This function returns TRUE if the user has logged on to the Oracle Portal, otherwise it returns FALSE, and the user can only access the public components.
logged_on	It is similar to the is_logged_on method, but it returns a number: 1 if the user is logged on and 0 if the user is not logged on.
get_sessionid	This function returns the session ID of the current session.
get_login_time	This function returns the login time of the current user (as date datatype).
get_ip_address	This function returns the IP address of the client machine.
get_nls_language	This function returns the language of the browser (e.g., us).
get_public_user	This function returns the public username, which is used by Oracle Portal users if they do not log on to the Oracle Portal.
get_sso_schema	This function returns the SSO schema name (e.g., PORTAL30_SSO).
get_proxy_server	This function returns the name of the proxy server used, if any.
get_image_path	This function returns the virtual path defined in the Oracle HTTP Server and can be used to store the images of Oracle Portal components (e.g., /images/). An image file name can be passed to the function to return the image file name qualified by the virtual path. You can use this function in your code to refer to the images to become independent from the middle tier settings.
get_proc_path	This function returns the fully qualified Oracle Portal URL from a relative URL.
get_server_protocol	This function returns HTTP or HTTPS.
get_sso_proc_protocol	This function returns the fully qualified Login Server URL from a relative URL.
get_server_name	This function returns the server name.
get_dad_name	This function returns the DAD name.

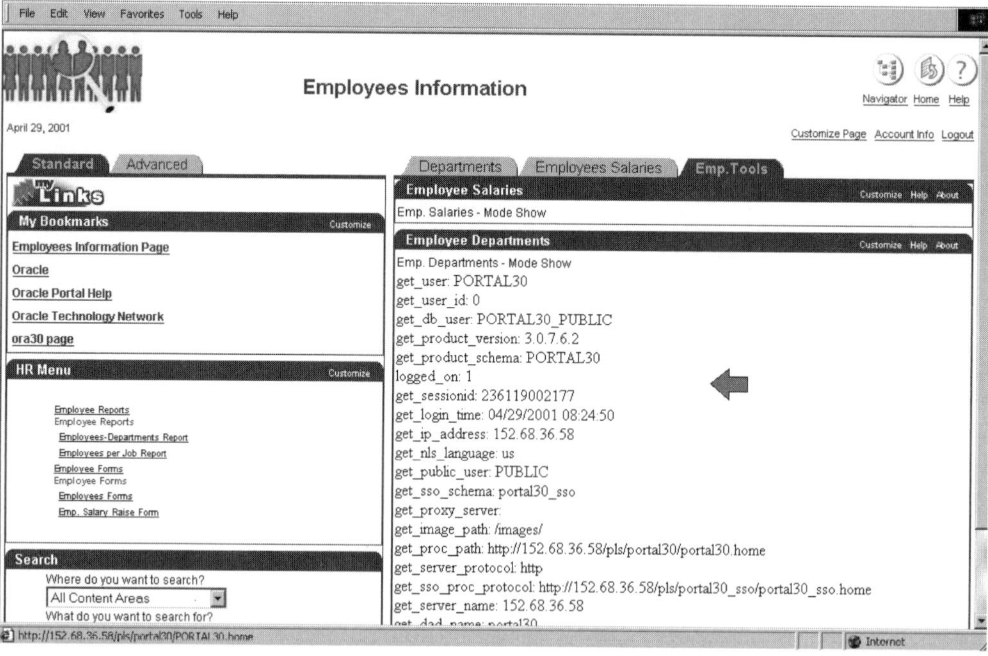

Figure 14.9 wwctx_api Package Methods Test.

created_by field of the portlet record, which is sent back by the get_portlet_info provider function.

You can add the following lines of code to the show procedure of the department portlet to test the wwctx_api package methods (Figure 14.9).

```
htp.print('<BR>' || 'get_user: '
      || wwctx_api.get_user || '<BR>');
htp.print('get_user_id: ' || to_char(wwctx_api.get_user_id)
      || '<BR>');
htp.p('get_db_user: ' || wwctx_api.get_db_user
      || '<BR>');
htp.p('get_product_version: '
      || wwctx_api.get_product_version || '<BR>');
htp.p('get_product_schema: ' || wwctx_api.get_product_schema
      || '<BR>');
htp.p('logged_on: ' || to_char(wwctx_api.logged_on)
      || '<BR>');
htp.p('get_sessionid: ' || wwctx_api.get_sessionid
      || '<BR>');
```

```
htp.p('get_login_time: '
      || to_char(wwctx_api.get_login_time,'MM/DD/YYYY HH24:MI:SS')
      || '<BR>');
htp.p('get_ip_address: ' || wwctx_api.get_ip_address
      || '<BR>');
htp.p('get_nls_language: ' || wwctx_api.get_nls_language
      || '<BR>');
htp.p('get_public_user: ' || wwctx_api.get_public_user
      || '<BR>');
htp.p('get_sso_schema: ' || wwctx_api.get_sso_schema
      || '<BR>');
htp.p('get_proxy_server: ' || wwctx_api.get_proxy_server
      || '<BR>');
htp.p('get_image_path: ' || wwctx_api.get_image_path
      || '<BR>');
htp.p('get_proc_path: ' ||
      wwctx_api.get_proc_path ( 'home', 'portal30') || '<BR>');
htp.p('get_server_protocol: ' || wwctx_api.get_server_protocol
      || '<BR>');
htp.p('get_sso_proc_protocol: '
      || wwctx_api.get_sso_proc_path ('home', 'portal30_sso' )
      || '<BR>');
htp.p('get_server_name: ' || wwctx_api.get_server_name
      || '<BR>');
htp.p('get_dad_name: ' || wwctx_api.get_dad_name
      || '<BR>');
```

Note

The full source code for the employee provider with the previous code added to the department portlet can be found on the CD-ROM.

Session Storage

The communication protocol used on the World Wide Web is hypertext transfer protocol. HTTP is a stateless protocol, thus, when you type a URL into your Web browser and hit the Enter key, the browser sends a request to the Web server to retrieve this page. Once the Web server sends the page contents back to the browser, the connection between the browser and the Web server is closed. So, by default the Web browser does not have enough information to be able to distinguish between clients.

Oracle Portal provides developers with a mechanism for storing data temporarily, to be shared across different modules of Oracle Portal. This mechanism is a server-side solution, which reduces the usage of client-side solutions, such as cookies. This section starts with an introduction to client-side session storage (i.e., cookies), and then introduces the session storage API.

Cookies in Oracle Portal

Many developers implement client-side session storage by using cookies. A cookie is a file kept in the client machine and maintained by the Web browser to hold data in encrypted format. A popular reason for using cookies is the storage of the username and password. Usually, for the user to log onto a secure Web site, he or she needs to authenticate by entering his or her username and password. By using cookies, the user can choose not to re-enter the authentication information the next time he or she visits the same Web site (assuming that the user did not log out in between).

The Oracle Portal product uses cookies to keep information about the Oracle Portal users and their authentication.

Session Storage API

Each portal user session has a unique identifier, which is used in the Oracle Portal session storage tables. The session data is temporarily stored inside the database until the user logs out, then it is removed. The Session Storage API allows you to store application-specific information related to the current user session.

Storing and retrieving session data temporarily into and from the database is done through an object called the Application Session Object. The portlet developers can use its methods to load the object, set its attributes, get its attribute values, and save its information.

The Application Session Object (wwsto_api_session)

The Application Session Object is a PL/SQL object (i.e., PL/SQL TYPE), which contains private attributes (i.e., they cannot be manipulated directly). To access these attributes, you need to use the object access methods. Also, the Application Session Object contains static methods and instance methods. Static methods belong to the object itself rather than its instances. So, you can use the static method even though there is no instance of that object created. This is the opposite of instance methods where you need to have an instance of the object first, to be able to call the instance method.

Note

You can get the attributes and methods information of the PL/SQL type by querying the following data dictionary views from the PORTAL30 schema: USER_TYPE_ATTRS and USER_TYPE_METHODS, respectively.

Table 14.2 wwsto_api_session Type Attributes

Attribute Name	Description
_id	The session object ID
_session_id	The Oracle Portal session_id (i.e., wwctx_api.get_sessionid)
_domain	Domain name of the session object
_sub_domain	Subdomain name of the session object
_element_data	Of type wwsto_session_elements

The Private Session Object Attributes Table 14.2 describes the wwsto_api_session attributes. The implementation steps of the Application Session Object are

1. Load the session object.
2. Set the contents of the object using the set methods or retrieve the contents using the get methods.
3. Save the session object.

The functions used to perform these steps are covered next.

Load_session Method The load_session method returns an instance of the application session object. It has the following specification:

```
static function load_session
(
      p_domain in varchar2,
      p_sub_domain in varchar2
)
return wwsto_api_session;
```

The domain and subdomain are used to categorize the storage object created by the function. Then you need both parameters to locate the session object.

Save_session Method The save_session method saves the session object to the database (i.e., Oracle Portal node). It has no parameters.

Drop_session Method The drop_session method deletes the session object. It has the following specification:

```
static procedure drop_session
(
```

```
        p_domain in varchar2,
        p_sub_domain in varchar2
);
```

SET Methods The SET methods allow you to set the values of the Session Object attributes. The p_name parameter is the case-sensitive attribute name. The following attributes setting methods are available.

- set_attribute: Depending on the data type of the method's second parameter, the attribute data type is chosen and the value is assigned. It has the following specifications:

```
member procedure set_attribute
(
        p_name in varchar2,
        p_value in date
);
member procedure set_attribute
(
        p_name in varchar2,
        p_value in varchar2
);
member procedure set_attribute
(
        p_name in varchar2,
        p_value in number
);
```

- set_attribute_as_string: This procedure is used to set NLS-specific values to attributes. It has the following specification:

```
member procedure set_attribute_as_string
(
        p_name in varchar2,
        p_value in varchar2,
        p_language in varchar2,
        p_type_name in varchar2 default 'STRING'
);
```

GET Methods The GET methods allow you to get the values of the attributes of the Session Object.

- get_attribute_as_date has the following specification:

```
member function get_attribute_as_date
(
      p_name in varchar2
)
return date;
```

- get_attribute_as_number has the following specification:

```
member function get_attribute_as_number
(
      p_name in varchar2
)
return number;
```

- get_attribute_as_varchar2 has the following specification:

```
member function get_attribute_as_varchar2
(
      p_name in varchar2
)
return varchar2;
```

- get_attribute_as_string has the following specification:

```
member function get_attribute_as_string
(
      p_name in varchar2,
      p_language in varchar2,
      p_type_name in varchar2 default 'STRING'
)
return varchar2;
```

Sample Portlet

The easiest way to demonstrate the session storage is to build a simple portlet that utilizes the session object to display how many times the portlet has been displayed. Follow the next steps in order to try using the session storage object in a new or existing coded portlet.

1. In the portlet package body, declare two constants. A good place to declare your constants is at the beginning of the package body, because it is easy to spot them:

```
DOMAIN constant varchar2(32) := 'wdwop';
SUBDOMAIN constant varchar2(32) := 'ch14';
```

2. In the show procedure of the portlet package body, add the following declarations; one is for the session storage object and the other is just the counter.

```
l_session_obj portal30.wwsto_api_session;
l_cnt integer := 0;
```

3. In the show procedure of the portlet package body, add the following code. The code loads a new storage session with the domain and subdomain declared in step 1, then it gets the counter attribute value. The first time the portlet is displayed, the get_attribute_as_number function returns NULL, and the NVL PL/SQL function converts the NULL value to zero so it can be incremented. Once the l_cnt is incremented, the attribute is set to the new value and the session object is saved, so the next time the get_attribute function runs, it picks up the latest value.

```
l_session_obj := portal30.wwsto_api_session.load_session (
                   DOMAIN, SUBDOMAIN
                   );
l_cnt := nvl(
      l_session_obj.get_attribute_as_number ('l_cnt'), 0
      );
l_cnt := l_cnt + 1;
l_session_obj.set_attribute ('l_cnt', l_cnt);
l_session_obj.save_session;
htp.p ('Portlet has been displayed '|| lpad(to_char(l_cnt),6,
'0') || ' times');
```

End-User Personalization (Preference Storage) API

One of the main advantages of Oracle Portal is that its end-users have the ability to customize their portal pages to their own needs. This ability is included as an out-of-the-box feature with application components portlets, content area components, and so on. When you build your own portlets, you are expected to give the end-users the same level of customization capabilities they have with out-of-the-box portlets.

Note

On the companion CD-ROM, you can find the source code of a provider, named services provider, which has both the codes mentioned in the book for the end-user personalization API and session storage API.

End-User Personalization Characteristics

- The user preferences (i.e., customizations) are saved persistently inside the database. If the end-user logs out and logs on again, his or her customizations (e.g., portlet title) are still in place.
- The preferences data structure is a tree, because a tree has a root node and each node in the tree can have zero or more siblings. The actual preferences values are saved in the leaves of the tree. And to get to any node in the tree, you need to follow a path from the root.
- The preferences are unique to each portlet instance. For example, if the same portlet is added twice to the same page, the end-user can customize each and give them different titles.
- The preferences hierarchy can be shared between multiple levels: users, groups, and system.

You can create a preference hierarchy for each portlet using two packages:

- WWPRE_API_NAME: Contains procedures used in creating and deleting the preferences paths and entries.
- WWPRE_API_VALUES: Contains procedures and functions used in setting and getting values of the preferences.

WWPRE_API_NAME Package

This package contains the following four procedures.

CREATE_PATH This procedure takes a varchar2 as an argument to create the Preference Path. Once created, paths and names can be deleted, but they cannot be modified. If the path MYEIP.Emps.Reports already exists, and a call is made to create the path MYEIP.Emps .Reports.Forms, only the segment "Forms" is created.

CREATE_NAME This procedure has the following specification:

```
procedure create_name
(
      p_path in varchar2,
      p_name in varchar2,
      p_description in varchar2,
      p_type_name in varchar2,
      p_language in varchar2
);
```

Here is an example:

```
wwpre_api_name.create_name
(
        p_path => 'MYEIP.EMPS.REPORTS',
        p_name => 'NumOfRows',
        p_type_name => 'NUMBER',
        p_description => 'Number of Rows displayed',
        p_language => wwctx_api.get_nls_language
);
```

DELETE_PATH This procedure deletes a specific path, all names under it, and all preferences values associated with the names.

DELETE_NAME This procedure deletes a preference name and the value associated with the name under a given path.

WWPRE_API_VALUE Package

The package contains the following set of procedures to assign values to preferences:

1. SET_VALUE_AS_DATE
2. SET_VALUE_AS_NUMBER
3. SET_VALUE_AS_VARCHAR2
4. SET_VALUE_AS_STRING

These procedures have similar specifications, such as:

```
procedure set_value_as_varchar2
(
      p_path in varchar2,
      p_name in varchar2,
      p_level_type in varchar2,
      p_level_name in varchar2,
      p_value in varchar2,
      p_commit in boolean default TRUE
);
```

The P_LEVEL_TYPE is the level at which the value is stored. It can be one of three values: USER_LEVEL_TYPE, GROUP_LEVEL_TYPE, and SYSTEM_LEVEL_TYPE. The default value is the USER_LEVEL_TYPE.

The P_LEVEL_NAME is a username, a group name, or null in case of system level. The default is the name of the user currently logged on.

P_COMMIT specifies when the value is committed. If TRUE, this procedure commits the value. If FALSE, callers of this API procedure need to commit the changes. It makes sense to set it to FALSE if you do not want the preference setting to take place if you decided to roll back your transaction. SET_VALUE_AS_STRING procedure has an extra parameter, which is the language.

The package contains the following get functions to retrieve the values of preferences:

5. GET_VALUE_AS_DATE
6. GET_VALUE_AS_NUMBER
7. GET_VALUE_AS_VARCHAR2
8. GET_VALUE_AS_STRING

These functions have similar specifications, such as:

```
function get_value_as_varchar2
(
        p_path in varchar2,
        p_name in varchar2,
        p_level_type in varchar2,
        p_level_name in varchar2
);
```

How Can You Use the End-User Personalization API?

1. Create the preference paths using the wwpre_api_name.create_path method.
2. Create the preference names (i.e., tree leaves) using the wwpre_api_name.create_name method.
3. Use the wwpre_api_value.set_value_as_varchar2, set_value_as_number, or set_value_as _date methods to set the preferences values.
4. Whenever you want to retrieve a preference value, you can use the wwpre_api_value .get_value_as_varchar2, get_value_as_number, or get_value_as_date methods to get the preferences values by providing the preference name and path.

Sample Portlet

To demonstrate the end-user personalization API, you can build a simple portlet that allows the end-user to customize the portlet title. The following steps describe the code pieces that need to be added to implement customizing a portlet title and saving it inside the preferences store. For a complete list of the code, please refer to the CD-ROM for this book.

1. In the beginning of the portlet package body, declare a constant to hold the leading part of the portlet preference path. This leading part should be unique with all the coded portlets you register with one Oracle Portal node.

```
MYEIP_PREF_PATH constant varchar2(200)  := 'HR.PORTAL';
```

2. In the register procedure of the portlet package, declare a local variable to hold the full preference path of the portlet.

```
l_preference_path varchar2(255) :=
    MYEIP_PREF_PATH || p_portlet_instance.reference_path;
```

3. In the same procedure, create your preferences hierarchy. Start by creating the paths, then the names.

```
wwpre_api_name.create_path( p_path=> l_preference_path );
wwpre_api_name.create_name (
      p_path              => l_preference_path,
      p_name              => 'portlet_title',
      p_description       => 'Portlet Title',
      p_type_name         => 'STRING',
      p_language          => wwctx_api.get_nls_language );
```

4. In MODE_SHOW_EDIT mode inside the show procedure of the portlet package, you should add the following local variable declaration to hold the portlet title value retrieved from the preference store.

```
l_portlet_title varchar2 (255);
```

5. In the MODE_SHOW_EDIT processing, get the portlet title preference value. You should display a text item that holds the current portlet title, and the user can enter a new portlet title. You also should display push buttons to accept or cancel the customization changes.

```
l_portlet_title := wwpre_api_value.get_value_as_varchar2(
      p_path => MYEIP_PREF_PATH || p_preference_path,
      p_name => 'portlet_title',
      p_level_type => wwpre_api_value.USER_LEVEL_TYPE,
      p_level_name => wwctx_api.get_user
);
```

6. In the MODE_SHOW_EDIT processing, if the user clicks on the "Apply" button or the "OK" button, the following code needs to be added, to save the new portlet_title value into the preferences store.

```
wwpre_api_value.set_value_as_varchar2(
    p_path       => l_preference_Path,
    p_name       => 'portlet_title',
    p_level_type => wwpre_api_value.USER_LEVEL_TYPE,
```

```
        p_level_name => wwctx_api.get_user,
        p_value      => portlet_title
    );
```

7. Finally, in the MODE_SHOW mode of the show procedure, you can set the title of portlets to the value of the portlet_title preference.

```
l_portlet_title varchar2(200);
begin
      if p_portlet_record.has_title_region
      then
            l_portlet_info := services_provider.get_portlet(
            p_provider_id => p_portlet_record.provider_id,
            p_portlet_id => p_portlet_record.portlet_id,
            p_language => p_portlet_record.language
      );
      l_portlet_title :=
            wwpre_api_value.get_value_as_varchar2(
                  p_path => MYEIP_PREF_PATH ||
                  p_portlet_record.reference_path,
                  p_name => 'portlet_title',
                  p_level_type =>
                        wwpre_api_value.USER_LEVEL_TYPE,
                  p_level_name => wwctx_api.get_user
            );
      wwui_api_portlet.draw_portlet_header(
            p_provider_id   =>
                  p_portlet_record.provider_id,
            p_portlet_id    =>
                  p_portlet_record.portlet_id,
            p_title         => l_portlet_title,
            p_has_details   => false,
            p_has_edit      => true,
            p_has_help      => false,
            p_has_about     => false,
            p_referencepath =>
            p_portlet_record.reference_path,
            p_back_url => p_portlet_record.page_url
            );
      end if;
...
```

Next, Chapter 15 explores building Web providers.

CHAPTER 15

Portal Development Kit and Web Providers

Introduction

You might have external Web applications that do not reside in an Oracle database. You can write programs that communicate with these external Web applications and that allow you to integrate them into your Oracle Portal. These programs are called Web providers. Web providers can be written in any language, like C, C++, Perl, Java, JSP, ASP, and so on. They may use any Web technology, like servlets, CGI, and FCGI. The only requirement these Web providers have to fulfill is that they must be accessible through HTTP and return HTML or XML. Web providers offer the same functionality as database providers, such as session storage, end-user personalization, and so on. For example, you might choose Java to write a Web provider that integrates an existing weather Web site into your Oracle Portal.

This chapter begins with an exploration of Oracle Portal Development Kit (PDK) and discusses how the PDK can help you develop Web providers and their portlets (which are called Web portlets). Next, the chapter introduces you to building Web providers and their portlets using Java servlets and JSP. This chapter is not meant to be a Java servlet or JSP programming tutorial. If you are not familiar with either, you will still be able to set up and test the examples in this chapter; but to be able to add your own code and build new Web providers from scratch, you need to be able to program in Java and have some familiarity with Java servlets and, optionally, JSPs.

Also, in this chapter you are asked to create a couple of simple and short XML files. You do not need to know XML to get the basic understanding of how the XML file is structured.

The Portal Development Kit

The PDK is a group of code samples and documentation that help you to develop providers. You can download the latest version of the PDK from the Oracle Technology Network (OTN) Web site, *http://technet.oracle.com;* a new version of the PDK is released every month or so. Using PDK can give you a head start in understanding Web providers and help building your first provider.

The Portal Development Kit Download

The PDK has many different components; this chapter is only concerned with the Java Portal Development Kit (JPDK) because it is needed to implement the code examples in this chapter.

Start by downloading the PDK from the OTN Web site. Save the downloaded zipped file (e.g., pdkmay.zip) into a new directory (e.g., c:\portal). Next, uncompress all the contents of the zipped file into the new directory. In Microsoft Windows you can uncompress it by double clicking on it. In UNIX you can uncompress it by executing the unzip command. You can uncompress the file into the same new directory that you just created. Uncompressing the zipped file creates all the PDK files under one directory (i.e., c:\portal\pdk).

JPDK Setup

After you download and unzip the PDK, you can start the JPDK setup by following these steps:

1. Because the JPDK setup requires editing a couple of the Oracle HTTP server (e.g., Apache) configuration files, I recommend that you back up these configuration files. These files are jserv.properties (Windows: <iAS_ORACLE_HOME>\Apache\Jserv\conf\jserv.properties; UNIX: <iAS_ORACLE_HOME>/Apache/Jserv/etc/jserv.properties) and zone.properties (Windows: <iAS_ORACLE_HOME>\Apache\Jserv\servlets\zone.properties; UNIX: <iAS_ORACLE_HOME>/Apache/Jserv/etc/zones.properties).

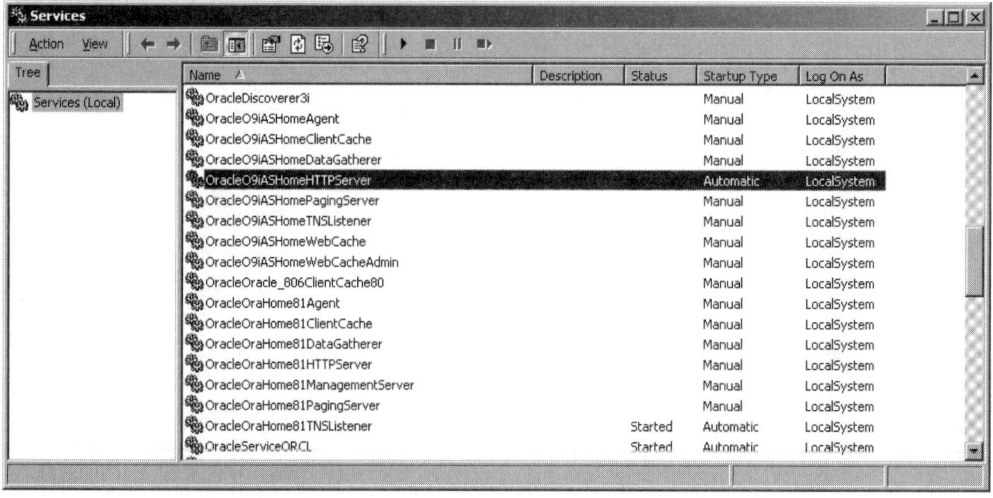

Figure 15.1 Stop Oracle HTTP Server: Windows 2000: Control Panel: Administrative Tools: Services.

2. Stop the Oracle HTTP Server. On Microsoft Windows, you can stop the HTTP server from the control panel services (Figure 15.1) or from the DOS prompt using the **Apache.exe** command (Figure 15.2). You can make sure that the Oracle HTTP server is down by looking for any of the Oracle HTTP server processes: Apache, Apache, and Java. These processes are found when the Oracle HTTP server is running (Figure 15.3).

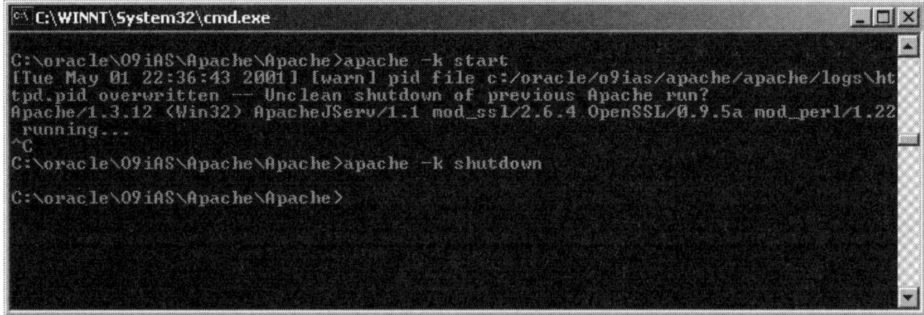

Figure 15.2 Stop Oracle HTTP Server: Windows 2000: DOS Prompt.

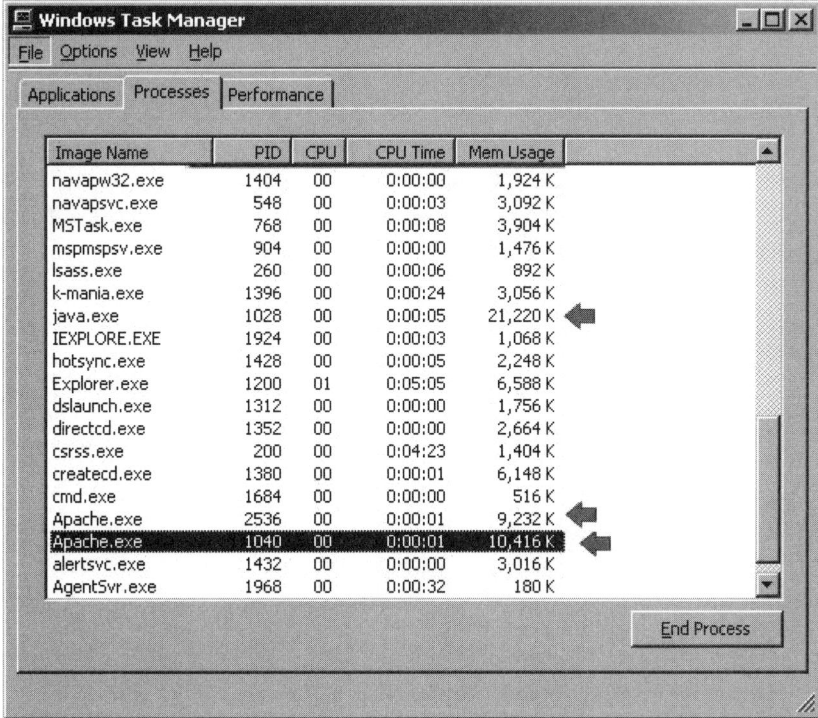

Figure 15.3 Oracle HTTP Server Processes: Windows 2000 Task Manager.

3. Add the following lines to your jserv.properties file. Add them to the wrapper.classpath existing lines, which are located normally at the end of the file. By adding these two lines, you are adding the two JAR (i.e., Java Archive) files to the CLASSPATH environment value passed to the JVM. The provider.jar files contain the JPDK Java class files needed to develop new Java Web providers. The sample.jar file contains the Java class files of a sample Web provider that generates a group of Web portlets. The sample provider is used later to test that the JPDK setup is performed correctly.

```
wrapper.classpath=C:\portal\pdk\jpdk\lib\provider.jar
wrapper.classpath=C:\portal\pdk\jpdk\lib\samples.jar
```

   Remember to change the directories if you decide not to unzip the PDK zipped file into c:\portal. The source code of the Java classes of the provider.jar can be found under the PDK unzipped directory (e.g., c:\portal\pdk\jpdk\src\oracle\portal\provider\v1). You can also access the source code of the sample Java classes either from the source directory (e.g., c:\portal\pdk\jpdk\src\oracle\portal\sample) or from the JPDK HTML documentation (e.g., c:\portal\pdk\jpdk\installing.feedback.portlet.html).
4. In the zone.properties file, under the "Servlet Aliases" section, add the following line:

```
servlet.sample.code=oracle.portal.provider.v1.http.HttpProvider
```

   This line specifies the Java class file that acts as the code of the sample Java servlet. The Java class file name is HttpProvider; it resides in the provider.jar file. The HttpProvider is also called the Web Provider Adapter, which is explained in more detail in a later section. Later on, when you run the sample provider (i.e., Java servlet), Apache looks for the class file HttpProvider in the provider.jar file under the location hierarchy oracle\portal\provider\v1\http.
5. In the zone.properties file, under the "Aliased Servlet Init Aliases" section, add the following line:

```
servlet.sample.initArgs=provider_root=c:\portal\pdk\jpdk
\providers\sample, sessiontimeout=1800000, debuglevel - 1
```

   This line specifies the argument passed to the sample provider Java servlet. The first parameter is the location of the provider.xml file needed by the provider to get the descriptions of the provider Web portlets. The second parameter sets the session timeout for the provider servlet. The value specified for this parameter needs to be the same as the value of the session.timeout parameter in the "Class loader" section in the same zone.properties file. By default it is 1,800,000 milliseconds (i.e., 30 minutes).

6. For the PDK JSP examples to work, you need to create a new directory (i.e., jpdk) to hold the JSP code. For simplicity, create this directory under the Apache Document Root. By default, in Microsoft Windows, it is <iAS_ORACLE_HOME>\Apache\Apache\htdocs directory. If you want, you can change your document root by editing the httpd.conf file and changing the DocumentRoot value and stopping and restarting the Oracle HTTP server.

   Next, copy all the contents of c:\portal\pdk\jpdk\htdocs to <iAS_ORACLE_HOME> \Apache\Apache\htdocs\jpdk.

Note

The root directory is accessed when you use the server name as your URL without adding a virtual path (i.e., alias). For example, when you type the URL *http://myportal.elmallah.com* without specifying any file names, Apache retrieves the index.html file from the DocumentRoot directory. If needed, you can change Apache's default file name from index.html to something else by changing the DirectoryIndex entry in the httpd.conf file.

---

7. Open the provider.xml file that is located under the root directory of the sample provider (i.e., c:\portal\pdk\jpdk\providers\sample\provider.xml). Check that the virtualRoot entry is "/jpdk/" and the physicalRoot entry is "<iAS_ORACLE_HOME>\Apache\Apache \htdocs\jpdk\". These entries are pointing to the location of the JSP directories you copied in the previous step (Figure 15.4).

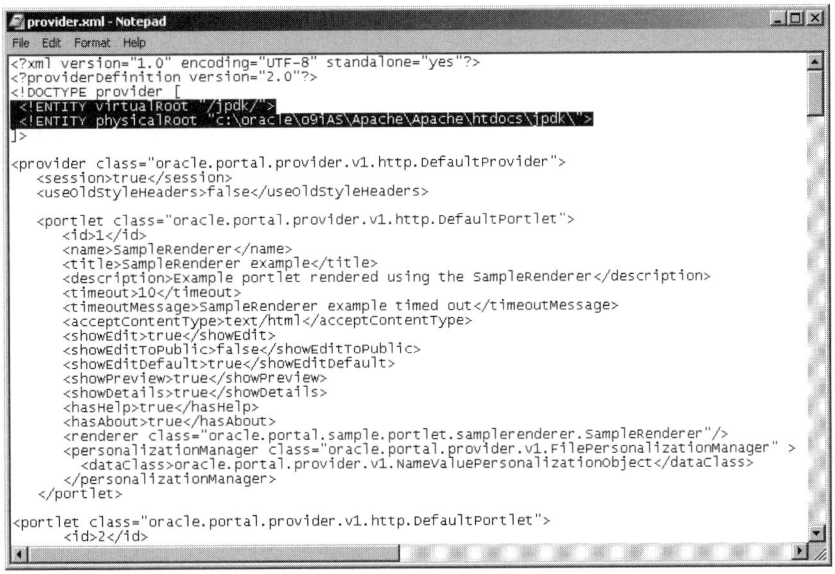

```
provider.xml - Notepad
File  Edit  Format  Help
<?xml version="1.0" encoding="UTF-8" standalone="yes"?>
<?providerDefinition version="2.0"?>
<!DOCTYPE provider [
 <!ENTITY virtualRoot "/jpdk/">
 <!ENTITY physicalRoot "c:\oracle\o9iAS\Apache\Apache\htdocs\jpdk\">
]>

<provider class="oracle.portal.provider.v1.http.DefaultProvider">
   <session>true</session>
   <useOldStyleHeaders>false</useOldStyleHeaders>

   <portlet class="oracle.portal.provider.v1.http.DefaultPortlet">
      <id>1</id>
      <name>SampleRenderer</name>
      <title>SampleRenderer example</title>
      <description>Example portlet rendered using the SampleRenderer</description>
      <timeout>10</timeout>
      <timeoutMessage>SampleRenderer example timed out</timeoutMessage>
      <acceptContentType>text/html</acceptContentType>
      <showEdit>true</showEdit>
      <showEditToPublic>false</showEditToPublic>
      <showEditDefault>true</showEditDefault>
      <showPreview>true</showPreview>
      <showDetails>true</showDetails>
      <hasHelp>true</hasHelp>
      <hasAbout>true</hasAbout>
      <renderer class="oracle.portal.sample.portlet.samplerenderer.SampleRenderer"/>
      <personalizationManager class="oracle.portal.provider.v1.FilePersonalizationManager" >
        <dataClass>oracle.portal.provider.v1.NameValuePersonalizationObject</dataClass>
      </personalizationManager>
   </portlet>

<portlet class="oracle.portal.provider.v1.http.DefaultPortlet">
      <id>2</id>
```

Figure 15.4 Provider.xml of the JPDK Sample Provider.

8. Start the Oracle HTTP server. On Microsoft Windows, you can start it by starting its service or you can start it from DOS (Figure 15.5).
9. Test the sample Java servlet by typing the following URL in your browser:

```
http://<hostname>:<portno>/servlets/sample
```

Also, you can use "servlet" instead of servlets. The sample provider's test page should be displayed (Figure 15.6).

```
C:\WINNT\System32\cmd.exe - apache -k start
C:\oracle\09iAS\Apache\Apache>apache -k start
Apache/1.3.12 (Win32) ApacheJServ/1.1 mod_ssl/2.6.4 OpenSSL/0.9.5a mod_perl/1.22
 running...
```

Figure 15.5 Starting the Oracle HTTP Server from DOS.

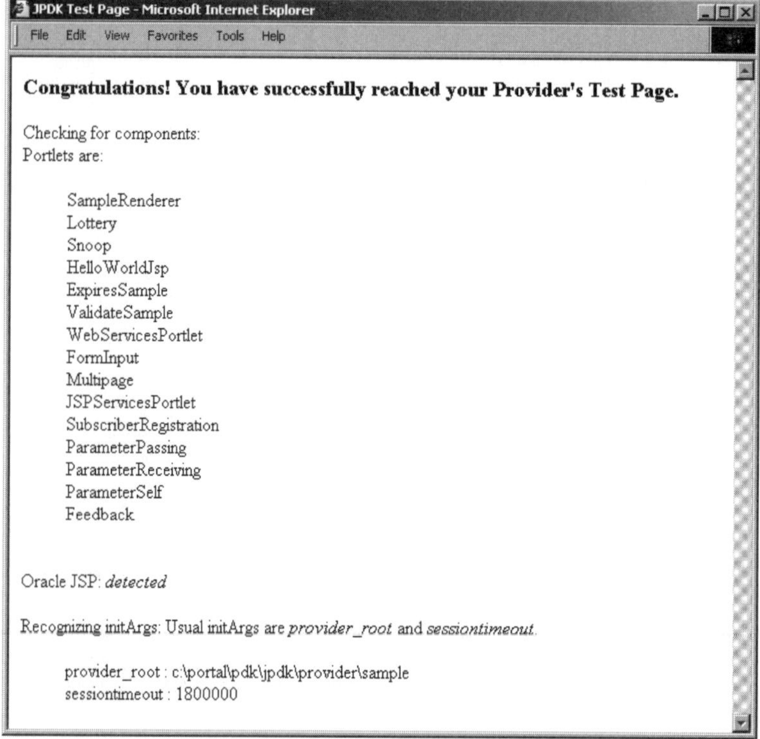

Figure 15.6 Testing the Sample Provider Java Servlet.

10. Now that you have tested that the sample Java servlet is set up correctly, you are ready to register it as a Web provider, and then you will be able to add its portlets to your pages. To register a Web provider, you need to follow similar steps to the ones followed in registering a database provider, but instead of specifying a database schema name and a procedure name, you specify the URL of the servlet. From the Administer tab on the Oracle Portal home page, click on the "Add a Portlet Provider" link in the Provider portlet (Figure 15.7).
11. Fill out the sample Provider Information (Figure 15.8 and Figure 15.9). You can choose its name, display name, timeout, and timeout message. Next specify the following field values:

    - Implementation Style: Web
    - Provider Login Frequency: Once Per User Session
    - Register On Remote Nodes: No
    - URL: *http://<hostname>:<portno>/servlet/sample* (replace the hostname with your server name)

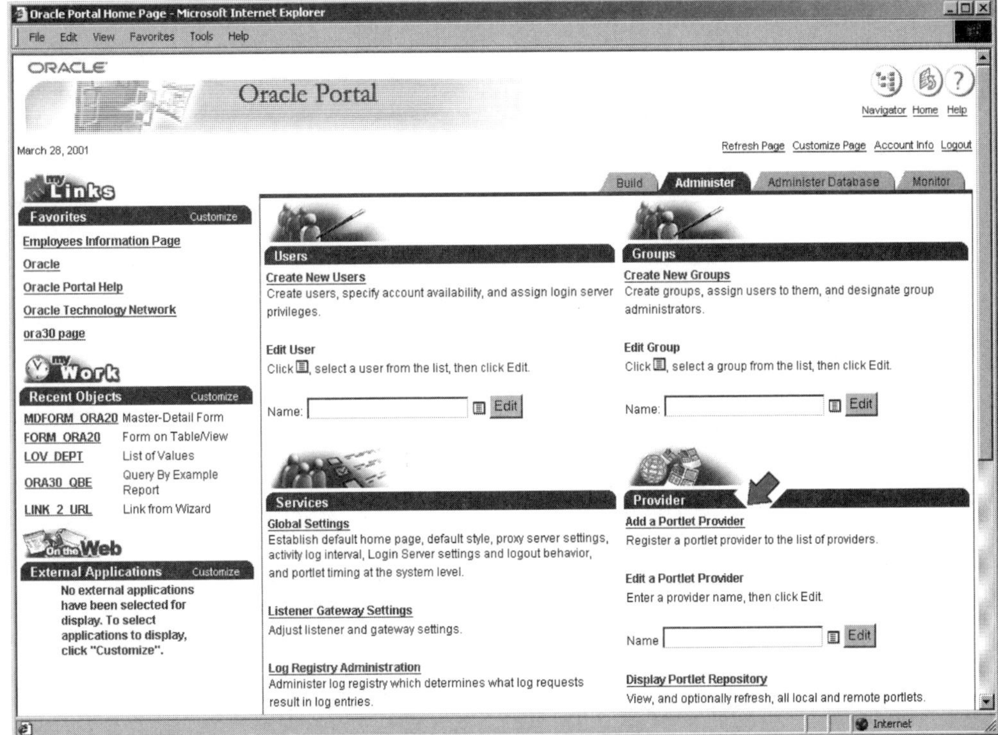

Figure 15.7 Oracle Portal Home Page: Administer Tab.

File Edit View Favorites Tools Help

Create Provider ?

Apply | OK | Cancel

Provider Information

Enter a unique name for the provider, the timeout time (in seconds) and a timeout message. The timeout message is presented to the user when a portlet takes longer than the specified time to execute.

Oracle Portal Node	PORTAL30_11249
Name	PDKSampleWebProvider
Display Name	100
Timeout	10 seconds
Timeout Message	PDKSampleWebProvider Application Timeout
Implementation Style	Web
Provider Login Frequency	Once Per User Session
Register On Remote Nodes	No

Hint: Choose Yes to allow providers on the local node to be registered on remote nodes.

Database Providers

This section is relevant only for Database providers. Register the name of the schema containing the provider implementation and the name of the package or class that implements its functionality.

Owning Schema

Package Name

Web Providers

This section is relevant only for Web Providers.

URL http://myportal/servlet/sample

Figure 15.8 Registering the JPDK Sample Web Provider (top).

File Edit View Favorites Tools Help

implementation and the name of the package or class that implements its functionality.

Owning Schema

Package Name

Web Providers

This section is relevant only for Web Providers.

URL http://myportal/servlet/sample

Specify how the user's identity will be set by the Portal when communicating with the Web provider.

- (•) The user has the same identity in the Web providers application as in the Single Sign-On identity.
- ( ) The user's identity needs to be mapped to a different name in the Web provider's application, and/or the Web provider requires an external application login for establishment of a browser session. If selecting this option, specify the external application ID below.

External Application ID

Provider Key

Hint: The provider key is passed to the Web provider where it is used to uniquely identify the requester.

Encryption Key

Hint: The encryption key is used for encrypting calls to the provider. If an encryption key is entered, a provider key must be entered.

Require Proxy No

Hint: Choose Yes to use a proxy server to make calls to the Web provider. You can specify a proxy server on the Global Settings page.

Done Internet

Figure 15.9 Registering the JPDK Sample Web Provider (bottom).

12. You can start adding some of the portlets to your pages, first to test that the provider is working, and second to get some ideas of what you can do with Web providers. The Portlet Repository should have the new provider portlets (Figure 15.10).
13. Add some of the sample portlets under the Sample Web Provider to one of your pages (Figure 15.11).

The Web Provider Architecture

The portal framework communicates with the provider over HTTP and uses the Simple Object Access Protocol (SOAP) and XML to send and receive structured data to and from the Web providers (Figure 15.12). The Web providers can reside in the same server that hosts the Oracle HTTP server or it can reside in another remote Web server.

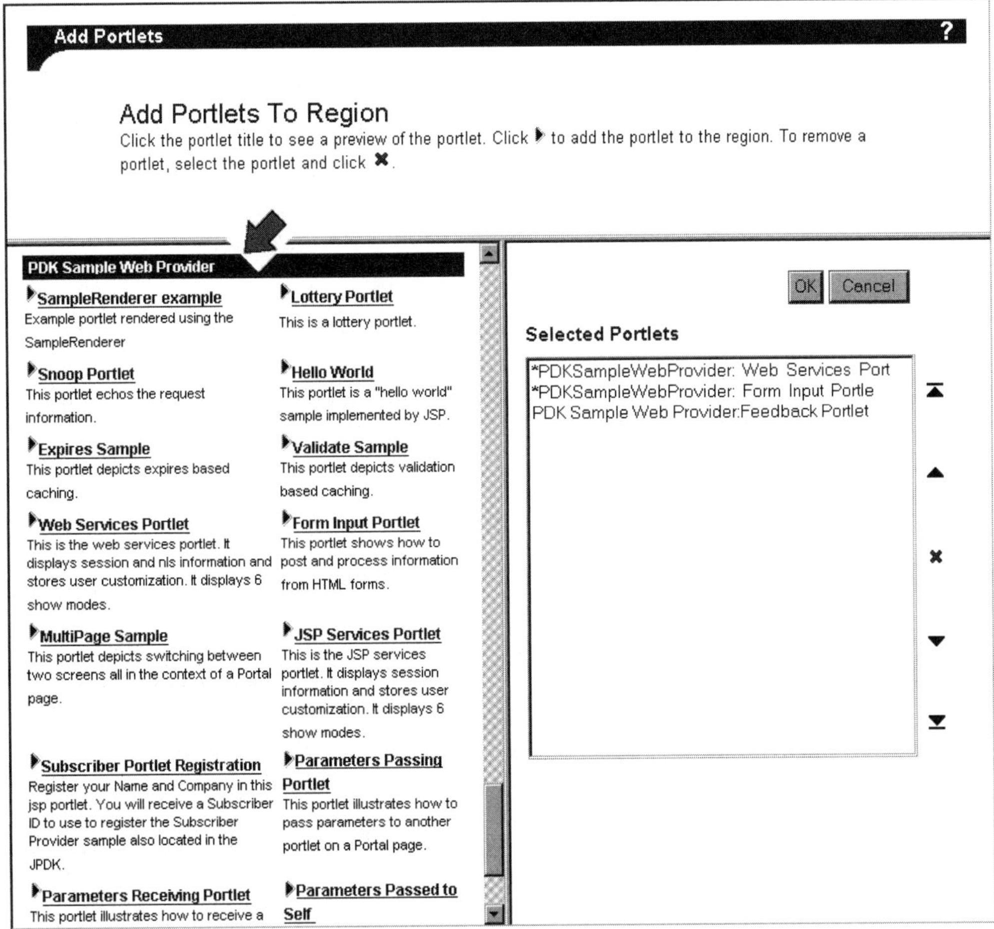

Figure 15.10 Portlet Repository: JPDK Sample Web Provider Portlets.

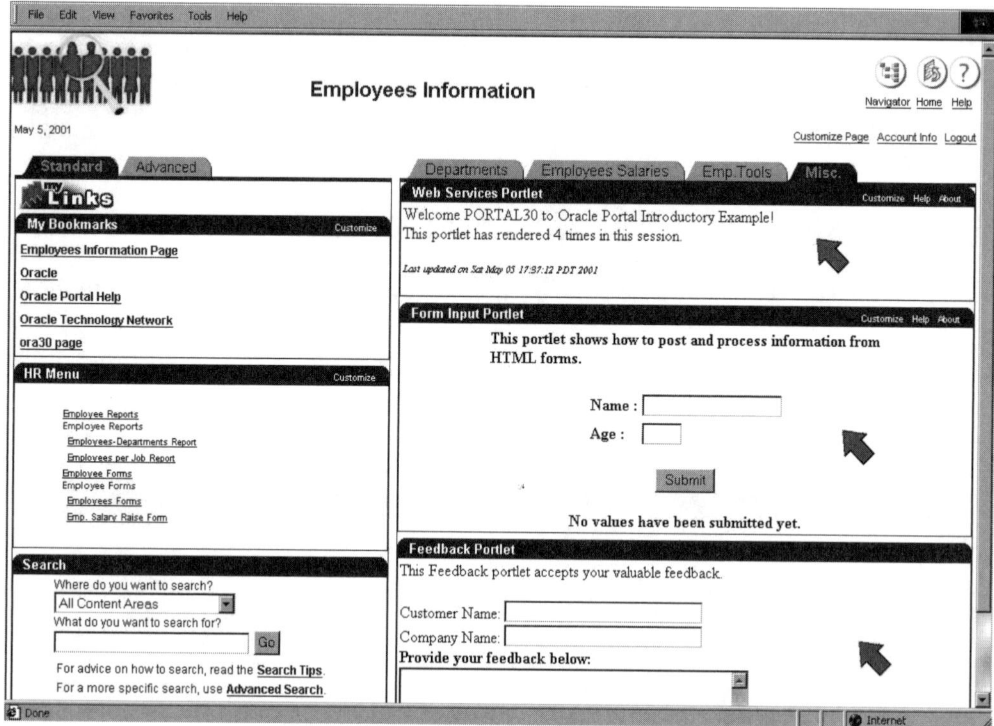

Figure 15.11 Employees Information Page.

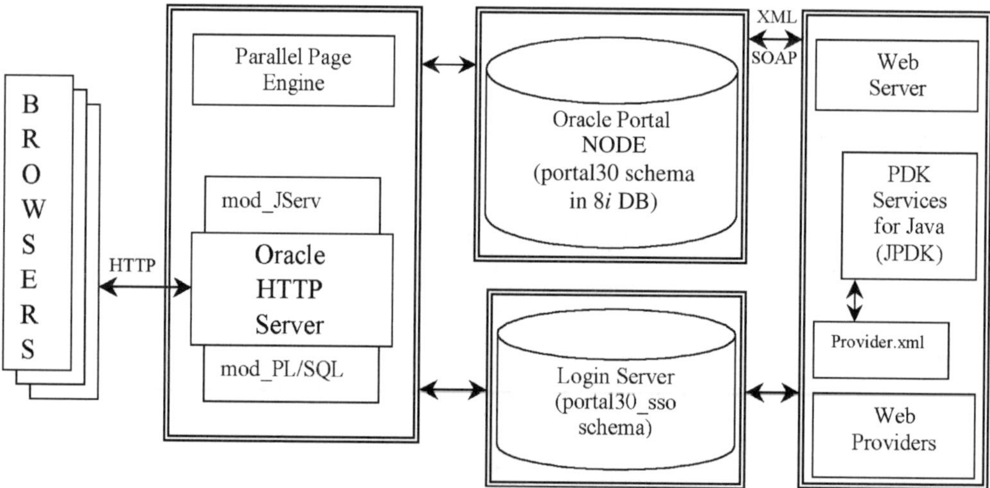

Figure 15.12 Oracle Web Provider Architecture.

Note

SOAP is an XML-based, lightweight protocol for exchange of information in a distributed environment. You can find more information about SOAP at *http://www.w3.org/TR/SOAP/*.

This is what happens when you request a Web portlet:

- The page request arrives at the portal from the client browser through Oracle HTTP server *powered by Apache* (part of Oracle9*i* Application Server).
- The portal Parallel Page Engine (PPE) realizes that the page contains a Web portlet. The PPE contacts the portal node to get the Web provider information (URL, timeout information, etc.). Also, the Login Server can be contacted to get the Single Sign-On authentication information.
- The portal makes an HTTP call to the remote Web provider.
- The Web provider calls the portlet methods to generate its HTML/XML output.
- The PPE collects all the output of all the page portlets and sends the consolidated page output back to the browser through the Oracle HTTP server.

Each of the double lined boxes in Figure 15.12 represents a logical component in the O9*i*AS Portal with Web providers architecture. Each of these boxes can reside on a separate hardware server or it can share the same server with other boxes.

PDK Services for Java (JPDK)

The main purpose of the PDK Services for Java (JPDK) is to simplify the provider/portlet implementation. So, it becomes easier on Java developers to build Java Web providers. The JPDK has four components:

1. The Provider Adapter: Its class name is oracle.portal.provider.v1.http.HttpProvider. It handles the HTTP communications.
2. The Provider Interfaces: A Java interface is an abstract class describing the public methods that a class implements and their calling signatures (number of parameters and parameters data types, etc.) without including anything about how those methods are implemented. The Provider Interfaces specify the Java API methods that are expected by the portal and hence need to be implemented by the Web provider.
3. The Provider Runtime: It provides a base implementation of the Provider Interfaces.
4. The Provider Utilities: It provides methods that simplify the portlet rendering.

The following sections describe each JPDK component in more detail.

The Web Provider Adapter

The Provider Adapter is responsible for receiving the portal requests, unmarshaling the details, locating the target provider, calling the provider API to perform the function, and marshaling the results into the HTTP response. Both Oracle Portal and the Web provider communicate directly with the Provider Adapter.

The Web Provider Interfaces

There are five Web provider interfaces.

1. Provider interface describes the provider methods. Its class file is oracle.portal.provider.v1.Provider.
2. Portlet interface describes the provider portlets. Its class file is oracle.portal.provider.v1.Portlet.
3. PortletRenderer interface describes the rendering method of a portlet instance. Its class file is oracle.portal.provider.v1.PortletRenderer.
4. PortletPersonalizationManager interface describes methods for creating, setting, and retrieving the customization data of a portlet. Its class file is oracle.portal.provider.v1.PortletPersonalizationManager.
5. PortletSecurityManager interface authenticates users to access the portlet. Its class file is oracle.portal.provider.v1.PortletSecurityManager.

The Web Provider Runtime

Provider Runtime provides a base implementation that follows the specification of the Web Provider Interfaces. The Provider Runtime includes a set of default classes that implement each one of the Web Provider Interfaces for a provider called DefaultProvider. These classes reduce the development work for a provider by implementing the common functions associated with a particular portal request. For developers to code their own providers, they do not have to implement all the interfaces; they can subclass and override only the methods that need to be customized to their needs. The Provider Runtime includes a class file for each of the Web Provider Interfaces.

The Web Provider Utilities

Provider Utilities provide methods for simplifying the rendering of portlets. The utilities include methods for constructing valid links (hrefs), rendering the portlet's title bar, rendering HTML forms that work within a portal page, and supporting portlet caching. Its implementation class is oracle.portal.provider.v1.http.HttpPortletRendererUtil.

The provider.xml file

The provider.xml file is a static file that stores information about a provider and its portlets. The Provider Interface implementation parses the provider.xml file to create a portlet instance (Java object) for each portlet listed in it; this behavior allows you to add new portlets without affecting the providers already registered with Oracle Portal.

Implementing a Web Portlet Using Java Servlets

This section demonstrates how to create a Web portlet using Java servlets. Java servlets are server-based Java programs (i.e., reside and run in a Web server/middle tier).

Write the Portlet Java Servlet Code

The first step is to write the portlet class where you need to implement the PortletRenderer interface. This interface contains the render method that needs to be implemented within your portlet class.

```
public class EmpStocksRenderer implements PortletRenderer {}
```

The only method you are forced to have is the render method.

```
public void render ( PortletRenderRequest pr )
```

Create the EmpStocksPortlet.java file to be the Java source file of a simple Web portlet.

```
import oracle.portal.provider.v1.*;
import java.io.*;

public class EmpStocksPortlet implements PortletRenderer {

    public EmpStocksPortlet() {
    }

    public void render ( PortletRenderRequest pr )
        throws PortletException, AccessControlException {

        try {
            String user = pr.getUser().getName();
            PrintWriter out = pr.getWriter("text/html");
```

```
15
16                // Starts the Portlet rendering
17
18                PortletRendererUtil.renderPortletHeader(pr,
                  out, null);
19
20                if (user != null) {
21                out.println("<b> Stocks from " + user +
                  " Portfolio</b>");
22            }
23            else {
24                out.println("<b> User is not logged on! </b>");
25            }
26
27            // Ends the portlet rendering
28
29            PortletRendererUtil.renderPortletFooter( pr, out );
30        }
31        catch (IllegalArgumentException ie) {
32                throw new PortletException( ie );
33        }
34        catch (java.io.IOException ioe) {
35                throw new PortletException(ioe);
36        }
37    }
38 }
```

EmpStocksPortlet.java

Note

The Java language is case-sensitive. You need to make sure that the Java source file name matches the Java class name (line 4) as well as the constructor name (line 6).

Save the Java source file to a directory (e.g., c:\portal), and then compile the java file to a class file (Figure 15.13). You need the Java compiler (i.e., **javac.exe**) that is part of the Java 2 Software Development Kit (SDK). You can download the Java 2 SDK from *http://www.javasoft.com.* You need to include the provider.jar file into your CLASSPATH environment variable, because the Java compiler searches this file for the imported classes in line 1. Next, zip the

```
C:\portal>set CLASSPATH=c:\portal\pdk\jpdk\lib\provider.jar
C:\portal>c:\jdk13\bin\javac EmpStocksPortlet.java
C:\portal>
```

Figure 15.13 Compiling the EmpStocksPortlet.java File.

generated EmpStocksPortlet.class file into EmpStocksPortlet.jar file in the same directory. You can use Winzip (downloadable from *www.winzip.com*) to zip the class file into a JAR file.

Create a provider.xml File

The second step is to create a new provider.xml file. Using a text editor (e.g., Notepad in Microsoft Windows or vi in UNIX) add the following lines to a new text file, and then save it under the name provider.xml. For simplicity, save the file in the same directory as the EmpStocksPortlet.java file.

```
<provider class="oracle.portal.provider.v1.http.Default
          Provider" session="true">
   <portlet class="oracle.portal.provider.v1.http.Default
          Portlet" version="1" >
      <id>1</id>
      <name>EmpStocksPortlet</name>
      <title>Employee Stocks Portlet</title>
      <description>A sample web portlet</description>
      <timeout>10</timeout>
      <timeoutMsg>EmpStocksPortlet Timed out</timeoutMsg>
      <acceptContentTypes>
         <item>text/html</item>
      </acceptContentTypes>
      <portletRenderer class="EmpStocksPortlet" />
   </portlet>
</provider>
```

provider.xml

Note

The ID acts as the primary key of the Web providers. Each provider entry in a provider.xml file has to have a unique ID value.

Update jserv.properties and zone.properties Files

The third step is to add an entry for the new portlet to jserv.properties.

```
wrapper.classpath=C:\portal\EmpStocksPortlet.jar
```

Next, add an entry for the new portlet to zone.properties. Under the Servlet Aliases section, add the following:

```
servlet.EmpStocks.code=oracle.portal.provider.v1.http.Http
Provider
```

The provider_root argument needs to point to the directory where the provider.xml resides. Under the Aliased Servlet Init Parameters section, add the following:

```
servlet.EmpStocks.initArgs=provider_root=C:\portal,session
timeout=1800000, debuglevel = 1
```

Next, stop and restart the Oracle HTTP server.

Test the Servlet Alias

Test the new alias in the browser by typing the following URL:

```
http://<hostname>/servlet/EmpStocks
```

You should receive a test page telling you that the Java class file EmpStocksPortlet is found and runnable (Figure 15.14).

Register a New Web Provider

Now you can register a new provider that calls this servlet alias. Its alias is *http://<hostname>/servlet/EmpStocksPortlet* (Figure 15.15). Next you can add the EmpStocksPortlet to one of your portal pages (Figure 15.16 and Figure 15.17). You can change the output of the portlet by adding your own code to line 21 of the EmpStocksPortlet.java. You can also add code to access the databases through JDBC driver.

Implementing a Web Portlet Using JSP

This section demonstrates how to create a Web portlet using Java Server Pages (JSP). JSP technology allows developers to mix static HTML code with the dynamic output of Java servlets.

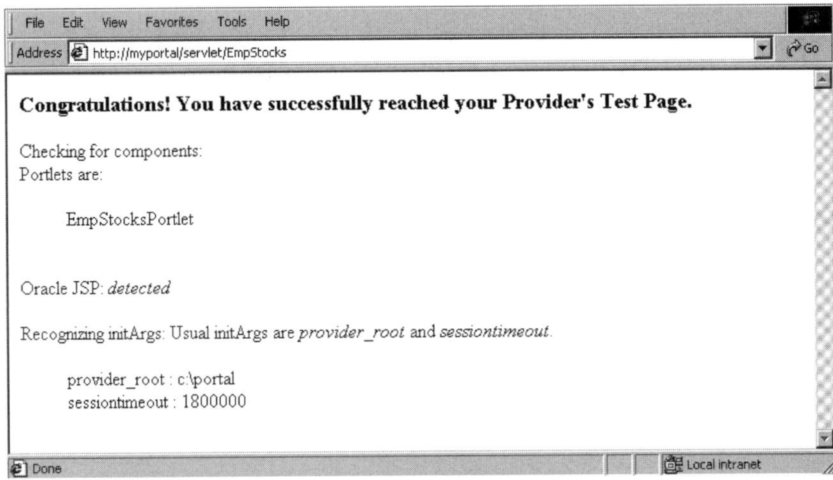

Figure 15.14 EmpStocksportlet Servlet Alias Test.

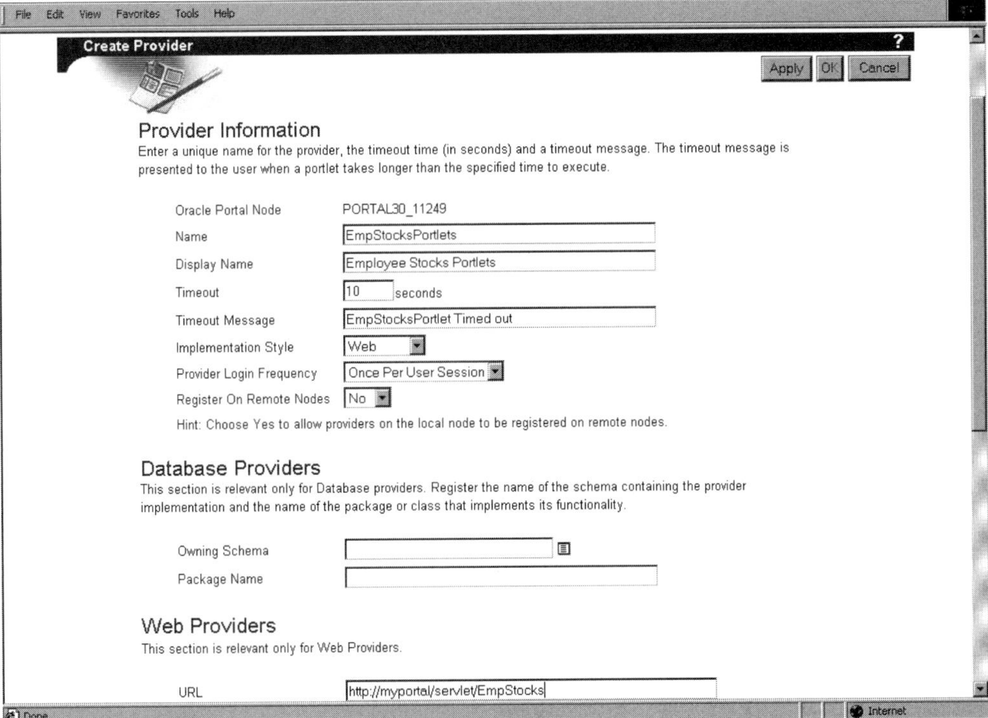

Figure 15.15 Registering the EmpStocksPortlet Web Provider.

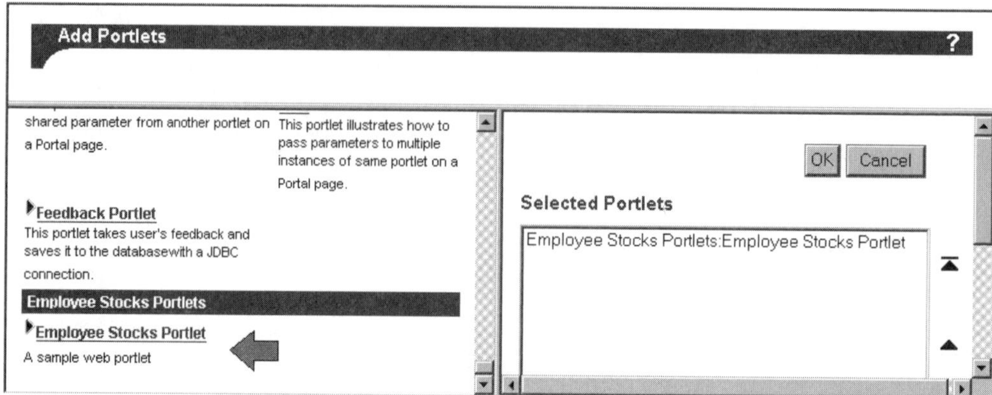

Figure 15.16 Portlet Repository.

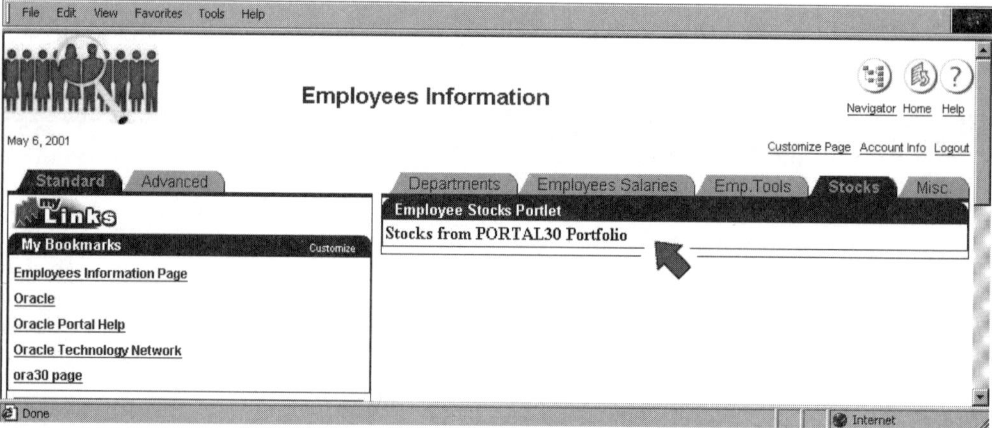

Figure 15.17 Portal Page Display.

Write the JSP Code

Create a new text file named EmpBenefitsPortlet.jsp that contains the following code:

```
<%@page import = "oracle.portal.provider.v1.*, oracle
.portal.provider.v1.http.*" %>
<%
  PortletRenderRequest portletRequest = (PortletRender
  Request)
  request.getAttribute(HttpProvider.PORTLET_RENDER_REQUEST);
%>
```

```
<br>
   Contact Andalos Benefits Inc. for all of your Benefits
questions
<br><br>
You are logged on as:
<b>
  <%= portletRequest.getUser().getName() %>
</b>
<br>
<h6>
   <b> Page URL:</b>
   <i> <%= portletRequest.getPageURL() %> </i>
</h6>
```

EmpBenefitsPortlet.jsp

Save the EmpBenefitsPortlet.jsp file under a new directory (e.g., c:\portal\jsp).

Add an Apache Alias (Virtual Path)

Add a new Apache alias to point to the location of your JSP file. To add the Apache alias, add the following line to your Httpd.conf file:

```
Alias /JSPportlets/ "c:\portal\jsp/"
```

Create a New provider.xml File

This newly created provider.xml file is needed to point to your new portlet provider. Add the following code to a new file, and, for simplicity, save it under the same directory holding your portlet JSP file (i.e., c:\portal\jsp). Make sure that the name of your JSP file specified in the <showpage> tag is exactly the same name as your JSP file name (including the case).

```
<provider class="oracle.portal.provider.v1.http.Default
          Provider"
          session="true">
   <portlet class="oracle.portal.provider.v1.http.Default
           Portlet" version="1" >
      <id>1</id>
      <name>EmpBenefitsPortlets</name>
      <title>Employees Benefits Portlet</title>
      <description>JSP Web Portlet</description>
      <timeout>10</timeout>
```

```
        <timeoutMsg>EmpBenefitsPortlet timed out</timeoutMsg>
        <showEdit>false</showEdit>
        <showEditDefault>false</showEditDefault>
        <showPreview>false</showPreview>
        <showDetails>false</showDetails>
        <hasHelp>false</hasHelp>
        <hasAbout>false</hasAbout>
        <acceptContentTypes>
            <item>text/html</item>
        </acceptContentTypes>
        <portletRenderer
            class="oracle.portal.provider.v1.http.Page
            Renderer" >
            <appPath>/JSPportlets</appPath>
            <appRoot>C:\portal\jsp</appRoot>
            <showPage>EmpBenefitsPortlet.jsp</showPage>
        </portletRenderer>
    </portlet>
</provider>
```

provider.xml

Update the zone.properties File

Add the following line to the Servlet Aliases section of your zone.properties file:

```
servlet.EmpBenefits.code=oracle.portal.provider.v1.http.Http
Provider
```

Next, add the following line to the Aliased Servlet Init Parameters section of the zone .properties:

```
servlet.EmpBenefits.initArgs=provider_root=c:\portal\jsp,
sessiontimeout=1800000, debuglevel = 1
```

The provider_root argument points to the location of the JSP portlet JSP file.

Test Apache Alias and Servlet Alias

Stop and start the Oracle HTTP server. Test your Apache alias (e.g., JSPportlets) by typing the following URL in your browser:

```
http://myportal/JSPportlets/provider.xml
```

Because the provider.xml resides in the physical path of the alias, this URL displays the XML file in the browser (Figure 15.18). Test your servlet alias by typing the following URL in your browser (Figure 15.19):

```
http://myportal/servlet/EmpBenefits
```

Register a New JSP Web Provider

Register your new JSP Web provider with Oracle 9*i*AS Portal (Figure 15.20). Specify the following information:

- Name: EmpBenefitsPortlets
- Display Name: Employees Benefits Portlets
- Timeout: 10
- Timeout Message: EmpBenefitsPortlet timed out
- Implementation Style: Web
- Provider Login Frequency: Once Per User Session

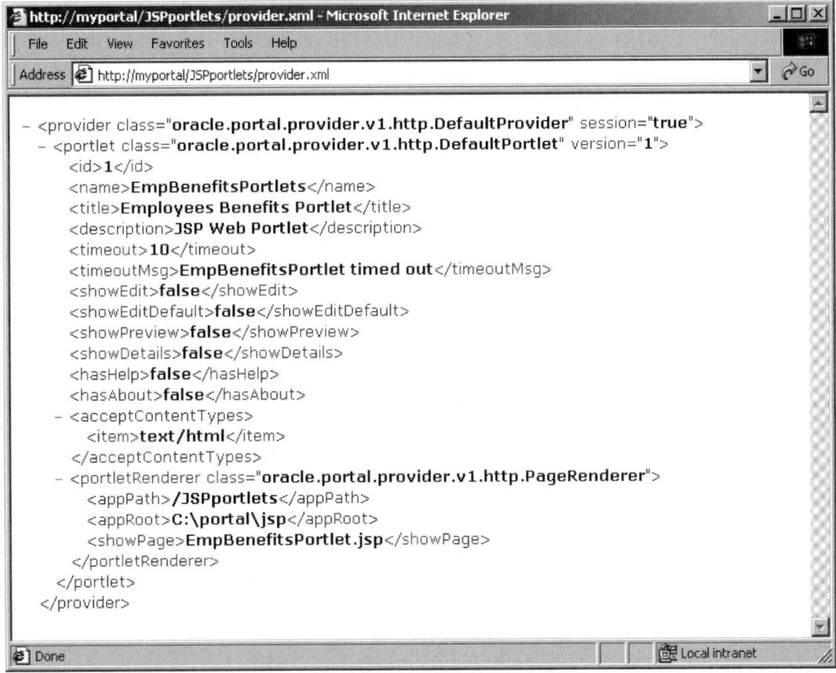

Figure 15.18 Testing the Apache Alias.

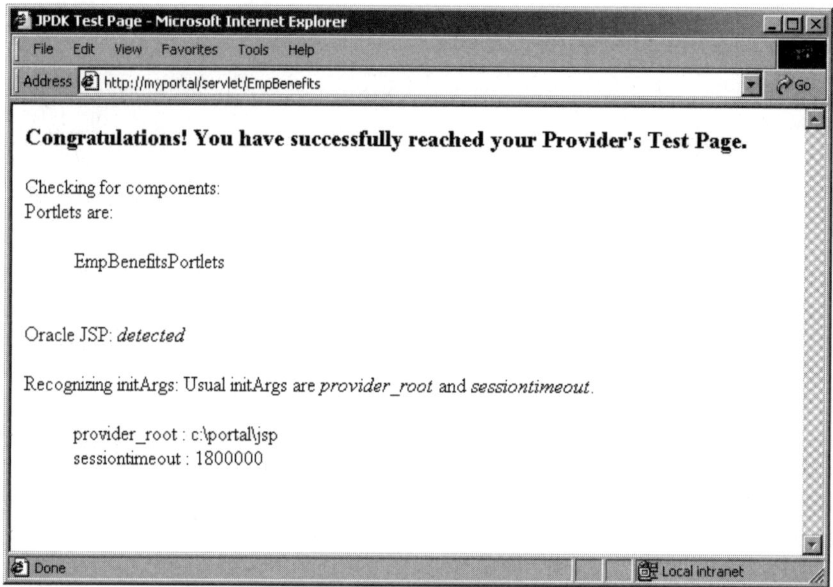

Figure 15.19 Testing the JSP Servlet Alias.

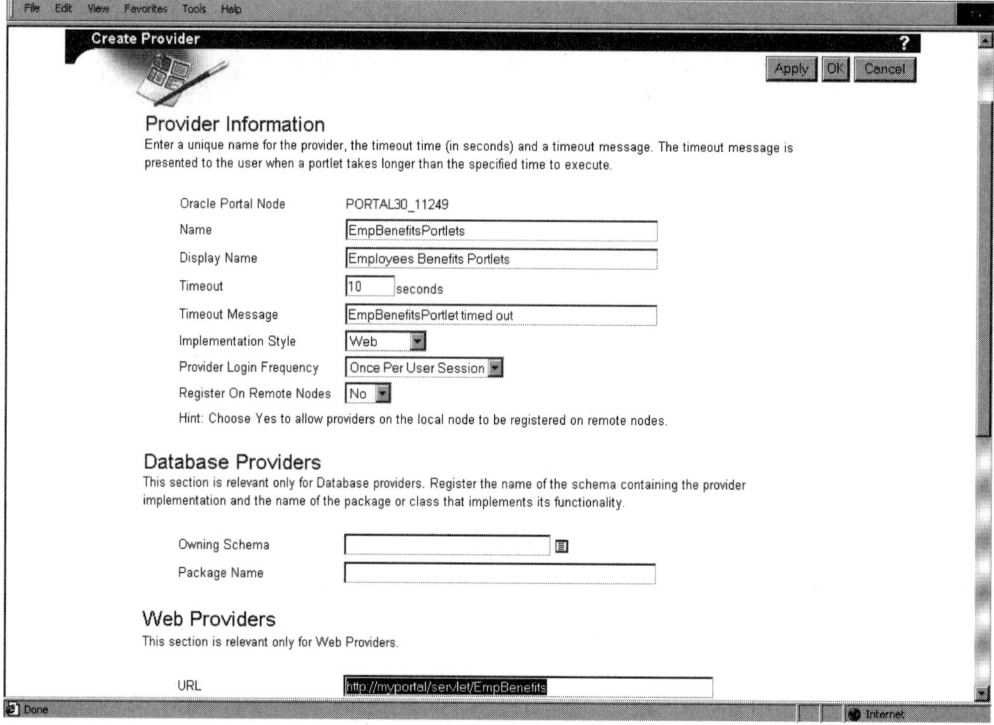

Figure 15.20 Register JSP Web Provider.

- Register On Remote Nodes: No
- URL: *http://myportal/servlet/EmpBenefits*

Add the JSP Web Portlet

Now you can add the portlet to one of your portal pages (Figure 15.21 and Figure 15.22). You can learn more about the JPDK by accessing the Java API Reference available in the PDK.

Next, Chapter 16 explores integrating other Oracle products into Oracle Portal.

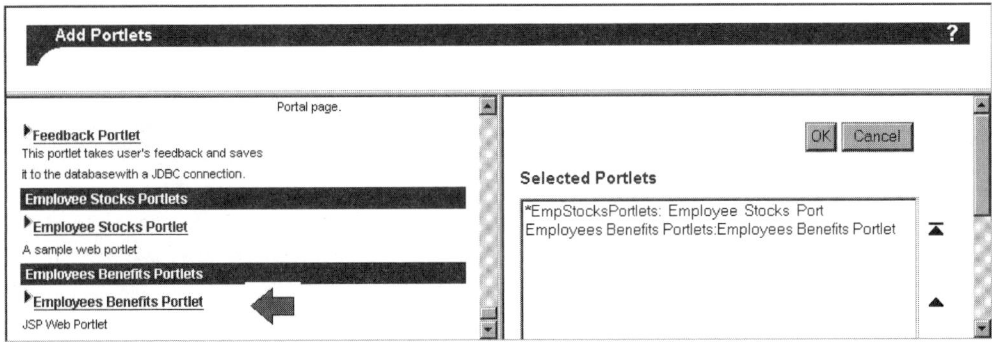

Figure 15.21 Portlet Repository.

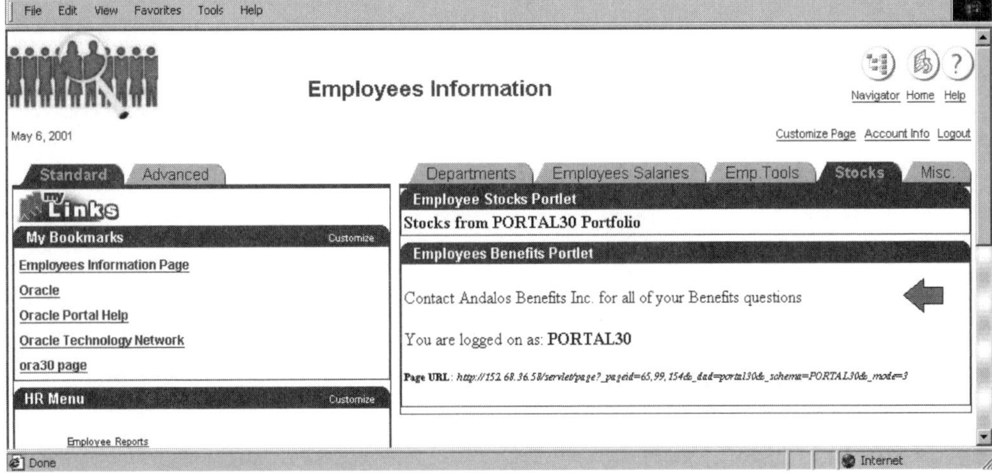

Figure 15.22 Portal Page Display.

CHAPTER 16

Integrating Oracle Products into Oracle9*i*AS Portal

Introduction

This chapter explains how to integrate Oracle Portal with one of Oracle's powerful server options, Oracle *inter*Media Text, and with three of the most popular Oracle development tools, Oracle Forms, Oracle Reports, and Oracle Discoverer. This chapter also explains how to configure LDAP authentication with Oracle Portal.

Integrating Oracle *inter*Media Text

Chapter 9 described the basic and advanced search capability of Oracle Portal. This section describes how you can set up and configure the *inter*Media Text option to use more sophisticated searching techniques with Oracle Portal.

Note

Oracle *inter*Media Text has a new name, which is just "Oracle Text." In earlier versions it is called Oracle Context.

The Oracle database *inter*Media Text option provides searching, retrieval, and viewing capabilities for text stored inside an Oracle database. In addition, the *inter*Media Text option provides concept searching and theme analysis of documents.

To perform searches using the *inter*Media Text option, a special index is created, and then standard SQL statements can be used. You can also use the supplied *inter*Media Text PL/SQL packages for more advanced features such as document presentation and thesaurus maintenance.

If *inter*Media Text is installed and enabled on Oracle Portal, a basic or advanced search operation tries to find the specified search words in the contents of the uploaded documents and the first pages of URL items. So, with *inter*Media Text, Oracle Portal searches through file items such as PDF files, PowerPoint presentations, and Word documents, as well as URLs, text, and HTML items.

The next section explains in detail how to install and configure *inter*Media Text to be used in Oracle Portal.

Installing *inter*Media Text in the Database

Before using *inter*Media Text inside Oracle Portal, your Oracle Portal database (i.e., the portal node) has to have the *inter*Media Text option. To check that your database has the *inter*-Media Text option, you can try logging on the database using username CTXSYS and default password CTXSYS (Figure 16.1). Note that the number of objects might vary depending on the version of the database. The Oracle Database Configuration Assistant creates this user when the *inter*Media Text option is selected (by default it is selected; Figure 16.2).

If the CTXSYS user does not exist, you need to check if the *inter*Media Text option is installed in the database ORACLE_HOME. Use the Oracle Universal Installer (OUI) to check that the option is installed (Figure 16.3). If the option is not installed, you need to install the *inter*Media Text option from the Oracle database CD. Choose the Custom installation type (Figure 16.4). Next, you need to manually add the *inter*Media Text option to your existing database. The manual process is explained in Chapter 20. One point worth mentioning here is that you need to set your database shared_pool_size initialization parameter to at least 116M's for the *inter*-Media to work properly.

Important

If the database is upgraded from 7.3 or 8.0 and it had the ConText option, make sure to remove the text_enable parameter from the init.ora file or set it to false. It is no longer used in Oracle8*i* and higher and will actually prevent the *inter*Media Text from working properly.

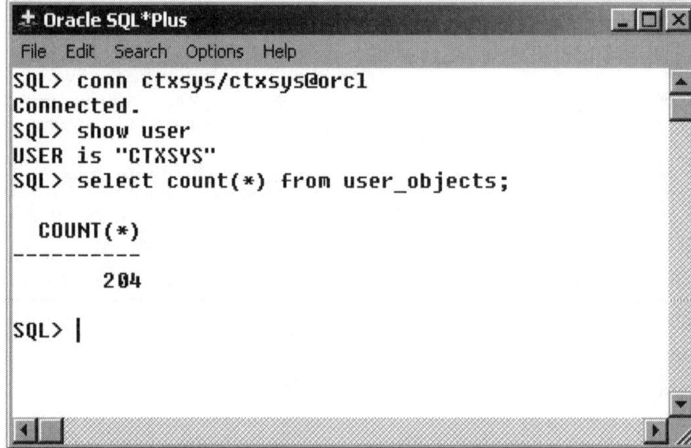

Figure 16.1
Checking that the Database has the *inter*Media Text Option.

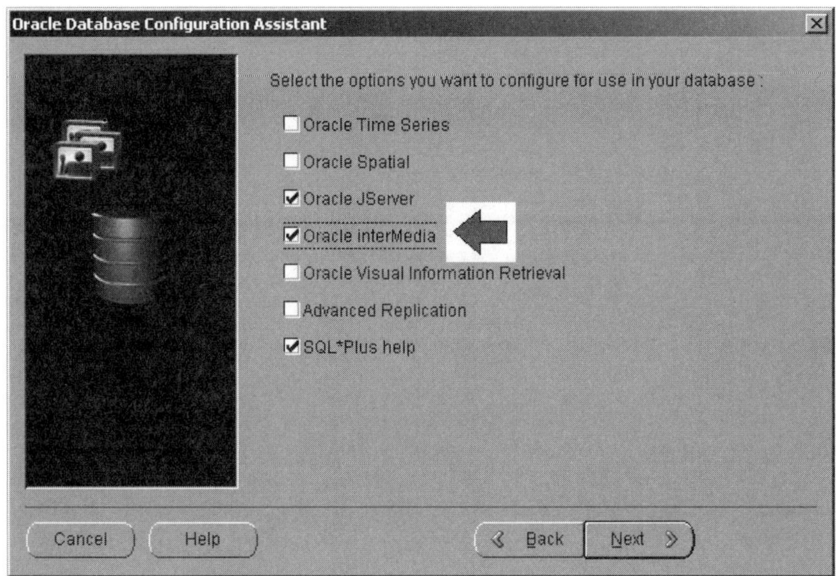

Figure 16.2 Adding the *inter*Media Option When Creating a New Database Using the Database Configuration Assistant.

For the *inter*Media Text feature to work with Oracle Database in UNIX, the LD_LIBRARY _PATH environment variable needs to be set before starting the Oracle Database and Net8 Listener.

UNIX Korn Shell (ksh)

```
LD_LIBRARY_PATH=$LD_LIBRARY_PATH:$ORACLE_HOME/ctx/lib
export LD_LIBRARY_PATH
```

UNIX C-Shell (csh)

```
setenv LD_LIBRARY_PATH ${LD_LIBRARY_PATH}:${ORACLE_HOME}/ctx/lib
```

If your database version is 8.1.6, you must configure the `listener.ora` and `tnsnames.ora` files in your Oracle8*i* Home directory to support the *inter*Media Text external procedures calls. If you are running Oracle8*i* Release 8.1.7, you can ignore this section, because 8.1.7 databases do not use external procedures to perform document filtering, and they use the database server processes (i.e., shadow).

Edit the `listener.ora` file to have a similar LISTENER entry to the following:

```
LISTENER =
       (DESCRIPTION_LIST =
```

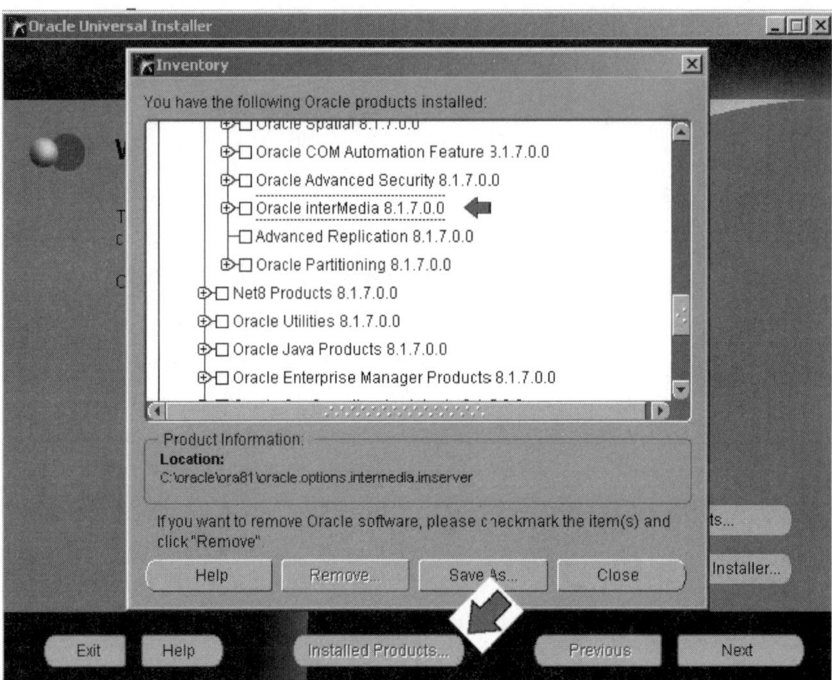

Figure 16.3 Oracle Universal Installer: Installed Products.

```
            (DESCRIPTION =
                    (ADDRESS_LIST =
                            (ADDRESS =  (PROTOCOL = IPC)
                                        (KEY = EXTPROC0)
                            )
                    )
                    (ADDRESS_LIST =
                            (ADDRESS =  (PROTOCOL = TCP)
                                        (HOST = myportal)
                                        (PORT=1521)
                            )
                    )
            )
    )
```

Also, in the SID_LIST_LISTENER definition, add the following:

```
    (SID_DESC =
```

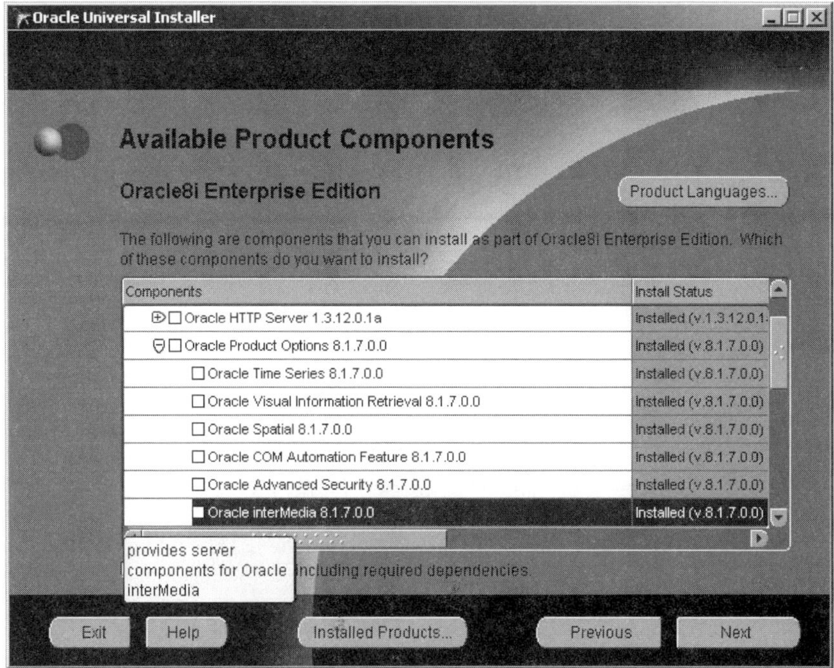

Figure 16.4 Running Oracle Universal Installer to Install the Oracle *inter*Media Option.

```
        (SID_NAME=PLSExtProc)
        (PROGRAM=extproc)
    )
```

You need to reload the listener.ora configuration file by executing the following command in the DOS or UNIX prompt:

```
lsnrctl reload
```

Add the following lines to the end of your tnsnames.ora file, to have a net service entry for EXTPROC0 in the database server's tnsnames.ora file. Use SID rather than SERVICE_NAME in the CONNECT_DATA section. For example:

```
extproc_connection_data =
        (DESCRIPTION=
              (ADDRESS_LIST =
                    (ADDRESS=   (PROTOCOL=IPC)
                                (KEY=EXTPROC0)
```

```
                    )
            )
            (CONNECT_DATA=
                    (SID=PLSExtProc)
                    (PRESENTATION = RO)
            )
    )
```

Test the *inter*Media Net Configuration

You can test the *inter*Media configuration by executing the following commands in SQL*Plus (Figure 16.5). If you get errors, double check your Net8 configuration changes. To further test that the *inter*Media is installed and set up correctly, create a test table, insert a few data inside the table, and perform a context query (Figure 16.6).

Setting up *inter*Media Text in Oracle Portal

Now that the *inter*Media Text option is configured in the database, this section shows how Oracle Portal can be configured to use the *inter*Media Text.

Important

You must log in as the portal administrator to set up the Oracle Portal search features.

There are four main steps for setting up *inter*Media Text in Oracle Portal:

1. Set up the global settings.
2. Enable *inter*Media Text search.

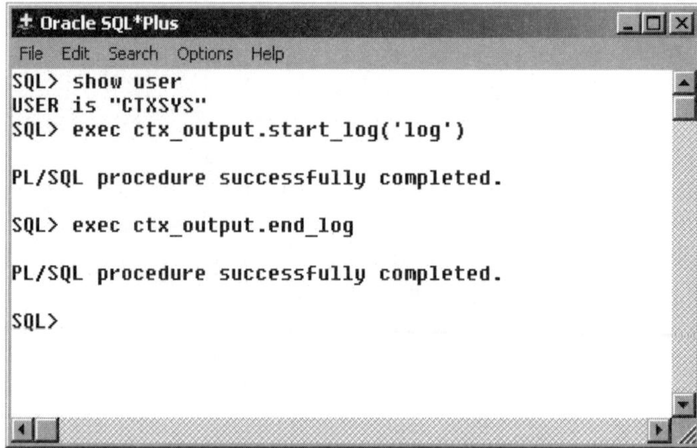

Figure 16.5 Testing *inter*Media Net Configuration.

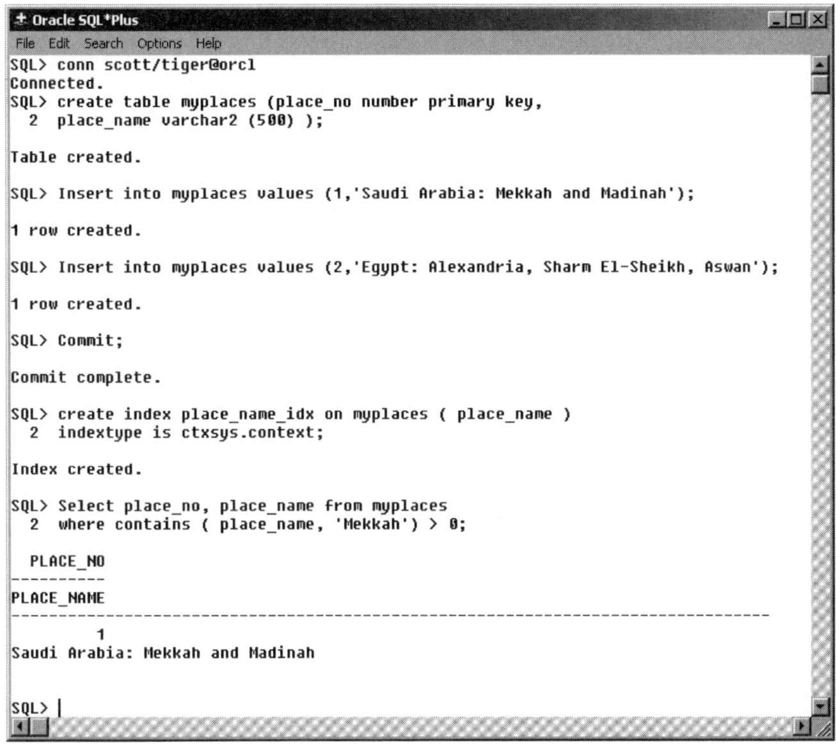

Figure 16.6 Testing *inter*Media Query.

3. Create the *inter*Media Text indexes.
4. Maintain the *inter*Media Text indexes.

To simplify testing the Oracle *inter*Media in Oracle Portal, create a file item that will hold a word document file inside your Employee HR Documents content area. When you create the text indexes, the document will be indexed, and hence you will be able to search for any word inside the Word Document.

1. Set up the Global Settings

This step is required only if you have a proxy server that is used to connect you to the Internet. You can enter your proxy server information through the "Global Settings" link in the Services portlet. Refer to Figure 13.4 and Figure 13.5.

Note

You do not need to prefix the proxy server name with "http://".

---

2. Enable *inter*Media Text Search

Before creating the *inter*Media Text indexes, you need to configure the *inter*Media Text settings in Oracle Portal.

In the Services portlet, click on the "Search Settings" link (Figure 16.7). Select "Enable *inter*Media Text Searching" to make *inter*Media Text searching available in portal content areas. Select "Enable Themes And Gists" to create a theme and gist for each item returned by the search.

Note

A theme shows the nouns and verbs that occur most frequently within the item. A gist displays a brief summary of the item, derived from how frequently those nouns and verbs appear.

In the Hits Per Page field, enter the number of search results to display on each Search Results page. For example, if you specify 10, the first ten results are displayed on the first Search Results page, the next ten on the second page, and so on.

In the URL field enter the URL of the search engine for users to extend their search to the Internet if they don't find the information they need in your content areas. The URL must be fully

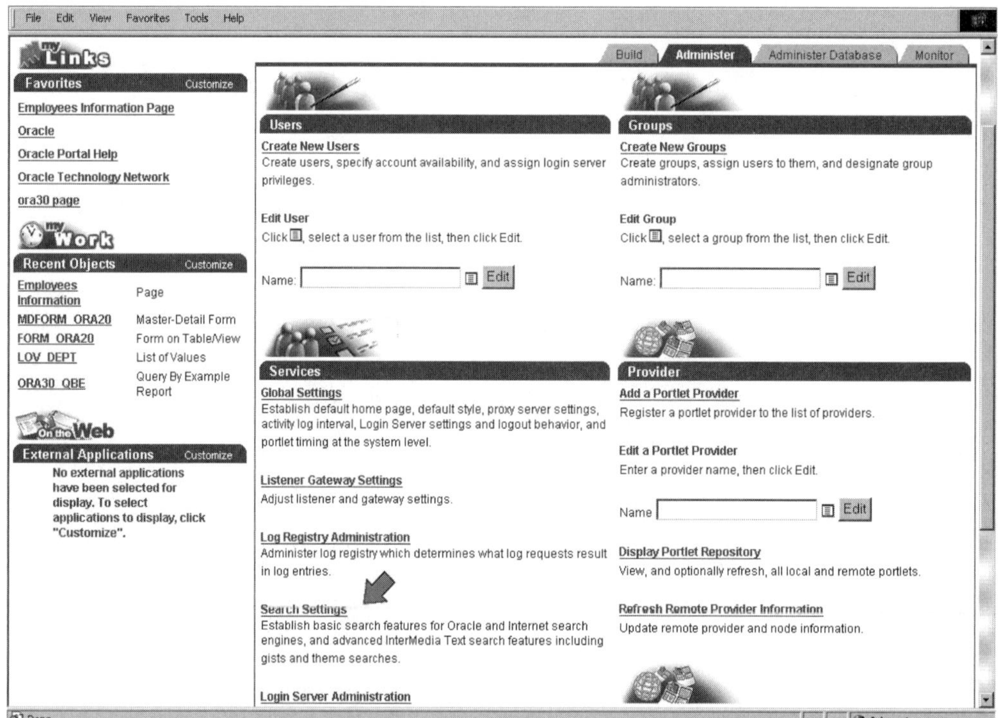

Figure 16.7 Oracle Portal Home Page: Administer Tab: Services Portlet.

Figure 16.8 Search Properties: Enabling *inter*Media Text.

formed and include any associated parameters, along with the final equal sign (=) for passing the search words. For example, to use Yahoo as the Internet search engine, enter

```
http://search.yahoo.com/search?p=
```

In the Link Text field, enter the text that users click to access the Internet search engine and send it their search criteria. This text is displayed as a link on the Search Results page and allows users to perform Internet searches outside your content areas.

In the Highlight Text Color list, choose the color to highlight the search words in the HTML renditions of the items returned by the search. In the Highlight Text Style list, choose the style to apply to the search words in the HTML renditions of the items returned by the search. Click "OK" (Figure 16.8).

3. Create the *inter*Media Text Indexes

To create the *inter*Media Text index, you need to perform the following tasks. First, execute the following procedure in SQL*Plus as the portal schema owner (i.e., portal30; Figure 16.9):

```
wwv_context_util.grantCtxRole(USER);
```

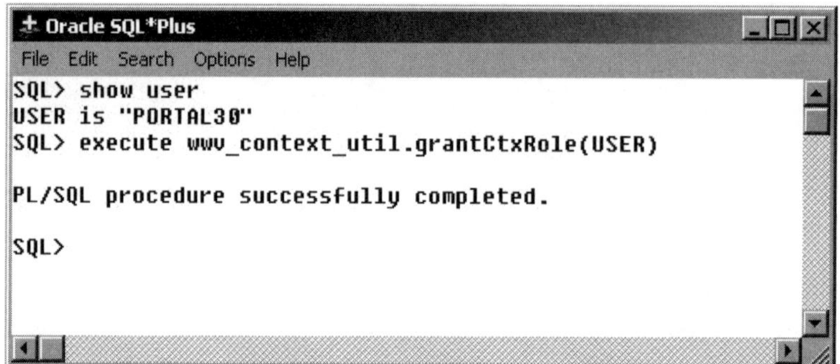

Figure 16.9 Granting the Context Role to the Portal Schema Owner.

Second, set the "Enable Connection Pooling" property to No in the Portal30 DAD. The easiest way to edit the DAD properties is to go to the Oracle HTTP Server home page (Figure 16.10), and then click on the "mod_plsql" link. The "mod_plsql" link takes you to the PL/SQL gateway configuration menu (URL: *http://<hostname>/pls/portal30/admin_/gateway.htm;* Figure 16.11). Click on the "Gateway Database Access Descriptor Settings" link.

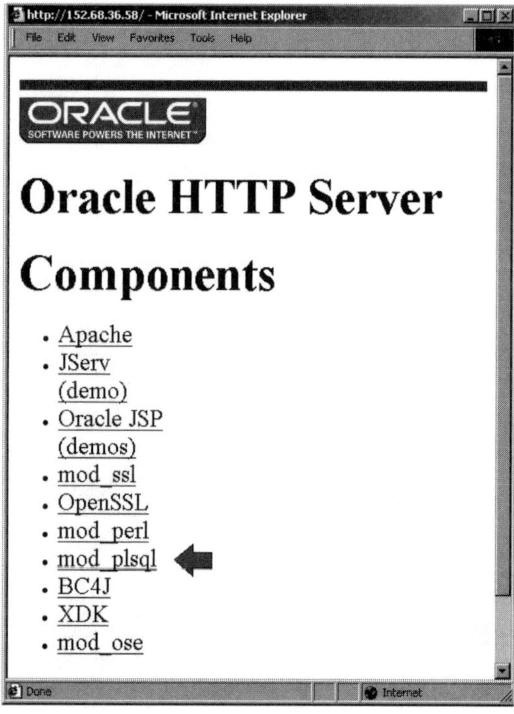

Figure 16.10 Oracle HTTP Server *powered by Apache* Home Page.

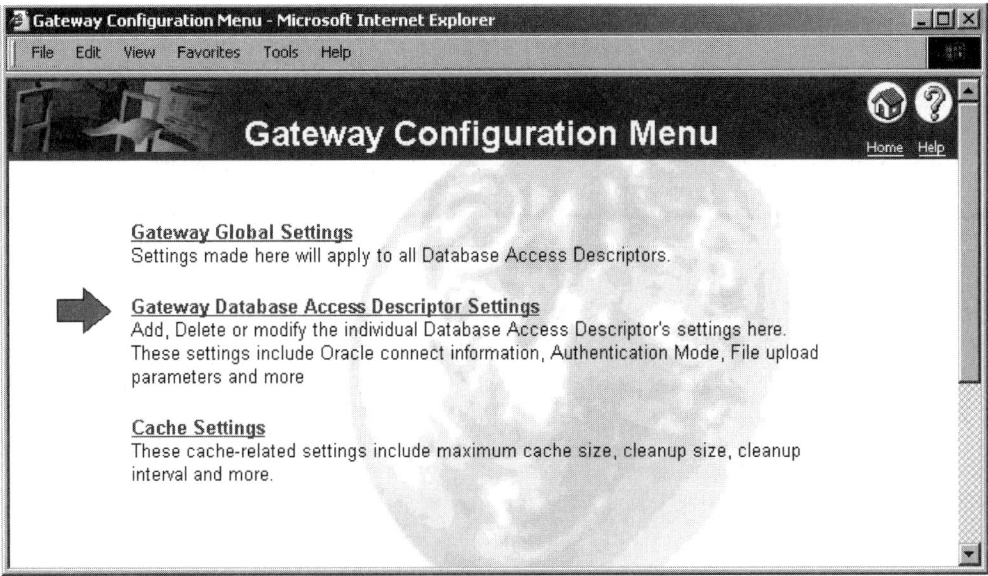

Figure 16.11 Gateway Configuration Menu.

Note

In Oracle Portal version 3.0.9, the Oracle HTTP Server home page is slightly changed to add more description to each component. The "mod_plsql" is called "Mod_plsql Configuration Menu".

Edit the properties of the Portal30 DAD by clicking on its Edit icon (Figure 16.12). Change the "Enable Connection Pooling" property to No (Figure 16.13).

Note

Setting the connection-pooling step is required in Oracle Database 8.1.7 and Portal 3.0.7. In future Oracle Portal releases, this setting might not be required.

Now you are ready to create the *inter*Media Text index by clicking on the "Create Index" button in the Search Settings page. If the creation is okay, you will get a message saying that the index is created on the server (Figure 16.14).

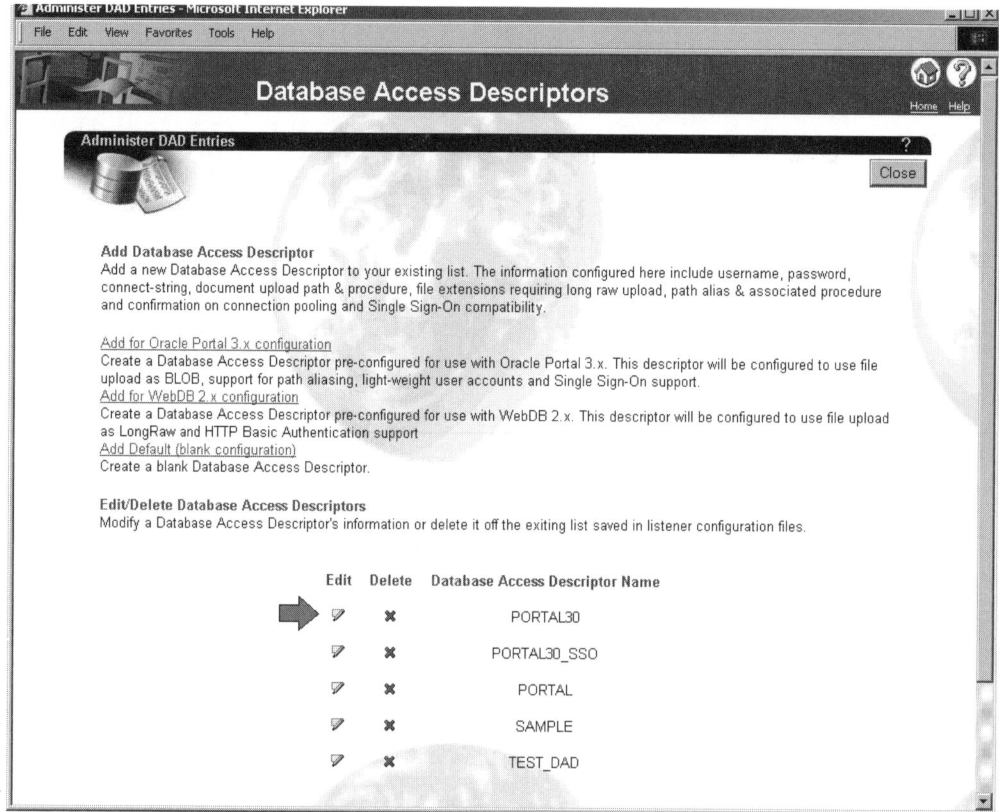

Figure 16.12 Gateway Configuration Menu.

Note

The time required for creating indexes varies depending on the number of items you have in your content areas. If you have just a few small content areas that are relatively small in size, it should only take a couple of minutes.

Next, the "Create Index" button displays "Drop Index" title instead (Figure 16.15). Also, you can create the indexes manually by running the SQL script `ctxcrind.sql` in SQL*Plus as the portal schema owner. The script can be found under <iAS_ORACLE_HOME>\portal30\admin\plsql\wws. You might need to edit the script to add the Oracle Database service name to the connect statement (i.e., @ORCL). Table 16.1 shows the indexes created.

Database Access Descriptor - Microsoft Internet Explorer

File Edit View Favorites Tools Help

Oracle User Name portal30

Oracle Password **************************

Oracle Connect String orcl

Authentication Mode

Select the authentication mode to be used for validating access through this DAD. For Oracle Portal 3.0, the use of Single Sign-on authentication is required. For WebDB 2.x, the use of Basic authentication is required. Please consult the documentation for information of the remaining three authentication modes: Global Owa, Custom Owa, and Per Package.

Authentication Mode Single Sign-On

Session Cookie

In most cases, the session cookie name should be left blank. A session cookie name must be specified only for Oracle Portal 3.0 instances that need to participate in a distributed Oracle Portal environment. For those Oracle Portal 3.0 nodes you want to seamlessly participate as a federated cluster, please ensure that the session cookie name for all of the participating nodes is the same. Independent Oracle Portal nodes need to use distinct session cookies.

Session Cookie Name

Session State

This setting determines whether database package/session state is preserved or is reset for each database request. For WebDB 2.x and Oracle Portal 3.0, this parameter must be set to No, resulting in the session state getting reset for each request.

Create a Stateful Session? No

Connection Pool Parameters

For maximum performance, keep the gateway's database connection pooling on.

Enable Connection Pooling? No

Default(Home)Page

This procedure will be called if no procedure name is specified in the URL.

Figure 16.13 Database Access Descriptor.

Figure 16.14 *inter*Media Text Indexes Creation.

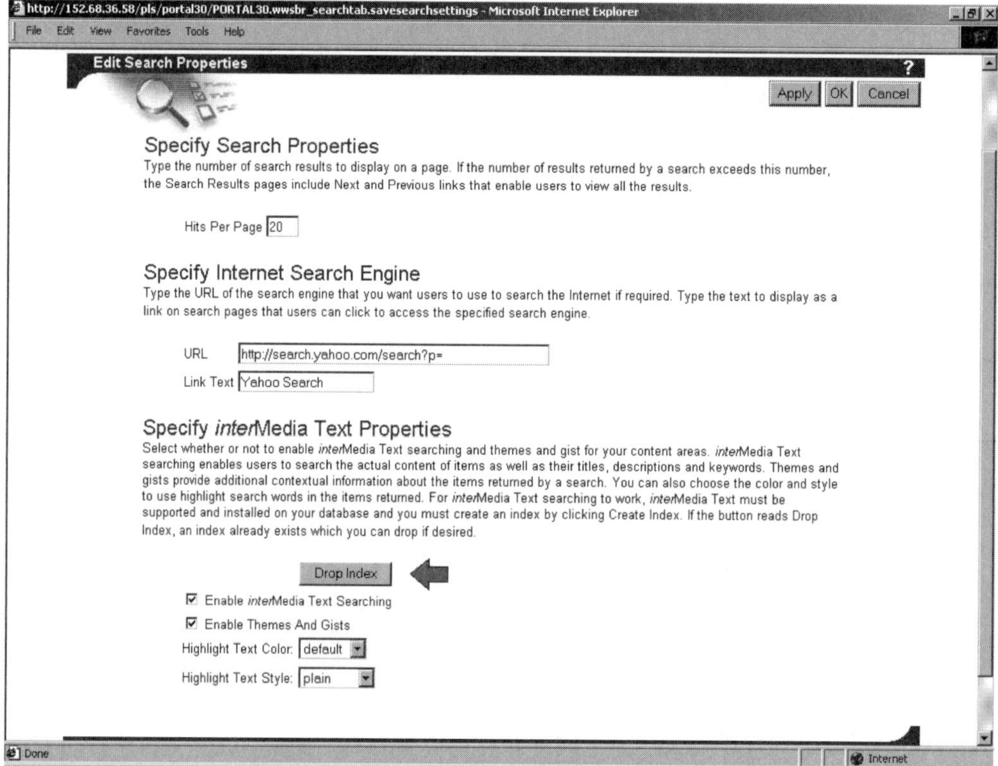

Figure 16.15 *inter*Media Text Indexes Creation.

Table 16.1 *inter*Media Text Indexes Created on the Content Area

Index Name	Index Function
WWSBR_CORNER_CTX_INDX	Index based on folders
WWSBR_DOC_CTX_INDX	Index based on the items' file name
WWSBR_PERSP_CTX_INDX	Index based on perspectives
WWSBR_THING_CTX_INDX	Index based on items
WWSBR_TOPIC_CTX_INDX	Index based on categories
WWSBR_URL_CTX_INDX	Index based on the items' Uniform Resource Locator (URL)

4. Maintain the *inter*Media Text Indexes

*inter*Media Text lets you create a text index (an inverted index) on documents stored in the database. Updating an inverted index requires heavy processing, so changes to a text column are queued and processed in batch. This is referred to as synchronizing the text index.

Note

An inverted index stores tokens and the documents in which these tokens occur.

After creating your *inter*Media Text index, you'll need to come up with a strategy for maintaining the index. Using *inter*Media Text, you have full control over how often each text index is synchronized. You can choose to synchronize every few seconds if it is important for the application to reflect text changes quickly in the index. Or, you can choose to synchronize once every few days for more efficient use of resources and a more optimal index.

Synchronize the *inter*Media Text Index(es) You need to install the `ctx_schedule` package to be able to automatically synchronize the *inter*Media Text index from SQL*Plus. As of Oracle Database 8.1.7, the `ctx_schedule` package is not available in the database by default; you need to create it manually by getting the source code of the package from *http://metalink.oracle.com.*

Log on to SQL*Plus as CTXSYS user, and then run the following commands:

```
exec ctx_schedule.startup( 'emp_ca_idx', 'SYNC', 3 ) ;
exec ctx_schedule.startup( 'emp_ca_idx', 'OPTIMIZE FAST', 180) ;
```

In this example the index `emp_ca_idx` is synchronized every 3 minutes and is optimized every 3 hours. This is true even if the database is shut down and restarted. You will need to replace `emp_ca_idx` with each of the Oracle Portal text indexes.

Stop the *inter*Media Text Index(es) Maintenance To stop the index maintenance, log on to SQL*Plus and run the following commands:

```
exec ctx_schedule.stop ( 'emp_ca_idx' ) ;
exec ctx_schedule.stop ( 'emp_ca_idx', 'OPTIMIZE FAST' ) ;
```

`ctx_schedule.stop` assumes that the operation to be stopped is 'SYNC', unless you specify otherwise.

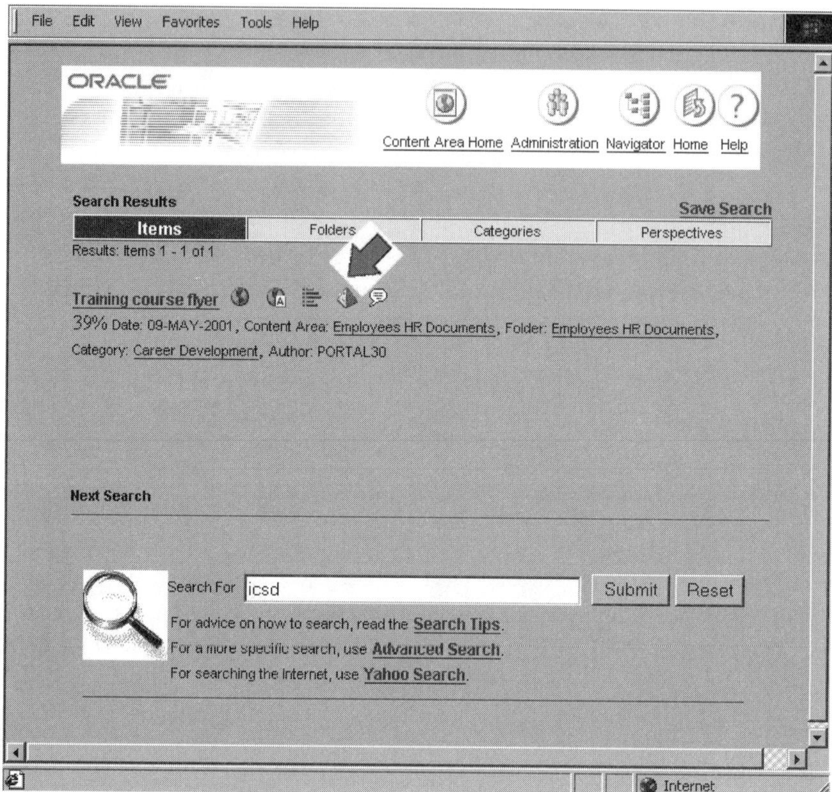

Figure 16.16 Search Results with *inter*Media Text Enabled.

Update the *inter*Media Text Index(es) If you added an item after creating the *inter*-Media Text, and you do not have a scheduled index maintenance, you can do a one-shot update for each one of the six indexes by issuing the following command:

```
ALTER INDEX <indexname> REBUILD ONLINE PARAMETERS ('SYNC')
```

If you want new text to be searched near-immediately (every five seconds), consider using the drbgdml.sql script located in

```
<iAS_ORACLE_HOME>\ctx\sample\script\drbgdml.sql
```

Drop the *inter*Media Text Index(es) In the Services portlet, click "Search Settings". In the *inter*Media Text Properties section, click "Drop Index". Then, the *inter*Media Text indexes are dropped from the server.

You can also drop the *inter*Media Text indexes by running the `ctxdrind.sql` script in

Oracle SQL*Plus and logging in as the Oracle Portal schema owner. The script exists in <iAS_ORACLE_HOME>\portal30\admin\plsql\wws.

Performing *inter*Media Text Search

Because the *inter*Media Text is enabled in Oracle Portal and the Text index is created, when a user performs a basic search, all the uploaded items of type file, text, or URL are searched as well.

From the Search Results page (Figure 16.16), you can choose any of the following icons to view the resulting search item differently:

- View an HTML version of the file.
- View an HTML version of the file with search terms highlighted in the color and font set in the search settings.
- View major themes in a chart (document theme analysis; Figure 16.17).
- View a short summary about the file's content (gist).

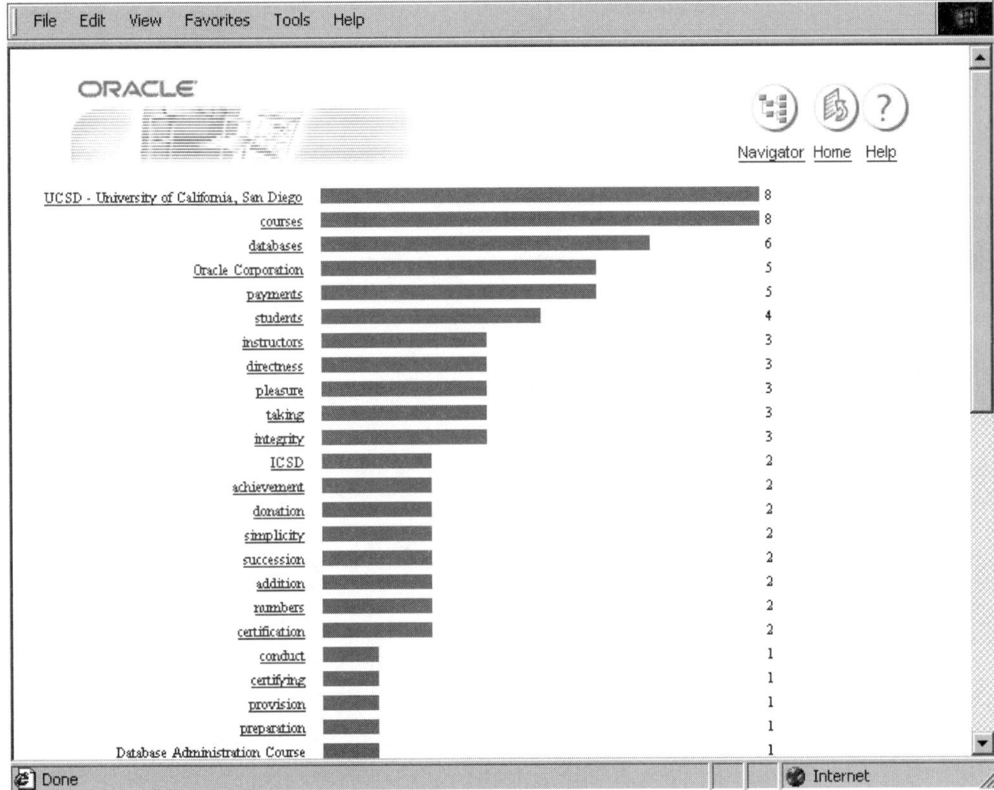

Figure 16.17 The Theme Analysis of a Search Result.

*Inter*Media Search Operators

When *inter*Media Text is enabled in Oracle Portal and an index is created, users can use a set of new operators added to the default search operator (i.e., Contains All, Contains Any; explained in Table 9.1). Now the operator list has the *inter*Media operators as well (Figure 16.18). Table 16.2 describes these operators.

Integrating Oracle9*i*AS Forms

Oracle Forms and Oracle Reports were part of Oracle Developer/2000 Suite; now they are part of Oracle 9*i* Development Suite. You develop forms (with fmb file extension) and reports (with rdf file extension) modules under GUI platforms (e.g., Microsoft Windows). Next, you can deploy your forms (fmx) and reports (rdf and rep) on the Web using Oracle Forms Server and Oracle Reports Server, respectively. These servers are part of the O9*i*AS Enterprise Edition, and their names are O9*i*AS Form Services and O9*i*AS Report Services. This section shows you how to configure Oracle Forms to run on the Web and how to integrate it into Oracle Portal.

Table 16.2 *inter*Media Text Operators

Operator	Description
Near	Returns a score based on the proximity of the specified words in the content. A higher score is returned for content with the specified words closer together and a lower score is returned for words farther apart.
Soundex (All)	Expands a Contains All search to include words that sound similar to the specified words. This allows comparison of words that are spelled differently but sound alike in English.
Soundex (Any)	Expands a Contains Any search to include words that sound similar to the specified words. This allows comparison of words that are spelled differently but sound alike in English.
Fuzzy (All)	Expands a Contains All search to include words that are spelled similarly to the specified words. This is helpful for finding more accurate results when there are frequent misspellings in the content.
Fuzzy (Any)	Expands a Contains Any search to include words that are spelled similarly to the specified words. This is helpful for finding more accurate results when there are frequent misspellings in the content.

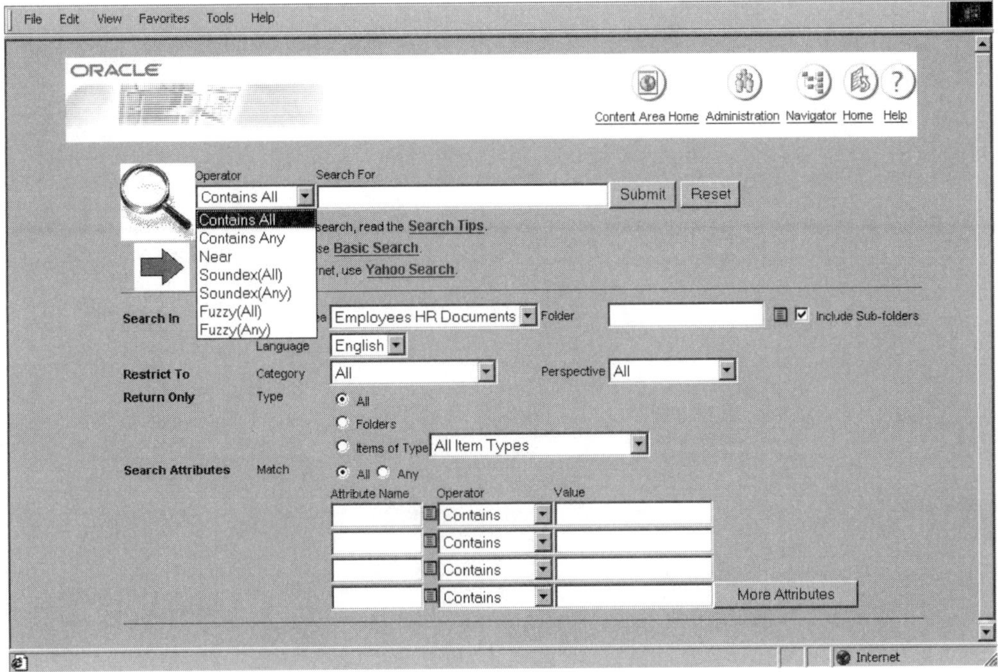

Figure 16.18 Advanced Search with the *inter*Media Text Operators.

Installing and Configuring O9*i*AS Form Services

The Form Services are installed as part of Oracle9*i* Application Server (1.0.2) Enterprise Edition. Form and Report Services reside in a different ORACLE_HOME. This book refers to this ORACLE_HOME by <6i_ORACLE_HOME>; on UNIX it is <iAS_ORACLE_HOME>/6iserver; and on Windows, if <iAS_ORACLE_HOME> is c:\oracle\o9ias, the <6i_ORACLE_HOME> is on a separate directory, c:\oracle\806.

Configuring O9*i*AS 1.0.2 Form Services is relatively easy, because the installation creates all the settings by default. At the end of the installation, the installer starts both the Forms Server and Reports Server. On Microsoft Windows, you can double check that both services are running by checking the NT services (Figure 16.19). On UNIX you can check for the service using the "ps" command.

The easiest way to test running a form is to type the following URL:

```
http://<Hostname>:<portno>/dev60html/runform.htm
```

where `<portno>` is the Oracle HTTP Server *powered by Apache* port.

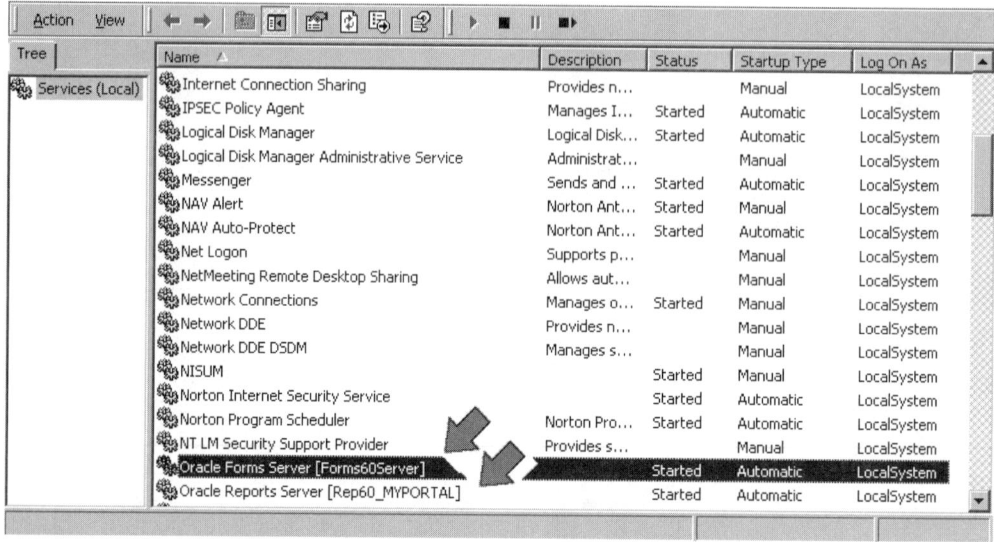

Figure 16.19 Checking the Form Service and Report Services on Windows.

You do not need to change the form default values or specify a user ID, because this form does not need to connect to a database. "dev60html" is an alias (i.e., virtual path) that is defined in the configuration file: <6i_ORACLE_HOME>\conf\6iserver.conf (Figure 16.20).

Note

If your hostname doesn't have a domain name, you might need to remove the postfixed ".".

When you click on the "Run form" button, the test.fmx form runs in a different browser window (Figure 16.21). Note the URL generated to run the text.fmx:

```
http://<Hostname>:<portno>/dev60cgi/ifcgi60.exe?form=test.fm
x&userid=&otherparams=useSDI=yes&lookAndFeel=generic&color
Scheme=teal
```

Note

The first time you run a form on the Web, you will be prompted to install a browser plug-in (i.e., Jinitiator).

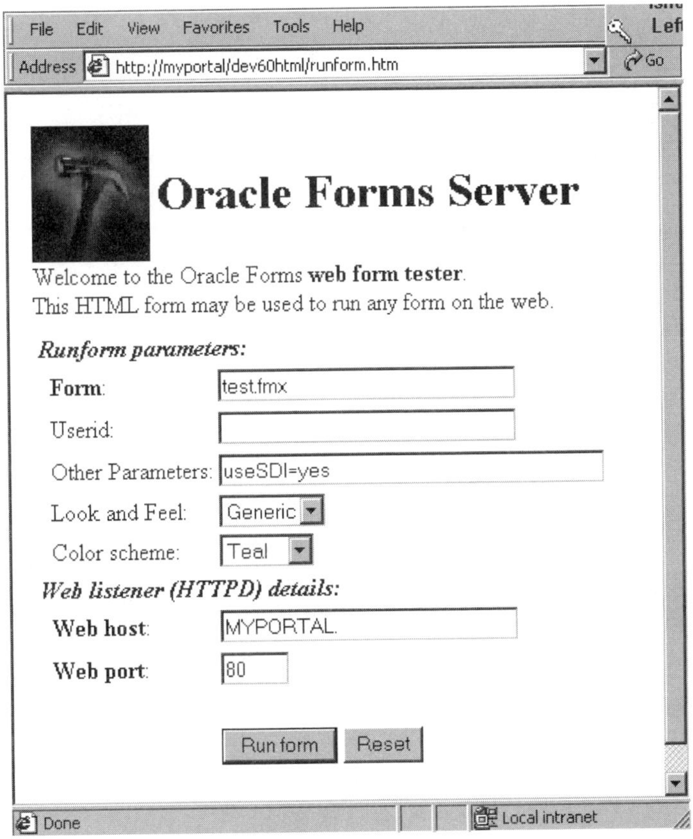

Figure 16.20 Checking the Form Service.

Note

In Forms6*i*, there is an easier way to specify the form run-time parameters instead of specifying them in the URL. You need to edit the file <6i_ORACLE_HOME>\forms60 \server\formsweb.cfg file and add a new application section for your form(s).

Now that you have tested your Forms Server, you need to test integrating a form into your portal. If you have an existing form you can use it, otherwise you need to start by building a simple form—you need the form builder to create your form. After you create your new form, you need to generate its FMX file and move it to a directory in your environment variable FORMS60_PATH. By default the FORM60_PATH contains c:\Oracle\806\FORMS60 (where the test.fmx resides; Figure 16.22). If you added a new directory (e.g., c:\portal\forms) to the FORMS60_PATH, you must stop and restart your Forms Server.

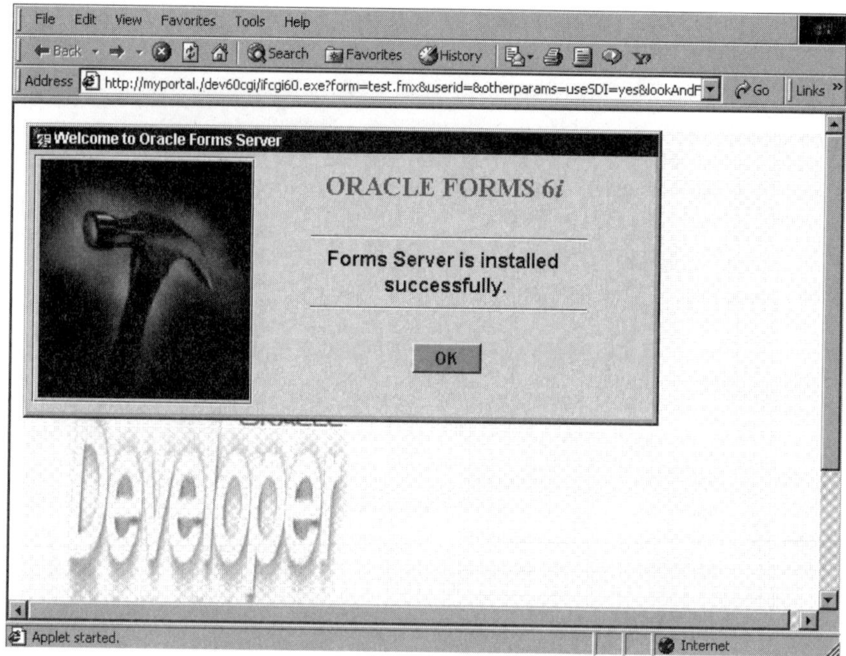

Figure 16.21 Test.fmx Runtime.

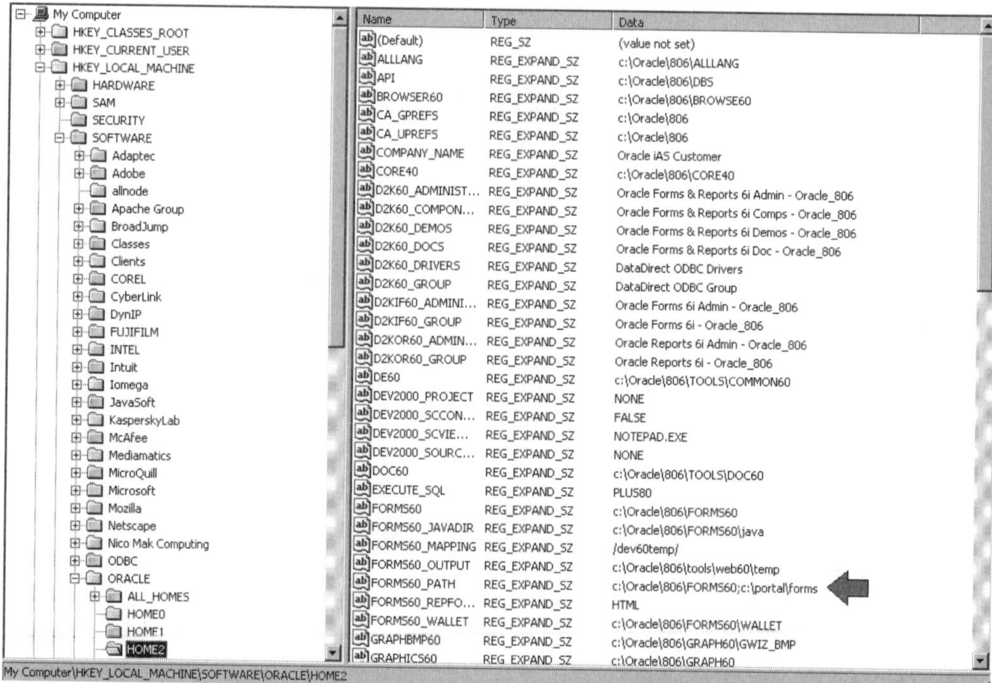

Figure 16.22 Running a Sample Web Form.

Also, you need to add an entry for the database to which the form will connect (e.g., ORCL) to the tnsnames.ora under the <6i_ORACLE_HOME>\net80\admin. Test the form on the Web by issuing the URL

```
http://<Hostname>:<portno>/dev60cgi/ifcgi60.exe?form=coun
tries.fmx&userid=myeip_owner/myeip_owner@orcl&separate
Frame=false
```

If that runs, the form is displayed within the browser window (Figure 16.23).

Creating a Content Area for the Form

One way of publishing your form in Oracle Portal is to use Content Areas. Start by creating a new content area in the Oracle Portal Navigator (Figure 16.24). Create a new container

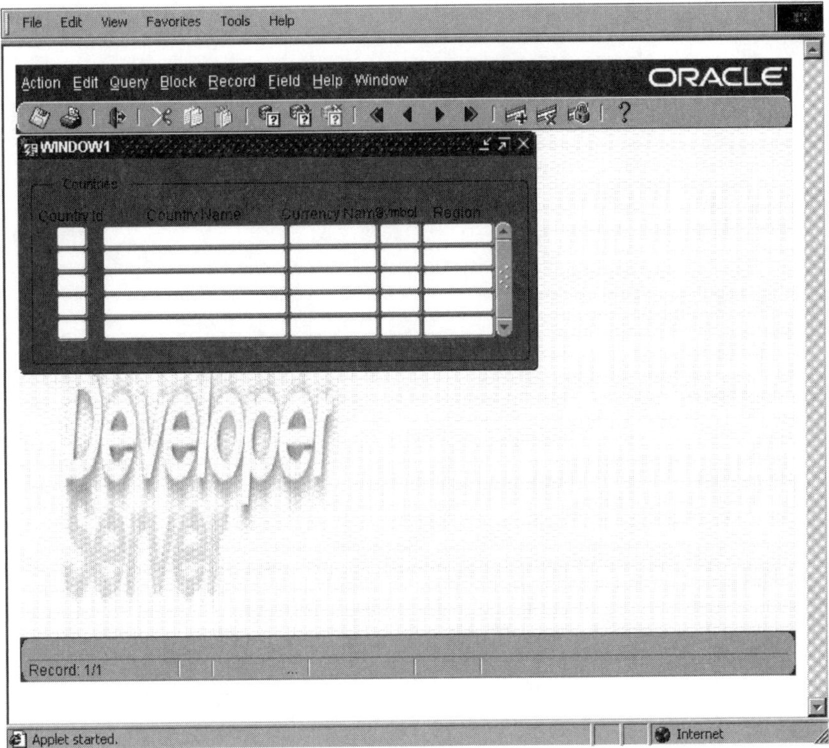

Figure 16.23 Running a Sample Web Form.

File Edit View Favorites Tools Help

ORACLE

Navigator Home Help

Create Content Area

Create Close

Content Area Properties

Enter a name, which is used internally, and a display name, which appears on the Navigator and throughout the product. Choose the language in which to create the content area, and assign an administrator. The name should not contain spaces or special characters.

Name	myEIP_forms
Display Name	myEIP Forms
Default Language	English
Content Area Administrator	PORTAL30

Figure 16.24 Create a New Content Area.

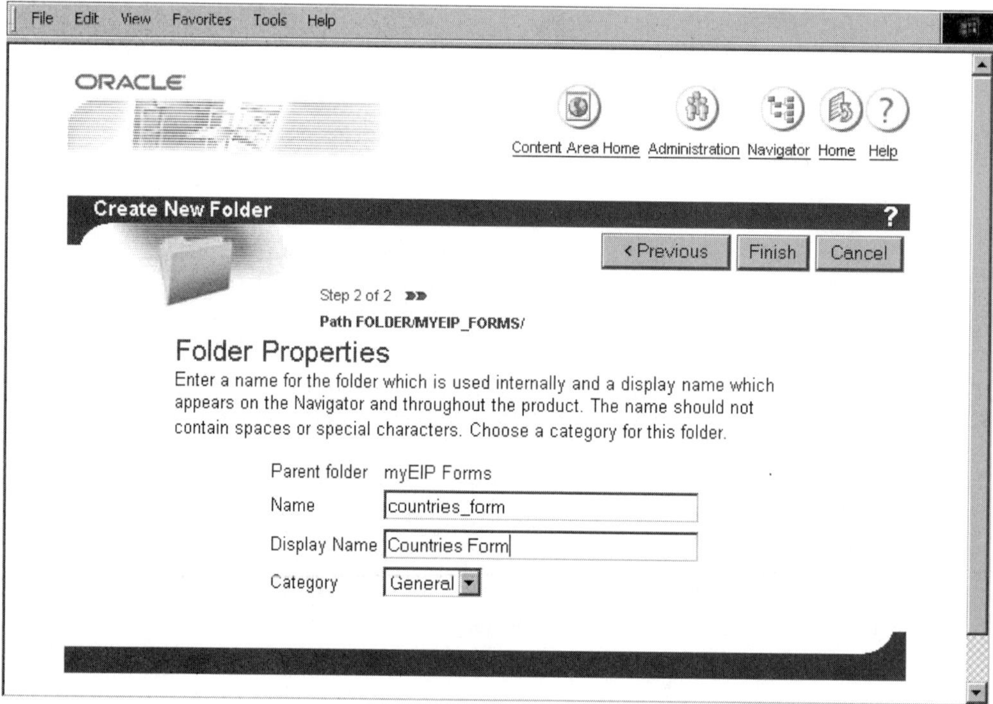

Figure 16.25 Creating a New Container Folder in the Content Area (1 of 2).

folder in the new content area (Figure 16.25). Next, edit the new folder properties to publish it as a portlet (Figure 16.26 and Figure 16.27). In that folder create a URL item and specify the same URL you used to test the form earlier (Figure 16.28). In the secondary preferences for that item, specify that it should be displayed directly in a folder (Figure 16.29). Now, your new folder in the content area should look like Figure 16.30.

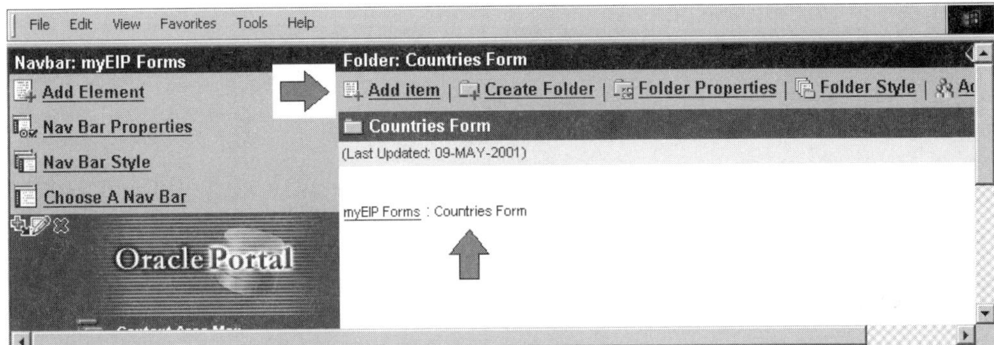

Figure 16.26 Creating a New Container Folder in the Content Area (2 of 2).

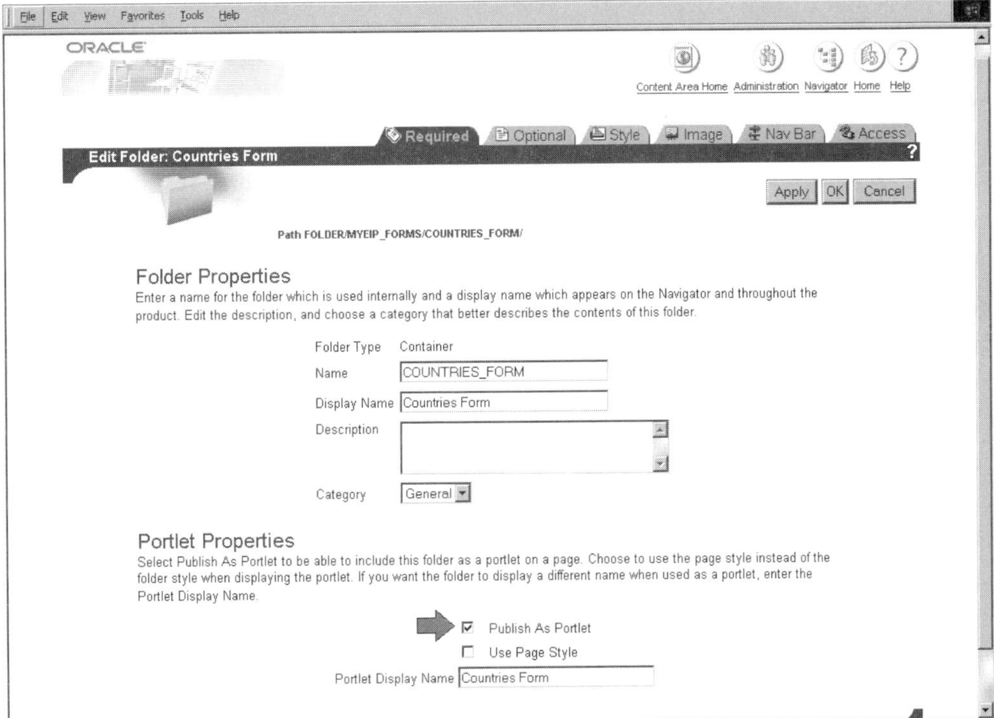

Figure 16.27 Edit the New Folder Properties: Publish As Portlet.

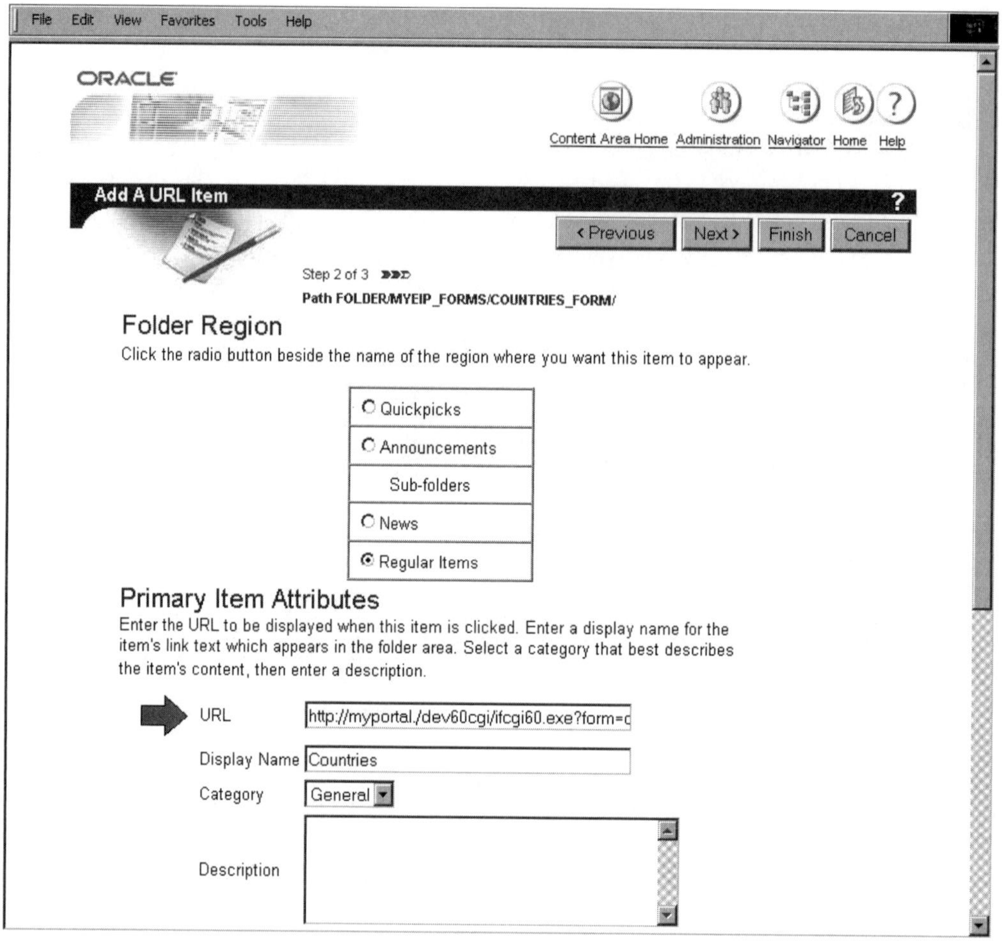

File Edit View Favorites Tools Help
ORACLE
Content Area Home Administration Navigator Home Help
Add A URL Item
< Previous
Next >
Finish
Cancel
Step 2 of 3
Path FOLDER/MYEIP_FORMS/COUNTRIES_FORM/
Folder Region
Click the radio button beside the name of the region where you want this item to appear.
Quickpicks
Announcements
Sub-folders
News
Regular Items
Primary Item Attributes
Enter the URL to be displayed when this item is clicked. Enter a display name for the item's link text which appears in the folder area. Select a category that best describes the item's content, then enter a description.
URL
http://myportal./dev60cgi/ifcgi60.exe?form=c
Display Name
Countries
Category
General
Description

Figure 16.28 Creating a URL Item: Primary Tab: Primary Item Attributes.

File Edit View Favorites Tools Help
Hide Item
Display Options
Choose how to display the results of the URL item: in the right pane of the browser window, directly below the item's display name, in your current browser window (no navigation bar), or in another browser window.
Link That Displays Item In Folder Area
Item Displayed Directly In Folder Area
Link That Displays Item In Full Browser Window
Link That Displays Item In New Browser Window

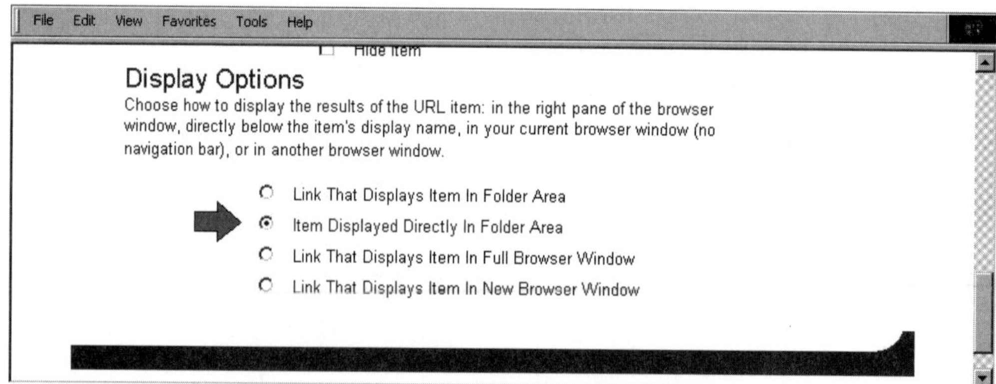

Figure 16.29 Creating an Item: Secondary Tab: Display Options.

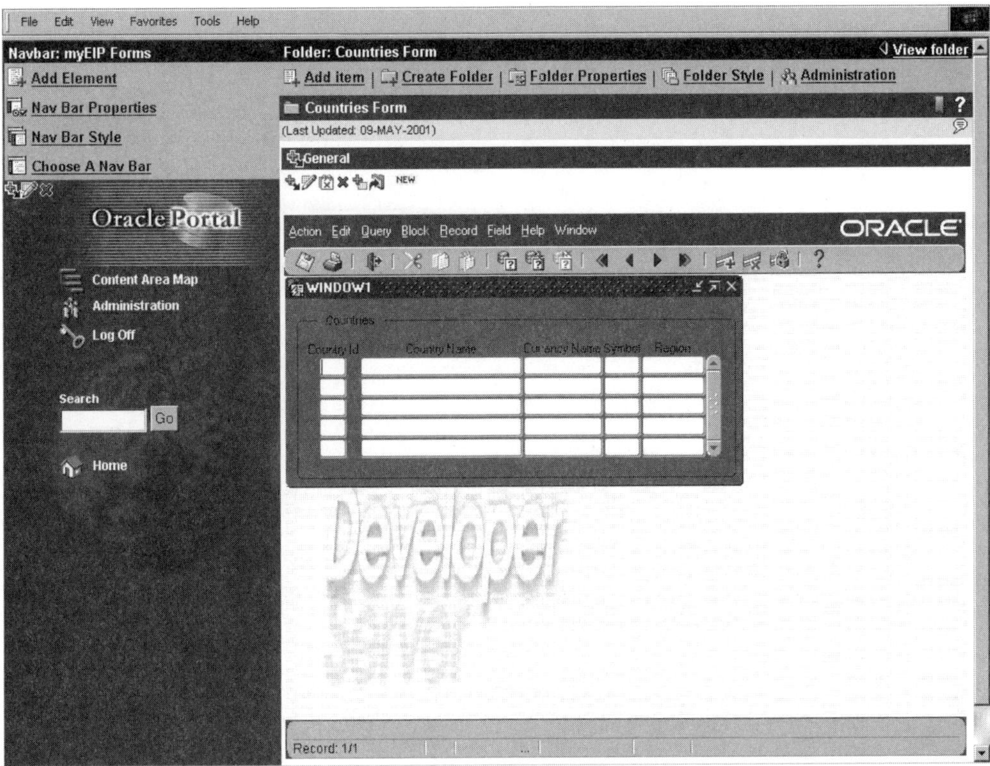

Figure 16.30 Content Area New Folder.

Add the Form Portlet to a Page

Add the folder as a portlet to one of your pages (Figure 16.31). Click on the "Edit Defaults" link of that portlet and choose only the form item region to be displayed (i.e., Regular items; Figure 16.32 and Figure 16.33). The form should be displayed within the page as a portlet (Figure 16.34).

Note

In Oracle Portal version 3.0.9, an "edit" link is displayed in the folder portlet that allows the user to edit the content area folder from within the page. You can hide this link if you want to by editing the defaults of the portlet.

This forms server implementation is called the CGI implementation. The disadvantage in the previous example is that the username and password are hard-coded in the item URL. Another alternative is to use the Forms Servlet implementation. You need to apply the Developer6*i* patch 5 or later for the servlet implementation to work smoothly. The forms servlet can be added as an

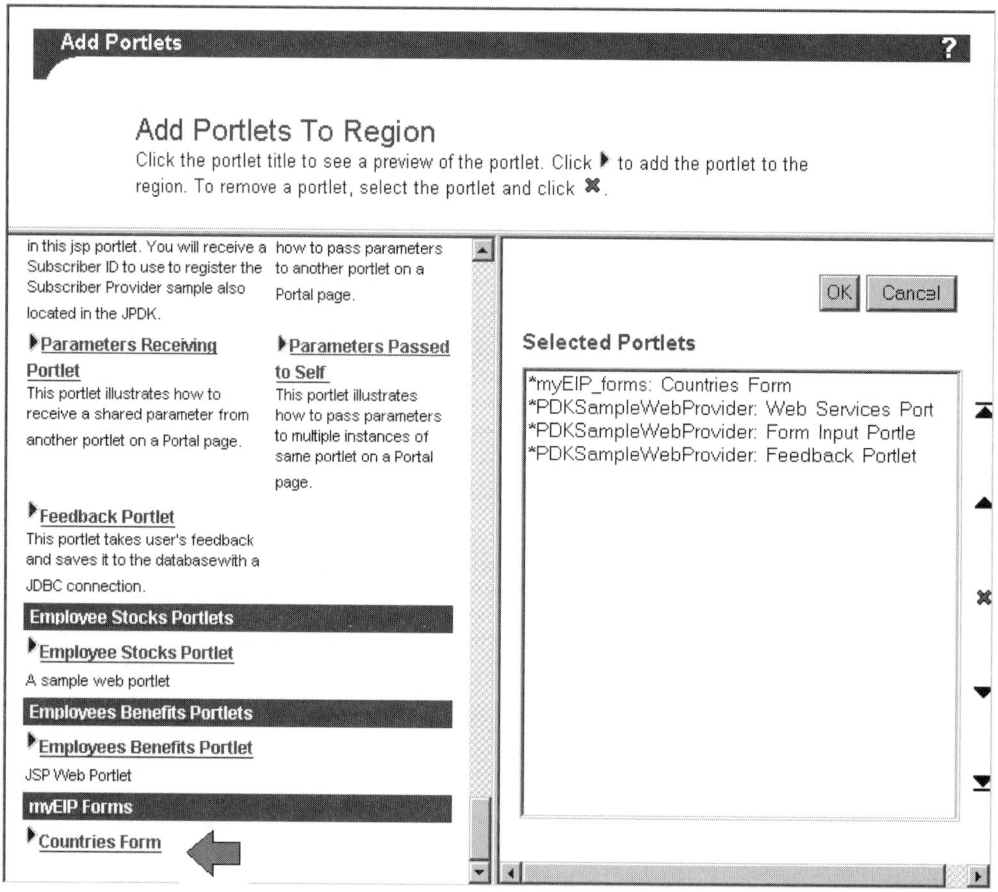

Add Portlets

Add Portlets To Region

Click the portlet title to see a preview of the portlet. Click ▶ to add the portlet to the region. To remove a portlet, select the portlet and click ✖.

in this jsp portlet. You will receive a Subscriber ID to use to register the Subscriber Provider sample also located in the JPDK.

how to pass parameters to another portlet on a Portal page.

▶**Parameters Receiving Portlet**
This portlet illustrates how to receive a shared parameter from another portlet on a Portal page.

▶**Parameters Passed to Self**
This portlet illustrates how to pass parameters to multiple instances of same portlet on a Portal page.

▶**Feedback Portlet**
This portlet takes user's feedback and saves it to the databasewith a JDBC connection.

Employee Stocks Portlets

▶**Employee Stocks Portlet**
A sample web portlet

Employees Benefits Portlets

▶**Employees Benefits Portlet**
JSP Web Portlet

myEIP Forms

▶**Countries Form**

OK Cancel

Selected Portlets

*myEIP_forms: Countries Form
*PDKSampleWebProvider: Web Services Port
*PDKSampleWebProvider: Form Input Portle
*PDKSampleWebProvider: Feedback Portlet

Figure 16.31 Portlet Repository: Adding the Form Portlet.

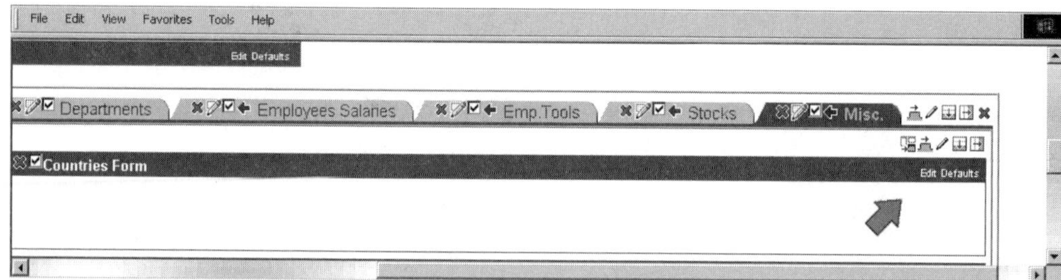

Figure 16.32 Edit the Portlet Defaults (1 of 2).

File Edit View Favorites Tools Help

ORACLE

Navigator Home Help

Customize Folder Portlet

Apply | OK | Cancel

Folder Portlet Settings

Use the Folder Regions check boxes to select one or more regions to display in the portlet. If you clicked Customize on the portlet banner, you are the only one who will see the selections you make. If you clicked Edit Defaults, the selections you make will be visible to everyone who sees this page.

Display Name: Countries Form

Folder Regions:

- [ ] Quickpicks
- [ ] Announcements
- [ ] Sub-folders
- [ ] News
- [x] Regular Items

Figure 16.33 Edit the Portlet Defaults (2 of 2).

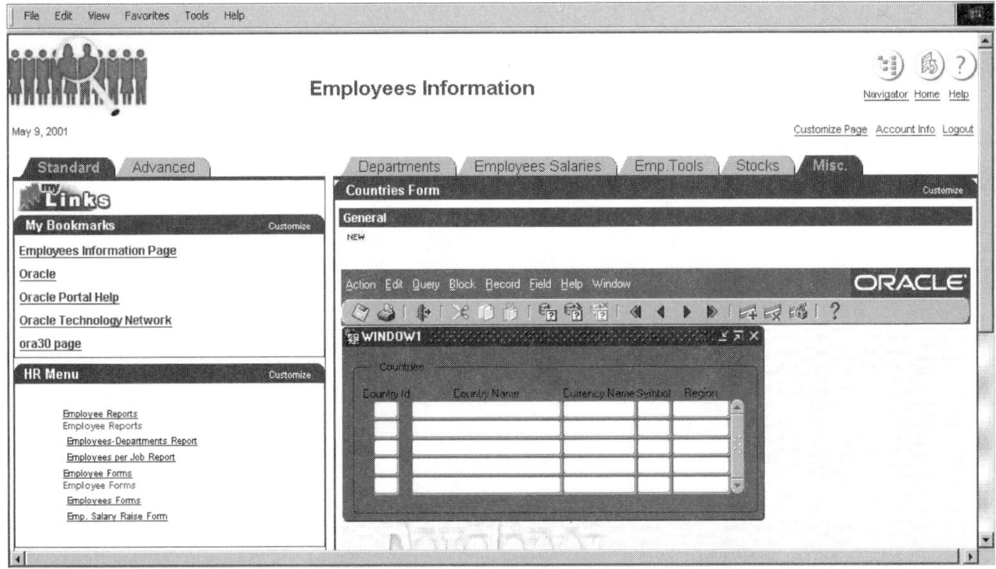

Figure 16.34 Displaying the Portal Page. (You can hide the General banner by editing the content area style. Click on the Folder Layout tab, edit the Regular Items region, and unselect the "Display Region Banner" check box.)

external Single Sign-On application to Oracle Portal, which means you do not need to hard-code the username or password in the form URL. For more information on the forms servlet implementation, refer to O9*i*AS Forms documentation.

Integrating Oracle9*i*AS Reports

Reports Server is a multi-threaded server that has the ability to have multiple threads servicing a large number of end-users requests to generate reports.

Installing and Configuring O9*i*AS Report Services

The Report Services are installed as part of Oracle9*i* Application Server (1.0.2) Enterprise Edition. The easiest way to test running a report is to type the following URL:

```
http://<Hostname>:<portno>/dev60html/runrep.htm
```

Change the database service name from test to your service name (e.g., orcl; Figure 16.35). When you click on the "Run Report" button, the test.rdf report runs in a different browser window (Figure 16.36). Note the URL generated to run the text.fmx:

```
http://myportal/dev60cgi/rwcgi60.exe?server=Rep60_MYPORTAL&r
eport=test.rdf&userid=scott/tiger@orcl&destype=cache&desfor
mat=HTML
```

Note

If you get the error message "Oracle Reports Server CGI—Unable to communicate with the Reports Server" when you try to run a report on the Web, add the following line to your jserv.properties file and then restart your HTTP server:

```
wrap.env=TNS_ADMIN=c:\oracle\806\net80\admin
```

Now that you have tested the reports server, you can try running one of your existing reports on the Web, or you can build a simple report using the Developer6*i* Reports Builder that is part of the Oracle9*i* Development Suite (DS) CD Pack. For practice, you can use the Report wizard to build a matrix report that runs against the SCOTT.EMP table to display the number of employees per job per department. You can name the report `job_dept.rdf` and put it under a subdirectory `c:\portal\reports`. To be able to run the report on the Web without specifying the directory where the report resides, you need to add the directory to the REPORTS60_PATH (Figure 16.37) and restart the reports server service. The URL to run the report looks like the following:

```
http://<Hostname>:<portno>/dev60cgi/rwcgi60.exe?server=Rep60
_<Hostname>&report=job_dept.rdf&userid=scott/tiger@orcl&des
type=cache&desformat=HTML
```

Figure 16.38 shows a sample output of the `job_dept.rdf` report. From the Reports Builder, you can generate the `job_dept.rep` report file that contains no PL/SQL source code and use it instead of the `job_dept.rdf` in the URL. You can also change the desformat parameter in the URL from HTML to PDF or XML to generate an Acrobat PDF or XML output.

You can add the report as a portlet to one of your pages by following the same steps performed earlier for adding a form:

1. Create a folder in one of your content areas.
2. Publish the folder as a provider.
3. Add a URL item to the new folder.
4. Set the display option for the new item to be displayed directly in the folder area.
5. Add the new URL item in your folder as a portlet to one of your pages.

Figure 16.35 Oracle Reports Web Testing Page.

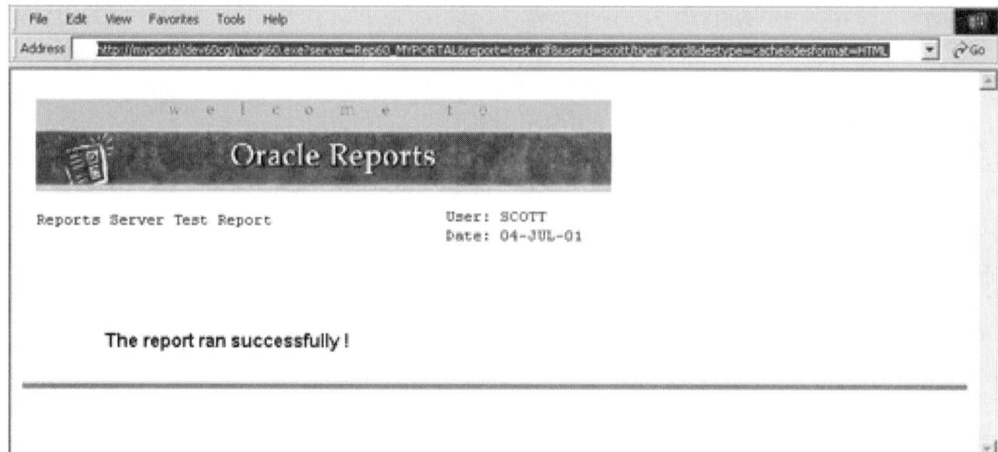

Figure 16.36 Test.rdf Runtime.

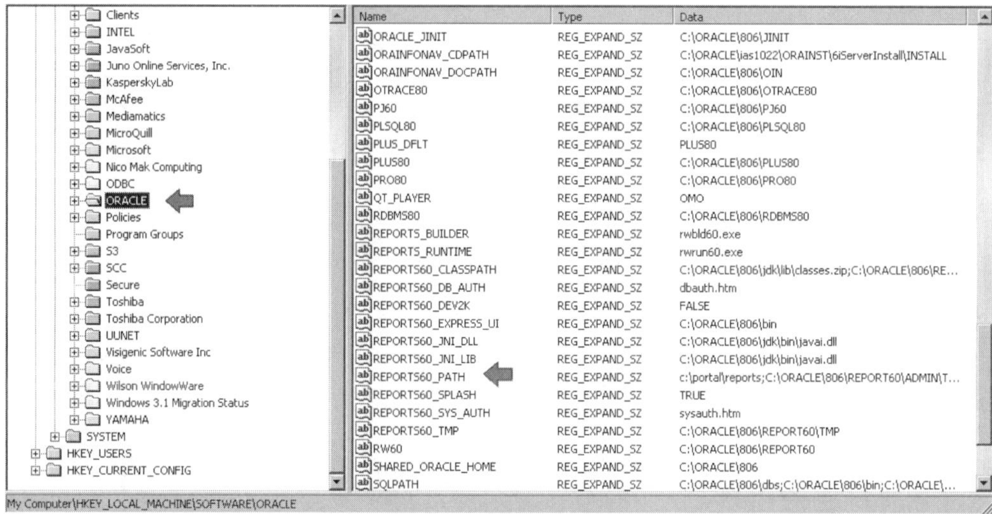

Figure 16.37 Windows Regedit: REPORTS60_PATH Value.

The disadvantage in the previous technique is that the username and password are hard-coded in the item URL. An alternative is to use the Reports security features in Portal 3.0. These features are available out of the box in Portal version 3.0.9 and higher. In earlier versions of Oracle Portal, you need to run the script `rwwwvins.sql` to set the features; this script is available under the <6*i*_ORACLE_HOME> (e.g., `c:\oracle\806\report60\server\security\`). Start integrating Reports into Portal by clicking on the "Oracle Reports Security Settings" link under the Administer tab of the Oracle Portal home page (Figure 16.39). The Oracle Reports Security page is displayed (Figure 16.40).

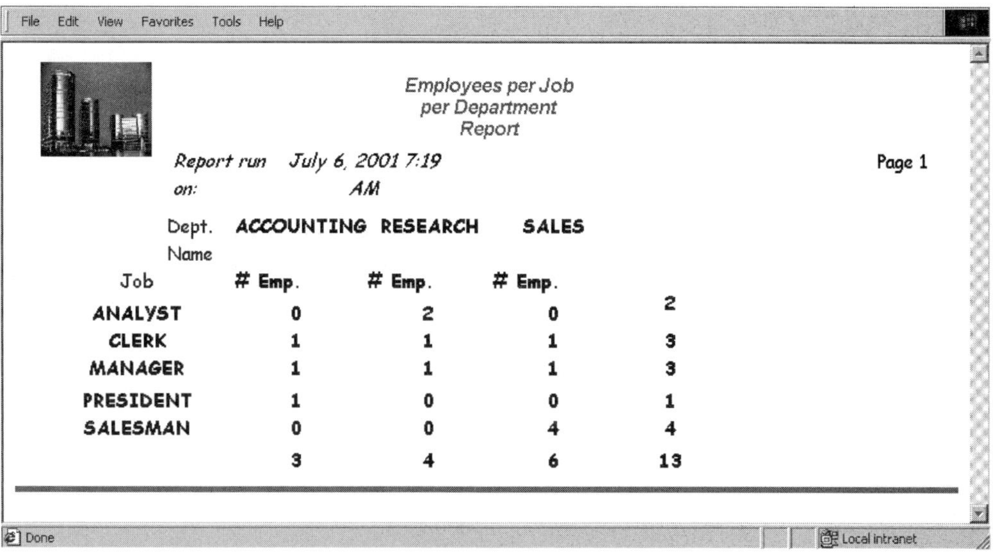

Figure 16.38 Sample Matrix Report: job_dept.rdf.

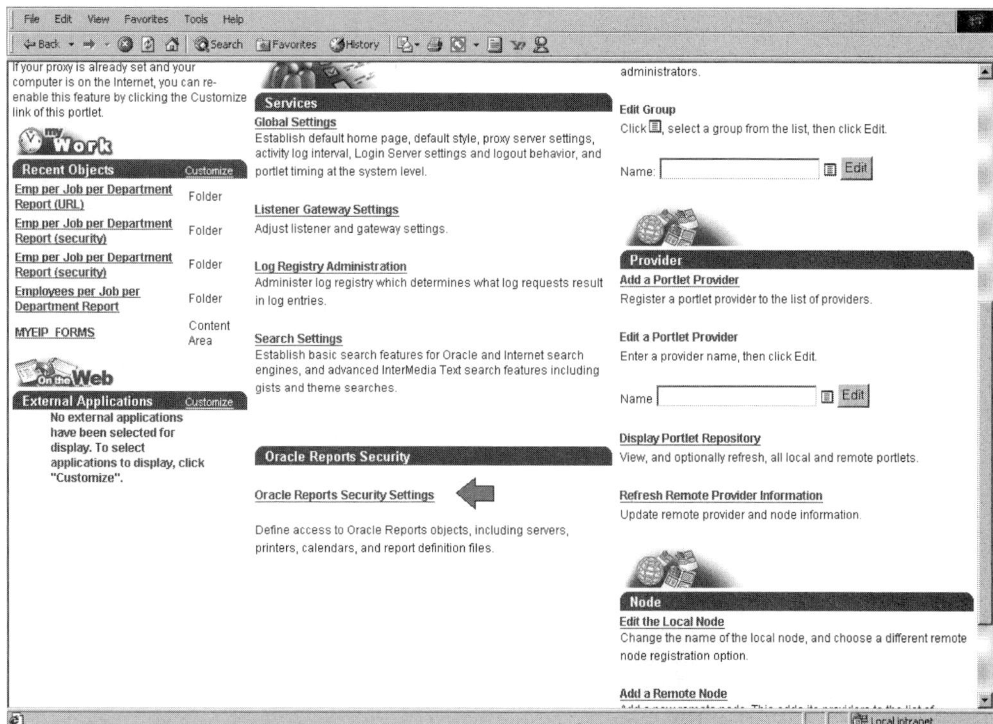

Figure 16.39 Oracle Portal Home Page: Administer Tab: Oracle Reports Security.

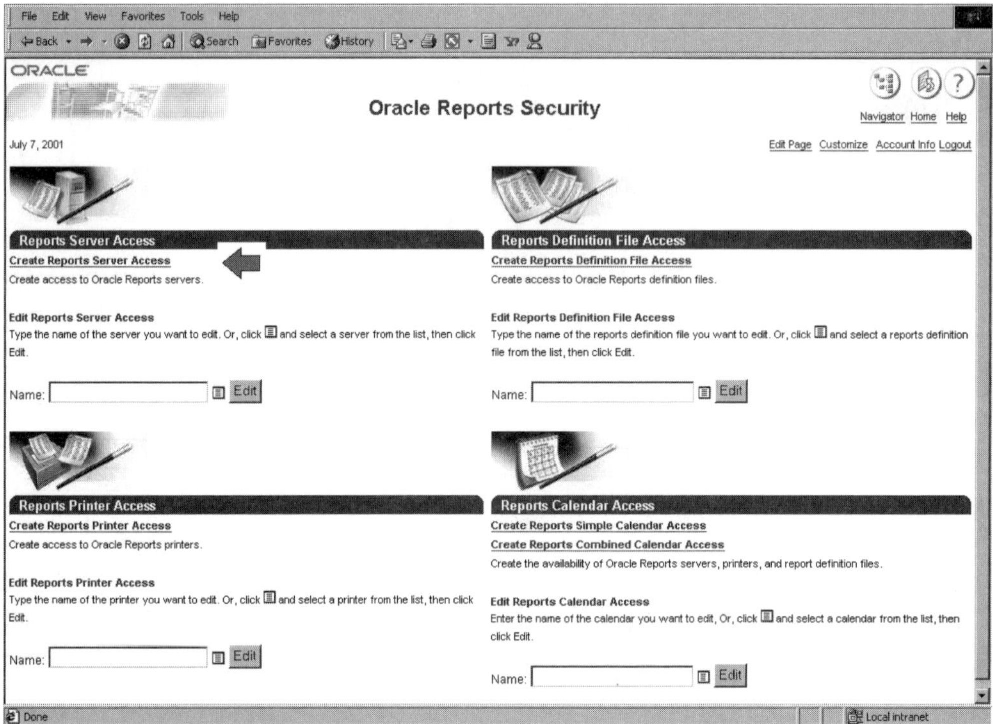

Figure 16.40 Oracle Reports Security Page.

The first step is to create a reports server entry in Oracle Portal by clicking on "Create Reports Server Access" and specify the reports server properties (Figure 16.41). The TNS name is the reports server name (i.e., REP60_<Hostname>) and the Oracle Reports Web Gateway URL should point to your Reports Server CGI executable (i.e., `http://<Hostname>:<portno>/dev60cgi/rwcgi60.exe`).

In the next step specify the users and groups who will have access to this reports server. The third and final step, where you associate an existing availability calendar with the reports server, is optional. The availability calendar allows the portal administrator to restrict the availability of this reports server for specific days or times.

When the reports server is created, you can create an entry to the report that you need to run from Oracle Portal. In the first step click on the "Create Reports Definition File Access" link in the Oracle Reports Security page to specify the report properties (Figure 16.42). Choose an application that will hold this report as a component, specify a report name, choose a report server (i.e., REP60_<Hostname>), and finally specify the report file name (i.e., `job_dept.rdf`).

In step two of the report creation steps, you can specify who can access this report. In step three you can optionally specify the report availability calendar. In step four you can choose one or more destination types and formats for this report (Figure 16.43).

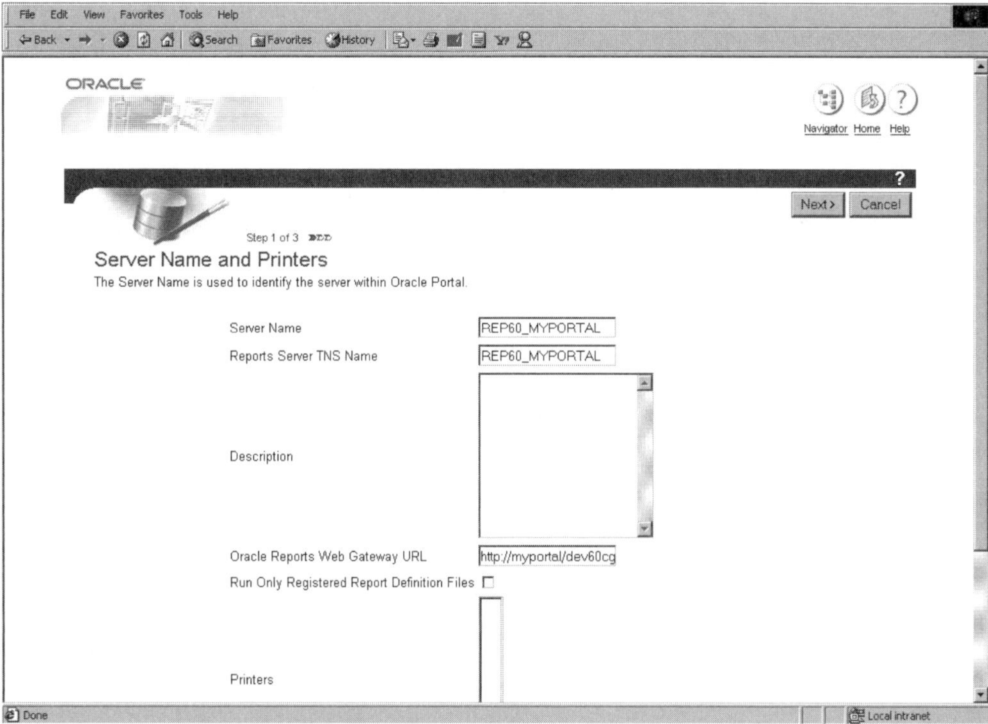

Figure 16.41 Create Report Server Access: Step 1 of 3.

If the report has parameters, you can specify a List of Values to these parameters in step five, and, finally, you can specify a validation trigger to be executed before the report is executed; if the trigger returns a TRUE value then the report will be run. When the report is created, you can add it as an Application Component item to one of your content area folders that can be published as a portlet (Figure 16.44).

Integration Discoverer

Oracle9*i*AS Discoverer is a business intelligence tool for analyzing data. There are two Oracle9*i*AS Discoverer components included in the Oracle9*i* Application Server suite: Oracle9*i*AS Discoverer Plus and Oracle9*i*AS Discoverer Viewer. With Discoverer Plus, business professionals can get and analyze data in a company's database using Wizard dialogs and menus. The Oracle9*i*AS Discoverer Viewer is a tool for viewing workbooks created by Discoverer Plus users.

To use the Discoverer Plus or the Discoverer Viewer, the Discoverer End User Layer (EUL) schema has to be created first. The EUL can be created using the Discoverer Administration Edition, which is part of the Oracle9*i* Development Suite (O9*i*DS). If you do not have an existing

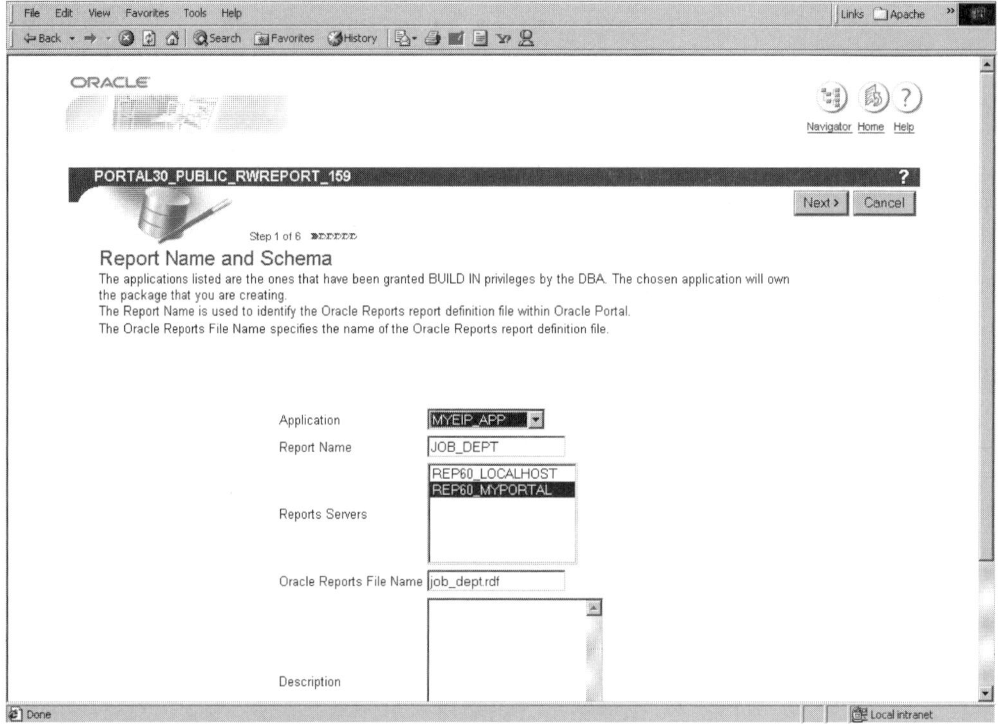

Figure 16.42 Create Reports Definition File Access: Step 1 of 6.

Discoverer workbook, you need to create one by running Discoverer Plus using the following URL (Figure 16.45):

```
http://<Hostname>:<portno>/discwb4/html/english/welcome.htm
```

When you have created the workbook, you can view it from the Discoverer Viewer using the following URL (Figure 16.46):

```
http://<Hostname>:<portno>/discoverer4i/viewer
```

To integrate your Discoverer workbook into Oracle Portal, you can add a URL item into a content area folder that is published as a portlet. This URL item is pointing to the workbook displayed in the Discoverer4*i* Viewer, the URL to your workbook in Discoverer Viewer should be similar to the following:

```
http://<Hostname>:<portno>/discoverer4i/viewer?ac=disc~40
orcl&eul=DISC&nlsl=en-us&wb=test
```

where the EUL schema owner is DISC and the workbook name is test.

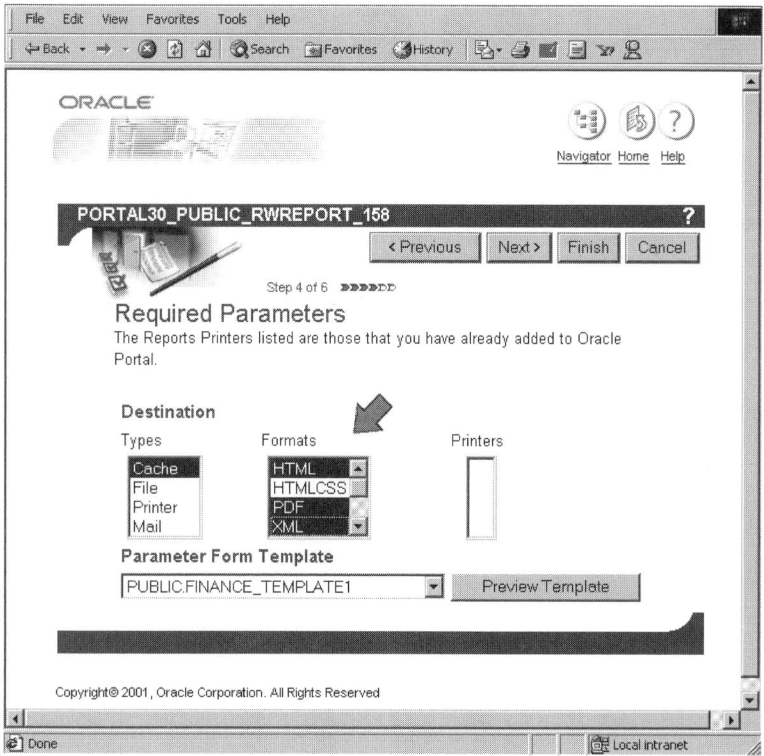

Figure 16.43 Create Reports Definition File Access: Step 4 of 6.

Another option to integrate Discoverer4*i* into your Oracle Portal is to add Discoverer as an Oracle External Application to avoid hard-coding the user information in the workbook URL that is to add the Discoverer as an external application. Click on the "Administer External Applications" link in the Login Server Administration Portlet in the Administer tab of the Oracle Portal home page (Figure 16.47).

Create a new external application for the Discoverer Viewer; specify its properties as the following (Figure 16.48):

1. Login URL: http://<Hostname>:<portno>/discoverer4i/viewer
2. User Name/ID Field Name: us
3. Password Field Name: pw
4. Additional Fields:
   Field Name: db, Field Value: <Discoverer EUL Database> (e.g., ORCL)
   Field Name: lc, Field Value: false
   Field Name: in, Field Value: dwb
   Field Name: _in, Field Value: dwb

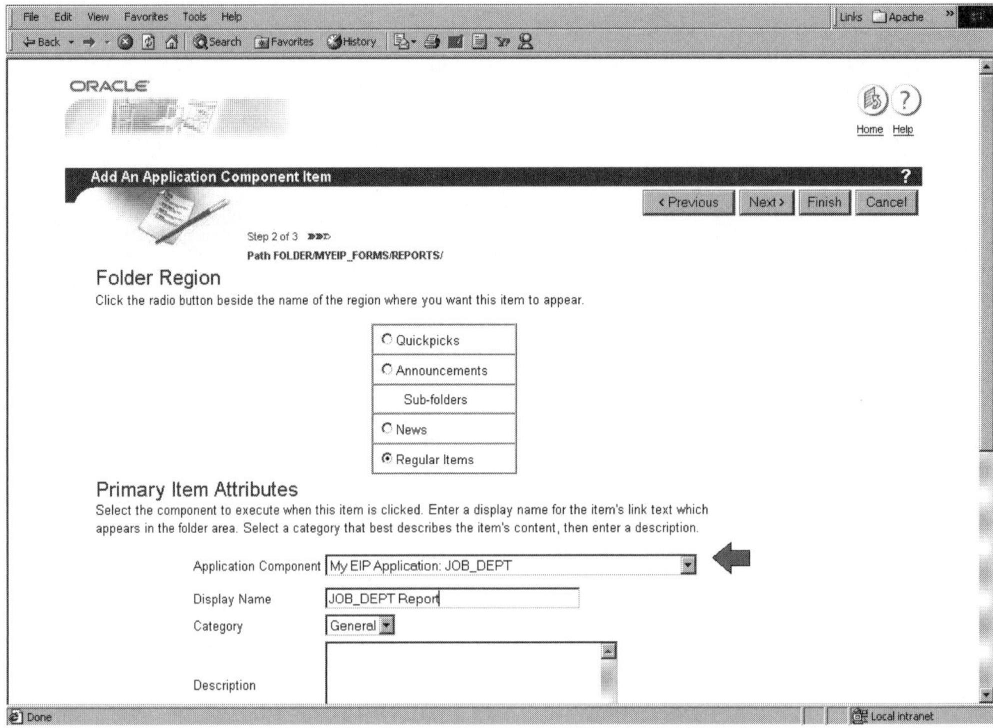

Figure 16.44 Create an Application Component Item in a Content Area Folder.

When the Discoverer external application is created, you can add the external applications portlet to your page. The external applications portlet is available under the Login Server Provider in the Portlet Repository. Figure 16.49 shows the Portlet Repository of Portal version 3.0.9. When the External Applications portlet is added to the page, you can click on the "Edit Defaults" link of the portlet to display only the link to the Discoverer Viewer (Figure 16.50).

Oracle Internet Directory LDAP Authentication

As mentioned in Chapter 12, you can use Oracle Internet Directory (OiD), which is an LDAP 3.0 compliant directory, to authenticate users externally to Oracle9*i*AS Portal. OiD needs the Oracle8*i* 8.1.6.2 or 8.1.7 database instance. It is preferred that you create a dedicated instance just for the OiD; the installer, while installing the OiD, creates this instance automatically. This section demonstrates using OiD version 2.1.1 with O9*i*AS Portal version 3.0.9. Also for simplicity, this section installs the OiD instance in the same server as the Oracle9*i*AS, but you can install the OiD instance and the Oracle Portal Login Server in a different machine from the Oracle9*i*AS.

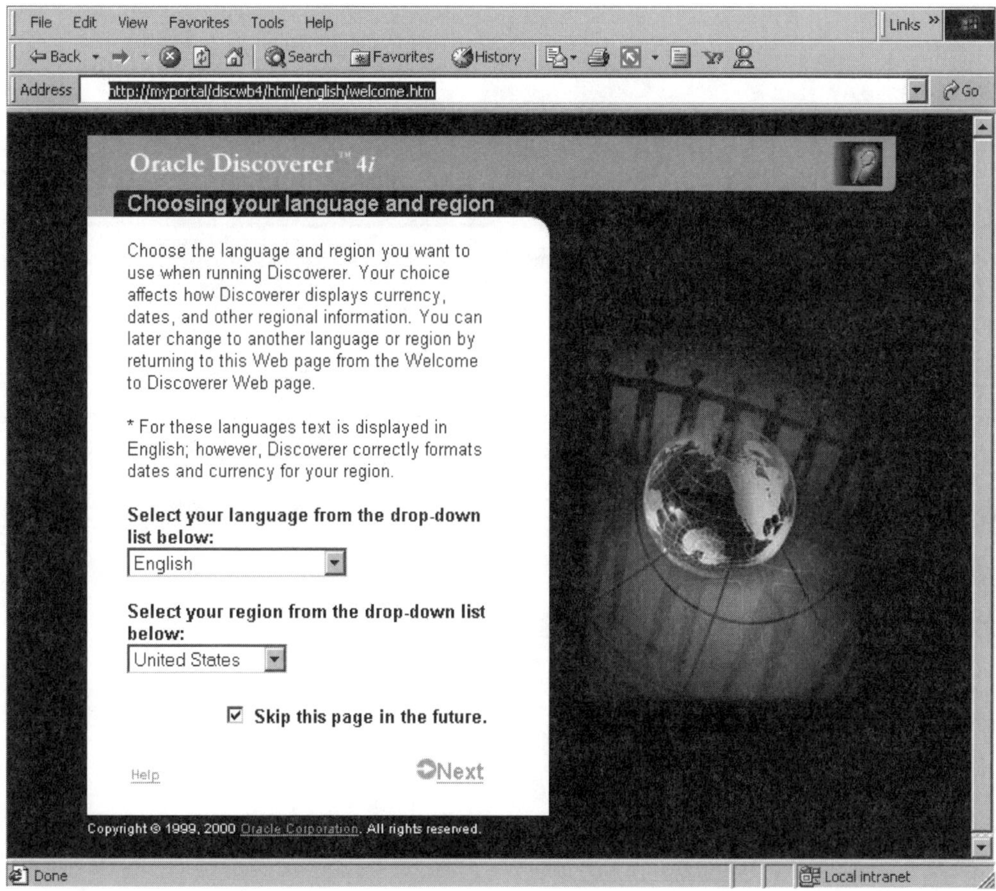

Figure 16.45 Running Discoverer 4*i* Plus.

Note

This section does not explain in detail the LDAP concepts, the OiD architecture, or its terminology. For more information about LDAP and OiD, refer to the OiD manuals.

Oracle Internet Directory Installation

To start the OiD installation, insert the Oracle8*i* database 8.1.7 CD-ROM. The welcome screen is displayed, then you need to choose the "Oracle8*i* Management and Integration 8.1.7.0.0"

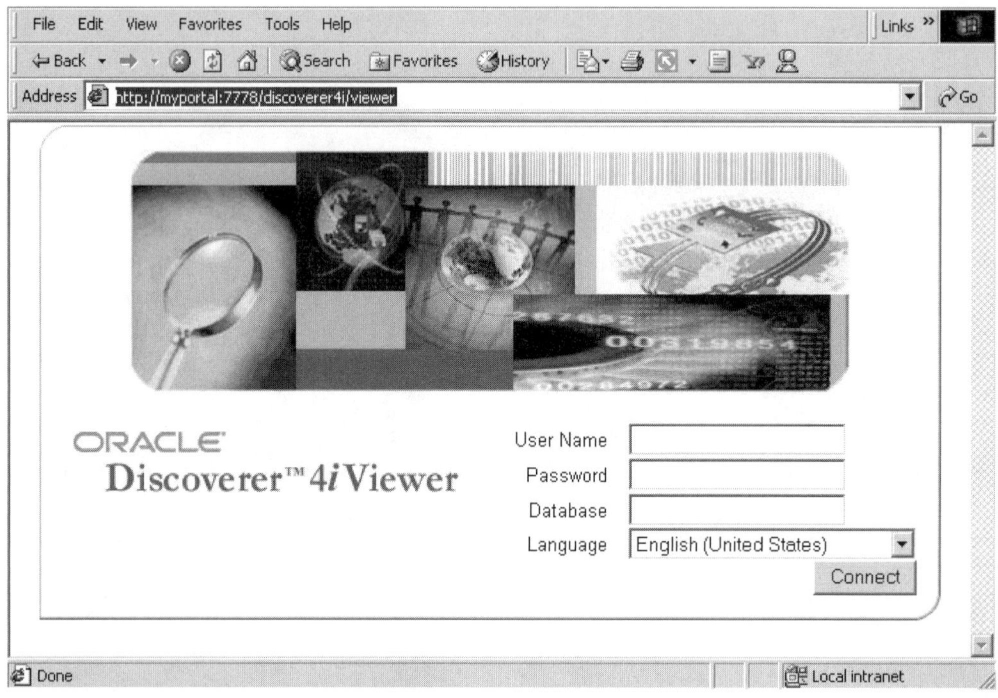

Figure 16.46 Running Discoverer4*i* Viewer.

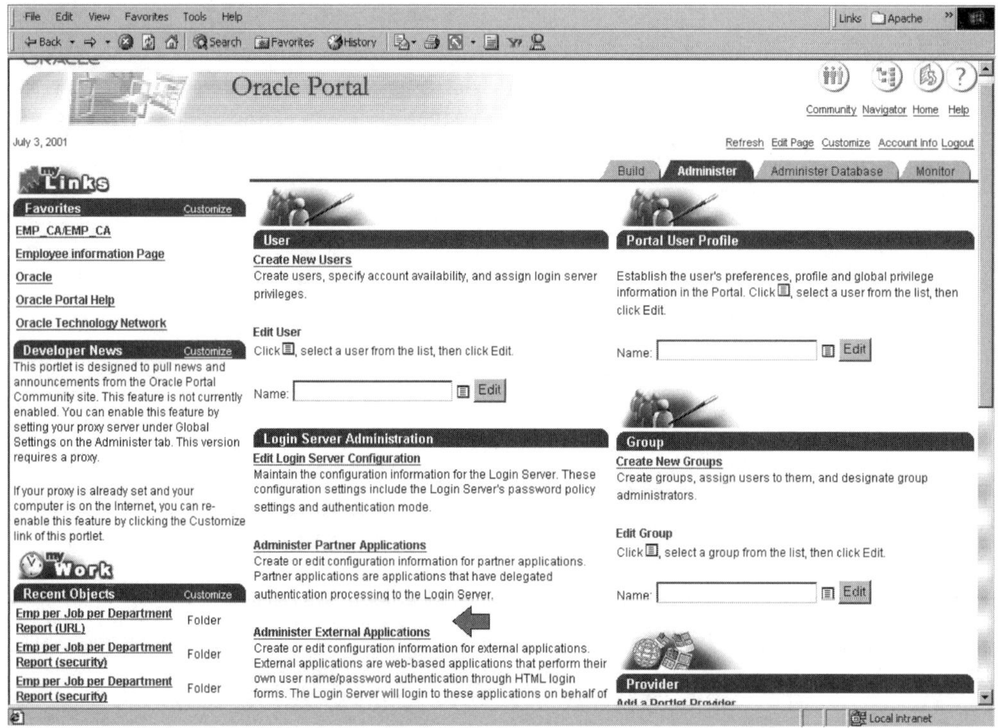

Figure 16.47 Oracle Portal Home Page: Administer Tab: Login Server Administration Portlet.

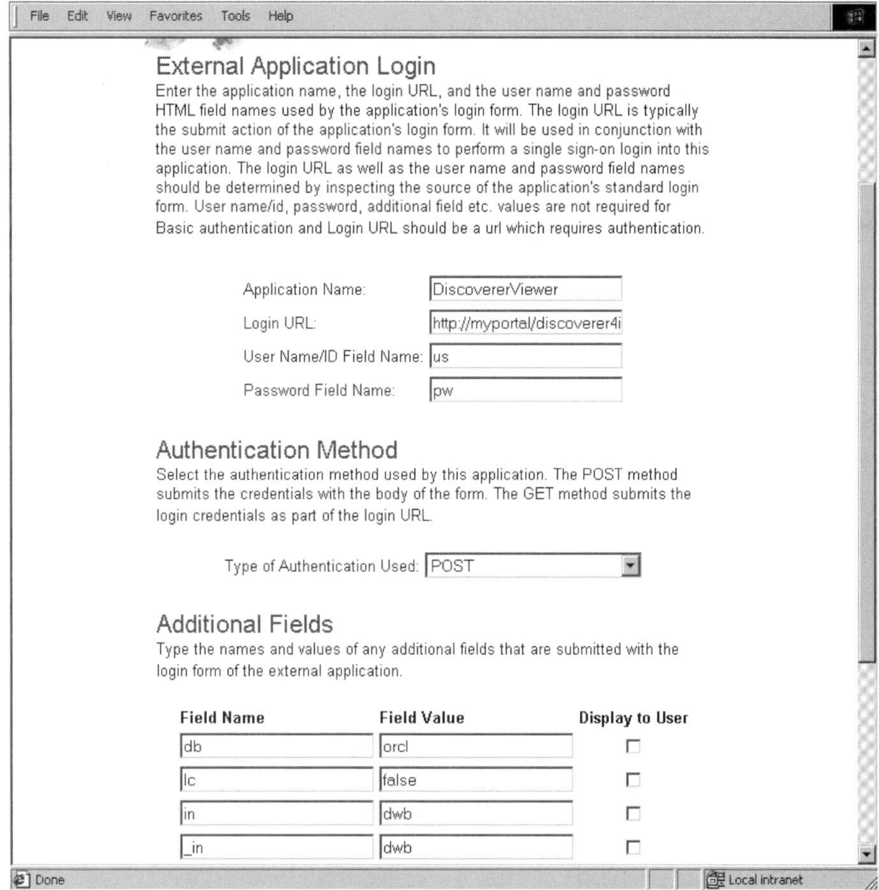

Figure 16.48 Add an External Application Login.

option (Figure 16.51). Next, choose the "Oracle Internet Directory" option (Figure 16.52). If you have a local existing 8*i* database instance, the installer asks if you want to use it for OiD or if you want to create a new one (Figure 16.53). The OiD database instance has to have the UTF8 character set. When you click "Next", the installer asks you for an SID for the new instance (e.g., OID) and then starts installing the OiD executables. When the installer finishes installing the executables, it starts the OiD Configuration Assistant to create the new database instance (Figure 16.54) and to create the OiD schema objects.

When the installation finishes, the OiD instance is created and a new service is added in the services and started. This new service is called "OracleDirectoryService" (Figure 16.55). To verify that the Oracle Internet Directory is working, you can run the Oracle Directory Manager to connect to the directory service (Figure 16.56). The first time the manager runs, it will display the message in Figure 16.57. To log in to OiD Manager, enter the super username: orcladmin; password: welcome; and server: the hostname where you have installed the OiD and where the direc-

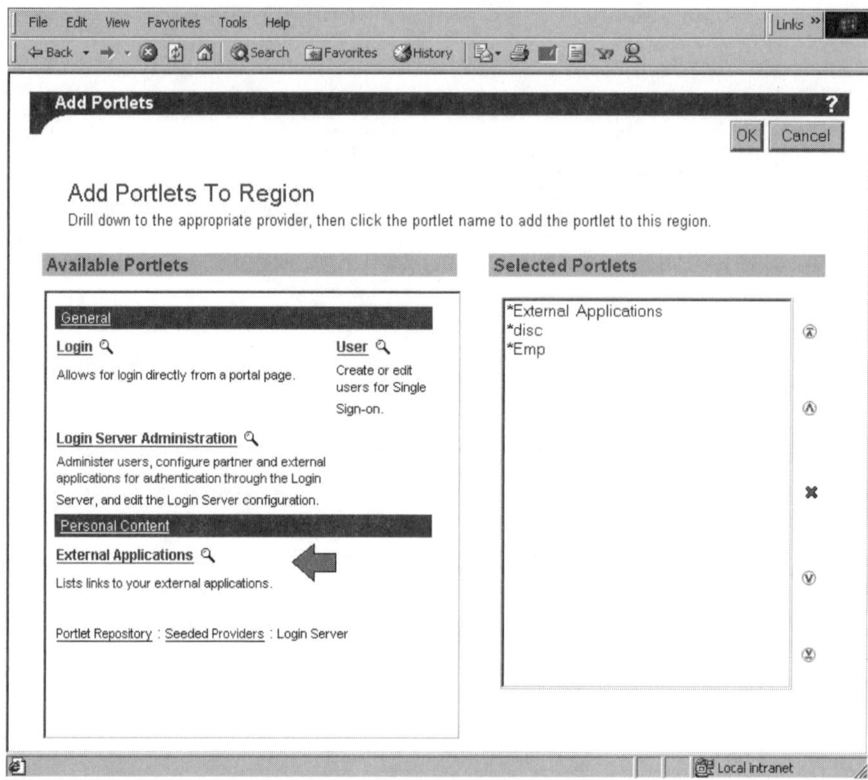

Figure 16.49 Portlet Repository: Login Server Provider.

tory service is running (Figure 16.58). If the server name is not displayed by default, you need to click on the "Select Server" button on the left side of the "Server" Field to display the LDAP servers (Figure 16.59), where you can add your hostname as a server manually. When logged in successfully, you should see the screen in Figure 16.60.

Configuring O9*i*AS Portal for External Authentication

You need to perform the following steps to configure Oracle9*i*AS Portal to use Oracle Internet Directory in authenticating users, so when a user specifies his or her username and password to log into Portal, Portal will verify the user information in Oracle Internet Directory and allow the user to log in.

Step 1

Copy the file <iAS_ORACLE_HOME>\portal30\admin\plsql\sso\ssoxldap.dll from the O9*i*AS Portal machine to the <DB_ORACLE_HOME>\bin\ssoxldap.dll in the Oracle Internet Directory machine.

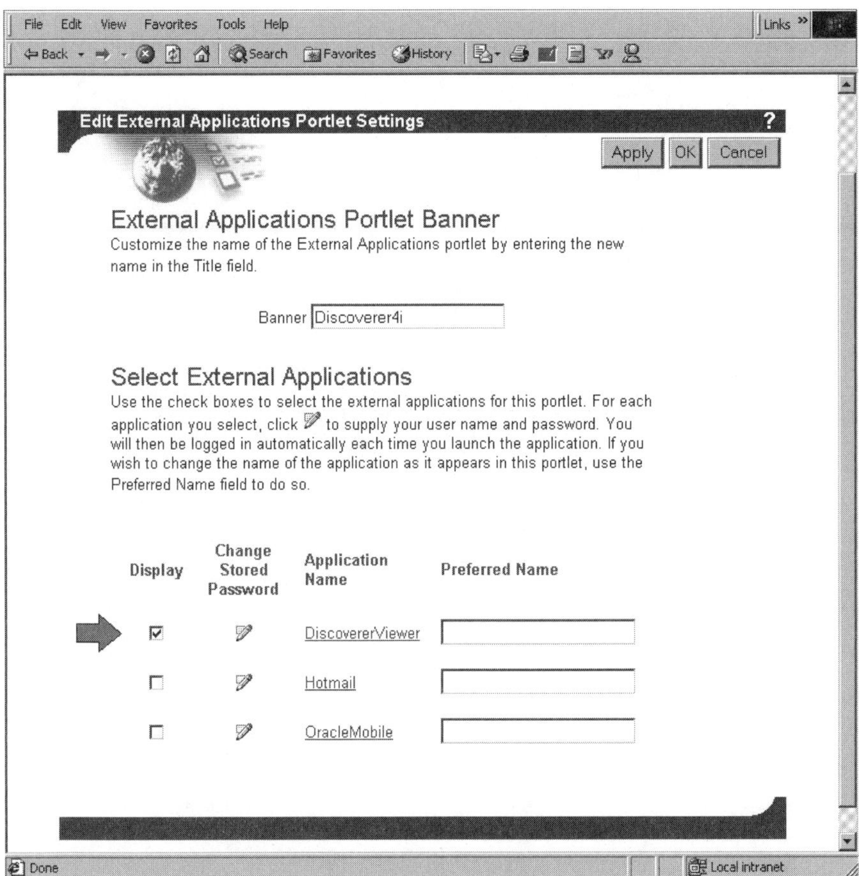

Figure 16.50 External Applications: Edit Defaults.

Step 2

Log into the Portal Login Server schema (i.e., PORTAL30_SSO) using SQL*Plus and run the following command to create the external library, change "c:\Oracle\Ora81" with your OiD ORACLE-HOME:

```
create or replace library auth_ext as
'C:\Oracle\Ora81\bin\ssoxldap.dll';
```

Step 3

When a user tries to log into Oracle Portal, the Login Server schema makes LDAP API calls (external procedure calls) to the LDAP directory. The database that the Login Server (PORTAL30_SSO) resides in must have a configured TNS listener for external procedure

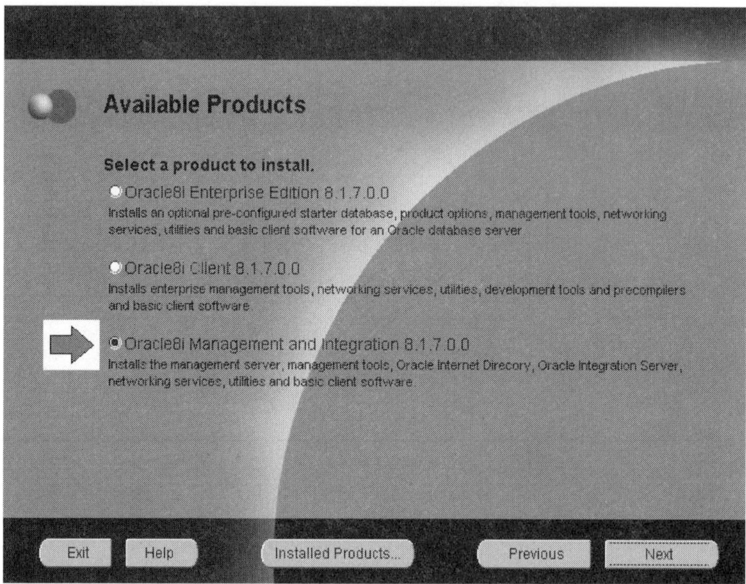

Figure 16.51 Oracle8*i* Database 8.1.7 Installation: Available Products.

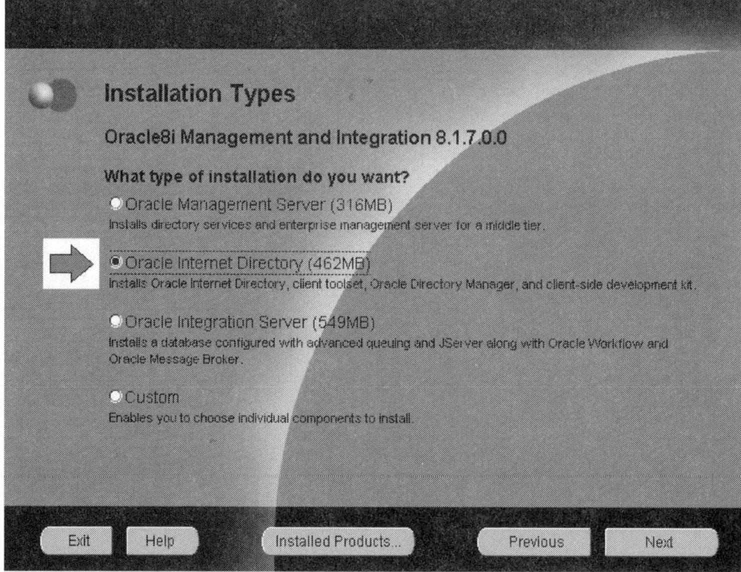

Figure 16.52 Oracle8*i* Database 8.1.7 Installation: Installation Types.

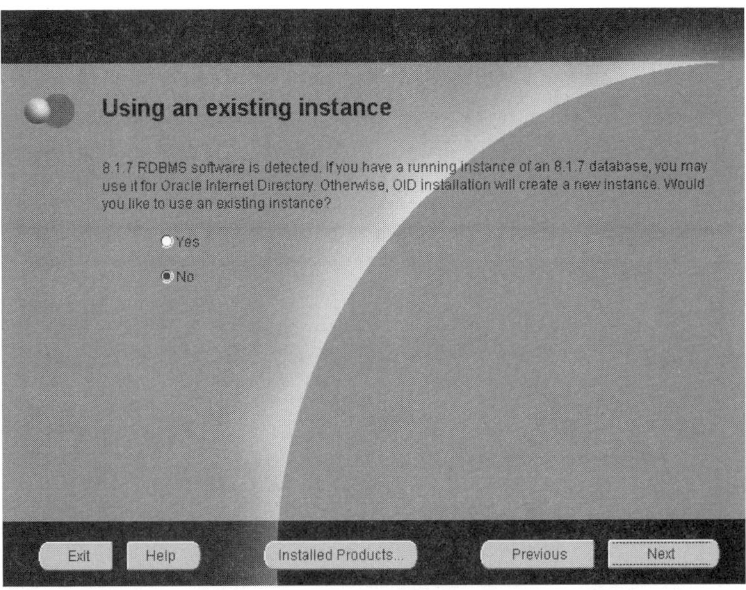

Figure 16.53 Oracle8i 8.1.7 OiD Installation: Using an Existing Instance.

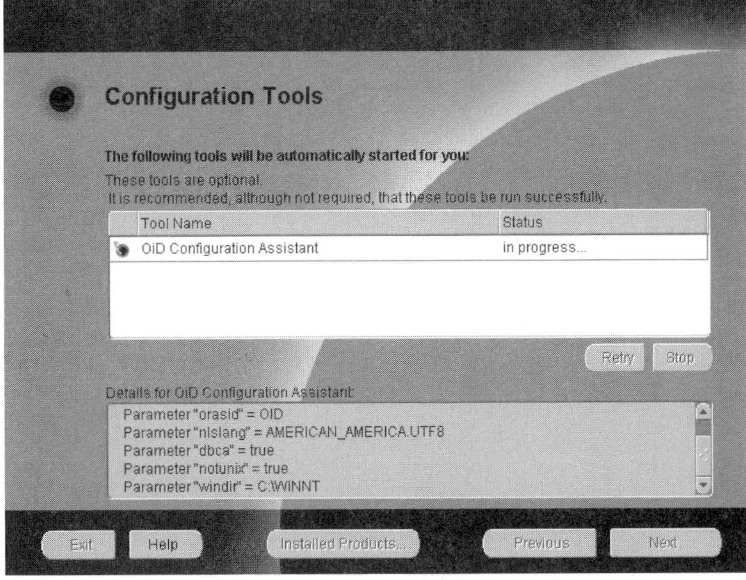

Figure 16.54 Oracle8i 8.1.7 OiD Installation: OiD Configuration Assistant.

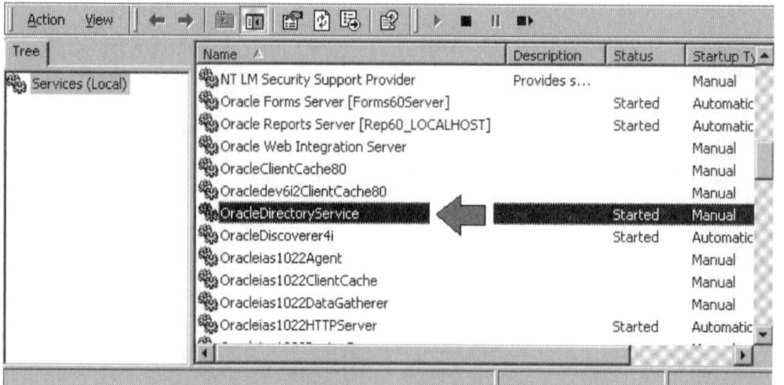

Figure 16.55
Windows 2000: Control Panel Services: OracleDirectoryService.

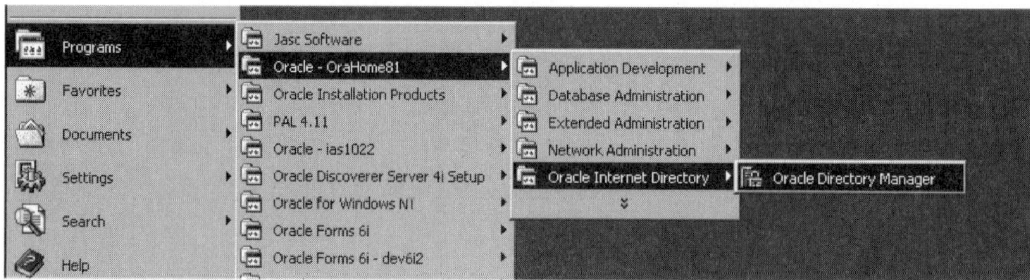

Figure 16.56 Starting Oracle Directory Manager.

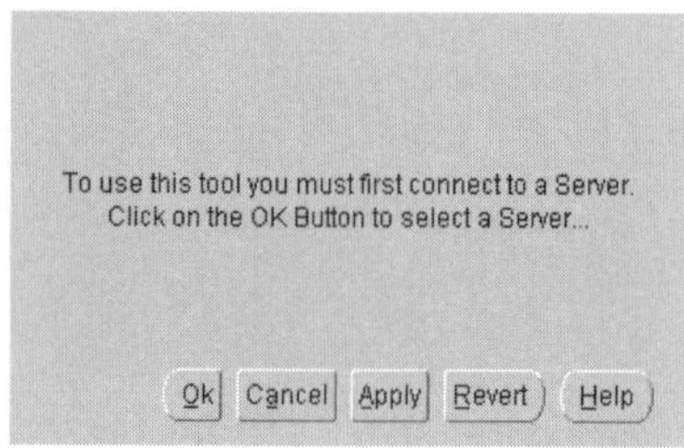

Figure 16.57
Oracle Directory Manager Connection Message.

(PLSExtProc) calls. In Oracle8*i* the listener should be configured by default for external procedure calls. Check the <DB_ORACLE_HOME>\network\admin\listener.ora file to make sure that it has an EXTPROC0 entry, such as:

```
LISTENER =
  (DESCRIPTION_LIST =
```

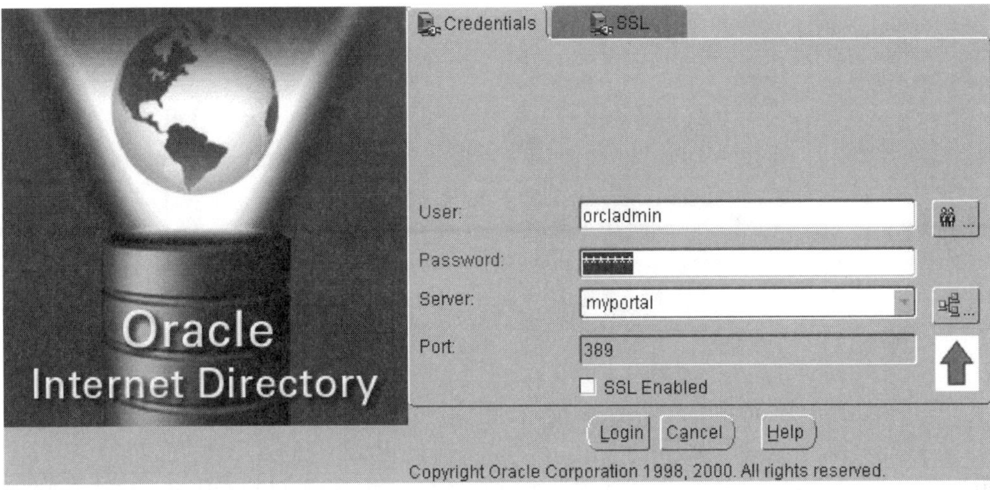

Figure 16.58 Oracle Directory Manager: Login.

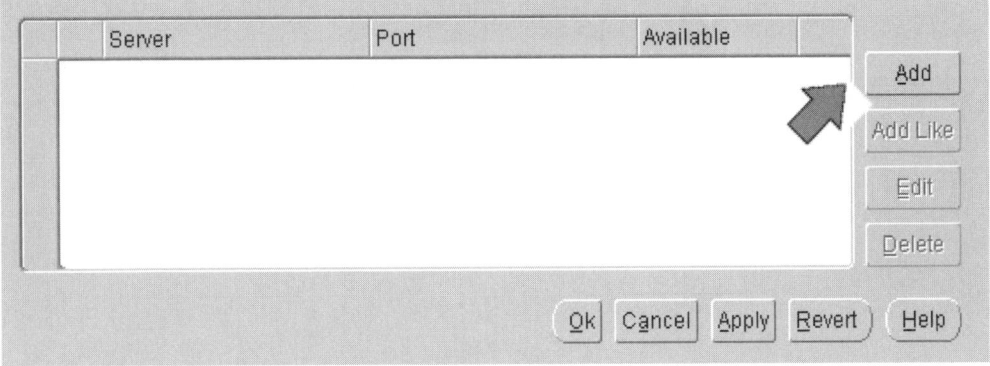

Figure 16.59 Oracle Directory Manager: LDAP Servers.

```
    (DESCRIPTION =
      (ADDRESS_LIST =
        (ADDRESS = (PROTOCOL = IPC)(KEY = EXTPROC0))
      )
      (ADDRESS_LIST =
        (ADDRESS = (PROTOCOL = TCP)(HOST = myportal)
            (PORT = 1521))
      )
)
```

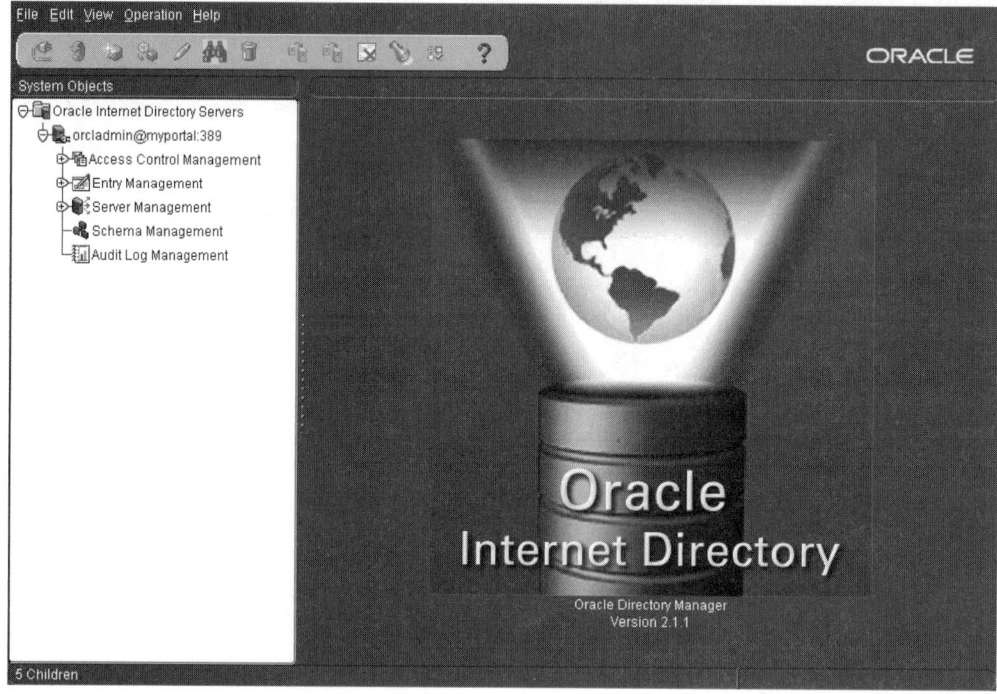

Figure 16.60 Oracle Directory Manager.

```
      (DESCRIPTION =
        (PROTOCOL_STACK =
          (PRESENTATION = GIOP)
          (SESSION = RAW)
        )
        (ADDRESS = (PROTOCOL = TCP)(HOST = myportal)(PORT =
        2481))
      )
    )
  SID_LIST_LISTENER =
    (SID_LIST =
      (SID_DESC =
        (SID_NAME - PLSExtProc)
        (ORACLE_HOME = C:\oracle\ora81)
        (PROGRAM = extproc)
      )
      (SID_DESC =
```

```
        (GLOBAL_DBNAME = ORCL)
        (ORACLE_HOME = C:\oracle\ora81)
        (SID_NAME = ORCL)
      )
      (SID_DESC =
        (GLOBAL_DBNAME = OID)
        (ORACLE_HOME = C:\oracle\ora81)
        (SID_NAME = OID)
      )
    )
```

Also, the <DB_ORACLE_HOME>\network\admin\tnsnames.ora file should have an EXTPROC _CONNECTION_DATA entry, such as:

```
EXTPROC_CONNECTION_DATA =
  (DESCRIPTION =
    (ADDRESS_LIST =
      (ADDRESS = (PROTOCOL = IPC)(KEY = EXTPROC0))
    )
    (CONNECT_DATA =
      (SID = PLSExtProc)
      (PRESENTATION = RO)
    )
  )
```

To test the PLSExtProc entry, you can run the "lsnrctl" command; you should see the PLSExtProc entry.

Step 4

Now you are ready to switch the Portal Login Server to external LDAP authentication mode. Log into the PORTAL30_SSO schema through SQL*Plus and run the <iAS_ORACLE_HOME>\portal30\admin\plsql\sso\ssoldap.sql script (Figure 16.61). The script prompts you for the following:

- Host: your OiD server; for example, myportal.
- Port: the OiD port number; default port number is 389.
- Search Base: You need to specify exactly the following text: "cn=Login Server (portal30_sso)".
- Unique Attribute: cn
- Bind DN: You need to specify the following text: "cn=orcladmin".
- Bind Password: welcome.

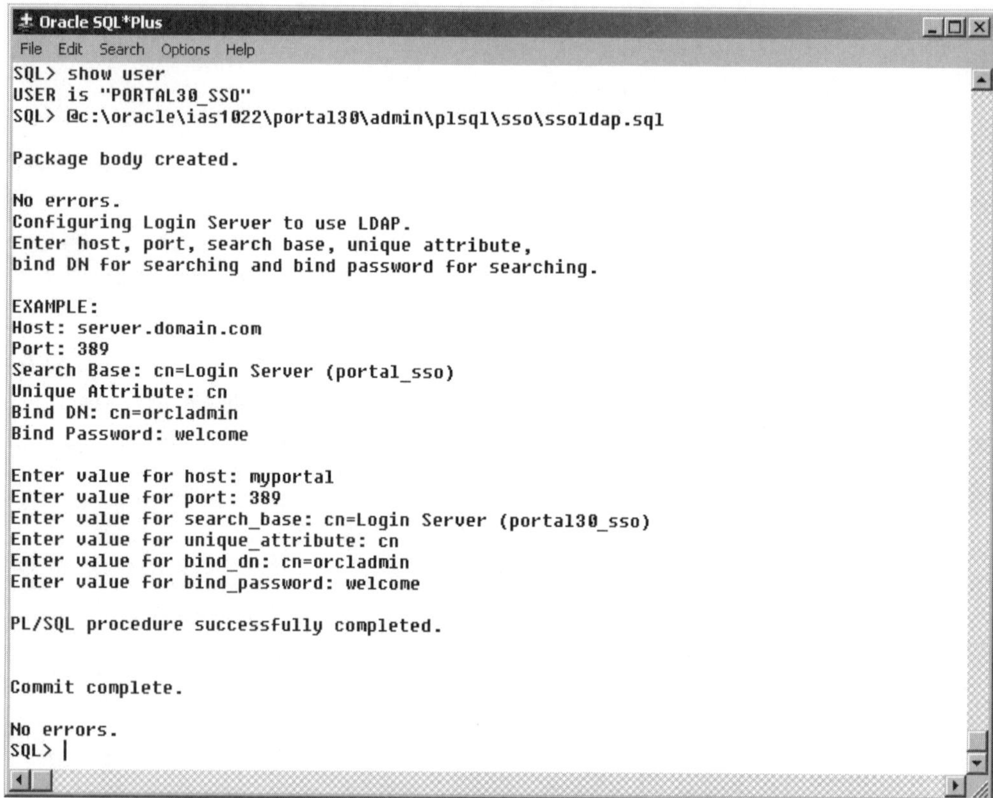
```
SQL> show user
USER is "PORTAL30_SSO"
SQL> @c:\oracle\ias1022\portal30\admin\plsql\sso\ssoldap.sql

Package body created.

No errors.
Configuring Login Server to use LDAP.
Enter host, port, search base, unique attribute,
bind DN for searching and bind password for searching.

EXAMPLE:
Host: server.domain.com
Port: 389
Search Base: cn=Login Server (portal_sso)
Unique Attribute: cn
Bind DN: cn=orcladmin
Bind Password: welcome

Enter value for host: myportal
Enter value for port: 389
Enter value for search_base: cn=Login Server (portal30_sso)
Enter value for unique_attribute: cn
Enter value for bind_dn: cn=orcladmin
Enter value for bind_password: welcome

PL/SQL procedure successfully completed.


Commit complete.

No errors.
SQL> |
```

Figure 16.61 Running the SSOLDAP Script to Switch the Login Server to External LDAP Authentication Mode.

If you get the error WWC-41655 when trying to log into Oracle Portal, check the values specified for the `ssoldap` script. The values are case- and whitespace-sensitive. To query the values from the database, execute the following query in the SSO schema (i.e., PORTAL30_SSO):

```
set pagesize 1000
select * from wwsso_ext_configuration_info$;
```

Note

You can revert back to Portal local-repository (i.e., internal) authentication by running the script `ssolocal.sql`.

Step 5

You need to populate the OiD LDAP directory with entries from your login server's local repository. Oracle provides a script that you can run to migrate the accounts to the LDAP directory along with their privileges. This script is `ssoldif.sql`, which needs to run as Login Server schema. This script creates an LDIF file containing the user accounts that are available currently in the Login Server.

Before you run the script you need to indicate to the database the file location where the `ssoldif.sql` script can generate the LDIF file; this can be achieved by adding the following line to your Oracle Login Server database instance `init.ora` file and bouncing the instance:

```
UTL_FILE_DIR = c:\Oracle\Ora81\admin\udump
```

When the instance is up again, log in as PORTAL30_SSO using SQL*Plus and run the script <iAS_ORACLE_HOME>\portal30\admin\plsql\sso\ssoldif (Figure 16.62).

The text file `users.ldif` should be generated to directory `c:\oracle\admin\ORCL\udump`. A sample portion of the `users.ldif` file looks like the following:

```
dn: cn=Login Server (portal30_sso)
cn: Login Server (portal30_sso)
description: Central Authentication Authority
```

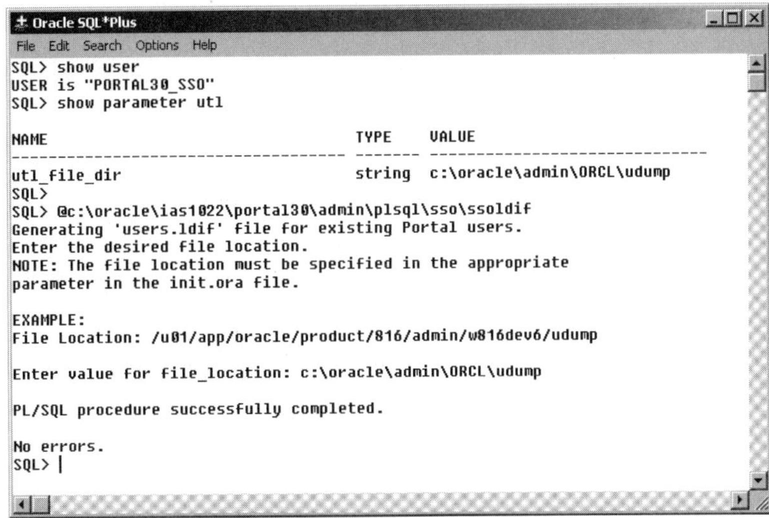

Figure 16.62 Running the SSOLDIF Script to Generate the Login Server Local Repository Users.

```
objectClass: top
objectClass: applicationProcess

dn: cn=PORTAL30_SSO, cn=Login Server (portal30_sso)
sn: PORTAL30_SSO
cn: PORTAL30_SSO
userPassword: portal30_sso
objectClass: top
objectClass: person

dn: cn=PORTAL30_SSO_ADMIN, cn=Login Server (portal30_sso)
sn: PORTAL30_SSO_ADMIN
cn: PORTAL30_SSO_ADMIN
userPassword: portal30_sso_admin
objectClass: top
objectClass: person

dn: cn=PUBLIC, cn=Login Server (portal30_sso)
sn: PUBLIC
cn: PUBLIC
userPassword: public
objectClass: top
objectClass: person

dn: cn=PORTAL30, cn=Login Server (portal30_sso)
sn: PORTAL30
cn: PORTAL30
userPassword: portal30
objectClass: top
objectClass: person

dn: cn=PORTAL30_ADMIN, cn=Login Server (portal30_sso)
sn: PORTAL30_ADMIN
cn: PORTAL30_ADMIN
userPassword: portal30_admin
objectClass: top
objectClass: person

dn: cn=ALFAROUK, cn=Login Server (portal30_sso)
sn: ALFAROUK
cn: ALFAROUK
```

```
userPassword: alfarouk
objectClass: top
objectClass: person
```

You need to add the entries of the `users.ldif` to the LDAP directory using the Oracle Internet Directory's `ldapadd` command line utility. Go to DOS and execute the following commands, replacing "myportal" with your hostname that has the OiD directory server:

```
cd c:\oracle\admin\ORCL\udump
ldapadd -h myportal -p 389 -D cn=orcladmin -w welcome -f users.ldif
```

Now you can log into Oracle Portal and this will use the LDAP directory. You can create new users in the Oracle Directory Manager. The easiest way to create a new user is to create it like an existing user (Figure 16.63). You need to provide the following fields to define the new account: cn, dn, sn, userpassword (Figure 16.64). When the user is created, you can try to log into Oracle Portal using the new user. Note that the password is case-sensitive.

Chapter 17 covers Oracle9*i*AS Portal UNIX installation.

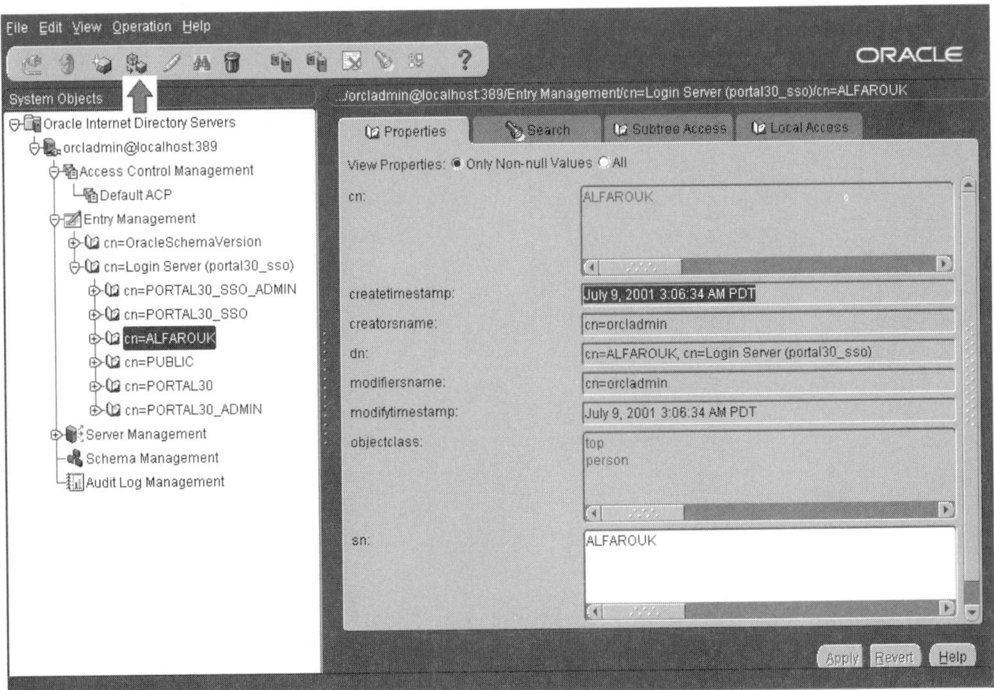

Figure 16.63 Oracle Directory Manager: Entry Management: Display User.

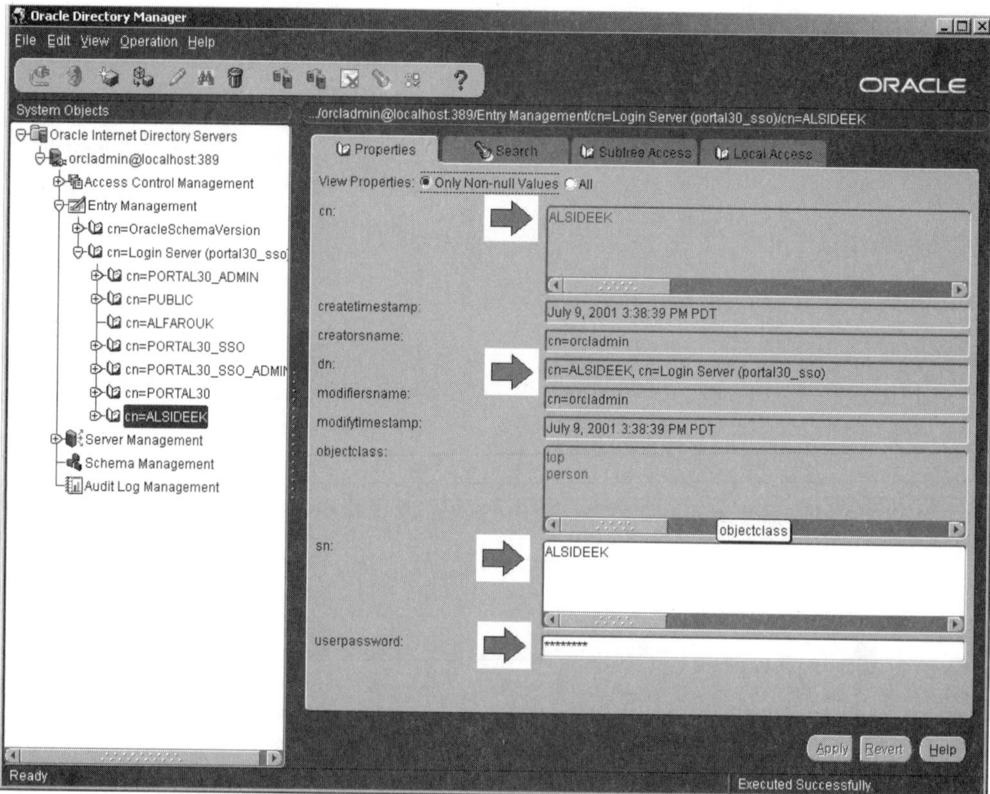

Figure 16.64 Oracle Directory Manager: Entry Management: Add a New User.

PART IV

Oracle Portal for the DBA

CHAPTER 17

Installing Oracle9*i*AS and Configuring Oracle Portal on UNIX

Introduction

We have already covered installation on Microsoft Windows NT/2000. This chapter covers the installation of the 8.1.7 database and O9*i*AS 1.0.2.x on a UNIX operating system. This chapter assumes that you have some knowledge of at least one UNIX operating system and its commands, so it does not explain in detail each UNIX command or the differences between UNIX shells. Sparc Solaris 8 is used as a sample in this chapter, because of its big market share as an operating system for database servers, Web servers, and application servers. With minor modifications, the installation steps can be applied to other UNIX operating systems such as Linux, AIX, and HP/UX.

Database Installation

You can skip this section if you already have an existing database instance up and running.

Preinstallation Steps

Before you start the installation, you need to read both the release notes and the installation guides of your platform for the certified operating system versions required and patches and hardware recommendations. This section describes the main preinstallation steps.

Note

Most of the database and O9*i* Application Server installation steps are similar to the Windows NT/2000 installation steps covered earlier in this book. The following steps concentrate on the UNIX-specific steps.

---

1. Change the UNIX Kernel parameters. You need to increase the values of some of the Kernel parameters for the operating system to be able to accommodate the database (such as the SGA). Some of these parameters' values depend on the database version, how many databases you will have, and how many users will be connecting to each. For example, for a Solaris Sparc server that will hold two 8.1.7 databases, each with a couple of hundred users, the following lines need to be added to the /etc/system:

```
set shmsys:shminfo_shmmax=4294967295
set shmsys:shminfo_shmmin=1
set shmsys:shminfo_shmmni=100
set shmsys:shminfo_shmseg=50
set semsys:seminfo_semmni=100
set semsys:seminfo_semmsl=500
set semsys:seminfo_semmns=2000
set semsys:seminfo_semopm=100
set semsys:seminfo_semvmx=32767
```

   The server has to be rebooted for these values to take effect. You need to refer to the installation guide of your Oracle database version on your specific platform for the exact values and calculation formulas for these parameters.
2. Create the UNIX groups: oinstall and dba. You can create these two groups using the "admintool" GUI UNIX tool or using the "groupadd" UNIX command. The oinstall group will have all the UNIX users who can install and uninstall Oracle software. The dba group will have all the UNIX users who are SYSDBA database users (to start up, shut down, and recover the databases).
3. I recommend that you have a separate file system (i.e., mount point such as /u01) to hold your ORACLE_HOME of your Oracle software. You should also create other mount points (e.g., /u02, /u03, /u04) to hold your database files and to be able to mirror your online redo log files and control files across them. These mount points need to be owned by the oracle UNIX user and the dba UNIX group. You can create the mount points as UNIX super user root, then change their ownership by executing the following UNIX commands:

```
chown oracle:dba u01
chown oracle:dba u02
chown oracle:dba u03
chown oracle:dba u04
```

4. Create the UNIX user oracle, which will be the UNIX owner of the Oracle Database Server installation files. You can use either the "admintool" or "useradd" command. Set the primary group of the oracle user to be "oinstall" and the "dba" group as secondary. You can set its home directory as /u01/app/oracle/product/8.1.7.

5. Add the Oracle environment variables settings to your UNIX oracle user environment. For example, in Korn Shell (i.e., ksh), you can set the variables inside the ".profile" file in the home directory of the UNIX user.

```
ORACLE_BASE=/u01/app/oracle
export ORACLE_BASE
ORACLE_HOME=$ORACLE_BASE/product/8.1.7
export ORACLE_HOME
ORACLE_SID=op30
export ORACLE_SID
PATH=/usr/bin:/etc:/usr/ccs/bin:/usr/openwin/bin:/usr/ucb:/
     user/local/bin:$ORACLE_HOME/bin
export PATH
DISPLAY=kortobah:0.0
export DISPLAY
```

   Replace "kortobah" in the DISPLAY parameter with the machine name from which you will be doing the installation. Replace the directory name "8.1.7" with your database version. Replace the "op30" with your chosen ORACLE_SID for your Oracle Portal instance.
6. Mount the Database CD-ROM. In Solaris 8 the CD-ROM is mounted automatically when inserted under the /cdrom file system (i.e., /cdrom/oracle8i).

Installation Steps

1. Log in as UNIX user oracle (to make sure that the environment variables are in effect), and then start the Oracle Universal Installer by running the following commands:

```
cd /cdrom/oracle8i
./runInstaller
```

2. When the OUI starts, you need to provide the oinstall UNIX group name (Figure 17.1). If the installer does not start, double check your DISPLAY environment setting and make sure that the workstation you are using is added to the server xhost list; if not you need to add it using the following command:

```
xhost +<workstationname>
```

3. OUI asks you to run the $ORACLE_HOME/orainstRoot.sh script as UNIX user root. You need to open a new shell (i.e., terminal window) and log in as root to run the script and then click on the "Retry" button (Figure 17.2).
4. The OUI will create a new database with the name defined in the environment variable OR-

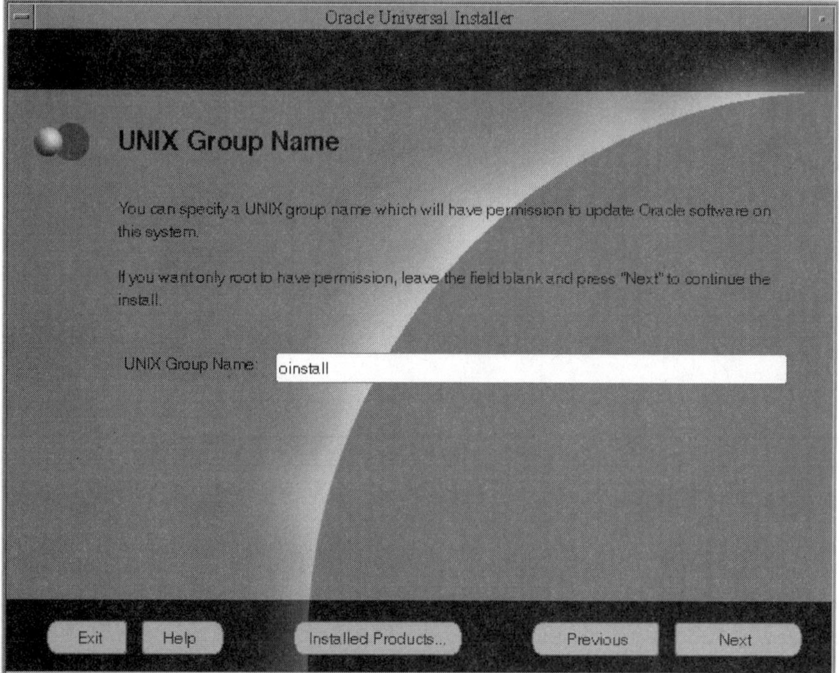

Figure 17.1 OUI: UNIX Group Name.

ACLE_SID. The OUI prompts you for the location of your database files (Figure 17.3). For a better performance, place the database files into a different file system than the Oracle software.

5. The rest of the installation steps are similar to the steps covered in the database on Windows installation, until the software installation is over. The OUI asks you to run the root.sh script (under $ORACLE_HOME) as the root UNIX user. It is a good idea to have a local user binary directory if you do not have one already (i.e., /usr/local/bin), because the root.sh script prompts you for its directory name. The script creates the file /var/opt/oracle/oratab that should have a line for each database in your server, so the dbstart and dbshut scripts (under $ORACLE_HOME/bin) can be used to start and shut down more than one database.
6. You need to automate the start up and shut down procedures of the database by adding a script to be called by UNIX after the operating system startup and before the shutdown. You can get more information by reading the database installation guide and the database administration reference for the UNIX platform.
7. Add an entry for your database in the $ORACLE_HOME/network/tnsnames.ora (i.e., op30). Next, check connecting to the database by running the following command:

```
sqlplus scott/tiger@op30
```

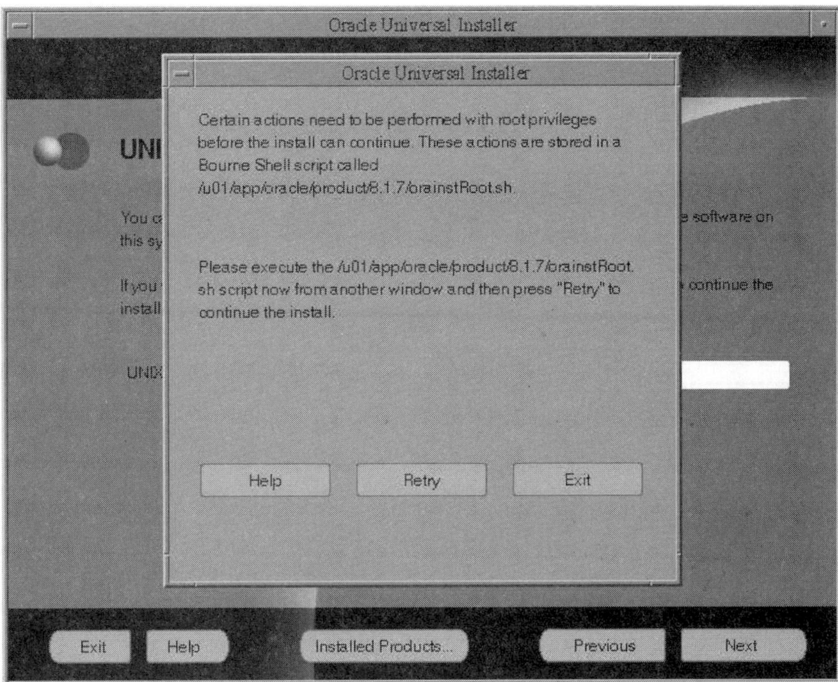

Figure 17.2 OUI: orainstRoot.sh.

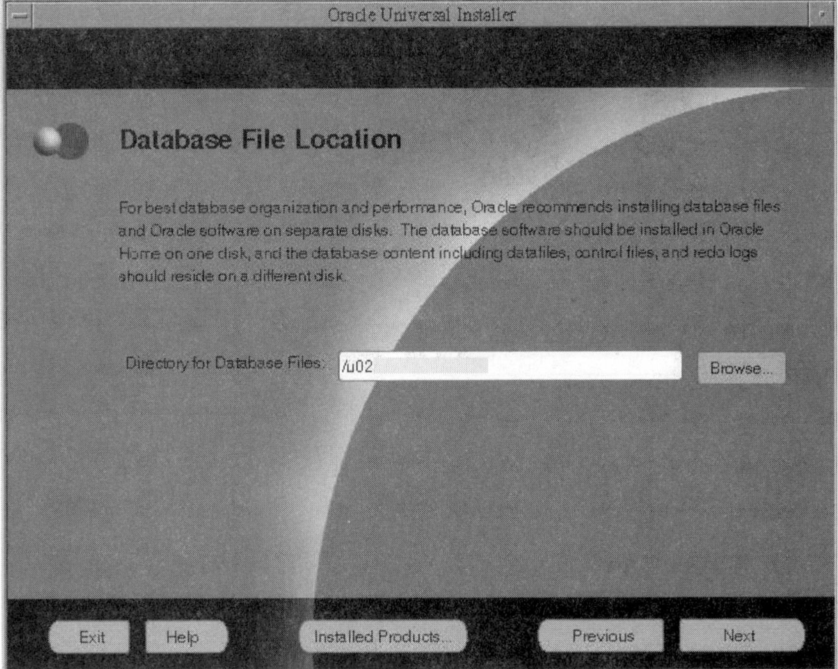

Figure 17.3 OUI: Database File Location.

Oracle9*i*AS Installation

Now that you have a database instance up and running, you can start the Oracle9*i*AS installation. The examples used in this section are taken from O9*i*AS 1.0.2.1 (i.e., Oracle9*i*AS Portal 3.0.8) installation on Sparc Solaris 8. Before you start the installation, you need to read both the release notes and the installation guides of your platform for the certified operating system versions required and patches and hardware recommendations.

Preinstallation Steps

Before you start the installation, you need to perform the following steps:

1. Create the UNIX groups: oinstall and dba, if they do not exist.
2. Create a new UNIX user o9*i*as, which will be the UNIX owner of the O9*i*AS installation files. You can use the database UNIX user (i.e., oracle) to be the owner but maintaining the environment variables will be an overhead. Set the primary group of the o9*i*as UNIX user to "oinstall" and its secondary group to be "dba". You can set its home directory to be /u01 /app/oracle/product/1.0.2.1.
3. Edit the ".profile" of the user o9*i*as to include the following:

```
ORACLE_BASE=/u01/app/oracle
export ORACLE_BASE
ORACLE_HOME=$ORACLE_BASE/product/1.0.2.1
export ORACLE_HOME
PATH=/usr/bin:/etc:/usr/ccs/bin:/usr/openwin/bin:/usr/ucb:$
      ORACLE_HOME/bin:$ORACLE_HOME/Apache/Apache/bin
export PATH
LD_LIBRARY_PATH=$ORACLE_HOME/lib
export LD_LIBRARY_PATH
DISPLAY kortobah:0.0
export DISPLAY
```

This chapter refers to the ORACLE_HOME of the Oracle9*i* Application Server by <iAS_ORACLE_HOME>, so it is not confused with the database ORACLE_HOME.

The recommended init.ora parameters in Table 2.1 need to be applied to the portal database. Also, you need to create new tablespaces and add free space to the SYSTEM tablespace to have similar storage layout to Figure 2.24.

You can use the DBA Studio to perform administrative tasks on your database. To start the DBA Studio, log in as the UNIX oracle user and execute the following command:

```
oemapp dbastudio
```

Installation Steps

When you insert the first O9*i*AS CD-ROM, it should automatically be mounted; if not, then you need to mount it manually using the UNIX "mount" command. Next, log in as the "o9ias" UNIX user and run the Oracle Universal Installer, by changing the current directory to the CD-ROM mount point, and execute the following command:

```
./runInstaller
```

1. The OUI displays the installation overview screen where you can click on the "help" button for more information (Figure 17.4). Next, it prompts you for the UNIX installation group name (i.e., oinstall), then for the installation location (i.e., /u01/app/oracle/procut/1.0.2.1).
2. Next you need to choose an installation type (Figure 17.5). The O9*i*AS version 1.0.2.1 first installation type is called "Minimal"; this is equivalent to the O9*i*AS version 1.0.2.0 "Oracle HTTP Server only" installation.
3. Next, you can deselect the components that you do not want to install in the component configuration and startup screen (Figure 17.6).
4. The installation and configuration of O9*i*AS Database Cache and Web Cache are not

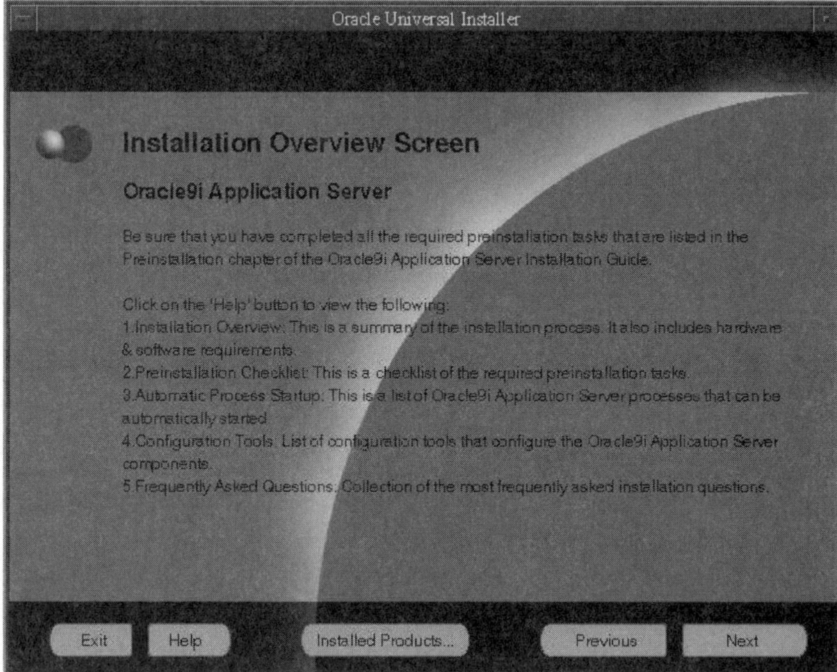

Figure 17.4 OUI: O9*i*AS 1.0.2.1 Installation Overview.

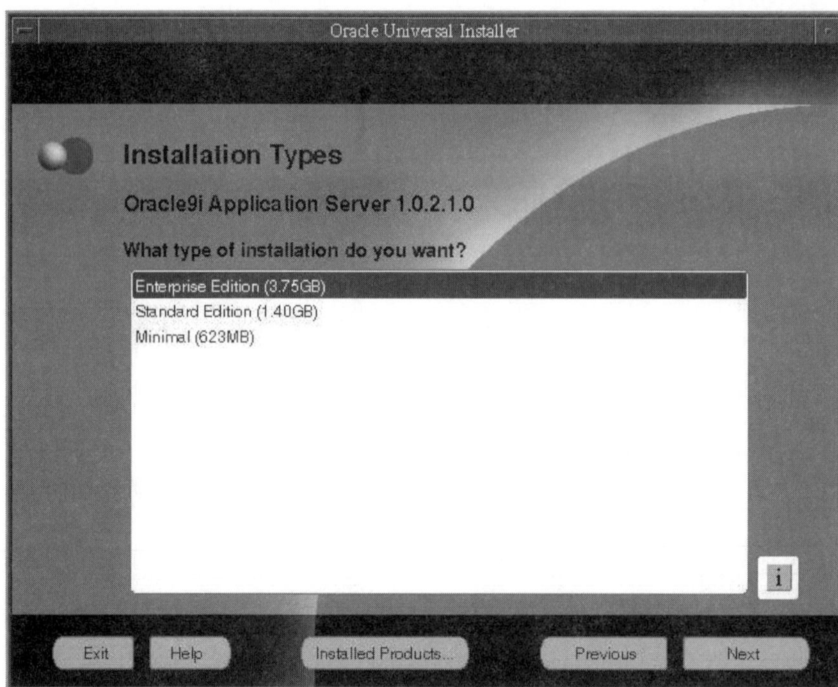

Figure 17.5 OUI: O9*i*AS 1.0.2.1 Installation Types.

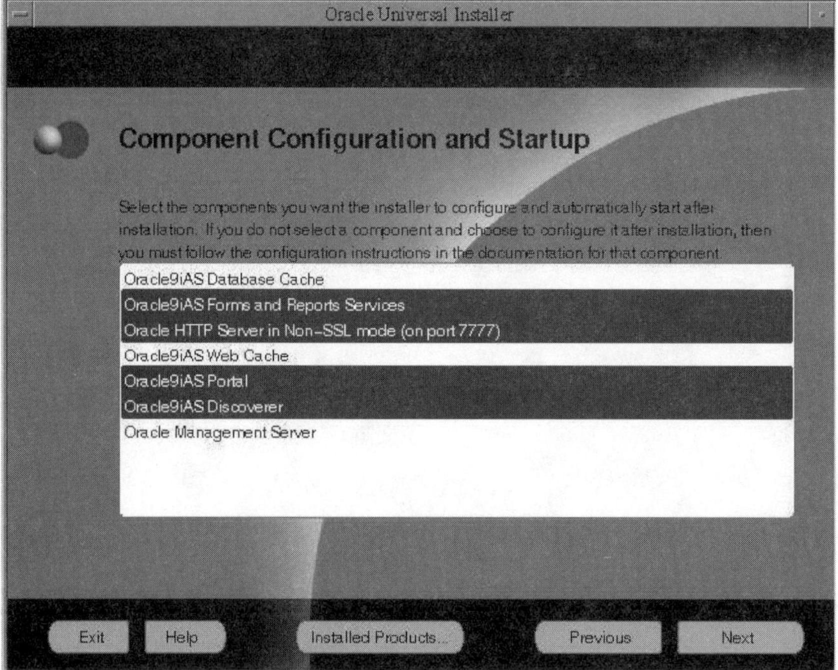

Figure 17.6 OUI: O9*i*AS 1.0.2.1 Enterprise Installation: Component Configuration and Startup.

covered in this book, but you might need to provide connection information to an origin database (database to be cached; Figure 17.7 and Figure 17.8). If you unselect the Database Cache from the component list, this information is not used in the installation.

5. The next step is to specify the portal Data Access Descriptor information (PORTAL30).
6. Next you specify the Login Server Data Access Descriptor (PORTAL30_SSO).

Note

If you are installing O9*i*AS 1.0.2.0 on Linux, you need to specify the location of the JDK. If you do not have an installed JDK, you can download a JDK version for Linux from Internet sites such as http://www.blackdown.org.

---

7. The next step is to provide the repository information for Oracle9*i* Application Server Wireless Edition (formerly known as Oracle Portal-to-Go). It is a good idea to provide the information needed for the installer to create the O9*i*AS Wireless repository even if you are not planning on using it. The reason is that you might get errors in the installation when the installer tries to create the repository with an empty username.

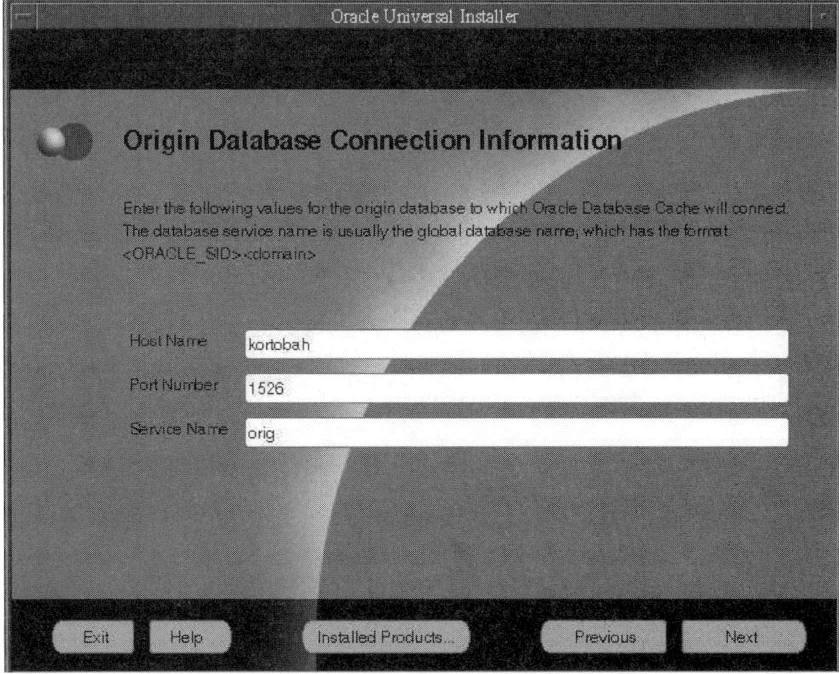

Figure 17.7 OUI: O9*i*AS 1.0.2.1 Origin Database Connection Information.

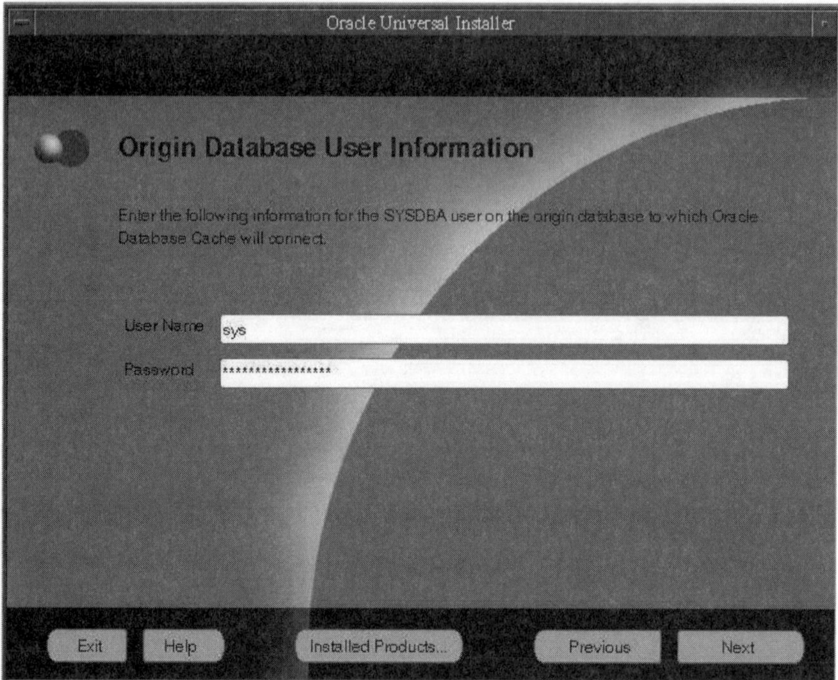

Figure 17.8 OUI: O9*i*AS 1.0.2.1 Origin Database User Information.

You can use any username to be the owner of your Oracle9*i* Application Server Wireless Edition repository, as long as it is a valid Oracle database username, and it does not already exist in the database.

For the installer to create the Oracle9*i* Application Server Wireless Edition repository owner, it needs to connect as a DBA account, so it will prompt you for the SYSTEM account password. Now, the installation is ready to proceed by giving you a summary list of the products to be installed. The installation might take from 30 minutes to 1.5 hours depending on your hardware. Oracle9*i*AS 1.0.2.1 has five CDs, and you will be asked to mount each one of them (maybe not in sequential order, so you need to check carefully the number of the CD requested). When you are prompted for another CD, make sure that your existing session current directory is not inside the CD-ROM file system. Next, unmount/eject the current CD-ROM, insert the requested one, and click "OK".

OUI will ask you to run the <iAS_ORACLE_HOME>/root.sh script by the root UNIX user (Figure 17.9). Once the O9*i*AS executables and files are installed to the <iAS_ORACLE_HOME>, the installer starts the configuration assistants (i.e., Net8, OPCA, etc.).

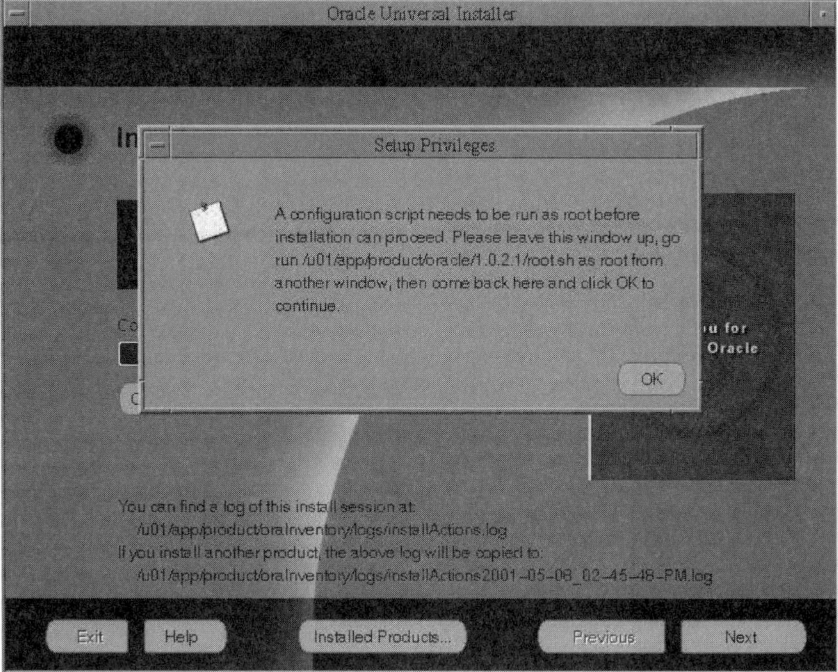

Figure 17.9 OUI: Setup Privileges.

Also, the installer starts the Apache server on port 7777 (the default port number of Apache in non-SSL mode on UNIX), Forms Server, and Reports Server. The installer starts the Oracle Portal 3.0 Configuration Assistant. The configuration assistant steps are very similar to the ones covered earlier for Windows NT/2000. Once the installation is finished, you can test that the Oracle HTTP server is working by typing the following URL into your browser: http://<Hostname>:7777.

You can click on the "mod_plsql" to test that the "pls" virtual path is working fine. One of the new features of Oracle Portal 3.0.8 (O9*i*AS 1.0.2.1) is that the DAD configuration page is protected (i.e., secured). You need to log in to Oracle Portal to be able to access the DADs configuration. In Oracle Portal 3.0.7 (O9*i*AS 1.0.2.0) and earlier, the DADs configurations are accessible to the public (but not the passwords).

Before testing your Oracle Portal, you need to add an entry into your <iAS_ORACLE_HOME>/network/admin/tnsnames.ora to point to the database. You can test the connection to the portal instance by running the sqlplus from your o9ias UNIX user. If you get a successful connection, you are ready to go to the Oracle Portal home page, http://<Hostname>:7777/pls. If you are running into any errors, please refer to Chapter 20 for installation troubleshooting.

If you will be using Oracle9*i*AS Form and Report Services, the OUI should start both automatically. You can start these services manually using the following commands:

```
cd /u01/app/oracle/product/1.0.2.1/6iserver
./forms60_server start
./reports60_server start
```

Chapter 18 describes some Oracle Portal administration tasks.

CHAPTER 18

Oracle Portal Administration and Migration

Introduction

This chapter describes some of the important Oracle Portal administration tasks and their scripts (i.e., commands) that come with Oracle Portal. The chapter first explains ssodatan and ssodatax scripts. Next, the chapter covers how you can export and import contents to and from Oracle Portal. Also, the chapter covers how to set up National Language Support in Oracle Portal. The second half of the chapter explains the process of migrating portal instances to newer versions and describes how you can set up and use Dynamic Services in Oracle 9*i*AS Portal.

Administration Scripts

This section explains different scripts that are provided as part of the Oracle Portal installation.

ssodatan

This script is used to associate an Oracle Portal node to a Login Server. It is located in <iAS_ORACLE_HOME>\portal30\admin\plsql. The script is called automatically by the Oracle9*i* Application Server installation. You need to run it in case there is an error in that association or change of the server name. Refer to some of the cases in Chapter 20. Running this script completely removes any existing configuration information in the Login Server configuration tables and replaces it with the information specified in the script parameters. If you are associating a portal node with an existing Login Server that contains configuration information you want to retain, use the ssodatax, which is described next.

```
ssodatan.cmd -w <portal_url> -l <login_server_url> [-s
<portal_schema>] [-p <portal_password>] [-o <sso_schema>]
[-d <sso_password>] [-c <portal_connect_string>]
```

Parameters Description

-w <PORTAL_URL> PORTAL_URL points to the Oracle Portal node DAD. It includes the full domain name with the host, prefixed by "http://" and appended by a forward slash (/). If Oracle HTTP server *powered by Apache* is listening on a different port number than the default (i.e., 80), you must specify the port number in the Oracle Portal URL.

-l <LOGIN_SERVER_URL> LOGIN_SERVER_URL points to the Login Server host and DAD. It includes the full domain name with the host, prefixed by "http://" and appended by a forward slash "/".

-s <PORTAL_SCHEMA> The Oracle database schema contains the Oracle Portal installation (database objects). Its default value is portal30.

-p <PORTAL_PASSWORD> The Oracle database password of the Oracle Portal schema has a default value of <PORTAL_SCHEMA>.

-o <SSO_SCHEMA> The Oracle database schema for the Login Server objects has a default value of <portal_schema>_SSO.

-d <SSO_PASSWORD> The Oracle database password for the Login Server schema has a default value of <sso_schema>.

-c <PORTAL_CONNECT_STRING> This is the connect string for the database in which the Oracle Portal schema is installed. You may skip this parameter if the Oracle Portal node instance is local and the ORACLE_SID environmental variable is set to the Oracle Portal Database SID. Its default value is null.

In Oracle Portal 3.0.8 and higher (9*i*AS 1.0.2.1), you can use the script to configure a standalone Login Server by the following syntax:

```
ssodatan -loginserver -l <login_server_url> [-o <sso_schema>]
[-d <sso_password>] [-c <portal_connect_string>]
```

Do not use the -w, -s, -p, and -e options with the loginserver parameter.

Also, in Portal 3.0.8 and higher there is another parameter, -e <PSTORE_SCHEMA>. This is the Oracle database password for access to the password store objects.

```
C:\>set ORACLE_HOME=c:\oracle\o9ias

C:\>cd \oracle\o9ias\portal30\admin\plsql

C:\oracle\O9iAS\portal30\admin\plsql>ssodatan -w http://152.68.36.58/pls/portal3
0/ -l http://152.68.36.58/pls/portal30_sso/ -s portal30 -p portal30 -o portal30_
sso -d portal30_sso -c orcl
Associating WebDB to the Login Server
Begining WebDB association to new Login Server"
...webdb_url:              http://152.68.36.58/pls/portal30/
...login_server_url:       http://152.68.36.58/pls/portal30_sso/
...webdb_schema:           portal30
...webdb_password:         ************
...sso_schema:             portal30_sso
...sso_password:           ************
...webdb_connect_string: orcl

SQL*Plus: Release 8.1.7.0.0 - Production on Thu May 10 22:09:02 2001

(c) Copyright 2000 Oracle Corporation.  All rights reserved.


Connected to:
Oracle8i Enterprise Edition Release 8.1.7.0.0 - Production
With the Partitioning option
JServer Release 8.1.7.0.0 - Production

SQL> exit;
Disconnected from Oracle8i Enterprise Edition Release 8.1.7.0.0 - Production
With the Partitioning option
JServer Release 8.1.7.0.0 - Production

SQL*Plus: Release 8.1.7.0.0 - Production on Thu May 10 22:09:11 2001

(c) Copyright 2000 Oracle Corporation.  All rights reserved.


Connected to:
Oracle8i Enterprise Edition Release 8.1.7.0.0 - Production
With the Partitioning option
JServer Release 8.1.7.0.0 - Production

SQL> exit;
Disconnected from Oracle8i Enterprise Edition Release 8.1.7.0.0 - Production
With the Partitioning option
JServer Release 8.1.7.0.0 - Production

SQL*Plus: Release 8.1.7.0.0 - Production on Thu May 10 22:09:18 2001

(c) Copyright 2000 Oracle Corporation.  All rights reserved.


Connected to:
```

Figure 18.1 Sample ssodatan Command Output.

Figure 18.1 shows a sample run of the script on Microsoft Windows NT, using an IP address and the default port 80.

ssodatax

This script is used to add an additional configuration entry to the portal to allow additional Oracle HTTP servers to access the portal node or additional Partner Applications to access the Login Server.

```
ssodatax -i <portal_site_id> -t <portal_site_token> -k
<encryption_key> -w <portal_url> -l <login_server_url>
```

```
[-s <portal_schema>] [-p <portal_password>] [-v <cookie_
version>] [-o <sso_schema>] [-c <connect_string>]
```

Parameters Description

-i <PORTAL_SITE_ID> The ID is automatically set when a Partner Application (including the Oracle Portal installation) is added. It is used by the Login Server to identify the Partner Application.

-t <PORTAL_SITE_TOKEN> The token is automatically set when a Partner Application (including Oracle Portal installation) is added. It is used by the Login Server to identify the Partner Application. The Partner Application must use the application token to identify itself to the Login Server to this node when requesting authentication.

-k <ENCRYPTION_KEY> When a user tries to log into this Oracle Portal node using Single Sign-On, the Login Server generates a cookie that indicates a user's identity and whether the user has been authenticated. This key is used to encrypt the login cookie.

-v <COOKIE_VERSION> The cookie version that is used by the Login Server has a default value of "v1.0".

-w , -l , -s, -p, -o, -c are the same as the ssodatan script.

In Oracle Portal 3.0.8 and later, the following parameters have been added:

-e <PSTORE_SCHEMA> The Oracle database schema used to access the Password Store objects has a default value of <SSO_SCHEMA>_PS.

-r <PSTORE_PASSWORD> The Oracle database password for Password Store access schema has a default value of <PSTORE_SCHEMA>.

-b <PSTORE_DBLINK> The name of the database link used to connect the Oracle Portal schema to the Password Store access schema in another database instance has a default value of <PORTAL_SCHEMA>_DBLINK.

-n <PS_CONNECT_STRING> The connect string used to connect to the Password Store access schema on a remote database has a default value of null.

-remove portal_host This is used to remove the enabler configuration entry associated with the specified portal host.

An example of using this script is covered later in Chapter 19, which is used in setting up a multinode portal environment.

Export and Import Scripts

Often, you need to move contents from one portal environment to another, for example, from your development node to your production node. The content of a page determines what needs to be exported and imported. If the page contains application component portlets, then the application(s) needs to be exported/imported. If the page contains folder(s) portlets or navigation bars portlets, then their content area(s) need to be exported/imported.

This section first explains the export commands in the order that they should be executed. Then it explains the import commands in the order of their execution as well.

Note

Performing exports and imports between different versions is not supported. You have to upgrade the earlier release to the newer release prior to exporting or importing its contents.

The export and import scripts can be found in <iAS_ORACLE _HOME>\portal30\admin\plsql\wwu.

Note

The scripts parameters are explained for each script, and each parameter is explained at least once. If you cannot find the parameter description for a certain script, please refer to an earlier script with the same parameter.

---

ssoexp (ssoexp.cmd for NT and ssoexp.csh for UNIX)

It exports the Login Server information (i.e., mainly the list of users) from the Login Server schema specified in the command.

```
ssoexp.cmd [-s <sso_schema>] [-p <sso_password>] [-d <dump_
file_name>] [-c <connect_string>]
```

-s <SSO_SCHEMA> The Oracle schema name for the Portal Login Server has a default value of PORTAL30_SSO.

-p <SSO_PASSWORD> The Oracle schema password for the Portal Login Server has a default value of <SSO_SCHEMA>.

-d <DUMP_FILE_NAME> The export dump filename has a default value of sso.dmp.

-c <CONNECT_STRING> An optional parameter, this is the connect string of your Oracle Portal database.

```
C:\oracle\O9iAS\portal30\admin\plsql\www>set ORACLE_HOME=c:\oracle\o9ias

C:\oracle\O9iAS\portal30\admin\plsql\www>ssoexp -s portal30_sso -p portal30_sso -d myeip_sso.dmp -c orcl
Begining Oracle Login Server User Export
...sso_schema:        portal30_sso
...sso_password:      *************
...dump_file_name:    myeip_sso.dmp
...connect_string:    orcl

SQL*Plus: Release 8.1.7.0.0 - Production on Thu May 10 22:06:08 2001

(c) Copyright 2000 Oracle Corporation.  All rights reserved.

Connected to:
Oracle8i Enterprise Edition Release 8.1.7.0.0 - Production
With the Partitioning option
JServer Release 8.1.7.0.0 - Production

Extracting Login Server Data to transport tables...
Activity Log:
    Clearing any existing SSO data from transport tables
        Truncating table WWUTL_SSO_TX_PERSON$
    Truncating table WWUTL_SSO_TRANSPORT_TABLE$
Begin extracting SSO data of Portal...
Extracting SSO data...
    ... 8rows extracted
Disconnected from Oracle8i Enterprise Edition Release 8.1.7.0.0 - Production
With the Partitioning option
JServer Release 8.1.7.0.0 - Production

Export: Release 8.1.7.0.0 - Production on Thu May 10 22:06:19 2001

(c) Copyright 2000 Oracle Corporation.  All rights reserved.

Connected to: Oracle8i Enterprise Edition Release 8.1.7.0.0 - Production
With the Partitioning option
JServer Release 8.1.7.0.0 - Production
Export done in WE8ISO8859P1 character set and WE8ISO8859P1 NCHAR character set
Note: indexes on tables will not be exported
Note: constraints on tables will not be exported

About to export specified tables via Conventional Path ...
. . exporting table      WWUTL_SSO_TRANSPORT_TABLE$          1 rows exported
. . exporting table            WWUTL_SSO_TX_PERSON$          8 rows exported
Export terminated successfully without warnings.
Export of Login Server User Information Complete
C:\oracle\O9iAS\portal30\admin\plsql\www>
```

Figure 18.2 Sample ssoexp Script Output.

Figure 18.2 shows a sample run of the ssoexp script.

secexp (secexp.cmd /secexp.csh)

This script exports security information.

```
secexp.cmd -s <portal_schema> [-p <portal_password>]
[-g <global_priv>] [-d <dump_file_name>] [-c <connect_
string>]
```

-s <PORTAL_SCHEMA> This is the Oracle schema name for Portal Security (e.g., portal30).

-p <PORTAL_PASSWORD> The Oracle schema password for Portal Security has a default value of <PORTAL_SCHEMA>.

-g <GLOBAL_PRIV> Set this parameter to ON to export the global privileges, or to OFF to not export the global privileges. The default value is OFF.

-d <DUMP_FILE_NAME> The generated dump file name has a default value of "security.dmp".

-c <CONNECT_STRING> An optional parameter, this is the connect string of your Oracle Portal database.

Figure 18.3 shows a sample run of the secexp script.

contexp (contexp.cmd /contexp.csh)

This command exports content areas one at a time. It requires you to know the name of the content area (not its display name). You can edit the content area to obtain the name.

```
contexp.cmd -s <portal_schema> [-p <portal_password>]
-a <content_area_name> [-d <dump_file_name>]
[-c <connect_string>]
```

-s <PORTAL_SCHEMA> This is the Oracle database account for the portal user that will perform the export.

-p <PORTAL_PASSWORD> The Oracle database password for the Portal user has a default value of <portal_schema>.

-a <CONTENT_AREA_NAME> This is the content area name to be exported.

-d <DUMP_FILE_NAME> The dump file name generated has a default value of "cont-area.dmp".

-c <CONNECT_STRING> An optional parameter, this is the connect string of your Oracle Portal database.

-security This parameter makes the script export the content area security into a dump file named "security.dmp".

-page This parameter makes the script export the content area page into a dump file named "pobpage.dmp".

Figure 18.4 shows part of a sample run of the contexp script.

```
C:\oracle\O9iAS\portal30\admin\plsql\wwu>secexp -s portal30 -p portal30 -g on -d myeip_sec.dmp -c orcl
Begining Portal Security Export
...portal_schema:       portal30
...portal_password:     *************
...dump_file_name:      myeip_sec.dmp
...connect_string:      orcl

SQL*Plus: Release 8.1.7.0.0 - Production on Thu May 10 22:23:16 2001
(c) Copyright 2000 Oracle Corporation.  All rights reserved.
Connected to:
Oracle8i Enterprise Edition Release 8.1.7.0.0 - Production
With the Partitioning option
JServer Release 8.1.7.0.0 - Production

Extracting Security Data to transport tables...
Activity Log:
   Clearing any existing security data from transport tables
      Truncating table WWUTL_SEC_TX_GROUP$
      Truncating table WWUTL_SEC_TX_MEMBER$
      Truncating table WWUTL_SEC_TX_SYS_PRIV$
      Truncating table WWUTL_SEC_TX_PERSON$
   Truncating table WWUTL_SEC_TRANSPORT_TABLE$
Begin extracting security data of Portal
Extracting Security Data...
Global Privilege export flag set to: on... (ON = export global privilege, OFF = do not export global privilege)
   ...Extracting Users...
   ...8 rows extracted
   ...Extracting Groups...
   ...6 rows extracted
   ...Extracting Members...
   ...20 rows extracted
   ...Extracting Group Ownerships...
   ...15 rows extracted
   ...Extracting Global Privileges...
   ...30 rows extracted
Disconnected from Oracle8i Enterprise Edition Release 8.1.7.0.0 - Production
With the Partitioning option
JServer Release 8.1.7.0.0 - Production
Export: Release 8.1.7.0.0 - Production on Thu May 10 22:23:30 2001
(c) Copyright 2000 Oracle Corporation.  All rights reserved.
Connected to: Oracle8i Enterprise Edition Release 8.1.7.0.0 - Production
With the Partitioning option
JServer Release 8.1.7.0.0 - Production
Export done in WE8ISO8859P1 character set and WE8ISO8859P1 NCHAR character set
Note: indexes on tables will not be exported
Note: constraints on tables will not be exported

About to export specified tables via Conventional Path ...
. . exporting table    WWUTL_SEC_TRANSPORT_TABLE$        4 rows exported
. . exporting table        WWUTL_SEC_TX_GROUP$        6 rows exported
. . exporting table       WWUTL_SEC_TX_MEMBER$        20 rows exported
. . exporting table      WWUTL_SEC_TX_SYS_PRIV$        45 rows exported
. . exporting table       WWUTL_SEC_TX_PERSON$        8 rows exported
Export terminated successfully without warnings.
Export of Security Data Complete.
```

Figure 18.3 Sample secexp script Output.

```
C:\oracle\O9iAS\portal30\admin\plsql\wwu>contexp -s portal30 -p portal30 -a emp_ca -d emp_ca.dmp -c orcl -security
Begining Portal Security Export
...portal_schema:      portal30
...portal_password:    *************
...dump_file_name:     security.dmp
...connect_string:     orcl

Extracting Security Data to transport tables...
Activity Log:
   Clearing any existing security data from transport tables
      Truncating table WWUTL_SEC_TX_GROUP$
      Truncating table WWUTL_SEC_TX_MEMBER$
      Truncating table WWUTL_SEC_TX_SYS_PRIV$
      Truncating table WWUTL_SEC_TX_PERSON$
   Truncating table WWUTL_SEC_TRANSPORT_TABLE$
Begin extracting security data of Portal
Extracting Security Data...
Global Privilege export flag set to: on... (ON = export global privilege, OFF = do not export global privilege)
   ...Extracting Users...
   ...8 rows extracted
   ...Extracting Groups...
   ...6 rows extracted
   ...Extracting Members...
   ...20 rows extracted
   ...Extracting Group Ownerships...
   ...15 rows extracted
   ...Extracting Global Privileges...
   ...30 rows extracted
Disconnected from Oracle8i Enterprise Edition Release 8.1.7.0.0 - Production
Connected to: Oracle8i Enterprise Edition Release 8.1.7.0.0 - Production
Note: indexes on tables will not be exported
Note: constraints on tables will not be exported

About to export specified tables via Conventional Path ...
. . exporting table     WWUTL_SEC_TRANSPORT_TABLE$        4 rows exported
. . exporting table          WWUTL_SEC_TX_GROUP$         6 rows exported
. . exporting table         WWUTL_SEC_TX_MEMBER$        20 rows exported
. . exporting table       WWUTL_SEC_TX_SYS_PRIV$        45 rows exported
. . exporting table         WWUTL_SEC_TX_PERSON$         8 rows exported
Export terminated successfully without warnings.
Export of Security Data Complete
Begining Portal Content Area Export
...portal_schema:      portal30
...portal_password:    *************
...content_area_name:  emp_ca
...dump_file_name:     emp_ca.dmp
...connect_string:     orcl

Connected to:
Oracle8i Enterprise Edition Release 8.1.7.0.0 - Production
JServer Release 8.1.7.0.0 - Production

Extracting Site Data to transport tables...
Activity Log:
   Clearing any existing data from transport tables
   Truncating table WWUTL_NLS_TX_STRINGS$
      Truncating table WWUTL_SBR_TX_SITES$
      Truncating table WWUTL_SBR_TX_SITE_LANGUAGES$
      Truncating table WWUTL_DOC_TX_DOCUMENT$
      Truncating table WWUTL_SBR_TX_TOPICS$
      Truncating table WWUTL_SBR_TX_PERSPECTIVES$
            ...
      Truncating table WWUTL_SBR_TX_PORTLET$
      Truncating table WWUTL_PRO_TX_PROVIDERS$
      Truncating table WWUTL_SBR_TX_GROUP$
      Truncating table WWUTL_SBR_TX_SYS_PRIV$
   Truncating table WWUTL_SBR_TRANSPORT_TABLE$
Site found with name = 'emp_ca'
Extracting Site data...
   Extracting Site (Core) data
      Extracting Site Data from WWUTL_SBR_TX_SITES$
      Extracting Site Data from WWUTL_SBR_TX_SITE_LANGUAGES$
```

Figure 18.4 Sample contexp script Output.

Exporting Applications

You can export applications one at a time. From the Oracle Portal home page, go to the navigator, and then click on the Applications tab, then the "Export" link next to the desired application (Figure 18.5). Oracle Portal displays a list of the components to be exported, along with a link to download a text file containing the SQL*Plus and PL/SQL source code to import the application (Figure 18.6 and Figure 18.7). The generated SQL script is your application export file. If you need to import your application in another Oracle Portal node, you need to run this script while connected to portal instance using SQL*Plus.

Pageexp (pageexp.cmd/pageexp.csh)

This script exports pages one at a time. You need to know the internal name of the page (not its display name).

```
pageexp.cmd -s <portal_schema> [-p <portal_password>]
-n <page_name> [-d <dump_file_name>] [-security]
[-c <connect_string>]
```

-s <PORTAL_SCHEMA> This is the Oracle database account for portal user.

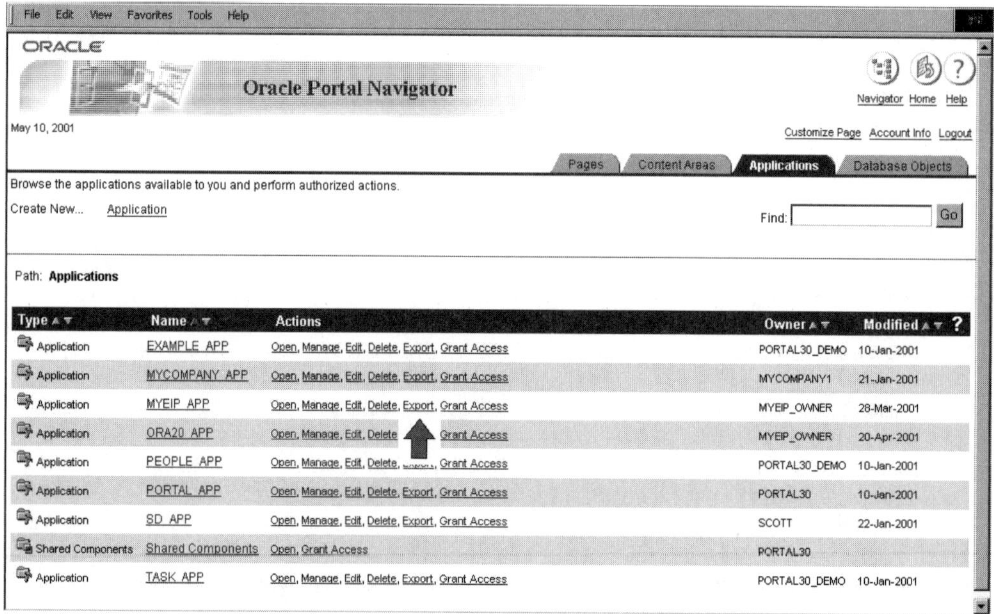

Figure 18.5 Oracle Portal Navigator: Application Export Action.

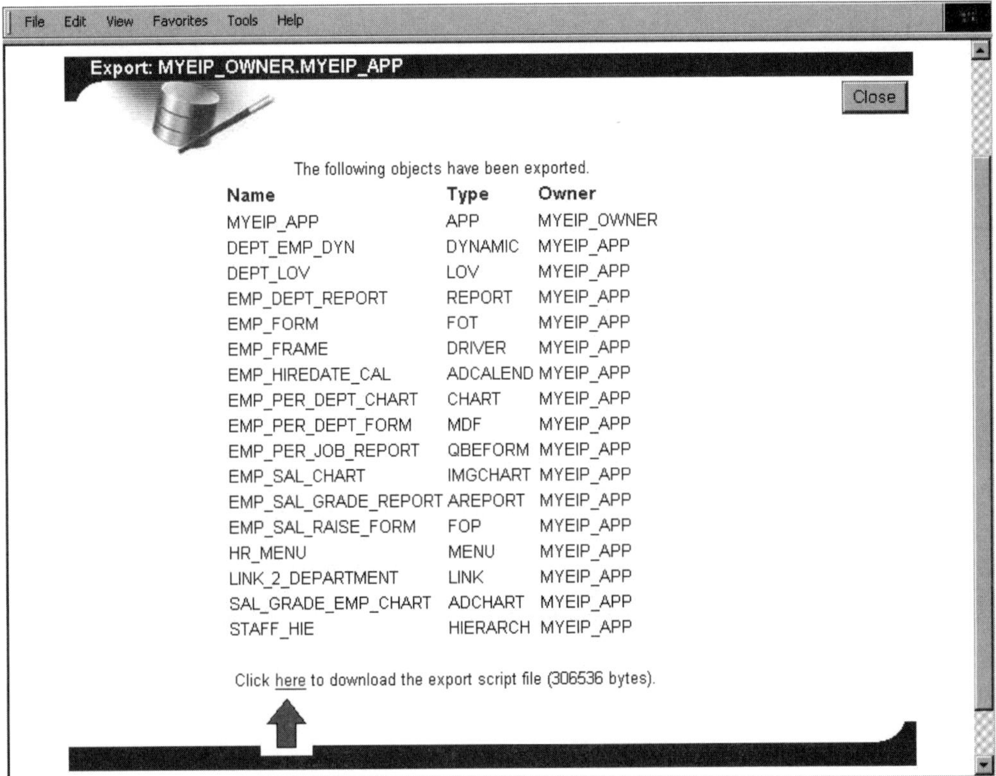

Figure 18.6 Application Export List.

-p <PORTAL_PASSWORD> The Oracle database password for the portal user has a default value of <PORTAL_SCHEMA>.

-n <PAGE_NAME> This is the portal page to be exported.

-d <DUMP_FILE_NAME> The dump file name has a default value of "pobpage.dmp".

-security This parameter exports the portal page security to a dump file named "security.dmp".

-c <CONNECT_STRING> An optional parameter, this is the connect string of your Oracle Portal database.

Figure 18.8 shows part of a sample run of the pageexp script.

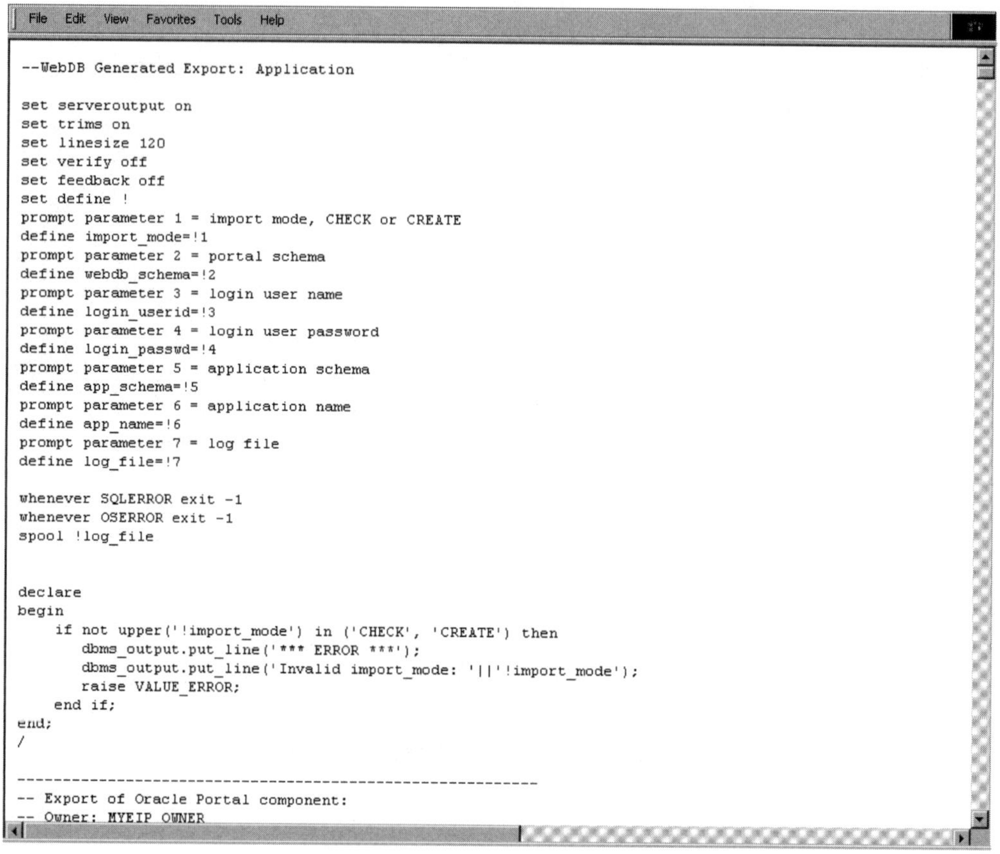

```
File Edit View Favorites Tools Help

--WebDB Generated Export: Application

set serveroutput on
set trims on
set linesize 120
set verify off
set feedback off
set define !
prompt parameter 1 = import mode, CHECK or CREATE
define import_mode=!1
prompt parameter 2 = portal schema
define webdb_schema=!2
prompt parameter 3 = login user name
define login_userid=!3
prompt parameter 4 = login user password
define login_passwd=!4
prompt parameter 5 = application schema
define app_schema=!5
prompt parameter 6 = application name
define app_name=!6
prompt parameter 7 = log file
define log_file=!7

whenever SQLERROR exit -1
whenever OSERROR exit -1
spool !log_file


declare
begin
    if not upper('!import_mode') in ('CHECK', 'CREATE') then
       dbms_output.put_line('*** ERROR ***');
       dbms_output.put_line('Invalid import_mode: '||'!import_mode');
       raise VALUE_ERROR;
    end if;
end;
/

-----------------------------------------------------------
-- Export of Oracle Portal component:
-- Owner: MYEIP_OWNER
```

Figure 18.7 Application Export Code.

ssoimp (ssoimp.cmd /ssoimp.csh)

The script is used to import Login Server information.

```
ssoimp.cmd -s <sso_schema> [-p sso_password]
[-o <from_sso_schema>] [-m <merge_mode>] [-u <db_user_mode>]
[-d <dump_file_name>] [-c <connect_string>]
```

-s <SSO_SCHEMA> This is the Oracle schema name for Login Server.

-p <SSO_PASSWORD> The Oracle schema password for Login Server has a default value of <SSO_SCHEMA>.

-o <FROM_SSO_SCHEMA> The Oracle schema name for Login Server from which the Login Server was exported has a default value of <SSO_SCHEMA>.

```
C:\oracle\O9iAS\portal30\admin\plsql\wwu>pageexp -s portal30 -p portal30 -n employee_page -d emp_page.dmp -c orcl
Begining Portal Page Export
...portal_schema:       portal30
...portal_password:     *************
...page_name:           employee_page
...dump_file_name:      emp_page.dmp
...connect_string:      orcl

SQL*Plus: Release 8.1.7.0.0 - Production on Thu May 10 23:36:07 2001
(c) Copyright 2000 Oracle Corporation.  All rights reserved.
Connected to:
Oracle8i Enterprise Edition Release 8.1.7.0.0 - Production

Initialize the transport tables

PL/SQL procedure successfully completed.

Disconnected from Oracle8i Enterprise Edition Release 8.1.7.0.0 - Production
SQL*Plus: Release 8.1.7.0.0 - Production on Thu May 10 23:36:15 2001
(c) Copyright 2000 Oracle Corporation.  All rights reserved.
Connected to:
Oracle8i Enterprise Edition Release 8.1.7.0.0 - Production
JServer Release 8.1.7.0.0 - Production

Extracting Portal Page Data for Export...
Disconnected from Oracle8i Enterprise Edition Release 8.1.7.0.0 - Production

Export: Release 8.1.7.0.0 - Production on Thu May 10 23:36:32 2001

Connected to: Oracle8i Enterprise Edition Release 8.1.7.0.0 - Production
JServer Release 8.1.7.0.0 - Production
Export done in WE8ISO8859P1 character set and WE8ISO8859P1 NCHAR character set
Note: indexes on tables will not be exported
Note: constraints on tables will not be exported

About to export specified tables via Conventional Path ...
. . exporting table     WWUTL_POB_TX_DOCUMENT$       5 rows exported
. . exporting table     WWUTL_POB_TX_NLS$          148 rows exported
. . exporting table     WWUTL_POB_TX_PRE_PATH$       7 rows exported
. . exporting table     WWUTL_POB_TX_PRE_NAME$      62 rows exported
. . exporting table     WWUTL_POB_TX_PRE_VALUE$     71 rows exported
Export terminated successfully without warnings.
Export of employee_page Complete
```

Figure 18.8 Sample page Export.

-m <MERGE_MODE> Set the mode used for merging imported data to "reuse" to reuse existing objects instead of importing them, or set it to "check" to check for conflicts and print a report. Its default value is "check".

-u <DB_USER_MODE> Set the mode used for specifying how to handle database schema information in the Login Server to "public_user" to always set all database schemas to PUBLIC_USER, or set it to "database_user" to set all the database schemas to the database username, and only set to PUBLIC_USER if the referenced schema could not be found. Its default value is "database_user".

-d <DUMP_FILE_NAME> The dump file name to be imported has a default value of "sso.dmp".

-c <CONNECT_STRING> An optional parameter, this is the connect string to your Oracle Portal database.

secimp (secimp.cmd /secimp.csh)

This script imports security information.

```
secimp.cmd -s <portal_schema> [-p <portal_password>]
[-o <from_portal_schema>] [-m <merge_mode>]
[-u <db_user_mode>] [-d <dump_file_name>] [-c <connect_
string>]
```

-o <FROM_PORTAL_SCHEMA> The Oracle schema name for Portal Security from which the Security was exported has a default value of <PORTAL_SCHEMA>.

-m <MERGE_MODE> Set the mode used for merging imported data to "reuse" to reuse existing objects instead of importing them, or set it to "check" to check for conflicts and print a report. Its default value is "check".

-u <DB_USER_MODE> This is similar to the ssoimp.

appimp (appimp.cmd /appimp.csh)

Import applications one at a time.

```
appimp.cmd [-s <portal_schema>] [-p <portal_password>]
[-m <import mode>] [-t <app_schema>] [-a <app_name>]
-f <script_file_name> [-c <connect_string>]
```

-t <APP_SCHEMA> This is the schema in which the application will be created. The default is the schema name in the used script.

-a <APP_NAME> The name of the application to be imported has a default value of the name in the used script.

-f <SCRIPT_FILE_NAME> This is the application script file name that was exported earlier.

-security Import portal security with this parameter.

contimp (contimp.cmd /contimp.csh)

Import content areas one at a time.

```
contimp.cmd -s <portal_schema> [-p <portal_password>]
```

```
[-o <from_portal_schema>] [-d <dump_file_name>] [-m <merge_mode>]
[-u <db_user_mode>] [-d <dump_file_name>]
[-c <connect_string>] [-security] [page]
```

-o <FROM_PORTAL_SCHEMA> The Oracle Database account for portal user from where the content area was exported has a default value of <PORTAL_SCHEMA>.

-m <MERGE_MODE> Set it to "check" to check for conflicts and print a report, or set it to "reuse" to reuse existing objects instead of importing them, or set it to "new" to create new objects. Its default value is "check".

-security This parameter is used to import the portal security from security.dmp file.

-page This parameter is used to import the content area page from pobpage.dmp file.

pageimp (pageimp.cmd/pageimp.csh)

Import pages one at a time.

```
pageimp <-s portal_schema> [-p <portal_password>]
[-o <from_portal_schema>] [-m <import mode>]
[-d <dump_file_name>] [-security] [-u <db_user_mode>]
[-c <connect_string>]
.
```

-o <FROM_PORTAL_SCHEMA> The Oracle schema name from which page was exported has a default value of <PORTAL_SCHEMA>.

-d <DUMP_FILE_NAME> The dump file name of the page import has a default value of "pobpage.dmp".

Supporting NLS in Oracle Portal

This section explains how you can add more languages to the Oracle Portal. Oracle Portal is installed with English by default. Table 18.1 lists the languages supported in Oracle Portal 3.0.

Before you run the langinst script to load other languages, you need to run the following script as Portal30:

```
<iAS_ORACLE_HOME>\portal30\admin\plsql\nlsres\ctl\us
      \wwvseedus.sql
```

Table 18.1 Languages Supported in Oracle Portal

Language	Language Appreciation
Arabic	ar
Czech	cs
German	D
Danish	dk
Spanish	E
Greek	el
French	F
Hebrew	iw
Hungarian	hu
Italian	I
Japanese	ja
Korean	ko
Norwegian	N
Dutch	nl
Polish	pl
Portuguese	pt
Brazilan Portuguese	ptb
Romanian	ro
Russian	ru
Swedish	S
Finnish	sf
Slovak	sk
Thai	th
Turkish	Tr
Simplified Chinese	zhs
Traditional Chinese	zht

langinst Script

To install another language, you need to run this script from <iAS_ORACLE_HOME> \portal30\admin\plsql directory. This shell script installs the string resources for a specific language. It uses SQL*Plus and SQL Loader to install the strings.

```
langinst.cmd [-s <portal_schema>] [-p portal_password]
[-o sso_schema] [-d sso_password] [-c connect_string]
-l language [-available]

Example: langinst.cmd -s portal30 -p portal30 -o
portal30_sso -c orcl -l f -available
```

-s <PORTAL_SCHEMA> The Oracle database schema for the portal database objects has a default value of PORTAL30.

-p <PORTAL_PASSWORD> The Oracle database password for the portal schema has a default value of <PORTAL_SCHEMA>.

-o <SSO_SCHEMA> The Oracle database schema for Login Server objects has a default value of <PORTAL_SCHEMA>_SSO.

-d <SSO_PASSWORD> The Oracle database password for Login Server schema has a default value of <SSO_SCHEMA>.

-l <LANGUAGE> This is the abbreviation of the language to be installed. The default value is "us".

-available An optional parameter—if used, the language will be available for user translations.

For an example, to load the Arabic language, the Oracle Portal database needs an Arabic character set, such as AR8MSWIN1256, AR8ISO8859P6, and so on. Next, you need to perform the langinst command:

```
langinst -s portal30 -p portal30 -o portal30_sso -d
portal30_sso -c orcl -l ar -available
```

Languages that are displayed from right to left on the screen (e.g., Arabic) are also known as BiDi (bidirectional) languages. For BiDi languages you need to run a script to update some Oracle Portal metadata to provide proper graphics support for some of the required images. You need to log in as Portal30 using SQL*Plus and run the following script:

```
<iAS_ORACLE_HOME>\portal30\admin\plsql\nlsres\imginst.sql
```

Choosing a Language

You can choose your desired language and also enable users to choose their desired language by adding the Set Language portlet to portal pages. This portlet is available under the Oracle Portal provider under Utilities. It displays all of the languages currently installed (Figure 18.9). For Arabic, you need a browser with Arabic text support, such as Microsoft Internet 5.x on Windows 2000 Professional with Arabic Language loaded.

Note

In earlier versions than Oracle Portal 3.0.9, you can choose your portal language by changing your browser's language. You do not need to do that in Portal 3.0.9.

Important

The Login Server automatically displays a list of installed languages on its login page, which determines the language used for the Login Server independent of the language chosen in the Set Language portlet.

Oracle Portal Migration

This part of the chapter explains how to upgrade Oracle Portal (WebDB) version 2.2 Web sites to Oracle Portal 3.0 contents. This process also demonstrates upgrading a portal instance from one 3.0 version to a later 3.0 version.

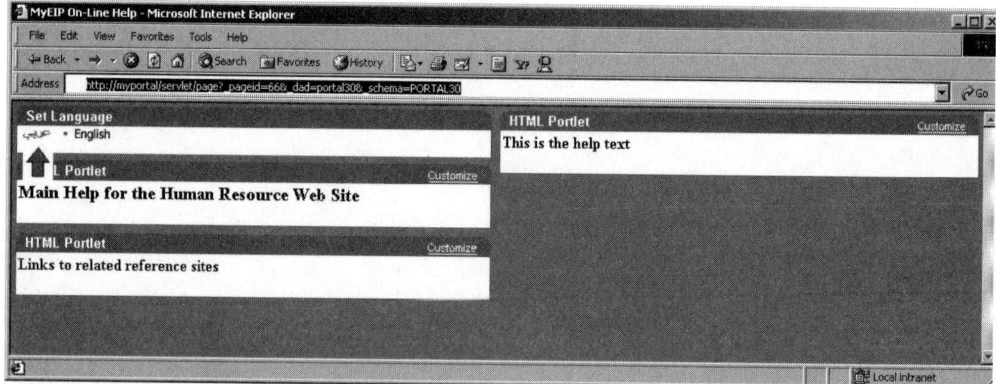

Figure 18.9 Set Language Portlet.

Note

Oracle Portal 3.0 content areas are called Sites in WebDB 2.2.

Table 18.2 lists Oracle9*i*AS versions and the Oracle Portal version shipped with each version. The upgrade script to a certain version of Oracle Portal is available as a separate download from Oracle Technology Network. This part illustrates the migration process, by describing how to migrate an existing WebDB 2.2 Web site to Oracle Portal 3.0.8. This upgrade process has two main steps: The first upgrade is to 3.0.6, and the second upgrade is from 3.0.6 to 3.0.8.

Table 18.2 Oracle9*i* Application Server and Portal Versions

Oracle9*i* Application Server Version	Oracle Portal Version
1.0.2.2	3.0.9
1.0.2.1	3.0.8
1.0.2.0.1 Solaris	3.0.7
1.0.2.0 NT/2000	3.0.7
1.0.2.0 Solaris	3.0.6.5

Important

You can download the upgrade scripts from http://technet.oracle.com/support/products/iportal/listing.htm.

Note

If you have an earlier version than WebDB 2.2, you will need to upgrade to 2.2 first.

In WebDB 2.x, the applications and sites reside in different schemas. In Oracle Portal 3.0, the product inhabits a single schema, regardless of the number of content areas, pages, or applications you create. So, for every WebDB 2.2 installation, a different schema is created. If you are using more than one schema in your WebDB environment, you will need to run the upgrade script for each schema, and each run will result in a new Oracle Portal 3.0 schema along with its login server schema. Then if you want you can export one schema and import it into the other, to consolidate your new upgraded Oracle Portal into one node.

WebDB 2.2 to Oracle Portal 3.0.6.6 Upgrade

As mentioned in the introduction, you have two sets of upgrade scripts to run to take you to 3.0.8. This is your first set of scripts that will take you to a midpoint, which is 3.0.6.6.

Step 1: Upgrade Requirements

The following requirements need to be met:

- A database instance, 8.1.7 Standard Edition, 8.1.7 Enterprise Edition or 8.1.6.2 Enterprise Edition accessible through SQL Net
- The SYS password of this database
- 150MB of free space in the SYSTEM tablespace and 150MB of free space in the WebDB default tablespace in this database
- Init.ora parameters:
    - max_enabled_roles = 30 (recommended)
    - open_cursors = 100 (recommended)
    - compatible = 8.1.0 (or above)
    - java_pool_size = 20971520 (minimum)
    - shared_pool_size = 15728640

Step 2: Oracle HTTP Server Installation

Install Oracle9*i* Application Server version 1.0.2 into a new Oracle Home. Choose "The Oracle HTTP Server Only" installation type. Once the O9*i*AS installation finishes, the Oracle Portal configuration assistant starts. Because you are upgrading your current WebDB 2.2 to Oracle Portal 3.0, you do not need to create a new Oracle Portal, so cancel the Oracle Portal configuration assistant.

Step 3: DADs Creation

You need to create two Data Access Descriptors (DADs) in the new O9*i*AS 1.0.2: one for the upgraded Portal DAD and another for the Single-Sign-On (SSO) DAD. For each WebDB site you need to create two DADs as well. You can create a PORTAL DAD by going to

```
http://<Hostname>:<portno>/pls/admin_/gateway.htm
```

Specify the DAD name (e.g., webdb); schema name, which is the one you need to upgrade (e.g., webdb); Oracle username; Oracle password; and Oracle connect string.

Create an SSO DAD, specify the DAD name (e.g., webdb_sso), schema name (e.g., webdb_sso), which is the one you need to upgrade; Oracle username; Oracle password; Oracle connect string; and the default home page (e.g., webdb_sso.wwsso_home.home). You can also add these two DADs manually by editing the file <iAS_ORACLE_HOME>\Apache\modplsql\cfg\wdbsvr.app. Also, you need to add an entry to the <iAS_ORACLE_HOME>\network\admin\tnsnames.ora to point to the WebDB database.

Step 4: Back Up WebDB 2.2

It is always a good idea to back up your WebDB 2.2 before the upgrade. You can perform this backup using a full database export.

Step 5: Run the Upgrade Script

Unzip and extract the Oracle Portal upgrade zip/tar file (i.e., `306upg_nt.zip`, which is downloadable from the Oracle Technology Network) into a local directory. The upgrade script `wupgrade` has the following syntax:

```
wupgrade.cmd -s <schema_name> -p <schema_password>
-u <sys_password> [-c <connect_string>] [-l <log_file_name>]
```

Table 18.3 Upgrade Script Parameters Descriptions

Parameter	Description
schema_name	Name of the database schema in which your existing Oracle Portal is installed
schema_password	Password for the above schema
sys_password	Password for the SYS user of the database on which the above schema is located
connect_string (optional)	Connect string for the database in which the above schema is installed
log_file_name (optional)	Name of the file where the output of the wupgrade script is written. If no file name is given, the output writes to wupgrade.log.

Note

A connect string/TNS Alias is not required if you have the database on the same machine and your ORACLE environment variables (ORACLE_SID, ORACLE_HOME, PATH, etc.) are pointing to that database.

A sample run of the upgrade script is in Figure 18.10. You need to set the environment variable ORACLE_HOME to point to the new O9*i*AS Oracle Home before running the upgrade scripts. When you run the upgrade script, you must answer a series of questions:

```
C:\book\upg\306>
C:\book\upg\306>
C:\book\upg\306>
C:\book\upg\306>wupgrade.cmd -s webdb -p webdb -u change_on_install -l upgrade.l
og

Welcome to the Oracle Portal 3.0 Production Upgrade

This script can be used to upgrade the following products to
Oracle Portal 3.0 Production:
WebDB 2.2 Sitebuilder and Webview
Oracle Portal 3.0 Early Adopters Release (3.0.6.3.3)
Note: Upgrade from WebDB 3.0 Beta (3.0.3.3.3, 3.0.3.3.5) is not supported.
The script will lead you through the upgrade step by step.


Before beginning the upgrade, it is important you export your existing
product schema as a backup.

Have you exported your existing WebDB schema? (Y/N): y


Analyzing the Product Schema...
Identifying Single Sign-On Login Server Schemas

no rows selected

Enter the name of the schema to use for the Login Server from the above list,
or just hit return to create a new one or use a remote one:
Do you want to create a new Login Server schema in this database? (Y/N): y
Enter the name of the Login Server schema to create: webdb_sso
Specify the URL prefix for web access to the Portal (WebDB schema).
Example: http://server.domain.com:80/pls/DAD/
url:http://152.68.36.58/pls/webdb/
Specify the URL prefix for web access to the Login Server.
Example: http://server.domain.com:80/pls/DAD_SSO/
url:http://152.68.36.58/pls/webdb_sso/_
```

Figure 18.10 3.0.6 Upgrade Script Sample Run (1 of 2).

1. Have you exported your existing WebDB schema? (Y/N)
   Enter "Y" if you have exported your existing WebDB 2.2 schema and site schema and are ready to upgrade the WebDB schema. Enter "N" if you have not exported your WebDB 2.2 schema. The upgrade process stops.
2. Enter the name of the schema to use for the Login Server from the above list, or just hit return to create a new one or use a remote one.
3. Do you want to create a new Login Server schema in this database? (Y/N):
   Enter "Y" if you want to install a new Login Server. Enter "N" if you do not want to install a new Login Server.

4. Enter the name of the Login Server schema to create.
5. Specify the URL prefix for Web access to the Portal (WebDB schema).
   For example:

   ```
   http://<Hostname>:<portno>/pls/webdb/
   ```

   Use the Portal DAD defined when you created a portal DAD in step 3.
6. Specify the URL prefix for Web access to the Login Server.
   For example:

   ```
   http://<Hostname>:<portno>/pls/webdb_sso/
   ```

   Use the SSO DAD defined when you created an SSO DAD in step 3.

Note

If you have multiple WebDB 2.2 sites, install the Login Server once for all sites. One Login Server can authenticate users to partner applications for more than one Oracle Portal installation.

---

7. Enter the tablespace name where the WebDB schema resides.
8. Enter the tablespace name for the temporary tablespace.
9. Enter the tablespace name for the document tablespace.
10. Is this information correct? (Y/N)
    Enter "Y" to proceed with the upgrade. Enter "N" to abort the upgrade and rerun the upgrade script (Figure 18.11).

    The URLs (for steps 5 and 6) are in the format:

    ```
    http://<Hostname>:<portno>/pls/<DAD>/
    ```

However, the hostname and port number must match the ServerName stored in the Oracle HTTP Server. If it does not, the Portal login results in an error. The ServerName in the Oracle HTTP Server is sometimes stored as host instead of host.domain. If this is the case, using the URLs in the specified format would not match the values obtained from the Oracle HTTP Server. You could not connect to the portal. You can solve this problem in one of three ways:

- If your Oracle HTTP Server is not using the domain name, you may change the ServerName in the `httpd.conf` file stored in the Apache/conf directory in your Oracle HTTP Server installation. Then restart the Oracle HTTP Server.

```
Enter the name of the schema to use for the Login Server from the above list,
or just hit return to create a new one or use a remote one:
Do you want to create a new Login Server schema in this database? (Y/N): y
Enter the name of the Login Server schema to create: webdb_sso
Specify the URL prefix for web access to the Portal (WebDB schema).
Example: http://server.domain.com:80/pls/DAD/
url:http://152.68.36.58/pls/webdb/
Specify the URL prefix for web access to the Login Server.
Example: http://server.domain.com:80/pls/DAD_SSO/
url:http://152.68.36.58/pls/webdb_sso/
Enter the tablespace name where the user schema resides :webdb22
Enter the tablespace name for temp tablespace : temp

The following details have been determined:

RDBMS Version: 8.1.7.0.0
WebDB/Portal Version: 2.2.0.0.5 - WEBVIEW
Oracle PL/SQL Toolkit Schema: SYS, version: UNKNOWN
Login Server Schema: Create new schema WEBDB_SSO
URL prefix for the Portal is    http://152.68.36.58/pls/webdb/
URL prefix for Login Server is  http://152.68.36.58/pls/webdb_sso/
Upgrade needed on obfuscation and cryptographic toolkits - Y
Upgrade needed on Oracle PL/SQL Toolkit  - Y


Schema Name                           : webdb
Schema Password (Entered)             : webdb
Schema Password (With Connect String): webdb
SSO Schema                            : WEBDB_SSO
SSO Password (Entered)                : WEBDB_SSO
SSO Password (With Connect String)    : WEBDB_SSO
Connect String                        :
Is this information correct (Y/N): y
">>> Installing dbms_obfuscation_toolkit and dbms_crypto_toolkit ..."
8.1.7 Detected - Not loading DBMS_OBFUSCATION_TOOLKIT
">>> Installing OWA packages into SYS schema..."

PL/SQL procedure successfully completed.


Package created.


Package body created.

No errors.

Grant succeeded.
```

Figure 18.11 3.0.6 Upgrade Script Sample Run (2 of 2).

- Specify just the host and exclude the domain while running the upgrade. This is provided the ServerName on the Oracle HTTP Server has been stored without the domain name.
- After upgrading, run the `ssodatan.cmd` script (provided with the distribution package) and supply the URLs so that you are compatible with the ServerName on the Oracle HTTP Server.

I recommend that you do not use the machine during the upgrade. Generally, it takes between two and four hours for an upgrade. The exact amount of time needed depends on the size of your portal applications and sites as well as the speed of the machine.

Step 7: Check the Log File

Open the log with a text editor. The default name for the log is wupgrade.log. It is located in the same directory as the `wupgrade` script. Check for errors.

Step 8: Access the Upgraded Oracle Portal

You are now ready to access your upgraded portal. Make sure your Oracle HTTP Server is up and running. Point your browser to

```
http://<Hostname>:<portno>/pls/<DAD>
```

where

<Hostname> is the machine where the Oracle HTTP Server is running.
<portno> is the port at which the Oracle HTTP Server is listening.
<DAD> is the Portal DAD name you entered for your upgraded Portal (i.e., webdb).

Oracle Portal 3.0.6.6 to 3.0.8 Upgrade

Now because you have a 3.0.6 Oracle Portal, you can perform the next step, which is upgrading it to version 3.0.8.

Step 1: Upgrade Requirements

Same as step 1 in WebDB 2.2 to 3.0.6.6 upgrade.

Step 2: Backup

It is a good idea to back up your upgraded 3.0.6.6 just in case the upgrade to 3.0.8 fails and you want to repeat the upgrade to 3.0.8 again.

Step 3: Run the Upgrade Script

Unzip and extract the Oracle Portal upgrade zip/tar file (i.e., `308upg_nt.zip`, which is downloadable from the Oracle Technology Network) into the local directory. The upgrade script has the following syntax:

```
pupgrade.cmd [-s <schema_name>] [-p <password>] [-u <sys_password>]
[c <connect_string>] [-m <upgrade_mode>] [-l <log_file_name>]
```

The script parameters are similar to the upgrade script parameters for the WebDB 2.2 to Portal 3.0.6.6 upgrade. The addition is the upgrade_mode flag. When used in the command, you can only perform an upgrade for the Login Server schema; the default is upgrading both portal schema and login server. Figure 18.12 shows a sample run of the upgrade script.

```
C:\book\upg\308>pupgrade.cmd  -m both -s webdb -p webdb -u change_on_install -c
orcl -l upgrade.log

C:\book\upg\308>echo off
'#Initialize' is not recognized as an internal or external command,
operable program or batch file.

Welcome to the Oracle Portal Production Upgrade

The script will lead you through the upgrade step by step.


Before beginning the upgrade, it is important you export your existing
product schema as a backup.

Have you exported your existing schema? (Y/N): y
Enter the name of the login server schema that you would like to upgrade(Default
=PORTAL30_SSO): webdb_sso
Enter the password for webdb_sso (Default=webdb_sso):
Enter the password for the SYS user of your loginserver database(Default=CHANGE_
ON_INSTALL):
Enter the connect string to the login server database (Default=orcl):
```

Figure 18.12 3.0.8 Upgrade Script Sample Run (1 of 2).

When you run the upgrade script, you must answer a series of questions, which vary slightly depending on the type of upgrade you are performing. The recommended upgrade is to upgrade both the Portal Schema and Login Server Schema at the same time.

1. Have you exported your existing schema? (Y/N)
   Enter "Y" if you have completed a backup and are ready to upgrade the Oracle Portal schema. Enter "N" if you have not completed a backup of your schema. The upgrade process stops.
2. Select the schema to use for the Login Server from the above list, or press return to create a new one or use a remote one (e.g., webdb_sso).
3. Enter the password for the Login Server schema (e.g., webdb_sso).
4. Enter the name of the password store schema you would like to create (default: webdb_sso_PS).
5. Enter the connect string to the login server database.
6. Is this information correct? (Y/N)
   Enter "Y" to proceed with the upgrade. Enter "N" to abort the upgrade and rerun the upgrade script (Figure 18.13).

You will need to keep an eye on the tablespaces (e.g., SYSTEM, USERS) while the script is running to make sure that they are not running out of space.

Step 6: Check the Log

Open the log with a text editor. The default name for the log is pupgrade.log. It is located in the same directory as the `pupgrade` script. Check for errors.

```
'#Initialize' is not recognized as an internal or external command,
operable program or batch file.

Welcome to the Oracle Portal Production Upgrade

The script will lead you through the upgrade step by step.


Before beginning the upgrade, it is important you export your existing
product schema as a backup.

Have you exported your existing schema? (Y/N): y
Enter the name of the login server schema that you would like to upgrade(Default
=PORTAL30_SSO): webdb_sso
Enter the password for webdb_sso (Default=webdb_sso):
Enter the password for the SYS user of your loginserver database(Default=CHANGE_
ON_INSTALL):
Enter the connect string to the login server database (Default=orcl):
Enter the name of the password store schema you would like to create(Default=web
db_sso_PS):
Enter the password for the above schema (Default=webdb_SSO_PS):

The following details have been determined:

Upgrade Mode : both
Log File Name: upgrade.log
RDBMS Version: 8.1.7
Portal Version: 3.0.6.6.6
Oracle PL/SQL Toolkit Schema: SYS, version: 3.0.0.0.0
Schema Details.....
------ ------------
Name           : webdb
Password       : *************
Connect String : orcl
Sys Password   : *************
Login Server Schema Details.....
----- ------ ------ -----------
Name           : webdb_sso
Password       : ************
Connect String : orcl
Sys Password   : ************
Password Store Schema Details.....
-------- ----- ------ ------------
Name           : webdb_SSO_PS
Password       : ***************
Connect String : orcl
Upgrade needed on obfuscation and cryptographic toolkits - Y
Upgrade needed on Oracle PL/SQL Toolkit  - Y
```

Figure 18.13 3.0.8 Upgrade Script Sample Run (2 of 2).

Step 7: Access the Upgraded Portal

You are now ready to access your upgraded portal. Make sure your Oracle HTTP Server is up and running. Point your browser to

```
http://<Hostname>:<portno>/pls/webdb
```

Dynamic Services in Oracle Portal

As a feature of Oracle8*i,* Oracle Dynamic Services is a Java-based programmatic framework for incorporating, managing, and deploying Internet and Intranet services. Using the Internet as the information source, Oracle Dynamic Services makes it easy for application developers to rapidly incorporate valuable services from Web sites, local databases, and proprietary systems into their applications.

Dynamic Services Installation

You need Oracle8*i* Enterprise Edition Release 8.1.6.2, Oracle8*i* Standard Edition, or Enterprise Edition Release 8.1.7 to install and use Oracle Dynamic Services. You can download the latest version of Dynamic Services from technet.oracle.com, and unzip the zip/tar file into the ds directory under your <DB_ORACLE_HOME>.

DSSYS Schema Creation

Go to DOS and run the following commands to create the DSSYS schema:

```
cd <DB_ORACLE_HOME>\ds\sql
sqlplus sys/change_on_install
SQL> @dsinstall.sql
```

Once the script finishes, you can verify the installation of the schema by trying to reconnect to the database as the DSSYS/DSSYS. Also, check the generated <DB_ORACLE_HOME>\bin\dsinstall.log for errors.

After the installation is complete, you must first configure and run the DSAdmin utility before you can register and execute services. You must first edit the dsadmin (Solaris) or dsadmin.bat (Windows) file to specify the correct <DB_ORACLE_HOME> before using the DSAdmin utility. The `dsadmin.bat` file is located under <DB_ORACLE_HOME>\ds\bin\.

Configuring Dynamic Services Proxy Settings

In order to connect to services located outside of a firewall, you must first configure the Dynamic Services proxy settings. To do this, you need to run the following commands:

```
sqlplus dssys/dssys@orcl
set serveroutput on
exec ds_properties.show()
exec ds_properties.setProperty('proxyHost','<www-your
complete proxy name>')
exec ds_properties.setProperty('proxySet','true')
```

Configuring and Testing DSADMIN

You need to open the <DB_ORACLE_HOME>\ds\etc\dsadmin\DSAdminConfig.xml file and change the DS_URL element of the Direct connection descriptor to point to the database instance (e.g., ORCL) that hosts Oracle Dynamic Services:

```
<DS_CONNECTION_DESCRIPTOR name="Direct">
<annotation>
-| For Nickname "Direct":
| These are specifications of the Direct Driver class
+| that will be used as well as the URL to be used with it
</annotation>
<DS_DRIVER>oracle.ds.driver.DSDirectDriver</DS_DRIVER>
<DS_URL>jdbc:oracle:thin:@myportal:1521:ORCL</DS_URL>
</DS_CONNECTION_DESCRIPTOR>
```

Then you can test running dsadmin to make sure that its configuration is correct but without performing any commands (Figure 18.14).

Installing Dynamic Services Web Provider Kit for Oracle9*i*AS Portal

You need to install the Dynamic Services Web Provider Kit to be able to build a portal provider that uses the Dynamic Services. You can download the Dynamic Services Web Provider Kit from the Oracle Technology Network. Then, unzip the tar/zip file into the <DB_ORACLE_HOME>\ds directory. Then perform the following steps.

Setting the DSGATEWAY Schema

Go to DOS and perform the following commands:

```
cd <DB_ORACLE_HOME>\ds\sql\gateway
sqlplus sys/change_on_install @dswebprovider_install.sql

sqlplus dssys/<dssys-password>;
grant dsuser_role to dsgateway;
```

Dynamic Services Web Provider Servlet Configuration

1. Create the directory

   ```
   <iAS_ORACLE_HOME>\Apache\Jserv\zones\dswebprovider
   ```

2. Copy <DB_ORACLE_HOME>\ds\conf\nt\dswebprovider.properties file to the above directory. Modify the copied file `dswebprovider.properties`.

   - Change the directory of `dsgw.jar`, `dswp.jar`, and `provider.jar` in the repositories parameter to point to the jar file in the Dynamic Services installation, for example:

     ```
     repositories=<DB_ORACLE_HOME>\ds\lib\provider.jar,
     <DB_ORACLE_HOME>\ds\lib\dswp.jar, <DB_ORACLE_HOME>\ds\
     lib\dsgw.jar
     ```

```
C:\oracle\ora81\ds\bin>dsadmin.bat
Using default config file: c:\oracle\ora81/ds/etc/dsadmin/DSAdminConfig.xml
/=================================================\
| Dynamic Services Command Line Administration Tool |
\=================================================/

        Enter UserName: DSSYS

        Enter Password: DSSYS

        Enter the DSConnection nickname to be used:
        1) Direct
        Please Choose the nickname: [1]
        DS Connection nickname used: Direct
        Opening DSConnection....... Done

Oracle Dynamic Services: Release 8.1.7.1.0 - Production (build 20010430)

Copyright (c) Oracle Corporation 2001.  All Rights Reserved.

        Available Commands
        ------------------
        Reg  (R): Registry Operations
        Prop (P): Shell Properties
        Exec (E): Execution Operations
        Connect (C): Connect to Dynamic Services Engine

        Exit (X): Exit from the DSAdminShell
        Quit (Q): Quit from the DSAdminShell

DSAdminShell> x
Closing Connection...DSREG.close: ...
DSREG.close: ... Done
Done

C:\oracle\ora81\ds\bin>_
```

Figure 18.14 Testing dsadmin.

- Modify the servlet initial parameter GWCTX_DBURL to point to your Oracle database instance where your DSGATEWAY schema is installed.

```
servlets.default.initArgs=GWCTX_DBURL=jdbc:oracle:thin:
@myportal:1521:ORCL
```

3. Modify *<iAS_ORACLE_HOME>*\Apache\Jserv\conf\jserv.conf to add a virtual path dswebprovider by adding the following lines to the ApJServMount area:

```
# Dynamic services mountpoint
ApJServMount /dswebprovider /dswebprovider
```

For Oracle Portal version 3.0.9, put this line instead:

```
ApJServGroupMount /dswebprovider balance://group1/
  dswebprovider
```

4. Modify <*iAS_ORACLE_HOME*>\ Apache\Jserv\conf\jserv.properties as follows:

   a. Include all jar files in <*DB_ORACLE_HOME*>\ds\lib into wrapper.classes ahead of all the predefined classpaths. For example:

```
# Dynamic services classes

wrapper.classpath=${DB_ORACLE_HOME}\ds\lib\ds.jar

wrapper.classpath=${DB_ORACLE_HOME}\ds\lib\jcert.jar

wrapper.classpath=${DB_ORACLE_HOME}\ds\lib\jndi.jar

wrapper.classpath=${DB_ORACLE_HOME}\ds\lib\jnet.jar

wrapper.classpath=${DB_ORACLE_HOME}\ds\lib\jsse.jar

wrapper.classpath=${DB_ORACLE_HOME}\ds\lib\ldap.jar

wrapper.classpath=${DB_ORACLE_HOME}\ds\lib\xsu12.jar

wrapper.classpath=${DB_ORACLE_HOME}\ds\lib\sax2.jar

wrapper.classpath=${DB_ORACLE_HOME}\ds\lib\oraclexsql
      .jar

wrapper.classpath=${DB_ORACLE_HOME}\ds\lib\providerutil
      .jar

wrapper.classpath=${DB_ORACLE_HOME}\ds\lib\xmlparserv2
      .jar

wrapper.classpath=${DB_ORACLE_HOME}\ds\lib\xschema.jar

# DS portal jar file

wrapper.classpath=${DB_ORACLE_HOME}\ds\lib\dswp.jar

wrapper.classpath=${DB_ORACLE_HOME}\ds\lib\dsgw.jar

wrapper.classpath=${DB_ORACLE_HOME}\ds\lib\provider.jar
```

   b. Make sure that the following line is commented out (prefixed by "#"):

```
# wrapper.classpath=<iAS_ORACLE_HOME>\rdbms\jlib\
  aqapi11.jar
```

Add the following line:

```
wrapper.classpath=<iAS_ORACLE_HOME>\rdbms\jlib\aqapi.jar
```

c. Add the new zone of dswebprovider, for example:

```
zones=root,dswebprovider
```

d. Comment out the conflicting classpaths including the following:

```
#wrapper.classpath=<iAS_ORACLE_HOME>\Apache\BC4J\lib
      \oraclexmsql.jar
#wrapper.classpath=<iAS_ORACLE_HOME>\Apache\BC4J\lib
      \jndi.jar
#wrapper.classpath=<iAS_ORACLE_HOME>\xdk\lib
      \oraclexsql.jar
#wrapper.classpath=<iAS_ORACLE_ HOME>\xdk\lib
      \xmlparserv2.jar
#wrapper.classpath=<ORACLE_PORTAL_HOME>\xdk\lib\xsu12.jar
#wrapper.classpath=<ORACLE_PORTAL_HOME>\xdk\lib\sax2.jar
#wrapper.classpath=<ORACLE_PORTAL_HOME>\xdk\lib
#wrapper.classpath=<ORACLE_PORTAL_HOME>\jlib\javax-
      ssl-1_2.jar
#wrapper.classpath=<ORACLE_PORTAL_HOME>\jlib\jssl-1_2.jar
#wrapper.classpath=${ORACLE_PORTAL_HOME}\jdbc\lib\classes
      111.zip
```

5. Now you can restart the Oracle HTTP Server *powered by Apache* and test the servlet by typing the following URL (Figure 18.15):

```
http://<Hostname>:<portno>/dswebprovider/DSWebProvider
```

Configuring the Dynamic Services Web Provider Administrator's Tool in Oracle Portal

1. Go to DOS and run the `dsgateway_mgt_service_install.dss` script using the following commands:

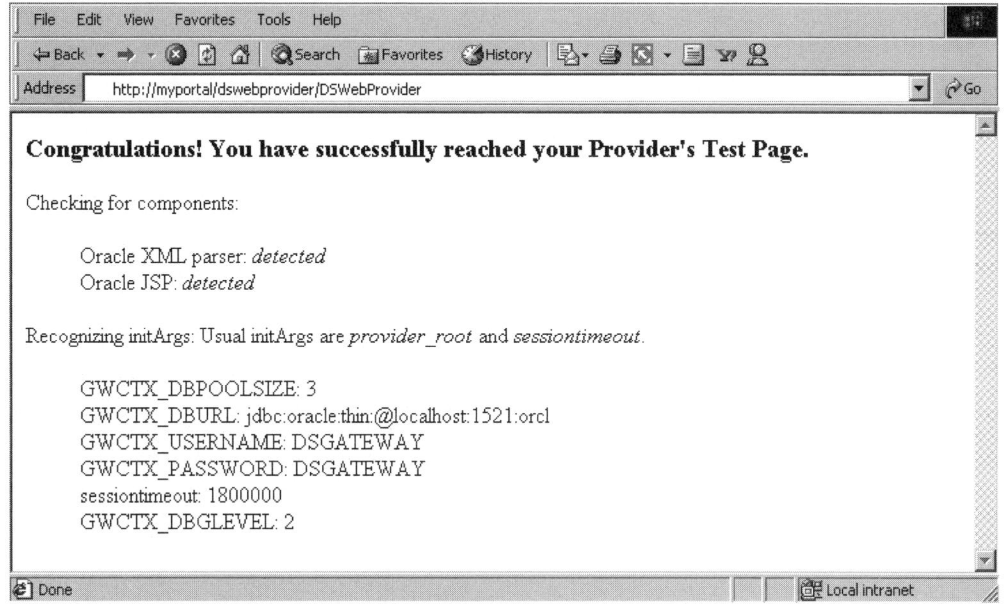

Figure 18.15 Running the DSWebProvider Servlet.

```
SET PATH=C:\oracle\ias1022\Apache\jdk\jre\bin;%ORACLE_HOME%
      \bin;%PATH%
cd c:\oracle\ora81\ds
.\bin\dsadmin -u dssys/dssys@Direct -i etc\dswebprovider
      \services\dsgateway_mgt_service_install.dss
```

2. Connect to the Dynamic Services database using sqlplus as dsgateway user and execute the following SQL commands:

```
UPDATE DSGatewayContext D SET D.DS_CONNURL =
'jdbc:oracle:thin:@myportal:1521:ORCL'
WHERE D.GWCTXID = 'DSProviderAdmin'
/

UPDATE DSGatewayContext D SET D.DSGATEWAYHELPERURL =
'http://myportal/dswebprovider/oracle.ds.gateway.portal.
DSPortalHelperServlet'
WHERE D.GWCTXID = 'DSProviderAdmin'
```

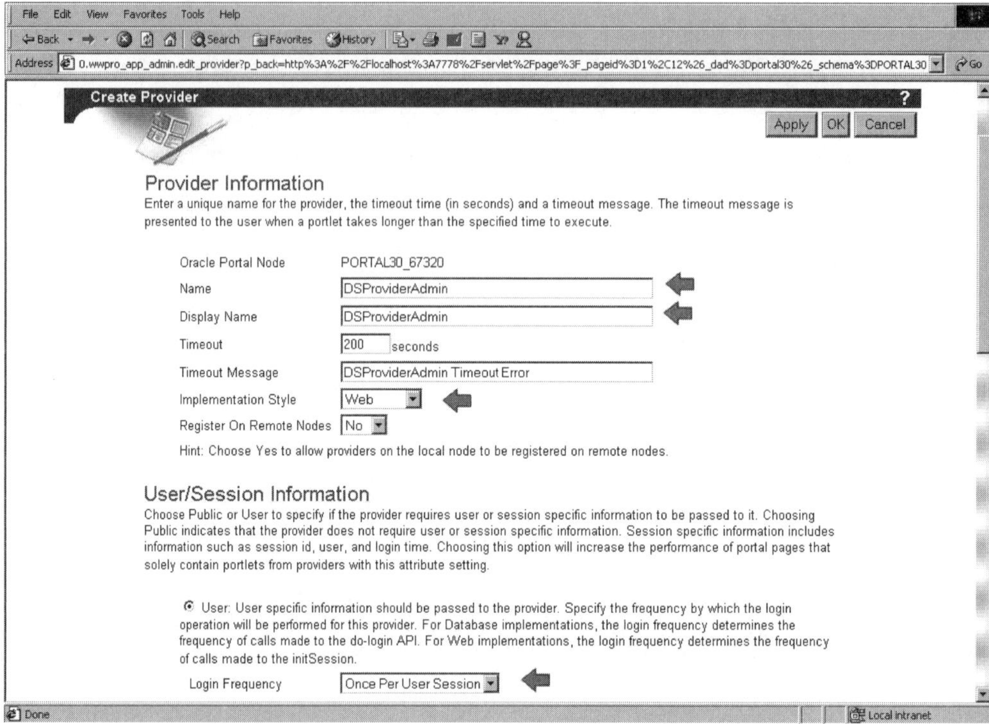

Figure 18.16 Registering the DSProviderAdmin Provider (1 of 2).

```
/

commit;
```

3. Register the Dynamic Services Web Provider Administrator portlets in Oracle Portal (Figure 18.16, Figure 18.17) by adding a new portlet provider with the following values:

   - Name: DSProviderAdmin
   - Display Name: DSProviderAdmin
   - Timeout: 100
   - Timeout Message: DSProviderAdmin Timeout Error
   - Implementation Style: Web
   - Register On Remote Nodes: No
   - Provider Logon Frequency: Once Per User Session
   - URL: http://myportal/dswebprovider/DSWebProvider
   - Provider Key: DSProviderAdmin

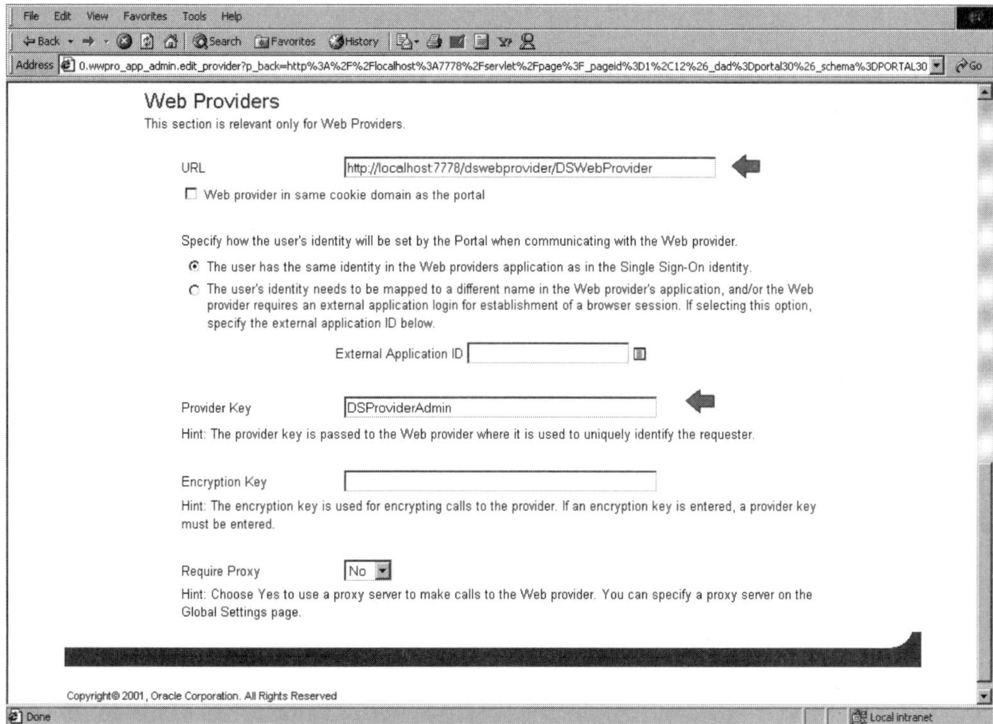

Figure 18.17 Registering the DSProviderAdmin Provider (2 of 2).

4. Create a DS ProviderAdmin portal page and add the following two portlets from the DSProviderAdmin provider (Figure 18.18, Figure 18.19):

    - Dynamic Services Provider Keys
    - Customized Dynamic Services Portlet Profiles

    After you have added these two portlets to the page, edit the defaults for a portlet. Even though the portlets do not have any customization parameters, the customize action is still necessary for initialization. When the two portlets are added, your page should look like Figure 18.20.

Create a Sample Dynamic Services Portlet

Now that you have installed the Dynamic Services and configured the Dynamic Services Web Provider Kit, you are ready to start building a new Dynamic Services portlet by performing the following steps.

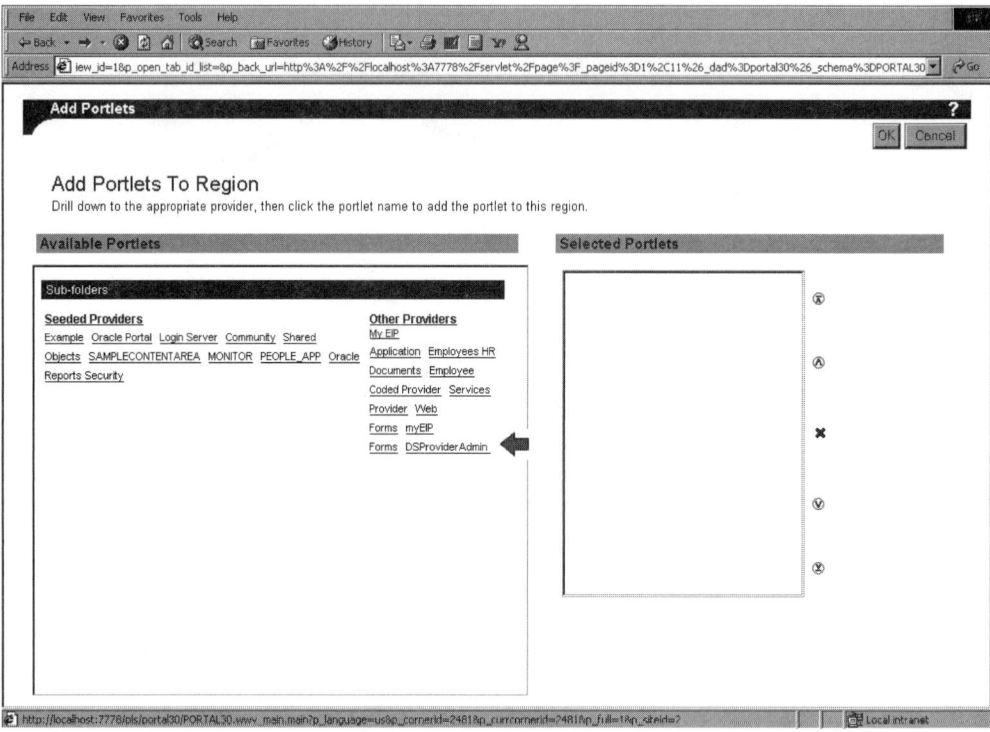

Figure 18.18 Portlet Repository: DSProviderAdmin.

Configuring and Running the Dynamic Services Creation Assistant

The Dynamic Services Creation Assistant (DSCA) is a graphical tool for defining Dynamic Services. You can download the creation assistance and uncompress it under `c:\oracle\ora81\ds`, which will create a directory "dsca".

Note

You will need the JAVAtm 2 SDK, which you can download from *www.javasoft.com.*

Edit file <DB_ORACLE_HOME>\ds\dsca\bin\dsca.bat to modify the environment variables to reflect your configuration. It should look similar to the following:

```
@echo off
@setlocal

rem ------ Please customize the following-----------
rem                1> ORACLE_HOME
```

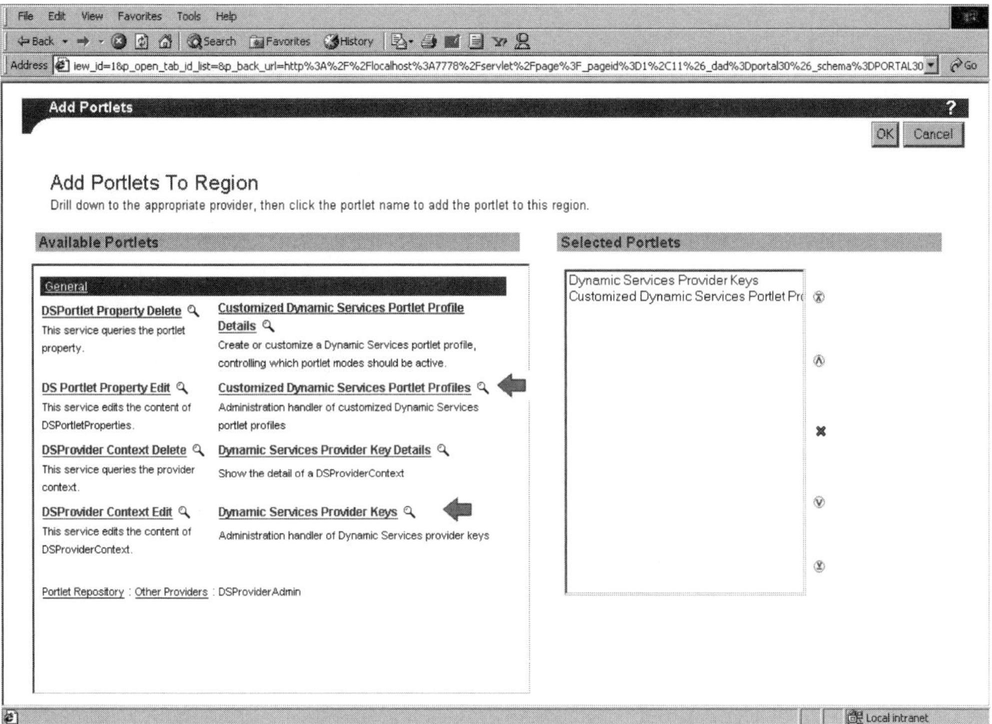

Figure 18.19 Portlet Repository: DSProviderAdmin Portlets.

```
rem                   2> DS_HOME
rem                   3> DSCA_HOME
rem                   4> PROXY_SET, PROXY_HOST, PROXY_PORT
rem           5> JDK_HOME
rem           NOTE: if not using JDK 1.2, please also customize
              JDK_CLASSPATH

rem ----------------- set up running environment
rem  if Oracle database is not installed, then set ORACLE_
     HOME to be the parent
rem       directory of DS_HOME
set ORACLE_HOME=c:\oracle\ora81

rem - Modify the path in the next two lines to specify the
    location of the kits
set DS_HOME=c:\oracle\ora81\ds
set DSCA_HOME=c:\oracle\ora81\ds\dsca
```

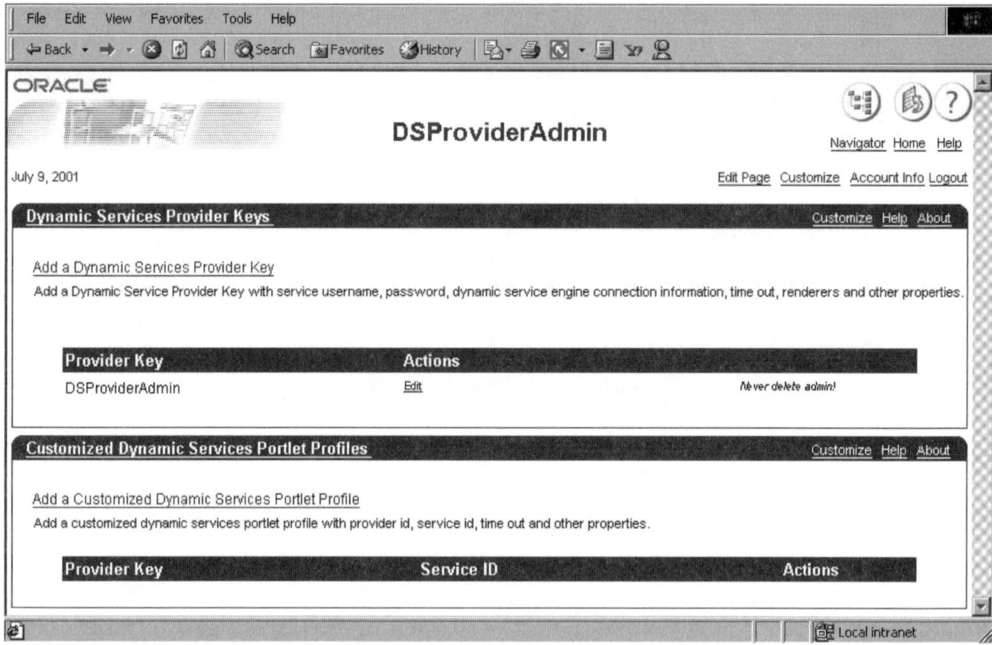

Figure 18.20 DSProviderAdmin Page.

```
set DSCA_JAVAMX=-mx128m

rem ---------- set up JDK environment
set JDK_HOME="c:\jdk1.2.2"
set path=%JDK_HOME%\bin

rem ---------- set up Proxy
set PROXY_SET=true
set PROXY_HOST=www-proxy.us.oracle.com
set PROXY_PORT=80

rem ------------- setup classpath
set
JDK_CLASSPATH=%JDK_HOME%\lib\dt.jar;%JDK_HOME%\lib\jvm.lib;
%JDK_HOME%\lib\methodtracer.jar;%JDK_HOME%\lib\tools.jar
set DSCA_XML_CLASSPATH=%DSCA_HOME%\lib\xmlcomp.jar;%DS_
HOME%\lib\xmlparserv2.jar
```

```
set DSCA_EWT_CLASSPATH=%DSCA_HOME%\lib\ewtcompat-opt-3_3_
15.zip;%DSCA_HOME%\lib\ewt-opt-3_3_15.zip;%DSCA_HOME%\lib
\help-3_1_8.jar;%DSCA_HOME%\lib\oracle_ice-4_06_6.jar;
%DSCA_HOME%\lib\share-opt-1_0_8.zip
set
DSCA_SUN_CLASSPATH=%DSCA_HOME%\lib\swingall.jar;%DSCA_HOME%
\lib\jcert.jar;%DSCA_HOME%\lib\jnet.jar;%DSCA_HOME%\lib
\jsse.jar
set
DSCA_ENGINE_CLASSPATH=%DS_HOME%\lib\ds.jar;%DSCA_HOME%\lib\
aqapi.jar;%DSCA_HOME%\lib\jmscommon.jar

set
DSCA_CLASSPATH=%JDK_CLASSPATH%;%DSCA_HOME%\bin;%DSCA_XML_
CLASSPATH%;%DSCA_EWT_CLASSPATH%;%DSCA_SUN_CLASSPATH%;%DSCA_
ENGINE_CLASSPATH%

rem ----------- execute
java %DSCA_JAVAMX% -classpath %DSCA_CLASSPATH% -DORACLE_
HOME=%ORACLE_HOME% -DproxySet=%PROXY_SET% -DproxyHost=
%PROXY_HOST% -DproxyPort=%PROXY_PORT% oracle.ds.dsca.
DscaCreateAssistantApp

endlocal
```

To run the Dynamic Services Creation Assistant, execute the batch or script file:

```
<DB_ORACLE_HOME>\ds\dsca\bin\dsca.bat
```

The sample service that we will be creating will use the Web page at *http://quote.yahoo.com* (Figure 18.21) to get stock quote information. This is a typical Web page that is used by Yahoo users to enter stock symbols. Yahoo will respond with a Web page that has the information on the user-supplied stock symbol. Later, we will deliver this information to Oracle Portal as a portlet.

DSCA will read the HTML forms that exist on the *http://quote.yahoo.com* page. To create a portlet using Dynamic Services, it is necessary to know the HTML form, and what the fields mean. For this Web page, we can know from reading the HTML form in a browser that the form sends two fields to Yahoo: "s" for the stock symbol, and "d", which corresponds to a list of the kinds of Web page results that this Yahoo HTML form can return. It is useful to go to a browser first and look at the HTML form (that is, view the HTML source).

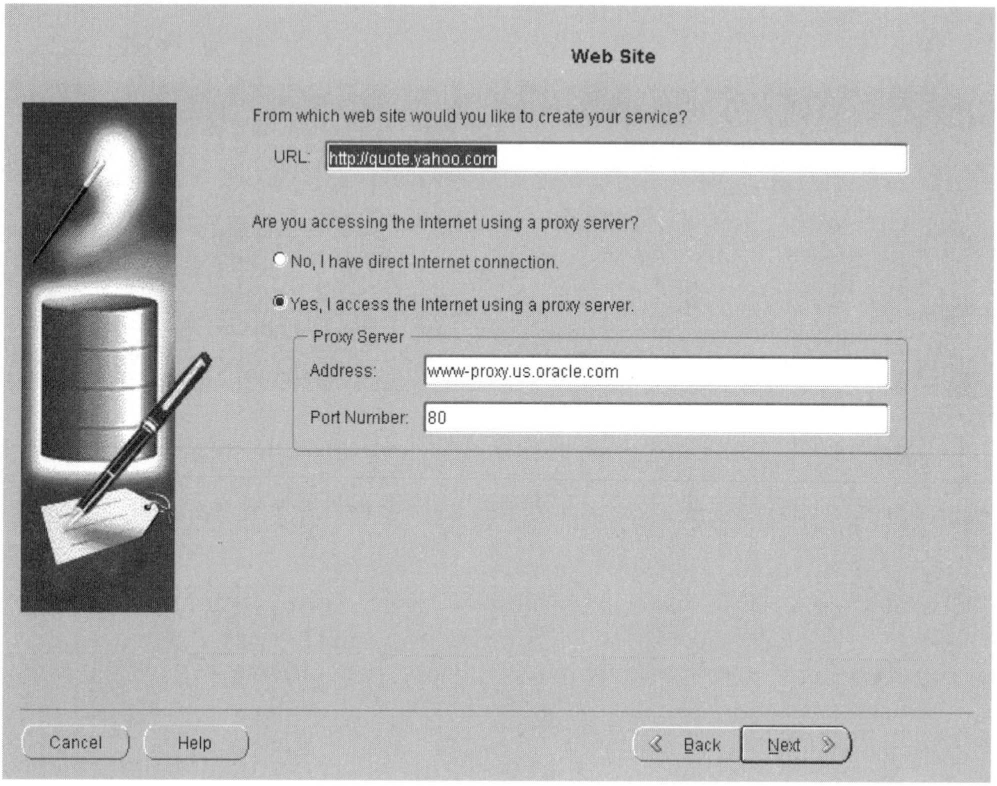

Figure 18.21 Dynamic Services Creation Assistant: Web Site.

Now, you can provide more descriptive names for the fields, and you can mark a field as hidden (in this case, its default value is used). These descriptive fields cannot contain spaces (Figure 18.22).

You can enter any sample input for the stock ticker (Figure 18.23). DSCA sends the HTML form information (ORCL for the "s" field and the default v1 for the "d" field) to the Yahoo Web page *http://quote.yahoo.com/q,* obtains the resulting Web page in HTML form, and transforms it from HTML to XHTML. The transformation to XHTML is performed to ensure the returned information is well formed to make subsequent processing of the returned information easier. The service result node window is displayed to allow you to select the node from which you can select the result information (Figure 18.24).

We now search the XHTML tree for the results you want to capture from the resulting Web page. You can search for the stock symbol ORCL by entering ORCL in the Find field and then choose the table row as the result node. You should also enter a node name that indicates what kind of information is in this node (e.g., Stock_Quote).

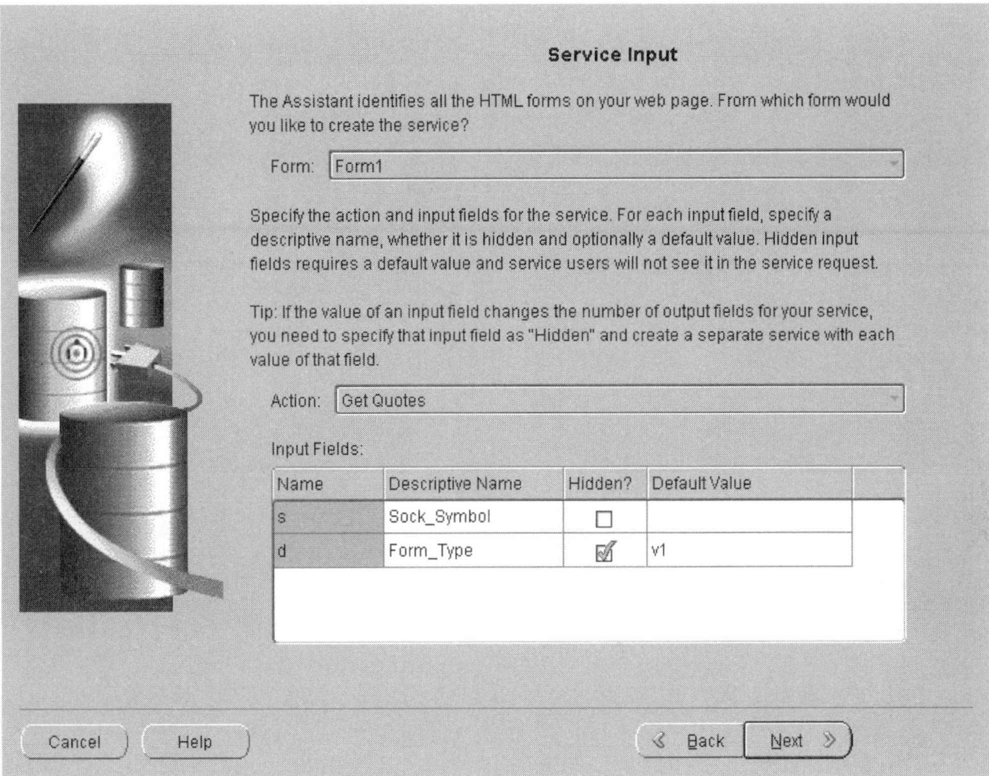

Figure 18.22 Dynamic Services Creation Assistant: Service Input.

In the next step you will identify the individual fields containing the data you want to display in the portlet. After you select the table cells you want, enter descriptive field names for the cells (Figure 18.25). The information entered on the next step (Figure 18.26) is used to identify and categorize the service. The following information about this service is entered:

- Service Name: Yahoo Stock Service
- Service ID [The unique name that will be used to refer to this service in Dynamic Services; this field is defined as a standard universal resource name (URN)]: urn:com.yahoo:stock.quote
- Description: Sample Dynamic Service
- Release Date: The default is the current date.
- Version: The version number of the service (e.g., 1.1)
- Service Update URL: Where the service provider is expected to maintain the current definition of services they provide (e.g., *http://www.oracle.com/Ds/yahoostockquote.zip*)

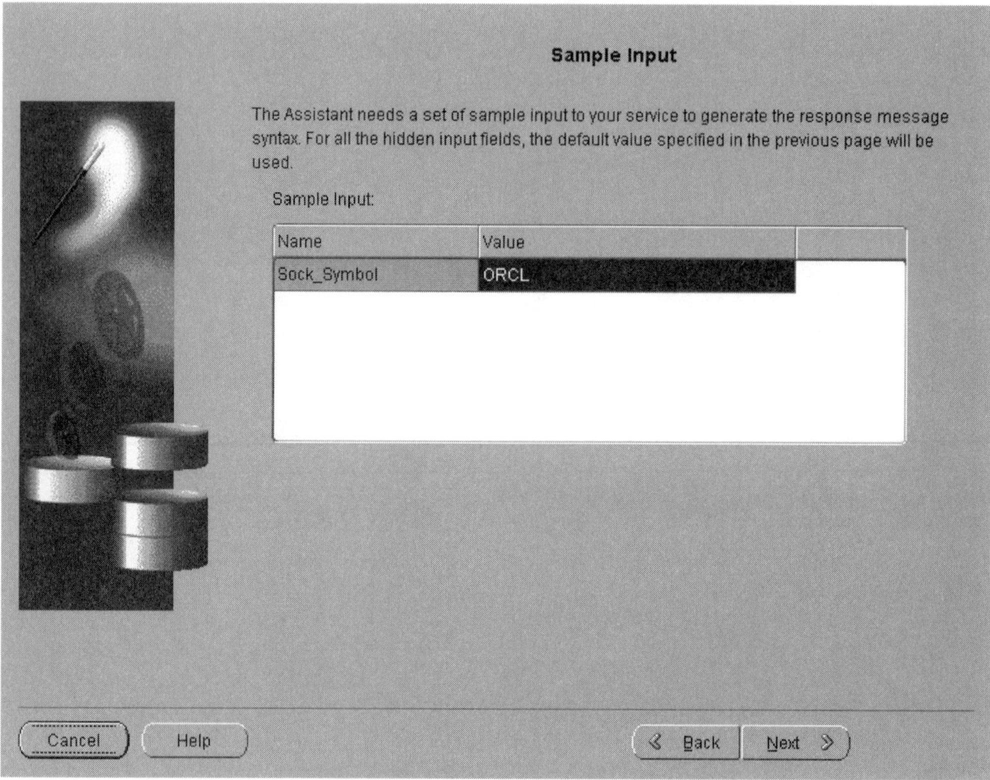

Figure 18.23 Dynamic Services Creation Assistant: Sample Input.

- Category [This is the Lightweight Directory Access Protocol (LDAP) category of the service. It is in a reverse tree format]: cn=stock, cn=finance, cn=business
- Related Keywords (These keywords can be used to search for services): stock

In the next step you supply the service provider information, which is used to identify who has created this service, how to contact them, and so on. (Figure 18.27). Try to provide information for all the fields to avoid errors when you register the service. Now the assistant can generate the service into definition files under <DB_ORACLE_HOME>\ds\dsca (Figure 18.28).

Registering the Service Using the Dynamic Services Administrator Utility

1. Start by running the dsadmin:

```
cd <DB_ORACLE_HOME>\Ds
.\bin\dsadmin -u dssys/dssys@Direct
```

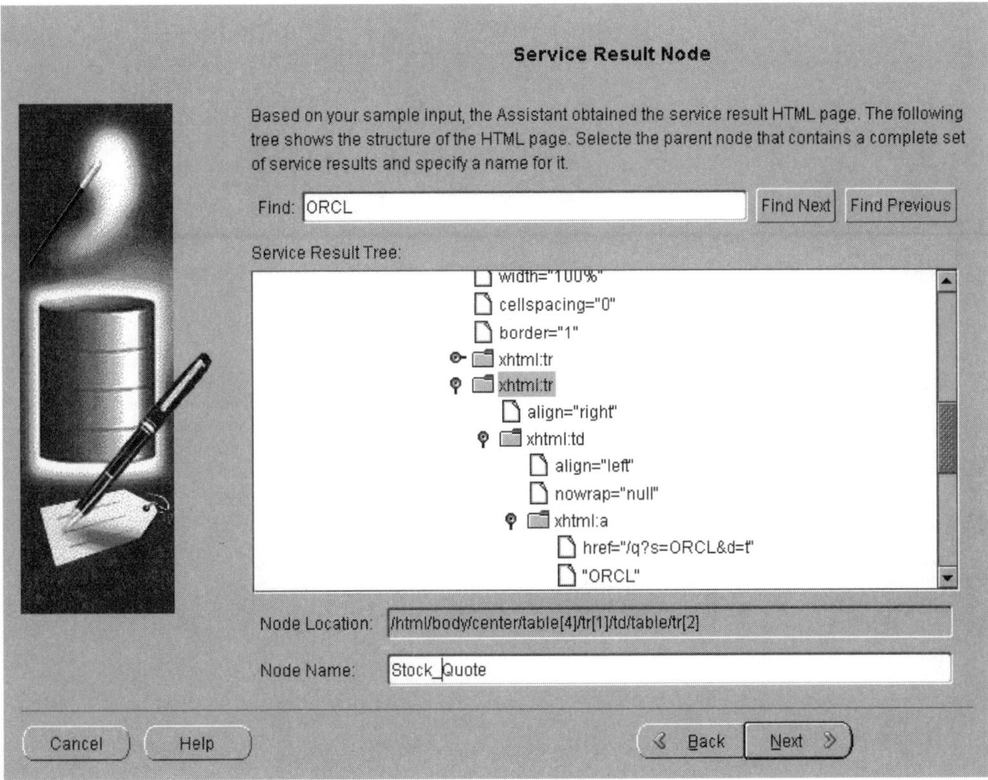

Figure 18.24 Dynamic Services Creation Assistant: Service Result Node.

2. Register the categories in the registry service tree of the DSAdmin shell (Figure 18.29):

   - DSAdminShell.Registry.Service> ac "cn=business"
   - DSAdminShell.Registry.Service> ac "cn=finance,cn=business"
   - DSAdminShell.Registry.Service> ac "cn=stock,cn=finance,cn=business"

3. After registering the categories, return to the DSAdmin shell root by entering "x" at the service management subshell and "x" at registry operations. Enter registry operations by entering "r" and then manage services by entering "s". When registering the service with the "r" command in this shell, you need to specify the directory tree root that was created with the Dynamic Services Creation Assistant previously (i.e., `c:\oracle\ora81\ds\dsca\serviceDefinition\Yahoo_Stock_Service`).
4. Before you can execute the newly created service through Oracle Portal, you must grant execution privileges to the service to the user that will be defined as a consumer application.

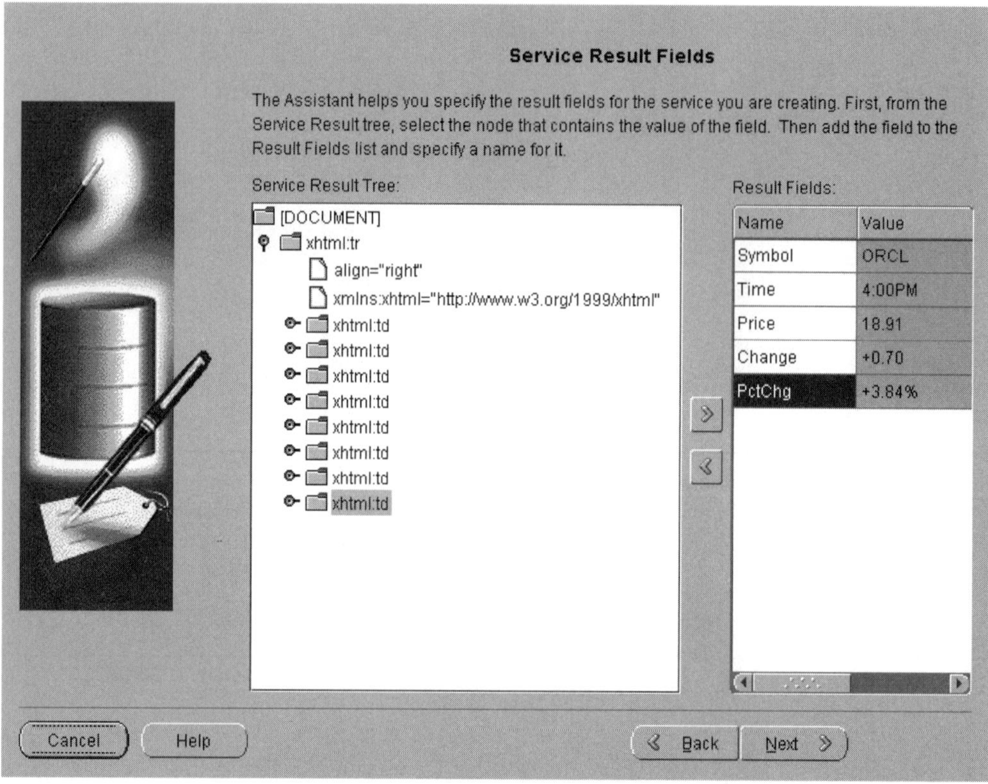

Figure 18.25 Dynamic Services Creation Assistant: Service Result Fields.

This user must first be granted the DSUSER_ROLE privilege. To grant this role log into PL/SQL as DSSYS and type "GRANT DSUSER_ROLE to scott;".

5. Then, return to the dsadmin shell and register SCOTT as a Dynamic Services consumer application. To get to the consumer application subshell of dsadmin, enter "x" at the service management subshell to return to the registry operations subshell, and enter "c" to enter the consumer application management subshell. Enter "a" to add a consumer application and scott as the user. Choose "g" to grant privileges, and then "1" to grant privileges to a service. The user "scott" is entered as the name of the user to grant privileges to, and then the number of the newly created service (e.g., 9) is entered from the list of services that is displayed (e.g., Figure 18.30).

At this point, the Portal Dynamic Services administration page that was created when the Dynamic Services Web provider was installed can be used to create a Web provider for the SCOTT username. First log into Oracle Portal as Portal30, and open the Dynamic Services

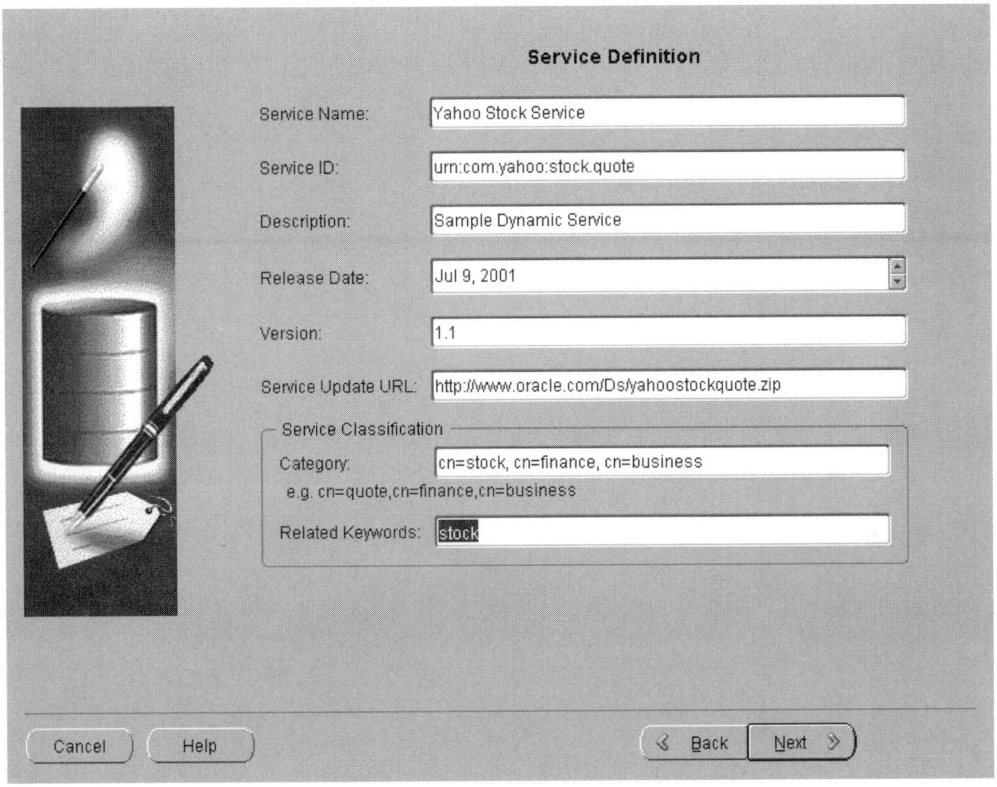

Figure 18.26 Dynamic Services Creation Assistant: Service Definition.

Administration page. Click on "Add a Dynamic Services Provider Key", and enter the following parameters (Figure 18.31):

- Key: ScottKey
- Username: Scott
- Password: tiger
- Connection URL: Change this to reflect a connect string to the database where dynamic services is installed. For example,

```
jdbc:oracle:thin:@myportal:1521:orcl
```

- Provider Helper URL: Change the host information to reflect where Oracle Portal is installed:

```
http://<Hostname>:<portno>/dswebprovider/oracle.ds.
  gateway.portal.DSPortalHelperServlet
```

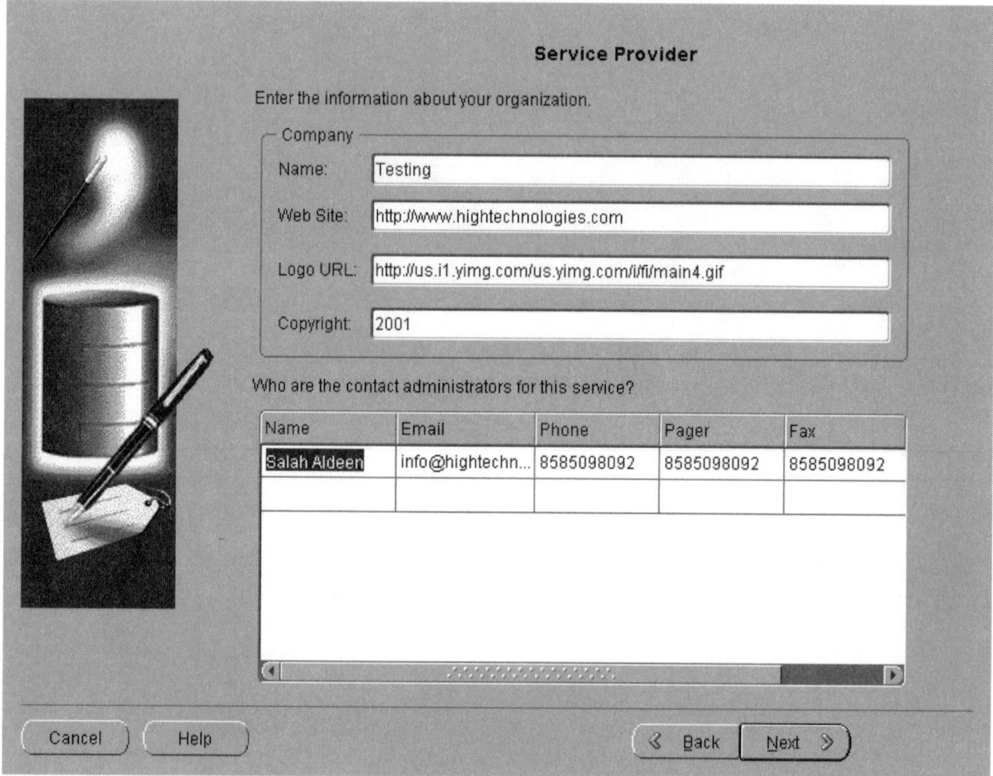

Figure 18.27 Dynamic Services Creation Assistant: Service Provider.

Click the "Add" button and make sure that the new provider key is displayed in the Dynamic Services Provider Keys portlet (Figure 18.32). Then you need to restart the Apache server.

After the restart, return to the Oracle Portal and add a new portlet provider that corresponds to the new Provider Key (i.e., ScottKey). Enter the following information to define the Portal Provider (Figure 18.33, Figure 18.34):

- Name: ScottKey
- Display Name: ScottKey
- Timeout: 200
- Timeout Message: Timeout
- Implementation Style: Web
- Register On Remote Nodes: No
- Provider Login Frequency : Once Per User Session

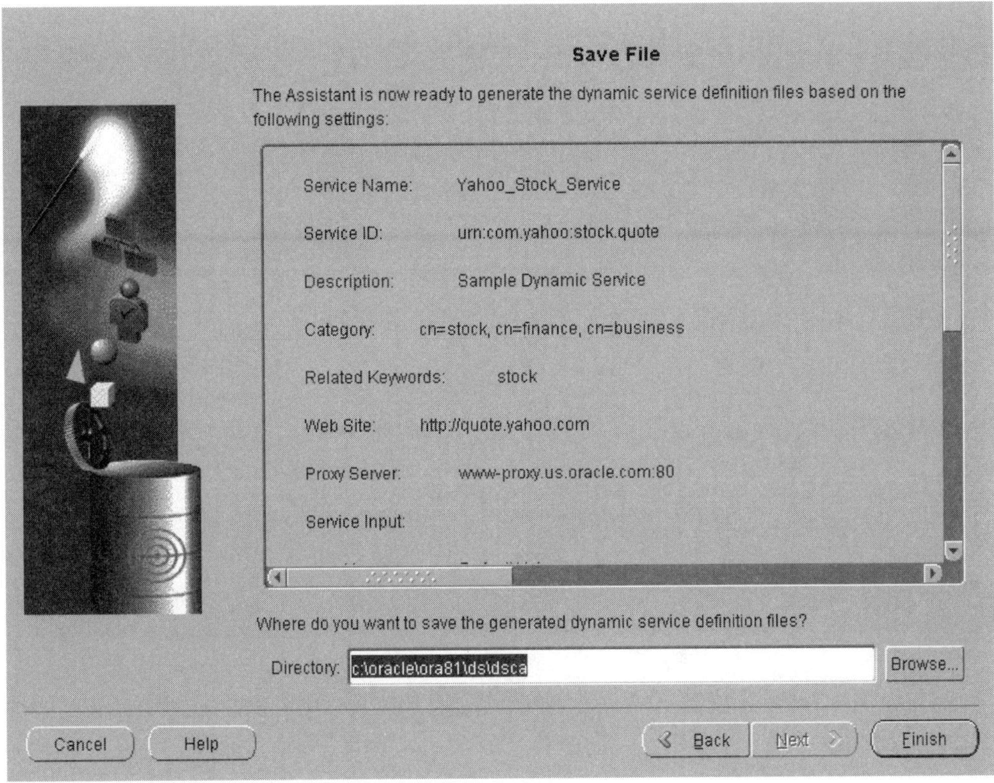

Figure 18.28 Dynamic Services Creation Assistant: Save File.

- URL: http://<Hostname>:<portno>/dswebprovider/DSWebProvider
- Provider Key: ScottKey

After registering the provider key as a portlet provider, you need to associate the particular Dynamic Service (i.e., Stock Quote) with this ScottKey provider by adding a new Customized Dynamic Services Portlet Profile. Click on the "Add a Customized Dynamic Services Portlet Profile" link in the Dynamic Services Administration page. Enter the following parameters (Figure 18.35):

- Key: ScottKey
- Service ID: urn:com.yahoo:stock.quote

When the profile is added successfully, it should be displayed in "Customized Dynamic Services Portlet Profiles" (Figure 18.36). Now, you can add the Stock Quote portlet from the ScottKey

```
C:\oracle\ora81\ds>.\bin\dsadmin -u dssys/dssys@Direct
Using default config file: c:\oracle\ora81/ds/etc/dsadmin/DSAdminConfig.xml
/================================================\
| Dynamic Services Command Line Administration Tool |
\================================================/

        Opening DSConnection....... Done

Oracle Dynamic Services: Release 8.1.7.1.0 - Production (build 20010430)

Copyright (c) Oracle Corporation 2001.  All Rights Reserved.

        Available Commands
        ------------------

        Reg  (R): Registry Operations
        Prop (P): Shell Properties
        Exec (E): Execution Operations
        Connect (C): Connect to Dynamic Services Engine

        Exit (X): Exit from the DSAdminShell
        Quit (Q): Quit from the DSAdminShell

DSAdminShell> R

Entering Registry Operation Subshell

        Available Commands
        ------------------

        Consumer (C): Manage Consumer Applications
        Service  (S): Manage Services
        Engine   (E): Manage Engine Instances
        General  (G): General Administration

        Exit     (X): Return to Top Level Shell
        Quit     (Q): Quit from DSAdminShell

DSAdminShell.Registry> S

Entering Service Operation Subshell

        Available Commands
        ------------------

        Register    (R): Register a Service
        Deregister  (D): Deregister a Service
        Reregister (RR): Reregister a Service
        Lookup      (L): Lookup by Service ID
        Search      (S): Search by Category or Keywords
        AddCat     (AC): Add a Service Category
        RemoveCat  (RC): Remove a Service Category

        Exit        (X): Return to Registry Shell
        Quit        (Q): Quit from DSAdminShell

DSAdminShell.Registry.Service> ac "cn=business"

        Please input the Category name to Add:  Adding Category <cn=business>...DSREG.addCategory: cn=business...
DSRP_DB.addCategory: cn=business... returns
DSREG.addCategory: cn=business... Done
```

Figure 18.29 dsadmin: Register Categories.

provider to one of your portal pages (Figure 18.37, Figure 18.38). You can edit the defaults of the stock quote portlet to choose another stock symbol (Figure 18.39). Finally, the portlet should be displayed in your portal page displaying the stock information of the symbol you chose (Figure 18.40).

Chapter 19 discusses the scalability of Oracle9*i*AS Portal.

```
Entering Consumer Operation Subshell

        Available Commands
        ------------------
        Add               (A): Add Consumer Application
        Remove            (R): Remove Consumer Application
        Grant             (G): Grant Privileges
        Revoke            (K): Revoke Privileges
        AddProp          (AP): Add a Property
        RemoveProp       (RP): Remove a Property
        GetProp          (GP): Get a Property
        ListConsumers    (LC): Get all consumer application names
        ListServices     (LS): Get all service IDs that a consumer
                               application has service privilege
        ListProperties   (LP): Get all properties of a service for
                               a consumer application

        Exit    (X): Return to Registry Shell
        Quit    (Q): Quit from DSAdminShell

DSAdminShell.Registry.Consumer> a

        Please input the name of the user to be Added: scott
        Adding User <scott>...DSREG.addUser: scott...
DSRP_DB.addUser: scott... returns
DSREG.addUser: scott... Done
Done

DSAdminShell.Registry.Consumer> g

        Please input the name of the user to grant to: scott

        1> Service
        2> Administrative
        Please input the type of privilege: [1] 1

DSREG.search: 2 - *...
DSREG.search: 2 - *... Done
        1> urn:com.oracle:dsportletproperty.delete
        2> urn:com.oracle:dsportletproperty.details
        3> urn:com.oracle:dsportletproperty.edit
        4> urn:com.oracle:dsportletproperty.query
        5> urn:com.oracle:dsprovidercontext.delete
        6> urn:com.oracle:dsprovidercontext.details
        7> urn:com.oracle:dsprovidercontext.edit
        8> urn:com.oracle:dsprovidercontext.query
        9> urn:com.yahoo:stock.quote

        Please Chuose ID of a Service to Grant to scott: [1] 9

        Granting Privilege on Service "urn:com.yahoo:stock.quote" to <scott>...DSREG.grantServicePrivilege: scott - ur
com.yahoo:stock.quote...
DSRP_DB.getProperty: [username=scott; serviceID=NA; property=DSUPR$TYPE; modifier=NA]... returns
DSRP_DB.grantServicePrivilege: scott - urn:com.yahoo:stock.quote... returns
DSREG.grantServicePrivilege: scott - urn:com.yahoo:stock.quote... Done
Done

DSAdminShell.Registry.Consumer> _
```

Figure 18.30 dsadmin: Grant the Stock Quote Service to User Scott.

File Edit View Favorites Tools Help

Address q/ns:GWCTXID=-18/ns:DetailsReq/ns:RedirectUrl=http%3A%2F%2Flocalhost%3A7778%2Fservlet%2Fpage%3F_pageid%3D77%26_dad%3Dportal30%26_schema%3DPORTAL30

Add Cancel

Please restart the listener after adding a new provider key before registering the provider.

Add Dynamic Services Provider

Key	ScottKey

Dynamic Services Connection Information

Username	scott
Password	*****
Driver	oracle.ds.driver.DSDirectDriver
Connection URL	jdbc:oracle:thin:@localhost:1521:orcl
Connection pool size	5

Default Time Out Settings

Time out value	100
Time out message	Warning: Connection Timed out

Customize Portlet Rendering Parameters

Type	HTML
Resource	oracle/ds/gateway/portal/input2html.xsl

Show Portlet Rendering Parameters

Type	HTML

Done Local intranet

Figure 18.31 Portal Dynamic Services Administration Page: Adding a New Provider Key.

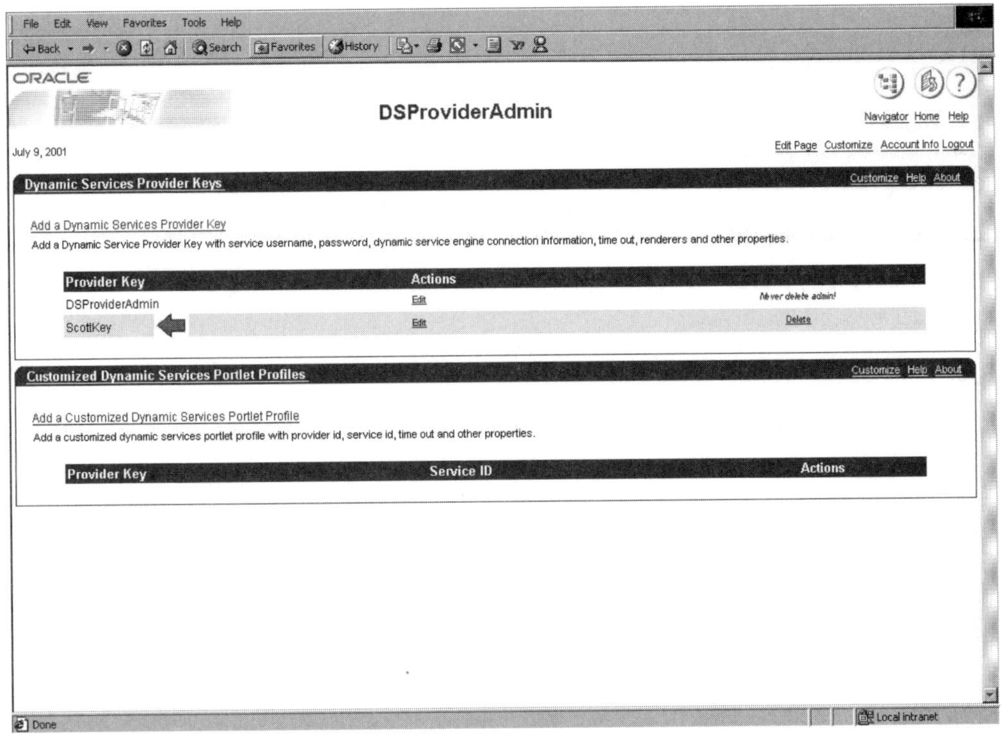

Figure 18.32 Portal Dynamic Services Administration Page: Dynamic Services Provider Keys.

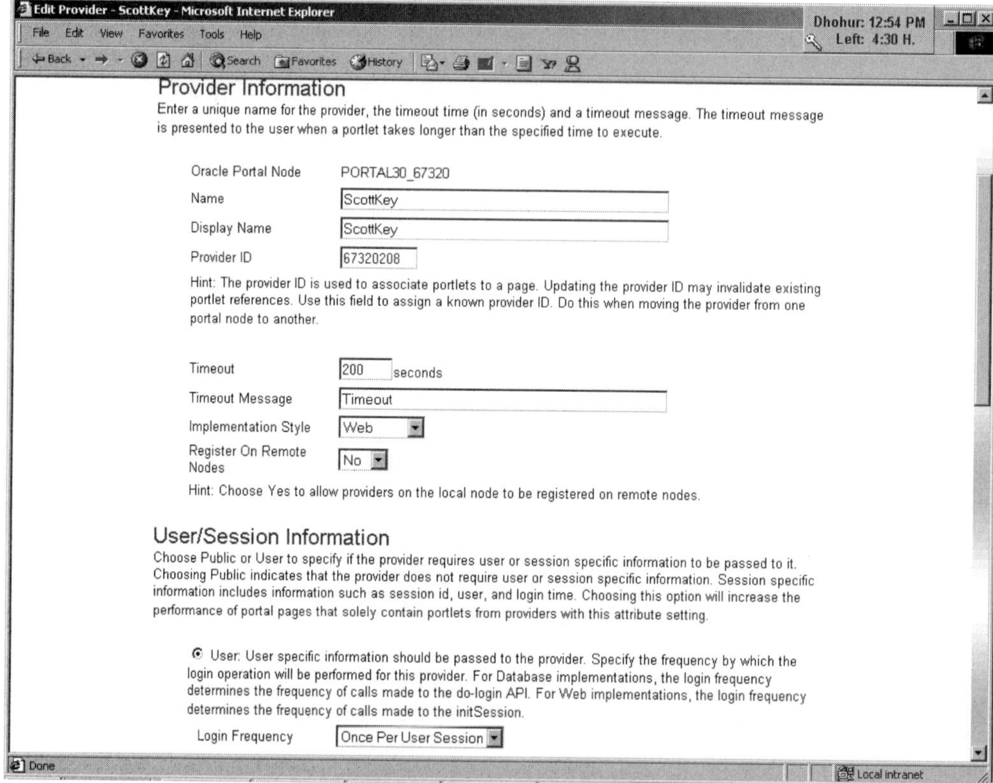

Figure 18.33 Registering the ScottKey Provider (1 of 2).

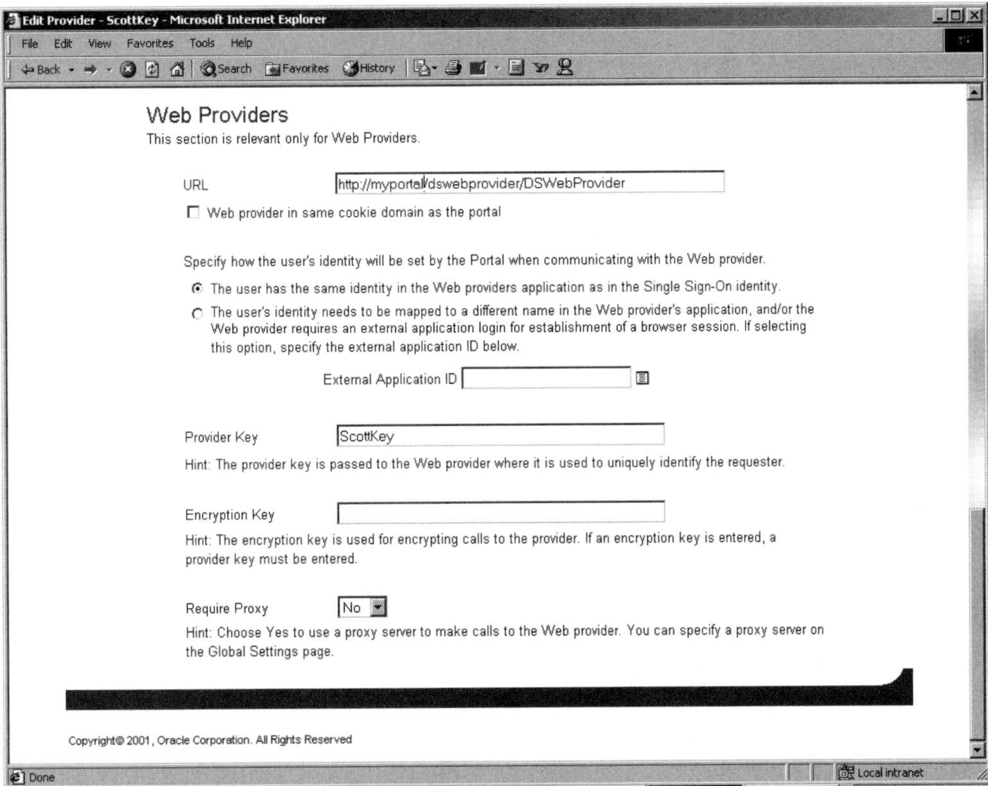

Figure 18.34 Registering the ScottKey Provider (2 of 2).

File Edit View Favorites Tools Help

Add Cancel

Please refresh the portlet repository after customizing a Dynamic Services portlet profile to make the customization effective.

Dynamic Services Provider

Key	ScottKey
Service ID	urn:com.yahoo:stock.quote

Time Out Settings

Timeout value	100
Timeout Message	timeout

Portlet Modes Settings

showEdit	true
showEditDefaults	true
hasHelp	true
hasAbout	true
showPreview	true
showDetails	true
hasShowForm	none

Done Local intranet

Figure 18.35 Adding a Customized Dynamic Services Portlet Profile.

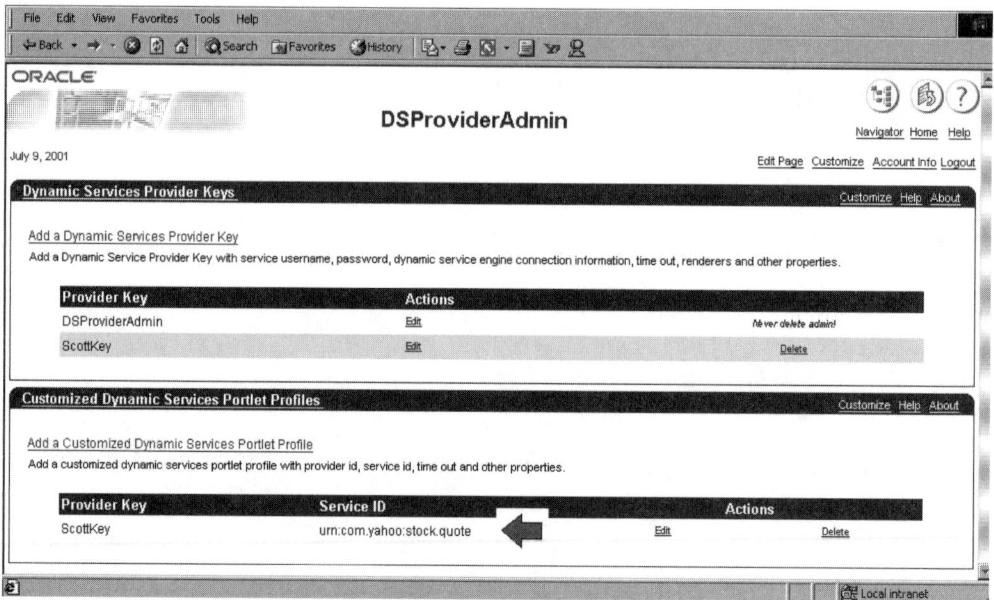

Figure 18.36 Portal Dynamic Services Administration Page: Customized Dynamic Services Portlet Profiles.

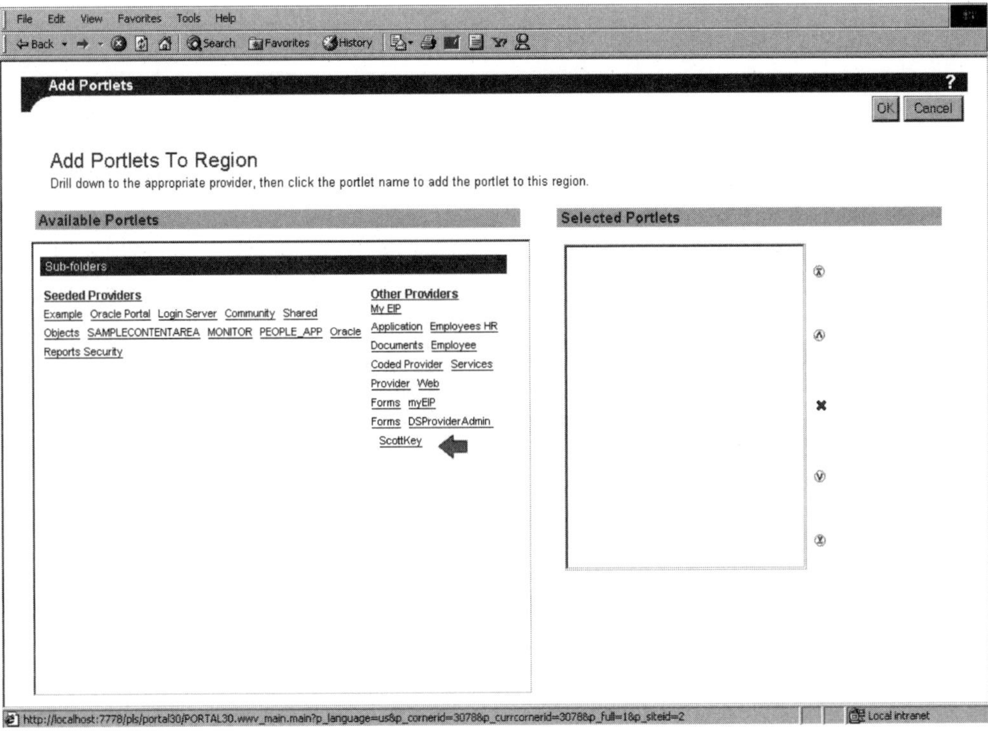

Figure 18.37 Portlet Repository: ScottKey Provider.

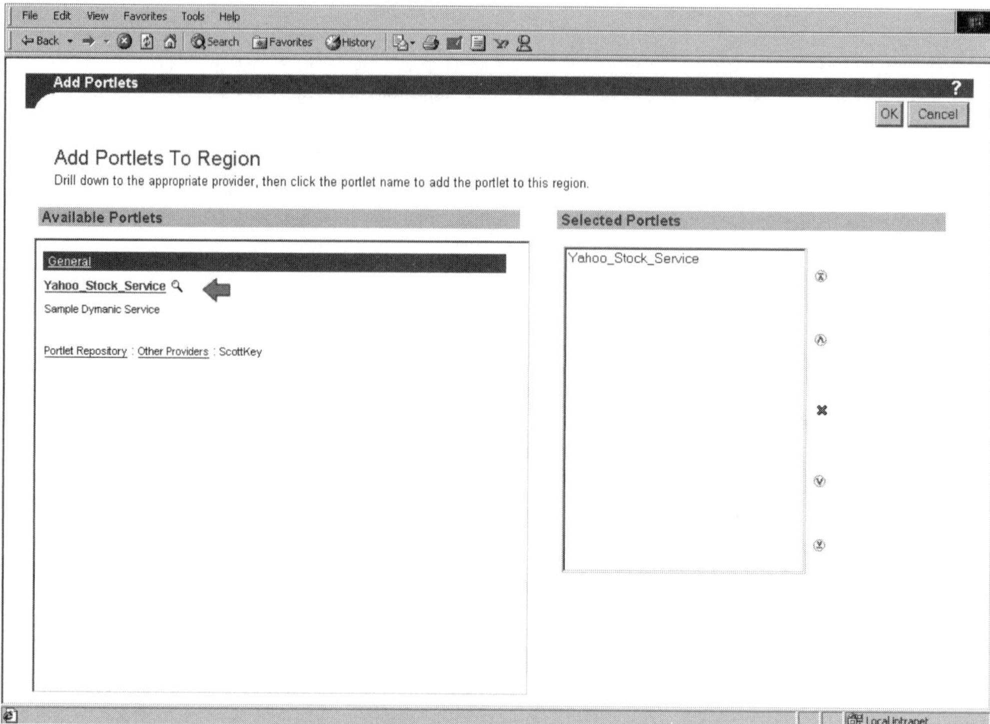

Figure 18.38 Portlet Repository: ScottKey Provider.

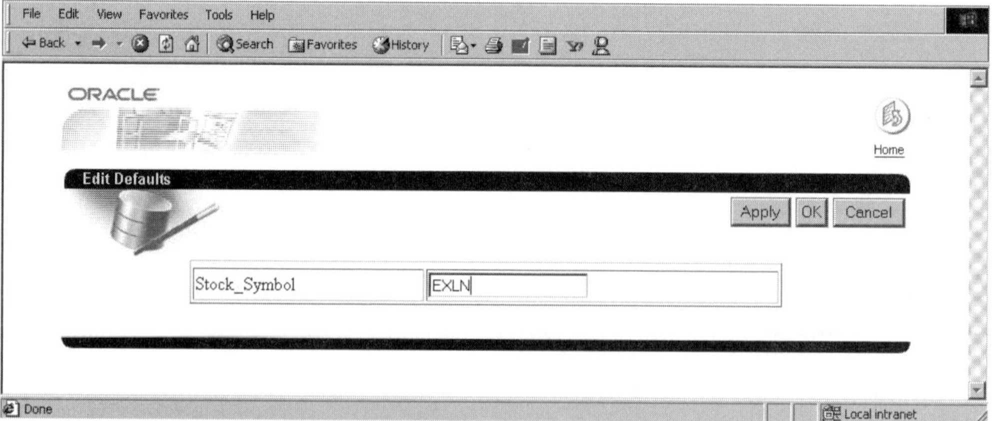

Figure 18.39 Yahoo Stock Service: Edit Defaults.

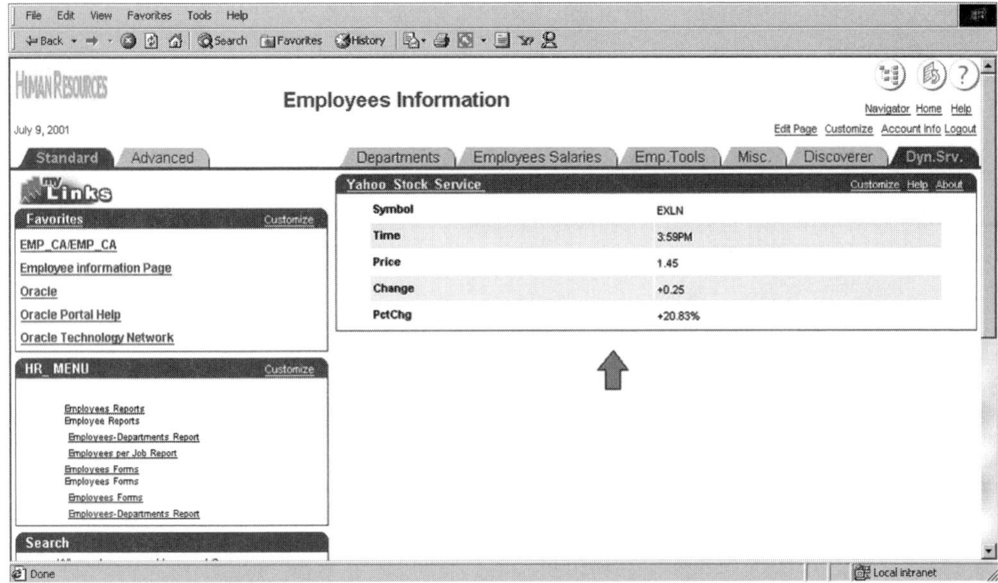

Figure 18.40 Page Display: Yahoo Stock Service Portlet.

CHAPTER 19

Scaling and Tuning Oracle9*i*AS Portal

Introduction

This chapter shows you how to add additional Oracle Portal nodes to scale your Oracle9*i*AS Portal environment This chapter also discusses some Oracle9*i*AS tuning topics.

Distributed Oracle Portal Installation

A distributed environment refers to several installations of Oracle Portal to create a multi-node environment. There are many benefits to such an environment, such as the ability to share portlet provider information across all nodes, as well as increased scalability, availability, and system throughput.

What Is a Node?

In a distributed Oracle Portal environment, each node is a complete Oracle Portal installation that resides in a separate database instance and is configured to operate in a distributed manner. Each node in the system may operate either independently or in conjunction with the other nodes. The node containing the page that you are currently viewing is considered the *local* node. All other installations are considered *remote* nodes. However, a page in Oracle Portal can contain portlets that were created on either the local or remote nodes.

Node registration refers to associating nodes to each other so that they may be able to share information. Node registration is done by completing a set of configuration steps. These steps are discussed later in this chapter.

Benefits of a Distributed Oracle Portal Environment

A distributed or multi-node Oracle Portal environment provides the following benefits over a single-node environment.

Portlet Provider Information Sharing

In a distributed Oracle Portal environment, provider information can be shared across nodes. During node registration, provider registration also occurs. When a provider is registered on a remote node, the portlets for that provider are populated in the node's Portlet Repository, which allows you to build pages with portlets residing on remote nodes. In addition to sharing provider information, the distributed environment also lets you group providers accordingly.

Higher Availability

When provider registration occurs, the provider registry information is replicated on the remote node. Only the provider registry information is replicated, not the actual provider implementation. The provider implementation package resides only on the host node of that provider. A page may consist of portlets from any number of nodes that participate in the distributed environment. When such a page is rendered, the portlets are executed on the host node of each of the portlet providers (the node where the provider implementation package resides).

For example, consider the following scenario, which can occur in a multi-Oracle Portal node environment: A page consists of portlet 1, which resides on node A, and portlet 2, which resides on node B. When the page is rendered, portlet 1 is executed on node A and portlet 2 is executed on node B. Such a scenario enables you to access multiple machines with significantly increased performance and increased system throughput because the rendering of a page is distributed among several database instances. The execution of the portlets on the different databases is done in parallel.

The distributed environment provides high availability. If one node fails, the other nodes would continue to process with full access except on portlets residing on the failed node.

Node Requirements

You must meet the following node requirements for configuring a distributed Oracle Portal architecture.

Common Cookie Domain

The cookie domain for the Oracle Portal session cookie must be common for all nodes that participate in the distributed Oracle Portal environment. If the cookie domain is changed on one node, it must be changed on all other nodes. Otherwise, the Oracle Portal nodes in your environment will not function in a distributed manner.

Oracle HTTP Server *powered by Apache* Configuration

Any other node that exists in the network and for which a communication path has been established may access a portlet provider that resides on a node. The Oracle HTTP server *powered by Apache* is responsible for establishing a communication path and for displaying portlets for each node.

You can choose either of the following scenarios in your distributed environment:

- Have multiple Oracle HTTP servers *powered by Apache* running, one for each node.
- Have a single Oracle HTTP server *powered by Apache* running and accessible by all nodes.

When communicating between browsers, the Oracle Portal session cookie is sent to each portlet execution request. Also, the cookie domain consists of the `<host.domain:port>`. When using multiple Oracle HTTP servers, this results in a different `<host.domain:port>`. Only one node will have the same cookie domain as the Login Server. Thus, in this case, when the user tries to access a node by clicking a portlet's URL, the Oracle Portal session cookie will *not* be sent by the browser. To resolve this situation, a common cookie domain name is required. To do this, you *must* run the `ctxckupd.sql` script on all nodes in your distributed environment.

In an Oracle Portal distributed environment, each Oracle HTTP server *powered by Apache* must have a Database Access Descriptor (DAD) configuration for each of the portal nodes that participate in the distributed system.

Common Login Server

All the nodes that participate in the distributed Oracle Portal environment must use the same Login Server. Otherwise, you may encounter a run-time error if a node that is registered to participate in the distributed Oracle Portal environment is not using the same Login Server as the other nodes. In this case, you would fail to log onto the Oracle Portal node via Single Sign-On (SSO) and not have access to the portlets on that node.

Symmetric Node Registration

All nodes included in the distributed architecture must be symmetrically registered between them. For example, if the distributed Oracle Portal environment consists of three nodes (A, B, and C), make sure that the following registrations exist:

- Node A is registered on B and C.
- Node B is registered on A and C.
- Node C is registered on A and B.

URLs in Portlets

If you are creating your own custom portlets using the Oracle Portal Development Kit (PDK), you must use absolute URLs (not relative URLs) for portlets destined to be run in a distributed Oracle Portal environment.

Setting up a Distributed Oracle Portal Environment

This section describes the process for setting up a distributed Oracle Portal environment. For the purpose of the following example, the environment will consist of two nodes: node A and node B. Ensure that you have the required privileges on the nodes and on the Login Server before performing the steps to set up your portal environment.

- You must have Full Administrator privileges on the Login Server to change any of its settings.
- You must be an Oracle Portal Administrator to access the Administer tab of the Oracle Portal home page.

Step 1: Create Oracle Portal Nodes

To participate in a distributed Oracle Portal environment, you must have at least two Oracle Portal installations, one for node A and the other for node B. To create a node, install Oracle Portal as instructed earlier. You will need to perform an installation of Oracle Portal for each node you want to have in your distributed environment.

Step 2: Create Same Cookie Domain

To resolve the issue of a different `<host.domain:port>` configuration for each node, the same cookie domain *must* exist across nodes in a distributed Oracle Portal environment in order for the Oracle Portal session cookie to be sent successfully by the browser. The solution is to run the `ctxckupd.sql` script on all the nodes in your distributed Oracle Portal environment.

To create the same cookie domain on all nodes, perform the following steps:

1. If you have an Oracle HTTP server *powered by Apache* running on the computer on which your node is located, stop the server from a command prompt or from the services.

Note

Be sure that the two nodes are created on two different databases because the distributed Oracle Portal functionality is not supported on nodes that exist on the same database.

Note

This step applies only if your distributed Oracle Portal environment is running multiple Oracle HTTP servers *powered by Apache*. If you are running only one Oracle HTTP server, you can skip this step.

---

2. On the database where your node is installed, log on to SQL*Plus with the Oracle Portal schema owner (i.e., PORTAL30). Then run the `ctxckupd.sql`, and, when prompted, enter the domain name for the session cookie as required.
3. Repeat these steps for all other remote nodes in your distributed Oracle Portal environment.

Step 3: Edit Oracle Portal DADs

A distributed Oracle Portal environment requires that each node has a separate Database Access Descriptor (DAD) for each Oracle HTTP server *powered by Apache.* Also, the Session Cookie Name field in the DAD configuration must be the same across nodes. Upon installation, a DAD is created for each node. This step requires you to edit the DAD on each node and specify a common cookie name across nodes.

Important

In a distributed Oracle Portal environment, there should be only one Login Server.

Access DAD Configuration Page DADs are created from the Database Access Descriptor configuration page in Oracle Portal, which you can access in either of the following two ways:

- Method one: In the Services portlet, click "Listener Gateway Settings". By default, the Services portlet is located on the Oracle Portal home page's Administer tab. Next, click on "Gateway Database Access Descriptor Settings". Then, in the Edit/Delete Database Access Descriptors section, click the Edit icon next to the node's DAD entry. The DAD configuration page is displayed.
- Method two: In your browser, go directly to the following URL:

```
http://<hostname.domain>:<portno>/pls/admin_/dadentries.htm
```

Then, in the Edit/Delete Database Access Descriptors section, click the "Edit" icon next to the node's DAD entry.

Configuration Provide the same cookie name for Oracle Portal nodes in your distributed environment:

1. From the appropriate node's Database Access Descriptor configuration page, edit the DAD for node A. In the Session Cookie Name field, enter a name.

   Example: `master_portal_session_cookie`.

2. From the appropriate node's Database Access Descriptor configuration page, edit the DAD for node B. In the Session Cookie Name field, enter the same cookie name you entered for node A.

   Example: `master_portal_session_cookie`.

3. From the Login Server's Database Access Descriptor configuration page, edit the DAD for the Login Server of node A. A Login Server DAD is appended with _SSO in its name. In the Session Cookie Name field, enter a cookie name that is different from the name given for node A and node B.

   Example: `master_portal_sso_session_cookie`.

Step 4: Associate Nodes with the Same Login Server

For the purpose of our example, we must make node A and node B share the same Login Server. Otherwise, any node that is not sharing the same Login Server as the other nodes in the distributed environment will fail when performing any type of distributed functionality.

Important

It is very important that the Session Cookie is the same for both (all) DADs in your distributed environment, except for the Login Server. The cookie is used by the Oracle Portal security subsystem to perform session establishment and authentication during Single Sign-On. It is very important to use a different name for the Session Cookie because the Login Server uses its own cookie. If the same name was used as that of Oracle Portal, the Login Server resulting in Oracle Portal authentication failures would overwrite the Oracle Portal session cookie.

This step must be performed to ensure that all nodes in your distributed Oracle Portal environment share the same Login Server. When installing Oracle Portal with the Oracle Universal Installer (OUI), each node is installed with its own Login Server. Therefore, when installing multiple nodes, they do not, by default, share the same Login Server.

Associate Node A with the Login Server of Node A

1. Start a command line prompt.
2. Change to the <iAS_ORACLE_HOME>\portal30\admin\plsql directory in which Oracle Portal for node A is installed.
3. Enter the following command to associate a node to the Login Server:

Example:

```
ssodatan -w http://myportal:80/pls/portal30/
-l http://myportal:80/pls/portal30_sso/ -s portal30 -p
portal30 -o portal30_sso -c orcl
```

By default, the OUI installs the first node and associates it to the appropriate Login Server. It is safe to skip this step unless you intend on editing the default Login Server association.

4. Enter the script parameters as you would if node A were to function in a single-node environment.

Register Node A as a Partner Application to the Login Server of Node B

1. In the Services portlet, click Login Server Administration. By default, the Services portlet is located on the Oracle Portal home page's Administer tab.
2. Click "Administer Partner Applications".
3. Click "Add Partner Application".
4. Enter the following information on the Partner Application page:

    - Name: `Oracle Portal`
    - Home URL: `http://Bnodeportal/pls/<node B DAD>/<node B schema>.home`
    - Success URL: `http://Bnodeportal/pls/<node B DAD>/<node B schema>.wwsec_app_priv.process_signon`

Important

The DAD name <node B DAD> must be specified in lowercase characters.

---

5. Click "Apply". The Edit Partner Application page is displayed.

Edit Partner Application On the page that appears, you'll need to copy exactly the following information, which you will require to run the script in the next step. For example:

- ID: 1323
- Token: G06U7W36
- Encryption Key: a21255e6b139ca34

Associate Node B with the Login Server of Node A

1. Start a command line prompt.
2. Change to the `<iAS_ORACLE_HOME>\portal30\admin\plsql` directory in which Oracle Portal for node A is installed.
3. Enter the following command to associate a node to a specific Login Server:

```
ssodatax -i 1234 -t A1B2C3 -k X9Y8Z7 -w
http://Bnodeportal:80/pls/portal30/
-l http://myportal:80/pls/portal30_sso/ -s portal30
-v v1.0 -o portal30_sso -c orcl
```

For a detailed list of ssodatax command parameters, refer to Chapter 18.

4. Enter the script parameters as required.

You have completed this step. Node A and node B are associated to the same Login Server.

Step 5: Create a User on the Login Server with Administrator Privileges

In this step you need to create a user on the Login Server with full administrator privileges on node B. This user must be the schema owner of node B.

1. In the Services portlet click "Login Server Administration". By default, the Services portlet is located on the Oracle Portal home page's Administer tab.
2. Click "Administer Users".
3. Click "Create New Users".
4. Enter the configuration information as required.
5. Click "Create".

A new user for the Login Server is created.

- User Name <schema_of_node_B>
- Password <schema_of_node_B>
- Confirm Password <schema_of_node_B>

Step 6: Discover the Name of Each Node

1. In Oracle Portal, log onto node A as required by entering the username and password.
2. In the Node portlet, click "Edit the Local Node." By default, the Node portlet is located on the Oracle Portal home page's Administer tab.

3. Write down the name of the local node.
4. Close all open browser windows.
5. Open a new browser window and repeat these steps for node B.

Step 7: Register Nodes between Themselves

1. While on node B, register node A to node B (see Table 19.1).

    - In the Node portlet, click "Add a Remote Node". By default, the Node portlet is located on the Oracle Portal home page's Administer tab.
    - Enter the configuration information for node A as required on the configuration page.

Important

You must close all browser windows before accessing node B in order for the Oracle Portal session cookie that was created by node A to expire and perform authentication on the appropriate node (node B).

Table 19.1 Node A to Node B Registration Information

Field	Description
Remote Node Name	Name of the remote node (node A) obtained in step 6
Oracle Portal Database User	The schema owner for node A
Oracle Portal Database Password	The schema password for node A
Database Link Name	Oracle recommends that you leave this field blank. The default name will be used when the database link is created on this page. Note that the default name is not displayed on this page.
TNS Name	The TNS Name alias (connect string) for the database on which node A is installed
Remote Oracle Portal DAD	The DAD for node A created in step 3
Remote Listener URL	The machine name on which the Oracle HTTP server *powered by Apache* is installed
Remote Listener Port	The port on which the Oracle HTTP server *powered by Apache* is running for that node

2. Click "OK".
3. Quit all the browser windows.
4. Repeat these steps to register node B to node A.

When this step is completed successfully, the Oracle Portal nodes are fully configured to operate in the distributed environment.

Step 8: Refresh the Portlet Repository for Each Node

Other nodes can use the node providers that are configured for a distributed Oracle Portal environment. However, the Portlet Repository needs to be refreshed on each node to see the providers and portlets created on remote nodes.

To refresh the Portlet Repository, perform the following steps:

1. From the Oracle Portal home page, click from the shortcut bar to access the navigator.
2. In the navigator, click the Content Areas tab.
3. In the Name column, click "Portlet Repository". The Portlet Repository Content Area is displayed.
4. Click "Refresh" in the upper right corner of the page.

Once this step is completed, the distributed portlets appear in the Portlet Repository. The providers that are not local (i.e., remote) are easily identifiable by their names, which are prefixed with the name of the node to which they belong. The distributed portlets are now displayed on the Add Portlets page and can be used when creating a page.

5. Repeat these steps for each node in your distributed Oracle Portal environment.

Important

This operation may take a few minutes to complete because the Portlet Repository is refreshed for all the providers that are registered on the node.

Step 9: Create Additional Nodes

You can always create additional nodes to participate in the distributed Oracle Portal environment. For example, to register node C, complete the following steps in the order presented: The registration of nodes must be symmetric. In addition, it is important to register the new node, in this case node C, on an existing node, either node A or node B, before registering an existing node on the new node. This is required to maintain the cookie encryption key used by the other nodes of the distributed environment.

1. Create node C on a different database from that of node A and node B.
2. Create a DAD for node C.
3. Associate node C with the Login Server used by node A and node B.
4. Create a user for node C on the Login Server.
5. Register node C on node A.
6. Register node C on node B.
7. Register node A on node C.
8. Register node B on node C.
9. Refresh the Portlet Repository on node A, B, and C.

O9*i*AS Performance Tuning

This section introduces Application Server tuning. Let's start by defining performance tuning.

When Do You Tune for Performance?

Performance tuning must be integrated into all the software development and deployment phases, rather than considered just before going into production. You must anticipate performance requirements during application analysis and design, and balance the costs and benefits for optimal performance.

Optimizing HTTP Server Performance

This section provides information on improving the Oracle HTTP server's performance.

Configuring the ThreadsPerChild Parameter

The ThreadsPerChild parameter in the httpd.conf file specifies the number of requests that can be handled concurrently by the HTTP server. Requests in excess of the ThreadsPerChild parameter value wait in the TCP/IP queue.

Configuring ThreadsPerChild for Servlet Requests

If the HTTP server will handle servlets exclusively, then the ThreadsPerChild parameter value must be much smaller than the number of concurrent requests that the JServ process can service. If a JServ process is handling all the requests it can (as specified by security.maxConnections in the jserv.properties file), then a delay occurs when the HTTP server tries to establish a connection to it. To prevent the corresponding increase in latency, set ThreadsPerChild to half the number of requests that all of the JServ processes can handle. For example, suppose you have four JServ processes, and each has a security.maxConnections value of 10. The total number of requests that the JServ processes can handle is 40, so set ThreadsPerChild to 20.

Configuring ThreadsPerChild for Static Page Requests

The more concurrent threads you make available to handle requests, the more requests your server can process. But be aware that with too many threads, under high load, requests will be handled more slowly and the server will consume more system resources. For example, if you have four CPUs, set ThreadsPerChild to 80. If, with this setting, CPU utilization does not exceed 85%, you can increase ThreadsPerChild, but ensure that the available threads are in use. You can determine this using the mod_status utility.

Enabling SSL Session Caching

The Oracle HTTP server caches a client's SSL session information by default. With session caching, only the first connection to the server incurs high latency. The SSLSessionCacheTimeout directive in httpd.conf determines how long the server keeps a session alive (the default is 300 seconds). The session information is kept in a file. You can specify where to keep the session information using the SSLSessionCache directive. Multiple Oracle HTTP server processes can use the file. The duration of an SSL session is unrelated to the use of HTTP persistent connections.

Understanding Performance Implications of Logging

This section discusses the performance implications of using access logging and the `HostNameLookups` directive.

Access Logging For static page requests, access logging of the default fields results in a performance overhead.

HostNameLookups By default, the HostNameLookups directive is set to OFF. The server writes the IP addresses of incoming requests to the log files. When HostNameLookups is set to ON, the server queries the DNS system on the Internet to find the hostname associated with the IP address of each request, then writes the hostnames to the log.

Depending on the server load and the network connectivity to your DNS server, the performance cost of the DNS lookup could be high. Unless you really need to have hostnames in your logs in real time, it is best to log IP addresses.

Benefits of the HTTP/1.1 Protocol

The Oracle HTTP server can use HTTP/1.1. Netscape Navigator release 4.0 still uses HTTP/1.0, with some 1.1 features, such as persistent connections. Internet Explorer uses

HTTP/1.1. The performance benefit of persistent connections comes from reducing the overhead of establishing and tearing down a connection for each request. A persistent connection accepts multiple get requests from the browser.

For a small static page request, the connection latency can equal or exceed the time to fulfill the request after the connection is established, so using persistent connections can result in major performance gains.

Supporting Persistent Connections If your users' browsers support persistent connections (the default behavior of HTTP/1.1), you can support them on the server using the KeepAlive directives in the Oracle HTTP server. (Some browsers that do not support all HTTP/1.1 features do support persistent connections; for example, recent versions of Netscape.)

Persistent connections can improve total response time for a Web interaction that involves multiple HTTP requests, because, most of the time, the delay of setting up a connection only happens once. Consider the total time required, without persistent connections, for a client to retrieve a Web page with three images from the server. With persistent connections, the response time for the same request is reduced.

Another benefit of persistent connections is reduction of the workload on the server. Because the server need not repeat the work to set up the connection with a client, it is free to perform other work.

Oracle Portal Caching

As the portal pages are generated dynamically by executing procedures in the Oracle Portal node or by communicating with information providers, assembling an Oracle Portal page, which includes a fairly large number of these sources, can be expensive (from CPU and I/O point of view). Therefore, caching becomes vital for maintaining good response times.

The middle-tier is the decision maker in determining if a page definition and its contents exist in the portal cache. If they do exist, then the following checks are performed to determine if this cached copy can be used.

- Validation-based caching
- Time-based caching

Validation-Based Caching

When a page is requested to be displayed by the user, the page engine checks the cache and the Oracle Portal Repository or provider to see if the cache copy needs to be refreshed (by comparing timestamps). That ensures that the Oracle Portal user is always seeing the latest information. This technique is most suitable if the contents of the pages change frequently, and you need to provide users with up-to-date information.

Time-Based Caching

In time-based caching, the cache entries reside in the cache for a specific time. This usually results in a better overall performance, especially with a relatively long expiration period. On the other hand, the disadvantage is that the longer the expiration period, the more probability that users might be seeing old information.

Chapter 20 provides troubleshooting information on installing and configuring Oracle Portal.

PART V

Oracle9*i* Application Server/Portal FAQs and Troubleshooting

CHAPTER 20

Installation and Configuration

Introduction

This chapter provides answers to some of the frequently asked questions related to the installation of Oracle9*i* Application Server and the configuration of Oracle Portal.

Q: Where is the PL/SQL Web Toolkit?

In WebDB 2.x the PL/SQL Web Toolkit is owned by a separate database user, usually named OAS_PUBLIC. This PL/SQL Web Toolkit is a group of PL/SQL stored packages (procedures and functions), which was part of the older generation of Oracle9*i* Application Server (i.e., Oracle Application Server or OAS). These PL/SQL stored packages are mainly used to generate HTML. In Oracle Portal 3.0 the PL/SQL Web Toolkit is created under the SYS database user. You can check the owner of one of the PL/SQL Web Toolkit packages (e.g., HTP), by executing the following SQL statement while connected to the Oracle Portal database as SYS or SYSTEM:

```
SELECT       OWNER, OBJECT_TYPE
FROM         DBA_OBJECTS
WHERE OBJECT_NAME = 'HTP';
```

Starting with Oracle Server 8.1.7 and higher, the PL/SQL Web Toolkit is included as part of the database data dictionary packages. And hence, in the Oracle9*i*AS/Portal 3.0.7–3.0.9, you are prompted to overwrite the 8.1.7 database PL/SQL Web Toolkit with the portal toolkit. A future version of Oracle Portal might totally rely on the fact that the database has the PL/SQL Web Toolkit, and it might not install its own.

Q: I get the following error when I try to log in to Oracle Portal: "WWC-41439: You cannot log in because there is no configuration information stored in the enabler configuration table."

This error happens because the Oracle Portal is trying to perform the Single Sign-On operation but cannot find the appropriate entry in the enabler configuration table PORTAL30_SSO.WWSEC_ENABLER_CONFIG_INFO$.

After installing Oracle Portal 3.0, this table should have one record. The value stored in column LSNR_TOKEN should match the hostname and port number in the "login" link URL. Check your login URL by just moving your cursor on the login link (without clicking); the URL is displayed on the status line of your browser (Figure 20.1).

The first portion of the login URL has the following format:

```
http://<Hostname>:<portno>/pls/<DADname>/<PortalSchema>
.wwsec_app_priv.login..... 25.wwsec_app_priv.login?
```

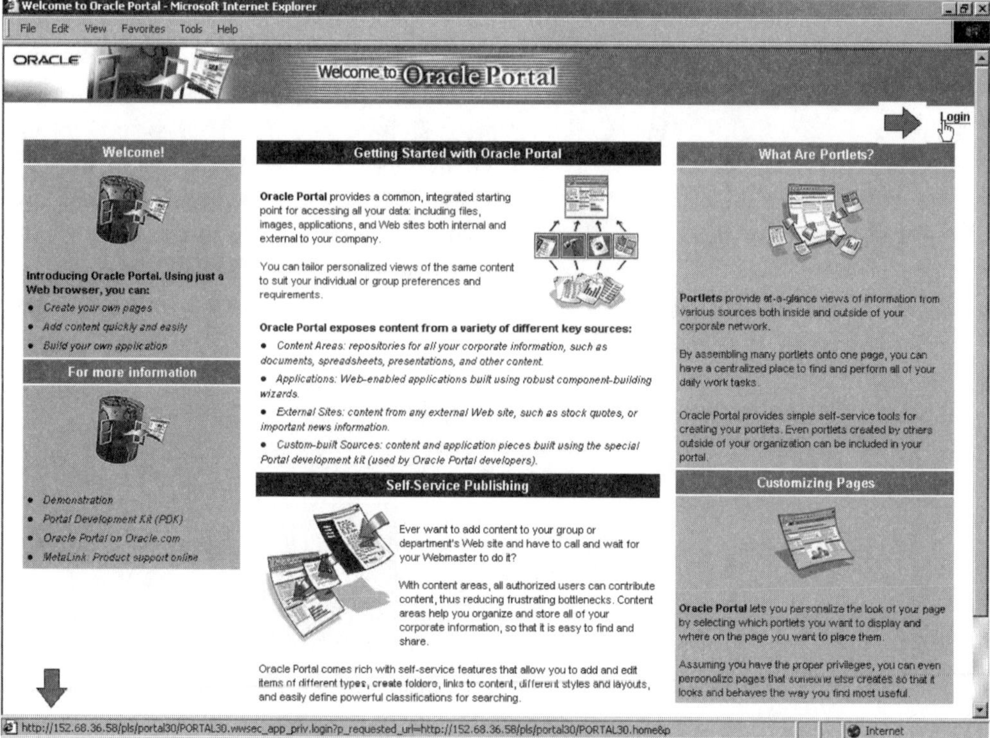

Figure 20.1 Oracle Portal Login URL.

```
SQL> show user
USER is "PORTAL30_SSO"
SQL> desc WWSEC_ENABLER_CONFIG_INFO$
 Name                                      Null?    Type
 ----------------------------------------- -------- ----------------------------
 LSNR_TOKEN                                NOT NULL VARCHAR2(255)
 SITE_TOKEN                                         VARCHAR2(255)
 SITE_ID                                            VARCHAR2(255)
 LS_LOGIN_URL                              NOT NULL VARCHAR2(1000)
 URLCOOKIE_VERSION                         NOT NULL VARCHAR2(80)
 ENCRYPTION_KEY                            NOT NULL VARCHAR2(1000)
 ENCRYPTION_MASK_PRE                       NOT NULL VARCHAR2(1000)
 ENCRYPTION_MASK_POST                      NOT NULL VARCHAR2(1000)
 URL_COOKIE_IP_CHECK                                VARCHAR2(1)

SQL> ed
Wrote file afiedt.buf

  1  SELECT LSNR_TOKEN, LS_LOGIN_URL
  2* FROM WWSEC_ENABLER_CONFIG_INFO$
SQL> /

LSNR_TOKEN
--------------------------------------------------------------------------------
LS_LOGIN_URL
--------------------------------------------------------------------------------
152.68.36.58
http://152.68.36.58/pls/portal30_sso/portal30_sso.wwsso_app_admin.ls_login

SQL> |
```

Figure 20.2 WWSEC_ENABLER_CONFIG_INFO$.

Next, select the value of the listener token column in the WWSEC_ENABLER_CONFIG_INFO$ table (Figure 20.2). The LSNR_TOKEN value should match the host-name in the Login URL. If not, then you most likely are running into one of the following scenarios:

1. The enabler table has no records. This could have been caused by the loadjava utility's failure to load a Java class called "SSOHash" during the install. If this class is not loaded, then a lot of the Login Server data is not loaded and hence the enabler table is not populated. To confirm that the class is not loaded, execute the following SQL statement as the portal schema owner:

```
select object_name from user_objects
where object_type = 'JAVA CLASS'
and object_name like '%SSOHash%';
```

You can try to fix this problem by loading the class manually using the following command from the operating system prompt:

```
loadjava -resolve -user <PORTAL_SCHEMA>/
<PORTAL_SCHEMA>@<CONNECT> SSOHash.class
```

If this does not solve the problem, you might need to reinstall after making sure that your database has the Java option and all the prerequisites mentioned in the preinstallation steps in Chapter 2 are performed. Check that your init.ora java_pool_size is greater than 20MB.

2. The Login link has the hostname with no domain and the LSNR_TOKEN has the hostname with the domain name (i.e., hostname.domainname). This typically occurs because there is an alias defined in Oracle HTTP server (Apache) configuration, which makes it translate the hostname.domainname to just hostname. The fix is to remove the alias.
3. If the hostname in the login URL does not have the domain name, and the value of the LSNR_TOKEN has the domain name, then you need to add the default domain name to the Apache configuration file.
4. If the value of the column LSNR_TOKEN has the port number 80, but the login URL does not, you need to run ssodatan without specifying the port number (i.e., 80). Also, when accessing the portal through the browser, don't specify the port number 80.
5. Otherwise if the hostname in the login URL does not match the value of the LSNR_TOKEN column in the enabler table, you need to rerun the ssodatan script with the correct hostname.

Q: I am trying to access the gateway settings page:
http://hostname/pls/admin_/gateway.htm
but I am getting the following error: "No DAD configuration Found".

The DAD configuration file wdbsvr.app does not have a Default DAD entry. You need to explicitly specify a valid DAD name in the URL to access the Gateway configuration menu page. Use http://<Hostname>/pls/<DADname>/admin_/gateway.htm (e.g., http://myportal/pls/portal30/admin_/gateway.htm) instead of http://<Hostname>/pls/admin_/gateway.htm.

To be able to use the Gateway configuration menu URL without specifying the DAD, click on the "Gateway Global Setting" link and set the Default Database Access Descriptor.

Q: I have just installed Oracle Portal and I am getting errors accessing Oracle Portal home page or logging into Oracle Portal.

Check for invalid objects and generate a script to compile these objects. For example, the following SQL script generates SQL statements that compile invalid package bodies.

```
SELECT 'ALTER PACKAGE '||OBJECT_NAME||' COMPILE BODY;'
FROM   USER_OBJECTS
```

```
WHERE  STATUS <> 'VALID'
AND    OBJECT_TYPE = 'PACKAGE BODY'
ORDER  BY OBJECT_NAME
```

Q: I got an error while installing Oracle Portal and I need to reinstall.

If you run into problems installing the software, you might need to drop the Oracle Portal schema using the Oracle Portal Configuration Assistant and then reinstall. You need to stop the Oracle HTTP listener (i.e., Apache) from the control panel services before you start the "drop" procedure. Check the install.log file for errors that happened in the drop procedure. If your Oracle Portal node resides in a database instance by itself, you might consider deleting and recreating the whole database. Dropping the Oracle Portal schema and the Login schema usually takes a long time due to the large number of objects under each schema. You can use the Oracle Database Configuration Assistant to drop the database and recreate it. It might be worth it to copy the init.ora file of the Oracle Portal database before deleting it, and then copying it over the new database once created, rather than changing the initialization parameters again.

Q: I want to install and configure Oracle HTTP server (i.e., Apache) on a separate machine by itself (which is different from the Oracle Portal node), but the installation keeps asking me to configure Oracle Portal.

You can just install the Oracle HTTP server without configuring the Oracle Portal by canceling the Oracle Portal Configuration Assistant. Then you need to run the ssodatan script on the Oracle Portal machine to configure it with the new HTTP server.

Q: Where are the documents uploaded into Portal 3.0 saved?

In Oracle Portal 3.0 the document table name is specified in the PORTAL30 DAD properties. By default, it is portal30.wwdoc_document. You can change this table to any other table as long as the new table conforms to the document table definition. This definition can be found in the Oracle9*i* Application Server documentation (Oracle HTTP Server *powered by Apache*: Using the PL/SQL Gateway Manual).

Q: How can I implement password management, such as setting the user password expiration period, in Oracle Portal?

Password expiration can be set in the Login Server Configuration Settings page on the Login Server. You can also disallow users from changing their password to the ones currently in use, if they were forced to change their password.

Q: Does Oracle Portal 3.0.7, 3.0.8, or 3.0.9 NT work on Microsoft NT 4.0 and Windows 2000?

Oracle Portal 3.0.7, 3.0.8, and 3.0.9, as part of O9*i*AS 1.0.2 and 1.0.2.1, are certified against both Microsoft Windows NT 4.0 and Microsoft Windows 2000.

Q: While trying to access an Oracle Portal Page, I got timeout errors, and some of the portlets are not rendered. Why?

Edit the zone.properties file under <iAS_ORACLE_HOME>\Apache\Jserv\servlets in MS Windows, and under <iAS_ORACLE_HOME>/Apache/Jserv/etc/ in UNIX platforms. Set

servlet.page.initArgs=requesttime=100

This parameter defines the Oracle Portal Page Parallel Rendered timeout in seconds. Save the file, restart your Apache server, and retry displaying the same page(s).

Also check your Oracle9*i*AS Portal proxy settings under the global settings in the services portlet in the Administer tab.

Q: How can I secure my O9*i*AS Portal using SSL?

To set SSL you need first to get a certificate from one of the SSL Certificate Authorities, such as VeriSign, then you need to configure the Oracle HTTP Server *powered by Apache* for SSL and then configure O9*i*AS Portal. Certificates are encrypted files that allow a client and server to pass sensitive data without the fear of that data being read by unauthorized clients.

There are two types of certificates: 40-bit and 128-bit certificate. The 128-bit certificate is more secure and more expensive than the 40-bit certificate. The first step in getting the certificate is to generate an RSA private key for your host using the openssl utility. The command has the following format:

```
<iAS_ORACLE_HOME>\<Apache\open_ssl\bin\openssl genrsa
-des3 -rand <file1>:<file2>:<file3>:<file4>:<file5>
-out <Hostname>.key 1024
```

where Hostname is your fully qualified domain name (e.g., www.elmallah.com), and the five files are the names of five large and random files from the server hard disk. Because of the des option, the command will ask you for a pass phrase. You need to remember this phrase, because your certificate is useless without it. The command generates a 1024-

bit RSA Private Key and stores it in the file `<Hostname>.key` (e.g., www.elmallah .com.key).

The second step in getting the certificate is to generate the Certificate Signing Request (CSR) file, using the following command:

```
<iAS_ORACLE_HOME>\<Apache\open_ssl\bin\openssl req
-new -key <Hostname>.key -out <Hostname>.csr
```

Specify your fully qualified domain name when the command prompts you for the "Common Name". The contents of the generated CSR file (e.g., www.elmallah.com.csr) are what you need to paste into the appropriate fields in the certificate online request from the certificate authority (e.g., from *verisign.com*). The certificate authority should email you the certificate file (i.e., `<Hostname>.crt`). Some certificate authority companies will send you a CA Certificate File as well.

Now you are ready to configure Apache for SSL, assuming the following locations for your files:

```
<iAS_ORACLE_HOME>\Apache\Apache\conf\ssl.crt\<Hostname>.crt
<iAS_ORACLE_HOME>\Apache\Apache\conf\ssl.key\<Hostname>.key
<iAS_ORACLE_HOME>\Apache\Apache\conf\ssl.crt\<Hostname>.ca
```

The first step to configure Apache for SSL is to edit the configuration file <iAS_ORACLE _HOME>\Apache\Apache\conf\httpd.conf. You need to modify and uncomment the following entries:

- SSLCertificateFile: This is the certificate file.
- SSLCertificateKeyFile: This is the Key file that contains the key to decrypt your certificate.
- SSLCACertificateFile: This is the CA Certificate file if you receive one from your certificate provider (e.g., VeriSign).

The second step in configuring Apache for SSL is to set up the Apache port numbers to work with the certificates in httpd.conf. The default port number used is 443. The third step in configuring Apache for SSL is to edit the <iAS_ORACLE_HOME>\Apache\Jserv \conf\zone.properties file and add the following entries:

```
servlet.page.initArgs=httpsports=443
servlet.page.initArgs=requesttime=30
```

Now you are ready to start the Apache. In Windows stop and start the service. In UNIX run the following command:

```
httpdsctl startssl
```

If it starts successfully, then try to access your secure page:

```
https://<Hostname>:443
```

You should get a browser warning stating that you are entering a secure site. The final stage in configuring SSL is to run the ssodatan command to configure Oracle Portal to use the SSL URLs:

```
ssodatan -w https://<Hostname>:443/pls/portal30/ -l
https://<Hostname>:443/pls/portal30_sso/ -s portal30 -o
portal30_sso -c orcl
```

Check that you can access Portal via SSL:

```
https://<Hostname>:443/pls/portal30
```

Q: How can I export/import applications between different versions of Oracle9*i*AS Portal?

This feature is not supported as of versions 3.0.6–3.0.9.

Q: How can I remove an Oracle Portal user lockout (assuming no LDAP authentication)?

Try running the following SQL as user PORTAL30_SSO:

```
begin
    wwsso_ls_private.test_ip_flag := 1;
    wwsso_ls_private.test_ip_addr := 'INTERNAL';
    wwsso_ls_private.unlock_user_account
        (p_user=>upper('&User'));
end;
/
```

Q: How do I create an alias for the Portal URL?

You can use the Redirect directives in the httpd.conf file.

Q: Can I export/import pages with child pages?

This feature is only supported in version 3.0.8 and later.

Q: How can Internet Explorer be configured optimally for Oracle Portal?

Choose Internet Options from the IE Tools dropdown menu. Click the "Settings" button in the Temporary Internet files region. Choose the "Every visit to the page" option. Next, under the Advanced tab select the "Use HTTP 1.1 through proxy connections" check box.

Q: On Windows, when I try to access the portal home page, I receive the following error: Apache.exe—Entry Point Not Found: The procedure entry point snlpcgtsvrbynm could not be located in the dynamic link library oranl8.dll.

Stop all Oracle services and then modify the DEFAULT_HOME entry in the Windows Registry:

MyComputer/HKEY_LOCAL_MACHINE/SOFTWARE/Oracle/ALL_HOMES/

to point to the Oracle9*i* Application Server Oracle Home.

Q: How do I add the *inter*Media Text option (Oracle Text) manually to the 8*i* Database?

In the instance initialization parameter file, check that the value of the text_enable parameter is false. Next, create a tablespace DRSYS to be the default tablespace for the new user CTXSYS (Oracle Text schema). On UNIX, the environment variable LD_LIBRARY_PATH must be set to <DB_ORACLE_HOME>\lib:<DB_ORACLE_HOME>\ctx\lib. Next, you need to perform the following commands:

```
cd <DB_ORACLE_HOME>\ctx\admin
set ORACLE_SID=orcl
sqlplus sys/change_on_install
@dr0csys.sql ctxsys drsys temp
conn ctxsys/ctxsys
@dr0inst.sql <DB_ORACLE_HOME>\ctx\lib\libctxx8.so
```

When the scripts are done, check that the user ctxsys has the Oracle Text Object:

```
column library_name format a8
column file_spec format a60
select library_name,file_spec,dynamic,status from
    user_libraries;
```

The final step is to create the default lexer, wordlist, and stoplist:

```
sqlplus ctxsys/ctxsys
@<DB_ORACLE_HOME>\ctx\admin\defaults\drdefus.sql
```

Q: I get the following error when I am installing 9*i*AS 1.0.2.2 on MS Windows 2000 after I have installed 8.1.7 database in the same machine: "Runtime exception occurred during execution of this query."

You need to uninstall the Oracle HTTP Server *powered by Apache* from your 8.1.7 Oracle Home. First, use the Oracle Universal Installer to deinstall it, then you need to remove the Apache directory under the 8.1.7 Oracle Home. Then you need to reinstall O9*i*AS 1.0.2.2.

Chapter 21 presents a FAQ list regarding Oracle Portal development.

CHAPTER 21

Development

Introduction

This chapter provides answers to some of the frequently asked questions related to development using Oracle Portal.

Q: How do I implement a multiple-selection-URL list of values in a portlet where I can choose one or more URLs from a list of URLs. For example, how do I provide my Web site end-user with the ability to pick one or more products from a list of the product's URL list?

One possible implementation of this requirement is to use a table to store the list of URLs. For practice, you can create a PRODUCTS table that has an ID column, a description column, and a URL column. Grant select on this table to public or to user Portal30_public because it is the schema that portal users use to connect to the Oracle Portal instance by default. Then, create a dynamic LOV, and, finally, create a report on an SQL query.

1. Create a dynamic LOV on the PRODUCTS table based on the following query:

```
SELECT    PRODUCT_DESC,     PRODUCT_ID
FROM      PRODUCTS
```

   Leave the default format as "Check Box".

2. Create a Report from SQL query, using the following query:

```
SELECT    '<A HREF=http://' || PRODUCT_URL ||
          '>' || PRODUCT_DESC || '</A>' "URL"
FROM      PRODUCTS
WHERE     PRODUCT_ID   IN    :PRODUCTS_IDS_P
```

On the Column Formatting tab, set the "Display as" to HTML. On the Customization Form Display Options tab, for the PRODUCTS_IDS_P parameter, set its prompt and its default value. Then, select your LOV and set the display LOV to Combo Box. Uncheck all of the Formatting Options: Output Format, Maximum Rows, and so on.

Hint: Make sure that you set the default value to some valid entry, otherwise the report will show nothing when first viewed as a portlet from the portal.

3. Set the access of the report to "Publish To Portal".

You can now add this report to your portal page and use the "Customize" option for users to select which links they want to see. You could use a Multiple Select format for the LOV instead of the Check Box.

Q: Is there a way to dynamically control which fields are displayed in Oracle Portal Application Components (e.g., Forms)? For example, can the same form display and hide different fields based on the logged-in user?

Unfortunately, this functionality cannot be implemented as of Oracle Portal version 3.0.6, but it might be added into a future release.

Q: How can I set the default value to a parameter in an Oracle Portal Application Component (e.g., Report)?

In practice, create a report from SQL:

```
SELECT    *
FROM      CUSTOMERS
WHERE     CUSTOMER_CITY = :CITY_P;
```

In the Parameter Setting screen, set the default value for the bind variable CITY_P as ALEXANDRIA. So, each time the parameter page is displayed, 'ALEXANDRIA' is displayed in the text field. A user can change the value and run the report, or just use it as the default value.

Q: How can the presentation of folders be changed? For example, how can both the image of the globe on the left pane and the Oracle logo be eliminated?

In the Folder Properties, you can change the folder image, navigation bar, and style. The style gives you very detailed control over the folder's visual appearance. You can also modify the Content Area page to add portlets and other visual elements. From the navigator, select Content Areas, edit properties for the selected Content Area, then click on the Page tab.

Q: How can the "Customize" link in an Oracle Portal page be hidden?

You can click on the "Edit Defaults" link while editing the page and uncheck the "Display Customize Page link" check box. Or, you can revoke the right to customize the page from users by going to the Access tab of the Page properties. Or you can switch off the whole banner of the page by editing the main tab of the Page properties.

Q: How can the "Customize" link in the HTML portlet be hidden?

There is no mechanism for hiding the portlet "Customize" link without switching off its header. You can hide the portlet header by editing its Region properties and unchecking the portlet header display check box. There are some exceptions to this. For example, in Oracle Portal 3.0.9, you can hide the "Customize" link of a content area folder portlet by editing the defaults of the portlet and unselecting the "Display Customize Link" check box.

Q: A Login Portlet on a Public page is published. When the page is displayed, a user can log in, but the same login page is displayed after the user is logged in. How can the user be directed to another page with a successful login?

By default, once the user is authenticated the browser redirects to the page on which the portlet requested is placed, unless a different URL is specified in the portlet customization. So, after you add the Login portlet to your page, click on the "Customize" link to specify a fully qualified URL for the "On Success URL" field. Also, you can use a relative URL, such as portal30.home, to go to the Portal30 home page.

Q: A perspective is defined in the shared objects under contents areas and published as a portlet, then a Content Area is created and items are inserted with this perspective. Next, when a page is created the portlet corresponding to the perspective is inserted in that page. If the page style is changed, then the "Customize" link in the perspective portlet header is clicked to select all documents with that shared perspective. Documents will appear in the default style of Oracle Portal. Can the style of the portlet be changed to the same style as that of the page?

No, perspectives are rendered using the "Main Site Style" defined in the shared objects. Currently, there is no way to specify a different style. The workaround is to update this style to the look and feel you want. To update/change this style, navigate to the styles under "Shared Objects," and, as a portal administrator, you can edit the "Main Site Style".

Q: Can the "User Default Style" for pages be set at the user level rather than group level?

There is no default style for an individual user as of 3.0.9. A way to work around this is that each user can create his or her own group and then assign him- or herself to the group and then designate this group as the default group.

Q: How do I bulk load document files into portal?

You can use the new zip file item to bulk load documents.

Q: Where can I increase the portlet timeout setting?

For database portlets, you can set the timeout in the portlet record. For Web portlets, you can increase the timeout in the provider.xml.

Q: Can an Oracle Portal form be created on any database view?

An Oracle Portal form cannot be built on a view that has any of the following:

- DISTINCT operator
- Aggregate functions like AVG, COUNT, MAX, MIN
- GROUP BY, HAVING, START WITH, CONNECT BY clauses

Q: Can a portal page include a link without creating a folder to hold it?

Yes, here are two possible implementations:

1. Create a shared public navigation bar in the content area portion of the product and add the URL elements to it. URL elements can have images and rollover images if needed. Then, the navigation bar can be published as a portlet and added to the page.
2. If just simple links are needed, they can be added to the page banner. You can customize the page's banner to add links.

Q: A Content Area is created with items in Announcements and Quick Picks. In the root Folder Properties, the "Publish As Portlet" check box is checked. Then, the contents are added as a portlet to display only the Announcements and all other areas are deselected.

When the page is displayed—while still logged in as the page owner—the Announcements items are the only items displayed. However, when the page is viewed publicly, both Announcements and Quick Picks are displayed. How can I hide the Quick Picks from the public access?

You would need to edit the default properties for the root folder portlet to display only the Announcements regions for all users by clicking on the "Customize" link, when viewing the page, then clicking on the "Edit Defaults" link of the folder portlet. Only set the Announcements region to be displayed.

Q: Can the images be turned off in some of the standard portlets in Oracle Portal, such as the Favorites Portlet, which comes with "My Links" image?

The image of the "Favorites Portlet" is a ml_us.gif located in the images directory of the Apache. You can overwrite that image with a 1-pixel transparent image (i.e., pobtrans.gif), which exists in the same directory. For example, you can use the following command:

```
c> copy pobtrans.gif ml_us.gif
```

You can do the same for other portlets' images, such as:

- the Recent Objects Portlet; its image is mw_us.gif.
- the External Applications; its image is otw_us.gif.
- the Page Portlet; its image is pg_us.gif.
- the Content Areas Portlet; its image is ca_us.gif.

Q: How can I develop a report of items awaiting approval in Oracle Portal Content Areas?

Build a report on the following SELECT statement:

```
SELECT DISTINCT
      c.title folder_title, a.title, a.itemtype, a.author,
      a.description, a.createdate, a.expiredate, b.name site_name,
      d.title perspective_title, d.description perspective_desc
FROM siteup_test.wwv_things a,
      wwsbr_sites$ b,
      wwv_corners c,
      wwv_perspectives d,
      wwv_thingsperspectives e
WHERE a.siteid = b.id
AND         a.iscurrentversion=1
AND         a.active in (0, -2)
```

```
                /* 0 is awaiting approval,
                  -2 is awaiting approval but have been
                     deleted */
AND             a.cornerid = c.id
AND             a.siteid = c.siteid
AND             a.language = 'us'
AND             a.id = e.thingid(+)
AND             e.perspectiveid = d.id(+);
```

Note that this does not take into account the privilege checks, which means that all the items awaiting approval will be displayed when this query is run. The items awaiting approval are items created by user(s) who have been granted "Create with Approval" in the content area folder(s) access list.

Q: A report is created in Oracle Portal on a table that contains a BLOB column. When the report is run, a link to the image is displayed. How can the image be displayed within the report itself?

In the Report wizard in the "Display Options" section, check the "Embed Intermedia Rich Content in the Report" check box. Then, create the report. The intermedia objects will be shown "in place" rather than as links.

Q: How can I install the URL Portlet to display a whole Internet site in my portal page?

The URL Portlet is part of the PDK. Refer to Chapter 13 for more information about the PDK. You need to expand the URLPortlet.zip file into a directory (e.g., C:\portal\pdk\plsql\url). Go to DOS and set the ORACLE_HOME to point to your O9*i*AS directory. Next, you need to run URL Portlet install script file (for NT: urlinstl.cmd, Solaris/UNIX : urlinstl):

```
urlinstl.cmd -w portal30 -wp portal30 -s pdk04 -p pdk04
     -c orcl
```

where PDK04 is the user created in Chapter 13. Next, you need to register the database provider url_provider. Specify the schema as PDK04 and the implementation package name is url_provider. The provider has a portlet "URL portlet" that you can add to any of your pages and customize by specifying the URL you want to display.

Q: How can I install the Excite Portlets to add Excite.com information to Oracle Portal pages?

You need to run the script insexcpr.sql from the PDK files under the plsql\excite directory.

Q: How can I build a custom form application component layout?

In the custom layout form page in the Create Form wizard, you can specify the HTML code for the header, body, and footer sections of the form. You can use the sample HTML code. Note that the column labels are specified by the suffix ".LABEL" (e.g., #EMPNO.LABEL#_) and the column values are specified by the suffix .ITEM (e.g., #EMPNO.ITEM#).

Q: How do I pass the username of the logged-in user to a field in a portal form?

Use the following expression: #portal30.wwctx_api.get_user.

Q: What is the URL to run an application component with parameters?

The format of the URL to run an application component in full-page mode with parameters is

```
http://<Hostname>:<portno>
/pls/portal30/<ApplicationSchema>.<ComponentName>
.SHOW?p_arg_names=<ParameterName>&p_arg_values=
<ParameterValue>
```

For example:

```
http://myportal/pls/portal30/MYEIP_OWNER.EMP_SAL_GRADE_
REPORT.SHOW?p_arg_names=department_no&p_arg_values=30
```

An example for the URL to display the component customization page is

```
http://localhost:7778/pls/portal30/MYEIP_OWNER.EMP_SAL_
GRADE_REPORT.SHOW_PARMS
```

PART VI

Appendices

APPENDIX A

Oracle Portal Glossary

This appendix provides definitions to the most commonly used Oracle Portal terms.

API Application Program Interface: a set of routines, protocols, and tools for building software applications.

Application A named group of components, such as forms, charts, reports, and so on.

Application Component A graphical user interface component, such as a form or a chart that is part of an application. It is implemented using a stored PL/SQL package created inside the component application's schema.

CCS Cascading Style Sheets: a simple mechanism for adding style (e.g., fonts, colors, spacing) to Web documents.

Concurrency The ability to handle multiple requests simultaneously. Threads and processes are examples of concurrency mechanisms.

Content Area Oracle Portal's way of organizing contents, facilitating the self-service publishing. It is called Sites in WebDB 2.2.

Content Area Style The interface settings of the content area, such as the background colors.

Contention Competition for resources.

DAD Database Access Descriptor: holds the username, password, and database connect string used by the Oracle9*i*AS PL/SQL module to connect to the database.

Database Provider The code written in PL/SQL or Java and saved in the database, aggregating data from other databases and providing the aggregated data to portlets through the portal API.

DB Database.

DES Data Encryption Standard: a popular symmetric-key encryption method. It is standardized by ANSI and it uses a 56-bit key.

DNS Domain Name System: an Internet service that translates domain names into IP addresses.

Dynamic Services A separate Oracle product that can be installed and configured on top of the Oracle database server to provide information to Oracle Portal.

ERD Entity-Relationship Diagram: a popular methodology used to model the system data.

GUI Graphical User Interface.

HTTP Hypertext Transfer Protocol: the underlying protocol used by the World Wide Web.

HTTPS Secure HTTP (S-HTTP): an extension to the HTTP protocol to support sending data securely over the World Wide Web.

***i*AS** Internet Application Server is the middle-tier suite from Oracle that includes both Oracle HTTP Server *powered by Apache* and Oracle Portal. It is referred to as O9*i*AS, Oracle9*i* AS, and Oracle9*i* Application Server.

***inter*Media Text** An option of the Oracle database server that allows you to search documents saved inside the database; its search capability can be utilized by Oracle Portal. It is also known as Oracle Text.

JAR Java Archive: a file format used to bundle all components required by a Java applet.

JVM Java Virtual Machine: a platform-independent programming language that converts Java bytecode into machine language and executes it.

Latency The time that one system component spends waiting for another component in order to complete the entire task. In networking context latency is defined as the travel time of a packet from source to destination.

Navigation Bar A part of the Oracle Portal content area to facilitate the movement between different pieces of the Content Area.

NLS National Language Support: where Oracle products can support multiple languages.

O9*i*AS Oracle9*i* Application Server.

OiD Oracle internet Directory: an Oracle directory service product that is LDAP 3.0 compliant and can be utilized by Oracle Portal. It is also used by the Oracle9*i* Dynamic Services.

Oracle HTTP Server *powered by Apache* Apache application server bundled with Oracle modules (such as mod_plsql).

OUI Oracle Universal Installer: the installer program shipped with the latest Oracle products (such as DB EE 8.1.7, O9*i*AS, etc.).

Page Style The layout setting that defines how the page will look, such as the page background images, text colors, and so on.

PDK Portal Development Kit: a separate piece of the Oracle Portal that is shipped and updated separately and more frequently than the Oracle Portal product itself. It provides the Oracle Portal developer with samples and the API needed to build customized programmable portlets.

Response Time The time between the submission of a request and the receipt of the response.

RSA Key A public-key encryption technology developed by RSA Data Security, Inc. The acronym stands for Rivest, Shamir, and Adelman, the inventors of the technique. The RSA algorithm has become the de facto standard for industrial-strength encryption, especially for data sent over the Internet. It is built into many software products, including Netscape Navigator and Microsoft Internet Explorer.

Scalability The ability to easily add resources to or remove resources from a system. A system can be called scalable if it can handle increasing numbers of requests by adding more resources to it, to maintain good response time and throughput.

SOAP Simple Object Access Protocol: used by Web providers to communicate with Oracle Portal.

SSL Secure Sockets Layer: a protocol developed by Netscape for transmitting private documents via the Internet. SSL works by using a public key to encrypt data that's transferred over the SSL connection.

Think Time The time the user is not engaged in actual use of the processor.

Throughput The number of requests processed per unit of time.

URL Uniform Resource Locator: the global address of documents and other resources on the World Wide Web.

Web Provider A separate program developed using a Web language such as Java, Perl, and so forth to integrate other Web sites existing currently in the environment.

WYSIWYG What You See Is What You Get: A WYSIWYG application is one that enables you to see on the display screen exactly what will appear when the document is printed.

APPENDIX B

Importing the CD-ROM Portal Application, Content Area, and Page

Introduction

This appendix describes the import steps of the sample portal used in the book, which is available on the companion CD-ROM under the export folder. The same instructions can be found in the `import_steps.txt` file.

The portal on the CD-ROM was developed and exported using O9*i*AS Portal version 3.0.9.8.0; it needs O9*i*AS Portal version 3.0.9.x.x to be imported.

Installation Steps

1. Connect to the Oracle Portal instance using SQL*Plus as the SYSTEM user to create the MYEIP_OWNER application schema:

   ```
   sqlplus system/manager@orcl

   create user myeip_owner identified by myeip_owner default
   tablespace users temporary tablespace temp;

   grant connect,resource to myeip_owner;
   ```

2. Connect to the Oracle Portal instance using SQL*Plus as SCOTT:

   ```
   sqlplus scott/tiger@orcl

   grant select,insert,update,delete on salgrade to
   myeip_owner,portal30_public;
   ```

3. If needed, edit the file `emp_item_type_proc.sql` to change the portal schema and its password (i.e., `portal30/portal30`) before running it:

```
SQL> @<source_dir>\ch08\emp_item_type_proc
```

For example,

```
SQL> @d:\source\ch08\emp_item_type_proc
```

4. Go to the operating system prompt (i.e., DOS), and set the ORACLE_HOME environment variable to the iAS_ORACLE_HOME. For example,

```
C> set ORACLE_HOME=c:\oracle\ias1022
```

5. Set the ORACLE_SID environment variable to the Oracle Portal database SID. For example,

```
C> set ORACLE_SID=ORCL
```

6. Change directory to <iAS_ORACLE_HOME>\portal30\admin\plsql\wwu. For example,

```
C> cd C:\oracle\ias1022\portal30\admin\plsql\wwu
```

7. Run the following command:

```
appimp.cmd -s <portal_schema> -p <portal_password> -o
PORTAL30 -m CREATE -f <export_dir>\myeip_app_export_
app.sql -c <connect_string>
```

For example,

```
c> appimp.cmd -s portal30 -p portal30 -o PORTAL30 -m
CREATE -f d:\export\myeip_app_export.sql -c orcl
```

8. Run the following command:

```
contimp.cmd -s <portal_schema> -p <portal_password> -o
PORTAL30 -m reuse -d <export_dir>\emp_ca_export.dmp -c
<connect_string>
```

For example,

```
c> contimp.cmd -s portal30 -p portal30 -o PORTAL30 -m
reuse -d d:\export\emp_ca_export.dmp -c orcl
```

9. Run the following command:

```
pageimp.cmd -s <portal_schema> -p <portal_password> -o
PORTAL30 -m reuse -d <export_dir>\employee_page_export
.dmp -c <connect_string>
```

For example,

```
c> pageimp.cmd -s portal30 -p portal30 -o PORTAL30 -m
reuse -d d:\export\employee_page_export.dmp -c orcl
```

Now you can access the application, content area, and page from Oracle Portal Navigator.

Installation and Troubleshooting Tips

- For the emp_form Form component to work correctly, you need to edit the form, and choose a different template in the Form Text tab. Next, save the form and test it. Read Chapter 7 to create your own template and then assign it to the form.
- If you get a "no data found" error when you try to run the STAFF_HIE hierarchy component, try editing the component: in the column conditions delete the first condition.
- For the portlets under the Emp.Tools tab in the Employees Information page to be displayed, you need to configure and register their providers as explained in Chapters 13 and 14.
- If you get "Timeout for content" errors on any of the Content Area folder portlets, check your Apache log file and your Portal Proxy settings.
- If the image chart application component is not showing, check your `jserv.log` file for errors.
- If the custom Employee item in the Employee Content Area is not displaying "King" employee information, check that the employee number property of the item is set to value 7839. Also, check that the Employee custom item procedure parameter is passed correctly. Refer to the "Extending Item Types" section in Chapter 8.

Index

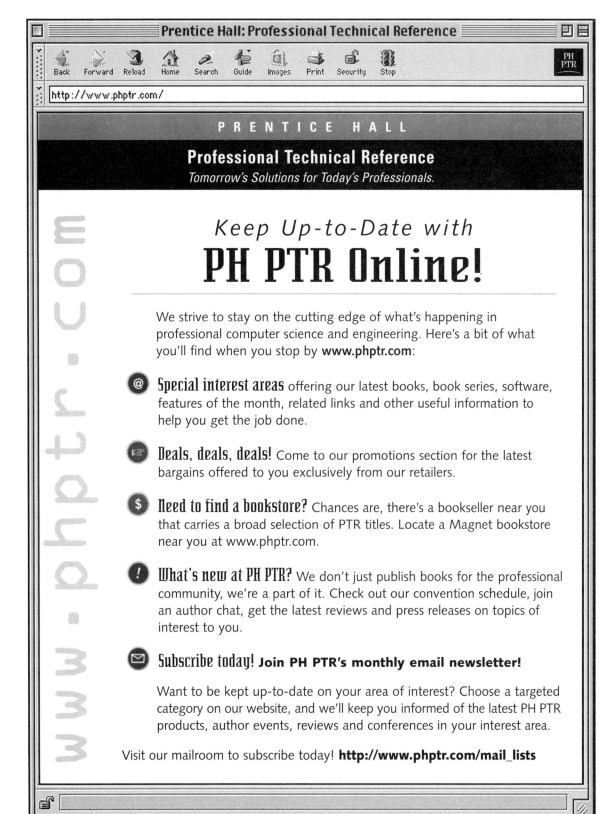

LICENSE AGREEMENT AND LIMITED WARRANTY

READ THE FOLLOWING TERMS AND CONDITIONS CAREFULLY BEFORE OPENING THIS SOFTWARE PACKAGE. THIS LEGAL DOCUMENT IS AN AGREEMENT BETWEEN YOU AND PRENTICE-HALL, INC. (THE "COMPANY"). BY OPENING THIS SEALED SOFTWARE PACKAGE, YOU ARE AGREEING TO BE BOUND BY THESE TERMS AND CONDITIONS. IF YOU DO NOT AGREE WITH THESE TERMS AND CONDITIONS, DO NOT OPEN THE SOFTWARE PACKAGE. PROMPTLY RETURN THE UNOPENED SOFTWARE PACKAGE AND ALL ACCOMPANYING ITEMS TO THE PLACE YOU OBTAINED THEM FOR A FULL REFUND OF ANY SUMS YOU HAVE PAID.

1. **GRANT OF LICENSE:** In consideration of your payment of the license fee, which is part of the price you paid for this product, and your agreement to abide by the terms and conditions of this Agreement, the Company grants to you a nonexclusive right to use and display the copy of the enclosed software program (hereinafter the "software") on a single computer (i.e., with a single CPU) at a single location so long as you comply with the terms of this Agreement. The Company reserves all rights not expressly granted to you under this Agreement.

2. **OWNERSHIP OF SOFTWARE:** You own only the magnetic or physical media (the enclosed software) on which the software is recorded or fixed, but the Company retains all the rights, title, and ownership to the software recorded on the original software copy(ies) and all subsequent copies of the software, regardless of the form or media on which the original or other copies may exist. This license is not a sale of the original software or any copy to you.

3. **COPY RESTRICTIONS:** This software and the accompanying printed materials and user manual (the "Documentation") are the subject of copyright. You may <u>not</u> copy the Documentation or the software, except that you may make a single copy of the software for backup or archival purposes only. You may be held legally responsible for any copying or copyright infringement which is caused or encouraged by your failure to abide by the terms of this restriction.

4. **USE RESTRICTIONS:** You may <u>not</u> network the software or otherwise use it on more than one computer or computer terminal at the same time. You may physically transfer the software from one computer to another provided that the software is used on only one computer at a time. You may <u>not</u> distribute copies of the software or Documentation to others. You may <u>not</u> reverse engineer, disassemble, decompile, modify, adapt, translate, or create derivative works based on the software or the Documentation without the prior written consent of the Company.

5. **TRANSFER RESTRICTIONS:** The enclosed software is licensed only to you and may <u>not</u> be transferred to any one else without the prior written consent of the Company. Any unauthorized transfer of the software shall result in the immediate termination of this Agreement.

6. **TERMINATION:** This license is effective until terminated. This license will terminate automatically without notice from the Company and become null and void if you fail to comply with any provisions or limitations of this license. Upon termination, you shall destroy the Documentation and all copies of the software. All provisions of this Agreement as to warranties, limitation of liability, remedies or damages, and our ownership rights shall survive termination.

7. **MISCELLANEOUS:** This Agreement shall be construed in accordance with the laws of the United States of America and the State of New York and shall benefit the Company, its affiliates, and assignees.

8. **LIMITED WARRANTY AND DISCLAIMER OF WARRANTY:** The Company warrants that the software, when properly used in accordance with the Documentation, will operate in substantial conformity with the description of the software set forth in the Documentation. The Company does not warrant that the software will meet your requirements or that the operation of the software will be uninterrupted or error-free. The Company warrants that the media on which the software is delivered shall be free from defects in materials and workmanship under normal use

for a period of thirty (30) days from the date of your purchase. Your only remedy and the Company's only obligation under these limited warranties is, at the Company's option, return of the warranted item for a refund of any amounts paid by you or replacement of the item. Any replacement of software or media under the warranties shall not extend the original warranty period. The limited warranty set forth above shall not apply to any software which the Company determines in good faith has been subject to misuse, neglect, improper installation, repair, alteration, or damage by you. EXCEPT FOR THE EXPRESSED WARRANTIES SET FORTH ABOVE, THE COMPANY DISCLAIMS ALL WARRANTIES, EXPRESS OR IMPLIED, INCLUDING WITHOUT LIMITATION, THE IMPLIED WARRANTIES OF MERCHANTABILITY AND FITNESS FOR A PARTICULAR PURPOSE. EXCEPT FOR THE EXPRESS WARRANTY SET FORTH ABOVE, THE COMPANY DOES NOT WARRANT, GUARANTEE, OR MAKE ANY REPRESENTATION REGARDING THE USE OR THE RESULTS OF THE USE OF THE SOFTWARE IN TERMS OF ITS CORRECTNESS, ACCURACY, RELIABILITY, CURRENTNESS, OR OTHERWISE.

IN NO EVENT, SHALL THE COMPANY OR ITS EMPLOYEES, AGENTS, SUPPLIERS, OR CONTRACTORS BE LIABLE FOR ANY INCIDENTAL, INDIRECT, SPECIAL, OR CONSEQUENTIAL DAMAGES ARISING OUT OF OR IN CONNECTION WITH THE LICENSE GRANTED UNDER THIS AGREEMENT, OR FOR LOSS OF USE, LOSS OF DATA, LOSS OF INCOME OR PROFIT, OR OTHER LOSSES, SUSTAINED AS A RESULT OF INJURY TO ANY PERSON, OR LOSS OF OR DAMAGE TO PROPERTY, OR CLAIMS OF THIRD PARTIES, EVEN IF THE COMPANY OR AN AUTHORIZED REPRESENTATIVE OF THE COMPANY HAS BEEN ADVISED OF THE POSSIBILITY OF SUCH DAMAGES. IN NO EVENT SHALL LIABILITY OF THE COMPANY FOR DAMAGES WITH RESPECT TO THE SOFTWARE EXCEED THE AMOUNTS ACTUALLY PAID BY YOU, IF ANY, FOR THE SOFTWARE.

SOME JURISDICTIONS DO NOT ALLOW THE LIMITATION OF IMPLIED WARRANTIES OR LIABILITY FOR INCIDENTAL, INDIRECT, SPECIAL, OR CONSEQUENTIAL DAMAGES, SO THE ABOVE LIMITATIONS MAY NOT ALWAYS APPLY. THE WARRANTIES IN THIS AGREEMENT GIVE YOU SPECIFIC LEGAL RIGHTS AND YOU MAY ALSO HAVE OTHER RIGHTS WHICH VARY IN ACCORDANCE WITH LOCAL LAW.

ACKNOWLEDGMENT

YOU ACKNOWLEDGE THAT YOU HAVE READ THIS AGREEMENT, UNDERSTAND IT, AND AGREE TO BE BOUND BY ITS TERMS AND CONDITIONS. YOU ALSO AGREE THAT THIS AGREEMENT IS THE COMPLETE AND EXCLUSIVE STATEMENT OF THE AGREEMENT BETWEEN YOU AND THE COMPANY AND SUPERSEDES ALL PROPOSALS OR PRIOR AGREEMENTS, ORAL, OR WRITTEN, AND ANY OTHER COMMUNICATIONS BETWEEN YOU AND THE COMPANY OR ANY REPRESENTATIVE OF THE COMPANY RELATING TO THE SUBJECT MATTER OF THIS AGREEMENT.

Should you have any questions concerning this Agreement or if you wish to contact the Company for any reason, please contact in writing at the address below.

Robin Short
Prentice Hall PTR
One Lake Street
Upper Saddle River, New Jersey 07458

About the CD-ROM

The CD-ROM included with *Web Development with Oracle Portal* contains the following three folders:

1. Artwork: This folder contains some of the images used in the book examples.
2. Source: This folder contains the source code of the book examples, with a subfolder for each chapter that has source code.
3. Export: This folder contains the export files of the sample portal used in the book.

System Requirements

The CD-ROM can be used on Microsoft Windows® 95/98/NT®.

License Agreement

Use of the software accompanying *Web Development with Oracle Portal* is subject to the terms of the License Agreement and Limited Warranty, found on the previous page.

Technical Support

Prentice Hall does not offer technical support for any of the programs on the CD-ROM. However, if the CD-ROM is damaged, you may obtain a replacement copy by sending an email that describes the problem to: disc_exchange@prenhall.com.